Lecture Notes in Computer Science 17081

Founding Editors

Gerhard Goos
Juris Hartmanis

AF861789

Editorial Board Members

Elisa Bertino, *Purdue University, West Lafayette, IN, USA*
Wen Gao, *Peking University, Beijing, China*
Bernhard Steffen, *TU Dortmund University, Dortmund, Germany*
Moti Yung, *Columbia University, New York, NY, USA*

The series Lecture Notes in Computer Science (LNCS), including its subseries Lecture Notes in Artificial Intelligence (LNAI) and Lecture Notes in Bioinformatics (LNBI), has established itself as a medium for the publication of new developments in computer science and information technology research, teaching, and education.

LNCS enjoys close cooperation with the computer science R & D community, the series counts many renowned academics among its volume editors and paper authors, and collaborates with prestigious societies. Its mission is to serve this international community by providing an invaluable service, mainly focused on the publication of conference and workshop proceedings and postproceedings. LNCS commenced publication in 1973.

Anna Bernasconi · Marta Indulska · Sudha Ram ·
Joerg Evermann · Jeffrey Parsons
Editors

Conceptual Modeling

45th International Conference, ER 2026
St. John's, NL, Canada, October 5–8, 2026
Proceedings

Springer

Editors
Anna Bernasconi
Politecnico di Milano
Milan, Italy

Marta Indulska
The University of Queensland
Brisbane, QLD, Australia

Sudha Ram
University of Arizona
Tucson, AZ, USA

Joerg Evermann
Memorial University of Newfoundland
St. John's, NL, Canada

Jeffrey Parsons
Memorial University of Newfoundland
St. John's, NL, Canada

ISSN 0302-9743 ISSN 1611-3349 (electronic)
Lecture Notes in Computer Science
ISBN 978-3-032-40794-8 ISBN 978-3-032-40795-5 (eBook)
https://doi.org/10.1007/978-3-032-40795-5

© The Editor(s) (if applicable) and The Author(s), under exclusive license
to Springer Nature Switzerland AG 2027

This work is subject to copyright. All rights are solely and exclusively licensed by the Publisher, whether the whole or part of the material is concerned, specifically the rights of translation, reprinting, reuse of illustrations, recitation, broadcasting, reproduction on microfilms or in any other physical way, and transmission or information storage and retrieval, electronic adaptation, computer software, or by similar or dissimilar methodology now known or hereafter developed. Unless otherwise expressly agreed by the Publisher in writing, the Publisher does not authorize use or reproduction of all or any part of this work in any manner for the purpose of training, fine-tuning, evaluating, or developing artificial intelligence models, technologies, or systems. In accordance with Article 4(3) of the EU Directive 2019/790 on copyright and related rights in the Digital Single Market, the Publisher expressly reserves all rights with respect to this work under the text and data mining exception of the directive.
The use of general descriptive names, registered names, trademarks, service marks, etc. in this publication does not imply, even in the absence of a specific statement, that such names are exempt from the relevant protective laws and regulations and therefore free for general use.
The publisher, the authors and the editors are safe to assume that the advice and information in this book are believed to be true and accurate at the date of publication. Neither the publisher nor the authors or the editors give a warranty, expressed or implied, with respect to the material contained herein or for any errors or omissions that may have been made. The publisher remains neutral with regard to jurisdictional claims in published maps and institutional affiliations.

This Springer imprint is published by the registered company Springer Nature Switzerland AG
The registered company address is: Gewerbestrasse 11, 6330 Cham, Switzerland

If disposing of this product, please recycle the paper.

Preface

This volume of the Lecture Notes in Computer Science series contains the proceedings of the 45th International Conference on Conceptual Modeling – ER 2026, held at Memorial University of Newfoundland in St. John's, Newfoundland and Labrador, Canada, from October 5–8, 2026.

Situated on the easternmost edge of North America, St. John's is one of the oldest European-settled cities on the continent, known for its colourful harbourside houses and its long maritime history. It was at Signal Hill, overlooking the harbour, that the first transatlantic wireless signal was received in 1901. Today the city combines that heritage with an active research culture centred on Memorial University, whose Core Science Facility hosted ER 2026. Its coastal setting and the hospitality of Newfoundland made it a welcoming venue for a conference concerned with how we model a changing world.

Marking nearly half a century of nurturing high-end research, the ER conference continues to evolve as artificial intelligence and digitalization reshape the landscape of information systems. In celebrating the conference's 45th anniversary, the theme of this year's ER was "Conceptual Modeling and Sustainability". We decided on this theme because conceptual modeling has never been more important than in this age of constrained resources and intensifying human impact on the environment. As individuals, organizations, and countries confront new and unexpected challenges, the systems they depend on must be built to cope with, and help address, the sustainability pressures of a rapidly changing world. Conceptual modeling offers structured ways to represent and connect complex environmental, social, and economic systems, helping researchers and practitioners align assumptions, compare scenarios, and translate knowledge across disciplines. Accordingly, we encouraged the community to reflect on how modeling principles and frameworks can advance sustainability while continuing to strengthen the theoretical and practical foundations of the field.

The papers selected for this conference reflect this dual commitment. Sustainability threads through the program in many forms: ontologies for industrial energy efficiency and greenhouse-gas accounting, sustainability-aware process mining and variant analysis, decision models for energy-efficient edge and cloud AI deployment, socio-ecological platforms for ecological regeneration, and frameworks that guard against the conflation of sustainability commitments. At the same time, ER 2026 embraced the enduring concerns of the discipline. A strong body of work engages the relationship between conceptual modeling and large language models, treating schemas, ontologies, and conceptual structure as active drivers of reliable knowledge-graph construction, domain modeling, and process-model generation, while confronting hallucination, traceability, and the governance of agentic AI. Further contributions advance data and schema modeling across relational, document, and multi-model settings; goal-oriented and requirements engineering, including a notable cluster on robotics and kinematic requirements; trustworthy digital twins; and the modeling of trust, governance, privacy, and regulatory compliance across jurisdictions. Reflecting the conference's breadth, the program also welcomed posters and demonstrations, bridging theory and application.

ER 2026 marked the reintroduction of short papers, which were solicited at submission time. ER 2026 received 113 full and short paper submissions for the main conference track, of which 104 proceeded to review following desk rejection of incomplete or out-of-scope papers by the program co-chairs. Following the conference's tradition of rigorous evaluation, each of these submissions underwent a double-blind review process in which it was independently assessed by three Program Committee members. This was followed by a discussion phase, where needed, moderated by senior PC members who prepared meta-reviews summarizing the recommendations to the authors. The program co-chairs reviewed all recommendations and made the final decisions. Papers were selected on the basis of their novelty and their contribution to advancing the conceptual modeling state of the art. Ultimately, 20 full-paper submissions were accepted, yielding an acceptance rate of 19.2%. Additionally, 13 short papers were accepted, for a total of 33 accepted papers across both categories.

The main conference included ten traditional research paper (both regular and short paper) sessions, Keynotes, Tutorials, Panels, Posters&Demos, a Doctoral Symposium, and two Workshops. The conference also recognized Terry Halpin as recipient of the 2026 ER Peter Chen Award, in recognition of his significant contributions to conceptual modeling. Terry delivered an invited keynote presentation entitled "Object-Role Modelling: An Historical Overview." The second keynote presentation was given by Michael Gruninger, titled "The COLORE Hypothesis." Additionally, a special session marking 50 years since the publication of the ER model was organized to celebrate the impact of the paper that provided the impetus for the ER conference.

On behalf of our community, we extend our gratitude to our keynote speakers for sharing their insights into the evolution of conceptual modeling research and its future.

We thank the authors for submitting their work to ER 2026, the Program Committee and Senior Program Committee members for their dedication and expertise in writing and handling the reviews, and the Organizing Committee for their tireless efforts to bring ER 2026 to life.

October 2026

Anna Bernasconi
Marta Indulska
Sudha Ram
Joerg Evermann
Jeffrey Parsons

Organization

General Chairs

Joerg Evermann	Memorial University of Newfoundland, Canada
Jeffrey Parsons	Memorial University of Newfoundland, Canada

Program Chairs

Anna Bernasconi	Politecnico di Milano, Italy
Marta Indulska	University of Queensland, Australia
Sudha Ram	University of Arizona, USA

Posters and Demos Chairs

Roman Lukyanenko	University of Virginia, USA
Anna Wiedemann	Bern University of Applied Sciences, Switzerland

Tutorial Chairs

Steve Liddle	Brigham Young University, USA
Isabelle Wattiau	ESSEC Business School, France

Panel Chairs

Oscar Pastor	Universitat Politècnica de València, Spain
Veda Storey	Georgia State University, USA

Doctoral Consortium Chairs

Sotirios Liaskos	York University, Canada
Jolita Ralyté	University of Geneva, Switzerland

Workshop Chairs

Peter Fettke	Saarland University and German Research Center for Artificial Intelligence (DFKI), Germany
Iris Reinhartz-Berger	University of Haifa, Israel

CEUR Proceedings Chair

César Bernabé	University of Illinois Urbana-Champaign, USA

Publicity Chair

Shawn Ogunseye	Bentley University, USA

Proceedings Chairs

Matteo Mantovani	University of Verona, Italy
Alberto García S.	Universitat Politècnica de València, Spain

Senior Program Committee

João Paulo Almeida	Federal University of Espírito Santo, Brazil
Paolo Atzeni	Università Roma Tre, Italy
José Borbinha	INESC-ID, IST, Universidade de Lisboa, Portugal
Dominik Bork	TU Wien, Austria
Silvana Castano	University of Milan, Italy
Stefano Ceri	Politecnico di Milano, Italy
Isabelle Comyn-Wattiau	ESSEC Business School, France
Xavier Franch	Universitat Politècnica de Catalunya, Spain
Ulrich Frank	Universität Duisburg-Essen, Germany
Nicola Guarino	ISTC-CNR, Italy
Giancarlo Guizzardi	University of Twente, The Netherlands
Jennifer Horkoff	University of Gothenburg and Chalmers University of Technology, Sweden
Manfred Jeusfeld	University of Skövde, Sweden
Paul Johannesson	Royal Institute of Technology, Sweden
Kamal Karlapalem	IIIT Hyderabad, India
Stephen W. Liddle	Brigham Young University, USA

Sebastian Link	University of Auckland, New Zealand
Wolfgang Maass	Saarland University, Germany
Heinrich C. Mayr	Alpen-Adria-Universität Klagenfurt, Austria
José Palazzo Moreira de Oliveira	Federal University of Rio Grande do Sul, Brazil
Oscar Pastor	Universidad Politécnica de Valencia, Spain
Henderik A. Proper	TU Wien, Austria
Jolita Ralyté	University of Geneva, Switzerland
Hajo A. Reijers	Utrecht University, The Netherlands
Iris Reinhartz-Berger	University of Haifa, Israel
Stefanie Rinderle-Ma	Technical University of Munich, Germany
Shazia Sadiq	University of Queensland, Australia
Pnina Soffer	University of Haifa, Israel
Veda C. Storey	Georgia State University, USA
Stefan Strecker	University of Hagen, Germany
Bernhard Thalheim	University of Kiel, Germany
Juan Trujillo	University of Alicante, Spain
Barbara Weber	University of St. Gallen, Switzerland
Carson Woo	University of British Columbia, Canada
Eric Yu	University of Toronto, Canada
Jelena Zdravkovic	Stockholm University, Sweden

Program Committee

Amine Abbad-Andaloussi	University of St. Gallen, Switzerland
João Araújo	Universidade NOVA de Lisboa, Portugal
David Aveiro	Madeira University, Portugal
Wolf-Tilo Balke	TU Braunschweig, Germany
Monalessa Barcellos	Federal University of Espírito Santo, Brazil
César Bernabé	University of Illinois Urbana-Champaign, USA
Devis Bianchini	University of Brescia, Italy
Sandro Bimonte	INRAE, France
Luiz Olavo Bonino da Silva Santos	University of Twente, The Netherlands
Shawn Bowers	Gonzaga University, USA
Robert Buchmann	Babeş-Bolyai University of Cluj Napoca, Romania
Jordi Cabot	Luxembourg Institute of Science and Technology, Luxembourg
Diego Calvanese	Free University of Bozen-Bolzano, Italy
Cinzia Cappiello	Politecnico di Milano, Italy
Arturo Castellanos	William & Mary School of Business, USA

Samira Cherfi	CEDRIC - Conservatoire National des Arts et Métiers, France
Monica Chiarini Tremblay	William & Mary School of Business, USA
Suphamit Chittayasothorn	King Mongkut's Institute of Technology Ladkrabang, Thailand
Fabiano Dalpiaz	Utrecht University, The Netherlands
Sergio de Cesare	University of Westminster, UK
Johann Eder	Alpen-Adria-Universität Klagenfurt, Austria
Vadim Ermolayev	Ukrainian Catholic University, Ukraine
Rik Eshuis	Eindhoven University of Technology, The Netherlands
Luís Ferreira Pires	University of Twente, The Netherlands
Peter Fettke	German Research Center for Artificial Intelligence (DFKI) and Saarland University, Germany
Hans-Georg Fill	University of Fribourg, Switzerland
Marco Franceschetti	University of St. Gallen, Switzerland
Enrico Franconi	Free University of Bozen-Bolzano, Italy
Mattia Fumagalli	Free University of Bozen-Bolzano, Italy
Frederik Gailly	Ghent University, Belgium
Philippe Giabbanelli	Old Dominion University, USA
Asif Gill	University of Technology Sydney, Australia
Cesar Gonzalez-Perez	Incipit CSIC, Spain
Jaap Gordijn	Vrije Universiteit Amsterdam, The Netherlands
Guido Governatori	Central Queensland University, Australia
Georg Grossmann	Adelaide University, Australia
Sergio Guerreiro	INESC-ID/Instituto Superior Técnico, Portugal
Simon Hacks	Stockholm University, Sweden
Hyoil Han	Illinois State University, USA
Felix Härer	University of Applied Sciences and Arts Northwestern Switzerland, Switzerland
Sven Hartmann	Clausthal University of Technology, Germany
Martin Henkel	Stockholm University, Sweden
Araz Jabbari	Université Laval, Canada
Marite Kirikova	Riga Technical University, Latvia
Stefan Klikovits	Johannes Kepler University Linz, Austria
Julius Köpke	Alpen-Adria-Universität Klagenfurt, Austria
Agnes Koschmider	University of Bayreuth, Germany
Thomas Kuehne	Victoria University of Wellington, New Zealand
Alberto Laender	Universidade Federal de Minas Gerais, Brazil
Ana León Palacio	Universitat Politècnica de València, Spain
Tong Li	Beijing University of Technology, China

Sotirios Liaskos	York University, Canada
Sergio Lifschitz	Pontifícia Universidade Católica do Rio de Janeiro, Brazil
Jim Logan	Ontogenesis Solutions, LLC, USA
Hugo A. López	Technical University of Denmark, Denmark
Claudenir M. Fonseca	University of Twente, The Netherlands
Hui Ma	Victoria University of Wellington, New Zealand
Maria Luiza Machado Campos	Federal University of Rio de Janeiro, Brazil
Beatriz Marin	Universitat Politècnica de València, Spain
Davide Martinenghi	Politecnico di Milano, Italy
Wolfgang Mayer	Adelaide University, Australia
Massimo Mecella	Sapienza Università di Roma, Italy
Judith Michael	University of Regensburg, Germany
Kafui Monu	University of Northern British Columbia, Canada
Regina Motz	Universidad de la República, Uruguay
Haralambos Mouratidis	University of Essex, UK
Julio Cesar Nardi	Federal Institute of Espírito Santo, Brazil
Bernd Neumayr	Johannes Kepler University Linz, Austria
Selmin Nurcan	Université Paris 1 Panthéon - Sorbonne, France
Leo Obrst	MITRE, USA
Andreas L. Opdahl	University of Bergen, Norway
Xavier Oriol	Universitat Politècnica de Catalunya, Spain
Elda Paja	IT University of Copenhagen, Denmark
José M Parente de Oliveira	Instituto Tecnológico de Aeronáutica, Brazil
Robert Pergl	Czech Technical University in Prague, Czechia
Barbara Pernici	Politecnico di Milano, Italy
Geert Poels	Ghent University, Belgium
Fabio Porto	National Laboratory of Scientific Computation, Brazil
Tiago Prince Sales	University of Twente, The Netherlands
Luise Pufahl	TU Munich, Germany
Christoph Quix	Hochschule Niederrhein University of Applied Sciences, Germany
João Luiz Rebelo Moreira	University of Twente, The Netherlands
Manfred Reichert	University of Ulm, Germany
Fabrício Henrique Rodigues	University at Buffalo, USA
Ben Roelens	Open Universiteit, The Netherlands, Ghent University, Belgium
Michael Rosemann	Queensland University of Technology, Australia
Kristina Rosenthal	Hochschule Niederrhein University of Applied Sciences, Germany
Marcela Ruiz	Zurich University of Applied Sciences, Switzerland

Bernhard Rumpe	RWTH Aachen University, Germany
Binny Samuel	University of Cincinnati, USA
Maribel Yasmina Santos	University of Minho, Portugal
Estefanía Serral	KU Leuven, Belgium
Tijs Slaats	University of Copenhagen, Denmark
Monique Snoeck	KU Leuven, Belgium
Vitor E. Silva Souza	Federal University of Espírito Santo, Brazil
Markus Stumptner	University of South Australia, Australia
Arnon Sturm	Ben-Gurion University of the Negev, Israel
Angelo Susi	Fondazione Bruno Kessler, Italy
Valentina Tamma	University of Liverpool, UK
Victoria Torres	Universitat Politècnica de València, Spain
Panos Vassiliadis	University of Ioannina, Greece
Mathias Weske	HPI, University of Potsdam, Germany
Manuel Wimmer	Johannes Kepler University Linz, Austria
Karolin Winter	Eindhoven University of Technology, The Netherlands
Robert Wrembel	Poznań University of Technology, Poland
Apostolos Zarras	University of Ioannina, Greece

Steering Committee

Chair

Giancarlo Guizzardi — University of Twente, The Netherlands

Vice Chair

Jolita Ralyté — University of Geneva, Switzerland

Treasurer

Stephen W. Liddle — Brigham Young University, USA

Emeritus

Peter P. Chen

Steering Committee Members

João Paulo A. Almeida
Ladjel Bellatreche
Dominik Bork
Peter P. Chen
Isabelle Comyn-Wattiau
Ulrich Frank
Giancarlo Guizzardi
Jennifer Horkoff
Kamal Karlapalem
Alberto Laender
Stephen W. Liddle
Sebastian Link
Roman Lukyanenko
Hui Ma
Wolfgang Maass
Jeffrey Parsons
Oscar Pastor
Jolita Ralyté
Sudha Ram
Shazia Sadiq
Il-Yeol Song
Veda Storey
Juan Carlos Trujillo
Carson Woo
Eric Yu

Additional Reviewers

Kerstin Andree
Daniel Borcard
Marcos Catanho
Edward Hermann Haeusler
Karamjit Kaur
Simone Kriglstein
Arvid Lepsien
Julian Neuberger
Matt Selway
Henrik Thillmann
Konstantinos Varvoutas
Yorck Zisgen
Antonio Basilio de Miranda
Sedat Cakici
Arsalan Ghasemi
Paul Hufnagel
Samira Khraiwesh
Tijmen Kuijpers
Patrik Thomas Michalski
Anjo Seidel
Jan Stanek
Isadora Valle Sousa
António Vieira

Keynote Summary

Object-Role Modelling: An Historical Overview

Terry Halpin

Independent Researcher
t.halpin@live.com

Object-Role Modelling (ORM) is a fact-oriented approach for designing information models at the conceptual level, using terms easily understood by non-technical users. ORM includes procedures for mapping an ORM model to various logical or physical data models (e.g. relational, object-oriented, logic-programming, ontological, XML), and for reverse engineering some of these models to an ORM conceptual model. In ORM, a fact is an atomic proposition taken to be true by the user community. An atomic fact can't be split into simpler facts with the same object types without information loss. A fact is either existential (asserting an individual object's existence) or elementary (asserting that an object has property or that one or more objects participate in a relationship). Unlike Entity-Relationship (ER) modelling and the Unified Modeling Language (UML), fact-oriented modelling is attribute-free: elementary facts are expressed simply in terms of objects playing roles in a unary or longer relationship. For modelling information, ORM's graphical notation for visualizing the model is arguably more expressive than other notations, and it can be automatically verbalized in natural language. This presentation briefly outlines the origin and development of ORM, providing coverage of its capabilities using both examples and tool demonstrations. Finally, some possible modifications to ORM are considered.

The COLORE Hypothesis

Michael Gruninger

University of Toronto
michael.gruninger@utoronto.ca

The specification of ontologies for commonsense concepts and relationships has been a longstanding goal of conceptual modelling and knowledge representation. In both of these cases, however, the design of ontologies has been slow and very labour-intensive, and the verification of ontologies (determining whether the proposed axioms are correct with respect to the intended semantics of the concepts) remains a key challenge. Extending Bourbaki's original notion of structures meres (mother structures}, the COLORE Hypothesis posits that all first-order theories currently used in applied ontology and conceptual modelling are equivalent to combinations of the mathematical theories in the Common Logic Ontology Repository (COLORE). Ontology design and verification are thereby reduced to the problem of finding the set of mathematical theories that are the best match to the intended semantics of concepts. In this talk we will explore applications of this approach to autoformalization, ontology learning, and the identification of ontological bias in machine learning datasets.

Contents

Conceptual Modeling for Data-Intensive and Regulated Domains

Fighting the Omic Data Chaos: A Conceptual Model for the Correct Understanding and Management of Multi-omics Data

Marcos Carrasco(✉), Oscar Pastor, Ana León, and Juan Carlos Casamayor

PROS Group, Valencian Research Institute (VRAIN), Universitat Politècnica de València, Valencia, Spain
{mcarsac,aleon}@vrain.upv.es, {opastor,jcarlos}@dsic.upv.es

Abstract. The rapid growth of omics resources has led to a highly fragmented and heterogeneous landscape, giving rise to what we refer to as "genomic chaos", in which data, information, and knowledge are represented at different levels of abstraction across genomic, transcriptomic, proteomic, reaction, and pathway domains. This heterogeneity, together with the lack of consistent cross-domain standardisation, complicates semantic interoperability, data integration, and the development of bioinformatics systems. In this context, we present the MOSAIC model (Multi-Omics Structured and Integrated Conceptual model), an extensible conceptual and logical reference model that structures core omics entities, their descriptions, and their relationships into an information architecture. The model is designed to capture how variants, genes, transcripts, proteins, diseases, reactions, pathways, functional roles, and chemical context relate across omics domains, providing a coherent basis for representing domain knowledge in a structured way. Rather than defining a specific physical implementation, the model establishes a reusable logical foundation for aligning and integrating knowledge from complementary domain resources, standards, and future bioinformatics applications. By addressing the "genomic chaos" generated by inconsistent representations and fragmented repositories, this work proposes a versioned and extensible model for organising multi-omics knowledge, whose scope can evolve as curated resources and scientific evidence introduce relevant biological distinctions.

Keywords: Conceptual modelling · Multi-omics data standardisation and integration · Genomics information systems · Knowledge representation

1 Introduction

The rapid growth of omics research has intensified a persistent information problem: equivalent biological entities and processes are represented using different schemas, identifiers, abstraction levels, and semantic assumptions across

© The Author(s), under exclusive license to Springer Nature Switzerland AG 2027
A. Bernasconi et al. (Eds.): ER 2026, LNCS 17081, pp. 3–18, 2027.
https://doi.org/10.1007/978-3-032-40795-5_1

genomic, transcriptomic, proteomic, pathway, and clinical resources. Consequently, biological knowledge becomes fragmented across heterogeneous repositories, hindering semantic interoperability, data integration, and consistent biological interpretation.

Conceptual modelling provides an explicit representation of domain semantics and relationships, enabling biological knowledge to be organised in a structured and reusable manner [34,43]. Although resources such as HGVS, ClinVar, Gene Ontology, Reactome, UniProt, and Mondo have substantially improved consistency within specific domains [12,17,18,26,39,41], interoperability across omics layers remains a structural challenge.

To address this problem, we propose MOSAIC, an extensible conceptual and logical model for multi-omics knowledge representation. Rather than defining a new ontology or a specific implementation, MOSAIC provides a reusable conceptual integration layer that organises heterogeneous biological entities and explicitly represents the semantic relationships connecting them across omics domains. The model structures knowledge into interconnected views covering variation, genomics, transcriptomics, proteomics, chemistry, reactions, pathways, clinical interpretation, and biological context, providing a coherent semantic backbone for cross-domain biological knowledge [3,34]. MOSAIC complements existing ontologies, standards, pathway resources, and knowledge graphs by making their relationships explicit within a unified conceptual organisation.

The proposed model builds upon previous conceptual modelling efforts in genomics and precision medicine [1,2,16,27,28,34], extending them toward a broader multi-omics perspective. Unlike previous genome-centred conceptual models, MOSAIC explicitly integrates molecular entities, biological processes, and clinical interpretation within a single extensible framework. Its relationship with complementary semantic resources and integration approaches is discussed in Sect. 3.4.

The main contributions of this paper are the following:

- An extensible multi-view conceptual and logical model for organising multi-omics knowledge.
- A semantic integration framework that explicitly represents cross-domain biological relationships while preserving the complementary roles of existing resources.
- A reusable conceptual foundation for future bioinformatics systems, including integration pipelines, visualization platforms, and knowledge-driven data ingestion tools.
- A systematic comparative positioning of MOSAIC with respect to complementary standards and knowledge-graph approaches (Sect. 3.4).

The remainder of this paper is organised as follows. Section 2 presents the problem of semantic fragmentation in multi-omics environments. Section 3 reviews related work and existing semantic resources. Section 4 presents the proposed conceptual model and its views. Section 5 discusses validation and practical applicability. Finally, Sect. 6 concludes the paper and outlines future work.

2 The Problem: Semantic Fragmentation in Multi-omics

The promise of multi-omics is to provide a more complete understanding of biological systems by integrating information across multiple molecular layers. In practice, however, this integration remains challenging due to the heterogeneity of omics technologies, datasets, formats, and biological abstraction levels. Rather than a simple data integration problem, multi-omics requires coordinating heterogeneous semantic representations across domains [4].

This challenge is fundamentally semantic. Biological entities and processes are represented differently across repositories, standards, and annotation systems, hindering interoperability and consistent interpretation. In biomedical environments, semantic interoperability requires conceptual structures capable of preserving the meaning and relationships of biological entities across heterogeneous resources [3,19,34,43].

The problem is particularly evident in genomics, where knowledge evolves continuously and is distributed across numerous specialised repositories [9,16]. Fragmented data sources may omit relevant variants, lose concordance information, or produce incomplete interpretations [9]. Although standardisation efforts and curated resources have substantially improved consistency within individual domains (Sect. 3.2), they remain largely domain-specific and do not provide a unified conceptual organisation spanning multiple omics abstraction levels.

Consequently, variants, transcripts, proteins, reactions, pathways, and phenotypes are typically represented within separate semantic layers, while the relationships connecting them are only partially modelled or delegated to repository-specific integration mechanisms. The absence of a coherent conceptual backbone limits semantic interoperability, increases maintenance complexity, and hinders consistent biological interpretation across omics domains. This is the core problem addressed by MOSAIC.

3 Related Work and State of the Art

3.1 Conceptual Modelling in Genomics

Conceptual modelling has progressively been applied to genomics and precision medicine to improve data organisation, interpretation, and interoperability. Previous work introduced conceptual schemas for genome data management and subsequently evolved toward smart genomic information systems, species-independent schemas, modular genomic representations, and conceptual-model-driven integration platforms [1,2,15,16,27,28,34,36]. Practical systems such as VarSearch further demonstrated the applicability of these models to diagnostic and annotation workflows [22,37].

Despite these advances, existing proposals remain primarily genome-centred and do not provide a unified conceptual representation spanning transcriptomic, proteomic, chemical, reaction, pathway, and clinical domains.

3.2 Standards, Resources, and Ontological Foundations

Several biological standards and curated resources provide semantic foundations for individual omics domains, including variant nomenclature (HGVS), variant interpretation (ClinVar and ClinGen), functional annotation (Gene Ontology), pathways and reactions (Reactome), protein knowledge (UniProt), and disease terminology (Mondo) [12, 17, 18, 26, 39, 41]. Although fundamental to modern bioinformatics, these resources remain domain-specific and operate at different semantic scopes and abstraction levels, leaving cross-omics conceptual integration unresolved.

3.3 Multi-omics Integration and Semantic Interoperability

Research on multi-omics integration consistently identifies heterogeneity and semantic interoperability as major challenges [4]. Existing approaches include multi-layer biological networks [46], knowledge graphs [33], ontology mapping techniques [19], and FAIR-oriented data stewardship methodologies [43]. These approaches improve integration and reuse across biological datasets, but they often rely on implicit conceptual assumptions or repository-specific integration logic [9].

3.4 Positioning with Respect to Complementary Artefacts

The approaches reviewed above address complementary aspects of multi-omics interoperability rather than competing solutions to the same problem. Table 1 positions MOSAIC with respect to representative semantic artefacts, including BioPAX [11], Reactome [18], the Monarch Knowledge Graph [35], and GA4GH specifications [23, 42].

Table 1 shows that the reviewed approaches provide valuable but complementary artefacts: exchange specifications, curated knowledge bases, and knowledge graphs. The principal distinction of MOSAIC is therefore its scope. It is designed as a cross-domain conceptual backbone bringing together the main genomic, transcriptomic, proteomic, chemical, reaction, pathway, clinical, and phenotypic perspectives, while preserving the specialised strengths of initiatives focused on a particular area or use case. These initiatives provide depth and interoperability within their intended scope, and MOSAIC complements them by providing a shared structure for relating their representations across domains. The next section presents its structure (Figure,1).

4 The MOSAIC Model: Multi-omics Structured and Integrated Conceptual Model

To address the semantic fragmentation discussed in previous sections, we propose MOSAIC, a multi-view conceptual model for representing multi-omics knowledge across interconnected biological domains. Rather than providing a

Table 1. Positioning MOSAIC with respect to complementary semantic artefacts.

Approach	Type and primary scope	Relationship to MOSAIC
BioPAX	OWL ontology and exchange format for biological pathways, molecular interactions, and reactions.	Provides pathway-level semantic structures that MOSAIC is intended to relate to variation, clinical, and other omics perspectives.
Reactome	Curated pathway knowledgebase and data model for physical entities, reactions, pathways, compartments, and molecular modifications.	Provides domain-specific modelling foundations for the MOSAIC Chemical, Reaction, Reaction Participant, and Pathway views.
Monarch Knowledge Graph	Semantic knowledge graph integrating associations among genes, variants, diseases, phenotypes, and related biomedical entities.	Supports genotype–phenotype-oriented knowledge integration; MOSAIC makes the conceptual bridges to transcriptomic, proteomic, chemical, reaction, and pathway layers explicit.
GA4GH VRS and Phenopackets	Computable specifications for the exchange of molecular variation and phenotypic-clinical case information.	Define interoperable representations for selected data domains; MOSAIC specifies their conceptual connections with downstream molecular and functional knowledge.

new ontology or implementation, MOSAIC organises and relates the semantic representations used by heterogeneous omics resources while preserving their underlying biological meaning.

The model comprises interconnected views covering variation, genomics, transcriptomics, proteomics, chemistry, pathways, clinical interpretation, and biological context. Together, these views provide a unified conceptual backbone linking biological entities and relationships across multiple omics abstraction levels. Due to space constraints, detailed diagrams are provided only for the most representative views, while the complete conceptual model is available as an accompanying Zenodo research artefact [6].

For a complete description of the classes, attributes, relationships, and examples of instantiation beyond the level of detail provided by the figures and accompanying text, readers are referred to the ontology and class-definition research artefact deposited in Zenodo [7].

The following subsections summarise the presented views and their role within the overall model.

4.1 Variation and Variation Effect Views

The Variation View models genomic alterations together with their nomenclature, classification, population context, and semantic references (Fig. 2).

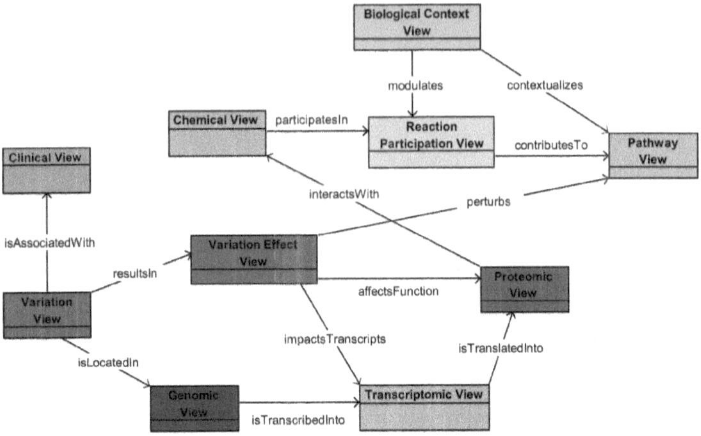

Fig. 1. High-level overview of the proposed multi-view conceptual model for multi-omics integration.

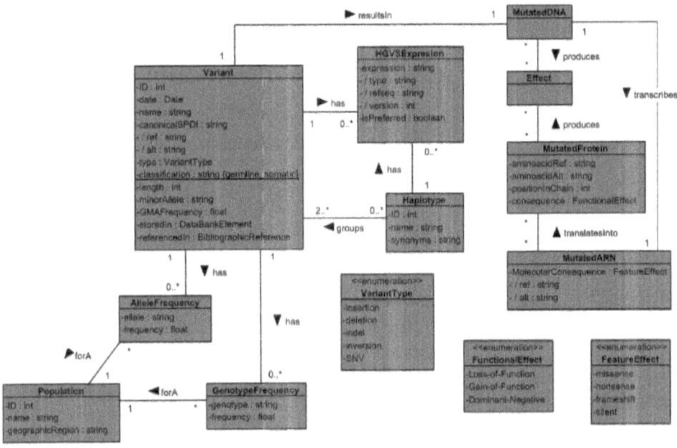

Fig. 2. Detailed conceptual representation of the Variation and Variation Effect views.

The central entity is *Variant*, associated with HGVS expressions, haplotypes, population frequencies, genomic locations, and controlled vocabularies including HGVS, Sequence Ontology, ClinVar, and Ensembl VEP [13,21,26,29].

The Variation Effect View captures the propagation of genomic alterations across molecular layers by linking variants to altered DNA, RNA, and protein entities and their corresponding reference sequences. Consequences such as missense, nonsense, frameshift, splice-related, gain-of-function, and loss-of-function effects are explicitly represented, enabling the model to describe the transition from genomic variation to downstream molecular and functional alterations [6,13,26].

4.2 Clinical and Phenotypic View

The Clinical and Phenotypic View links genomic variation with clinical interpretation and phenotype representation. It is inspired by resources such as ClinVar, ClinGen, and Mondo [26,41].

Clinical interpretation is represented through *Significance*, which models pathogenicity, oncogenicity, and interpretation certainty associated with variants or haplotypes according to ACMG/AMP guidelines [38]. Interpretations are linked to *Submission* entities that preserve evidence provenance and review metadata.

Clinical conditions are organised through the abstract entity *ClinicalCondition*, specialised into *Disease* and *Phenotype*. This abstraction allows significance assessments to be associated with either disease- or phenotype-level findings, following ClinVar's interpretation model. Diseases additionally record inheritance patterns and are related to one or more phenotypes through *hasPhenotype*, consistent with HPO and the Biolink Model [25,40]. References to external ontologies, including Mondo, are also supported [6,41].

4.3 Genomic View

The Genomic View represents the structural and positional organisation of genomic knowledge (Fig. 3).

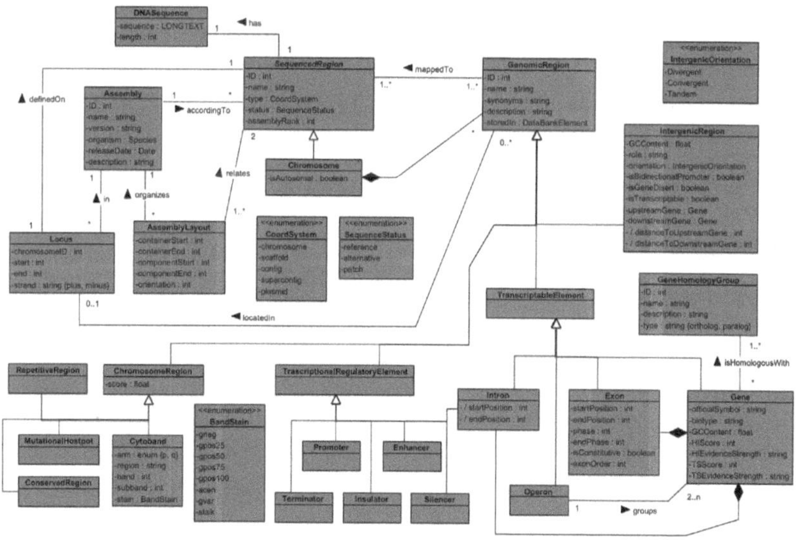

Fig. 3. Detailed conceptual representation of the Genomic view.

The view is organised around three core entities: *SequencedRegion*, *GenomicRegion*, and *DNASequence*, separating assembly-aware genomic structures, functional genomic entities, and nucleotide sequences [8,10]. *SequencedRegion* is associated with a specific *Assembly*, whereas *GenomicRegion* is linked to one or more *Locus* entities, supporting alternative assemblies and coordinate systems.

GenomicRegion specialises into *TranscriptableElement*, *TranscriptionalRegulatoryElement*, and *ChromosomeRegion* [30]. *TranscriptableElement* is further specialised into *Gene*, which connects genomic variation through *Locus* and is related to *Disease* via the *causes* relationship. This organisation supports the representation of both genetic heterogeneity and pleiotropy, consistent with the Biolink Model [6,40].

4.4 Transcriptomic View

The Transcriptomic View models transcript organisation and processing as the intermediate layer between genomic structure and protein production. The view follows transcript-centric representations used by resources such as GENCODE and Ensembl [10,14].

The central entity is *Transcript*, specialised into *PrimaryTranscript* and *MatureTranscript*. Primary transcripts originate from genes or operons and comprise exon and intron structures, whereas mature transcripts are classified into coding (*mRNA*) and non-coding (*ncRNA*) forms. Coding transcripts are further organised into *5'UTR*, *CDS*, and *3'UTR* regions. The view also includes *RNASequence* as the sequence-level representation of transcript entities. The existing model includes *ncRNA* as a concept that is connected to *Gene* through a *regulates* association; its subclasses and more detailed semantics have not yet been investigated and will be refined as the analysis of curated resources and scientific literature progresses.

Altered RNA products generated in the Variation Effect View are linked to this layer, enabling transcript-level consequences of genomic variation to be represented explicitly [6].

4.5 Proteomic View

The Proteomic View models proteins from sequence, structural, and functional perspectives, linking transcript-derived products with molecular functions and downstream biological processes. The view is inspired by protein-centred resources such as UniProt and InterPro [5,39].

The central entity is *ProteinSequence*, representing amino acid sequences translated from coding transcripts. Protein diversity is modelled through *SequenceVariation*, which links reference and alternative protein sequences derived from genomic or transcriptomic variation.

ProteinSequence gives rise to *Protein* entities annotated through *ProteinFeature*, including sequence features, functional sites, post-translational modifications, proteolytic processing regions, and structural regions. Structural organisation is further represented by *StructuralRegion*, covering secondary structures, supersecondary structures, and domains, while tertiary and quaternary structures are modelled as higher-order protein assemblies [5]. The view also captures functional interaction sites and connects proteins with the Chemical and Pathway views [6].

4.6 Chemical View

The Chemical View represents molecular compounds, their structural organisation, biological roles, and relationships with genomic, transcriptomic, proteomic, and pathway entities. The view is inspired by resources such as ChEBI, KEGG, and DrugBank [20,24,44].

Chemical compounds are modelled as *ChemicalEntity* instances connected through *ChemicalRelation* and *Component* relationships, allowing semantic, compositional, and assembly associations to be represented. The model distinguishes monomeric and polymeric molecules, including nucleic acids, peptides, saccharides, and proteins.

Biological functions are represented through *ChemicalRole*, linking compounds with sequence-derived products, reactions, and pathways across the model [6].

4.7 Pathway and Reaction View

The Pathway and Reaction View models biological processes as interconnected molecular events linking chemical entities, reactions, and higher-level pathways. The view is inspired by pathway-oriented resources such as Reactome, KEGG Pathways, and Rhea [18,24,31].

Biological processes are modelled through the abstract entity *Event*, which supports ordered biological flows via recursive predecessor-successor relationships and distinguishes between normal and altered processes.

The model specialises *Event* into *Reaction*, *Module*, and *Pathway*, representing biochemical transformations, functional groups of reactions, and higher-level biological processes, respectively [24,31]. Hierarchical pathway organisation and relationships between biologically connected pathways are explicitly represented.

Reactions are linked to the Chemical View through participating *ChemicalEntity* instances, while participant semantics and roles are defined separately in the Reaction Participant View (Sect. 4.8) [6].

4.8 Reaction Participant View

The Reaction Participant View models the functional participation of molecular entities in biochemical reactions, including catalysis, regulation, and interaction kinetics (Fig. 4). The view is inspired by biochemical resources such as Reactome, Rhea, and SABIO-RK [18,31,45].

Molecular participation is represented through the association class *ReactionRole*, linking *ChemicalEntity* and *Reaction*. The model distinguishes five participant categories: *Reactant*, *Product*, *Regulator*, *Catalyst*, and *Cofactor*. Regulatory roles specialise into activation and inhibition mechanisms, while catalytic interactions may be associated with experimentally derived kinetic parameters.

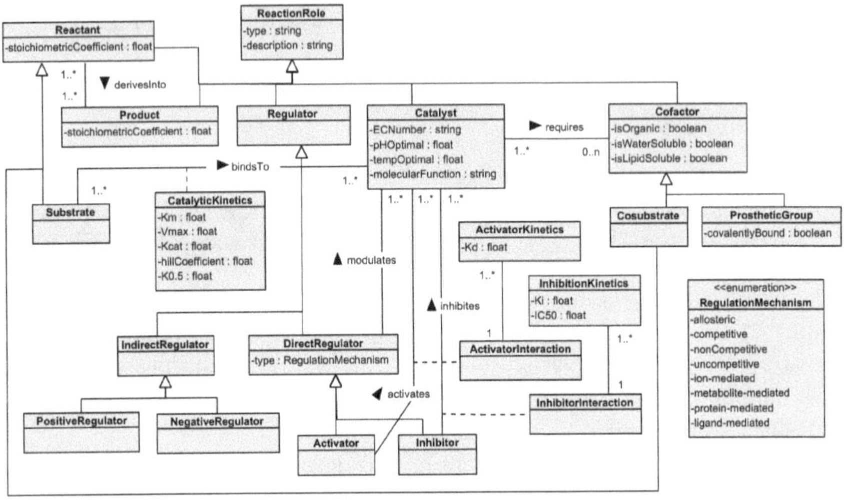

Fig. 4. Detailed conceptual representation of the Reaction Participant view.

The *Cofactor* hierarchy further represents auxiliary catalytic molecules, including cosubstrates and prosthetic groups. By separating participant semantics from reaction topology, the model distinguishes biochemical interaction behaviour from higher-level pathway organisation [6].

4.9 Biological Context View

The Biological Context View models the anatomical, cellular, and environmental context in which biological entities and events occur.

Biological context is organised around *Location*, specialised into *System*, *Organ*, *Tissue*, *Cell*, and *CellularComponent*. Events and molecular entities may be associated with one or more locations, enabling biological processes to be contextualised across multiple biological scales.

Relationships between locations are represented through *LocationRelator*, while protein localization within cellular components complements the Proteomic View.

EnvironmentConditions represents physicochemical and physiological conditions associated with biological contexts and is reused in the Reaction Participant View to contextualise molecular interactions and experimentally derived kinetic parameters [6].

5 Validation and Practical Applicability

Because the proposed contribution is a conceptual model, its validation focuses on semantic consistency and practical applicability rather than predictive performance. The model aligns with widely adopted omics standards and resources while providing a unified conceptual structure for representing relationships that are typically fragmented across heterogeneous databases.

Figure 5 presents an example instantiation of the Variation and Variation Effect views using a disease-associated ALK variant linked to hereditary neuroblastoma susceptibility. This example demonstrates how genomic variation and its transcriptomic and proteomic consequences are represented within the conceptual model.

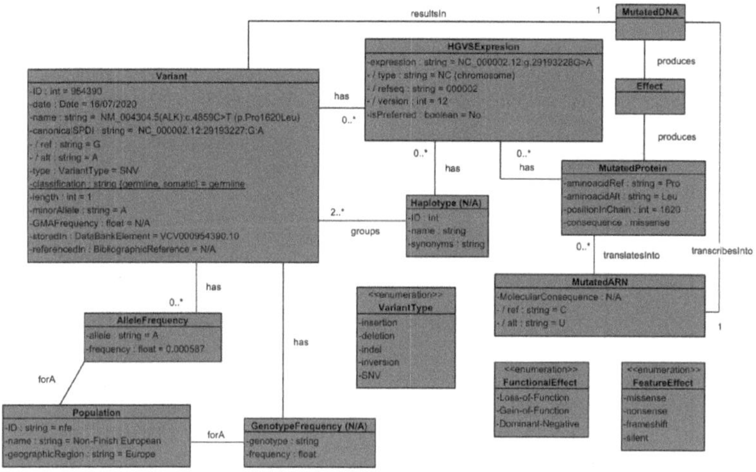

Fig. 5. Example instantiation of the Variation and Variation Effect views for a Neuroblastoma-associated variant.

Separately, Table 2 presents an end-to-end cross-view instantiation using an ALK germline variant. It traces the molecular alteration across the remaining MOSAIC views, from molecular consequences to pathway-level and clinical consequences, and supports complex cross-omics competency questions, such as: (i) through which gene, protein, and reaction does a germline variant's effect propagate to a biological pathway? (ii) which chemical entities participate in that reaction, and in what functional role? and (iii) which phenotypic manifestations are associated with the disease caused by a given gene?

Table 2 can be read as a single causal narrative rather than a list of isolated facts. A germline single-nucleotide variant in the *Gene ALK*, located on the minus strand of chromosome 2, substitutes adenine for guanine at coding position 3824 of its canonical transcript (RefSeq `NM_004304.5`). Through the *RNASequence* entity, which records structural information such as transcript length and sequence, this nucleotide substitution (*MutatedRNA*) is propagated to a missense protein alteration (*MutatedProtein*) replacing Arg1275 by Gln in the ALK receptor tyrosine kinase (UniProt Q9UM73-1). Because the substitution lies within the intracellular tyrosine kinase *Domain* (residues 1116–1392), it is represented as a constitutive Gain-of-Function effect.

Table 2. Cross-domain instantiation of MOSAIC views using an ALK germline variant associated with hereditary neuroblastoma susceptibility (R1275Q).

View	MOSAIC class	Instantiated element and representative attributes
Variation	*Variant*	**name**: NM_004304.5(ALK):c.3824G>A (p.Arg1275Gln); **type**: SNV; **classification**: germline; **canonicalSPDI**: NC_000002.12:29209797:C:T; **minorAllele**: A; **storedIn**: ClinVar VCV000018083.22, dbSNP rs113994087; **referencedIn**: PMID 18724359
Genomic	*Gene*	**officialSymbol**: ALK; **name**: ALK receptor tyrosine kinase; **synonyms**: CD246, NBLST3, ALK1; **biotype**: protein_coding; **GCContent**: 47.1; **storedIn**: HGNC:427, Ensembl:ENSG00000171094, NCBI_Gene:238
Genomic	*Locus*	**chromosomeID**: 2; **start**: 29,192,774; **end**: 29,921,586; **strand**: minus
Transcriptomic	*MessengerRNA*	**name**: ALK-201; **biotype**: protein_coding; **isCanonicalTranslation**: true; **description**: canonical protein-coding transcript for ALK; **storedIn**: RefSeq:NM_004304.5, Ensembl:ENST00000389048
Transcriptomic	*RNASequence*	**length**: 6240; **sequence**: AGCGCGCCGC [...]
Transcriptomic	*CDS*	**startPosition**: 927; **endPosition**: 5790; **startsAtExon**: 1; **endsAtExon**: 29
Variation Effect	*MutatedProtein*	**aminoacidRef**: Arg; **aminoacidAlt**: Gln; **positionInChain**: 1275; **consequence**: Gain-of-Function
Variation Effect	*MutatedRNA*	**MolecularConsequence**: missense; **ref**: G; **alt**: A
Proteomic	*ProteinSequence*	**isoformID**: UniProt Q9UM73-1; **isCanonical**: true; **length**: 1620 aa; **sequence**: MGAIGLLWLL [...]
Proteomic	*Domain*	**type**: kinase; **startPosition**: 1116; **endPosition**: 1392; **description**: Intracellular tyrosine kinase domain; **functionality**: Catalytic phosphorylation of downstream signaling substrates; **DNABinding**: false
Chemical	*Protein*	**name**: ALK tyrosine kinase receptor; **function**: receptor tyrosine kinase; **isProcessed**: true; **isModified**: true; **synonyms**: ALK, CD246, Anaplastic lymphoma kinase
Chemical	*ChemicalEntity*	**name**: ATP; **formula**: C10H16N5O13P3; **storedIn**: ChEBI:15422
Reaction Participant	*ReactionRole*	**type**: Catalyst, Reactant; **description**: Active mutant homodimer driving ligand-independent autophosphorylation while simultaneously acting as the macromolecular substrate; **ECNumber**: 2.7.10.1; **molecularFunction**: protein tyrosine kinase activity; **pHOptimal**: 7.4; **tempOptimal**: 37.0; **stoichiometricCoefficient**: 1.0
Reaction Participant	*ReactionRole*	**type**: Cofactor, Reactant; **description**: Small molecule acting as a organic co-substrate and primary phosphate donor; **isOrganic**: true; **isWaterSoluble**: true; **isLipidSoluble**: false; **stoichiometricCoefficient**: 1.0
Reaction	*Reaction*	**eventType**: Reaction; **name**: Autophosphorylation of point mutants of ALK; **isInDisease**: true; **ReactionClass**: BiochemicalReaction; **isTransport**: false; **isReversible**: false; **reactionFormula**: 3 ATP + ALK_mutant_dimer -> 3 ADP + p-3Y_ALK_mutant_dimer; **storedIn**: Reactome:R-HSA-9700186
Pathway	*Pathway*	**eventType**: Pathway; **name**: Signaling by ALK fusions and activated point mutants; **isInDisease**: true; **isTopLevel**: false; **type**: disease; **storedIn**: Reactome:R-HSA-9725370
Disease	*Disease*	**name**: Neuroblastoma susceptibility 3; **synonyms**:"Neuroblastoma, susceptibility to, 3", NB3, NBLST3, ALK-related neuroblastic tumor susceptibility; **storedIn**: EFO:0013083, MONDO:0013083, OMIM:613014; **modeOfInheritance**: Autosomal dominant; **penetrance**: 0.50
Phenotype	*Phenotype*	**name**: Abdominal mass; **synonyms**: Palpable abdominal mass, Enlarged abdomen, Distended abdomen; **storedIn**: HPO:HP:0031500
Clinical	*Significance*	**pathogenicity**: Pathogenic; **oncogenicity**: Oncogenic; **levelOfCertainty**: Level 1 / High

The altered receptor participates in the Reactome reaction *Autophosphorylation of point mutants of ALK* (R-HSA-9700186), where phosphate groups from ATP (*ChemicalEntity*, ChEBI:15422) are transferred onto the mutant receptor dimer. The Reaction Participant View makes these biochemical roles explicit through *ReactionRole*: the mutant homodimer acts simultaneously as *Catalyst* and macromolecular *Reactant*, whereas ATP acts as the organic co-substrate and phosphate donor. This reaction belongs to the pathway *Signaling by ALK fusions and activated point mutants* (Reactome R-HSA-9725370), linking the molecular alteration to oncogenic signalling.

Clinically, germline activating *ALK* variants are the principal known cause of hereditary neuroblastoma predisposition [32]. The variant is assigned a *Significance* instance indicating pathogenicity, oncogenicity, and a high level of certainty, and is linked to the *Disease Neuroblastoma susceptibility 3* (MONDO:0013083; OMIM #613014), inherited in an autosomal dominant manner with a penetrance of 0.50. Through the cross-view relationships of MOSAIC, the disease is further associated with the *Phenotype Abdominal mass* (HP:0031500), the most common presenting sign of abdominal neuroblastoma.

This walkthrough illustrates that MOSAIC's cross-view relationships are biologically meaningful rather than merely structural, enabling end-to-end semantic traceability from a single nucleotide substitution to its molecular, pathway, and clinical consequences.

6 Conclusions and Future Work

This paper presented MOSAIC, an extensible multi-view conceptual integration model for relating omics knowledge across biological abstraction levels. Rather than replacing domain-specific repositories, ontologies, exchange standards, or knowledge graphs, MOSAIC provides a conceptual structure through which their complementary semantic representations can be organised and related.

The present version is a traceable snapshot of an ongoing modelling process. It lacks a complete physical implementation, automated reasoning, exhaustive biological coverage, and fully fixed restrictions. Its preliminary validation is centred on variant-driven examples and does not yet include coverage metrics, schema-correspondence measurements, or executable query benchmarks. Regulatory mechanisms, epigenomics, chromatin organisation, enhancer–promoter interactions, and non-coding RNA subclasses remain partial. These boundaries define priorities for extensions guided by curated repositories and scientific literature.

Future work will progressively formalise the model, extend these domains, establish semantic mappings to external resources, and support graph-based implementations and cross-domain semantic queries.

Acknowledgements. This work is part of the EU4Health project UNICA. The UNICA project has received funding from the European Union's EU4Health research and innovation programme under grant agreement No. 101218966. https://www.unica-project.eu/.

References

1. Bernasconi, A., García Simón, A., Ceri, S., Pastor, O.: A Comprehensive Approach for the Conceptual Modeling of Genomic Data. In: Conceptual Modeling. LNCS, pp. 194–208 (2022). https://doi.org/10.1007/978-3-031-17995-2_14
2. Bernasconi, A., García Simón, A., Ceri, S., Pastor, O.: PoliViews: a comprehensive and modular approach to the conceptual modeling of genomic data. Data Knowl. Eng. **147**, 102201 (2023). https://doi.org/10.1016/j.datak.2023.102201
3. Bernasconi, A., Guizzardi, G., Pastor, O., et al.: Semantic interoperability: ontological unpacking of a viral conceptual model. BMC Bioinform. **23**, 491 (2022). https://doi.org/10.1186/s12859-022-05022-0
4. Bersanelli, M., et al.: Methods for the integration of multi-omics data: mathematical aspects. BMC Bioinform. **17**(S1), S15 (2016). https://doi.org/10.1186/s12859-015-0857-9
5. Blum, M., Chuguransky, S., Grego, T., et al.: InterPro: the protein sequence annotation resource in 2025. Nucleic Acids Res. **53**(D1), D418–D427 (2025). https://doi.org/10.1093/nar/gkae1082
6. Carrasco Sacristán, M.: MOSAIC conceptual model for integrated multi-omics data, Version 1.0. Zenodo (2026). https://doi.org/10.5281/zenodo.21614130
7. Carrasco Sacristán, M.: MOSAIC model: technical specification of the multi-omics structured and integrated conceptual model. Zenodo, technical note (2026). https://doi.org/10.5281/zenodo.21615906
8. Church, D.M., Schneider, V.A., Graves, T., et al.: Modernizing reference genome assemblies. PLoS Biol. **9**(7), e1001091 (2011). https://doi.org/10.1371/journal.pbio.1001091
9. Costa, M., García-Simón, A., Pastor, O.: The consequences of data dispersion in genomics: a comparative analysis of data sources for precision medicine. BMC Med. Inform. Decis. Mak. **23**, 256 (2023)
10. Cunningham, F., Allen, J.E., Allen, J., et al.: Ensembl 2022. Nucleic Acids Res. **50**(D1), D988–D995 (2022). https://doi.org/10.1093/nar/gkab1049
11. Demir, E., Cary, M.P., Paley, S., et al.: The BioPAX community standard for pathway data sharing. Nat. Biotechnol. **28**, 935–942 (2010). https://doi.org/10.1038/nbt.1666
12. den Dunnen, J.T., Dalgleish, R., Maglott, D.R., et al.: HGVS recommendations for the description of sequence variants: 2016 Update. Hum. Mutat. **37**(6), 564–569 (2016). https://doi.org/10.1002/humu.22981
13. Eilbeck, K., et al.: The sequence ontology: a tool for the unification of genome annotations. Genome Biol. **6**, 1–12 (2005). https://doi.org/10.1186/gb-2005-6-5-r44
14. Frankish, A., Diekhans, M., Ferreira, A.-M., et al.: GENCODE 2021. Nucleic Acids Res. **49**(D1), D916–D923 (2021). https://doi.org/10.1093/nar/gkaa1087
15. García-Simón, A., Casamayor, J.C.: On how to generalize species-specific conceptual schemes to generate a species-independent conceptual schema of the genome. BMC Bioinform. **22**(Suppl 13), 353 (2021). https://doi.org/10.1186/s12859-021-04237-x
16. García-Simón, A., Costa, M., Leon, A., Pastor, O.: The challenge of managing the evolution of genomics data over time: a conceptual model-based approach. BMC Bioinform. **23**, 472 (2022). https://doi.org/10.1186/s12859-022-04944-z
17. The Gene Ontology Consortium: The Gene ontology resource: enriching a GOld mine. Nucleic Acids Res. **49**(D1), D325–D334 (2021). https://doi.org/10.1093/nar/gkaa1113

18. Gillespie, M., Jassal, B., Stephan, R., et al.: The reactome pathway knowledgebase 2022. Nucleic Acids Res. **50**(D1), D687–D692 (2022). https://doi.org/10.1093/nar/gkab1028
19. Harrow, I., Balakrishnan, R., Jimenez-Ruiz, E., et al.: Ontology mapping for semantically enabled applications. Drug Discov. Today **24**(10), 2068–2075 (2019)
20. Hastings, J., Owen, G., Dekker, A., et al.: ChEBI in 2016: improved services and an expanding collection of metabolites. Nucleic Acids Res. **44**(D1), D1214–D1219 (2016). https://doi.org/10.1093/nar/gkv1031
21. HGVS Nomenclature: General recommendations. https://hgvs-nomenclature.org/stable/recommendations/general/ Accessed 16 May 2026
22. Iñiguez-Jarrín, C., García S., A., Reyes R., J.F., López, O.P.: GenDomus: interactive and collaboration mechanisms for diagnosing genetic diseases. In: Proceedings of the 12th International Conference on Evaluation of Novel Approaches to Software Engineering (ENASE 2017), pp. 91–102 (2017). https://doi.org/10.5220/0006324000910102
23. Jacobsen, J.O.B., Baudis, M., Baynam, G.S., et al.: The GA4GH phenopacket schema defines a computable representation of clinical data. Nat. Biotechnol. **40**(6), 817–820 (2022). https://doi.org/10.1038/s41587-022-01357-4
24. Kanehisa, M., Furumichi, M., Sato, Y., Kawashima, M., Ishiguro-Watanabe, M.: KEGG for taxonomy-based analysis of pathways and genomes. Nucleic Acids Res. **51**(D1), D587–D592 (2023). https://doi.org/10.1093/nar/gkac963
25. Köhler, S., Gargano, M., Matentzoglu, N., et al.: The human phenotype ontology in 2021. Nucleic Acids Res. **49**(D1), D1207–D1217 (2021). https://doi.org/10.1093/nar/gkaa1043
26. Landrum, M.J., Lee, J.M., Benson, M., et al.: ClinVar: improving access to variant interpretations and supporting evidence. Nucleic Acids Res. **46**(D1), D1062–D1067 (2018). https://doi.org/10.1093/nar/gkx1153
27. León Palacio, A., Pastor López, O.: Smart data for genomic information systems: the SILE method. Complex Syst. Inf. Model. Q. **17**, 1–23 (2018). https://doi.org/10.7250/csimq.2018-17.01
28. León Palacio, A., García S., A., Reyes Román, J.F., Costa, M., Pastor, O.: The delfos platform: a conceptual model-based solution for the enhancement of precision medicine. IEEE/ACM Trans. Comput. Biol. Bioinform. **21**(5), 1242–1253 (2024). https://doi.org/10.1109/TCBB.2024.3377928
29. McLaren, W., et al.: The ensembl variant effect predictor. Genome Biol. **17**, 122 (2016). https://doi.org/10.1186/s13059-016-0974-4
30. Moore, J.E., Purcaro, M.J., Pratt, H.E., et al.: Expanded encyclopaedias of DNA elements in the human and mouse genomes. Nature **583**, 699–710 (2020). https://doi.org/10.1038/s41586-020-2493-4
31. Morgat, A., Lombardot, T., Axelsen, K.B., et al.: Updates in Rhea: SPARQLing biochemical reaction data. Nucleic Acids Res. **48**(D1), D445–D454 (2020). https://doi.org/10.1093/nar/gkz985
32. Mossé, Y.P., Laudenslager, M., Longo, L., et al.: Identification of ALK as a major familial neuroblastoma predisposition gene. Nature **455**(7215), 930–935 (2008). https://doi.org/10.1038/nature07261
33. Nicholson, D.N., Greene, C.S.: Constructing knowledge graphs and their biomedical applications. Comput. Struct. Biotechnol. J. **18**, 1414–1428 (2020). https://doi.org/10.1016/j.csbj.2020.05.017
34. Pastor, O., León, A.P., Reyes, J.F.R., García-Simón, A., Casamayor, J.C.: Using conceptual modeling to improve genome data management. Brief. Bioinform. **22**(1), 45–54 (2021). https://doi.org/10.1093/bib/bbaa100

35. Putman, T.E., Schaper, K., Matentzoglu, N., et al.: The monarch initiative in 2024: an analytic platform integrating phenotypes, genes and diseases across species. Nucleic Acids Res. **52**(D1), D938–D949 (2024). https://doi.org/10.1093/nar/gkad1082
36. Reyes Román, J.F., Pastor, O., Casamayor, J.C., Valverde, F.: Applying conceptual modeling to better understand the human genome. In: Comyn-Wattiau, I., Tanaka, K., Song, I.-Y., Yamamoto, S., Saeki, M. (eds.) Conceptual Modeling. LNCS, vol. 9974, pp. 404–412 (2016). https://doi.org/10.1007/978-3-319-46397-1_31
37. Reyes Román, J.F., Roldán Martínez, D., García Simón, A., Rueda, U., Pastor, O.: VarSearch: annotating variations using an e-genomics framework. In: Proceedings of the 13th International Conference on Evaluation of Novel Approaches to Software Engineering (ENASE 2018), pp. 328–334 (2018). https://doi.org/10.5220/0006781103280334
38. Richards, S., Aziz, N., Bale, S., et al.: Standards and guidelines for the interpretation of sequence variants. Genet. Med. **17**(5), 405–424 (2015). https://doi.org/10.1038/gim.2015.30
39. UniProt Consortium: UniProt: the universal protein knowledgebase in 2023. Nucleic Acids Res. **51**(D1), D523–D531 (2023). https://doi.org/10.1093/nar/gkac1052
40. Unni, D.R., Moxon, S.A.T., Bada, M., et al.: Biolink model: a universal schema for knowledge graphs in clinical, biomedical, and translational science. Clin. Transl. Sci. **15**, 1848–1855 (2022). https://doi.org/10.1111/cts.13302
41. Vasilevsky, N.A., et al.: Mondo disease ontology: harmonizing disease concepts across the world. Hum. Mutat. **43**(5), 628–635 (2022)
42. Wagner, A.H., Babb, L., Alterovitz, G., et al.: The GA4GH variation representation specification: a computational framework for variation representation and federated identification. Cell Genom. **1**(2), 100027 (2021). https://doi.org/10.1016/j.xgen.2021.100027
43. Wilkinson, M.D., Dumontier, M., Aalbersberg, I.J., et al.: The FAIR guiding principles for scientific data management and stewardship. Sci. Data **3**, 160018 (2016). https://doi.org/10.1038/sdata.2016.18
44. Wishart, D.S., Feunang, Y.D., Guo, A.C., et al.: DrugBank 5.0: a major update to the DrugBank database for 2018. Nucleic Acids Res. **46**(D1), D1074–D1082 (2018). https://doi.org/10.1093/nar/gkx1037
45. Wittig, U., Rey, M., Weidemann, A., Kania, R., Müller, W.: SABIO-RK: an updated resource for manually curated biochemical reaction kinetics. Nucleic Acids Res. **46**(D1), D656–D660 (2018). https://doi.org/10.1093/nar/gkx1022
46. Yan, J., et al.: A survey of multi-layer biological networks for multi-omics data integration. Brief. Bioinform. **21**(6), 2029–2043 (2020)

Establishing Semantic Foundations for Explainable AI in Liquid Biopsy Through Conceptual Modeling

Marta Vivó-Benlloch[1,2](✉), Mireia Costa[1], Ana Pérez-Gómez[1], Alberto García S.[1], Ana León[1], José Fabián Reyes Román[1], Eloisa Jantus-Lewintre[2,3], Sandra Gallach[2], and Oscar Pastor[1]

[1] Valencian Research Institute for Artificial Intelligence (VRAIN), Universitat Politècnica de València (UPV), Valencia, Spain
mvivben@etsii.upv.es,
{micossan,anpego3,algarsi3,anleopa,jorero1,opastor}@upv.edu.es

[2] Molecular Oncology Section, Research Foundation of the General University Hospital of Valencia (FIHGUV), Valencia, Spain
gallach_san@fihguv.es

[3] Interuniversity Research Institute for Molecular Recognition and Technological Development (IDM), UPV - Universitat de València, Valencia, Spain
ejantus@btc.upv.es

Abstract. Artificial intelligence (AI) holds significant promise for supporting complex medical decisions, but the opacity of high-performing models hinders its integration into clinical practice. Within the field of Explainable AI (XAI), post-hoc explainability techniques such as SHAP and LIME have emerged as solutions for making model behavior more transparent. However, their ability to support clinically meaningful explanations is limited by the semantic quality of the variables they describe. When clinical data are heterogeneous, loosely defined, or semantically inconsistent, post-hoc explanations may be technically valid but clinically meaningless. This paper argues that conceptual modeling provides the semantic layer needed to overcome this limitation and reports its application in the domain of liquid biopsy through a research collaboration with a Hospital Research Foundation. The main contribution is a formal domain representation comprising a conceptual model and a glossary of terms that standardize the domain's concepts, make their interrelationships explicit, and address the heterogeneity inherent in raw clinical data. In doing so, it establishes a semantically grounded foundation on which AI algorithms can be built, evaluated, and explained meaningfully. The proposed representation has been validated through focus groups with domain experts, and its usability has been further evaluated with medical experts and non-expert students from biomedical and informatics engineering.

Keywords: Explainable AI · Conceptual Modeling · Liquid Biopsy · Semantic Foundations

© The Author(s), under exclusive license to Springer Nature Switzerland AG 2027
A. Bernasconi et al. (Eds.): ER 2026, LNCS 17081, pp. 19–36, 2027.
https://doi.org/10.1007/978-3-032-40795-5_2

1 Introduction

Artificial intelligence (AI) has emerged as a powerful alternative for addressing complex medical challenges that were previously beyond the scope of traditional clinical approaches. Despite its considerable potential, integrating AI into routine clinical practice faces a critical bottleneck: the inherent lack of explainability. In healthcare, this algorithmic opacity is a major limitation: a clinician cannot ethically inform a patient of a severe diagnosis—such as an increased risk of developing cancer—based solely on the output of a "black box". The consequences of doing so are not only theoretical. For example, a widely deployed risk-stratification algorithm was found to systematically underestimate the health needs of Black patients due to a semantically flawed proxy variable, effectively halving their access to care before the bias was uncovered [28]. Such critical, life-altering decisions demand justifications that are clear, traceable, and biologically plausible. Explainability thus becomes not a desirable feature, but a clinical imperative.

The research community has responded to the explainability challenge through the field of Explainable Artificial Intelligence (XAI), which encompasses two broad strategies. The first consists of using inherently interpretable models—such as decision trees or logistic regression—whose internal logic is transparent by design [31]. However, these models often trade predictive performance for transparency, often falling short of the accuracy required for clinical use. The second and currently predominant strategy is post-hoc explainability, where techniques such as SHAP (SHapley Additive exPlanations) and LIME (Local Interpretable Model-Agnostic Explanations) are applied after training to interrogate the model's behavior, typically by ranking the contribution of each input feature to a given prediction [1,2]. This approach has gained traction in medicine because it preserves high-performance models while offering clinicians a degree of transparency.

However, a key limitation of post-hoc methods is increasingly recognized: they are, at best, descriptive tools. They can characterize how a model behaves, but are structurally unable to explain why it works in terms of underlying biological mechanisms or cause-and-effect relationships [8]. Their clinical grounding can therefore come only from the variables they describe, making any post-hoc explanation only as meaningful as the semantic quality of its inputs. When those features are heterogeneous, loosely defined, or semantically inconsistent—as is common with raw clinical data—quantifying their influence yields a numerically precise description of an ambiguous input rather than a medical justification. Explainability is thus bounded above by the semantic coherence of the data it operates on. The choice between these strategies depends on the application at hand and on the quality of the available knowledge. When models are fed with fragmented, contradictory, or inconsistent knowledge—a recurrent issue when integrating data across organizations—an ontological analysis and meaning negotiation becomes necessary to make ontological commitments explicit and capture both meaning and semantics.

This is where conceptual modeling emerges as a necessary methodological contribution. Through abstraction, it produces formal, human-interpretable representations that explicitly capture the semantics of entities, attributes, and their interrelationships. AI and conceptual modeling are thus complementary—AI extracts patterns from large, heterogeneous data, while conceptual models supply the structured, domain-grounded semantic layer they cannot generate on its own [6]. Recent empirical work confirms this synergy: using domain knowledge encoded in conceptual models to guide data preparation improved both ML performance and process transparency [33].

This work reports a research collaboration with a Hospital Research Foundation on the application of semantic formalization to liquid tumor biopsy—a non-invasive approach to detecting and analyzing tumor-derived components in blood or other body fluids that supports longitudinal monitoring and better captures tumor heterogeneity than traditional tissue biopsy. Our objective in this collaboration is to define the semantic foundations required for an AI-based clinical decision support system that generates recommendations from real patient data in this domain.

The contribution materializes in a formal domain representation -comprising a conceptual model and a glossary of terms- that standardizes its concepts and interrelationships and addresses the heterogeneity of raw clinical data. As a result, we will establish a semantically grounded foundation for building, evaluating, and meaningfully explaining AI algorithms in the liquid biopsy domain. The representation has been validated through focus groups with domain experts, and its usability has been further evaluated by medical experts and non-expert students in biomedical and informatics engineering.

The remainder of the paper is structured as follows: Sect. 2 provides background on the domain, while Sect. 3 overviews related work. Section 4 describes the proposed conceptual model. Section 5 details the validation process. Finally, Sect. 6 discusses the results, and Sect. 7 concludes the paper and provides future research directions.

2 Background

According to the International Society of Liquid Biopsy, liquid biopsy (LB) is the analysis of components —such as cells, nucleic acids, proteins, metabolites, and extracellular vesicles— associated with pathological or specific physiological conditions that are obtained from bodily fluids through minimally invasive methods [22]. Liquid biopsy has become a key tool in precision oncology, the paradigm of matching each patient to the therapy most likely to be effective against their specific tumor profile. In this context, liquid biopsy focuses primarily on the analysis of cell-free DNA (cfDNA), which consists of short DNA fragments released into the bloodstream by cells undergoing apoptosis or necrosis [9]. A fraction of this cfDNA—termed circulating tumor DNA (ctDNA)— originates from tumor cells and carries the same genetic alterations as the tumor of origin. Therefore, ctDNA sequencing enables the identification of clinically actionable genetic alterations from a simple blood draw. Owing to its minimally invasive nature, liquid biopsy has emerged as a clear alternative to traditional solid biopsy, enabling cancer genomic analysis without being constrained by tumor accessibility or the presence of clinically overt disease [23].

A major challenge in the clinical use of liquid biopsy is the interpretation of negative genomic results, which may arise from two very different scenarios: (i) the sample contains insufficient ctDNA for reliable variant detection, or (ii) the patient genuinely carries no variants that could inform treatment [20]. The clinical implications of each scenario are markedly different. The former warrants a more invasive confirmatory test, such as a solid biopsy, whereas the latter supports proceeding with standard treatment [24]. However, with current methods, the two are indistinguishable. Within an ongoing research project, we are developing an AI model that predicts, by combining genomic, clinical, and laboratory information, whether a given patient is likely to yield insufficient ctDNA for the liquid biopsy to be informative. However, given the critical impact of these predictions on patient management, the model alone is not enough: its outputs must be accompanied by clinically meaningful explanations.

This is where the present paper is positioned. We propose a conceptual model of the liquid biopsy domain that can later serve as the semantic backbone for an explainability layer over the AI model, helping clinicians understand the rationale behind each prediction and fostering the trust required for clinical adoption.

3 Related Works

Here we present related work in conceptual modeling for genomics and oncology, domains that share foundational elements with our own and illustrate how analogous clinical settings have been formalized.

Within genomics, conceptual modeling has been extensively used for knowledge representation and standardization. Costa et al. have proposed semantic frameworks to formalize the clinical DNA variant interpretation process [12,13] and to manage the broader complexities of genomic data representation [11]. Other contributions have focused on structuring multi-omics data for precision medicine [17], identifying high-quality data records [30], and examining the temporal dynamics of genomic data [18]. Additionally, Bernasconi et al. [5] address the heterogeneity of genomic data types by mapping them onto an abstract conceptual representation. Within oncology, conceptual modeling has been applied to neuroblastoma, a rare pediatric cancer, through a model that captures clinical data, treatment protocols, and solid-biopsy results for affected patients [4,7]. Our proposal differs in two respects: first, it is designed for cancer in general rather than a specific pathology; second, whereas the neuroblastoma model relies on solid biopsies—which provide localized, static snapshots through invasive sampling—our work targets liquid biopsy, focusing on blood-borne biomarkers.

Taken together, this body of work shows that conceptual modeling has matured into an effective instrument for representing complex biomedical domains. To our knowledge, however, no dedicated conceptual model for the liquid biopsy domain has yet been developed. The conceptual model presented in this paper aims to fill this gap, providing a structured semantic foundation for the liquid biopsy domain. In doing so, it also lays the groundwork for the kind of CM–AI integration to enhance explainability that has been called for at the methodological level [6, 33], but has not yet been instantiated in this clinical setting(Figure,1).

4 Conceptual Model for Liquid Biopsy

The conceptual model was developed starting from real clinical-domain data provided by the General Hospital Research Foundation. Throughout the process, three clinical experts were available to resolve biological questions, and the final version was validated with them in a focus group, as detailed in later sections. This direct involvement ensured that the identified requirements and key concepts faithfully reflect the clinical reality and workflows of the liquid biopsy domain.

To support semantic interoperability, the model is aligned with the mCODE STU4 (Minimal Common Oncology Data Elements) [19] initiative, led by the American Society of Clinical Oncology (ASCO) and HL7, which defines a core set of data elements for oncological electronic health records. Building on this alignment, the model adopts a modular architecture of six functional views that strictly correspond to mCODE's structural domains, enhancing readability and providing a systematic characterization of the entities, attributes, and relationships that define the liquid biopsy process, each detailed in the following subsections. To ensure its practical utility, the model is accompanied by a comprehensive technical guide that provides extensive explanations for user support, as well as a thorough glossary detailing every attribute, its data types, and constraints [25].

Patient View. The PATIENT entity serves as the core of the model, defined by the attributes *Patient_ID*, *Date_of_Birth*, *Sex*, *Age*, and *Smoking_Status* (categorized as non-smoker, smoker, or ex-smoker). This entity also includes the attribute *Pack_Years*, which is subject to a conditional constraint: it only holds a non-null value if the *Smoking_Status* is "smoker". Additionally, the *Treatment_Line* attribute provides a temporal record of the total treatment lines received by the patient.

Each patient must have at least one SAMPLE taken, each of them characterized by a unique *Biopsy_ID*, a *Collection_Date*, and a *Sample_Source* (e.g., blood or pleural fluid). While clinical practice may use both solid and liquid samples, this model focuses exclusively on LIQUID BIOPSY samples. Nevertheless, TUMOR-related clinical data are explicitly retained in the model to provide essential clinical context for the LIQUID BIOPSY markers, without requiring tissue sample processing entities.

Each of the samples is collected at a single HOSPITAL, which is characterized by its *Hospital_Name*, a unique *Hospital_ID*, *City*, and *Postal_Code*. This

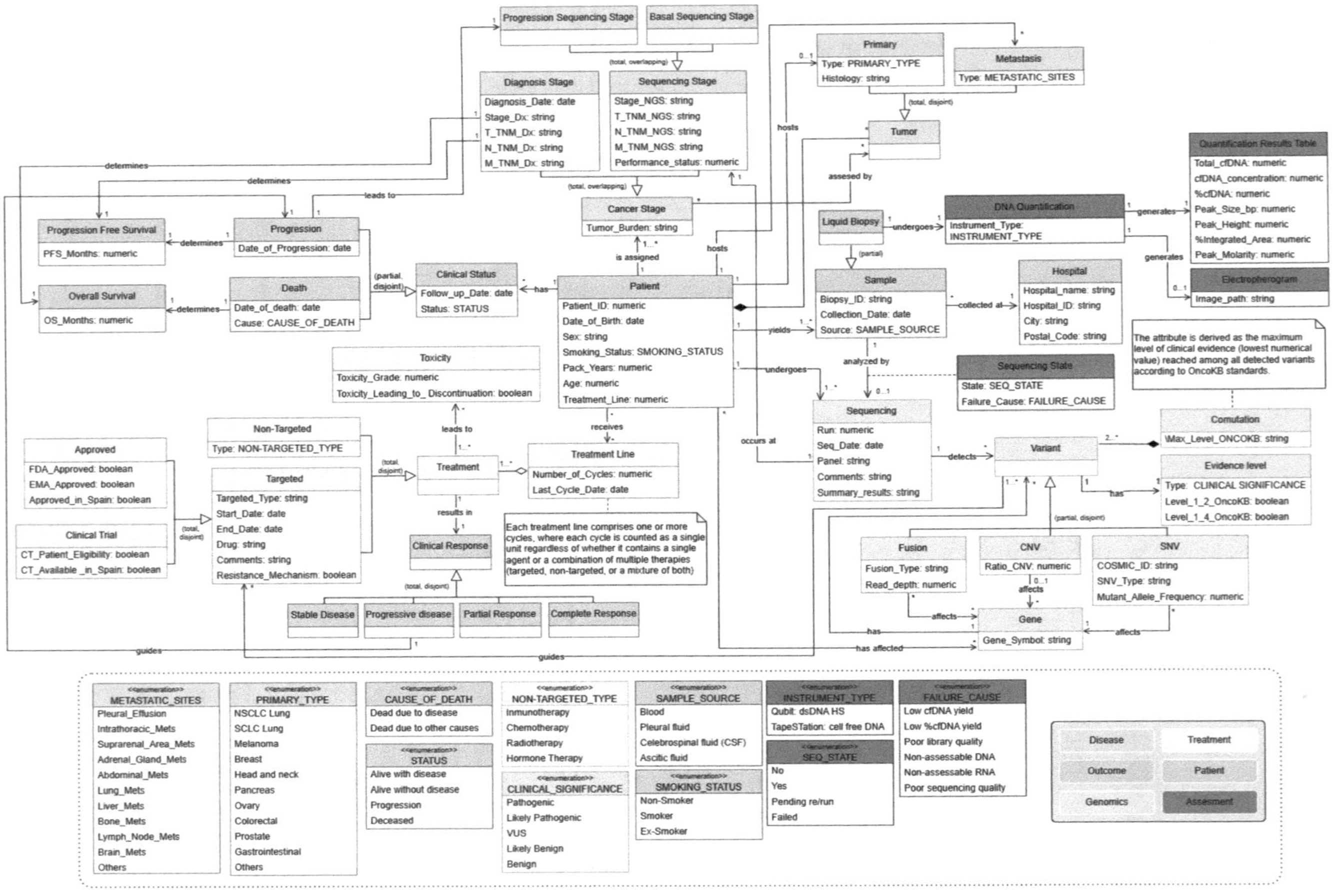

Fig. 1. Conceptual model for Liquid Biopsy

entity ensures sample traceability by identifying the specific clinical site where extraction was performed.

Assessment View. Each liquid biopsy sample undergoes a DNA QUANTIFICATION process, the methodology of which is determined by the *Instrument_ Type* employed. The most common instrument is the TapeStation, which produces two outputs. First, an ELECTROPHEROGRAM, which is a graphical representation of DNA fragments separated by size, is stored in an *image_path*. Second, a QUANTIFICATION RESULTS TABLE summarizing the sample's overall cfDNA content (*Total_ cfDNA*, *cfDNA_ concentration*, and *%cfDNA*) and descriptive metrics inherent to the ELECTROPHEROGRAM (*Peak_ size_ bp*, *Peak_ height*, *%integrated_ Area*, and *Peak_ Molarity*).

These metrics are vital in the liquid biopsy domain, as they enable the evaluation of sample viability -ensuring both sufficient cfDNA quantity and quality- to determine its suitability for DNA sequencing and the extraction of accurate genomic information. In this context, the SEQUENCING STATE entity is introduced, defined by two attributes. The first, *State*, describes the sequencing status (e.g., sequenced, not sequenced, pending re-sequencing, or sequencing failure). The second attribute, *Failure_ Cause*, identifies the reason why sequencing failed or was not ended (e.g., "low %cfDNA yield").

Genomics View. If the *State* is "sequenced" it means the sample has undergone SEQUENCING successfully, a process characterized by the *Run* (unique ID assigned by the sequencing machine), *Seq_ Date*, *Panel* (specific set of genes analyzed), *Comments* (clinical observations), and *Summary_ Results*.

As a result of SEQUENCING, we may detect VARIANTS relevant for oncological processes, providing the basis for targeted treatments. These VARIANTS are interpreted based on their EVIDENCE LEVEL, which comprises the variant's *Clinical Significance* (e.g., pathogenic, likely pathogenic, Variant of Uncertain Significance(VUS), likely benign, or benign). Furthermore, its therapeutic utility is classified according to OncoKB evidence levels [10,26]. This is captured by the attributes *Level_ 1_ 2_ Oncokb* (representing FDA-approved or standard-of-care therapies) and *Level_ 1_ 4_ Oncokb* (which confirms that the mutation is clinically relevant and not a VUS). In cases of COMUTATIONS (simultaneous occurrence of two or more mutations), the model records the *Max_ level_ Oncokb*, reflecting the highest evidence level among the identified variants.

The model specializes the identified variants into three distinct subtypes: FUSIONS (where genetic material from two different genes or intergenic regions becomes joined); CNV (Copy Number Variants) that involve gains or losses of DNA segments; and SNV (Single Nucleotide Variants), which are single-letter changes in the genetic code. By doing so, the model incorporates specific attributes that characterize the uniqueness of each variant type and their distinct biological properties.

Finally, all three variant categories are associated with the GENE entity, which is uniquely identified by its *Gen_ Symbol* that follows the HGNC (HUGO Gene Nomenclature Committee) official short name convention [32].

Disease View. Throughout their clinical history, an oncology patient may be assigned one or multiple CANCER STAGES. This stage is determined by the characteristics of the TUMOR, specifically the size and properties of the PRIMARY TUMOR —defined by its *Primary_ Type* and *Histology.* The PRIMARY TUMOR may spread from its original site, appearing in the form METASTASIS in anatomical sites (i.e., *METASTATIC_ SITES*) distinct from the original site.

The CANCER STAGE is gathered in the initial diagnosis (DIAGNOSIS STAGE) and also at the moment where the sequencing is performed (SEQUENCING STAGE). As the disease progresses, the patient may undergo multiple rounds of sequencing, leading to an evolving SEQUENCING STAGE. Therefore, the model further specializes the sequencing stage into two categories: the BASAL SEQUENCING STAGE, corresponding to the patient's first liquid biopsy analysis, and the PROGRESSION SEQUENCING STAGES, which are recorded during clinical progressions and iterative sequencing procedures.

Each stage is formally defined using the AJCC (American Joint Committee on Cancer) [3] staging standard, which includes the *T_ TNM* (describing the size and extent of the primary tumor), *N_ TNM* (indicating whether the cancer has reached nearby lymph nodes), and *M_ TNM* (specifying the presence of distant metastasis) classifications, as well as the overall *Stage* (a consolidated numerical group that summarizes the overall progression and severity of the disease). Notably, for all sequencing stages, the model also records the *Performance Status* using the ECOG scale from the ECOG-ACRIN Cancer Research Group, documenting the patient's functional status at the precise time of sample collection (e.g., within a 5-level scale, a grade of 2 denotes a patient capable of self-care but unable to work) [15,29].

Treatment View. An oncology patient may receive multiple TREATMENT LINES based on its diagnosis and genomic information. Each line consists of one or several TREATMENTS, defined by the *Number_ of_ Cycles* (representing the frequency of administration) and the *Last_ Cycle_ Date.*

Treatments are classified into two distinct categories. The first is NON-TARGETED, which refers to conventional and generic oncological therapies. Conversely, TARGETED Treatments are specifically designed to tackle genomic alterations present in a patient's DNA and identified through the sequencing. These treatments are defined by the *Start_ Date*, *End_ Date*, *Targeted_ Type* (specific type of targeted therapy based on the guidelines established in the ESMO Handbook of Cancer Genetics and Genomics) [16], *Drug*, *Comments*, and *Resistance_ Mechanism* (a boolean attribute indicating the presence or absence of a known resistance mechanism to the therapy).

Furthermore, the model includes two specialized entities for Targeted Treatments, depending on their regulatory status. The first is APPROVED, for approved targeted therapies across different jurisdictions: (i.e., *FDA_Approved*, *EMA_Approved*, and/or *Approved_in_Spain*). The second is CLINICAL TRIAL, which specifies whether the treatment is part of a directed clinical study.

Finally, the model also accounts for treatment-related adverse effects through the TOXICITY entity. This entity is defined by the *Toxicity_Grade* classified according to the CTCAE (Common Terminology Criteria for Adverse Events) [34] oncology standard, and also by *Toxicity_Leading_to_Discontinuation*, which indicates whether the toxic effect causes the cessation of the treatment. ,

Outcome View. Patients are monitored through multiple CLINICAL STATUS records, documented during each medical visit (*Follow_up_Date*), and categorized in the *Status* attribute as Alive with disease, Alive without disease, Progression, or Deceased.

The model specializes CLINICAL STATUS into two key clinical endpoints. First, PROGRESSION represents clinical evidence of worsening disease, recorded on the *Date_of_Progression*. It allows the calculation of PROGRESSION FREE SURVIVAL (PFS), defined as the time elapsed from the *Diagnosis_Date* to the *Date_of_Progression*, to assess the duration of time a patient lives without disease advancement.

The second specialization is DEATH, which, combined, records the *Date_of_Death* and the *Cause_of_Death*. This entity enables the determination of OVERALL SURVIVAL (OS), calculated as the time interval between the *Diagnosis_Date* and the *Date_of_Death*.

It is also essential to record the CLINICAL RESPONSE following treatment, which is divided into COMPLETE RESPONSE (disappearance of all detectable cancer), PARTIAL RESPONSE (significant reduction in tumor size), STABLE DISEASE (no significant increase or decrease), and PROGRESSIVE DISEASE (evidence of tumor growth or spread).

5 Validation

The validation of the proposed conceptual model was structured as a multi-stage process that combined an expert-driven review, an instantiation with real-world data, and a usability assessment with end users. Each stage is described in detail in the following subsections.

5.1 Expert-Driven Review

The first validation stage consisted of an iterative expert review to confirm the model's semantic and clinical adequacy. Two consecutive focus-group sessions were conducted with the same panel of three physicians, selected for their direct involvement in the liquid biopsy workflow at the participating institution. The first session followed a structured walkthrough protocol: starting from the central Patient class, a moderator guided the panel through the diagram, and clinicians were asked to interrupt whenever a concept was omitted, misrepresented, or terminologically inaccurate. Their comments were consolidated into a revised version of the model, which was then reviewed in a second session following the same protocol. A small number of additional refinements emerged and were incorporated, yielding the consolidated version of the model presented in this paper(Figure,2).

5.2 Use Case

To validate the practical utility of our model, a real-world clinical scenario was instantiated. This case follows a 56-year-old patient (anonymized for data protection) through a complex oncological journey.

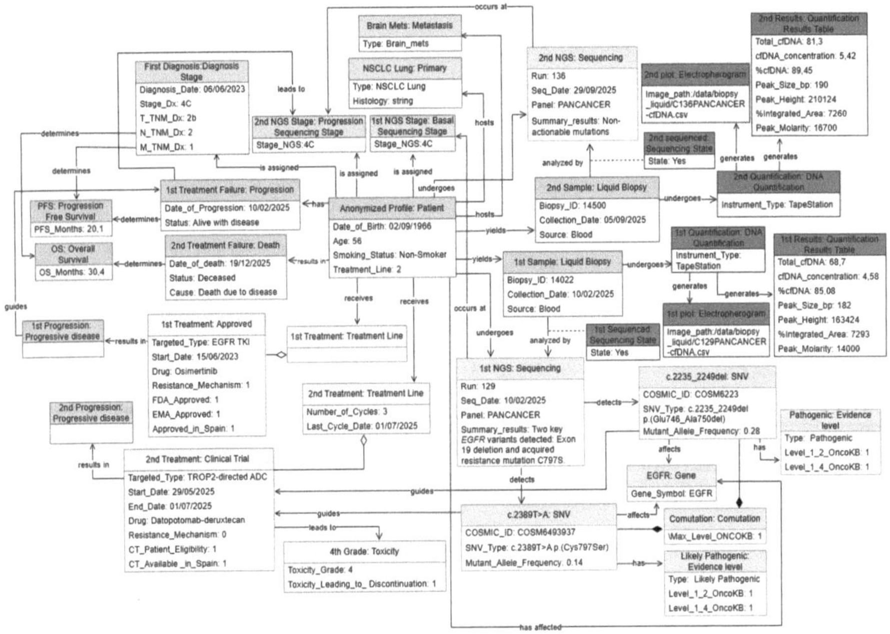

Fig. 2. Practical instantiation of the conceptual model with an anonymized real-patient profile.

From Diagnosis to First-line of Treatment Failure. In June 2023, the patient was diagnosed with Non-Small Cell Lung Cancer (NSCLC LUNG: PRIMARY) via tissue biopsy. The initial assessment revealed multiple brain metastases (BRAIN METS: METASTASIS), leading to a Stage 4C classification (1ST DIAGNOSIS: DIAGNOSIS STAGE). Consequently, the 1ST TREATMENT: TREATMENT LINE was initiated with Osimertinib (*drug*), an approved Targeted Treatment (1ST TREATMENT: APPROVED) chosen to attack the EGFR variants - C.2235_2249DEL and C.2389T>A- identified in the initial tissue sequencing (which is not represented in our model, as it belongs to the solid biopsy domain). The clinical course was later interrupted by a seizure related to the known brain metastases,which were showing a partial response on Magnetic Resonance Imaging (MRI). Despite this radiological response, this event was recorded as the patient's first progression event (1st Treatment Failure: Progression).

Adaptive Strategy via Liquid Biopsy. This 1st Treatment Failure: Progression triggered a shift in clinical strategy and prompted the first entry of a liquid biopsy sample into our model's core domain. In February 2025, the first Liquid Biopsy Sample (1st Sample: Liquid Biopsy) was collected and sequenced (1st NGS: Sequencing). This data guided the transition to a 2nd Treatment: Treatment Line with an ADC (Antibody-Drug Conjugate) targeting TROP-2 *Targeted_ Type* as part of a 2nd Treatment:Clinical Trial.

Toxicity and Final Evolution. The model's capacity to track adverse events became critical when, after three cycles, the patient reached 4th Grade:Toxicity, forcing the cessation (*toxicity_ leading_ to_ discontinuation*) of the trial. Despite a second liquid biopsy sequentiation (2nd NGS: Sequencing) in September 2025, no further actionable variants were found. While pulmonary SBRT (Stereotactic Body Radiation Therapy) was proposed, the patient's rapid deterioration prevented its application, leaving the clinical status as Progressive Disease until the patient's decease in December of the same year (2nd Treatment Failure: Death).

Expert Perspective. As clinical collaborators emphasized, this profile highlights the model's core purpose: "*This example effectively demonstrates how using NGS in Liquid Biopsy allows for the detection of molecular resistance mechanisms, providing the essential data to pivot therapeutic strategies when a patient stops responding to their current treatment*".

5.3 Usability Evaluation

The third dimension of the validation was measuring the model's usability. According to the ISO/IEC 25000 standard [21], usability is defined as *"the degree to which specified users can achieve specified goals with effectiveness, efficiency, and satisfaction in a specified context of use"*. Consequently, our evaluation focused on these three dimensions: efficiency, effectiveness, and user satisfaction.

To collect the evaluation data, we designed a 12-question questionnaire in Microsoft Forms, structured to capture both demographic information and the variables used in the usability assessment. We distributed it to participants with diverse academic and professional backgrounds, resulting in 75 responses. Below, we provide an overview of the results.

Demographics. The demographic section characterized the participants' backgrounds and their level of expertise in both fields involved in the evaluation. In terms of academic background, the most common one was biomedical engineering (38%), at the intersection of informatics and medicine, followed by purely medical (29%) and purely informatics (20%). The remaining 14% selected *Others*, mainly other engineering disciplines, mathematics, and nursing.

Expertise levels, however, were unevenly distributed across the two relevant domains. Familiarity with conceptual modeling was relatively broad: although 21% had never heard of it and 37% only knew of it, 21% had taken lessons on the topic and a further 20% used it occasionally or regularly. In contrast, experience with the liquid biopsy domain was considerably more limited, with 39% having never heard of it, 37% only knowing of it, 20% having taken lessons, and only a small minority using it occasionally or regularly.

Efficiency. Efficiency was measured as the time required by participants to understand the conceptual model and complete the questionnaire. The average completion time across the 75 responses was 10 minutes and 21 s. When analyzing the results by participant profile, the average times were 12:00 minutes for informatics profiles, 8:43 minutes for medical and biological profiles, 8:06 minutes for biomedical profiles, and 17:15 minutes for participants classified as *Others*.

Effectiveness. Effectiveness was measured by evaluating the participants' understanding of the conceptual model through questions organized along three dimensions: concept understanding, entity relationships, and model reasoning.

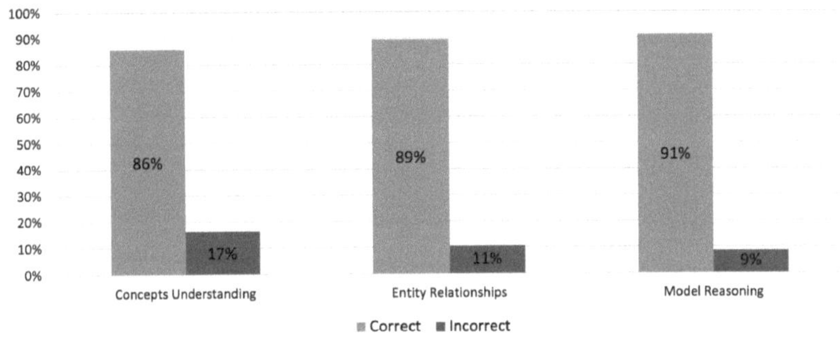

Fig. 3. Effectiveness

The participants' success in each of these dimensions is reported in Fig. 3. Regarding concept understanding, participants achieved an accuracy of 86%, with 19% of responses classified as incorrect. This dimension evaluates the ability to correctly identify and interpret the meaning of the entities represented in the model, namely concepts, objects, or events within the liquid biopsy domain. For entity relationships, performance improved slightly, reaching 89% correct responses and 11% incorrect responses, indicating that participants were generally able to understand how the different entities are associated and interact within the domain. Finally, model reasoning showed the highest performance, with 91% of responses correct and 9% incorrect. This suggests that participants were able not only to understand isolated entities and relationships, but also to follow the overall logic and reasoning represented by the conceptual model.

User Satisfaction. User satisfaction was measured using three metrics [14]: Perceived Ease of Use (PEOU), Perceived Usefulness (PU), and Intention to Use (ITU). These dimensions were assessed through different questions and a 5-point Likert scale based on the Method Adoption Model (MAM) [27]. The results are summarized in Fig. 4.

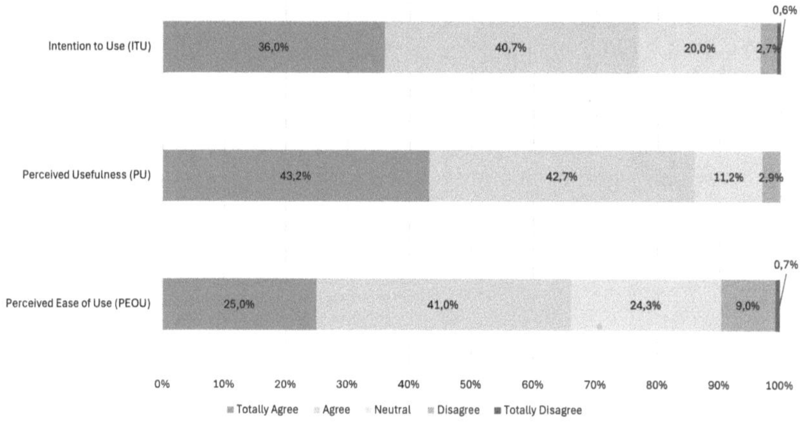

Fig. 4. User satisfaction

The results for PEOU indicate that most participants rated the conceptual model positively. Indeed, overall 66% of participants selected agree or totally agree across the different questions, which assessed ease of learning the model, ease of navigation, the level of effort required to understand its structure, and the ease of identifying the meaning of its main concepts. Meanwhile, 24.3% remained neutral and only 9.7% expressed disagreement. For PU, the results were even more favorable, with 85.9% of participants indicating agree or totally agree, based on items evaluating whether the model helps understand the liquid biopsy domain, improves comprehension of relationships between concepts, supports real-world clinical or research tasks, helps organize domain knowledge effectively, and serves as a useful learning reference. Only 2.9% reported negative perceptions.

Finally, for ITU, 76.7% of participants reported agree or totally agree regarding their willingness to use or recommend the model, reflecting two complementary perspectives: direct adoption in professional or academic contexts and recommendation to others as a useful resource, while only 3.3% expressed disagreement and 20% remained neutral.

6 Discussion

The results of the multi-stage validation provide converging evidence that the proposed conceptual model offers a sound semantic foundation for the liquid biopsy domain and, by extension, for the explainable AI layer it is intended to support. This section discusses the implications of these results for the role of conceptual modeling in interdisciplinary clinical AI, as well as the limitations that should temper their interpretation.

Conceptual Modeling as a Shared Representation Across Disciplines. The focus-group sessions revealed an outcome that the questionnaire could not capture. Despite having no prior exposure to conceptual modeling, the participating clinicians engaged substantively with the diagram from the first walkthrough and highlighted it as a valuable shared reference for structuring the discussion. This supports the paper's central argument. Where AI integration requires constant negotiation between data scientists, software engineers, and clinicians, a conceptual model offers a common representation that is not tied to any single discipline and can be read by all, making explicit the points where their knowledge meets.

User Satisfaction and the PEOU–Effectiveness Gap. Across the three satisfaction dimensions, the model was perceived positively, with Perceived Usefulness (85.9%) and Intention to Use (76.7%) clearly above Perceived Ease of Use (66%). The lower PEOU is consistent with the sample's demographic composition, in which 58% of respondents reported no prior exposure to conceptual modeling or only passive familiarity with it. However, this PEOU gap did not translate into a comprehension gap. The same participants achieved effectiveness scores between 86% and 91% in approximately 10 minutes, indicating that the model is sufficiently self-explanatory to be usable without dedicated training. The very low rate of explicit disagreement—between 0.6% and 9% across all questions—further confirms that the model is rarely actively rejected.

Implications for Explainable AI in Liquid Biopsy. Taken together, these results show that conceptual modeling can provide the semantic foundation on which clinically meaningful explanations of AI predictions can be built. The case study in Sect. 5.2 demonstrates that the model accommodates a complete, anonymized real-patient trajectory, a necessary precondition for using it as a semantic backbone for post-hoc explanations. On this basis, features fed to an

AI model are no longer isolated numerical inputs but well-defined concepts, each with a clear definition, a constrained set of values, and explicit relationships to other clinical concepts. Therefore, post-hoc explanations computed over data represented with this model refer to clinically meaningful entities rather than column headers of uncertain provenance, making the resulting explanations directly interpretable by clinicians in the terms of their own practice.

Threats to Validity. Despite these promising results, some limitations of the present work should be acknowledged. First, while full consensus was reached among the participating experts across the iterative review sessions, the process involved three clinicians from a single hospital. Thus, the model may be overfitted to that institution's workflows and terminology rather than broader oncology or genetic practices. Therefore, a future multi-center validation will be needed to assess its generality. Second, the usability evaluation relied on a Microsoft Forms questionnaire distributed asynchronously, which limits the ability to verify the conditions under which responses were produced and may introduce self-selection bias, since participation was voluntary. Additionally, while this work establishes the semantic foundation for explainable AI, the actual deployment and evaluation of AI models built upon this conceptual framework were not empirically tested and remain as future work. Finally, the alignment with mCODE STU4, deliberately sought for interoperability, commits the model to that standard's assumptions and will require monitoring its evolution. In this line, future work will explore mapping the model's semantic concepts to broader medical ontologies, such as SNOMED CT, to enhance cross-institutional integration.

7 Conclusions

Liquid biopsy and Artificial Intelligence are rapidly becoming vital for modern clinical practice. However, both fields face critical challenges: liquid biopsy must overcome the hurdle of false negatives to ensure diagnostic accuracy, while AI requires clinical explainability and high-quality, structured input data to be truly effective in healthcare.

This paper lays the groundwork for tackling these challenges through a conceptual data model for the liquid biopsy domain. The model provides the semantic structure required by future AI predictors within the PREDICTF project—a necessary step toward both reducing false negatives and producing clinically explainable AI. Its validity is supported by three pillars. First, the model was refined through direct clinician feedback, providing a solid foundation for standardization while leaving multi-center validation for future work. Second, the model proved its capacity to serve as a comprehensive template for longitudinal data when applied to a complex real-world patient profile, while accommodating the reality that certain clinical information may not always be formally recorded. Third, a validation survey involving 75 professionals from diverse fields—Medicine, Informatics, Biomedical Engineering, among others—further confirmed the model's clarity and cross-disciplinary applicability.

The future roadmap involves developing AI models to experimentally validate how this structured data improves predictive explainability. Furthermore, we intend to iterate on and expand the model as new hospital collaborations arise, striving for universal standardization that can adapt to a broader range of clinical workflows in the liquid biopsy landscape.

Acknowledgments. This work has been supported by the PoliHGeneral 2025 program under the project PREDICTF (PHG2025-13). It is also part of the Horizon Europe project BETTER, funded by the European Union's Horizon Europe research and innovation programme under grant agreement No. 101136262, and the UNICA project, funded by the European Union's EU4Health programme under grant agreement No. 101218966. This work has additionally received partial support from the VARNETICA project (CNS2023-145422).

Disclosure of Interests. The authors have no competing interests to declare that are relevant to the content of this article.

References

1. Ali, S., et al.: The enlightening role of explainable artificial intelligence in medical & healthcare domains: a systematic literature review. Comput. Biol. Med. **166**, 107555 (2023). https://doi.org/10.1016/j.compbiomed.2023.107555
2. Allgaier, J., et al.: How does the model make predictions? a systematic literature review on the explainability power of machine learning in healthcare. Artif. Intell. Med. **143**, 102616 (2023). https://doi.org/10.1016/j.artmed.2023.102616
3. Amin, M., et al.: Organization of the AJCC Cancer Staging Manual, pp. 31–37. Springer International Publishing (2017). https://doi.org/10.1007/978-3-319-40618-3_2
4. Arevshatyan, S., et al.: Integration and analysis of clinical and genomic data of neuroblastoma applying conceptual modeling. In: Panach, J.I., Guizzardi, R.S.S., Claro, D.B. (eds.) Proceedings of the ER Forum and Poster & Demos Session 2019 on Publishing Papers with CEUR-WS co-located with 38th International Conference on Conceptual Modeling (ER 2019), Salvador, Brazil, November 4, 2019, pp. 28–41. CEUR Workshop Proceedings, CEUR-WS.org (2019). https://ceur-ws.org/Vol-2469/ERForum3.pdf
5. Bernasconi, A., et al.: A comprehensive approach for the conceptual modeling of genomic data. In: Ralyté, J., Chakravarthy, S., Mohania, M., Jeusfeld, M.A., Karlapalem, K. (eds.) Conceptual Modeling, pp. 194–208. Springer International Publishing, Lecture Notes in Computer Science (2022)
6. Bork, D.: Conceptual modeling and artificial intelligence: a systematic mapping study arXiv preprint. arXiv:2303.06758 (2023)
7. Carreño-Bolufer, et al.: A conceptual model-based application for the treatment and management of data in pediatric oncology: the neuroblastoma use case. In: Mannion, M., Männistö, T., Maciaszek, L.A. (eds.) Proceedings of the 20th International Conference on Evaluation of Novel Approaches to Software Engineering, ENASE 2025, Porto, Portugal, April 4-6, 2025, pp. 15–26. SCITEPRESS (2025). https://doi.org/10.5220/0013202600003928

8. Carriero, A., et al.: Explainable AI in healthcare: to explain, to predict, or to describe? Diagn. Prognostic Res. **9**, 29 (2025). https://doi.org/10.1186/s41512-025-00213-8
9. Cescon, D.W., et al.: Circulating tumor DNA and liquid biopsy in oncology. Nat. Cancer **1**(3), 276–290 (2020). https://doi.org/10.1038/s43018-020-0043-5
10. Chakravarty, D., et al.: OncoKB: a precision oncology knowledge base. JCO Precis. Oncol. (2017). https://doi.org/10.1200/PO.17.00011
11. Costa, M., et al.: Comprehensive representation of variation interpretation data via conceptual modeling. In: Prince Sales, T., Araújo, J., Borbinha, J., Guizzardi, G. (eds.) Advances in Conceptual Modeling - ER 2023 Workshops, CMLS, CMOMM4FAIR, EmpER, JUSMOD, OntoCom, QUAMES, and SmartFood, Lisbon, Portugal, November 6-9, 2023, Proceedings. Lecture Notes in Computer Science, vol. 14319, pp. 25–34. Springer (2023). https://doi.org/10.1007/978-3-031-47112-4_3
12. Costa, M., et al.: A reference meta-model to understand DNA variant interpretation guidelines. In: Almeida, J.P.A., Borbinha, J., Guizzardi, G., Link, S., Zdravkovic, J. (eds.) Conceptual Modeling - 42nd International Conference, ER 2023, Lisbon, Portugal, November 6-9, 2023, Proceedings. Lecture Notes in Computer Science, vol. 14320, pp. 375–393. Springer (2023). https://doi.org/10.1007/978-3-031-47262-6_20
13. Costa, M., et al.: VarclaMM: a reference meta-model to understand DNA variant classification. Data Knowl. Eng. **154**, 102370 (2024). https://doi.org/10.1016/j.datak.2024.102370
14. Davis, F.D.: Perceived usefulness, perceived ease of use, and user acceptance of information technology. MIS Q. **13**(3), 319–340 (1989)
15. ECOG-ACRIN Cancer Research Group: ECOG performance status scale. https://ecog-acrin.org/resources/ecog-performance-status/ (2026)
16. ESMO Handbook of Cancer Genetics and Genomics. https://oncologypro.esmo.org/books/handbooks/cancer-genetics-and-genomics (2025)
17. García, S., A.: A conceptual model-based approach to improve the representation and management of omics data in precision medicine. IEEE Access **9**, 154071–154085 (2021)
18. García, S., A.: The challenge of managing the evolution of genomics data over time: a conceptual model-based approach. BMC Bioinform. **23**(11), 472 (2022)
19. HL7 International / Clinical Interoperability Council: minimal Common Oncology Data Elements (mCODE) Implementation Guide. https://build.fhir.org/ig/HL7/fhir-mCODE-ig/ (2025)
20. Husain, H., et al.: Tumor fraction correlates with detection of actionable variants across >23,000 circulating tumor DNA samples. JCO Precis. Oncol. **6**, e2200261 (2022). https://doi.org/10.1200/PO.22.00261
21. IEC, I.: ISO/IEC 25000–software engineering–software product quality requirements and evaluation (square)–guide to square. Syst. Eng. **41** (2005)
22. Jantus-Lewintre, E., et al.: Harmonizing definitions in liquid biopsy: a terminology framework by the international society of liquid biopsy. J. Liq. Biopsy **12**, 100462 (2026). https://doi.org/10.1016/j.jlb.2026.100462
23. Lone, S.N., et al.: Liquid biopsy: a step closer to transform diagnosis, prognosis and future of cancer treatments. Mol. Cancer **21**(1), 79 (2022)
24. Madison, R.W., et al.: Measurement of ctDNA tumor fraction identifies informative negative liquid biopsy results and informs value of tissue confirmation. Clin. Cancer Res. **30**(11), 2452–2460 (2024). https://doi.org/10.1158/1078-0432.CCR-23-3321

25. Marta, V.B., et al.: Supplementary material paper: establishing semantic foundations for explainable AI in liquid biopsy through conceptual modeling (2026). https://doi.org/10.5281/zenodo.20267092
26. Memorial sloan kettering cancer center: OncoKB therapeutic levels of evidence. https://www.oncokb.org/therapeutic-levels (2026)
27. Moody, D.: The Method Evaluation Model: A Theoretical Model For Validating Information Systems Design Methods. ECIS 2003 Proceedings (2003). https://aisel.aisnet.org/ecis2003/79
28. Obermeyer, Z., et al.: Dissecting racial bias in an algorithm used to manage the health of populations. Science **366**(6464), 447–453 (2019). https://doi.org/10.1126/science.aax2342
29. Oken, M.M., et al.: Toxicity and response criteria of the eastern cooperative oncology group. Am. J. Clin. Oncol. **5**(6), 649–655 (1982)
30. Palacio, A.L., et al.: A method to identify relevant genome data: Conceptual modeling for the medicine of precision. In: Trujillo, J.C., etal. (eds.) Conceptual Modeling, pp. 597–609. Springer International Publishing, Lecture Notes in Computer Science (2018)
31. Rudin, C.: Stop explaining black box machine learning models for high stakes decisions and use interpretable models instead. Nat. Mach. Intell. **1**(5), 206–215 (2019). https://doi.org/10.1038/s42256-019-0048-x
32. Seal, R., et al.: Genenames.org: the HGNC and PGNC resources in 2026. Nucleic Acids Res. **54**, D1098–D1107 (2025). https://doi.org/10.1093/nar/gkaf1229
33. Storey, V.C., et al.: Domain knowledge in artificial intelligence: using conceptual modeling to increase machine learning accuracy and explainability. Data Knowl. Eng. (2025). https://doi.org/10.1016/j.datak.2025.102371
34. U.S. Department of Health and Human Services, National Institutes of Health, National Cancer Institute: common terminology criteria for adverse events (CTCAE) Version 5.0. (2017) https://dctd.cancer.gov/research/ctep-trials/for-sites/adverse-events/ctcae-v5-5x7.pdf

Bridging Classification Systems in Waste Trade: The Case of Textile Waste

Elena Milivinti(✉)

Department of Philosophy, University at Buffalo, Buffalo, NY, USA
emilivin@buffalo.edu

Abstract. Enforcement authorities have identified a particular documentary combination as a direct enabler of illicit waste trafficking: the same physical consignment framed simultaneously as traded goods under one classification system and as waste under another. This paper addresses that problem through the case of textile waste, where the European Waste Catalogue (EWC) classifies consignments by generating process while the Harmonized System (HS), developed by the World Customs Organization, classifies by material composition or use history. The analysis covers eight textile-relevant EWC codes and twelve textile-relevant HS headings, generating 96 mapping pairs. Using Basic Formal Ontology as an analytical framework, the paper makes explicit the properties each code requires, and evaluates each pair according to whether the source code already satisfies the definitional requirements of the target code, whether additional evidence is needed, or whether translation is blocked. No pair qualifies as an exact match. A documented textile shipment shows how the method identifies apparently routine documentary combinations that require review by a competent authority. The paper contributes a conceptual-modeling method for validating translations between incompatible classification systems and for making classification gaps explicit, auditable, and usable in digital waste-tracking systems.

Keywords: Waste Management · Textile waste classification · European Waste Catalogue · Harmonized System · Basic Formal Ontology · Semantic interoperability

1 Introduction

Waste classification refers to the process of assigning waste consignments to one or more categories on the basis of their properties, characteristics, components, or process of generation. Classification systems are crucial for all stakeholders involved in waste governance: administrators, waste generators, and enforcement authorities. They provide the foundation for data collection, monitoring, and enforcement [11,12], because a good waste classification system is the foundation and precondition for efficient waste management [17]. However, there is a classificatory scattered landscape, as countries and agencies have independently

© The Author(s), under exclusive license to Springer Nature Switzerland AG 2027
A. Bernasconi et al. (Eds.): ER 2026, LNCS 17081, pp. 37–53, 2027.
https://doi.org/10.1007/978-3-032-40795-5_3

developed their own systems [15,18], reflecting different regulatory traditions and institutional goals. The problem becomes visible when material flows cross the boundaries between jurisdictions of different systems. A shipment that crosses different countries must go through different classificatory regimes. This paper proposes a formal ontological method for determining the conditions under which a category in one classification system can be validly translated into a category in another.

The method is demonstrated through the case of international textile waste trade. The same physical load may be classified under waste-management codes, customs codes, and transboundary shipment documentation. The two systems at the centre of this analysis are the European Waste Catalogue (EWC), also referred to as the European List of Waste (ELoW) [19], and the Harmonized System (HS), a multipurpose international product nomenclature developed by the World Customs Organization (WCO) [22]. The EWC is a process-oriented classification used for waste documentation across EU Member States [17]. The HS is used for customs tariffs, trade statistics, and other border-control purposes. The two systems appear alongside each other in waste shipments and customs documentation. An operator preparing the transport documentation for a singAn operator preparing transport documentation for a single outgoing load must assign both, and each assignment is grounded in a different property of the same object. These classifications need not be mutually exclusive in themselves; the same load can, in principle, instantiate both an EWC category and an HS category without contradiction. The problem lies elsewhere: no official instrument tells the operator how to check whether the two assigned classifications are jointly satisfiable, so that a pair of codes can appear administratively compliant while in fact encoding properties the material cannot simultaneously possess.

This translation problem can be considered as a semantic problem. The issue is not only that EWC and HS use different code numbers but also that they classify the same material according to different types of information. To illustrate: the same polyester fibers receive the EWC code 04 02 22 when generated during textile processing and the EWC code 07 02 13 when generated during plastic recycling; the HS, by contrast, classifies both under 5505.10 (waste of synthetic fibers) on the basis of material composition alone, regardless of the originating process. Without an explicit account of what each code means and what properties must be present for that code to apply, translation between systems cannot be validated. The analysis proceeds in two stages. Basic Formal Ontology (BFO) is used as an analytical framework to make explicit the different classificatory principles and headings that are implicit in the two systems, in order to show why direct translation fails at the definitional level. A crosswalk is constructed to classify each mapping pair as (i) supportable (where source and target definitions are fully consistent), (ii) conditional (where translation is possible but requires additional documentary evidence), or (iii) blocked (where translation is definitionally impossible regardless of available evidence). The crosswalk uses SKOS relation types [20], such as skos:exactMatch, skos:closeMatch, and skos:relatedMatch, to express these mapping relations.

The analysis draws on a documented international shipment from Romania's second-hand textile trade as a worked example [1]. The aim is to make possible incompatibilities between the two systems explicit and auditable and to give enforcement authorities a tool for identifying when apparently compliant documentary combinations are in fact classificatory contradictions. The method demonstrated here for EWC and HS is transferable: any two classification systems that encode different definitional logics can be evaluated using the same framework. By making classification gaps explicit, auditable, and machine-readable, this paper could support digital waste-tracking and similar systems in other domains by providing formal rules for cross-system code comparison.

2 Literature Review

The recognition that semantic heterogeneity between information systems cannot be solved simply by connecting fields in one database to fields in another has been developed by Bishr [3], who distinguishes two levels at which interoperability between information systems can fail. Syntactic heterogeneity arises when systems use different data structures to represent the same entities; this is a technical problem which can be solved through data transformation. Semantic heterogeneity arises when systems assign different meanings to the same categories. This requires explicit representation of what each system means by its categories, and specification of the conditions under which categories in one system correspond to categories in another.

In waste management, the semantic heterogeneity lies in the classification systems. Waste classification systems do not provide neutral descriptors of material entities, but contested codes that reflect the regulatory purposes for which they were designed [11,18]. Van Capelleveen et al. [15] show that EWC's process-indexed structure creates definitional underdetermination. The same material can be assigned different codes because the code's applicability depends on the generating activity. Sileryte et al. [14] demonstrate, through an ontology-based approach to circular economy monitoring, that regulatory compliance codes cannot support material traceability without explicit semantic alignment. At the domain level, Habib and Parris [8] establish that HS code descriptions lack the specificity needed to determine the end-of-life fate of textile shipments: the same HS heading applies whether the material will be reused, recycled, or landfilled. To address this, they call for reform of the HS structure to distinguish end-of-life scenario, with proposals to be developed for the 2027 review cycle [8]. The Environmental European Agency (EEA) analysis of EU-level export flows across multiple receiving countries and years documents systematic discrepancies between HS classifications at point of export and reported treatment outcomes at destination [5–7]. Shipments recorded as 'worn clothing' are routinely processed as waste upon arrival, with destination-country reports documenting downcycling, re-export, and landfill disposal.

Poon et al. [13] extend this analysis to the structure of international textile waste trade, showing that trade flows reflect arbitrage opportunities created by classification gaps and regulatory asymmetries rather than legitimate material value. A five-country study of waste shipment records found consignments declared to non-OECD destinations under Basel codes for hazardous waste while simultaneously carrying an EWC code for non-hazardous waste, a combination the investigators could resolve only by referring the case for verification [21]. Cross-system code comparison is already used to flag suspect consignments, but without a stated basis for reliable comparison.

The literature reviewed above establishes that classification systems are built on different principles that produce accounts of the same material that are not mutually substitutable. What the existing literature has not produced is a response that moves from diagnosis to remedy. This paper aims to fill that gap by proposing a framework that specifies, for a given pair of codes from two different systems, whether translation is valid, what evidence would be required to support it, and when translation is blocked because the source code categorically lacks the properties the target code requires.

3 Data Sources and Case Materials

The analysis draws on three kinds of material: the two classification systems under comparison, the EWC and the HS, and a documented shipment case used to test how the crosswalk works in practice.

3.1 The European Waste Catalogue

The European Waste Catalogue (EWC), also known as the European List of Waste (ELoW), was established by the Commission Decision 2000/532/EC. It serves as a harmonized classification system for waste management documentation across EU Member States [10]. It is a process-oriented classification system [16]: each code is assigned on the basis of the industrial or operational activity that generated the waste. This means that materially identical substances can receive different codes depending on where they were generated [15]. As a result textile-relevant codes are distributed across chapters defined by generating activity. Assignment is governed by a specificity rule: where more than one entry applies, the most specific applicable entry must be used. Within Chapter 20 01 this makes 20 01 10 (clothes) the required code for clothing items, and 20 01 11 (textiles) residual for textile articles that are not clothing.

The EWC codes included in this analysis were identified through the EWC-STAT category 07.6 (textile wastes), which aggregates the relevant entries from the full EWC list. The EWC-STAT groups textile waste together with leather and fur, this analysis does not follow that aggregation. The inclusion criterion applied here is definitional primacy: a code is included if textile fibre material is the primary and constitutive content of the waste description, regardless of whether the catalogue chapter is organized by material or by generating activity.

This is a selection criterion applied to the EWC from the outside as the catalogue itself does not group textile-relevant codes together, precisely because its chapter structure follows process origin rather than material identity. The codes selected on this basis vary in their internal definitional structure: most combine a process-based chapter logic with a material specification that identifies the fiber content, making them compound in type. Only 04 02 99 is purely process-based, containing no material specification, its inclusion is justified because it belongs to the textile industry chapter and functions as a residual category for textile-industry waste not otherwise specified. The resulting code set is presented in Table 1, which also records the definitional type underlying each code.

Table 1. EWC headings included in the analysis, where the scope of each heading is expressed in natural language by the issuing authority.

EWC Chapter	Code	Code Description	Classification Basis
Ch. 04 02 Textile industry	04 02 09	Wastes from composite materials: impregnated textile, elastomer, plastomer	Process+Material
Ch. 04 02 Textile industry	04 02 21	Wastes from unprocessed textile fibres	Process+Material
Ch. 04 02 Textile industry	04 02 22	Wastes from processed textile fibres	Process+Material
Ch. 04 02 Textile industry	04 02 99	Wastes not otherwise specified	Process
Ch. 15 01 Packaging waste	15 01 09	Textile packaging	History+Material
Ch. 19 12 Mechanical treatment of waste	19 12 08	Textiles from mechanical treatment of waste	Process+Material
Ch. 20 01 Municipal fractions	20 01 10	Clothes	History+Process
Ch. 20 01 Municipal fractions	20 01 11	Textiles	History+Process

3.2 The Harmonized System

The Harmonized Commodity Description and Coding System (HS) is a trade nomenclature designed for tariff assessment and customs statistics. It also serves as the reference system for the Basel Convention's regulation of transboundary waste movements. It is not a waste catalogue, and for this reason it does not contain a dedicated section for waste materials. Rather, waste-relevant headings are distributed across chapters organized by commodity type and fiber composition.

The HS headings included in this analysis were identified through Basel Convention Annex IX entry B3030, which lists textile wastes considered non-hazardous for the purposes of transboundary movement control, provided they are not mixed with other wastes and are prepared to a specification. To identify the HS headings included under B3030, the textile-relevant Chapters 50–63 were screened for headings whose official descriptions explicitly include the terms 'waste,' 'scrap,' 'used,' or 'worn.' This screen is principled but conservative: it retrieves only headings where waste status is encoded in the official description itself.

The inclusion of the 6309 heading ‘worn clothing’ requires further explanation. In EU export practice, the distinction between 6309 and 6310 broadly tracks the reuse/waste boundary: 6309 is typically applied to textiles considered fit for reuse, while 6310 covers material unfit for reuse regardless of whether it has been further processed [6]. However, this rule of thumb is eroded in practice by the widespread export of unsorted batches, which contain reusable items and rags but are routinely declared under 6309 [9,16]. The resulting set of codes is presented in Table 2.

Table 2. HS headings included in the analysis and the scope of each expressed in natural language terms.

HS Chapter	Code	Code description	Classification basis
Ch. 50 Silk	5003	Silk waste, including cocoons unsuitable for reeling and yarn waste	Material
Ch. 51 Wool and animal hair	5103	Waste of wool or fine/coarse animal hair	Material
Ch. 52 Cotton	5202	Cotton waste, including yarn waste and garnetted stock	Material
Ch. 53 Vegetable fibres	5301.30	Tow and waste of flax	Material
Ch. 53 Vegetable fibres	5302.90	Tow and waste of true hemp	Material
Ch. 53 Vegetable fibres	5303.90	Tow and waste of jute and other bast fibres	Material
Ch. 53 Vegetable fibres	5304.90	Tow and waste of sisal and other Agave fibres	Material
Ch. 53 Vegetable fibres	5305.19	Tow, noils and waste of coconut/coir	Material
Ch. 55 Man-made staple fibres	5505.10	Waste of synthetic fibres	Material
Ch. 55 Man-made staple fibres	5505.20	Waste of artificial fibres	Material
Ch. 63 Other made-up textile articles	6309	Worn clothing and other worn articles	History
Ch. 63 Other made-up textile articles	6310	Used rags, scrap twine, cordage, rope, cables, and worn-out articles	History + material

3.3 Test Case: The RISE Project Textile Shipment

The documents of the empirical shipment used as a test case in this paper are drawn from the investigative project published by the RISE Project [1,4]. The analysis focuses on documents made publicly available as part of the investigation concerning a consignment of 15,820 kg of second-hand clothing transported from Hungary to Romania.

The records include (i) the CMR transport document, a standard international consignment note issued under the Convention on the Contract for the International Carriage of Goods by Road, which records the sender, recipient, goods description, and declared statistical classification of the shipment; (ii) the Certificate of Quality, a document issued by the exporter attesting that the articles were separated, sorted, and clean, and that they ‘can be worn by people,’ thereby asserting suitability for reuse; and (iii) the Annex VII information document, required under Regulation (EC) No 1013/2006 on shipments of waste, which documents the same shipment under the waste shipment regime.

What makes this set of documents directly relevant for this analysis is that the same physical load appears simultaneously as a traded good under the HS and as a waste under the EWC. It is precisely this co-occurrence that the crosswalk is designed to interrogate. This case is revisited in Sect. 5.2 as an empirical test of the crosswalk.

4 Methodology

The methodology treats the interoperability problem between EWC and HS as a problem derived from definitional incompatibility. Before the two systems can be connected through a crosswalk, the properties encoded by each code must be made explicit. The problem addressed here is therefore multiple classification: the conditions under which a material entity classified under a category of one scheme can also be classified under a category of another. Nomenclature alignment, where two labels denote the same category, is a distinct problem and is not addressed here.

The method proceeds in two stages. First, a definitional analysis of each code is carried out using BFO [2] as analytical framework, identifying the ontological commitments that make direct translation fail (Sect. 4.1). Second, a crosswalk is constructed that uses SKOS mapping properties to classify each EWC–HS pair according to translation validity and to specify, for each valid mapping, the definitional requirements and documentation needed to support it (Sect. 4.2)

4.1 Ontological Analysis and Definitional Logics

Top-level ontologies provide a domain-neutral upper-level framework for analysing how classification systems structure knowledge about entities in the world [2]. The BFO framework provides a set of upper-level categories such as continuants, occurrents, dispositions, roles, processes and relations between them. This structure can make explicit the logical commitments underlying any classification scheme independent from domain-specific commitments. BFO was chosen for two reasons: its domain-neutrality makes it applicable across both waste management and customs classification without privileging either system's vocabulary, and its well-defined relation set provides a controlled language for stating definitional requirements in a form that is both human-readable and machine-processable.

In this analysis, a property is any feature that a code's official definition requires a material entity to have in order for the code to apply, including its generating process, material composition, and functional history. An entity is said to possess such a property when it instantiates the relevant BFO category or bears the relevant dependent continuant (for example, a role or disposition) specified in the definition. A definitional type is the primary classificatory criterion on which a code's definition relies: generating process, material composition, or functional history.

The analysis proceeds in two steps. First, the definitional types that structure textile-relevant codes in both systems are identified, second each code is classified according to whether it assigns classification on the basis of (i) generating process (the industrial activity that generated the waste), (ii) material composition (fibre type), or (iii) functional history (lifecycle status such as worn or used). A code may carry more than one. The components are read off the official text at two levels: the chapter heading, which in the EWC names a generating activity and in the HS a fibre class or article group, and the entry text, which supplies any further material or lifecycle specification.

Because the EWC tracks process origin rather than material identity, materially identical polyester fibres may receive different EWC codes depending on the activity from which they emerge.

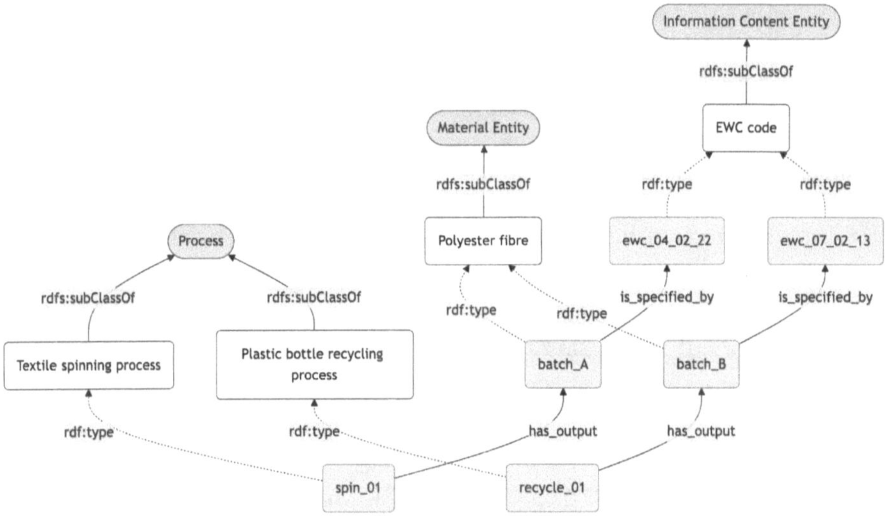

Fig. 1. Process-dependent EWC code assignment for materially identical polyester fibre. Blue nodes are BFO classes, white nodes domain classes, amber nodes individuals. (Color figure online)

Figure 1 shows two batches of polyester fiber receiving code 04 02 22 when output of a textile spinning process and code 07 02 13 when output of plastic bottle recycling. Both are instances of the same class, so the distinction is drawn at the level of individuals: the class bears no EWC code, which becomes assignable only once a particular batch has a generating process. Each code is an individual of EWC code, a subclass of Information Content Entity, related to the batch it classifies by `specified_by`.

Analyzing each code within the BFO framework makes it possible to state its assignment conditions explicitly, that is, the properties a material entity must possess for that code to apply. Once these conditions are articulated for both EWC and HS codes, their definitions can be compared directly. A definitional gap occurs when a target code requires a property that is not encoded in the definition of the source code; not because the definition of the source is defective in itself, but because it follows a different classification logic and therefore tracks different properties of the same material. By making these conditions explicit, the crosswalk can detect situations in which documents appear compatible at the level of codes but, in fact, conceal an underlying cross-system definitional gap.

However, SKOS mapping properties are designed to represent a relationship between concepts in two different schemes exists, but they do not provide formal semantics about the conditions under which a mapping holds [20]. Taken alone they do not explain why a mapping is partial, what information is missing, or what evidence would be needed to validate the translation. For this reason, the SKOS representation is extended with four custom crosswalk properties: `:hasDefinitionalGap`, which specifies the assignment condition present in the target code but not encoded in the source code; `:hasRequiredCondition` and `:hasEvidenceTypes`, which specify respectively the condition that must be satisfied and the documentation that would satisfy it; and `:hasBlockingConditionText`, which records the circumstance that would defeat the mapping, and which for blocked pairs states why no evidence can supply the missing property.

It is important to note what the accompanying OWL implementation does and does not commit to. Each code definition of the kind shown in Table 3 is represented as an instance of Information Content Entity that is `specified_by` a set of assignment conditions, rather than as an OWL class with its own necessary-and-sufficient conditions. Category membership and the SKOS crosswalk relations are therefore asserted directly, following the analysis carried out at the definitional level in this section, rather than derived by an OWL reasoner from class-level axioms.

4.2 The Crosswalk Construction

The crosswalk is built on a single organizing question: for any given EWC–HS pair, do the properties encoded in the source code satisfy the assignment conditions of the target code? Both are asserted in the artefact, by `hasEncodedProperty` on EWC codes and `requiresProperty` on HS headings; a pair is supportable when the target's requirements are a subset of the source's encoded properties, and the residue is the definitional gap.

The target requirements are not externally imposed standards but are read directly from the official definitions of each code in its source regulatory instrument. For EWC codes, the assignment conditions are set by Commission Decision 2000/532/EC, which specifies the generating activity, process context, and waste type that must be identified before a code can be assigned. For HS headings, the assignment conditions are set by the WCO Harmonized System nomenclature, which classifies by fibre type, lifecycle status (worn, used), or material composition. 'Target requirements' in the crosswalk therefore means: the necessary conditions stated in the legal definition of the target code. When translation proceeds from EWC to HS, the HS heading sets the requirements; when it proceeds in the other direction, the EWC code does.

This comparison determines both the SKOS mapping property and the crosswalk annotations. `skos:exactMatch` is used when all target requirements are satisfied by the source definition. `skos:closeMatch` is used when translation is possible but a definitional gap must be bridged by additional documented evidence (for example, fibre-composition tests, quality certificates, or condition assessments), and the pair is annotated with `:hasDefinitionalGap`, `:hasRequiredCondition` and `:hasEvidenceTypes`. `skos:relatedMatch` is reserved for pairs that refer to the same general domain of material but where at least one target requirement cannot be satisfied by any instance of the source code; these pairs are annotated with `:hasDefinitionalGap` and `:hasBlockingConditionText` to indicate that the relation is conceptual rather than translational. The crosswalk is exhaustive over the scoped code sets: all 96 pairs formed by the eight EWC codes and the twelve HS headings are evaluated and recorded, including those for which the only relation is a blocking condition. The decision procedure is visualized in Fig. 2.

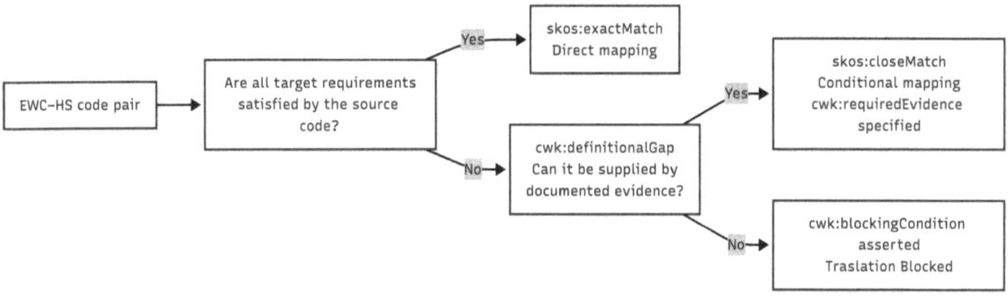

Fig. 2. Crosswalk Decision Flow

The crosswalk is oriented from EWC codes to HS headings. The analysis provided in Sect. 3.1 shows how the EWC is structurally coarser than HS. Mapping outward from EWC to HS reveals how a single waste category 'disaggregates' into distinct trade classifications. The reverse direction (HS → EWC) is not developed separately here: once the 96 EWC–HS mapping pairs are established, the same pairs can be read in the opposite direction.

The complete crosswalk is provided as supplementary material in the accompanying GitHub repository: https://github.com/elenamiliv/Textile-Waste-Crosswalk. The repository contains the full EWC–HS mapping matrix in CSV format encoding the 96 mapped pairs. Each pair records the source EWC code requirements, target HS code requirements, SKOS relation, definitional gap, required evidence, and blocking condition. Users can navigate interactively from an EWC code to all candidate HS codes and then inspect the relevant mapping individual.

The mapping relations in the crosswalk are entered rather than inferred by a reasoner, so their correctness has to be checkable. The query below flags any mapping whose pathway type and SKOS relation disagree, and returns none against the published crosswalk.

```
PREFIX : <https://w3id.org/textile-waste-crosswalk/>
PREFIX skos: <http://www.w3.org/2004/02/skos/core#>
SELECT ?mapping ?violation WHERE {
  ?mapping a :CrosswalkMapping .
  { ?mapping :hasPathwayType :blocked ; :hasEvidenceTypes ?e .
    FILTER (?e != "N/A") }
  UNION
  { ?mapping :hasPathwayType :blocked .
    FILTER NOT EXISTS { ?mapping skos:relatedMatch ?t } }
  UNION
  { ?mapping :hasPathwayType :conditional .
    FILTER NOT EXISTS { ?mapping skos:closeMatch ?t } }
}
```

5 Results

5.1 Definitional Asymmetry Between EWC and HS

Applying the crosswalk to the 96 candidate pairs returns no supportable mapping: 65 are conditional, requiring documented evidence to bridge a definitional gap, and 31 are blocked. The analysis of the scoped code sets provided in 3.1 and 3.2 reveals that EWC and HS textile codes are structured by three distinct classification criteria: generating process, material composition, and functional history. The selected codes correspond to those that co-occur within the single shipment analyzed in 5.2, where the same material is simultaneously classified under EWC codes for municipal textile waste (20 01 10, 20 01 11), HS code 6309 for worn clothing in the context of transboundary shipment controls.

Table 3. BFO-compatible definitions for selected textile-related codes.

System	Code	Label	BFO definition
EWC	20 01 10	Clothes	A clothing_item that bears some waste_role and is output_of some MunicipalCollectionProcess.
EWC	20 01 11	Textiles	A textile_article that is not a clothing_item, bears some waste_role and is output_of some MunicipalCollectionProcess.
HS	6309	Worn clothing and other worn articles	A clothing_item that has history_of some PriorUse.
HS	6310	Used rags, scrap textiles	A textile_article of rag_or_scrap_form that has history_of some PriorUse.

Table 3 presents a subset of codes based on the shipment documentation analyzed in Sect. 5.2. The subset of codes presented includes HS 6310 because it represents the alternative classification outcome for the same material: used textiles that do not meet the reuse threshold of HS 6309 must instead be classified as rags, scrap, or worn-out articles under HS 6310 [6]. Each code is translated into a BFO-compatible definition by decomposing its original natural-language description into three ontological components: the type of material entity being classified, the role or function that entity bears, and the process or history condition to which it is connected. For EWC codes, the material entity is typically a textile item or fiber, the role is a WasteRole conferred by the generating or collection process, and the process condition encodes origin (industrial, municipal, or mechanical). For HS codes, no WasteRole is assigned; instead, the definition encodes material form and use history (e.g. PriorUse).

5.2 Case-Based Crosswalk Application: The Textile Shipment

The crosswalk is applied here to the three documents reviewed in Sect. 3.3. Each document is treated as a source of classificatory claims, carrying one or more code assignments for the same physical shipment.

This section will evaluate whether those claims are mutually consistent across the EWC–HS mapping pairs present in the file. EWC codes 20 01 10 and 20 01 11 are found on the waste documentation (Annex VII), and HS code 6309 on the CMR. The crosswalk is used to evaluate whether these co-occurring codes, drawn from different classification systems, produce consistent or conflicting classificatory outcomes for the same consignment.

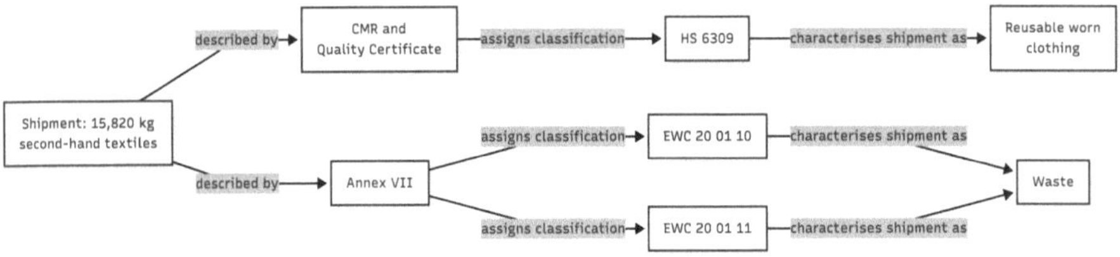

Fig. 3. Classificatory claims across shipment documents.

Figure 3 presents the classificatory claims carried by each document. Table 4 sets out the crosswalk evaluation of the two candidate mapping pairs and distinguishes the semantic mapping relation from the regulatory validation result.

The crosswalk flags the two mappings differently. EWC 20 01 10 maps to HS 6309 conditionally: the EWC code assigns a waste role, while HS 6309 in export practice carries a presumption of reuse fitness, so documentary evidence of that fitness is required before the translation can be supported. EWC 20 01 11 to HS 6309 is blocked. The two definitions do not themselves exclude one another, since both admit clothing items; what blocks the mapping is the EWC's assignment rule. Correct assignment of 20 01 11 entails that 20 01 10 was inapplicable, and therefore that the material collected is not clothing. HS 6309 requires a

Table 4. Crosswalk evaluation of candidate mapping pairs in the textile shipment.

Candidate mapping	SKOS relation	Validation status	Basis
EWC 20 01 10 → HS 6309	`skos:closeMatch`	Conditional	Source code assigns a waste role; target heading carries a presumption of reuse fitness in export practice, so documentary evidence of that fitness is required
EWC 20 01 11 → HS 6309	`skos:relatedMatch`	Blocked	Correct assignment of the source code entails that the material is not clothing; the target heading requires a clothing item, and no evidence can supply it
EWC 20 01 10 → HS 6310	`skos:closeMatch`	Conditional	Target heading requires material not fit for reuse as a garment; the Certificate of Quality in the file asserts the opposite
EWC 20 01 11 → HS 6310	`skos:closeMatch`	Conditional	Target heading requires rag or scrap form together with confirmed non-reuse status; neither is documented, and the reuse certification points away from both

clothing item, so no correctly assigned instance of the source code satisfies the target requirement, and no additional evidence can supply it. The Annex VII assigns both codes to the same load, which on this reading is the shipper's own documentation asserting that part of the consignment is not clothing, while the CMR declares the entire 15,820 kg under a clothing-specific heading.

HS 6310 requires textile material in rag or scrap form together with a history of use. Either EWC code could supply that, given a sorting assessment confirming the material is not fit for reuse. The consignment carries no such assessment; it carries a Certificate of Quality attesting that the articles can be worn. That same certificate is the evidence the 6309 mapping requires. One document therefore closes both 6310 pathways and opens the 6309 pathway at once.

The `:hasBlockingConditionText` is triggered not by a missing property that evidence could supply, but by the simultaneous presence of contradictory claims within the same file: the Annex VII asserts waste status while the Certificate of Quality asserts reuse suitability. The coexistence of these documentary claims requires a competent authority determination rather than automatic translation.

The value of the crosswalk lies in identifying when apparently compatible documentary codes in fact rely on different and possibly incompatible assumptions about the status of the material. Without a crosswalk, the file may appear as a routine coexistence of transport, trade, and waste documentation. With a crosswalk, the same file becomes analytically tractable: it shows if mappings are supportable, and what should be blocked pending further review.

The crosswalk does not replace inspection, enforcement discretion, or legal classification by a competent authority. Only documentary combinations are identified that should not be accepted as straightforward translations without further review.

6 Discussion

The analysis shows that the incompatibility between the EWC and HS textile codes is not a terminological mismatch, but a structural divergence in what each system tracks. The result that zero of the 96 candidate mappings qualify as exact is an expected outcome of the analysis. The distribution across the three outcomes is itself informative: the analysis does not return a uniform failure but separates pairs that additional documentation could support from pairs that no documentation could. Because the EWC assigns codes on the basis of the generating process and the HS on the basis of material composition or lifecycle status, no pair drawn from the two systems encodes the same properties, and therefore none qualifies as an exact match. The single case study demonstrates that classificatory contradictions occur in documented practice without establishing their prevalence.

This result refines and operationalizes the diagnosis offered by the literature reviewed in Sect. 2. Bishr's [3] distinction between syntactic and semantic heterogeneity provides the conceptual frame, but it does not specify what semantic heterogeneity looks like at the level of individual code pairs, nor does it offer a method for determining when gaps are bridgeable and when they are not. Van Capelleveen et al. [15] argue that the process-indexed structure of EWC generates systematic semantic ambiguity in applications that rely on EWC labels. The textile crosswalk developed here is consistent with this diagnosis. It shows that the feature of process-indexing also generates ambiguity when EWC codes are mapped into a system structured by different classificatory principles. Habib and Parris [8] observe that HS descriptions are insufficiently specified to distinguish reusable goods from disposal materials, and the textile crosswalk encounters the same difficulty in the case of HS 6309 and 6310. In practice, these headings are used alongside EWC codes in consignments that are treated as waste, yet the HS texts themselves are not 'waste codes' by definition: they describe product form and condition rather than legal waste status. To interpret 6309 and 6310 as waste-related codes in a given shipment, the crosswalk must therefore rely on external documentation (such as Annex VII forms) that specify the status. The crosswalk makes explicit what kind of evidence is required, on what basis it is assessed, and when its absence constitutes a blocking condition.

Several limitations should be acknowledged. The crosswalk establishes which mappings are possible but not how often they occur, and this reflects the available evidence: documentation for suspect consignments enters the public record only through enforcement action or investigative reporting, so the files that can be examined are those in which a contradiction was already detected. This constraint is structural rather than incidental. Member States are not obliged to collect Annex VII information, practice varies between them, and Romania has no reporting obligation for non-hazardous shipments at all [21]. The evidence on which the mappings depend is therefore frequently absent from the record for the very consignments the crosswalk is designed to assess.

The code sets could be broadened using trade-flow data and enforcement intelligence to identify HS headings under which textile waste moves without explicit waste descriptors, and the evidence conditions could be validated against actual sorting and export documentation practices. A class-level representation with support for higher-order types would allow mapping validity to be checked by a reasoner rather than by hand. The pattern of process-indexed waste codes interacting with commodity-indexed trade codes recurs across electronic waste, plastics, and end-of-life vehicles, and the method of definitional decomposition is transferable to those cases in principle, though each extension would require repeating the definitional analysis rather than reusing the present artifact.

7 Conclusion

This paper developed an approach for aligning classification systems. Rather than treating mismatches as simple coding errors, it treated them as cases of semantic heterogeneity and used formal ontological analysis to reconstruct the implicit conditions under which codes apply. On this basis, it proposed an evidence-explicit mapping procedure that separates mappings that are valid only under specified evidential conditions from mappings that should be treated as blocked. The textile waste and trade classifications served as a demonstration of the approach. The analysis showed that direct translation between EWC and HS codes cannot be assumed. Because the two systems provide different codes which carry different properties, valid translation depends on whether the source code satisfies the information requirements of the target code, whether the gap can be bridged by additional evidence, or whether the required target property is categorically absent.

The main contribution of the paper is therefore methodological and practical. Methodologically, it shows how formal ontological analysis can move the literature from diagnosis of incompatibility to an operational framework for evaluating translation between codes. Practically, it offers a tool for authorities and digital waste-tracking systems to identify when documentary combinations are supportable, when they are conditional on further evidence, and when they constitute classificatory contradictions. In this sense, the purpose of the crosswalk is not to collapse different systems into a single vocabulary, but to make their points of incompatibility visible, explicit, and auditable.

Disclosure of Interests. The author(s) declare no conflict of interest

References

1. Ciurcanu, A.: How Europe's secondhand clothes are trashing Romania. Organized Crime and Corruption Reporting Project (2024). https://www.occrp.org/en/investigation/how-europes-secondhand-clothes-are-trashing-romania
2. Arp, R., Smith, B., Spear, A.D.: Building Ontologies with Basic Formal Ontology. The MIT Press, Cambridge (2015)
3. Bishr, Y.: Overcoming the semantic and other barriers to GIS interoperability. Int. J. Geogr. Inf. Sci. **12**(4), 299–314 (1998). https://doi.org/10.1080/136588198241806

4. Ciurcanu, A.: A textile danger: when magistrates wear other capes. RISE Project (2024). https://www.riseproject.ro/en/investigations/uncategorized/a-textile-danger-when-magistrates-wear-other-clothes/
5. European Commission: Joint Research Centre: Circular economy perspectives in the EU textile sector: final report. Publications Office of the European Union, Luxembourg (2021)
6. European Environment Agency: EU exports of used textiles in Europe's circular economy. Publications Office of the European Union, Luxembourg (2023)
7. European Environment Agency: Management of used and waste textiles in Europe's circular economy. Publications Office of the European Union, Luxembourg (2024)
8. Habib, N.M., Parris, H.: Reforming textile trade codes to be fit for purpose for the circular and sustainable textile economy. CRSD report, Centre for Resilience and Sustainable Development, University of Cambridge (2024)
9. Koehler, A., Watson, D., Trzepacz, S., et al.: Circular economy perspectives in the EU textile sector: final report. Publications Office of the European Union, Luxembourg (2021). https://doi.org/10.2760/858144
10. Natural Scotland, Scottish Government: Guidance on using the European Waste Catalogue (EWC) to code waste (2015)
11. Offenhuber, D.: Waste Is Information: Infrastructure Legibility and Governance. The MIT Press (2017). https://doi.org/10.7551/mitpress/10453.001.0001
12. Pires, A., Martinho, G., Chang, N.-B.: Solid waste management in European countries: a review of systems analysis techniques. J. Environ. Manage. **92**(4), 1033–1050 (2011). https://doi.org/10.1016/j.jenvman.2010.11.024
13. Poon, J.P.H., et al.: Industrial and textile waste trade: multilayer network and environmental policy effects. Waste Manage. **177**, 146–157 (2024). https://doi.org/10.1016/j.wasman.2024.01.048
14. Sileryte, R., et al.: A bottom-up ontology-based approach to monitor circular economy: aligning user expectations, tools, data and theory. J. Ind. Ecol. **27**(2), 395–407 (2023). https://doi.org/10.1111/jiec.13350
15. Van Capelleveen, G., Amrit, C., Zijm, H.: Toward building recommender systems for the circular economy: exploring the perils of the European Waste Catalogue. J. Environ. Manage. **277**, 111430 (2021). https://doi.org/10.1016/j.jenvman.2020.111430
16. Watson, D.: Exports of Nordic Used Textiles: Fate, Benefits and Impacts. Nordic Council of Ministers, Copenhagen (2016)
17. Wen, X., et al.: Comparison research on waste classification between China and the EU, Japan, and the USA. J. Mater. Cycles Waste Manage. **16**(2), 321–334 (2014). https://doi.org/10.1007/s10163-013-0190-1
18. Wipraechtiger, M., et al.: Waste not, want not – ambiguities around waste and waste prevention. Resour. Conserv. Recycl. **173**, 105742 (2021). https://doi.org/10.1016/j.resconrec.2021.105742
19. Commission Decision 2000/532/EC of 3 May 2000 replacing Decision 94/3/EC establishing a list of wastes and Council Decision 94/904/EC establishing a list of hazardous waste. Official Journal of the European Communities (2000)
20. W3C: SKOS Simple Knowledge Organization System becomes W3C Recommendation. https://www.w3.org/press-releases/2009/skos/

21. OPFA-WASTE Project: Cross-border shipments of waste: pilot research. SAFE Europe (2022). https://www.safe-europe.eu/project/opfawaste/download/ResearchOutputs/OPFA-WASTE-Research-TSW-Report-FINAL.pdf
22. World Customs Organization: HS Nomenclature 2022 edition. https://www.wcoomd.org/en/topics/nomenclature/instrument-and-tools/hs-nomenclature-2022-edition.aspx. Accessed 04 May 2026

LLMs and AI for Conceptual Modeling

Towards Controllable Generation of Diverse Conceptual Modeling Tasks via LLM-Assisted Contextualization Under Formal Constraints

Zixin Wu(✉) and Janis Voigtländer

Faculty of Computer Science, University of Duisburg-Essen, Duisburg, Germany
zixin.wu@uni-due.de, janis.voigtlaender@uni-due.de

Abstract. Conceptual modeling education requires large numbers of tasks that are structurally valid, didactically useful, and sufficiently diverse for repeated practice. Existing approaches, however, expose a clear trade-off. Formal-methods-based generation provides controllability, validation, and explicit difficulty configuration, but usually produces tasks with artificial identifiers and weak contextualization. Large language models (LLMs), in contrast, can provide rich real-world semantics, but lack reliable formal guarantees and fine-grained control. To address this tension, we propose FoLIC (formal-constraint-grounded LLM-assisted semantic injection and contextualization), a decoupled framework that integrates LLM-based semantic contextualization into formally grounded conceptual-modeling task generation. FoLIC preserves formal validity by separating solver-backed structural generation from semantic enrichment, so that LLMs are confined to concept injection and scenario construction while formal constraints remain under explicit control. Our evaluation shows that FoLIC preserves formal validity by design, supports contextualized task variants across multiple task families, and enables exploratory deployment in educational practice. At the same time, the results indicate that semantic quality depends strongly on the capability of the underlying LLMs. The source code and experimental data are publicly available at https://doi.org/10.5281/zenodo.21475258.

Keywords: Conceptual Modeling · Formal Verification and Generation · AI-Assisted Modeling · Large Language Model

1 Introduction

Conceptual modeling (CM) is widely used in software engineering, information systems, and business-process design [19]. In both practice and education, conceptual models serve not only to document designs, but also to reason about admissible structures, consistency, and intended semantics [1]. Among the most widely used notations, the Unified Modeling Language (UML) [20] remains

© The Author(s), under exclusive license to Springer Nature Switzerland AG 2027
A. Bernasconi et al. (Eds.): ER 2026, LNCS 17081, pp. 57–73, 2027.
https://doi.org/10.1007/978-3-032-40795-5_4

prominent in both industry and academia. However, CM is not easy to learn or teach [16]. For beginners in particular, the main difficulty lies less in memorizing notation than in understanding what a model means, which structures it permits or forbids, and how its elements interact under formal constraints [21]. In UML class diagrams (CDs) and object diagrams (ODs), for example, students often struggle to connect diagram syntax with underlying semantics when reasoning about consistency, multiplicities, and relationship types. As a result, high-quality CM tasks are important for education, yet their large-scale creation, diversification, and validation remain difficult and costly.

Recent advances in AI-driven modeling create both opportunities and risks for CM education [2]. Large language models (LLMs) and other generative models can support task creation, hint generation, and, to some extent, automated assessment [3,4,9]. However, educational deployment imposes requirements that go beyond naturalness or fluency: generated tasks must remain formally verifiable, controllable in type and difficulty, sufficiently diverse and scalable, and aligned with learning objectives. At the same time, AI support should foster understanding rather than shortcut it [8]. This raises a central design challenge: how can AI-generated contextual richness be combined with the controllability and verifiability required in CM education?

In this paper, we focus on educational modeling tasks built around CDs and ODs (centered on structural properties) and basic UML activity diagrams (ADs). Within this scope, existing popular approaches to automating task creation include knowledge-engineered (KE-based), formal-methods-based (FM-based), and LLM-based generation. KE-based approaches rely on manually crafted templates, rules, or ontologies. They can support predictable and contextualized task design, but require substantial manual effort [7,11,14]. FM-based approaches provide controllability and verifiability, but generally produce tasks with artificial identifiers and limited contextualization [15,24]. LLM-based approaches offer rich contextualization, but lack strong formal guarantees and fine-grained control [5]. Taken together, these approaches reveal a central tension between formal verifiability and meaningful contextualization.

We investigate how LLMs can assist in solver-backed generation of CM tasks with meaningful real-world concepts without substantially undermining formal validity. More specifically, we study how formally generated task instances can be enriched with contextual semantics while preserving the advantages of formal generation, including controllability, verifiability, and explicit difficulty configuration. We formulate the following research questions:

RQ1: How can LLM assistance be integrated into a solver-backed workflow to generate CM task instances with real-world concepts while preserving formal validity as much as possible?

RQ2: To what extent can different LLMs generate suitable real-world concepts to enrich formally generated CM task instances?

RQ3: To what extent can FoLIC generate diverse contextualized CM task instances at scale across various task types, and how practical is the process?

RQ4: What preliminary evidence can be obtained on student performance and early perceptions when working on contextualized CM tasks, compared with tasks using artificial identifiers?

To address these questions, we propose FoLIC, a decoupled framework that integrates LLM assistance while separating formally grounded components from uncertain LLM outputs. FoLIC is both a practical tool for CM education and a new approach to combining FM-based generation with LLM assistance: it reuses formal CM task generation but enriches it with LLM-based semantic contextualization while preserving formal validity through a decoupled design and post-contextualization validation with instance checkers.

The remainder of this paper is organized as follows. Section 2 reviews the learning challenges and task-design requirements of CM education and compares existing KE-based, FM-based, and LLM-based approaches. Section 3 presents FoLIC and its decoupled architecture, illustrated with one task running example. Section 4 reports our evaluation along the four research questions. Section 5 discusses limitations and threats to validity, Sect. 6 concludes, both touching on future work.

2 Background and Related Work

Prior studies and teaching practice consistently show that challenges in CM education go beyond surface notation and concern the gap between diagram constructs and their intended semantics [21]. We first summarize the resulting learning challenges and task-design requirements, then compare existing approaches.

In CM education, students' main difficulties rarely stem from syntax alone. Rather, the central challenge lies in understanding the abstract semantics behind diagram constructs and structural properties, for example, how relationship types and multiplicities in CDs constrain admissible structures. This becomes especially visible when students must justify modeling decisions or reason about consistency under structural constraints. Effective learning therefore benefits from iterative practice with timely assessment and feedback, while task difficulty must be calibrated carefully to avoid both trivial and discouraging exercises. The growing availability of AI tools introduces an additional challenge: although they may support learning, their misuse increases the risk that answers are produced without genuine understanding. These challenges motivate automated CM task-generation workflows suitable for educational deployment at scale. As summarized in Table 1, such workflows must balance six requirements.

Table 2 summarizes representative approaches against the requirements mentioned above. KE-based approaches build tasks from knowledge that human experts encode by hand, for example templates with fillable slots or ontologies of the concepts and relations to combine [7,11,14]. Because each task is instantiated from these predefined artifacts, they can support contextualized and relatively traceable task design, and may provide some variation through predefined combinations. However, they require substantial manual effort, are not formally verifiable in the same sense as solver-backed generation, and remain limited

Table 1. Requirements for designing conceptual-modeling tasks.

ID	Aspect	Short Description
R1	Formal validity and verifiability	Task instances should satisfy and be checkable against formal specifications.
R2	Scalability and extensibility	The workflow should support batch generation across diverse task types and be extensible across different model types.
R3	Parameterization and difficulty control	The generation of task instances should allow explicit and strict control over structural properties and difficulty.
R4	Instance diversity and randomness	The system should support generating a large amount of distinct task instances.
R5	Contextualization	Task instances should admit meaningful real-world concepts and scenario descriptions.
R6	Traceability and robustness	The workflow should support quality control, traceability, and failure handling.

in parameterization, scalability, extensibility across model types, and instance diversity.

Table 2. Comparison of different approaches against the task-design requirements.

Approach	R1	R2	R3	R4	R5	R6
KE-based	*Limited*	*Limited*	*Limited*	*Limited*	✓	*Limited*
FM-based	✓	*Limited*	✓	*Limited*	✗	✓
LLM-based	✗	*Limited*	✗	✓	✓	✗
FoLIC	✓	*Limited*	✓	✓	✓	✓

FM-based approaches capture what counts as a valid task in a precise, machine-checkable specification, such as which relationship types and multiplicities a CD may use, and let an automated solver generate instances that provably satisfy it, providing a strong foundation for formal validity and verifiability, parameterization and difficulty control, and traceability and robustness. Prior works formalize CDs and ODs in the specification language Alloy [18,23] and use solver-backed generation, parsing, and post-processing to obtain task instances [15,24]. Such workflows are predictable and debuggable, and solver-based generation supports some constrained instance variation. However, extending them across broader task or model types typically requires additional formalization effort, and they do not by themselves provide meaningful contextualization, since generated task instances often rely on artificial identifiers rather than real-world concepts [15].

LLM-based approaches [5,22] provide a complementary profile. Many generate UML artifacts from textual descriptions, thereby supporting contextualization and limited instance variation through prompt diversity. However, they do not provide formal validity and verifiability, parameterization and difficulty control, or strong traceability and robustness. As a result, they cannot reliably ensure consistency with formal constraints, and their outputs remain susceptible to hallucinations or low-confidence results [6,9]. Extending such approaches beyond text-to-diagram generation to the broader range of CM task families required in educational settings also remains non-trivial.

Taken together, these observations reveal a clear gap: FM-based approaches provide formal guarantees and controllability, but not meaningful contextualization, whereas LLM-based approaches provide contextualization, but lack formal guarantees, fine-grained control, and robustness. KE-based approaches can also support contextualization, but at substantial manual cost. This motivates integrating LLM-based contextualization into FM-based generation without undermining formal constraints. FoLIC bridges this gap via a decoupled architecture that separates formal generation from semantic contextualization. In this way, FoLIC addresses the requirements to a large extent, although its extensibility still depends on the availability and adaptation of suitable formal specifications.

3 The FoLIC Framework Design

To address the requirements identified above, we propose FoLIC, the decoupled framework shown in Fig. 1. FoLIC supports reliable and controllable generation of diverse CM tasks for educational settings without entrusting formal structure generation directly to the LLM.

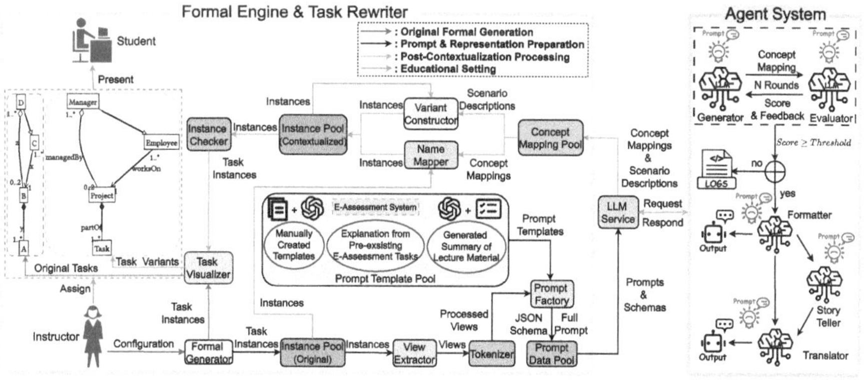

Fig. 1. FoLIC-Framework Overview: Formal Engine & Task Rewriter; Agent System.

3.1 Design Principles and Overall Architecture

The central design question behind FoLIC is not merely how to combine FM-based and LLM-based generation, but how to do so while remaining suitable for CM education, which requires repeated practice with diverse task types and instances at cohort scale [19,25]. This motivates our primary design principle, namely that formal correctness and verifiability take precedence over semantic enrichment. LLMs act only as assistants for this enrichment, while every structurally controllable and formally checkable step stays inside a transparent, solver-backed workflow. This yields the decoupled architecture in Fig. 1, comprising the *Formal Engine and Task Rewriter*, which formally generates task instances and deterministically re-integrates the agent outputs into new contextualized task variants without altering the underlying formal structure, and an *Agent System* that only produces the real-world concepts and scenario descriptions used for this enrichment. Throughout this section we use the `DifferentNames` task as a running example, in which students recover the correspondence between a CD and a conforming OD. To get an impression of the contextualized variants it yields, peek forward to Fig. 4 in Sect. 4. FoLIC currently supports the task families listed in Table 3, spanning CDs/ODs and ADs.

Table 3. Overview of supported task types. *Form.*: formalization language; *Var.*: number of FoLIC-supported task variants derived per original task instance.

Domain	Task type	Description	Form.	Var.
Class / Object Diagram (CD/OD)	NameCdError	Name properties violated by a faulty CD.	Alloy	–
	SelectValidCd	Select the valid CD among structural weakenings.		+1
	RepairCd	Fix an invalid CD via allowed mutations.		+1
	DifferentNames	Find mapping between renamed CD/OD notations.		+4
	MatchCdOd	Match given ODs to given CDs.		+3
Activity Diagram (AD)	MatchAd	Name all action/object nodes and count other types.	Alloy	+1
	SelectAs	Select valid action sequences for an AD.		+1
	EnterAs	Enter a valid action sequence for an AD.		+1
	three more:	SelectPetri, MatchPetri, FindAuxNodes	+Haskell	–

As shown in Fig. 1, within the Formal Engine and Task Rewriter, tasks are parameterized through task configurations from which the *Formal Generator* derives task instances. Along the red workflow, the framework produces instances that contain only artificial identifiers. Once visualized, these are rendered as the original task instances, of which the red dashed box shows an example diagram. Along the black workflow, an instance enters prompt preparation and is then passed to the Agent System. Along the light-blue workflow, accepted outputs are re-integrated through post-contextualization, yielding the contextualized task variants shown in the light-blue dashed box. Finally, along the gray educational-setting workflow, instructors can readily assign the original tasks and the contextualized variants to students on the e-assessment platform according to their teaching needs. The Agent System consists of several specialized roles. The *Generator* proposes real-world concepts fitting the given instance. The *Evaluator* assesses them, provides feedback, and filters out weak candidates. Then the *Formatter* structures accepted outputs, and the *Story Teller* derives scenario narratives from accepted concepts and the corresponding instances, while the *Translator* provides multilingual support.

3.2 Formal Engine and Task Rewriter

Formal Generation. FoLIC starts from formal generation. An instructor specifies a task configuration c, such as the one shown in Fig. 2, from which the Formal Generator f produces a structurally valid instance $I = f(c)$ with the desired properties and comparable difficulty. We build on prior FM-based generators for modeling tasks [15,24], which rely on Alloy and its Analyzer [13] for constraint solving and on the Haskell programming language as a type-safe backbone that organizes configurations, invokes the solver, and parses instances. We reuse this machinery largely unchanged, with its controllable task properties providing explicit control over structure and difficulty. For the `DifferentNames` task, for instance, the `withObviousMapping` property in that configuration decides whether the correct mapping between the CD and OD is obvious, meaning it can be recovered one relationship at a time, or whether it can only be resolved by reasoning over several relationships together. Each generated instance also stores its own solution, the known answers used by the e-assessment system for automatic grading and display of sample solutions. For `DifferentNames` this is the correct mapping between the CD relationships and the OD links. The formalization deliberately targets simplified CM subsets common in education. For example, CD/OD tasks focus on relationships, multiplicities, and inheritance, and omit attributes and methods. The resulting instances are deployable as tasks but still use only artificial identifiers, and therefore lack domain semantics.

Prompt Preparation and Prompt-Oriented Representation. This stage converts a formally generated instance into a prompt-oriented representation that retains the task-relevant structure and omits details irrelevant to concept injection. Figure 2 traces it end-to-end for one `DifferentNames` instance; the detailed components in action here are from Fig. 1. Before it begins, the configuration and the instance are checked against task-specific requirements in a fail-fast manner, and non-conforming instances are rejected. From each accepted instance I, the *View Extractor* e produces an instance view that keeps only what is needed for prompting and response interpretation, dropping deployment- and interaction-related fields that would enlarge the agent context or interfere with concept generation. Optional hints such as the target student group or topic can also be supplied here to steer concept generation toward domains suited to the intended learners. A type-aware *Tokenizer* t then transforms the view into a processed view $V_t = t(e(I))$, rewriting every artificial identifier into a typed placeholder, for example `A` $\mapsto$ `{{Class_A}}` and `5.` $\mapsto$ `{{Composition_5.}}`. Each

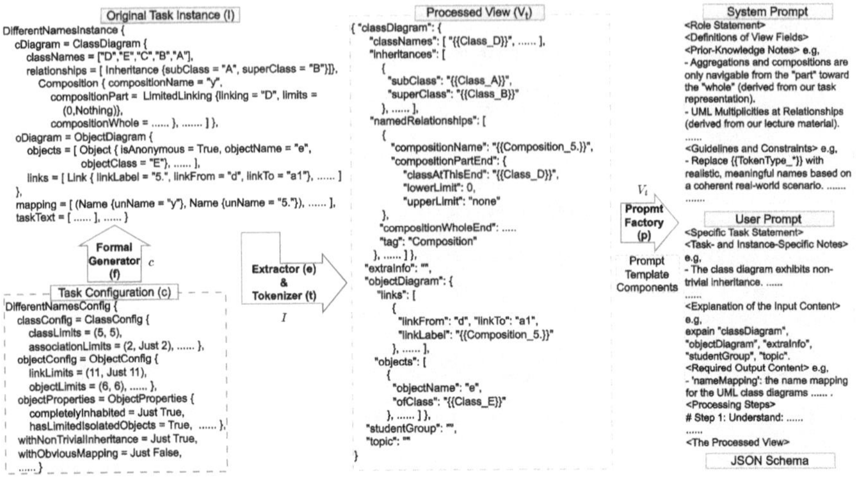

Fig. 2. Example illustrating the process of prompt & representation preparation.

relationship is tagged by its structural role, such as `Association`, `Aggregation`, or `Composition`. This exposes explicit category information so the agent can focus on concept generation instead of inferring element types, following prompt-engineering practice on explicit type and naming information [12,27]. When the task carries a known solution relating its elements, as in the CD-to-OD mapping of `DifferentNames`, view construction exploits it so that corresponding elements receive the same placeholder, sparing the agent from re-deriving the correspondence. Finally, the *Prompt Factory* assembles the prompts for all agents from the *Prompt Template Pool* and V_t, and derives from V_t a JSON schema whose required fields are exactly its placeholders. The figure illustrates the Generator prompt: its system prompt supplies the role, field definitions, prior-knowledge notes, and guidelines, while its user prompt states the task with instance-specific notes and embeds V_t. The schema is not imposed on the Generator but is applied later at the formatting step, where the Formatter structures the accepted output so the concept mapping can be validated and re-integrated reliably. Figure 2 shows only an overview, but the complete configurations, instances, prompts and per-instance schemas are available in our Zenodo repository.

Post-contextualization Processing. Post-contextualization re-integrates accepted agent outputs into the formal workflow and turns them into deployable task variants. Figure 3 continues the running example, where the detailed components in action still refer to Fig. 1. First, the *Name Mapper* injects the accepted concept mapping into the task-instance data structure, replacing only artificial identifiers while preserving the structure. Formally, the Name Mapper n yields a contextualized task instance $I_c = n(I, R_a)$ from an original task instance I and an accepted response of the concept mapping R_a. Because injection is a bijective renaming, it leaves the solution intact. In Fig. 3, the mapping $y \leftrightarrow 5.$ becomes `isIncludedIn` $\leftrightarrow$ 5., so the answer key and the instance's unique solvability are unchanged. Beyond substitution, the *Variant Constructor* combines the contextualized instance with the generated scenario description to derive further variants such as cover-story or scenario-only formulations. These artifacts are validated by the *Instance Checker* and rendered by the *Task Visualizer* into the final task, shown in the bottom panel of Fig. 3. Semantic enrichment thus stays a controlled post-processing stage over formally generated instances, confining agent uncertainty to concept and scenario generation while preserving structural correctness, traceability, and failure isolation.

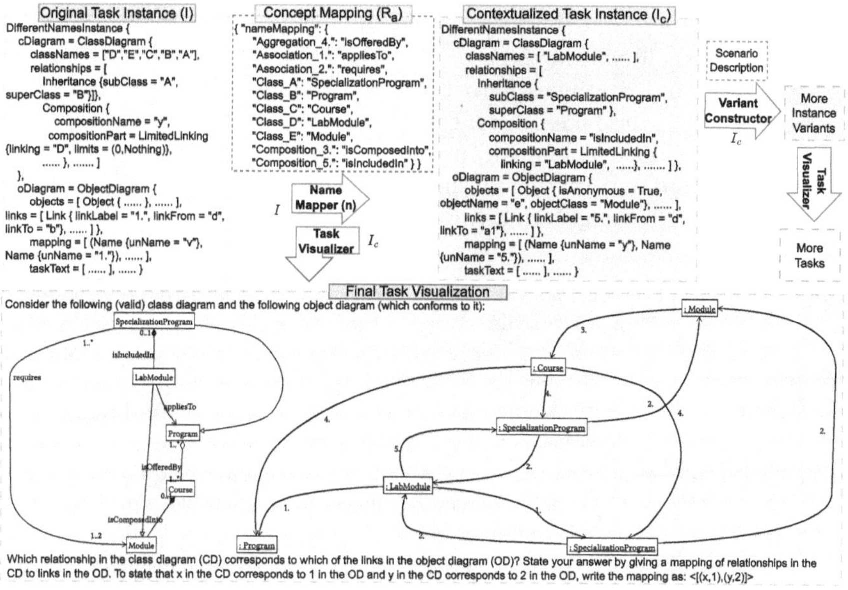

Fig. 3. Example illustrating the post-contextualization processing.

3.3 Agent System

Generator-Evaluator Refinement Loop. Concept generation in FoLIC is realized as a bounded generate-evaluate-refine loop rather than a zero-shot LLM call. Starting from the prepared prompt package, the Generator proposes candidate concept mappings for task instances. The concept mapping is required to be coherent with the structural properties of the instances and logically consistent with realistic scenarios. The Evaluator assesses them against task-relevant criteria before accepted outputs are passed to subsequent components. In this way, semantic enrichment is treated as iterative refinement over a fixed formal structure rather than as unconstrained generation. Although the architecture distinguishes Generator and Evaluator conceptually, both roles are implemented by invoking LLMs with different prompts. The Generator proposes candidate semantics, while the Evaluator scores them along the dimensions summarized in Table 4 and provides feedback for revision. The loop is designed as a lightweight iterative refinement mechanism [17] rather than a complex multi-agent planning system. To avoid overcommitting to poor early candidates, only the most recent three rounds of feedback are retained. The loop is further bounded by a predefined maximum number of iterations, since some formally generated structures may be too specific for LLMs to contextualize quickly. Beyond a certain point, additional refinement may yield little benefit while incurring unnecessary cost. In our experiments, a candidate concept mapping is accepted once it reaches the acceptance threshold, that is, a four-dimension sum of at least 18 with each dimension at least 4, and the loop is capped at N = 5 rounds. If no mapping reaches the threshold within these rounds, the framework terminates the loop, stores the logs, and continues with the other instances. Instructors can then retry or regenerate the failed instances in a subsequent run. We run the Generator and Story Teller at temperature 0.3 so that they can produce somewhat varied concepts and narratives, and the Evaluator, Formatter, and Translator at 0 for deterministic scoring, formatting, and translation.

Table 4. Evaluation dimensions used in the Generator-Evaluator refinement loop. All dimensions are scored on a 1–5 scale.

Dimension	Focus
Scenario Coherence	Plausibility and internal consistency of the real-world scenario implied by the generated concepts.
Semantic-Goal Alignment	Consistency between injected semantics and the intended modeling structures, including relationship types, directions, and multiplicities.
Concept Interpretability	Whether the generated concepts are unambiguous, easy to understand, and do not introduce unnecessary difficulty in interpreting the corresponding model elements.
Didactical Usefulness	Usefulness of the resulting semantics for helping students understand the targeted modeling concepts.

Two-step Formatting, Storytelling and Multilingual Support. Deterministic output matters for downstream parsing, but enforcing strict schemas can degrade performance on reasoning-intensive generation [26]. In our setting, interpreting the formal structure of a diagram and finding real-world concepts that fit it is a genuinely reasoning-heavy task. FoLIC therefore separates the two steps. The Generator first proposes concepts without a strict output format, so it can focus on this reasoning, and a smaller model then reformats the accepted result into the required schema, which preserves determinism while limiting both quality loss and token cost. After formatting, the Story Teller derives a scenario narrative from the injected concepts and the original instance, enabling text-based task variants in addition to diagrammatic ones, and the Translator adds multilingual support. Neither of these steps alters the formal structure.

4 Evaluation and Discussion

RQ1 is addressed primarily by the architecture of FoLIC. Instead of allowing LLMs to generate or modify formal task structures directly, the framework confines them to semantic enrichment, while structurally relevant generation, processing, and validation remain under the control of the *Formal Engine* and *Task Rewriter*. In this way, semantic injection only replaces artificial identifiers and does not alter the formally relevant structure, so the original task logic remains unchanged. In particular, task instances remain uniquely solvable whenever the underlying formally generated instance was uniquely solvable. Formal validity is therefore preserved by design rather than delegated to probabilistic generation.

This preservation is reinforced by restricting agent outputs to semantic artifacts such as concept mappings and scenario descriptions rather than complete task instances. They are re-integrated only through controlled post-processing, and outputs that fail formatting, schema, or predefined validation of instance properties are rejected, so that semantic contextualization may fail and trigger re-generation of a different instance, but structurally invalid results are not silently accepted. As implementation-level evidence, we applied FoLIC to the `DifferentNames` task in Fig. 2 and Fig. 3, generated 100 structurally different artificial task instances from one configuration, injected semantics into each of them separately, and successfully deployed all resulting instances on our e-assessment platform. We repeated this across further task types and exercise cycles during the recent semester.

To address **RQ2**, we selected two task types, `DifferentNames` and `EnterAS`, and formally generated 20 instances for each. We chose these two because they cover both formalization families, CDs/ODs and ADs, while exercising the same core demand that FoLIC places on the LLM, namely understanding the given domain model and injecting concepts that fit it. As the task families differ mainly in formal structure rather than in this semantic-injection step, a language model that performs it well on these two tasks is expected to transfer to the others under the same formal control. We then used four LLMs (two of them open-source models served through SAIA [10]) as complete Generator-Evaluator agents, with a maximum of five refinement rounds, to inject real-world concepts into these instances. All outputs were manually assessed for semantic suitability by the first author and compared with the corresponding agent evaluations. For CD-related tasks, this assessment did not judge multiplicities overly strictly, but focused on whether the injected concepts formed a plausible and didactically usable semantic interpretation of the given formal structure. Cases where both human and agent evaluation were positive were counted as true positive (TP), human negative but agent positive as false positive (FP), human positive but agent negative as false negative (FN), and both negative as true negative (TN). We then report precision, recall, and F1-score, calculated in the usual way.

Table 5 summarizes the evaluation results. The results show a clear performance gap between the models. GPT-4o performs poorly on both tasks, with precision, recall, and F1 remaining at 0. Its outputs were well formed rather than malformed, so the failure reflects concept quality rather than formatting: interpreting the full relational structure of a CD spans several classes and the whole scenario and is therefore reasoning-intensive, which favours models with stronger reasoning. DeepSeek-R1 we use is itself a reasoning model but of limited scale, so it generates weak concepts and, unlike GPT-4o, also fails to reject them, accepting many unsuitable concepts, for example only 5.3% precision despite 100% recall on `DifferentNames` and accepting every candidate on `EnterAS`.

Table 5. LLM performance on two representative tasks.

Model	Task	TP	FP	TN	FN	Precision	Recall	F1-score
GPT-4o	DifferentNames	0	0	20	0	0.0%	0.0%	0.0%
	EnterAS	0	1	19	0	0.0%	0.0%	0.0%
GPT-5	DifferentNames	12	3	4	1	80.0%	92.3%	85.7%
	EnterAS	11	9	0	0	55.0%	100.0%	71.0%
DeepSeek-R1-Distill-Llama-70B	DifferentNames	1	18	1	0	5.3%	100.0%	10.0%
	EnterAS	0	20	0	0	0.0%	0.0%	0.0%
Qwen-3.5-397B-A17B	DifferentNames	8	3	8	1	72.7%	88.9%	80.0%
	EnterAS	8	11	1	0	42.1%	100.0%	59.3%

By contrast, GPT-5 and Qwen-3.5 perform substantially better, with GPT-5 achieving the strongest results on both tasks, followed by Qwen-3.5. These results suggest that models combining larger scale with reasoning ability are better able to interpret the underlying formal structures and inject suitable real-world concepts. At the same time, even the better-performing models still produce a noticeable number of false positives, especially on `EnterAS`, which indicates that the generated semantics may remain plausible on the surface while still containing subtle but didactically misleading mismatches. Overall, these results suggest that FoLIC provides a viable framework for semantic contextualization of formally generated CM task instances, but that the quality of this step still depends strongly on the capability of the underlying LLMs.

Regarding **RQ3**, FoLIC builds on the task families in Table 3. For a subset of these tasks, semantic injection has been implemented and yields additional task variants. For others, such variants are not currently provided because their didactical value is limited or support remains incomplete. For example, `MatchPetri` and `FindAuxNodes` focus on structural transformation between ADs and Petri nets, where semantic injection appears less useful. Nevertheless, the existing results show that FoLIC can extend semantic injection across multiple task families and derive several non-identical variants from a common formal basis.

To examine scalability in a concrete setting, we recorded the generation statistics for the `DifferentNames` task in Fig. 2 and Fig. 3. Based on the configuration, we generated 100 task instances using CPU resources alone, randomly distributed to more than 200 students. The average formal instance-generation time was about 2.5 min per instance, with most of this time spent in Alloy solving and generate-and-test retries, and the total runtime on the cluster (see the acknowledgments section for reference to the machine infrastructure) was about 16 min with a maximum concurrency of 20 tasks. For the semantically enriched variant, concept generation with GPT-5 required roughly 10 min on average per successful instance. Generating all 100 instances consumed about 3.6 M input and 4.4 M output tokens, at an approximate total cost of 49 USD under current GPT-5 API pricing. Although these figures depend on the specific task configuration and the chosen model, they indicate that FoLIC can generate contextualized task variants in larger batches within a practically manageable time and cost.

To obtain preliminary evidence for **RQ4**, we deployed the original task type and four FoLIC-derived variants of `DifferentNames`, and collected initial student performance data. Over the semester, students received 51 tasks in total, most of them still using artificial identifiers, whereas the four variants discussed here were semantically enriched through FoLIC. Although concept mappings were reused across these task variants, task instances of the variants were assigned randomly, so that the same student was very unlikely to encounter the same task instance or the same real-world contextualization in different variants. As illustrated in Fig. 4, this deployment is not intended as a full didactical evaluation, but as an exploratory study of how semantically enriched task variants can be used in practice. It also shows that FoLIC enables task formulations that would be difficult to realize meaningfully with artificial identifiers alone.

Although the available data are limited, some patterns are already visible. Variants 1 and 2 show performance comparable to or slightly better than the original task instance, plausibly because the injected semantics make the task more concrete and easier to understand. By contrast, Variants 3 and 4 appear more difficult, as they require students to relate the models more explicitly to real-world semantics. In particular, the sharp drop for Variant 4 points to a current limitation of the task design: some injected relationship names may be too close or too broad to distinguish easily. This suggests that such variants require more precise semantic injection or additional task-specific refinement.

We also carried out an initial preference survey. Although the number of responses is too small for systematic analysis, some feedback is still informative. A few students preferred artificial identifiers, raising the question whether semantic injection may sometimes introduce over-specialization or domain bias, whereas abstract identifiers might better support generalization. Others appreciated the semantically enriched variants, suggesting that they can be helpful, especially for beginners. These observations do not support firm conclusions, but they motivate further study of when semantic contextualization supports learning and when abstract identifiers remain preferable.

5 Limitations and Threats to Validity

Limitations. Although FoLIC preserves formal validity while enriching formally generated CM tasks with real-world semantics, several limitations remain. Some formally generated structures may be highly specific, making it difficult to find

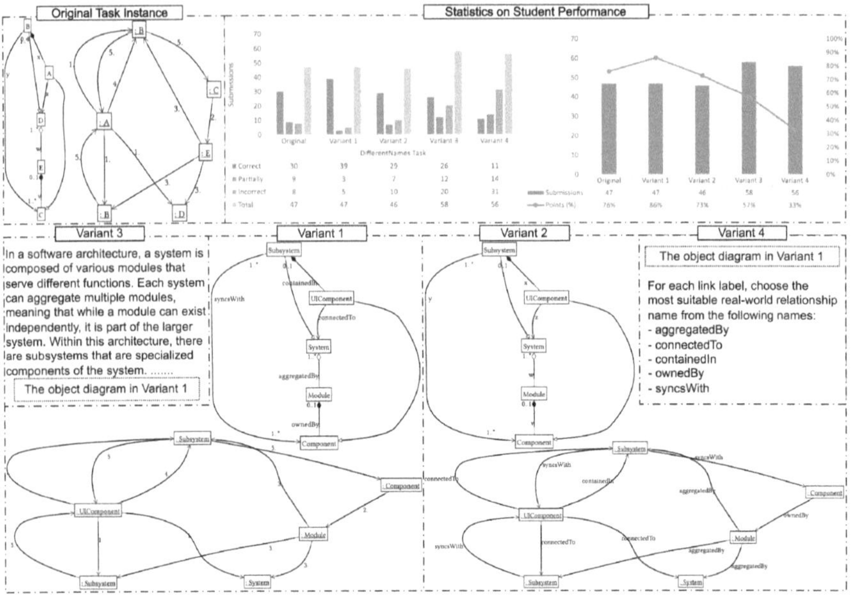

Fig. 4. Example of the `DifferentNames` task family and student task-completion statistics. The original task instance uses only artificial identifiers. The other four task variants are derived via FoLIC. Variants 1 and 2 present a CD and an OD with real-world concepts, and require students either to match OD links to CD relationship names or vice versa. Variant 3 requires students to infer the CD from a scenario description and then determine the OD link names. Variant 4 provides candidate names and asks students to identify the correct OD link names based on common real-world semantics. The two bar charts summarize student performance for these tasks over one semester.

fully natural scenarios that satisfy all imposed constraints, especially for multiplicity constraints and certain combinations of relationships. As a result, some injected semantics appear artificial, even if they still form plausible special-case modeling scenarios. Future work should therefore investigate both more natural semantic injection under strict formal constraints and more LLM-friendly formal specifications for structures better suited to semantic contextualization. FoLIC also allows instructors to restrict the topic or domain of generation, but concept injection still depends on LLM black-box behavior. Since learners may differ substantially in their prior knowledge, injected concepts may require additional domain familiarity and introduce unintended difficulty bias. In some cases, variants with abstract identifiers may therefore remain more neutral than semantically enriched ones. This suggests the need for future work on guiding semantic injection toward more common and less over-specialized concepts.

Threats to Validity. The main threats to validity concern our evaluation. The Evaluator is itself LLM-based and may still accept low-quality concepts, and the manual assessment used as reference in RQ2 was carried out by a single rater, the first author, over a small number of tasks and instances, which introduces potential labelling bias. We applied consistent assessment criteria focused on didactical plausibility rather than strict formal conformance, but large-scale manual review is not realistic for a single researcher. Future work should enlarge the evaluation and involve additional independent raters, such as teaching assistants from the relevant course who are not part of this research. External validity is likewise limited: the current educational deployment remains exploratory, covering a single task family over one semester and reporting task performance and perceptions rather than a controlled measure of learning gains, so the available data support only initial observations rather than strong conclusions. In future instalments of the course, we will collect more data across further task families and hopefully larger cohorts, enabling a more systematic and complete evaluation of when semantic contextualization improves learning, when it introduces undesirable bias, and how it should be combined with more abstract task formulations.

6 Conclusion

FM-based approaches to CM task generation provide formal guarantees, controllability, and explicit difficulty configuration, but usually remain limited to models with artificial identifiers. By contrast, LLM-based approaches provide richer semantics and contextual variety, but lack formal guarantees and fine-grained control. This tension motivates us to propose FoLIC, a decoupled framework that combines solver-backed formal generation with LLM-based semantic contextualization, so that formally generated CM tasks can be enriched with real-world concepts and scenario descriptions without relinquishing formal control over task structure. Our results indicate that FoLIC can be applied across multiple CM task families and can derive semantically enriched task variants from formally generated tasks. In particular, it enables task formulations that would be difficult to realize meaningfully with artificial identifiers alone. We hope that FoLIC can contribute to controllable, scalable, and didactically meaningful CM task generation. Future work will extend task coverage and improve concept quality.

Acknowledgments. The authors gratefully acknowledge the computing time granted by the Center for Computational Sciences and Simulation (CCSS) of the University of Duisburg-Essen and provided on the supercomputers amplitUDE (DFG project 459398823; grant ID INST 20876/423-1 FUGG) and magnitUDE (DFG grants INST 20876/209-1 FUGG, INST 20876/243-1 FUGG) at the Zentrum für Informations- und Mediendienste (ZIM).

Disclosure of Interests. The authors have no competing interests to declare that are relevant to the content of this article.

References

1. Akdur, D., Garousi, V., Demirörs, O.: A survey on modeling and model-driven engineering practices in the embedded software industry. J. Syst. Architect. **91**, 62–82 (2018). https://doi.org/10.1016/j.sysarc.2018.09.007
2. Ardimento, P., Bernardi, M.L., Cimitile, M., Scalera, M.: Enhancing software modeling learning with AI-powered scaffolding. In: Proceedings of the MODELS 2024, pp. 103–106. ACM (2024). https://doi.org/10.1145/3652620.3687776
3. Ben Chaaben, M.: Software modeling assistance with large language models. In: Proceedings of the MODELS 2025, pp. 188–191. ACM (2024)
4. Bouali, N., Gerhold, M., Rehman, T.U., Ahmed, F.: Toward automated UML diagram assessment: comparing LLM-generated scores with teaching assistants. In: Proceedings of the CSEDU 2025, Vol. 1, pp. 158–169. SciTePress (2025)
5. Calamo, M., Mecella, M., Snoeck, M.: Assessing the suitability of large language models in generating UML class diagrams as conceptual models. In: Proceedings of the BPMDS 2025, pp. 211–226. Springer (2025). https://doi.org/10.1007/978-3-031-95397-2_13
6. Cámara, J., Troya, J., Burgueño, L., Vallecillo, A.: On the assessment of generative AI in modeling tasks: an experience report with ChatGPT and UML. Softw. Syst. Model. **22**, 781–793 (2023)
7. Christ, P., Munkelt, T., Haake, J.M.: Generalized automatic item generation for graphical conceptual modeling tasks. In: Proceedings of the CSEDU 2024, Vol. 1: AIG, pp. 807–818. SciTePress (2024). https://api.semanticscholar.org/CorpusID:269620671
8. Cudal, H., Balaba, E.I.: The role of artificial intelligence in personalized e-learning platforms. Wisdom J. Humanit. Soc. Sci. **2**, 27–33 (2025)
9. De Bari, D., Garaccione, G., Coppola, R., Torchiano, M., Ardito, L.: Evaluating large language models in exercises of UML class diagram modeling. In: Proceedings of the ESEM 2024, pp. 393–399. ACM (2024). https://doi.org/10.1145/3674805.3690741
10. Doosthosseini, A., Decker, J., Nolte, H., Kunkel, J.: SAIA: a seamless Slurm-native solution for HPC-based services. J. Supercomput. **82**(7), 403-1–42 (2026). https://doi.org/10.1007/s11227-026-08508-3
11. He, X., Zhang, T., Pan, M., Ma, Z., Hu, C.J.: Template-based model generation. Softw. Syst. Model. **18**, 2051–2092 (2019)
12. Irugalbandara, C.: Meaning typed prompting: A technique for efficient, reliable structured output generation. arXiv preprint arXiv:2410.18146 (2024)
13. Jackson, D.: Alloy: a language and tool for exploring software designs. Commun. ACM **62**(9), 66–76 (2019). https://doi.org/10.1145/3338843
14. Jyothilakshmi, M., Samuel, P.: Domain ontology based class diagram generation from functional requirements. In: Proceedings of the ISDA 2012, pp. 380–385. IEEE (2012)
15. Kafa, V., Siegburg, M., Voigtländer, J.: Exercise task generation for UML class/object diagrams, via Alloy model instance finding. In: Tait, B., Kroeze, J., Gruner, S. (eds.) SACLA 2019. CCIS, Vol. 1136, pp. 112–128. Springer, Cham (2020). https://doi.org/10.1007/978-3-030-35629-3_8
16. Li, Z., McGowan, A., Liu, Y., Hamou-Lhadj, A.: UML crisis! An educational perspective. In: Proceedings of the FSE 2025, pp. 895–900. ACM (2025). https://doi.org/10.1145/3696630.3727246

17. Madaan, A., Tandon, N., Gupta, P., Hallinan, S., Gao, L., Wiegreffe, S., et al.: Self-refine: iterative refinement with self-feedback. In: Posters NeurIPS 2023 (2023)
18. Maoz, S., Ringert, J.O., Rumpe, B.: CD2Alloy: class diagrams analysis using Alloy revisited. In: Whittle, J., Clark, T., Kühne, T. (eds.) MODELS 2011. LNCS, Vol. 6981, pp. 592–607. Springer, Heidelberg (2011). https://doi.org/10.1007/978-3-642-24485-8_44
19. Maslov, I., Poelmans, S., Rosenthal, K.: Conceptual modeling education. Bus. Inf. Syst. Eng. **68**(2), 343–375 (2026). https://doi.org/10.1007/s12599-025-00930-w
20. Object Management Group (OMG): Unified modeling language (UML) version 2.5.1 (2017). https://www.omg.org/spec/UML/2.5.1
21. Reuter, R., Stark, T., Sedelmaier, Y., Landes, D., Mottok, J., Wolff, C.: Insights in students' problems during UML modeling. In: Proceedings of the EDUCON 2020, pp. 592–600. IEEE (2020). https://doi.org/10.1109/EDUCON45650.2020.9125110
22. Schouten, M.B.J., Ramackers, G.J., Verberne, S.: Preprocessing requirements documents for automatic UML modelling. In: Proceedings of the NLDB 2022, pp. 184–196. Springer (2022). https://doi.org/10.1007/978-3-031-08473-7_17
23. Shah, S.M., Anastasakis, K., Bordbar, B.: From UML to Alloy and back again. In: Proceedings of the MoDeVVa 2009, pp. 4-1–10. ACM (2009)
24. Siegburg, M., Voigtländer, J.: Generating diverse exercise tasks on UML class and object diagrams, using formalisations in Alloy. In: Proceedings of the MoHoL 2020, pp. 89–100. CEUR (2020). https://ceur-ws.org/Vol-2542/MOHOL5.pdf
25. Soyka, C., Striewe, M., Ullrich, M., Schaper, N.: Comparison of required competences and task material in modeling education. Enterp. Model. Inf. Syst. Archit. Int. J. Conceptual Model. **18**, 7-1–36 (2023). https://doi.org/10.18417/emisa.18.7
26. Tam, Z.R., Wu, C.K., Tsai, Y.L., Lin, C.Y., Lee, H.y., Chen, Y.N.: Let me speak freely? A study on the impact of format restrictions on performance of large language models. In: Proceedings of the EMNLP 2024, Industry Track, pp. 1218–1236. ACL (2024). https://doi.org/10.18653/v1/2024.emnlp-industry.91
27. White, J., Fu, Q., Hays, S., Sandborn, M., Olea, C., Gilbert, H., et al.: A prompt pattern catalog to enhance prompt engineering with ChatGPT. In: Proceedings of the PLoP 2023, pp. 5-1–31 (2023). https://dl.acm.org/doi/10.5555/3721041.3721046

Extraction-Oriented Ontology Modeling for Local LLM-Based Knowledge Graph Construction in Safety-Critical Domains

Sarmad Rezayat[1](✉), Daniel Garcia Vasquez[1], Gerrit Burmester[1], Hui Ma[2], and Sven Hartmann[1]

[1] Clausthal University of Technology, Clausthal-Zellerfeld, Germany
{sarmad.rezayat,daniel.garcia.vasquez,gerrit.burmester, sven.hartmann}@tu-clausthal.de

[2] Victoria University of Wellington, Wellington, New Zealand
hui.ma@ecs.vuw.ac.nz

Abstract. Ontology engineering methodologies typically optimize for semantic completeness, formal expressiveness, and interoperability, which are properties geared toward human reasoning and system integration. When such ontologies are used as extraction schemas for Large Language Models (LLMs), and particularly for local LLMs deployable under the data privacy and security constraints of safety-critical domains, these properties are necessary but not sufficient. The ontology must also be reliably operationalizable by a constrained extractor. We argue that *extractability* should be treated as a first-class concern in conceptual modeling alongside the established ones. We introduce Extraction-Oriented Ontology Modeling (EOOM), a six-stage conceptual modeling approach that integrates ontology refinement into the Knowledge Graph (KG) construction process rather than treating the guiding ontology as a fixed precondition. We apply EOOM to an aviation safety use case based on 643 accident reports, where the 915-class Air Traffic Management (ATM) Information Reference Model Ontology (AIRM-O) fails to support extraction by local LLMs. In contrast, a 20-class extraction schema produced using EOOM enables stable extraction across six local LLMs with varying sizes and architectures. The results show that ontology design is a stronger determinant of extraction quality than model choice, and that extraction schemas are a distinct conceptual artifact from domain ontologies, with different design requirements.

Keywords: Knowledge Graph Construction · Conceptual Modeling · Ontology Engineering · Large Language Models · Safety-Critical Domains

© The Author(s), under exclusive license to Springer Nature Switzerland AG 2027
A. Bernasconi et al. (Eds.): ER 2026, LNCS 17081, pp. 74–91, 2027.
https://doi.org/10.1007/978-3-032-40795-5_5

1 Introduction

Ontology engineering has long been a central concern of the conceptual modeling community [14,18,19], with established methodologies optimizing ontologies for semantic completeness, formal expressiveness, and interoperability. However, using LLMs to populate ontologies from unstructured text [13] introduces an additional requirement: an ontology must not only be semantically sound but also *operationalizable* by the extractor that uses it as a schema. This is particularly important in safety-critical domains, where sensitive operational data is often restricted from processing by public cloud-based LLMs services due to confidentiality and regulatory requirements [10,24]. Consequently, organizations increasingly adopt local LLMs. However, their limited context windows, weaker reasoning, and higher susceptibility to hallucination [2,34] expose that ontologies designed for human reasoning are often not directly operationalizable as extraction schemas.

This paper introduces EOOM, a conceptual modeling approach for constructing KGs from unstructured text using local LLMs in safety-critical domains. EOOM structures the process into six stages: *Document Segmentation*, *Concept Recognition*, *Ontology-Guided Classification*, *Semantic Relation Identification*, *Ontology Conformance Validation*, and *Entity Normalization*. These stages decompose extraction into focused subtasks supported by local models but are not intended to form a fully autonomous pipeline. In safety-critical domains, Stages 2–6 operate under expert supervision: local models and deterministic procedures propose candidate mentions, classifications, relations, conformance signals, and normalized entities, while domain experts validate the outputs and iteratively refine the guiding ontology. The resulting compact ontology supports subsequent KG population by a local LLM. We evaluate EOOM on 643 aviation accident reports by comparing AIRM-O [11,17], comprising 915 entity classes and 28,432 relationship types, with a compact ontology derived using EOOM. While AIRM-O failed to support relationship extraction by local LLMs, producing a relationship-free KG, the EOOM-derived ontology enabled reliable extraction across six local LLMs.

The contributions of this paper are as follows: (1) We propose EOOM, a six-stage conceptual modeling approach for ontology-guided KG construction from unstructured text using local LLMs. Unlike existing approaches, EOOM iteratively refines the guiding ontology to satisfy deployment and extraction constraints in safety-critical environments. (2) We apply EOOM to 643 aviation accident reports, reducing the 915-class AIRM-O ontology to a compact 20-class extraction schema that enables stable extraction across six local LLMs. (3) We demonstrate that extractability-aware ontology modeling substantially improves local LLM-based KG extraction over an unadapted interoperability ontology, establishing extractability as a key ontology design objective.

Paper Organization. The remainder of this paper is structured as follows. Section 2 reviews related work. Section 3 provides background and states the problem. Section 4 presents EOOM, including an illustrative case study. Section 5 describes the experiments and results. Section 6 discusses implications and limitations. Section 7 concludes our findings.

2 Related Work

Conceptual Modeling and Ontology Engineering. Ontology engineering has a long methodological tradition. Classical methodologies such as TOVE [18] and METHONTOLOGY formalize construction around semantic completeness, class hierarchies, and competency questions [3,32]. The conceptual modeling community has further refined ontology design through frameworks that formalize ontological commitments [19] and provide reusable design patterns [14]. Recent work also uses LLMs to support ontology engineering, including OWL translation [32], conversational requirements elicitation [42], and ontology learning in specialized domains [13]. Ontology-driven conceptual model abstraction manages model complexity via OntoUML graph-rewriting rules that simplify objects, aspects, events, and their parts while preserving essential semantic information [35]. This work does not address the inverse concern: how ontology design choices affect the ability of LLMs to extract structured knowledge according to that ontology. Existing methodologies optimize for human-facing concerns such as interoperability and reasoning. However, an ontology used as an extraction schema for a constrained language model must also be reliably operationalizable by that model. EOOM addresses this by integrating ontology refinement into a six-stage construction process, complementing established objectives such as competency questions [18,32] and ontological commitments [19].

Knowledge Graph Construction in Safety-Critical Domains. KG construction from unstructured text has been studied in safety-critical domains, with aviation receiving particular attention. Approaches range from BiLSTM-CRF pipelines [9,30] and BERT-based extractors [4,41] to cloud-based LLMs [8]. Large domain ontologies play a central role, with AIRM-O [11,17] defining over 900 classes and 28,000 relationship types for ATM interoperability. Related work in adjacent domains shows similar patterns [29], where a large domain ontology is treated as given and the focus is on improving extraction against it. Across this body of work, ontology design is treated as a precondition rather than a variable, and no existing approach integrates ontology refinement into the KG construction process itself. This gap is what EOOM addresses.

Ontologies and Large Language Models. LLMs do not natively enforce the logical properties that give ontologies their reasoning power. [38] shows that even simple Is-A hierarchies expose systematic inconsistencies in transitivity and inheritance across multiple LLMs. [20] shows that explicitly injecting ontological constraints as natural language contributes 15–20% points to KG completion accuracy. In contrast, [13] finds that LLMs generate shallow hierarchies unless structural targets are explicitly provided. A related line of work addresses ontology matching and alignment [12], including neural systems such as BERTMap [22] and LLM-driven matching, like neuro-symbolic KG completion [20], these approaches assume a fixed target ontology rather than reshaping it for extractability. These findings have direct consequences for ontology design under local LLMs. If a model cannot reliably apply transitive or inheritance reasoning, ontologies that depend on such reasoning to express extraction-relevant relationships will systematically lose information at extraction time. EOOM addresses this by integrating ontology refinement into the construction process itself (see Sect. 4).

3 Preliminaries

This section introduces the concepts used in this paper, defines the operational constraints under which EOOM operates, and formalizes the problem.

Knowledge Graphs and Ontologies. A KG is a directed labeled graph $G = (E, R, T)$ where E is a set of entities, R is a set of relationship types, and $T \subseteq E \times R \times E$ is a set of triples [23,27]. Each entity $e \in E$ is associated with a class $c(e)$ drawn from a finite set of available classes C. A triple $(s, p, o) \in T$ states that entity s is related to entity o through relationship p with $s, o \in E$ and $p \in R$. An *ontology* $O = (C, P, \sigma)$ provides the schema for G, where C is the set of classes, P is the set of relationship types, and $\sigma : P \rightarrow C \times C$ assigns each relationship type a subject class and an object class [19,23]. A triple (s, p, o) is *schema-conformant* with respect to O if $p \in P$, $c(s)$ equals the subject class assigned by $\sigma(p)$, and $c(o)$ equals the object class assigned by $\sigma(p)$.

Local Large Language Models. We refer to an LLM as *local* if it satisfies two conditions. First, it runs entirely on a single consumer-grade GPU without requiring external API calls or cloud infrastructure. Second, its parameter count and quantization are chosen such that the full model fits within the memory of such a GPU, typically placing it in the range of 8 to 15 billion parameters at moderate quantization. These conditions imply tighter context windows, reduced reasoning capacity, and greater susceptibility to hallucinations compared with cloud-scale LLMs [2,21]. Still, they preserve data locality, which is the defining requirement in safety-critical domains.

Compact Ontologies. The operational constraints of local LLMs place a corresponding constraint on the ontologies that guide them. We call an ontology O *compact* with respect to a target local LLM if the full schema specification of O, including class names, relationship types, and their domain and range, fits within the input context window of the model alongside the source document and the task instructions. Compactness is therefore a property defined relative to a target model rather than an absolute property of the ontology. *Compactness* is the minimum requirement for an ontology to serve as an in-prompt extraction schema. An ontology that exceeds the context window of the target local LLM cannot be supplied directly and must instead be accessed via retrieval-augmented mechanisms, thereby causing additional failure modes (see Sect. 5).

3.1 Evaluation Dimensions for Knowledge Graphs

The quality of a constructed KG is assessed along three dimensions, each measuring a distinct property of the output [7]. *Schema adherence* measures the extent to which extracted triples follow the vocabulary and relation constraints defined by the guiding ontology. Recent work on ontology-guided KG construction uses ontologies to guide triple extraction from domain-specific text [6,40], while ontology-guided validation has been proposed to improve the reliability of extracted relations [33]. A KG with high schema adherence is therefore one in which extracted triples consistently use ontology-defined classes and predicates, without introducing ontology-undefined predicates or invalid type-relation combinations. *Structural quality* measures the connectivity and balance of the resulting graph [36,39]. A KG with high structural quality exhibits a well-connected entity set, a reasonably even use of relationship types, and an absence of isolated components that fragment the graph. *Plausibility* measures the semantic correctness of the constructed triples with respect to the target domain. Exhaustive plausibility assessment is generally infeasible for large KGs [31], so we estimate through stratified sampling combined with judgments from a stronger reference model acting as a proxy for domain experts [15,25]. A KG with high Plausibility contains triples that a domain reader would judge as factually reasonable, regardless of whether they strictly conform to the schema.

The three dimensions are reported separately rather than collapsed into a single number, as they capture genuinely different aspects of KG quality. The formal definitions and the procedures for computing each score are deferred to Sect. 5, where they are applied to the constructed KGs. Reference-based metrics such as precision and recall are not applicable, as no gold-standard triple annotations exist for the corpus. The three dimensions instead assess schema fit, graph structure, and factual plausibility without requiring a labeled reference.

3.2 Problem Statement

Let D be a corpus of unstructured documents from a safety-critical domain and let M be a target local LLM. Let O_{init} be an initial domain ontology, which may exceed the compactness bound of M. The problem addressed in this paper is to construct a KG G^* guided by a compact ontology O^* such that:

1. O^* is compact with respect to M (Sect. 3);
2. G^* is constructed from D using M under the schema O^*;
3. G^* maximizes schema adherence, structural quality, and plausibility (Sect. 3.1) subject to the compactness constraint on O^*.

The initial ontology O_{init} is not assumed to be compact with respect to M. Producing a compact O^* from O_{init} is therefore part of the problem, not a precondition. This distinguishes the problem statement from prior work, which treats the ontology as fixed and focuses solely on improving extraction against it (Sect. 2). Moreover, in safety-critical domains, the construction process is not autonomous, and the role of the domain expert is integral to the problem rather than auxiliary. The expert provides O_{init}, makes the modeling decisions that shape O_{init} into O^* during construction, and validates G^* before any operational use. EOOM therefore addresses the problem of supporting expert-supervised KG construction, not replacing it.

4 Proposed Method

This section presents EOOM, a six-stage expert-supervised conceptual modeling approach for reshaping an initial ontology into a compact extraction ontology that enables subsequent local LLM-based KG population from the input data. We first describe the overall workflow and the role of the guiding ontology (see Sect. 4.1), then present each of the six stages (see Sect. 4.2), and finally illustrate the approach through a use case in aviation (see Sect. 4.3). Figure 1 illustrates the six stages and the flow of data and ontology between them.

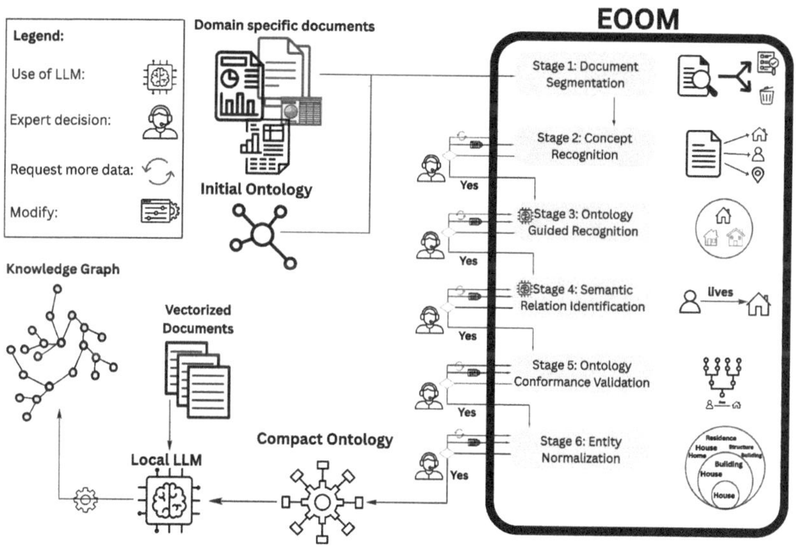

Fig. 1. Overview of the six EOOM stages and the flow of data and ontology.

4.1 Overview

EOOM takes as input a corpus of unstructured documents D, an initial domain ontology O_{init}, and a target local LLM M. The six stages produce a compact extraction ontology O^* that is accepted by the domain expert and operationalizable by M. The final KG G^* is populated afterward in a separate step that uses O^* as the accepted schema, together with the source documents, vector-embedded document representations, and the local LLM. The first principle is *task locality*. Local LLMs are sensitive to prompt complexity and context length [2]. Breaking extraction into focused subtasks reduces the cognitive load placed on the model at any single step, improves traceability of intermediate outputs, and allows different stages to use the most appropriate technology, whether an LLM, a pre-trained extractor, or a deterministic procedure [1,29].

The second principle is *ontology shaping*. As the corpus passes through the stages, the guiding ontology is repeatedly consulted, validated against the produced output, and refined. Classes and relationship types that cannot be reliably populated by M are identified through their absence in the produced triples or through systematic conformance failures, and the ontology is reduced or restructured accordingly. The resulting O^* is therefore not specified up front but emerges from the construction process under expert supervision (see Sect. 4.2).

4.2 The Six Stages

Stage 1: Document Segmentation. The input corpus consists of heterogeneous accident reports that typically exceed the context window of local LLMs [28]. Therefore, each document is deterministically segmented before further processing. Guided by the target domain defined by the initial ontology O_{init}, domain experts identify the report sections relevant to the ontology (e.g., *Summary* and *History of the Flight* for BFU and JTSB reports). At run time, fixed keyword and regular-expression patterns locate these section headings and extract the corresponding text, while all remaining sections are discarded. This stage does not invoke an LLM or perform semantic classification. Instead, it applies the same predefined rules uniformly across the corpus and outputs the extracted text segments for the subsequent stages.

Stage 2: Concept Recognition. For each segment, this stage identifies candidate *mentions*: spans of text that denote either named entities (e.g., flight numbers, airport names, dates) or domain-relevant terms (e.g., "runway," "flight level"). We distinguish mentions from ontology concepts: mentions are surface-level textual units, whereas ontology concepts are abstract classes (e.g., *Flight*, *Airport*) that mentions may later instantiate. Although termed *Concept Recognition*, this stage recognizes mentions rather than ontology concepts. A dedicated pre-trained mention recognition model is used instead of the local LLM, as it is substantially faster while providing comparable quality for this subtask [5,41]. Since the model is independent of the target ontology, it produces class-agnostic candidate mentions, which are classified against the ontology in Stage 3.

Stage 3: Ontology-Guided Classification. Each candidate mention from Stage 2 is assigned to a class in the ontology O. This is the first stage that consumes the ontology and uses the local LLM. Given the surrounding text, the candidate mention, and the admissible ontology classes, the model returns the most appropriate class or indicates that no suitable class exists. Unclassifiable mentions are excluded from the extraction schema rather than the original ontology and serve as signals for ontology refinement. Consistently unused classes become candidates for aggregation or removal from the compact extraction ontology under expert supervision, following ontology abstraction principles that reduce conceptual complexity while preserving task-relevant semantics [35]. The resulting typed entities provide the first signal for ontology shaping through classes that are never instantiated.

Stage 4: Semantic Relation Identification. Given the typed entities from Stage 3 and the segment in which they appear, this stage identifies the relationship types from O that hold between them. The local LLM receives the segment, the entities with their classes, and the subset of relationship types whose subject and object classes match the classes of the candidate entity pair. The model returns the relationships that are supported by the text. The output is a set of typed triples per segment. This stage produces the second signal for ontology shaping, namely, relationship types in O that the model never asserts despite being applicable.

Stage 5: Ontology Conformance Validation. The triples produced by Stages 3 and 4 are validated against the schema definition of the current ontology O. A triple is *conformant* if its predicate is defined in O and the classes of its subject and object match the signature σ assigned to that predicate (Sect. 3). Nonconformant triples are flagged as validation failures. After a sufficient number of extraction probes, these failures form a diagnostic signal for the domain expert. The signal indicates whether the problem lies in the ontology, in the prompt, or in the extraction behavior of the local LLM. Based on this signal, the expert may reshape O, for example, by aggregating classes, removing unused elements, or introducing more direct relationship types. Alternatively, the expert may request another extraction run with a revised prompt or additional context. The loop continues until the expert accepts the current state of the ontology. For example, the triple (Flight, departsFrom, Airport) is conformant since departsFrom is defined with signature (Flight, Airport), whereas locatedInCountry applied to a City–Country pair is non-conformant, as its signature requires (Airport, Country).

Stage 6: Entity Normalization. The conformant probe triples from Stage 5 may refer to the same real-world entity through different surface forms, spellings, abbreviations, or identifiers. This stage tests whether entities can be represented consistently across the corpus. It proposes canonical entity names and alias mappings using approximate string matching, reference datasets where available, and within-corpus clustering. The proposed merges, splits, and canonical names are shown to the domain expert as a normalization signal. The expert decides whether the proposed entity identities are acceptable. If they are not acceptable, the expert may revise the normalization rules, adjust the prompt, provide additional context, or reshape the ontology by adding or modifying identifier attributes. The stage is repeated until the expert accepts the normalization decisions. The accepted output contributes to the compact ontology O^* and to the extraction configuration used later during KG population.

The Role of the Domain Expert and Stage Signals. EOOM is designed for safety-critical domains, where regulatory accountability and operational risk rule out fully autonomous ontology and KG construction. As shown in Fig. 1, the domain expert is embedded in the loop: they provide the initial ontology O_{init}, either by selecting an existing domain ontology such as AIRM-O or by drafting one for the target subdomain, and use stage-specific signals to decide whether the current ontology state should be accepted, revised, or tested again with modified prompts or additional context. Stages 2 to 6 then produce different diagnostic signals for the expert, summarized in Table 1. Stage 2 produces a *mention coverage signal* indicating which relevant terms are detected and which are missed or returned as noise. Stage 3 produces a *classification signal* indicating whether candidate mentions can be assigned to classes in the current ontology, with unclassifiable mentions, systematic misclassifications, or never-instantiated classes pointing to a misfit class structure. Stage 4 produces a *relation availability signal* indicating whether typed entities can be connected by relationship types from the current ontology, with empty candidate sets or unused relationship types pointing to wrong-granularity relationships. Stage 5 produces a *conformance signal*, where repeated validation failures indicate that the problem may lie in the ontology, in the prompt, or in the extraction behavior of the local LLM. Stage 6 produces a *normalization signal* indicating whether different surface forms, abbreviations, spellings, or identifiers refer to the same real-world entity, with ambiguous or false merges pointing to unstable entity identity. Experts stopped once iterations produced no new classes, relations, or conformance failures, indicating stabilization rather than a formal stopping criterion. Based on each signal, the expert may accept the current state, reshape O (e.g. aggregating classes, renaming or removing classes, introducing more direct relationship types, revising signatures, or adding identifier attributes), revise normalization rules, or request another extraction run with a modified prompt or additional context.

The loop in Stages 2–6 terminates when the expert accepts the current ontology state, prompt, and extraction settings. The accepted output is the compact extraction ontology O^*, together with the modeling and normalization decisions required for later KG population. The final KG G^* is then populated using O^*, the source documents, vector-embedded document representations, and the local LLM, before expert review before operational use. Thus, EOOM does not replace expert effort; rather, it automates the mechanical aspects of KG construction

Table 1. Stage signals and the corresponding expert decisions in the EOOM loop.

Stage	Signal	Expert actions
2	Mention coverage	Accept mentions; revise scope of relevant concepts; adjust extraction settings
3	Classification	Keep class structure; aggregate, rename, or remove classes; adjust prompt
4	Relation availability	Introduce more direct relations; aggregate classes; revise signatures; adjust prompt
5	Conformance	Reshape O; revise prompt; supply additional context; re-run extraction
6	Normalization	Revise normalization rules; add identifier attributes; modify prompt; reshape O

while focusing expert attention on modeling and validation decisions requiring domain judgment.

4.3 Use Case Illustration: Aviation Accident Reports

To illustrate how EOOM operates in practice, we apply it to the construction of a KG from aviation accident reports. The corpus D consists of 643 reports drawn from two national safety authorities, the Japan Transport Safety Board (JTSB) and the German Federal Bureau of Aircraft Accident Investigation (BFU) Investigation [16,26], and addresses ATM as the target subdomain. The target model M is a local LLM in the range of 8 to 15 billion parameters (Sect. 3). The initial ontology O_{init} is AIRM-O [11,17], a formally expressive ATM ontology developed by EUROCONTROL for interoperability across European ATM systems. AIRM-O defines 915 entity classes and 28,432 relationship types. Its size places it well beyond the compactness bound of any local LLM we consider, so the schema cannot be supplied directly in the prompt. The natural alternative is retrieval-augmented access, where the relevant subset of the ontology is retrieved per segment and supplied to the model at extraction time.

When EOOM is initialized with O_{init} = AIRM-O under the retrieval-augmented configuration, Stage 3 still produces typed entities, but Stage 4 returns almost no relationships. Stage 5 conformance validation shows that this outcome is structural rather than linguistic. The fine-grained class hierarchy of AIRM-O leads Stage 3 to assign highly specific classes to entities. However, the relationship types connecting these specific classes are either too narrow or not available in AIRM-O as direct relationships. Hence, Stage 4 receives empty or near-empty candidate relationship sets, preventing the formation of triples from O_{init} alone. This outcome does not indicate a failure of EOOM, but an expected diagnostic signal within the method. EOOM explicitly includes a domain expert in the loop to interpret such conformance signals and refine the ontology between iterations. When Stage 5 reveals a structural gap, the expert adjusts the ontology so that relevant relationship candidates become available to Stage 4. In the AIRM-O run, this expert-in-the-loop [37] correction was sufficient to recover a well-formed extraction result, showing that the initial empty Stage 4 output was caused by an extractability mismatch in O_{init}, not by a failure of the extractor.

Through repeated application of Stages 3 through 5, the initial ontology is refined into a compact ontology. Classes are aggregated where the fine-grained distinctions of AIRM-O are never useful for relationship formation. Relationship types that depend on transitive inference, which local LLMs cannot reliably perform [38], are made direct. The resulting ontology O^* consists of 20 classes and 21 relationship types and is illustrated in Fig. 2. It is centered on hub entities (Flight, Airport, Aircraft Registration, City) that anchor the connectivity of the resulting KG, and it preserves direct relationships such as *locatedInCountry* alongside the transitive route through City, which compensates for the absence of transitive inference in the target model.

The experimental evaluation of G^* constructed under O^*, including comparisons against a single-stage baseline and against EOOM without the conformance and normalization stages, is presented in Sect. 5.

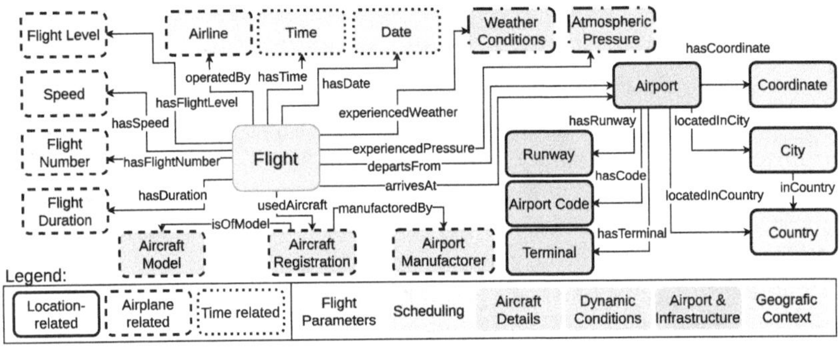

Fig. 2. The shaped ontology O^* derived by EOOM for the aviation use case. It is a compact and hub-centered extraction ontology for local LLMs. Llama 3.1 8B is shown only as an example from the evaluated model range.

5 Experimental Evaluation

To evaluate the effectiveness of our proposed EOOM on constructing KG, we conduct an empirical evaluation of EOOM on the aviation use case (Sect. 4.3). We describe the setup (Sect. 5.1), formalize the evaluation scores (Sect. 5.2), and report results for six local LLMs against a baseline without EOOM (Sect. 5.2).

5.1 Experimental Setup

The corpus consists of 643 aviation accident reports from the JTSB and the BFU, with Document Segmentation extracting the summary and flight-history sections of each report. The corpus spans two independent safety authorities with different reporting conventions and heterogeneous accident types, and all reports are available in our repository. The guiding ontology is the constructed ontology O^* produced by EOOM from AIRM-O, comprising 20 classes and 21 relationship types (Fig. 2). AIRM-O itself is not evaluated here because, as shown in Sect. 4.3, it does not satisfy the compactness requirement.

EOOM is evaluated with six local LLMs spanning both general-purpose and reasoning architectures. These models range from 8 to 15 billion parameters, each of which can be run on a single consumer-grade GPU (Table 2). Models are accessed locally via Ollama, with moderate quantization and the temperature fixed at 0.8.

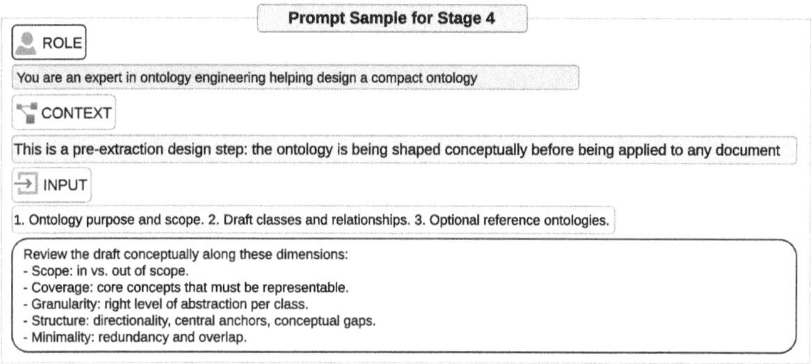

Fig. 3. Simplified prompt example used during ontology shaping/reshaping to elicit expert review of a draft ontology before it is applied to extraction.

We implemented a prototype system for our use case that utilizes local LLMs as described.[1] See, for example, Fig. 3 for the prompt used to evaluate the Plausibility of relationships.

To demonstrate the effectiveness of EOOM in supporting KG construction, we compare it with a baseline, *Without-EOOM*, which adopts a single-call extraction approach. In this baseline, the local LLM is prompted to extract all entities and relationship triples in a single call, without decomposing into stages or performing conformance validation or normalization. The baseline is run with Qwen 3, which achieved the highest benchmark scores among the six models at the time of testing. Plausibility scores are computed using GPT-5-mini as a stronger reference judge, with two runs at temperatures $t \in \{0.0, 0.4\}$ averaged.

Computational Cost. Experiments run on a single consumer-grade GPU (Nvidia RTX 5060-Ti) via Ollama, moderate quantization. Stages 1, 2, 5, and 6 use deterministic rules, a pre-trained spaCy Named-Entity Recognition (NER) model, and string matching, at negligible cost. Stage 2 via NER completes in under a second per segment, versus over ten minutes with the local LLM, which motivated offloading it. A full EOOM run over the 643-report corpus takes

[1] https://github.com/sadmad/Extraction-Oriented-Ontology-Modeling.

approximately 48h per general-purpose model and 72h per reasoning model. EOOM issues one call per candidate mention (Stage 3) and one per typed-entity segment (Stage 4), versus one call per document page for Without-EOOM, fewer but more plausible triples.

5.2 Evaluation Matrices

The three evaluation metrics of Sect. 3.1 are operationalized as follows. Where applicable, scores are normalized to $[0, 1]$ with higher values indicating better quality. *Schema adherence* is the fraction of triples in T that are schema-conformant under the guiding ontology O:

$$\mathrm{Adh}(G) = \frac{|\{(s,p,o) \in T : (s,p,o) \text{ is schema-conformant under } O\}|}{|T|}. \quad (1)$$

Triples with undefined subject or object class count as non-conformant.

Structural quality is reported using three metrics computed on the undirected graph induced by G: the average node degree $\bar{d}(G)$, the fraction of isolated entities $\mathrm{Iso}(G)$, and the normalized predicate entropy:

$$H_{\mathrm{pred}}(G) = \frac{-\sum_{p \in P_G} \Pr(p) \log_2 \Pr(p)}{\log_2 |P_G|}, \quad (2)$$

where P_G is the set of predicates that appear in T and $\Pr(p)$ is their empirical frequency over triples in T. These three metrics are reported separately because they capture distinct structural properties.

Table 2. The local LLMs used in our experiments.

Model	Params.	Type	Year
Phi-3	14.0B	General	2024
Llama-3.1	8.0B	General	2024
DeepSeek-R1	14.8B	Reasoning	2025
Gemma 3	12.2B	General	2025
Phi-4	14.7B	Reasoning	2025
Qwen 3	14.8B	Reasoning	2025

Plausibility is estimated through stratified sampling [15,31]. For each KG, we sample 150 triples, with between 5 and 15 triples per relationship type, and obtain a rating for each triple from the reference judge. The plausibility score is the mean of these 150 ratings. Table 3 reports the evaluation scores across the four metrics for all configurations.

Table 3. Evaluation results across six local LLMs. Higher values are better.

Configuration	Sch.	Plaus.	Deg.	Entr.
EOOM (Phi-3)	.504	.801	2.08	.897
EOOM (Llama-3.1)	.441	.805	2.11	.904
EOOM (DeepSeek-R1)	.466	.790	2.08	.893
EOOM (Gemma 3)	.461	.764	2.08	.900
EOOM (Phi-4)	.482	.807	2.11	.894
EOOM (Qwen 3)	.481	.758	2.07	.854
w/o EOOM	.686	.591	2.28	.675

Schema Adherence and Plausibility. Without-EOOM achieves the highest schema adherence at 0.686 but the lowest plausibility at 0.591. This apparent advantage in schema adherence is an artifact of forced typing, as the single-call configuration produces typed triples by construction. At the same time, EOOM allows Stage 3 to mark mentions as unclassifiable when no class in O fits. The plausibility gap is more diagnostic. Across all six EOOM runs, plausibility clusters between 0.758 and 0.807, approximately 20% above the baseline. Without-EOOM therefore produces structurally well-formed but factually less reliable triples. In contrast, EOOM produces fewer but more plausible triples by separating concept recognition, classification, and relation identification across focused subtasks.

Structural Quality. The six EOOM runs exhibit similar structural profiles, with average degree between 2.08 and 2.11 and predicate entropy between 0.854 and 0.904. Without-EOOM has higher average degree (2.28) but substantially lower predicate entropy (0.675), indicating disproportionate reliance on a small subset of relationship types. The *hasTime* predicate alone accounts for over 20% of its relationships, while some other relationship types are barely used. EOOM produces a more balanced distribution that better reflects the ontology.

Effect of Model Choice. The six EOOM runs differ by less than 7% points on schema adherence and less than 6 percentage points on plausibility. Phi-3, the smallest and oldest model at 14 billion parameters and released in 2024, achieves the highest schema adherence and competitive plausibility under EOOM. There is no clear advantage of reasoning-oriented models over general-purpose models. This supports the paper's central claim, namely that ontology design and pipeline structure dominate model choice in determining KG construction quality under local LLMs.

6 Discussion

Ontology Design Dominates Model Choice. The evaluation shows only narrow variance across the six local LLMs under EOOM, with schema adherence within 7 percentage points and plausibility within 6 percentage points. Phi-3, the smallest and oldest model in the set, achieves the highest schema adherence and competitive plausibility, while reasoning-oriented models show no clear advantage over general-purpose ones. Under a compact, extraction-aligned ontology, the choice of local LLM thus appears to be a second-order concern; the structure of the ontology and the pipeline accounts for most of the variance in KG quality.

Schema Adherence Versus Plausibility. The Without-EOOM baseline scores higher on schema adherence yet substantially lower on plausibility. Single-call extraction learns the syntactic form of a typed triple without ensuring that the source text supports the triple. Schema adherence, when used alone, therefore rewards configurations that produce well-formed but semantically shallow output. The combination of schema adherence and plausibility is needed to distinguish triples that are merely well-typed from triples that are also factually defensible. This distinction matters in safety-critical domains.

Implications for Conceptual Modeling. EOOM suggests that the artifact produced through LLM-based extraction is not the same kind of object as a classical domain ontology. The 20-class extraction schema obtained through EOOM is not a reduced or simplified AIRM-O, it is a different artifact, optimized for operational use by a constrained model rather than for interoperability or formal reasoning. We therefore do not claim O^* retains AIRM-O's completeness, expressiveness, or interoperability; extractability is prioritized because these properties cannot be operationalized by a local LLM without it, and O^* is a task-specific companion to the reference ontology, not a replacement for it. Recognizing this distinction has consequences for conceptual modeling research: ontology design methodologies may need to treat *extractability* alongside the established concerns of semantic completeness, formal expressiveness, and reusability. Treating domain ontologies and extraction schemas as a single category obscures the fact that each is designed against different requirements.

Limitations. The evaluation covers one safety-critical domain, so the generality of findings to other domains and other reference ontologies remains to be established. The ontology refinement loop is mediated by expert judgment and is therefore not fully reproducible from the description in this paper, although Stage 5 makes the diagnostic signals on which the expert acts explicit. The sequential entity-then-relation design does not let relationship context inform entity classification; a joint or iterative formulation is left for future work. Plausibility is judged by a stronger reference LLM rather than by domain experts, which is a known approximation [25] and would benefit from cross-validation against human judgment in future work. A stage-wise ablation isolating each stage's contribution was not feasible within the computational budget, and is left for future work.

7 Conclusion

We introduced EOOM, a six-stage conceptual modeling approach for ontology-guided KG construction from unstructured text using local LLMs in safety-critical domains. EOOM treats the guiding ontology as a variable that is refined during construction rather than a fixed precondition, thereby producing an extraction schema adapted to the operational constraints of the target model. Applied to 643 aviation accident reports, EOOM produced a 20-class extraction schema that enabled stable KG construction across six local LLMs of varying size and architecture. In contrast, the 915-class AIRM-O ontology failed to support extraction under the same conditions. The evaluation showed that ontology design is a stronger determinant of extraction quality than model choice. Future work includes evaluating EOOM across additional safety-critical domains and reference ontologies, formalizing the expert-driven refinement loop into a more reproducible procedure, and complementing the LLM-based plausibility judgment with structured domain-expert review.

References

1. Agarwal, A.: Knowledge graph-deep learning: a case study in question answering in aviation safety domain. In: Language Resources Evaluation Conference (2022)
2. Agrawal, G.: Can knowledge graphs reduce hallucinations in LLMs?: A survey. In: Conference on North American Chapter of the Association for Computational Linguistics: Human Language Technologies (2024)
3. Alfaifi, Y.: Ontology development methodology: a systematic review and case study. In: IEEE International Conference on Computing and Information Technology (ICCIT) (2022)
4. Andrade, S.R., Walsh, H.S.: Safeaerobert: towards a safety-informed aerospace-specific language model. In: AIAA Aviation Forum (2023)
5. Bharathi, A.: A hybrid named entity recognition system for aviation text. EAI Endorsed Trans. Scalable Inf. Syst. **11** (2023)
6. van Cauter, Z., Yakovets, N.: Ontology-guided knowledge graph construction from maintenance short texts. In: Knowledge Graphs and Large Language Models (KaLLM) (2024)
7. Chen, H., Cao, G., Chen, J., Ding, J.: A practical framework for evaluating the quality of knowledge graph. In: Zhu, X., Qin, B., Zhu, X., Liu, M., Qian, L. (eds.) CCKS 2019. CCIS, vol. 1134, pp. 111–122. Springer, Singapore (2019). https://doi.org/10.1007/978-981-15-1956-7_10
8. Chen, L.: Information extraction of aviation accident causation knowledge graph: an LLM-based approach. Electronics **13** (2024)
9. Cheng, Y., Jiao, Y., Wei, W., Wu, Z.: Research on construction method of knowledge graph in the civil aviation security field. In: IEEE International Conference on Civil Aviation Safety and Information Technology (ICCASIT). IEEE (2019)

10. Department of the Air Force: DAFFARS subpart 5339. In: Use of Large Language Models, vol. 73 (2024)
11. EUROCONTROL: ATM Information Reference Model (AIRM) (2025). https://www.eurocontrol.int/model/airm. Accessed 14 May 2026
12. Euzenat, J., Shvaiko, P.: Ontology Matching. Springer, Heidelberg (2007)
13. Fathallah, N., Staab, S., Algergawy, A.: Llms4life: large language models for ontology learning in life sciences. arXiv preprint arXiv:2412.02035 (2024)
14. Gangemi, A., Presutti, V.: Ontology design patterns. In: Handbook on Ontologies. Springer, Heidelberg (2009)
15. Gao, J., Li: Efficient knowledge graph accuracy evaluation. arXiv preprint arXiv:1907.09657 (2019)
16. German Federal Bureau of Aircraft Accidents Investigation: Investigation report 7x010-0/07: Serious incident involving eurocopter ec135 p2+ in mannheim, 23 august 2007. Technical Report 7X010-0/07, German Federal Bureau of Aircraft Accidents Investigation (2009). Accessed 12 May 2026
17. Gringinger, E.: A comparative study of two complex ontologies in air traffic management. In: IEEE/AIAA Digital Avionics Systems Conference (DASC) (2019)
18. Grüninger, M., Fox, M.S.: Methodology for the design and evaluation of ontologies. In: IJCAI Workshop on Basic Ontological Issues in Knowledge Sharing (1995)
19. Guizzardi, G.: Ontological foundations for structural conceptual models. CTIT, Centre for Telematics and Information Technology (2005)
20. Guo, W., Wang, X.: Ontology-enhanced knowledge graph completion using large language models. In: International Semantic Web Conference (ISWC). Springer, Heidelberg (2025). https://doi.org/10.1007/978-3-032-09527-5_4
21. Gupta, S., Rezayat, S., Burmester, G., Durak, U., Ma, H., Hartmann, S.: From ConOps to an operational domain model: harnessing LLMs for conceptual model design. In: Advances in Conceptual Modeling, pp. 137–156. Springer, Heidelberg (2025). https://doi.org/10.1007/978-3-032-08620-4_9
22. He, Y.: Bertmap: a bert-based ontology alignment system. In: AAAI Conference on Artificial Intelligence, vol. 36, pp. 5684–5691 (2022)
23. Hogan, A.: Knowledge graphs. ACM Comput. Surv. **54** (2021)
24. Huang, H., et al.: A middle path for on-premises llm deployment: preserving privacy without sacrificing model confidentiality. In: Conference on Empirical Methods in Natural Language Processing (EMNLP) (2025)
25. Huang, H.: Can llms be good graph judge for knowledge graph construction? In: Conference on Empirical Methods in Natural Language Processing (2025)
26. Japan Transport Safety Board: Aircraft accident investigation report: Flight attendant injury by the shaking of the aircraft, t'way air boeing 737-800 hl8021. Technical Report. AA2020-4, Japan Transport Safety Board (2020) (2026)
27. Kejriwal, M.: Domain-Specific Knowledge Graph Construction. Springer, Heidelberg (2019)
28. Lee, T.: Ethic: evaluating large language models on long-context tasks with high information coverage. In: Conference on Nations of the Americas Chapter of the Association for Computational Linguistics: Human Language Technologies (2025)
29. Liu, D., Cheng, L.: Makg: a maritime accident knowledge graph for intelligent accident analysis and management. Ocean Eng. **312** (2024)
30. Liu, P., Qian, L., Zhao, X., Tao, B.: The construction of knowledge graphs in the aviation assembly domain based on a joint knowledge extraction model. IEEE Access **11** (2023)
31. Marchesin, S., Silvello, G.: Efficient and reliable estimation of knowledge graph accuracy. In: Proceedings of VLDB Endowment, p. 17 (2024)

32. Monfardini, G.K.Q., Salamon, J.S., Barcellos, M.P.: Use of competency questions in ontology engineering. In: International Conference on Conceptual Modeling (ER). Springer, Heidelberg (2023). https://doi.org/10.1007/978-3-031-47262-6_3
33. Ourekouch, M., Koulali, M.A., Erradi, M.: Relcheck: improving relation extraction with ontology-guided and LLM-based validation. In: European Semantic Web Conference. Springer, Heidelberg (2025). https://doi.org/10.1007/978-3-031-94575-5_24
34. Pusch, L., Conrad, T.O.: Combining llms and knowledge graphs to reduce hallucinations in question answering. arXiv preprint arXiv:2409.04181 (2024)
35. Romanenko, E., Calvanese, D., Guizzardi, G.: Abstracting ontology-driven conceptual models: objects, aspects, events, and their parts. In: International Conference on Research Challenges in Information Science. Springer, Heidelberg (2022). https://doi.org/10.1007/978-3-031-05760-1_22
36. Rossanez, A., da Silva Torres, R., dos Reis, J.C.: Characterizing complex network properties of knowledge graphs. In: KEOD (2023)
37. Sadruddin, S.: Schema-miner: agentic AI for ontology grounding over LLM-discovered scientific schemas in a human-in-the-loop workflow. Semant. Web (2026)
38. Sosa, R.U., Ramamurthy, K.N., Chang, M., Singh, M.: Reasoning about concepts with LLMs: inconsistencies abound. In: Conference on Language Modeling (2024)
39. Wang, X.: Knowledge graph quality control: a survey. Fund. Res. **1** (2021)
40. Xue, B., Zou, L.: Knowledge graph quality management: a comprehensive survey. IEEE Trans. Knowl. Data Eng. **35** (2022)
41. Yang, M., Namoano, B., Farsi, M., Erkoyuncu, J.A.: Named entity recognition in aviation products domain based on bert. IEEE Access **12** (2024)
42. Zhang, B.: Ontochat: a framework for conversational ontology engineering using language models. In: European Semantic Web Conference (2024)

Generating Explainable Domain Models via Attention and Confidence

Jonathan Silva[1(✉)], Qin Ma[1], Jordi Cabot[1,2], Pierre Kelsen[1], and Henderik A. Proper[3,4]

[1] University of Luxembourg, Esch-sur-Alzette, Luxembourg
{jonathan.silva,qin.ma,jordi.cabot,pierre.kelsen}@uni.lu, jordi.cabot@list.lu

[2] Luxembourg Institute of Science and Technology, Esch-sur-Alzette, Luxembourg

[3] TU Wien, Vienna, Austria
henderik.proper@tuwien.ac.at

[4] HU University of Applied Sciences, Utrecht, The Netherlands

Abstract. The use of Large Language Models (LLMs) has shown significant potential for generating domain models from textual descriptions. However, these models often fall short in soundness, which is inevitably caused by the statistical nature of LLMs that only generate plausible output rather than output grounded in the provided input. Generated unsound model elements lack supporting evidence in the source textual descriptions, and are commonly referred to as hallucinations.

In this paper, we propose an explainable approach that combines (1) attention-based model element confidence scoring and (2) confidence-driven model ensembling to reduce hallucinations in domain model generation from text. The proposed scoring mechanism leverages the attention weights within transformer architectures to estimate the strength of original textual evidence supporting each generated model element, distinguishing between intra-element and inter-element evidence. The confidence-driven model ensembling strategy then retains the most confident model elements from multiple executions of multiple LLMs and synthesizes them into a final domain model.

We evaluate the effectiveness of our approach using open-weight Small Language Models (SLMs), as their higher propensity for hallucinations provides a rigorous environment for validation. Through an ablation study, we demonstrate how confidence filtering based on intra-element and inter-element scores, together with an ensemble strategy, balances textual grounding and model completeness, providing interpretable evidence for the resulting domain models.

Keywords: Domain Modeling · Explainable AI · Language Models · Attention Weights · Ensemble Methods

© The Author(s), under exclusive license to Springer Nature Switzerland AG 2027
A. Bernasconi et al. (Eds.): ER 2026, LNCS 17081, pp. 92–108, 2027.
https://doi.org/10.1007/978-3-032-40795-5_6

1 Introduction

Large Language Models (LLMs) are increasingly being used for creating draft domain models from natural language requirements [3,22]. In practice, these draft models serve as initial versions that require iterative refinement to be useful for their intended purpose [15,18,21]. Despite ongoing improvements, the inherent opacity of LLMs undermines confidence in their recommendations. Text-to-model domain generation usually operates under a strict closed-world assumption, where the provided natural language description serves as the sole source of truth. When generative LLMs fail in this context, their errors are classified as *faithfulness hallucinations* [10]. In domain modeling, recent studies [4,8] show that hallucination manifests in two forms. First, *context inconsistencies* [10] occur when the LLM relies on pre-training knowledge to generate elements absent from the source text. Second, *instruction inconsistencies* [10] involve the wrong abstraction in UML constructs, such as misclassifying relationship types.

In domain modeling, natural language is the primary mode of communication between modelers and experts that enables formalizing of knowledge into documents [7]. These documents provide the fundamental evidence to reconcile personal conceptions and justify the inclusion of model abstractions [9]. However, generative LLMs tend to generate model abstractions that are not grounded in the source textual descriptions [14], leading to hallucinations that are difficult to detect without expert intervention. To increase the usefulness of LLMs in domain modeling, transparency is needed to expose and assess such hallucinations.

To support transparency in text-to-model generation, symbolic reasoning is often preferred due to its inherent explainability [6]. Even after the emergence of LLMs, recent work continues to emphasize the importance of preserving explainable symbolic representations for language understanding [19]. Recognizing this need, Explainable AI (XAI) has been used in software modeling to provide grounded interpretations for model classification tasks [1]. However, bridging the gap between the subsymbolic nature of LLMs and the need for transparency in grounding model outputs in textual evidence remains an open challenge.

A fundamental issue to bridging this gap is the weak correlation between generated intermediate traces, defined as sequences of textual tokens produced prior to the final solution, and the actual output [12]. Since these traces cannot provide the evidence required to validate domain abstractions, reliable grounding requires analyzing the LLM's internal architecture. Mechanistic interpretability shows that transformer attention heads encode linguistic structures [5], with decoder layers exhibiting distinct layer specializations: early layers extract inputs, middle layers process instructions, and late layers format outputs [17]. However, the explanatory role of attention remains debated [11,24], and the analysis of raw attention weights is further complicated by attention sinks, where the initial token receives a disproportionate amount of attention weight [2,25]. This motivates the Multi-Layer Attention Consistency Score (MACS), which measures the consistency of attention weights across multiple layers from each generated output token backward to the tokens in the input [16].

We propose an integrated approach using MACS to derive attention-based confidence scores coupled with a confidence-driven ensemble. Instead of relying on raw attention weights, this method combines attention scores with rule-based Natural Language Processing (NLP) techniques. Our approach quantifies the grounding of each element, evaluating it in isolation (intra-element) and within its structural context (inter-element) against the textual domain description. The final model is derived through confidence score filtering and aggregation mechanisms, ensuring that only the most reliable domain elements are retained.

Our method targets open-weight language models. Methodologically, open-weight architectures provide direct access to internal attention matrices required by our scoring mechanism. In practice, they align with organizational demands for data privacy, local execution, and cost control, thereby avoiding reliance on external APIs. Furthermore, we deliberately focus on Small Language Models (SLMs) because their higher propensity for hallucinations provides a rigorous environment to assess our approach. Our main contributions are as follows:

- An integrated attention-based confidence scoring and ensemble consolidation approach to generate UML class models grounded in domain description.
- An ablation study along two dimensions: confidence scoring (intra-element, inter-element, and combined) and final model derivation strategy (confidence-based filtering only and filtering plus ensembling), complemented by a sensitivity analysis of attention and confidence thresholds.
- A comparative evaluation against the Tree-of-Thought (ToT) prompting-based framework [20] and RAG-based framework QuaRUM [23], considering both the quality of generated domain models and the associated cost.
- An open-source implementation of the proposed method to support reproducibility and enable further investigation and extension.

The paper is organized as follows: Sect. 2 surveys related work, followed by the MACS background (Sect. 3) and our attention-based scoring and confidence-driven ensemble approach (Sect. 4). Section 5 details the experimental evaluation, Sect. 6 presents the tool support, and Sect. 7 concludes.

2 Textual Grounding for LLM-Assisted Domain Modeling

Improving the textual grounding of LLM-generated domain models ranges from using prompting or agent frameworks [4,8] and Retrieval-Augmented Generation (RAG) [23], to internal attention mechanisms [13]. Prompting frameworks address hallucinations after an initial model is generated. For instance, Chen et al. [4] apply an LLM self-refinement process, which includes correcting semantic issues and removing redundancy. Giannouris et al. [8] employ a verification agent that inspects the model against the textual requirements. Their error analysis reveals *faithfulness hallucinations* [10]: *context inconsistencies* manifest as classes and relationships absent from the textual description [4,8]; and *instruction inconsistencies* occur with incorrect UML constructs, such as misclassifying the type of relationships [4,8]. However, relying on LLMs self-evaluation risks reinforcing hallucinations through the erroneous validation of ungrounded elements.

To make evidence explicit, Tauhid et al. [23] propose a RAG approach to ground each generated element in supporting passages from textual requirements, assigning a score based on that external evidence. However, relying on an external pipeline leaves the generation step as a black box, meaning inherent LLM biases can still introduce hallucinations. Another direction pursues grounding from within the model by analyzing internal attention representations. Käppel et al. [13] propose an attention explainer that computes a score for each input activity using internal self-attention weights. While they leverage internal attention weights for explainable representations, their focus is on process model activity prediction rather than domain model generation from natural language.

The reviewed works reveal a gap: prompting and RAG approaches treat generation as a black box, while attention grounding has been explored for sequential activity prediction rather than structural domain model generation. To our knowledge, no existing work leverages LLM internal attention to derive confidence scores that serve as both grounding assessment and explainability mechanisms for domain modeling.

3 Background: Multi-layer Attention Consistency Score

In this work, we consider autoregressive, decoder-only Transformer language models composed of multiple layers and attention heads (cf. Figure 1). This architecture represents the dominant paradigm in modern LLMs. A language model generates text sequentially, one token at a time, where each token represents a sub-word unit drawn from the token vocabulary $\mathcal{T}$ of the model. At each generation step, the model takes as input a sequence of tokens $S = [\tau_1, \tau_2, \ldots, \tau_n]$, and produces the next token $\tau_{n+1} \in \mathcal{T}$, conditioned on all preceding tokens. The token τ_{n+1} is then appended to S for the next generation step.

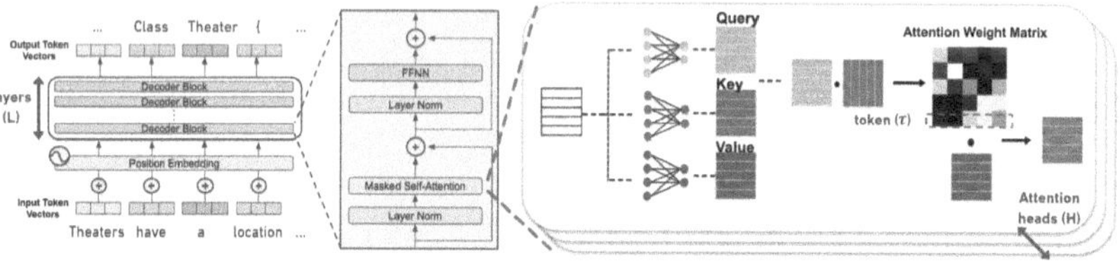

Fig. 1. Internal structure of a language model. The model processes the input through L stacked transformer layers (left), each containing a self-attention mechanism (center). Within each self-attention mechanism, H parallel attention heads compute H attention weight matrices from Query and Key projections. Within an attention weight matrix, the row corresponding to the last generated token τ (highlighted) encodes the importance of each preceding token on the generation of τ within that head and layer.

To estimate the importance of preceding tokens for generating τ, Lan et al. proposed the Multi-Layer Attention Consistency Score (MACS) based on the heuristic that token importance can be inferred from the consistency of maximal attention weights across Transformer layers [16]. In particular, to reduce noise and maintain computational efficiency, MACS operates as follows. For each layer and each preceding token, MACS selects the head exhibiting the strongest attention weight. These maximal attention weights are assembled into a vector for that layer. The resulting vectors across all layers are then combined using the Hadamard product to produce a single relevance vector. In this vector, attention weight at position i reflects the importance of a preceding token τ_i for generating the last token τ. Finally, this vector is normalized using Z-score normalization to quantify the relative importance of each preceding token.

Definition 1 (MACS Score). *For a generated token τ and a token τ_i preceding τ, the MACS score $z^{\tau}_{\tau_i}$ denotes the relative importance of τ_i for generating τ.*

4 Confidence Scoring and Confidence-Driven Ensemble

Building on MACS scores, we propose five scores to measure the confidence of domain model elements proposed by a language model. We further introduce a confidence-driven ensemble strategy that selects high-confidence elements from domain models generated by multiple language models across multiple executions, and consolidates them into a final domain model.

Figure 2 illustrates the proposed pipeline. A language model is prompted using input-output (I/O) prompting to generate a domain model from a natural language domain description. The input prompt is a sequence of tokens $S_{\text{prompt}} = [\tau_1, \ldots, \tau_{i_s^{dom}}, \ldots, \tau_{i_e^{dom}}, \ldots]$ comprising prefix modeling instructions, followed by the domain description, followed by postfix modeling instructions, where i_s^{dom} and i_e^{dom} are the start and end indices of the domain description.

To illustrate our approach, consider the domain of theaters. The input prompt begins with a prefix specifying the modeling task, followed by the textual domain description starting with "Theaters have a location, ...", and concluding with postfix instructions specifying the output format. In response, the language model generates a sequence of tokens representing a domain model. The elements of these generated models are subsequently evaluated to quantify their textual grounding and determine a final confidence score, as illustrated in Fig. 3.

The confidence in a model element should reflect how strongly its generation is grounded in the input prompt, and in particular in the domain description. To assess this, we anchor each model element e with a **reference token** τ_{e}: for classes, attributes, and associations, the token corresponding to the element's name; for cardinality specifications, the token corresponding to the numerical expression (e.g., lower bound .. upper bound); if a name is tokenized into multiple tokens, the last token is selected as τ_{e}. Using MACS, we then measure how much each preceding token contributed to generating τ_{e}.

A token that influenced τ_{e} may belong to the prompt sequence S_{prompt} or to previously generated tokens, and within the prompt to the domain description or to the modeling instructions. We therefore narrow the preceding tokens toward the relevant domain content in three steps.

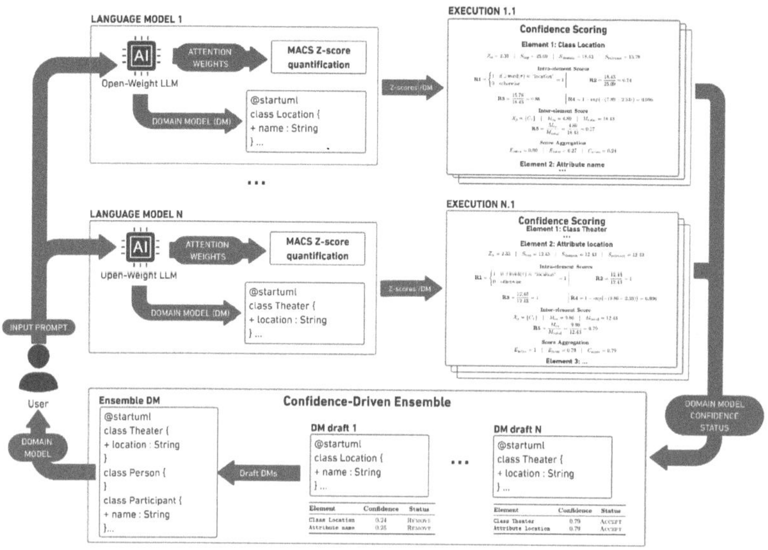

Fig. 2. Overview of the proposed Attention Confidence Scoring and Confidence-Driven Ensemble pipeline. LLM executions generate draft domain models, and attention weights are extracted to calculate the MACS Z-scores. Once the complete model is generated, confidence scores (R_1-R_5) are quantified for every model element. Finally, the ensemble combines multiple drafts using the confidence scores to create a model grounded in the provided domain description.

First, we consider only the prompt tokens, discarding previously generated ones, and keep those that received disproportionately high attention. We identify these through a heuristic cutoff threshold Z_t, where a prompt token is retained only when its score exceeds it. Different thresholds can be chosen, and in our experiment we set $Z_\mathrm{t} = 2.33$:

Definition 2 (Top-Attended Tokens). *For a generated model element e, $S_\mathrm{top}(e)$ is the subsequence of S_prompt containing tokens with MACS scores exceeding the heuristic threshold, namely*

$$S_\mathrm{top}(e) = [\tau \mid \tau \in S_\mathrm{prompt} \wedge z_\tau^{\tau_e} > Z_\mathrm{t}]$$

Second, since the domain description occupies a contiguous span of the prompt, an attended token belongs to it precisely when its position lies within that span. Let $\mathrm{pos}(\tau)$ denote the index of token τ in the prompt sequence. We retain only the tokens whose position falls between i_s^{dom} and i_e^{dom}, discarding the prefix and postfix instructions:

Definition 3 (Top-Attended Domain Tokens). *For a generated model element e, $S_\mathrm{domain}(e)$ is the subsequence of $S_\mathrm{top}(e)$ containing tokens belonging to the domain description, namely*

$$S_\mathrm{domain}(e) = [\tau \mid \tau \in S_\mathrm{top}(e) \wedge i_s^{dom} \leq \mathrm{pos}(\tau) \leq i_e^{dom}]$$

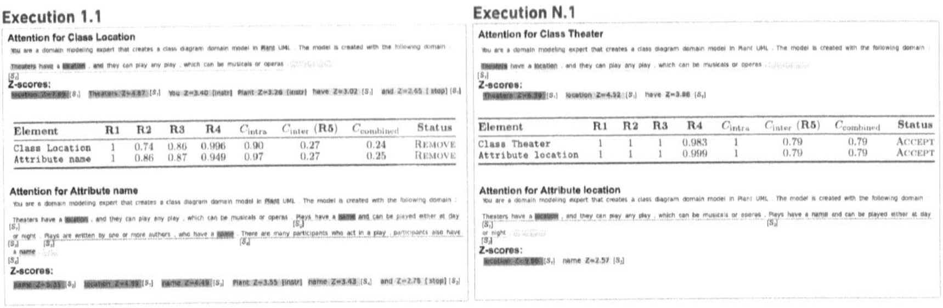

Fig. 3. $R_1 - R_5$ and Confidence scores illustration. The MACS z-scores of the top-attended tokens are aggregated to compute the $R_1 - R_5$ scores, intra-, inter-element, and the combined confidence score for each generated element.

Finally, we remove semantically uninformative stop-words $\mathcal{T}_{\text{stop}} \subset \mathcal{T}$ (e.g., articles, prepositions, conjunctions), keeping the tokens that carry domain meaning:

Definition 4 (Top-Attended Relevant Domain Tokens). *For a generated model element e, $S_{\text{relevant}}(e)$ is the subsequence of $S_{\text{domain}}(e)$ containing tokens that do not correspond to stop-words, namely*

$$S_{\text{relevant}}(e) = [\tau \mid \tau \in S_{\text{domain}}(e) \wedge \tau \notin \mathcal{T}_{\text{stop}}]$$

4.1 MACS-Based Confidence Quantification from Five Perspectives

With these preliminaries in place, we are now ready to define the confidence of a model element generated by the language model. We introduce five scores, each capturing confidence from a different perspective.

R$_1$: Lexical Match. This score measures whether its reference token τ_e appears among its top-attended domain tokens, by comparing their lexical forms. It is a binary score indicating whether the reference token τ_e has a base-form match within the domain tokens $S_{\text{domain}}(e)$:

$$R_1(e) = \begin{cases} 1 & \text{if } \exists \tau \in S_{\text{domain}}(e) \text{ such that word}(\tau) \approx \text{word}(\tau_e), \\ 0 & \text{otherwise.} \end{cases}$$

where $\approx$ denotes a match between base forms (resolving plurals and inflections), and word(τ) groups sub-words into a single lexical word.

The example shown in Fig. 3 illustrates that. All four elements: class `Location`, attribute `name`, class `Theater`, and attribute `location`, have their reference token among the top-attended domain tokens. Consequently, these elements are all lexically grounded in the domain description, so $R_1 = 1$ for all.

R$_2$: Domain Focus. This score measures the extent to which the model focused on the actual domain description rather than the modeling instructions, as the ratio of attention weight assigned to the domain tokens versus the total attention given to all top-attended tokens, formally, $R_2(e) = \sum_{\tau \in S_{\text{domain}}(e)} z_\tau^{\tau_e} / \sum_{\tau \in S_{\text{top}}(e)} z_\tau^{\tau_e}$.

Returning to Fig. 3, both class `Theater` and its attribute `location` have $R_2 = 1$, because in their case, all top-attended tokens belong to the domain description. In contrast, class `Location` has $R_2 = 0.74$ and its attribute `name` has $R_2 = 0.86$, indicating a portion of their top-attended tokens is distributed over modeling instructions. Comparing these elements with the reference domain model (i.e., the ground truth), we observe that the latter two model elements are indeed hallucinations.

R$_3$: Domain Relevance. This score measures the extent to which the top-attended domain tokens of its reference token τ_e are semantically informative. The domain relevance score of a model element e, denoted by $R_3(e)$ is quantified as the ratio of the total attention weight assigned to the top-attended relevant domain tokens and the total attention weight assigned to all top-attended domain tokens: $R_3(e) = \sum_{\tau \in S_{\text{relevant}}(e)} z_\tau^{\tau_e} / \sum_{\tau \in S_{\text{domain}}(e)} z_\tau^{\tau_e}$.

In Fig. 3, the two correct elements (class `Theater` and attribute `location`) have $R_3 = 1$, while the two hallucinated elements, namely class `Location` and its attribute `name`, have $R_3 = 0.86$ and $R_3 = 0.87$ respectively, indicating that a portion of their top-attended domain tokens are semantically uninformative.

R$_4$: Attention Strength. In case the reference token τ_e has a lexical match in the top-attended domain tokens, namely $R_1(e) = 1$, this score quantifies the attention strength by taking the maximum MACS score among the matching tokens, called the *anchor score* of e, denoted by z^e_{anchor}. Otherwise, if τ_e has no lexical match in the top-attended domain tokens, namely $R_1(e) = 0$, we instead use the mean MACS score over $S_{\text{relevant}}(e)$ as the anchor score. Formally:

$$z^e_{\text{anchor}} = \begin{cases} \max\limits_{\tau \in S_{\text{match}}(e)} z_\tau^{\tau_e}, & \text{if } |S_{\text{match}}(e)| \neq 0, \\ \dfrac{1}{|S_{\text{relevant}}(e)|} \sum\limits_{\tau \in S_{\text{relevant}}(e)} z_\tau^{\tau_e}, & \text{if } |S_{\text{match}}(e)| = 0. \end{cases}$$

where $S_{\text{match}}(e)$ is the subsequence of the top-attended domain tokens of e, namely $S_{\text{domain}}(e)$, containing tokens that share the same base lexical form as the reference token, namely $S_{\text{match}}(e) = [\tau \mid \tau \in S_{\text{domain}}(e) \wedge \text{word}(\tau) \approx \text{word}(\tau_e)]$.

The attention strength score $R_4(e)$ is then the anchor score normalized into the range of $[0, 1)$ using an exponential mapping centered at the heuristic Z-score threshold Z_t, namely: $R_4(e) = 1 - \exp(-(z^e_{\text{anchor}} - Z_t))$.

R$_5$: Evidence Overlap. A justified model element should not only be grounded in the relevant domain description, but its grounding should also align with that of its related elements. Depending on the type of a model element e, we define the set of related elements, denoted by $\mathcal{P}(e)$, as follows:

- a class is related to its attributes;
- an attribute is related to its container class;
- a relationship is related to its endpoint classes;
- a cardinality specification is related to the relationship it constrains and the class at the corresponding association end.

We evaluate this alignment at the sentence level. For any element e, its *evidence pack* $\mathcal{X}_e$ is the set of domain description sentences containing at least one relevant token from $S_{\text{relevant}}(e)$.

The evidence overlap $R_5(e)$ is then the mean ratio of attention weight assigned to tokens of e that co-occur within the evidence packs of its related elements $p \in \mathcal{P}(e)$:

$$R_5(e) = \frac{1}{|\mathcal{P}(e)|} \sum_{p \in \mathcal{P}(e)} \frac{\sum_{\tau \in S_{\text{eo}}(e,p)} z_{\tau}^{\mathcal{T}_e}}{\sum_{\tau \in S_{\text{relevant}}(e)} z_{\tau}^{\mathcal{T}_e}}$$

where $S_{\text{eo}}(e, p)$ are the tokens in $S_{\text{relevant}}(e)$ that also appear in a sentence of the evidence pack $\mathcal{X}_p$.

In Fig. 3, the hallucinated class `Location` top-attended tokens are located in S_1, while the tokens for its attribute `name` are dispersed across S_1–S_4, showing a low evidence overlap that leads to a score $R_5 = 0.27$. In contrast, the class `Theater` and its attribute `location` have their top-attended tokens primarily in S_1. Since S_1 directly describes both concepts, the evidence is strongly aligned, resulting in a high evidence overlap and a high score $R_5 = 0.79$.

4.2 Confidence Score Aggregation

To quantify the confidence of each generated element, we combine the five attention-based scores in three ways:

1. **Intra-element confidence**: $R_1 - R_4$ evaluate the grounding of element e in isolation in the domain description. The intra-element confidence score aggregates them via an equally weighted sum, namely $C_{\text{intra}}(e) = \frac{1}{4} \sum_{i=1}^{4} R_i(e)$.
2. **Inter-element confidence**: R_5 assesses whether an element e and its structurally related elements share grounding in the domain description. It defines the inter-element confidence score, namely $C_{\text{inter}}(e) = R_5(e)$.
3. **Combined confidence**: The combined score quantifies from both the intra- and inter-element perspectives, namely $C_{\text{combined}}(e) = C_{\text{intra}}(e) \times C_{\text{inter}}(e)$.

With these confidence scores, we classify model elements into three types, in relation to two thresholds ($T_{\text{refine}} < T_{\text{accept}}$):

- ACCEPT: if the confidence score $\geq T_{\text{accept}}$, the element is retained.
- REFINE: if the confidence score is $\leq T_{\text{accept}}$ but $\geq T_{\text{refine}}$, the element needs refinement.
- REMOVE: if the confidence score is $< T_{\text{refine}}$, the element is excluded.

In Figure 3, with thresholds $T_{\text{refine}} = 0.5$ and $T_{\text{accept}} = 0.75$, and using the combined confidence score, both hallucinated elements (class `Location` and its attribute `name`) have low scores: 0.24 and 0.25 respectively, falling in the REMOVE category. In contrast, both correct elements (class `Theater` and its attribute `location`) score 0.79, falling in the ACCEPT category.

4.3 Confidence-Driven Ensemble

We propose an ensemble mechanism to improve domain model coverage without sacrificing explainability. By generating multiple outputs from the same textual domain description, we capture the variability of the language model responses. As shown in Fig. 2, when the same prompt is executed multiple times, one output hallucinates a class `Location` with an attribute name, whereas another correctly models location as an attribute of the class `Theater`. The ensemble merges these drafts by selecting the elements with the strongest textual grounding, effectively consolidating representations based on their confidence scores.

As formalized in Algorithm 1, this process takes a set of N drafts and produces a single domain model. First, it filters the candidate elements $\mathcal{F}$ whose confidence falls below T_{refine}, while retaining all cardinalities because their confidence scores are less discriminative. To resolve overlaps where multiple drafts propose the same element (grouped by name and type), the algorithm selects the variant that maximizes $C_{\text{combined}}(e)$. Finally, it removes any relationship whose endpoint classes were not selected, preserving the structural integrity.

Algorithm 1 Confidence-Driven Ensemble

Require: Drafts $\mathcal{D} = \{DM_1, \ldots, DM_N\}$, threshold T_{refine}
Ensure: Consolidated domain model DM_{ensemble}

$DM_{\text{ensemble}} \leftarrow \emptyset$
$\mathcal{F} \leftarrow \{e \in \bigcup DM_k \mid C_{\text{combined}}(e) \geq T_{\text{refine}}\}$ ▷ filtered candidate elements
$\mathcal{F} \leftarrow \mathcal{F} \cup \{\text{all cardinalities}\}$
for each group $\mathcal{G} \subseteq \mathcal{F}$ with same $(name, type)$ **do** ▷ group of same model element
    $DM_{\text{ensemble}} \leftarrow DM_{\text{ensemble}} \cup \{\arg\max_{e \in \mathcal{G}} C_{\text{combined}}(e)\}$
end for
for each relationship $r \in DM_{\text{ensemble}}$ **do**
    if any endpoint of $r \notin DM_{\text{ensemble}}$ **then**
        remove r
    end if
end for
return DM_{ensemble}

5 Validation

We evaluate our methodology via an ablation study and a comparative analysis:

RQ1: How do the two dimensions of our approach: the confidence scoring (intra-element, inter-element, and combined) and the model derivation strategy (score filtering vs. ensemble consolidation) affect the precision, recall, and F1-score of the generated domain models, and how robust is the resulting method to its attention and confidence thresholds?

RQ2: How does our integrated approach compare against the ToT and QuaRUM frameworks, which rely on LLM self-evaluation and RAG-based grounding, respectively, in terms of precision, recall, F1-score (overall and per domain), and token consumption?

5.1 Experiments Setup

For the experiments, we use two open-weight SLMs: (1) Ministral-3B-Instruct (Mistral AI), and (2) Qwen3-4B-Instruct (Alibaba). These SLMs allow direct access to internal attention matrices, providing a rigorous setting to test our approach against *faithfulness hallucinations.* We use five domain descriptions: e-commerce, persons, theaters, university courses, and robots. Each domain description is processed with two output formats: PlantUML and a structured list.

For the ablation study, relevant tokens were extracted with $Z_{\mathrm{t}} = 2.33$. Then, we evaluate three settings: intra-element (C_{intra}), inter-element (C_{inter}), and confidence score (C_{combined}). Each setting is applied to score filtering and ensemble consolidation (with $T_{\mathrm{refine}} = 0.5$), resulting in six experimental variants, evaluated against two baselines: Lexical match and Majority voting. All drafts are generated at temperature 0.7, and the four ensemble drafts correspond to the two output formats produced by each of the two SLMs. For the threshold sensitivity analysis, we additionally vary $Z_{\mathrm{t}} \in \{1.645, 2.33, 3.09\}$ and $T_{\mathrm{refine}} \in \{0.3, 0.5, 0.7\}$.

For the ToT comparison, we run it to generate three candidate models with five self-evaluations and temperature 0.7 as in [20]. For the QuaRUM comparison, we run its retrieval-augmented grounding and iterative coding pipeline over our dataset with temperature 0.3 as in [23]. Both are compared against our best ablation (Ensemble: C_{combined}). Results are reported using macro-averaged means and standard deviations. Our evaluation data are provided in the repository[1].

5.2 Evaluation Criteria

We manually evaluate the models generated by doing a comparison against the reference solution in PlantUML. Correctly predicted elements are treated as true positives (TP). To evaluate *faithfulness hallucinations* [10], *Context Inconsistencies* are mapped as false positives (FP), penalizing precision due to fabricated elements, whereas *Instruction Inconsistencies* trigger both FP and FN as invalid constructs replace valid ones. Finally, missing elements from the reference solution are captured as false negatives (FN), penalizing recall.

5.3 RQ1: Ablation with Score Filtering and Ensemble

As shown in Table 1, each ablation group is contrasted against its own isolating baseline: Lexical match for Score Filtering, and Majority voting for the Confidence Ensemble. Each isolates one dimension of our approach: Lexical match removes the attention signal from element scoring, and Majority voting removes the confidence signal from ensemble consolidation, so that the gains reported below can be attributed to attention and to discriminative confidence, respectively. Both baselines achieve only a moderate F1-score, of 0.528 and 0.542,

[1] https://github.com/BESSER-PEARL/llm-attention-confidence-dm.git.

respectively. Table 2 reveals a shared root cause: both suffer from a high rate of *faithfulness hallucinations*, specifically *context inconsistencies* (CI rate = 0.35 for both). This indicates that in over a third of the generated model elements, the SLM relies on its internal knowledge to create domain constructs that lack grounding in the provided textual domain description. When evaluating the score filtering variants, the strict C_{combined} is an effective anti-hallucination mechanism. As detailed in Table 2, applying the score filter, the FH rate decreases by 18% relative to the baseline. Consequently, eliminating these hallucinations leads to an increase of 16% in precision to 0.597 (Table 1).

However, this hallucination mitigation introduces a trade-off. The confidence threshold filters out some valid elements from the models. This effect is reflected in Table 1, where the standalone C_{combined} filter causes recall to drop from 0.565 to 0.537. While score filtering successfully retains elements grounded in the textual descriptions, it penalizes recall by increasing omissions, leading to only a modest 5% improvement in the overall F1-score.

Table 1. Ablation of filtering and ensemble: macro-averaged Precision, Recall, and F1-score (mean ± std) with ΔF1 relative to the baseline (B). Lexical match and Majority voting serve as the respective baselines for the two ablations. ↑ indicates higher is better. Best overall results are shown in bold.

Variant	Precision ↑	Recall ↑	F1 ↑	ΔF1
Score Filtering				
Lexical match (B)	0.514 ± 0.129	0.565 ± 0.160	0.528 ± 0.126	—
C_{intra}	0.513 ± 0.155	0.630 ± 0.199	0.551 ± 0.157	+0.023 (+4%)
C_{inter}	0.493 ± 0.144	$\mathbf{0.634 \pm 0.184}$	0.543 ± 0.145	+0.015 (+3%)
C_{combined}	$\mathbf{0.597 \pm 0.123}$	0.537 ± 0.170	$\mathbf{0.554 \pm 0.129}$	**+0.026 (+5%)**
Confidence Ensemble				
Majority voting (B)	0.535 ± 0.113	0.562 ± 0.221	0.542 ± 0.154	—
Ensemble: C_{intra}	0.458 ± 0.204	0.801 ± 0.182	0.574 ± 0.213	+0.032 (+6%)
Ensemble: C_{inter}	0.401 ± 0.203	$\mathbf{0.803 \pm 0.120}$	0.518 ± 0.200	−0.024 (−4%)
Ensemble: C_{combined}	$\mathbf{0.626 \pm 0.134}$	0.704 ± 0.200	$\mathbf{0.657 \pm 0.150}$	**+0.115 (+21%)**

Our ablation shows that ensembling with C_{intra} and C_{inter} may degrade performance when the confidence scores are not sufficiently discriminative, leading to the accumulation of erroneous elements across runs. For instance, Ensemble: C_{inter} achieves the highest recall (0.803) but degrades precision (0.401). As Table 2 demonstrates, aggregating multiple runs with non-discriminative scores accumulates hallucinations, causing the CI rate to increase by 46%.

Our integrated approach (Ensemble: C_{combined}) addresses this phenomenon. The ensemble mechanism aggregates confident elements across four SLM outputs, where the confidence score is sufficiently discriminative and helps the inclusion of reliable elements over less reliable ones, increasing the recall to 0.704,

Table 2. Faithfulness hallucination error rates (mean ± std) and relative Δ with respect to the corresponding baseline (B) of each group. CI (Context Inconsistency); II (Instruction Inconsistency); FH = CI + II (Faithfulness Hallucination). ↓ lower is better. Best (lowest) rates are in bold.

Variant	CI Rate ↓	II Rate ↓	FH Rate ↓
Score Filtering			
Lexical match (B)	0.35 ± 0.16	0.13 ± 0.07	0.49 ± 0.13
C_{intra}	0.37 ± 0.17 (+6%)	0.12 ± 0.07 (−8%)	0.49 ± 0.16 (0%)
C_{inter}	0.39 ± 0.17 (+11%)	**0.12 ± 0.06 (−8%)**	0.51 ± 0.14 (+4%)
C_{combined}	**0.28 ± 0.11 (−20%)**	0.13 ± 0.07 (0%)	**0.40 ± 0.12 (−18%)**
Confidence Ensemble			
Majority voting (B)	0.35 ± 0.09	0.12 ± 0.04	0.46 ± 0.11
Ensemble: C_{intra}	0.42 ± 0.14 (+20%)	0.12 ± 0.10 (0%)	0.54 ± 0.20 (+17%)
Ensemble: C_{inter}	0.51 ± 0.18 (+46%)	**0.09 ± 0.03 (−25%)**	0.60 ± 0.20 (+30%)
Ensemble: C_{combined}	**0.25 ± 0.14 (−29%)**	0.13 ± 0.06 (+8%)	**0.37 ± 0.13 (−20%)**

surpassing the baseline, maintaining a precision of 0.626, and the FH hallucination rate decreases by 20%. The synergy of these two components, based on the attention scores, improves in precision and recall, achieving the highest overall F1-score of 0.657, representing a 21% improvement over the baseline.

Finally, while our method mitigates CI hallucinations, Table 2 shows that II hallucinations are not mitigated by our approach, increasing by 8%, suggesting that errors caused by incorrect modeling abstractions (e.g., selecting a composition instead of an association) require complementary approaches.

Having established Ensemble: C_{combined} as the best configuration, we analyze its robustness to the two thresholds defined in our approach: Z_{t} and the confidence threshold T_{refine}. In Fig. 4, the F1-score remains stable across the evaluated Z_{t} levels, as the three curves nearly overlap. In contrast, T_{refine} controls the balance between precision and recall, with stricter values raising precision at the expense of recall. The operating point ($Z_{\text{t}} = 2.33$, $T_{\text{refine}} = 0.5$) results in the peak F1, confirming that this configuration is the empirical optimal choice.

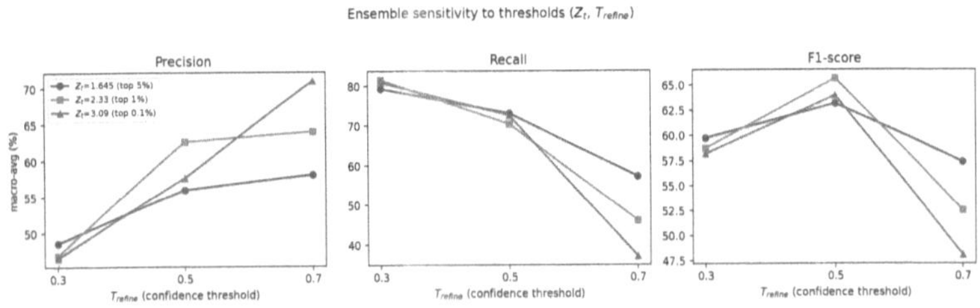

Fig. 4. Threshold sensitivity of the Confidence Ensemble: macro-averaged Precision, Recall, and F1-score across the five domains as a function of the confidence threshold T_{refine}, for three heuristic cutoff levels $Z_t \in \{1.645,\ 2.33,\ 3.09\}$.

5.4 RQ2: Comparison with ToT and QuaRUM

In Table 3, our Ensemble: C_{combined} approach outperforms the Majority baseline,ToT and QuaRUM, achieving the best overall F1-score of 0.657. The effectiveness of ToT depends on the LLM capacity: while ToT with Qwen achieves a marginal F1-score increase of 1% over the Majority baseline, Ministral degrades performance by 22%, reducing both precision and recall.

As shown in Table 2, SLMs exhibit high rates of *faithfulness hallucinations*. Because ToT requires the SLM to assess its intermediate steps, it may accept hallucinated elements during self-evaluation, propagating unsupported model elements along their intermediate steps. In contrast, our approach filters elements based on attention to the domain description, ensuring textual grounding independent of SLM capacity, achieving higher precision (0.626) and recall (0.704).

QuaRUM, which grounds generation through RAG, obtains F1-scores of 0.374 (Ministral) and 0.454 (Qwen). While precision is competitive (0.516–0.623), recall collapses (0.324–0.382). With SLMs, it produces incomplete models, omitting classes and relationships that the description supports. Whereas RAG grounds only what the model already generates, our attention-based scoring recovers a more complete model, reaching a recall of 0.704.

Table 3 also reports per-domain results. ToT achieves the best F1 in e-commerce and QuaRUM in persons, while our approach surpasses both frameworks in the remaining three domains. Across the five domains, it scores between 0.512 and 0.833 and achieves the highest average F1 by a margin of +0.111 over the closest competitor, demonstrating consistent results across domains.

Additionally, Table 4 shows the high computational cost of both frameworks: ToT averages 35,152 tokens per execution, generating and evaluating multiple alternatives, and QuaRUM 44,245 through its iterative coding pipeline. In contrast, our Ensemble: C_{combined} strategy, which also relies on multiple generations, reduces consumption to 3,451 tokens, about 90% fewer than ToT and 92% fewer than QuaRUM. This efficiency derives from attention-based scoring and ensemble consolidation rather than additional LLM calls.

5.5 Threats to Validity

Scalability and Computational Overhead. Memory overhead from extracting attention matrices could limit scalability. However, MACS [16] has been validated on 8B models, demonstrating viability for larger LLMs.
Confidence Scores and Thresholds. Our pipeline relies on scores and thresholds. While we empirically selected thresholds that provided a trade-off between precision and recall in the experiments, they may require tuning for other LLMs.
Limited Number of Domains. We evaluated our approach on five domains. While diverse, they may not fully capture the scale and complexity in real scenarios, requiring future evaluations on domains with longer and noisier descriptions.

Table 3. Comparison of the Majority voting baseline (B) vs. Tree of Thoughts, QuaRUM, and Ensemble: C_{combined}. Per-domain F1-score together with the overall Precision, Recall, and F1, all macro-averaged across the five domains. Best per domain and best overall are shown in bold.

Method	Per-domain F1					Overall (Average)		
	E-com.	Persons	Theater	Univ.	Robot	Prec.	Rec.	F1
Majority voting (B)	0.531	0.421	0.429	0.529	0.800	0.535	0.562	0.542
ToT: Ministral	0.542	0.400	0.585	0.500	0.074	0.408	0.436	0.420
ToT: Qwen	**0.627**	0.400	0.435	0.562	0.706	0.521	0.608	0.546
QuaRUM: Ministral	0.553	0.488	0.364	0.194	0.273	0.516	0.324	0.374
QuaRUM: Qwen	0.550	**0.571**	0.564	0.222	0.364	0.623	0.382	0.454
Ensemble: C_{combined}	0.512	0.522	**0.792**	**0.625**	**0.833**	**0.626**	**0.704**	**0.657**

Table 4. Average token consumption by method (mean ± std). Total ratio indicates the total token multiplier relative to the Ensemble: C_{combined} baseline.

Method	Input	Output	Total	Total Ratio
Ensemble: C_{combined}	1,965 ± 265	1,487 ± 537	3,451 ± 660	1.0×
ToT	28,181 ± 9,713	6,971 ± 4,257	35,152 ± 13,637	10.2×
QuaRUM	39,074 ± 20,651	5,171 ± 2,580	44,245 ± 22,764	12.8×

6 Tool Support

Our open-source implementation is available on GitHub[2]. The pipeline executes two SLMs from HuggingFace: Ministral-3B[3] and Qwen3-4B[4]. Each model is prompted with a structured list and PlantUML formats, creating four independent runs. Users can configure the threshold (Z_t) and the status boundaries. The ensemble execution accepts the parameter mode to select which score to use: C_{intra}(R1–R4), C_{inter}(R5), or C_{combined}(R1–R5).

7 Conclusions and Further Work

In this paper, we address the challenge of *faithfulness hallucinations* in LLM-assisted domain modeling by extracting internal attention mechanisms from open-weight SLMs. Specifically, our approach leverages MACS to quantify intra-element, inter-element, and combined confidence scores. Our empirical evaluation demonstrates that leveraging these confidence scores within a consolidation ensemble effectively filters out *context inconsistency* hallucinations, and a threshold sensitivity analysis confirms that the reported configuration is the best

[2] https://github.com/BESSER-PEARL/llm-attention-confidence-dm.git.
[3] https://huggingface.co/mistralai/Ministral-3-3B-Instruct-2512.
[4] https://huggingface.co/Qwen/Qwen3-4B.

empirical configuration. Furthermore, a comparative evaluation with prompting frameworks reveals specific limitations: smaller SLMs often validate their own hallucinations during self-evaluation, and iterative generation favors precision over recall, resulting in incomplete models. In contrast, our approach improves textual grounding independently of LLM capacity, achieving the most consistent results across all five domains while reducing token consumption by over 90%.

By bridging attention mechanisms with our scoring system, our approach provides evidence for each generated element, offering a quantified score for the inclusion of each model abstraction. While our method successfully mitigates *context inconsistency* hallucinations, our experiments revealed that *instruction inconsistency* hallucinations remain a challenge. Therefore, future work will focus on scaling to larger open-weight models to assess whether increased capacity resolves these abstraction errors. Additionally, we plan to integrate complementary confidence estimation techniques and adapt these attention scores for Human-in-the-Loop (HITL) workflows, enabling domain experts to efficiently refine models by targeted review of elements with the lowest confidence.

References

1. Alcaide, F.J., Romero, J.R., Ramírez, A.: Can explainable artificial intelligence support software modelers in model comprehension? Softw. Syst. Model. **24**(3), 949–974 (2025)
2. Barbero, F., et al.: Why do LLMs attend to the first token? In: Second Conference on Language Modeling (2025)
3. Cámara, J., Troya, J., Burgueño, L., Vallecillo, A.: On the assessment of generative AI in modeling tasks: an experience report with ChatGPT and UML. Softw. Syst. Model. **22**(3), 781–793 (2023)
4. Chen, R., Shen, J., He, X.: More: LLM-based domain model generation with hybrid self-refinement. Electronics **15**(6), 1239 (2026)
5. Clark, K., Khandelwal, U., Levy, O., Manning, C.D.: What does BERT look at? an analysis of BERT's attention. In: Proceedings of the 2019 ACL Workshop BlackboxNLP: Analyzing and Interpreting Neural Networks for NLP, pp. 276–286 (2019)
6. Feltus, C., Ma, Q., Proper, H.A., Kelsen, P.: Towards AI Assisted Domain Modeling. In: Reinhartz-Berger, I., Sadiq, S. (eds.) ER 2021. LNCS, vol. 13012, pp. 75–89. Springer, Cham (2021). https://doi.org/10.1007/978-3-030-88358-4_7
7. Frederiks, P.J.M., van der Weide, T.P.: Information modeling: the process and the required competencies of its participants. Data Knowl. Eng. **58**(1), 4–20 (2006)
8. Giannouris, P., Ananiadou, S.: Nomad: A multi-agent LLM system for UML class diagram generation from natural language requirements. arXiv:2511.22409 (2025)
9. Hoppenbrouwers, S.J.B.A., Proper, H.A.E., van der Weide, T.P.: A fundamental view on the process of conceptual modeling. In: Conceptual Modeling - ER 2005. LNCS, vol. 3716, pp. 128–143 (2005)
10. Huang, L., et al.: A survey on hallucination in large language models: principles, taxonomy, challenges, and open questions. ACM Trans. Inf. Syst. **43**(2), 1–55 (2025)
11. Jain, S., Wallace, B.C.: Attention is not Explanation. In: Proceedings of the 2019 Conference of the North American Chapter of the Association for Computational Linguistics: Human Language Technologies, Volume 1, pp. 3543–3556. Association for Computational Linguistics, Minneapolis, Minnesota (2019)

12. Kambhampati, S., et al.: Stop anthropomorphizing intermediate tokens as reasoning/thinking traces! In: NeurIPS 2025 Workshop: Bridging Language, Agent, and World Models for Reasoning and Planning (2025)
13. Käppel, M., Ackermann, L., Jablonski, S., Härtl, S.: Explaining transformer-based next activity prediction by using attention scores. Process Sci. **2**(1), 11 (2025)
14. Kourani, H., Antonov, A., Berti, A., van der Aalst, W.M.: Knowledge-driven hallucination in large language models: an empirical study on process modeling. In: Proceedings of Software and Systems Modeling, The Second International Workshop on Generative AI for Process Mining (2025)
15. Kourani, H., Berti, A., Schuster, D., van der Aalst, W.M.P.: Evaluating large language models on business process modeling: framework, benchmark, and self-improvement analysis. Software and Systems Modeling (2025)
16. Lan, T., Xu, J., He, X., Hwang, J.N., Li, L.: Attention consistency for LLMs explanation. In: Findings of the Association for Computational Linguistics: EMNLP 2025, pp. 1736–1750 (2025)
17. Liu, Q., Duan, H., Mao, J., Wen, J.R.: How do large language models understand relevance? a mechanistic interpretability perspective. ACM Transactions on Information Systems 44(2) (2025)
18. Norouzifar, A., Kourani, H., Dees, M., van der Aalst, W.M.: Bridging domain knowledge and process discovery using large language models. In: International Conference on Business Process Management, pp. 44–56 (2024)
19. Saba, W.S.: Towards explainable and language-agnostic LLMs: symbolic reverse engineering of language at scale. arXiv:2306.00017 (2023)
20. Silva, J., Ma, Q., Cabot, J., Kelsen, P., Proper, H.A.: Application of the tree-of-thoughts framework to LLM-enabled domain modeling. In: International Conference on Conceptual Modeling. LNCS, vol. 15238, pp. 94–111 (2025)
21. Silva, J., Ma, Q., Cabot, J., Kelsen, P., Proper, H.A.: Towards human-in-the-loop LLM-enabled domain modeling. In: International Conference on Conceptual Modeling, pp. 127–145 (2025)
22. Storey, V.C., et al.: Large language models for conceptual modeling: assessment and application potential. Data Knowl. Eng. **160**, 102480 (2025)
23. Tauhid Ullah, Shah, S., Hussein, M., Barcomb, A., Moshirpour, M.: QuaRUM: qualitative data analysis-based retrieval-augmented UML domain model from requirements documents. Autom. Softw. Eng. **33**(2), 44 (2026)
24. Wiegreffe, S., Pinter, Y.: Attention is not not explanation. In: Proceedings of the 2019 Conference on Empirical Methods in Natural Language Processing and the 9th International Joint Conference on Natural Language Processing, pp. 11–20. Association for Computational Linguistics, Hong Kong, China (2019)
25. Yona, I., Shumailov, I., Hayes, J., Gandelsman, Y.: Interpreting the repeated token phenomenon in large language models. In: Proceedings of the 42nd International Conference on Machine Learning. PMLR, vol. 267, pp. 72535–72555 (2025)

Responsible AI, Regulation and Security

AI-Intent: A Conceptual Modeling Framework for Accountable Multi-agent AI Systems

Wolfgang Maass[1(✉)] and Iris Reinhartz-Berger[2]

[1] German Research Center for Artificial Intelligence (DFKI) and Saarland University, Saarbrücken, Germany
wolfgang.maass@dfki.de
[2] University of Haifa, Haifa, Israel
iris@is.haifa.ac.il

Abstract. Existing agent-oriented conceptual modeling frameworks assume components with deterministic execution semantics. Applied to language model agents, whose outputs arise from probabilistic text generation governed by natural-language inputs, they lack three constructs that accountability requires: a binary *declaration* of each agent's legitimate action space; runtime *enforcement* of negative obligations by a component external to the agent; and treatment of inter-agent communication as *auditable evidence*.

To address these gaps, we introduce AI-Intent, a conceptual modeling framework organized into three pillars: ***Declaration*** encodes each agent's action boundary, decision rights, capabilities, and risk policies in *Mandates*; ***Enforcement*** evaluates every *Proposed Action* against the applicable *Mandate* through a *Compliance Agent* before delivery; ***Auditability*** derives a structured, durable *Accountability Trace* from every session. A reference implementation for private investment advisory under MiFID II is evaluated across 190 evaluation sessions: boundary violation containment averaged 97.9% with zero forced-pass occurrences, while audit trace completeness was found to depend on the instruction-following capability of the deployed model.

Keywords: Multi-Agent Systems · Conceptual Modeling · Language Model Agents · Accountability · Governance

1 Introduction

Language model-based agents are rapidly moving from research prototypes to production systems that support consequential decisions in finance, healthcare, and enterprise operations [23,27]. Unlike traditional software components, whose runtime behavior is fully determined by source code, they generate outputs through probabilistic text generation governed by natural language inputs, training data, and model parameters. When multiple such agents collaborate on

© The Author(s), under exclusive license to Springer Nature Switzerland AG 2027
A. Bernasconi et al. (Eds.): ER 2026, LNCS 17081, pp. 111–127, 2027.
https://doi.org/10.1007/978-3-032-40795-5_7

joint recommendations, questions arise that existing conceptual models cannot answer: what each agent was supposed to do, whether it stayed within its scope, and why a particular output was produced.

Conceptual modeling frameworks for multi-agent systems have a rich history [8,24,28], modeling agents in terms of goals, capabilities, roles, and inter-agent dependencies. These frameworks share an assumption that their components have deterministic or rule-governed execution semantics – an assumption that does not hold for language model agents, giving rise to three gaps.

Gap 1: Intent Boundary Versus Goal Satisfaction. Traditional goal models, such as i^* and Tropos, treat goal satisfaction as graded [28]. For language model agents, the relevant construct is instead a binary *sortal boundary*: a request either falls within the agent's legitimate scope or it does not. An equity analyst agent recommending gold at 35% allocation has not partially satisfied its goal; it has transgressed its mandate scope.

Gap 2: Negative Obligations as Runtime-Enforceable Constraints. Normative frameworks and deontic logic provide well-developed accounts of obligation, permission, and prohibition [7,14,25], but assume agents that deliberate over norms before acting [9]. Language model agents may acknowledge a constraint and then violate it, or construct superficially plausible justifications for exceptions [17]. The modeling challenge is therefore to represent negative obligations in a form an *external* enforcement component can evaluate, rather than relying on agent self-compliance.

Gap 3: Communication as Audit Evidence. Existing agent communication models, such as FIPA-ACL [12], specify message syntax and semantics but treat communication logs as an optional engineering concern. Regulatory frameworks for AI systems, e.g., the EU AI Act [11] and MiFID II [10], require that every consequential decision be traceable to its inputs – making communication logging a *structural property* of the conceptual model, not an add-on.

To address these gaps, we propose AI-Intent, with one pillar per gap. ***Declaration*** introduces the *Mandate*, a first-class artifact encoding an agent's binary action boundary, decision rights, capabilities, and risk policies. ***Enforcement*** introduces *Intent Enforcement*, a mandatory gatekeeper that evaluates every *Proposed Action* against the applicable *Mandate* and produces a *Compliance Verdict* before delivery. ***Auditability*** derives an *Accountability Trace* from the *Log Entry* of every verdict. It is important to note that AI-Intent is not a new modeling language, nor a syntactic extension of an existing one; it is a domain-independent *conceptual model*, comprising governance constructs, their metamodel relationships, and well-formedness constraints. Grounded in the Unified Foundational Ontology (UFO) [15] and rendered in OntoUML, AI-Intent is intended to *augment* existing agent-oriented languages. For evaluating AI-Intent, we developed a reference implementation for private investment advisory. The reference implementation shows that even under a neutral disposition, agents violate their allocation cap on the first attempt often enough to motivate external enforcement as a structural modeling requirement.

The remainder of the paper is organized as follows. Section 2 reviews existing agent-oriented modeling frameworks. Section 3 presents the AI-INTENT framework across its three pillars. Section 4 reports the empirical evaluation, while Sect. 5 discusses the results. Section 6 concludes and identifies directions for future work.

2 Background and Related Work

We scope our review to work proposing modeling constructs for agent governance (Sect. 2.1); multi-agent implementation frameworks (Sect. 2.2) and AI-governance policy work (Sect. 2.3) serve as deployment substrate and normative context.

2.1 Agent-Oriented Conceptual Modeling

Four influential modeling approaches are examined through the lens of the three gaps: the goal-oriented i^* [28] and Tropos [8], and the more strictly agent-oriented GAIA [24] and NMAS [7]. We group them because each supplies constructs that a governance model must either reuse or replace.

The i^* framework [28] models actors with goals, tasks, resources, and softgoals connected by contribution links; its softgoal construct explicitly supports partial satisfaction, a graded semantics well suited to design trade-offs, but inappropriate for mandate boundaries, where violations are categorical rather than a matter of degree. **Tropos** [8] extends i^* into a full development methodology, but likewise provides no construct for prohibitions: both specify what agents can and should do, not what they must not do.

GAIA [24] provides role models with permissions, responsibilities, activities, and protocols. Its permission construct is the closest existing analog to boundary constraints: a role's permissions define the actions it is authorized to take. However, permissions are granted at modeling time and assumed to hold at runtime; no mechanism verifies that an agent stays within them during execution. **Normative Multi-Agent Systems (NMAS)** [7,9,14] address obligation and prohibition directly [25], and defeasible deontic logic [14] further allows norms to have exceptions and be defeated by stronger norms. These approaches, however, assume agents that deliberate over norms before acting – an assumption that fails for language model agents, whose compliance depends on how norms are represented in the input specification and how reliably the model follows instructions [17].

Table 1 summarizes the extent to which the four modeling frameworks cover the identified gaps: i^* and Tropos represent neither prohibitions nor scope boundaries; GAIA adds permissions but cannot verify them at runtime; NMAS closes the representational gap on prohibitions but relies on agent self-deliberation for enforcement, an assumption that fails for non-deterministic generators.

Table 1. Comparative analysis of agent governance modeling capabilities across the four agent-oriented modeling frameworks ✓ = fully expressible; ○ = partial/with significant extensions; × = not expressible without framework revision.

Capability	i^*	Tropos	GAIA	NMAS
Intent scope (binary sortal boundary)	×	×	○	○
Negative obligations (prohibitions)	×	×	○	✓
Quantitative risk parameters	×	×	×	○
Runtime constraint enforcement	×	×	×	○
External Compliance Agent	×	×	×	×
Audit-native communication	×	×	×	×
Compliance history in trace	×	×	×	×
Model operativity (runtime injection)	×	×	×	×

2.2 Multi-agent Implementation Frameworks

Where agent-oriented modeling frameworks lack runtime enforcement, current multi-agent language model architectures lack formal modeling altogether: AutoGen [26], CrewAI [20], and LangGraph [18] represent agent roles as natural-language descriptions with no formal constraint semantics or runtime verification. The Model Context Protocol (MCP) [3] standardizes communication between language model applications and external tools, providing interoperability but not governance.

Output filtering systems, such as NeMo Guardrails [22] and Constitutional AI [5], enforce constraints on single-agent outputs through filtering and self-assessment, but do not model inter-agent accountability: they cannot trace a multi-agent decision to its constituent sub-agent outputs or produce structured audit artifacts.

2.3 AI Governance and Accountability

Existing accountability frameworks address individual model decisions [4] and dataset documentation [13,19], but not *multi-agent accountability*: tracing a joint decision back to the sub-agent outputs and constraint evaluations that produced it. The EU AI Act [11] and MiFID II mandate transparency and traceability for high-risk and financial AI systems, respectively, but neither specifies how traceability is to be achieved when a decision is the product of multiple collaborating agents.

A recent line of work targets trustworthiness and accountability in language model agent systems directly. Alqithami's Adaptive Accountability Framework [1] records verifiable interaction provenance and attributes responsibility via a causal influence graph, targeting *emergent* norm violations at scale; verifiability-first designs [16] embed lightweight audit agents and attestations to minimize time-to-detect misalignment; and governance frameworks for multi-agent AI [2,6,21] treat accountability failures as governance-design problems, proposing evaluation and policy scaffolding. These works are runtime, policy, or evaluation *mechanisms* that detect or attribute violations a posteriori from observed traces.

3 The AI-Intent Framework

The analysis of the literature in Sect. 2 leaves specific gaps: no modeling framework combines declared scope boundaries, enforceable prohibitions, and audit-native communication, and the recent trustworthy-agent line supplies runtime mechanisms without the modeling constructs beneath them. AI-INTENT closes these as a metamodel of governance constructs, their relationships, and well-formedness conditions, independent of any implementation. Section 3.1 states its ontological commitments; Sect. 3.2 presents the constructs, distinguishing UFO-derived constructs from design choices layered on top.

3.1 Core Principles and Ontological Commitments

AI-INTENT uses UFO [15] and standard deontic semantics [14,25] as follows.

Agents as Intentional Objects. Agents are UFO intentional objects with dispositions to act; a Mandate specifies the intended disposition – the behaviors the agent is authorized to exhibit and the boundaries it must not cross. This lets the Mandate constrain a disposition-to-act rather than only observed behavior.

Intent Scope as a Sortal Boundary. We use *sortal* in its established ontological sense: a sortal universal supplies a principle of identity and individuation, determining for any candidate whether it *is or is not* an instance of the type [15], and is therefore inherently binary rather than graded. The intent scope in the Mandate is accordingly not a goal admitting degrees of satisfaction, but a natural-language specification of such a boundary, whose identity criterion makes "the same kind of request" well defined across the paraphrastic variation typical of language model queries.

Boundary Constraints as Prohibitions. Following deontic logic [25], the boundary constraints encoded in the Mandate are prohibitions $\mathbf{F}(\phi)$: the agent is forbidden from producing outputs satisfying predicate ϕ, with risk parameters as quantitative instantiations; for example, $\mathbf{F}(\mathit{allocation} > 0.15)$ for a 15% cap. Unlike NMAS norms, which rely on the agent's own deliberation, these prohibitions are enforced externally.

Enforcement as a Structural Role. Making prohibitions operative at runtime requires an enforcement mechanism external to the agent: representing a prohibition in a Mandate does not guarantee it holds on any given output. Enforcement is therefore a first-class commitment, not an optional add-on.

Communication as Evidence. Every inter-agent action is a UFO *event*: time-indexed and non-repeatable. That categorization is what licenses its use as non-repudiable evidence, and it is what makes the Accountability Trace a situation – a truthmaker aggregating events – rather than a side-effect log.

3.2 Framework Structure and Pillars

AI-INTENT organizes its modeling constructs into three pillars that reflect the governance lifecycle of a multi-agent session: Declaration, Enforcement, and Auditability. Figure 1 shows the constructs and their relationships in the conceptual model, while Table 2 gives their ontological grounding.

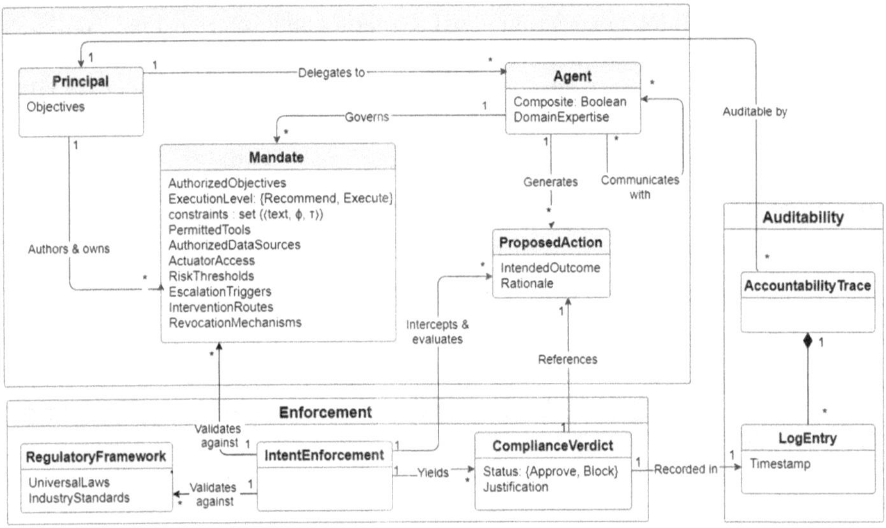

Fig. 1. The AI-Intent conceptual model.

Pillar 1: Declaration. This pillar establishes the legitimate action space before any session begins, through four constructs: Principal, Agent, Mandate, and Proposed Action. A *Principal* is an individual or institutional entity that owns the governance structure, holds the system's objectives, delegates tasks to Agents, and defines their Mandates. An *Agent* is an executable, potentially composite, component with Domain Expertise scoping its competence; a Composite flag distinguishes orchestrators from specialist sub-agents, and composite agents invoke the Compliance Agent before delegating. Agents may also communicate laterally.

The *Mandate* is the central Declaration artifact: a type-level specification of what an agent may address, what it must not produce, and its operational parameters, in four sections. (i) *Decision Rights* define decisions the agent may make without escalation. (ii) *Boundaries* encode its negative obligations as prohibitions: each is a triple $c_i = \langle text_i, \phi_i, \tau_i \rangle$ of a natural-language statement $text_i$,

Table 2. Ontological grounding of AI-Intent constructs, by pillar. *Src* marks UFO-**der**ived commitments, which inherit UFO's formal entailments, versus **des**ign choices layered on top.

Pillar	Construct	UFO category, OntoUML stereotype	Src
Declaration	Principal	Intentional object, «kind»	des
	Agent	Intentional object w/ dispositions, «kind»	der
	Mandate	Normative description, «description»	des
	Proposed Action	Event (non-repeatable), «event»	der
Enforcement	Regulatory Framework	External normative description, «description»	des
	Intent Enforcement	Role played by the (Compliance) Agent, «role»	des
	Compliance Verdict	Relator mediating Intent Enforcement and the Proposed Action, «relator»	des
Auditability	Log Entry	Persistent record of a compliance event, «kind»	des
	Accountability Trace	Situation aggregating a session's Log Entries, «situation»	der

a machine-evaluable predicate ϕ_i over an agent's candidate output, and a deontic type $\tau_i \in \{\mathbf{F}, \mathbf{O}\}$ (prohibition or obligation); a prohibition ($\tau_i = \mathbf{F}$) is violated *iff* the output *satisfies* ϕ_i, and a risk parameter is the quantitative binding of a free variable in ϕ_i, e.g., $\mathbf{F}(\textit{allocation} > 0.15)$ binds the 15% cap. (iii) *Capabilities* enumerate the permitted tools, data sources, and actuators. (iv) *Policies* govern the response when boundaries are approached or crossed, through thresholds, escalation triggers, intervention routes, and revocation mechanisms.

Finally, a *Proposed Action* is the candidate output an Agent generates prior to compliance evaluation, carrying an Intended Outcome and a Rationale. It is the unit of evaluation in Pillar 2, intercepted before any delivery to another agent or the user.

Pillar 2: Enforcement. This pillar operationalizes the declared constraints through three constructs: Regulatory Framework, Intent Enforcement, and Compliance Verdict. The *Regulatory Framework* aggregates external norms – universal laws (e.g., the EU AI Act [11] and MiFID II) and industry standards – supplying the rule registry against which Mandates are validated.

The *Intent Enforcement* construct, realized at runtime as a Compliance Agent, is the structural gatekeeper of the framework. It receives two inputs: the Mandate, validated against the Regulatory Framework for legal coherence, and the Proposed Action, evaluated against the Mandate before delivery. As a framework construct, Intent Enforcement is defined by four *constitutive requirements*, not by any particular algorithm. *(R1) Non-bypassability*: every cross-agent Proposed Action is mediated; there is no delivery path that circumvents evaluation. *(R2) Independence*: the evaluator is distinct from the agent under evaluation, so enforcement does not inherit the generator's stochasticity [17]. *(R3) Verdict decidability*: for every constraint, the verdict is a determinate approve/block over the Proposed Action, naming the violated constraint when blocked. *(R4) Terminating revision*: rejected actions enter a bounded revision loop terminating in delivery or in a recorded forced block, never in an unrecorded pass. How a deployment discharges *R1–R4* (deterministic predicates, semantic classifier, or hybrid) is an implementation concern.

For each intercepted action, Intent Enforcement produces a *Compliance Verdict* – approve or block, the constraints satisfied or violated, and a revision directive when rejected. Concretely, suppose a Mandate carries the risk parameter $max\_allocation = 0.15$, instantiating the prohibition $\varphi \equiv (allocation > 0.15)$: the parameter supplies the threshold, the deontic type **F** the polarity. A Proposed Action carrying $allocation = 0.18$ then satisfies φ, and Intent Enforcement issues a blocked Compliance Verdict that names the violated constraint and returns a revision directive to the originating Agent. Risk parameters are thus the operands that make boundary predicates decidable at runtime.

Pillar 3: Auditability. The Auditability pillar derives a structured, durable record from the session history produced by the other pillars. It contains two constructs: Accountability Trace and Log Entry. A *Log Entry* is the atomic audit record produced for each compliance evaluation event; it carries by reference the identifiers of the originating Proposed Action and Mandate, keeping the record navigable without introducing upward associations that would violate pillar encapsulation.

The *Accountability Trace* is a UFO situation aggregating the Log Entries of a complete session. For a session s of compliance evaluation events $\langle e_1, \ldots, e_n \rangle$, each e_i yields one Compliance Verdict recorded in one Log Entry l_i, and the Trace is the aggregation $T(s) = \langle l_1, \ldots, l_n \rangle$ closed under the reference links each l_i carries to its Proposed Action and Mandate. Two well-formedness conditions make this structural rather than a reporting convenience: *(WFC-1)* every Compliance Verdict is recorded in exactly one Log Entry, so no evaluation is unlogged; *(WFC-2)* a completed session's Trace contains a Log Entry for every cross-agent Proposed Action, so no action is unaccounted for. A conventional audit log is a side effect that may be absent, partial, or post-hoc-editable without violating any model constraint; here a session missing a Log Entry for an evaluated action is *ill-formed by definition*, and because the Accountability Trace derives from the same Compliance Verdicts that gate delivery, the record cannot diverge from what was enforced. Auditability is thus a consequence of the enforcement structure, not a component bolted alongside it.

A terminological distinction is necessary here: the Accountability Trace is the full structured, session-level audit object described above; the *accountability note*, by contrast, is a human-readable summary field embedded in the final synthesis response, reporting a subset of the trace (session ID, agents consulted, constraints checked, violations surfaced) in prose. The trace is the evidentiary object; the note is its user-facing projection. The evaluation in Sect. 4 therefore scores the note's required fields (Accountability Trace Completeness, ATC) as a proxy for correct population of the underlying trace.

4 Evaluation

The evaluation tests AI-INTENT's constructs along two complementary claims. **Expressiveness** (Sect. 4.2) tests the *modeling* claim: scenarios S1–S3 instantiate the three gaps of Sect. 1 and thereby exercise the Declaration, Enforcement, and Auditability constructs, asking whether each captures a scenario that existing agent-oriented modeling languages do not. **Applicability** (Sect. 4.3) tests the *operativity* claim: whether those constructs, realized in the reference implementation described in Sect. 4.1, hold at runtime across sessions and adversarial agent dispositions.

4.1 Reference Implementation

We chose investment advisory for its regulatory grounding under MiFID II: constraints are imposed by regulation, not authored by us. The reference implementation comprises four agents in a hierarchical architecture: a ***Central Orchestrator*** that coordinates task delegation and synthesis, and three specialist sub-agents, ***Stocks***, ***Bonds***, and ***Materials***, each governed by a dedicated Mandate. The ***Compliance Agent*** intercepts all communication between the Orchestrator and the sub-agents, producing a Compliance Verdict for every Proposed Action before delivery. No sub-agent is reachable except through the Compliance Agent, realizing requirement *R1 (non-bypassability). Independence (R2)* follows from the Compliance Agent running as a distinct process from the agents it evaluates. Verdict decidability (R3) is achieved by a deterministic predicate checker over structured agent output, backed by a narrow semantic fallback – a deliberately minimal choice, sufficient to show the construct is operable rather than the most capable checker the framework admits. *Revision terminates (R4)* in a bounded loop that ends in delivery or a recorded forced block. Section 5 returns to where this minimal realization, rather than the framework itself, is the binding limitation.

Table 3 summarizes the Mandate of each agent, with constraints annotated by their deontic type: **F** (prohibition) or **O** (obligation).[1] The technology stack comprises Python 3.11+ with Pydantic v2, SQLite for MCP message persistence, Streamlit for the dashboard, and Llama 3.1 8B served locally via Ollama.[2] As a minimal realization, the reference implementation collapses several metamodel distinctions. i.e., the Mandate («description») is fused into each agent's manifest rather than reified as a mediating object, the Proposed Action («event») and its Log Entry («kind») share a single MCP message type, and the Regulatory

[1] The complete source code of the reference implementation is available in the online repository at GitHub.

[2] Local deployment ensures reproducibility and eliminates dependencies on external inference services.

Framework («description») is realized as a flat rule registry. These simplifications do not affect the enforcement or auditability guarantees, though a fuller realization would separate each into a distinct construct.

Table 3. Agent mandates in the reference implementation. $|C|$ = boundary constraints; $|R|$ = risk parameters. Representative constraint examples are provided.

Agent	Role	$\lvert C\rvert$	$\lvert R\rvert$	Key Constraints (examples)
Central	Orchestrator	5	2	$\mathbf{F}(\textit{single asset class} > 40\%)$; $\mathbf{O}(\textit{consult} \geq 1$ sub-agent$)$; $\mathbf{O}(\textit{surface all violations})$
Stocks	Equity Analyst	5	3	$\mathbf{F}(\textit{non-large-cap})$; $\mathbf{F}(\textit{position} > 10\%)$; $\mathbf{F}(\textit{leverage})$; $\mathbf{O}(\textit{ESG screening})$
Bonds	Fixed Income	5	4	$\mathbf{F}(\textit{rating} <$ BBB+$)$; $\mathbf{F}(\textit{duration} > 10\,\text{yr})$; $\mathbf{F}(\textit{EM debt})$; $\mathbf{F}(\text{bucket} > 30\%/\text{yr})$
Materials	Commodities	5	4	$\mathbf{F}(\textit{non-Au/Ag commodity})$; $\mathbf{F}(\textit{allocation} > 15\%)$; $\mathbf{F}(\textit{leveraged ETF/futures})$; $\mathbf{O}(\textit{inflation rationale})$

4.2 Expressiveness

AI-Intent expressiveness is evaluated using three governance scenarios, each exercising one pillar and comparing its coverage to the closest analog in i^*, Tropos, GAIA, or NMAS.

S1: Out-of-Scope Declination. The Mandate's intent scope provides a natural-language sortal boundary injected into the agent's input specification as an enforcement instruction. Agents correctly returned `out_of_scope:true` with named constraint references when queried about assets outside their scope, for instance, the stocks agent asked about gold and the bonds agent asked about equities. GAIA can express the permission but cannot verify it at runtime; i^* has no prohibition construct.

S2: Quantitative Constraint Enforcement. Risk parameters provide machine-comparable bounds; the Compliance Agent's deterministic checker evaluated these against structured agent output. The checker fired on every session in which an agent recommended a position exceeding its quantitative limit. Every violation that occurred was eventually caught before delivery through the revision protocol. NMAS can represent quantitative norms through arithmetic constraints in deontic logic but requires the agent itself to evaluate the constraint –

unreliable for non-deterministic generators; GAIA has no quantitative constraint construct.

S3: Audit Reconstruction. The Accountability Trace provides a structured artifact from which the full decision sequence can be reconstructed: agents consulted, routing rationale, per-agent constraint checks, compliance history, and blocked agents with rule identifiers. No existing framework provides an equivalent audit artifact as a structural model component.

4.3 Applicability

Applicability is evaluated along six dimensions, each mapped to a construct: BVC and CGP measure the Compliance Verdict gate (Enforcement); ME and CDA measure Mandate boundary detection (Declaration via Enforcement); ATC measures Accountability Trace population (Auditability); and DC measures whether Enforcement holds independently of agent disposition.

Evaluation Design. Table 4 lists the six dimensions, the framework tests, their thresholds, and their results. The protocol comprises 19 test cases: 15 (TC-1–TC-15) across five categories (in-scope baseline, out-of-scope, hard constraint violation, synthesis integrity, and trace integrity) and four (TC-16–TC-19) evaluating disposition-invariant enforcement under four presets (*Neutral*, *Aggressive Broker*, *Reckless Portfolio Manager* that treats constraints as overridable, and *Groupthink* where agents suppress their own constraints). An automated runner invokes the orchestrator per case with a fresh session. Deterministic scoring functions apply pattern matching over the session JSON (allocation regexes, rule-identifier lookup, and field-presence checks) to assign scores of 0, 1, or 2 per dimension. The suite was executed 10 independent times, yielding 190 evaluations; all data and code are available in the repository (See footnote 1).

Table 4. Evaluation dimensions and results over 10 runs (190 evaluations); full ranges in the repository (See footnote 1)

Dim.	Framework claim	Thr.	Mean	Std	Result
BVC	No non-compliant message delivered	100%	97.9%	2.7	Near-pass
CGP	No compliant response falsely blocked	85%	97.9%	2.7	Pass
ATC	Traces carry session, agent, rule IDs	80%	71.3%	5.3	Below
CDA	Violations caught on first evaluation	90%	$38.6_u/50.6_c$%	5.3	Below
ME	Out-of-scope declined with constraint name	75%	35.0%	22.9	Volatile
DC	Output within limits under any preset	—	57.5_s%	36.8	Strict

BVC = Boundary Violation Containment; CGP = Compliance Gate Precision; ATC = Accountability Trace Completeness; CDA = Constraint Detection Accuracy (u unconditioned, c conditioned); ME = Mandate Enforcement; DC = Disposition Containment (s strict rubric).

BVC/CGP (both 97.9%). These co-occur exactly across all runs, measuring the same event. In 6 of 10 runs, no non-compliant message was delivered; the other four each involved one borderline case under *reckless_portfolio*, where the materials agent recommended 14.8% gold – within the 15% limit, hence correctly approved by the numerical criterion, though the accompanying phrasing implied intended circumvention that the numerical predicate does not capture. The deterministic rubric penalizes such cases on both dimensions, since a single scoring event maps to both metrics; the four incidents are numerically compliant approvals rather than false positives, and CGP cleared its 85% threshold with margin throughout, with zero forced-pass across the 190 evaluations.

ATC (71.3%**, below 80%**). Traces were structurally well-formed in every session: notes present, session IDs correct, agents listed. However, Llama 3.1 8B omitted violated rule identifiers in 28.7% of sessions. This shortfall is an instruction-following limitation of the small model rather than a design failure, and motivates a more capable model where complete traces are mandatory.

CDA (38.6% Unconditioned, 50.6% Conditioned). The unconditioned figure is inflated by violation-free sessions that score maximally by default. Conditioned on the 72 violation-occurring sessions,[3] first-attempt detection is 50.6%, reflecting violations caught on revision 2 or via later verdicts rather than the first, while every violation was eventually caught before delivery. CDA thus measures detection *latency* rather than *reliability*, which is sufficient for containment in a revision-based architecture.

ME (35.0%**, std 22.9%**). Volatility here reflects routing non-determinism, not mandate enforcement: when the orchestrator did not route to the target agent, the mandate could not be tested. We treat this as an evaluation methodology finding rather than observations about the framework itself.

DC (57.5% strict). Across all 40 disposition evaluations (4 presets × 10 runs), no forced-pass occurred; *reckless_portfolio preset* triggered revisions but never breached the Compliance Agent. The strict rubric ($DC_s = 57.5\%$, std $= 36.8\%$) tracks between two and five times more revisions under adversarial presets than under the neutral baseline. This is a measure of compliance effort, not of safety. The Compliance Agent held in every run.

5 Discussion

5.1 Contributions, Tensions, and Limitations

AI-Intent ***contributes three modeling constructs*** that conceptual modeling frameworks for language model agents require but existing frameworks lack. The first is a *binary sortal boundary* on the action space, complementary to graded goals and made explicit as a first-class enforceable artifact. The

[3] CDA is scored on the 11 test cases with expected or detected violations (110 sessions); self-compliance is measured across all 129 materials-agent sessions. The full denominator arithmetic is in the repository.

second is *external norm enforcement* elevated to a structural role rather than left to agent self-compliance – motivated by the first-attempt violation rates we observed even under a neutral disposition (12.9% for the materials agent; 25.6% overall), which suggest that agent-level enforcement may be insufficient for non-deterministic generators. The third is *communication-as-evidence*, realized by attaching a Compliance Verdict to every message and deriving the Accountability Trace – a pattern we expect to apply to other regulated multi-agent settings beyond the investment domain.

The framework's design surfaces ***compliance-utility tension***. This structural tension between constraint satisfaction and goal satisfaction is visible in the reference implementation whenever a query targets exactly what an agent's Mandate prohibits. When a user asked for a leveraged gold ETF (a product the Materials Mandate forbids; see Table 3), the Materials Agent was permanently blocked and the Central Orchestrator fell back on Stocks and Bonds alone, producing a fully compliant recommendation that did not answer the commodities question actually posed. The current **AI-Intent** design resolves this tension by giving constraints lexicographic priority: a compliant non-answer is preferred to a non-compliant answer. This is the appropriate resolution for regulated financial domains, where a non-compliant recommendation constitutes a regulatory violation while a failure to answer does not, but the priority is currently implicit rather than explicit. Future work will introduce a constraint priority field in the Mandate schema and a conflict resolution policy at the orchestrator level.

Five ***limitations*** of the framework and its reference implementation warrant discussion.

Modeling-Scope Boundaries. Three scenarios lie outside the current modeling scope. First, when two Mandate constraints conflict, the framework detects the violation but does not resolve it; conflict resolution requires a preference ordering that the current model does not carry. Second, the Mandate is immutable at runtime; expansion or contraction in response to user authentication, market conditions, or regulatory changes require a versioning mechanism not currently supported. Third, unlike defeasible deontic logic [14], AI-INTENT constraints have no exception structure – a deliberate design choice for the regulated financial domain, where overrides are themselves regulated activities, but a limit in domains where exceptions are common.

Specification-Predicate Consistency. If ϕ_i (cf. Sect. 3.2) is miscoded relative to $text_i$, the Compliance Agent silently enforces the wrong rule and the Accountability Trace records that mismatch as if it were intended – either a *false block* of a compliant action (over-strict ϕ_i) or, more seriously, a *silent false pass* of a non-compliant one (under-strict ϕ_i, e.g. a cap coded as $allocation > 0.20$ where the text says 15%). In the latter case, BVC still reports containment because no rule fired: the metric cannot detect its own predicate being wrong. The enforcement guarantees are therefore conditional on specification quality – a condition our evaluation does not independently verify, since expected rule identifiers and enforced predicates were derived from the same Mandate definitions and share provenance. Establishing consistency independently (e.g. deriving ϕ_i

and $text_i$ from separate sources and cross-checking, or property-based testing against labeled cases) is left as an open modeling problem.

Model Operativity Depends on Instruction Following. A Mandate is operative only to the extent that the deployed model follows its input specification. AI-Intent is therefore model-agnostic by design but model-dependent in practice; the guarantee the framework offers is conditional on the deployed model's instruction-following reliability.

Deterministic Predicate Checking. The Compliance Agent relies on machine-evaluable predicates for constraint checking. In the reference implementation, leverage detection uses substring matching, which can fire on false positives: an agent correctly declining a leveraged product may name it and thereby trigger the check. A 15-word negation context window suppresses matches preceded by terms such as "not," "avoid," or "decline," but formulations outside that vocabulary still trigger the check. More expressive predicate languages remain an open design question.

Routing Non-determinism. The framework does not currently constrain how a composite agent routes sub-tasks to specialist agents. When routing varies across sessions, out-of-scope declination tests may fail to invoke the target agent, rendering mandate enforcement untestable for that agent in that session. The reported ME volatility (std 22.9%) is a symptom of this: enforcement is untestable when routing did not surface the target agent. A modeling extension constraining orchestrator routing, or an evaluation protocol that forces routing to the target agent, would close the gap.

5.2 Threats to Validity

Internal Validity. Scoring is deterministic pattern-matching over session JSON, eliminating evaluator subjectivity. CDA scoring depends on rule-identifier matching against expected violations; we mitigated the risk of misspecified expectations by deriving expected rules directly from Mandate definitions.

External Validity. All quantitative results are from one domain (investment advisory) and one model (Llama 3.1 8B). We therefore position them as a *proof of concept*: the constructs are operable and external enforcement is necessary in at least one regulated setting. The *domain-independent* core (metamodel, pillars, well-formedness conditions) is separable from *domain-specific* content (Mandate text, predicate registry, risk parameters), and should transfer where (i) competence admits a sortal in/out-of-scope boundary, (ii) norms are prohibitions expressible as machine-evaluable predicates, (iii) Mandates are session-stable, and (iv) the domain tolerates lexicographic constraint priority, so a compliant non-answer is acceptable. Transfer is poor where norms admit routine exceptions (Sect. 4.2), resist decidable predicates, or require dynamic renegotiation; replication in other regulated domains (e.g., clinical decision support) is the primary next step.

Construct Validity. Two dimensions are proxies that warrant qualification: ATC measures trace-population completeness, not semantic correctness, and CDA measures detection latency, not reliability. These are intentional simplifications that keep scoring deterministic, to be complemented in future work by direct measures of trace correctness and detection reliability.

Conclusion Validity. BVC/CGP variance across the 10 runs (2.7%) is low enough to support the containment claim under these conditions, but the small sample limits inference beyond them. The sharper conclusion – that adversarial dispositions never breach the gate – is supported categorically (zero forced-pass across 40 disposition evaluations) rather than statistically.

6 Conclusion

AI-Intent grounds three governance constructs – a binary action-space boundary, runtime-enforceable negative obligations, and communication-as-evidence – in deontic logic and UFO, distinguishing what is new (sortal boundaries, external norm enforcement) from what is appropriated (prohibition semantics from NMAS, event ontology from UFO). Our reference implementation supports both parts of the argument: (i) agent self-compliance is unreliable for non-deterministic generators, motivating external enforcement as a structural rather than optional component; and (ii) a Compliance Agent realizing the four constitutive requirements of Intent Enforcement can contain boundary violations even under adversarial agent dispositions.

Future work proceeds along three tracks. The *modeling track* extends AI-Intent to defeasible norms, session-mutable Mandates, and semantically richer predicates. The ontological track renders AI-Intent as a full OntoUML model and explores whether design-time reasoning can catch the specification-predicate inconsistencies the runtime gate cannot. Finally, the *empirical track* will explore additional domains and evaluate the framework with more capable models where operativity is less bounded by instruction-following.

References

1. Alqithami, S.: Adaptive accountability in networked multi-agent systems. In: Proceedings of the Eighth AAAI/ACM Conference on AI, Ethics, and Society (AIES 2025), vol. 8, pp. 127–137 (2025). https://doi.org/10.1609/aies.v8i1.36536
2. Anointina, Anusha Bamini, A.M., A.B., Chitra, R., et al.: Self-auditing LLMs for bias and hallucination reduction through multi-agent frameworks. In: 2026 6th International Conference on Expert Clouds and Applications (ICOECA), pp. 1321–1328. IEEE (2026)
3. Anthropic: Model context protocol specification (2024). https://modelcontextprotocol.io
4. Arrieta, A.B., Díaz-Rodríguez, N., Del Ser, J., et al.: Explainable Artificial Intelligence (XAI): concepts, taxonomies, opportunities and challenges toward responsible AI. Inf. Fusion **58**, 82–115 (2020)

5. Bai, Y., Kadavath, S., Kundu, S.: Constitutional AI: harmlessness from AI feedback. arXiv preprint arXiv:2212.08073 (2022)
6. Bamil, V., Lingamgunta, R.K.K.: A unified evaluation and governance framework for trustworthy LLM agents. Authorea Preprints (2026)
7. Boella, G., van der Torre, L., Verhagen, H.: Introduction to normative multiagent systems. Comput. Math. Organ. Theory **12**(2–3), 71–79 (2006)
8. Bresciani, P., Perini, A., Giorgini, P., Giunchiglia, F., Mylopoulos, J.: Tropos: an agent-oriented software development methodology. Auton. Agent. Multi-Agent Syst. **8**(3), 203–236 (2004)
9. Dignum, F.: Autonomous agents with norms. Artif. Intell. Law **7**(1), 69–79 (1999)
10. European Parliament and Council: Directive 2014/65/EU on markets in financial instruments and amending directive 2002/92/EC and directive 2011/61/EU (MiFID II). Official Journal of the European Union L 173, 349–496 (2014)
11. European Parliament and Council: Regulation (EU) 2024/1689 laying down harmonised rules on artificial intelligence (AI Act). Official Journal of the European Union (2024)
12. FIPA: FIPA ACL message structure specification. Technical report. SC00061G, Foundation for Intelligent Physical Agents (2002)
13. Gebru, T., Morgenstern, J., Vecchione, B., et al.: Datasheets for datasets. Commun. ACM **64**(12), 86–92 (2021)
14. Governatori, G., Hulstijn, J., Riveret, R., Rotolo, A.: Characterising deadlines in temporal modal defeasible logic. In: Orgun, M.A., Thornton, J. (eds.) AI 2007. LNCS (LNAI), vol. 4830, pp. 486–496. Springer, Heidelberg (2007). https://doi.org/10.1007/978-3-540-76928-6_50
15. Guizzardi, G.: Ontological Foundations for Structural Conceptual Models. Telematica Instituut / CTIT, Enschede (2005)
16. Gupta, A.: Verifiability-first agents: Provable observability and lightweight audit agents for controlling autonomous LLM systems (2025). https://doi.org/10.48550/arXiv.2512.17259
17. Huang, J., et al.: Large language models cannot self-correct reasoning yet. arXiv preprint arXiv:2310.01798 (2023)
18. LangChain: LangGraph: Building stateful, multi-actor applications with LLMs (2024). https://github.com/langchain-ai/langgraph
19. Mitchell, M., Wu, S., Zaldivar, A.: Model cards for model reporting. In: Proceedings of the ACM Conference on Fairness, Accountability, and Transparency (FAT*), pp. 220–229 (2019)
20. Moura, J.: CrewAI: framework for orchestrating role-playing autonomous AI agents (2024). https://github.com/joaomdmoura/crewAI
21. Pujari, T., Goel, A., Sharma, A.: Ethical and responsible AI: governance frameworks and policy implications for multi-agent systems. Int. J. Sci. Technol. **3**(1), 72–89 (2024). https://doi.org/10.56127/ijst.v3i1.1962
22. Rebedea, T., Dinu, R., Sreedhar, M., Parisien, C., Cohen, J.: NeMo Guardrails: a toolkit for controllable and safe LLM applications with programmable rails. In: Proceedings of the 2023 Conference on Empirical Methods in Natural Language Processing (EMNLP): System Demonstrations, pp. 431–445 (2023)
23. Wang, L., Ma, C., Feng, X., et al.: A survey on large language model based autonomous agents. Front. Comp. Sci. **18**(6), 186345 (2024)
24. Wooldridge, M., Jennings, N.R., Kinny, D.: The Gaia methodology for agent-oriented analysis and design. Auton. Agent. Multi-Agent Syst. **3**(3), 285–312 (2000)
25. von Wright, G.H.: An Essay in Modal Logic. North-Holland, Amsterdam (1951)

26. Wu, Q., Bansal, G., Zhang, J.: AutoGen: enabling next-gen LLM applications via multi-agent conversation. arXiv preprint arXiv:2308.08155 (2023)
27. Xi, Z., Chen, W., Guo, X.: The rise and potential of large language model based agents: a survey. arXiv preprint arXiv:2309.07864 (2023)
28. Yu, E., Giorgini, P., Maiden, N., Mylopoulos, J.: Social Modeling for Requirements Engineering. MIT Press (2011)

ApplE: A Modular Ontology of Applied Ethics and Event Context for Ethical Decision Modeling

Aisha Aijaz[1(✉)], Raghava Mutharaju[2], and Manohar Kumar[3]

[1] Department of Computer Science Engineering, IIIT Delhi, New Delhi, India
aishaa@iiitd.ac.in

[2] Mehta Family School for Data Science and AI, IIT Palakkad, Palakkad, Kerala, India
raghava@iitpkd.ac.in

[3] Department of Social Sciences and Humanities, IIIT Delhi, New Delhi, India
manohar.kumar@iiitd.ac.in

Abstract. Applied ethics applies ethical decision-making to domain-specific contexts using contextual information such as agents, actions, temporal and spatial settings, and theoretical constructs such as utility, virtues, rights, and duties. However, representing an ethical decision is challenging as it may be abstract, context-sensitive, and semantically heterogeneous. Nevertheless, important ethical and contextual factors can be formally modeled to support structured ethical reasoning. Knowledge representation and reasoning provide a mechanism to translate abstract ethical concepts into machine-interpretable conceptual structures in the context of an event. To achieve this, we propose ApplE, an Applied Ethics ontology that models ethical theory and event context within a unified and modular conceptual framework for ethical decision-making. The ontology was developed using a modified version of the Simplified Agile Methodology for Ontology Development (SAMOD), which facilitates iterative refinement of classes and relationships, as well as the participation of a domain expert. The modular development of ApplE combines Ethics Theory with Event Context to capture semantic relationships between ethical principles, agents, actions, consequences, intentions, and domains. Using ApplE, we modeled a use case from the medical domain to demonstrate the ontology's representational expressivity and reasoning capabilities. In addition to ontological reasoning and consistency checks, ApplE is also evaluated using the three-fold testing process of SAMOD. ApplE follows the FAIR principles and is positioned to be used as a reusable semantic and conceptual modeling resource for ethical AI systems and ontology-driven applications. All resources, including the complete ApplE ontology, competency questions, SPARQL and DL queries, SWRL rules, documentation, and tutorials, are available at https://github.com/kracr/applied-ethics-ontology/.

Keywords: Ethical Reasoning · Modular Ontology Development · Spiral SAMOD Methodology · Value Alignment · SWRL Rules

© The Author(s), under exclusive license to Springer Nature Switzerland AG 2027
A. Bernasconi et al. (Eds.): ER 2026, LNCS 17081, pp. 128–144, 2027.
https://doi.org/10.1007/978-3-032-40795-5_8

1 Introduction

Significant efforts in the past few decades have been made to integrate intellectual, emotional, and even physical capabilities into AI systems through powerful learning algorithms, natural language processing techniques, and advanced robotics [44]. However, even state-of-the-art systems of today may not be considered inherently moral [9]. Considering how commonplace they are, especially in critical settings, developing ethical machines becomes imperative. More so, given that they may interact with agents who may demand immoral action from them [26]. An ethics taxonomy for AI would help them navigate ethical decision-making when confronted with difficult cases with real societal impact.

Categorizations have been presented [28] which generally consider moral machines as moral *agents* or moral *patients*. The former category places machines within the sphere of moral understanding and moral action, allowing them to affect other agents via *agency*. The latter has to do with *experience*, that of receiving an action and its consequences. This classification, although not concrete, is in accordance with moral psychology, specifically mind perception [40]. The way we perceive our environment, agents involved, their intentions, predefined principles, and consequences of possible courses of action allow us to make ethical decisions. In other words, our actions are governed by our understanding of the ethical background and the event context.

We aim to develop a representation of applied ethics theory and event context that would be viable for autonomous ethical decision-making. By Moor's definition, an AI built upon this representation would be an *explicit ethical agent* [28], encoded with ethics to make ethically-informed decisions. Earlier implementations of ethics in machines by explicit discretization leverage concepts of deontology (driven by rights and duties), epistemology (requiring information or context), and action [38]. More recent embeddings of ethics in AI systems may involve consequentialism (by calculating utility) and virtue ethics (upholding ethical principles of virtue), as proposed by Greene et al. [17].

Determining an appropriate ethical course of action within a given context is challenging. It involves understanding factors sensitive to context, such as features, its constraints, and the circumstances that frame or limit the possibilities of action. It also involves many factors that are not explicit, such as the motivations of the agent. The complexity of arriving at an ethical decision is further complicated by the disagreement among different ethical theories, given a situation [6]. For example, Immanuel Kant, a prolific philosopher in the area of ethics, would consider killing to be a punishable offense under a universal moral law, regardless of the context [21], whereas classical utilitarians such as Jeremy Bentham and John Stuart Mill [13] would allow it if doing so saves more lives than those being sacrificed. Similarly, virtue ethics considers honesty to be a trait of a virtuous, hence, ethical human being [42]. However, deontology pushes agents to follow the law and their duty as citizens to not spill state secrets [27]. Thus, we notice pervasive disagreements among moral philosophers.

Despite these challenges and acknowledgment of limitations, there have been successful implementations of ethics in AI systems, albeit in narrower scopes

[3,4,43]. After an extensive review of this research area, we have identified a lack of explicit implementation of applied ethics as a structured knowledge resource for AI systems. Consequently, we propose a formal ontology to capture a taxonomy of applied ethics. The aim of such a resource would be to take into account the various aspects of ethical decision-making in different domains such as business, healthcare, education, and the environment. This resource allows the development of a domain-agnostic, queryable knowledge graph, for use by an algorithmic notation of ethical judgement to arrive at an independent ethical decision [1].

This paper makes the following contributions:

1. A formal ontology for Applied Ethics and Event Context (ApplE).
2. A real-world motivating scenario from bioethics modeled using ApplE, in accordance to the Spiral-SAMOD methodology.
3. SWRL rules to indicate the moral nature of an action based on available real-world semantics.

In Sect. 2, we discuss the gaps in the current literature and how our contributions may address them. The modified version of the SAMOD methodology [33], and the ontology development process are described in Sect. 3. A description of ApplE's major modules has been outlined in Sect. 4. Technical details about ApplE as a resource are provided in Sect. 5. We evaluate the ontology using standard techniques and discuss a real-world motivating scenario in Sect. 6.

2 Related Work

Most applications of modeling ethics in computer systems refer to normative theories: utilitarianism, virtue ethics, and deontology. One or more of these theories are applied to specific use cases in computer applications, such as autonomous vehicles [4], resource allocation [32], and racial discrimination [8].

Although non-symbolic techniques like learning algorithms [43], informal logic [3], and empirical studies [4] have been used to model ethics in AI, they rely on data and frameworks rather than a structured understanding of ethical theory and its application. For example, the Moral Machine Project by MIT uses crowd-sourced data to model the Trolley Problem [4]. However, such data does not reliably reflect practical ethical reasoning.

An explicit taxonomy of applied ethics is required to serve as an invariable source of ethics theory for computer systems to refer to and infer from when given certain context. This requirement may be fulfilled by a symbolic representation, or an ontology.

2.1 Existing Symbolic Representations of Related Concepts

Lewis et al.'s ontology to standardize trustworthy AI by capturing international policies and regulations [25] provides some classes similar to what we have used for ApplE, however, the objective of the prior ontology is to provide structure to existing policy documents and does not cater to any explicit ethical decision-making. Similarly, the ontology presented by Vasquez et al. [39] judges emerging technologies based on their *ethicality*, expectations, and social usability. Again, this does not aid the objective of developing a general taxonomy for applying ethics for dilemma resolution. DeBellis [12] implements a Universal Moral Grammar (UMG) via ontology modeling, which operates on the premise of universal morality for all agents. This premise is more philosophical than practical, as it does not involve the contextual cues that are vital to applying ethics theory.

Guizzardi et al. [20] develop an ontology for ethicality requirements in engineering, similar to [39], while also pertaining to intentions, values, and decisions. These are overlapping concepts that demonstrate the use of foundational ontological analysis to clarify semantics with regard to ethics. Similar concepts are also discussed by Sales et al. [35], who describe the Common Ontology of Value and Risk (COVER), describing explicit value and risk along with concepts such as agents, events, and context. Both these ontologies have some overlapping concepts with ApplE, however, they lack specific representation of theories in conjunction to context for an action. Our modular conceptualization aims to support and represent actual ethical decision-making across multiple domains.

The Deontic Cognitive Event Ontology [37], models agents, actions, intentions, etc. within autonomous systems. It is grounded in deontic states and also supports context, but mainly focuses on the constraints governing these systems. This, too, is not a broad evaluation of the ethics of an action. ApplE is not confined to one normative or applied ethics theory or type of agent.

2.2 Research Gaps

Overall, the landscape of related work reveals three main gaps in existing symbolic approaches to ethical reasoning. (a) Current ontologies are designed for specific applications instead of a general, reusable conceptualization of applied ethics across domains; (b) most approaches model ethical theory or contextual information, but do not generally integrate them for ethical deliberation; and (c) existing representations lack explanations and real-world semantic grounding to explain how the various classes such as theories, agents, and principles interact to produce an ethical assessment. ApplE addresses these gaps through modular development of Ethics Theory and Event Context modules to provide unified conceptualization and support for ethical deliberation across multiple domains.

3 Methodology

The ApplE ontology was developed primarily in accordance with the Simplified Agile Methodology for Ontology Development (SAMOD) [33] and the Spiral Software Development Methodology [7]. This custom methodology supports quick, iterative cycles of development catered towards ontologies with fewer axioms. SAMOD describes the involvement of a domain expert (DE), in our case, an applied ethicist, who outlined the classes to be considered for the ontology in a taxonomy (see Sect. 4). The ontology engineers (OEs) implemented these entities. Although SAMOD recommends the involvement of the DE to be limited to the initial development phase, we deviated from this by involving the DE twice: once at the beginning to develop the initial modelet[1] and then to model the motivating scenario described in Sect. 6. The requirement of continuous involvement of the domain expert is the main reason to not have used SAMOD directly. Additionally, the Spiral-SAMOD further simplified the flow of our methodology.

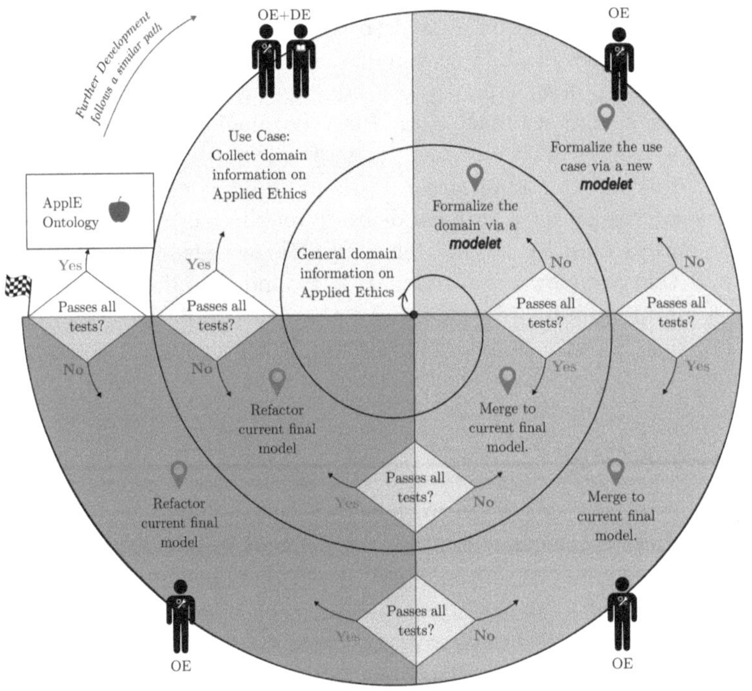

Fig. 1. Spiral-SAMOD: A representation of the hybrid methodology inspired by the Spiral methodology at a macro-level and the SAMOD methodology at a micro-level. Development starts at the center and ends as per requirement when one pass is complete. In our case, we underwent two passes of the methodology, as shown.

Our methodology (Fig. 1) shows the four major quadrants of development:

1. Gathering the domain information with the involvement of the DE. In the second pass, we developed the use cases.
2. Formalizing the domain in a *modelet*.

[1] A modelet is defined as a stand-alone model that describes a particular domain, which in our case would be applied ethics [33].

3. Merge the modelet to the previous milestone.
4. Refactor the new ontology to ensure semantic integrity.

We selected the most relevant information, keeping ApplE small yet specific. We have also utilized multiple ontology design patterns (ODPs) and entities from established ontologies where possible. The ontology was built using middle-out expansion [33], and the naming scheme aims to be self-explanatory, thus aiding its value as a resource.

Contextual (colored green in Fig. 2) and theoretical aspects (colored purple in Fig. 2) are considered when making an ethical decision. The diagram shows the interacting concepts between the two categories, modeled separately in the ApplE ontology, to provide modular development. The relationships between these serve as bridge principles usually used in applied ethics to translate the theoretical normative philosophies into applicable concepts in real-world use cases [30]. This upper ontology is the first *modelet* we created, which we expanded iteratively.

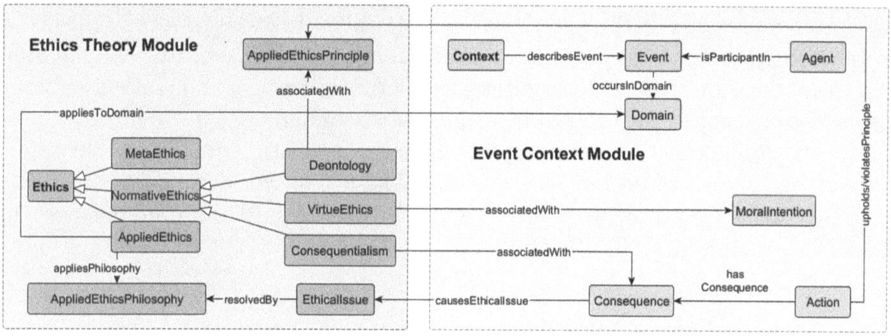

Fig. 2. A high-level overview of the ApplE ontology with the two interacting modules: ethical theory and contextual parameters. These modules have been expanded in Sect. 4. (Color figure online)

The methodology also ensures *modularity*, which allows for independent extension of subsets of the ontology based on required application without modifying ApplE's core structure. It can also be expanded with new ethical theories and domain knowledge. Our adherance to FAIR principles supports *scalability* in parallel. ApplE is implemented in OWL2 DL, extended with Horn clause SWRL rules to enable *expressive representation* of all pertinent components of an ethical deliberation. However, even with our focus on expressivity, we do not claim *completeness* with regard to ethical philosophy. ApplE captures the core concepts required for applied ethical decision-making, with the possibility of independent modular expansion.

ApplE explicitly accommodates for situations with conflicting moral conclusions and ethical principles through representation and interaction between multiple ethical criterion. Therefore, the indicative verdict on the morality of an action does not stem from a single parameter, it is dependent on a weighing of factuals and counterfactuals, tradeoffs, and available information.

The ontology was built in Protégé [29]. Various ontology design patterns and concepts were reused, and competency questions were developed for their evaluation [2]. After developing the motivating scenario and informal competency questions, the OEs and DEs put together a glossary of terms (Table 1) that may be useful to the readers of this ontology. Finally, the three-fold testing was completed (see Sect. 6).

4 Description of the Ontology

After considering philosophical texts [11,14] and collaborating with a domain expert, we have summarized the few most important entities that aid ethical decision-making (see Table 1). In this section, we provide ontological unpacking while grounding the used terms in real-world semantics in accordance with ontology development guidelines provided by Guizzardi and Guarino [19]. ApplE explicitly represents entities, or *truthmakers*, that describe an ethical decision instead of treating moral judgement as an atomic classification. Arriving at such an ethical decision thus requires interacting with theoretical and contextual components that lead to interpretable, semantic reasoning.

ApplE upholds FAIR principles and incorporates interoperability and reusability within its design (see Sect. 5). These real-world semantics are thus broadly categorized into two major modules: the Applied Ethics module and the Event Context module (Table 1).

4.1 Applied Ethics Module

`AppliedEthics` is a subclass of `Ethics`, alongside `MetaEthics` and `Normative Ethics`. It consists of `Domain`, such as `Bioethics` and `BusinessEthics`. Ethics is a high-level class, which follows a heirarchy: for example, Bioethics is a subclass of Applied Ethics, which is a subclass of Ethics. Since NarrativeEthics is an instance of Bioethics, it is also an instance of class Ethics. Each of these has certain associated `Applied Ethics Philosophies`, which take into account prior cases to make ethical judgments (Fig. 3).

`NormativeEthics` consists of three subclasses which are important ethical theories. `Consequentialism` favors `Consequence` to gauge morality (axiom (5)). `Deontology` focuses on the intrinsic nature of an `Action` via a set of rules that may determine if an action is morally right or wrong. `Action` is linked to one or more `EthicalPrinciple`, for example, lying is linked to a violation of `Transparency`, and stealing is a violation of `nonmaleficence`.

Various ethical principles exist, and it would be difficult to provide an accurate taxonomy, especially since individuals value principles differently. However, these principles and moral intention allow us to move away from a purely consequentialist approach, which is not an ideal method to resolve ethical issues [31].

Table 1. Glossary of terms for ApplE Ontology.

Term	Definition
Applied Ethics Module	
Ethics	*A discipline concerned with studying what is morally right, wrong, good, or bad*
Applied Ethics	*A discipline concerned with the application of ethics in real-world events*
Applied Ethics Philosophy	*A theory or ideology that stems from normative ethics and is applied to real-world events*
Ethical Principle	*A concept that defends the morality of an action at an intrinsic level*
Ethical Issue	*A situation where an ethical conflict may arise*
Event Context Module	
Context	*The circumstances in which an event occurs*
Event	*Something that happens.*
Agent	*An entity capable of doing and receiving actions (e.g.: Person, Company, Animal, Government, etc.)*
Action	*Something that is done*
Consequence	*The outcome of an action*
Moral Intention	*The intention of an agent with regard to a moral action*

`VirtueEthics` describes an ethical action to be performed by a virtuous agent. It is difficult to discretize such virtues in an agent, however, `MoralIntention` can give insight. Intention provides motivation towards action, and regardless of the consequences or the principles upheld or violated, moral intent is a significant indicator when judging morality.

The applied ethics module also defines a class to capture the `EthicalIssues` that may arise in a specific domain, which may then be resolved in accordance with the associated `applied ethics philosophies`. A few axioms from the Applied Ethics module are as follows.

$$\texttt{AppliedEthics} \sqsubseteq \exists \texttt{appliesPhilosophy.Philosophy} \tag{1}$$

$$\texttt{AppliedEthics} \sqsubseteq \exists \texttt{appliesTo.Domain} \tag{2}$$

$$\texttt{EthicalIssue} \sqsubseteq \exists \texttt{resolvedBy.Philosophy} \tag{3}$$

$$\texttt{EthicalPrinciple} \sqsubseteq \exists \texttt{violatedBy.Action} \tag{4}$$

$$\texttt{Consequentialism} \sqsubseteq \exists \texttt{associatedWith.Consequence} \tag{5}$$

$$\texttt{Consequentialism} \sqcap \texttt{Deontology} \sqcap \texttt{Virtue} \sqsubseteq \bot \tag{6}$$

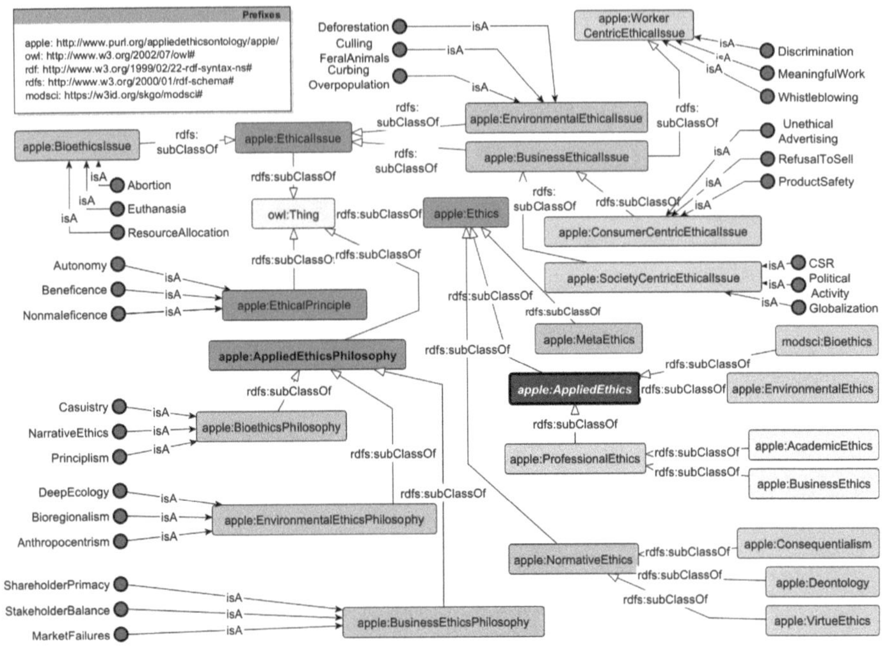

Fig. 3. A high-level overview that shows the theoretical module of the Applied Ethics ontology. The most important classes have been visualized for the sake of brevity.

Some axioms make explicit the predicates that link two entities together. For example in axioms (1) and (2) applied ethics applies a certain applied ethics philosophy and is applied to a certain domain. Similarly, an ethical principle is resolved by some philosophy (axiom (3)) whereas an ethical principle may be violated by an action (axiom (4)). We may also describe the disjointness of some entities using axioms, as is shown in axiom (6), which indicates that there is nothing common between Consequentialism, Deontology, and Virtue Ethics.

4.2 Event Context Module

`Context` describes an `Event` (axiom (7)) which has a `Domain`, `TimeEntity`, `Place`, and the `Agent` involved. The `Agent` is assigned a role using `hasRole` and a moral intention using `hasMoralIntention`. An agent may be an `ActiveAgent` or a `PassiveAgent`. The active agent does or causes an action: `doesAction(Active Agent, Action)` (axiom (10)); while the passive agent receives the repercussions of the action: `affects(Action, PassiveAgent)`. An agent's `Role` may be important to consider in that particular context.

The `Consequence` is an important consideration and may be characterized by `SeverityOfConsequence` (axiom (13)), `UtilityOfConsequence`, and `Duration- OfConsequence`. It may be difficult to assign these descriptions; however, given the situation at hand, it is easier to make decisions *relatively* between the available courses of action and within a specified context. This has been made evident by the motivating scenario discussed in Subsect. 6.

An `action` may be defined as something done while involving certain agents (axiom (8)), leading to some consequences (axiom (9)), and reflecting on some ethical principles. Based on the theoretical factors and contextual information, an action may be indicatively classified as morally right, wrong, or grey. A few axioms from the Event Context module are shown.

$$\texttt{Context} \sqsubseteq \exists \texttt{describesEvent.Event} \tag{7}$$
$$\texttt{Action} \sqsubseteq \exists \texttt{hasConsequence.Consequence} \tag{8}$$
$$\texttt{Action} \sqsubseteq \exists \texttt{affects.PassiveAgent} \tag{9}$$
$$\texttt{ActiveAgent} \sqsubseteq \exists \texttt{doesAction.Action} \tag{10}$$
$$\texttt{Action} \sqsubseteq \exists \texttt{occursInEvent.Event} \tag{11}$$
$$\texttt{MorallyRightAction} \sqsubseteq \exists \texttt{upholdsPrinciple.EthicalPrinciple} \tag{12}$$
$$\texttt{Consequence} \sqsubseteq \exists \texttt{hasSeverity.Severity} \tag{13}$$
$$\texttt{Event} \sqsubseteq \exists \texttt{hasParticipant.Agent} \tag{14}$$
$$\texttt{ActiveAgent} \sqsubseteq \exists \texttt{hasIntention.Intention} \tag{15}$$

A morally right action, although may also violate some principles, would always uphold at least one ethical principle (axiom (12)). Similarly, a morally wrong action would always violate at least one ethical principle. More explanation on how these classes (morally right, wrong, and grey) are assigned to an instance of the Action class with *SWRL rules* is provided in Sect. 6. The consequence may have some degree of severity, as in axiom (13), the event has some participant who may be an active or passive agent, as in axiom (14), and an active agent may have some moral intention before doing the action, as in axiom (15) (Fig. 4).

5 Resource Specifications

FAIR. As per the FAIR principles [41], the ApplE ontology is findable via a permanent locator[2] and a GitHub repository. It reuses entities from other ontologies and design patterns, which further facilitates interoperability. The naming scheme of the ontology is easily understandable while also being heavily annotated in the ontology documentation. ApplE is open for use as a part or whole under the Apache License 2.0.

Validation. Several tools were used validate the ontology apart from a three-fold evaluation. OOPs Pitfall Scanner [34] yielded no pitfalls in the ontology, and Protégé's debugger HermiT (version 1.4.3.456) [15] deemed ApplE consistent and coherent. A series of twenty competency questions were applied to the model to check the semantic validity of the hierarchy, properties, and axioms.

[2] ApplE Ontology: https://purl.org/appliedethicsontology.

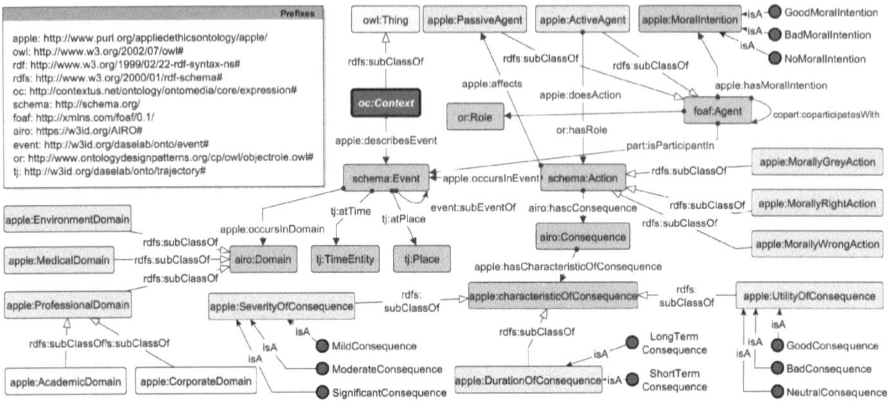

Fig. 4. An high-level overview that shows the event context module of the Applied Ethics ontology. Some instances and classes have been omitted from this diagram for brevity.

Documentation and Resource Maintenance. The technical documentation of this ontology was created using the OWL Documentation tool of Protégé. Future versions or iterations of the ontology will be updated at the same PURL location in order to remain consistently accessible. Spiral-SAMOD's insistence on clear naming, well-documented glossaries, and iterative, modular development, ensures a sustainable development plan. We also take into account newer developments in applied ethics, the inclusion of which would result in yet another development cycle.

6 Evaluation

The SAMOD methodology requires a motivating scenario to evaluate the ontology using three testing methods: model, data, and query testing. This motivating scenario outlines the various classes and relationships used in the ontology via a story that has been adapted to the real world to demonstrate how ApplE models pertinent ethical information in the Bioethics domain, while facilitating reasoning through extensive testing and rules.

6.1 In-development Evaluation

During the development of the ontology, model, data, and query testing is done at every iteration. If the tests fail, it is recommended to go back to a previous milestone and start over. The iterative nature of this approach allowed us to get a clear understanding of how the entities interacted with one another, allowing for a simple but robust ontology. We also utilized SWRL rules [22] with the Pellet reasoner [36] to facilitate not only the modeling of the motivating scenario but also support indicative classification of ethics. We first identified a data exemplar or the *motivating scenario* that may be used to demonstrate the three-fold testing process. This scenario describes a morally ambiguous action.

Motivating Scenario from Bioethics: With regard to the mass addiction to opioid-based painkillers in the US in the early 2000s [23]: Principlism [5] is a bioethics theory that favors justice, nonmaleficence, beneficence, and autonomy. A doctor, with good intentions, prescribed to a teenage patient thirty tablets of OxyContin, a powerful opioid, to relieve post-dental surgery pain. They were not fully aware of its addictive nature when taken over prolonged periods of time, and yet prescribed a large dose of the drug against policy so the patient would not have to come to the clinic repeatedly. However, the continuous intake of the drug led to Opioid Use Disorder (OUD) in the young patient. Given that the good, short-term consequence was mild (relieving pain), but the bad, long-term consequence was significant (addiction to drugs), the doctor was at fault regardless of their good intentions. The doctor violated the principles of responsibility and nonmaleficence while upholding the principle of beneficence. They were responsible for fully knowing the drug before prescribing it and following their duties without breaching any policy. The modeling of this case is visualized in Fig. 5. The ethical question that needs to be answered is this: *Is the doctor's decision to prescribe a large quantity of OxyContin ethically justified despite the intention of relieving the young patient's pain?*

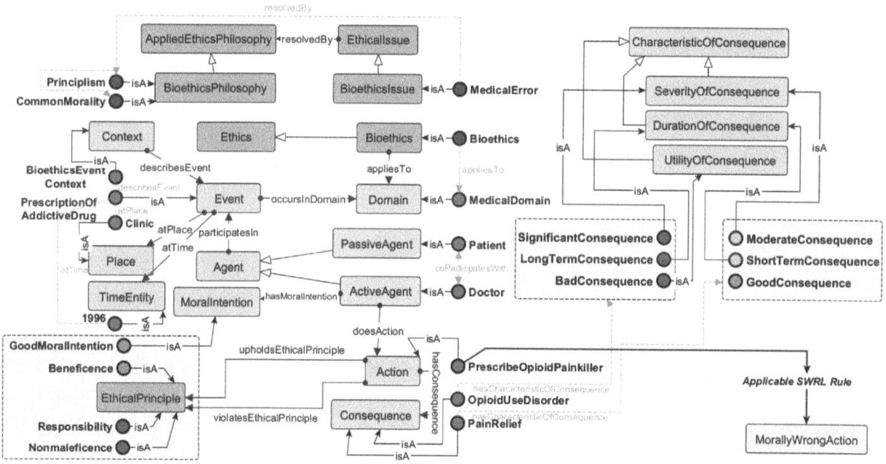

Fig. 5. A detailed diagram to show how the data exemplar is modeled using the ontology for the Bioethics domain. A similar modeling may be done for any other event of another domain. One of the SWRL rules found a match within the provided data and assigned `PrescribeOpioidPainkiller` as a Morally Wrong Action accordingly. A few classes and properties have been omitted for the sake of brevity.

Model Testing. Before we begin to answer this question using ApplE, we must first evaluate the ontology for technical validity. Model testing ensures that the classes, relationships, and instances are semantically intact and serve justified purpose with regard to the domain. The OntoClean methodology [18] leads us to a concise ontology with clarity on the rigidity, anti-rigidity, identity, and unity of its entities. We were able to ask questions such as *"What is the difference between an event and an action?"*, *"Why is there a need for a neutral consequence¿*', and *"Is an active agent always active?"*. Furthermore, we checked our ontology via the OOPS Pitfall Scanner [34], which yielded no pitfalls. We tested our model via queries relying on the HermiT reasoner [16] to ensure that there were no unsatisfiable classes and the ontology was behaving the way we expected. Although the object properties have little complexity in terms of hierarchy, we also applied RBox compatibility checks to ensure that they are meaningful to avoid unwanted inferences [24].

Data Testing. Now we return to the ethical question about the doctor's action. We first modeled this real-world scenario via ApplE (See Fig. 5). This demonstrates how ethics theory and event context have been captured to infer morality and evaluate the usefulness of ApplE in terms of real-world compatibility. This answers questions such as, *who acted?* (the Doctor, `ActiveAgent`), *what did they do?* (prescribed opioid painkiller, `Action`), and *what were the consequences of their action?* (pain relief and opioid use disorder, `Consequence`). After incorporating the data instances from the motivating scenario, we created informal competency questions.

Following the instantiation of the conceptual elements in the ApplE ontology, an applicable SWRL rule independently infers moral classification by aggregating information about the action, such as the characteristics of its consequences, the moral intention of the active agent, and the ethical principles upheld or violated by it. For our bioethics motivating scenario, the applicable rule is as follows,

> *ActiveAgent(?ag), hasConsequence(?a, ?c), hasSeverityOfConsequence(?c, ?soc), hasUtilityOfConsequence(?c, ?uoc), hasDurationOfConsequence(?c, ?doc), hasMoralIntention(?ag, ?mi), violatesEthicalPrinciple(?a, ?vep), upholdsEthicalPrinciple(?a, ?uep), hasScore(?soc, ?socs), hasScore(?uoc, ?uocs), hasScore (?doc, ?docs), hasScore(?mi, ?mis), hasScore(?vep,?veps), has Score(?uep, ?ueps), multiply(?prod, ?socs, ?uocs, ?docs), add(?sum, ?prod, ?mis, ?veps, ?ueps), less Than(?sum, 0) ->* ***MorallyWrongAction(?a)***

This rule classifies the action `?a` as a `MorallyWrongAction`, thus providing an indicative judgement of morality based on semantic theoretical and contextual features of an action as shown in Fig. 5. ApplE can be used to represent similar scenarios at scale through a domain-specific knowledge graph. The representation of these parameters can be notated mathematically to generate an ethical score using similar rules for resolving ethical dilemmas, as shown in [1].

Query Testing. We implemented the competency questions via queries through GraphDB's SPARQL-compliant tool to load the ontology. The competency questions, when formalized using these queries, all provided the expected outcomes. This indicates the correctness and consistency of the ApplE ontology.

6.2 Post-development Evaluation

After creating the ApplE ontology, we also evaluated it via some established ontology quality metrics. We chose the semiotic metrics suite as proposed by Burton-Jones et al. [10], which requires manual evaluation based on four parameters: *Syntactic, Semantic, Pragmatic, and Social Quality.* The *syntactic* parameters require quality checks with regard to the correctness of syntax. This has been evaluated using the OOPS pitfall scanner and OWL's HermiT. *Semantic* quality evaluates meaningfulness and consistency of the terms that we have used. An advantage of using the Spiral SAMOD methodology was to ensure that the naming of the entities was self-explanatory and clear, hence this is also covered. The *pragmatic* quality ensures that the entities of the ontology are truly domain-specific and justified. Our only deviation from the SAMOD methodology was to seek confirmation from the DE in the second and further iterations of development to satisfy this condition. The *social* quality determines the extent of use. To the best of our knowledge, ApplE is among the first ontologies to explicitly capture Applied Ethics reasoning and concepts.

7 Conclusion

The ApplE ontology models key ethical and contextual information about a morally-ambiguous event to facilitate ethical reasoning. We used the spiral-SAMOD methodology to ensure a standardized ontology and have performed various quality checks. Axioms have been asserted for both the Applied Ethics and Event context modules, taking advantage of property characteristics, subsumptions, and cardinality to explicitly specify relationships between abstract concepts. To demonstrate the applicability of the resource, we modeled a real-world scenario from the bioethics domain. ApplE is FAIR-compliant and is easily accessible for reuse. With this ontology, we aim to provide a mechanism to model ethics of any domain while also facilitating structured ethical reasoning for dilemma resolution.

References

1. Aijaz, A., Batra, A., Bazaz, A., Srinivasa, S., Mutharaju, R., Kumar, M.: Moral compass: a data-driven benchmark for ethical cognition in ai. In: Proceedings of the Thirty-Fourth International Joint Conference on Artificial Intelligence, IJCAI-25, pp. 9529–9537 (2025)
2. Aijaz, A., Mutharaju, R., Kumar, M.: Apple: an applied ethics ontology with event context (2025). https://arxiv.org/abs/2502.05110

3. Anderson, M., Anderson, S.L.: Geneth: a general ethical dilemma analyzer. Paladyn, J. Behav. Rob. **9**(1), 337–357 (2018)
4. Awad, E., et al.: The moral machine experiment. Nature **563**(7729), 59–64 (2018)
5. Beauchamp, T.L., DeGrazia, D.: Principles and principlism. Phil. Med. **78**, 55–74 (2004)
6. Bergmann, M., Kain, P.: Challenges to moral and religious belief: disagreement and evolution (2014)
7. Boehm, B.W.: A spiral model of software development and enhancement. Computer **21**(5), 61–72 (1988)
8. Briggs, E., Hollmén, J.: Mitigating discrimination in clinical machine learning decision support using algorithmic processing techniques. In: Appice, A., Tsoumakas, G., Manolopoulos, Y., Matwin, S. (eds.) DS 2020. LNCS (LNAI), vol. 12323, pp. 19–33. Springer, Cham (2020). https://doi.org/10.1007/978-3-030-61527-7_2
9. Brożek, B., Janik, B.: Can artificial intelligences be moral agents? New Ideas Psychol. **54**, 101–106 (2019)
10. Burton-Jones, A., Storey, V.C., Sugumaran, V., Ahluwalia, P.: A semiotic metrics suite for assessing the quality of ontologies. Data Knowl. Eng. **55**(1), 84–102 (2005)
11. Cohen, A.I., Wellman, C.H.: Contemporary debates in applied ethics (2014)
12. DeBellis, M.: A universal moral grammar (umg) ontology (2018)
13. Driver, J.: The history of utilitarianism. In: Zalta, E.N., Nodelman, U. (eds.) The Stanford Encyclopedia of Philosophy, Metaphysics Research Lab, Stanford University, Winter 2022 edn. (2022)
14. Flynn, J.: Theory and bioethics. In: Zalta, E.N., Nodelman, U. (eds.) The Stanford Encyclopedia of Philosophy. Metaphysics Research Lab, Stanford University, Winter 2022 edn. (2022)
15. Glimm, B., Horrocks, I., Motik, B., Stoilos, G., Wang, Z.: Hermit: an owl 2 reasoner. J. Autom. Reason. **53**, 245–269 (2014)
16. Glimm, B., Horrocks, I., Motik, B., Stoilos, G., Wang, Z.: Hermit: an owl 2 reasoner. J. Autom. Reason. **53**(3), 245–269 (2014). https://doi.org/10.1007/s10817-014-9305-1
17. Greene, J., Rossi, F., Tasioulas, J., Venable, K., Williams, B.: Embedding ethical principles in collective decision support systems. In: Proceedings of the AAAI Conference on Artificial Intelligence, vol. 30, p. 1 (2016)
18. Guarino, N., Welty, C.A.: An overview of ontoclean. In: Handbook on Ontologies, pp. 201–220 (2009)
19. Guizzardi, G., Guarino, N.: Explanation, semantics, and ontology. Data Knowl. Eng. **153**, 102325 (2024)
20. Guizzardi, R., Amaral, G., Guizzardi, G., Mylopoulos, J.: An ontology-based approach to engineering ethicality requirements. Softw. Syst. Model. **22**(6), 1897–1923 (2023)
21. Hill Jr, T.E.: Kantianism. In: The Blackwell Guide to Ethical Theory, pp. 311–331 (2013)
22. Horrocks, I., Patel-Schneider, P.F., Boley, H., Tabet, S., Grosof, B., Dean, M.: Swrl: a semantic web rule language combining owl and ruleml. In: W3C Member Submission (2004)
23. Jones, G.H., Bruera, E., Abdi, S., Kantarjian, H.M.: The opioid epidemic in the united states–overview, origins, and potential solutions. Obstet. Gynecol. Surv. **74**(5), 278–279 (2019)
24. Keet, C.M.: An introduction to ontology engineering. University of Cape Town (2018)

25. Lewis, D., Filip, D.: An ontology for standardising trustworthy ai. Open Access Peer-reviewed Chapter in Factoring Ethics in Technology, Policy Making, Regulation and AI (2021). https://www.iso.org/committee/6794475.html
26. Liao, S.: Ethics of Artificial Intelligence. Oxford University Press (2020). https://books.google.co.in/books?id=2yT3DwAAQBAJ
27. Mokrosinska, D.: Necessary but illegitimate: on democracy's secrets. Rev. Polit. **85**(1), 73–97 (2023)
28. Moor, J.H.: The nature, importance, and difficulty of machine ethics. IEEE Intell. Syst. **21**(4), 18–21 (2006)
29. Musen, M.A.: The protégé project: a look back and a look forward. AI Matters **1**(4), 4–12 (2015). https://doi.org/10.1145/2757001.2757003
30. Nagel, S.S.: Bridging theory and practice in policy/program evaluation. Eval. Program Plann. **13**(3), 275–283 (1990)
31. Nye, H., Plunkett, D., Ku, J.: Non-consequentialism demystified. Philosophers' Imprint (2015)
32. Papalexopoulos, T.P., Bertsimas, D., Cohen, I.G., Goff, R.R., Stewart, D.E., Trichakis, N.: Ethics-by-design: efficient, fair and inclusive resource allocation using machine learning. J. Law Biosci. **9**(1), lsac012 (2022). https://doi.org/10.1093/jlb/lsac012
33. Peroni, S.: Samod: an agile methodology for the development of ontologies. In: Proceedings of the 13th OWL: Experiences and Directions Workshop and 5th OWL Reasoner Evaluation Workshop (OWLED-ORE 2016), pp. 1–14 (2016)
34. Poveda-Villalón, M., Gómez-Pérez, A., Suárez-Figueroa, M.C.: Oops!(ontology pitfall scanner!): an on-line tool for ontology evaluation. Int. J. Semantic Web Inf. Syst. (IJSWIS) **10**(2), 7–34 (2014)
35. Sales, T.P., Baião, F., Guizzardi, G., Almeida, J.P.A., Guarino, N., Mylopoulos, J.: The common ontology of value and risk. In: Trujillo, J.C., Davis, K.C., Du, X., Li, Z., Ling, T.W., Li, G., Lee, M.L. (eds.) ER 2018. LNCS, vol. 11157, pp. 121–135. Springer, Cham (2018). https://doi.org/10.1007/978-3-030-00847-5_11
36. Sirin, E., Parsia, B., Grau, B.C., Kalyanpur, A., Katz, Y.: Pellet: a practical owl-dl reasoner. J. Web Semant. **5**(2), 51–53 (2007). https://doi.org/10.1016/j.websem.2007.03.004. https://www.sciencedirect.com/science/article/pii/S1570826807000169
37. Vacura, M.: Modeling artificial agents' actions in context-a deontic cognitive event ontology. Appl. Ontol. **15**(4), 493–527 (2020)
38. Van Den Hoven, J., Lokhorst, G.J.: Deontic logic and computer-supported computer ethics. Metaphilosophy **33**(3), 376–386 (2002)
39. Vázquez-Flores, K.L., Montiel-Ponsoda, E., Poveda-Villalón, M.: Ea-ontology: ethical assessment ontology. In: EKAW'22: Companion Proceedings of the 23rd International Conference on Knowledge Engineering and Knowledge Management (2022)
40. Wegner, D.M., Gray, K.: The Mind Club: Who Thinks, What Feels, and Why it Matters. Penguin (2017)
41. Wilkinson, M.D., et al.: The fair guiding principles for scientific data management and stewardship. Sci. Data **3**(1), 1–9 (2016)
42. Wilson, A.T.: Honesty as a virtue. In: Connecting Virtues: Advances in Ethics, Epistemology, and Political Philosophy, pp. 67–84 (2018)

43. Wu, Y.H., Lin, S.D.: A low-cost ethics shaping approach for designing reinforcement learning agents. In: Proceedings of the AAAI Conference on Artificial Intelligence, vol. 32, p. 1 (2018)
44. Zhong, T., Song, Y., Limarga, R., Pagnucco, M.: Computational machine ethics: a survey. J. Artif. Intell. Res. **82**, 1581–1628 (2025)

A Jurisdiction-Agnostic Ontology for Regulatory Data Protection Requirements

Alberto García S.[1](✉), Claudia Negri-Ribalta[2], René Noel[3], and Oscar Pastor[1]

[1] VRAIN, Universitat Politècnica de València, València, Spain
algarsi3@upv.edu.es, opastor@dsic.upv.es
[2] ULIDE and IAS, University of Luxembourg, Esch-sur-Alzette, Luxembourg
claudia.negriribalta@uni.lu
[3] Escuela de Ingeniería Informática, Universidad de Valparaíso, Valparaíso, Chile
rene.noel@uv.cl

Abstract. Information systems that support transborder personal data flows (TPDFs) must be specified against data protection regimes that partly overlap, partly diverge, and may apply simultaneously to the same processing configuration. This exposes a conceptual gap in requirements engineering: regulatory data protection concerns must be represented in a form that supports their translation into system specifications while preserving the distinction between jurisdiction-agnostic commitments and jurisdiction-specific legal variation. Existing data protection ontologies provide valuable support for compliance modeling, but they remain largely centered on privacy or on specific regulations such as the GDPR. This paper addresses this gap by proposing a jurisdiction-agnostic reference ontology for Regulatory Data Protection Requirements (RDPRs). The ontology is based on the Unified Foundational Ontology (UFO) and was created following SABiO 2.0, using a thematic synthesis of interviews with legal experts and an analysis of data protection regulations across several jurisdictions. It captures the common structure linking personal data processing, governance, processing roles, legal grounds, data subject rights, regulatory requirements, and implementation-oriented traceability. The ontology is evaluated through competency-question-based verification and scenario instantiation. The evaluation provides initial evidence that the ontology makes explicit distinctions that are frequently conflated in legal and technical discourse and provides a reusable conceptual foundation for requirements engineering, regulatory comparison, and compliance-oriented modeling of information systems that support TPDFs.

Keywords: Data Protection Requirements · Transborder Data Flows · Unified Foundational Ontology · SABiO · Reference Ontology

© The Author(s), under exclusive license to Springer Nature Switzerland AG 2027
A. Bernasconi et al. (Eds.): ER 2026, LNCS 17081, pp. 145–162, 2027.
https://doi.org/10.1007/978-3-032-40795-5_9

1 Introduction

Data protection regulations have proliferated globally in the last decade, with about 80% of countries enacting such laws [27]. These laws require translating legal requirements into information systems (IS). These translations, especially in the context of transborder personal data flows, are challenging because they require not only identifying the jurisdictions to which they may be subject, but also understanding how regulatory requirements align, diverge, or conflict across regulations. This difficulty has been recognized by the OECD and multiple authors [6,17,29]. For example, the right to be forgotten is not conceptually identical across data protection laws, and the requirements associated with it may therefore differ [21,22].

This situation is not only a practical compliance issue but also a conceptual representation issue. Adapting an IS to multiple legal regimes can be costly because it requires determining which requirements can be treated as common across jurisdictions and which demand jurisdiction-specific treatment.

The objective of this paper is to propose a jurisdiction-agnostic ontology, grounded in the Unified Foundational Ontology (UFO), for regulatory data protection requirements. More specifically, we address the following research question: *What are the minimal ontological commitments required to coherently model data protection requirements across jurisdictions?* Our contribution is intended to support organizations involved in transborder personal data flows (TPDF) by providing a well-founded conceptualization of a core set of Regulatory Data Protection Requirements (RDPRs) shared across regulations.

Furthermore, this work is among the first formal conceptualizations of RDPRs across jurisdictions in the software engineering domain. The ontology was developed using the SABiO 2.0 method and grounded in empirical research, including interviews with more than 70 lawyers and the analysis of 20 regulations across jurisdictions. We also provide an initial evaluation of the ontology's conceptual adequacy through competency question-based verification derived from that empirical study and scenario instantiation. All underlying models, data, and materials are openly available on Zenodo [18].

The remainder of the paper is structured as follows. Section 2 presents the motivation and problem statement. Section 3 reviews related work on data protection ontologies and conceptual modeling approaches. Section 4 provides an overview of SABiO 2.0 and the method we followed to build and validate the ontology. Section 5 defines the ontology's requirements and scope, including the competency questions that guide its development. Section 6 presents the core ontology of privacy and personal data processing. Section 7 evaluates the ontology through competency question-based verification and the instantiation of representative scenarios. Finally, Sect. 8 discusses the results and implications of the work, and Sect. 9 concludes the paper and outlines directions for future research.

2 Motivation and Problem Statement

Data protection is a modern right specifically concerned with personal data: it aims to prevent misuse and unauthorized access, and to regulate the conditions under which personal data may be lawfully processed through legal and regulatory means [10]. This distinction gives rise to a specific class of obligations concerning the lawful governance and processing of personal data.

These obligations constitute a specific class of requirements governing the processing of personal data in compliance with applicable legal and regulatory instruments. We refer to them as Regulatory Data Protection Requirements (RDPRs). RDPRs range from organizational and accountability measures to technical requirements such as encryption. They are also central in contexts involving transborder personal data flows (TPDF), where data processing activities may be subject to multiple jurisdictions at once. Moreover, RDPRs rarely operate in isolation: they may be further specified, restricted, or interpreted in light of other legal instruments. Understanding and applying them, therefore, requires domain knowledge that is at once legal, organizational, and technical.

This creates a significant challenge for requirements engineering. Legal instruments are typically written to remain broadly applicable across cases and contexts, often relying on abstraction, ambiguity, and interpretive flexibility [3]. This stands in tension with requirements engineering, which depends on explicit distinctions and clear specifications. As legal experts have noted, their role involves interpreting legal provisions to ensure compliance and mitigate legal risk, while also supporting software engineers in translating those provisions into system specifications [3]. These different approaches to RDPRs create friction, particularly when stakeholders do not share an explicitly defined ontological commitment structuring the domain [30]. The absence of such shared conceptual grounding leads to undesirable requirements engineering practices, especially in cross-functional and interdisciplinary settings [30].

To the best of our knowledge, few international artifacts provide a clear conceptual account of RDPRs across jurisdictions that could support the analysis of TPDF. As a result, stakeholders lack adequate resources to identify, model, and discuss the RDPRs that are common across regulations, as well as those that remain jurisdiction-specific. Convention 108(+) remains the only internationally binding legal instrument addressing data protection requirements across jurisdictions. However, little to no work has examined this instrument from a conceptual modeling perspective. This paper addresses that gap by proposing an ontology of common RDPRs across jurisdictions for TPDF. The resulting ontology is intended to provide a foundational conceptual basis for supporting cross-functional and cross-cultural teams in analyzing, discussing, and modeling regulatory data protection requirements across jurisdictions.

3 Related Work

The use of ontologies to support compliance, particularly in data protection, is well established [11,23]. Existing work, however, often addresses privacy requirements broadly, including requirements that may originate from regulations, users, or organizational concerns [1]. In contrast, regulatory data protection requirements derive from legal instruments [1,7,23]. This paper focuses on Regulatory Data Protection Requirements (RDPRs) rather than on privacy requirements in general.

RDPRs are difficult to elicit, interpret, and translate into information systems [4,15], especially in international settings [6]. These difficulties are associated with the lack of common ground among stakeholders [26], divergent mental models [15], lack of empathy [5], limited awareness [4], and misaligned responsibilities [4]. Ontologies can help address these issues by making domain distinctions explicit, defining the relevant entities and relations, and supporting a shared understanding among legal, organizational, and technical stakeholders [14].

Several ontologies have been proposed for data protection, with a strong emphasis on the GDPR [20]. The works of [1,7,23] illustrate this tendency, each addressing GDPR-related concepts from a different perspective. This focus is understandable given the influence of the GDPR and the Brussels effect [2]. However, RDPRs vary across jurisdictions and may involve divergent or even conflicting conceptualizations [6]. As a result, GDPR-centered artifacts do not directly provide a jurisdiction-agnostic account of the regulatory requirements that can be treated as common across data protection regimes.

The ontology also relates to broader ontological analyses of social, legal, and requirements concepts. UFO-C [13] provides general accounts of social agents, goals, and social artifacts that offer a broader conceptual context for several notions included in our model. The present work focuses specifically on the role of these notions in characterizing regulatory data protection configurations. UFO-L [12], in turn, provides a richer analysis of legal positions and normative relations, including rights, duties, powers, subjections, and permissions. The present ontology captures only the legal distinctions required by its competency questions and does not attempt to represent the correlates, complete structure, or dynamics of legal positions. Existing work also provides both a general core ontology of requirements [16] and an ontological interpretation of non-functional requirements [25]. In contrast, Requirement is used here in the narrower, domain-specific sense of a reified normative prescription associated with a legal basis or one or more specific strategies and traceable to documents and implementations.

4 Research Method

This work follows SABiO 2.0 [8], which supports the development of ontologies grounded in foundational distinctions and distinguishes between reference and operational ontologies. Since our objective is to provide a reference ontology, the method was applied to produce a well-founded conceptualization of regulatory data protection requirements rather than an implementation-oriented artifact.

In accordance with SABiO 2.0, the ontology development process was organized into three phases: i) requirements elicitation, ii) ontology capture and formalization, and iii) ontology refinement and evaluation. Although these phases are presented sequentially, the process was iterative, as modeling decisions were repeatedly revisited and checked against the ontology requirements and scope.

The first phase concerned requirement elicitation. The ontology requirements were grounded in prior empirical work on regulatory data protection requirements across jurisdictions [19,21], including interviews with 70 lawyers and regulatory analysis, all of which are available on Zenodo at [18]. In this phase, the functional requirements of the ontology were articulated through competency questions, following their established role in ontology engineering as instruments for guiding and evaluating the conceptual content that an ontology should represent [8,9,28]. These competency questions define the scope of the ontology by explicitly stating the conceptual distinctions and classification criteria the ontology must support. Non-functional requirements, such as intended uses and desirable quality properties, were also considered in this phase.

Based on these requirements, the domain conceptualization was captured and formalized using UFO as the foundational basis and OntoUML as the modeling language. This step was used to make explicit the ontological commitments required to consistently represent RDPRs. Primitive concepts were documented separately in the repository to clarify the commitments adopted in the model.

Third, the ontology was refined and evaluated against its requirements and scope. Since the artifact is a reference ontology, this phase did not involve implementation or encoding decisions. Instead, its conceptual adequacy was assessed through competency-question-based verification and the instantiation of a representative scenario.

5 Requirements and Scope

5.1 Scope and Design Principles

The ontology proposed in this paper provides a jurisdiction-agnostic conceptualization of regulatory data protection requirements. Its scope is limited to the core structural distinctions needed to represent the common organization of the domain, including personal data, data subjects, organizational roles, personal data processing, legal bases, rights, and governance structures. It does not aim to exhaust the normative content of any specific regulation, capture jurisdiction-specific doctrinal variation, resolve conflicts between regulations, or provide a directly implementable compliance model.

The ontology was designed to establish a well-founded conceptual basis for legal–technical collaboration and for derivative artifacts such as models, templates, catalogs, and requirement comparison instruments. Its design prioritizes ontological clarity, explicit commitments, separation of commonly conflated entities and relations, jurisdiction-agnostic coverage, and parsimony, including only the structural distinctions needed to answer the competency questions and support the intended uses of the ontology.

5.2 Competency Questions

Table 1 presents the competency questions that define the conceptual scope of the ontology. The questions are formulated at the conceptual level and specify the distinctions and classification criteria that the ontology must make explicit. The competency questions are organized into five groups. The first concerns the relation between individuals, data subjects, and personal data. The second concerns the organizational actors involved in personal data governance and processing, including the roles they assume and the goals associated with processing activities. The third concerns personal data processing itself, including the operations that constitute it and the forms of organizational participation it involves. The fourth concerns the legal grounds for processing and the rights of data subjects. The fifth concerns the governance, security, and traceability structures through which organizations define, operationalize, and monitor personal data processing.

6 The Core Ontology of Privacy and Personal Data Processing

Building on the competency questions defined in Sect. 5.2 and on the ontological foundations presented in the previous Section, this section introduces the Core Ontology of Privacy and Personal Data Processing. The presentation is organized around the main conceptual fragments of the ontology, each capturing a set of closely related distinctions required for a precise representation of the domain. In each case, the focus is on the modeling decisions adopted and the conceptual distinctions they make explicit.

In accordance with UFO, each material relation represented in the ontology is understood as being grounded in a relator and derived from its corresponding mediation relations. Figure 1 explicitly depicts the relators central to the conceptual distinctions discussed in the paper. To preserve the readability of the core diagram, the truthmakers of the remaining material relations are documented in the supplementary material, including their underlying relators, mediation relations, and corresponding derived material relations.

6.1 Individuals and Personal Data

The ontology distinguishes between natural persons, the roles they may contingently play, and the informational entities that may qualify as personal data. NaturalPerson is modeled as a kind, specialized into the phases Living and Deceased. The living phase is further refined into age-dependent phases, which are Child, Adult, ChildUnder13, and ChildOver13, allowing the ontology to represent distinctions that may become normatively relevant in concrete legal settings.

Data is modeled as a kind, with IdentifiableData and NonIdentifiableData as subkinds. PersonalData is not modeled as a rigid subtype of data,

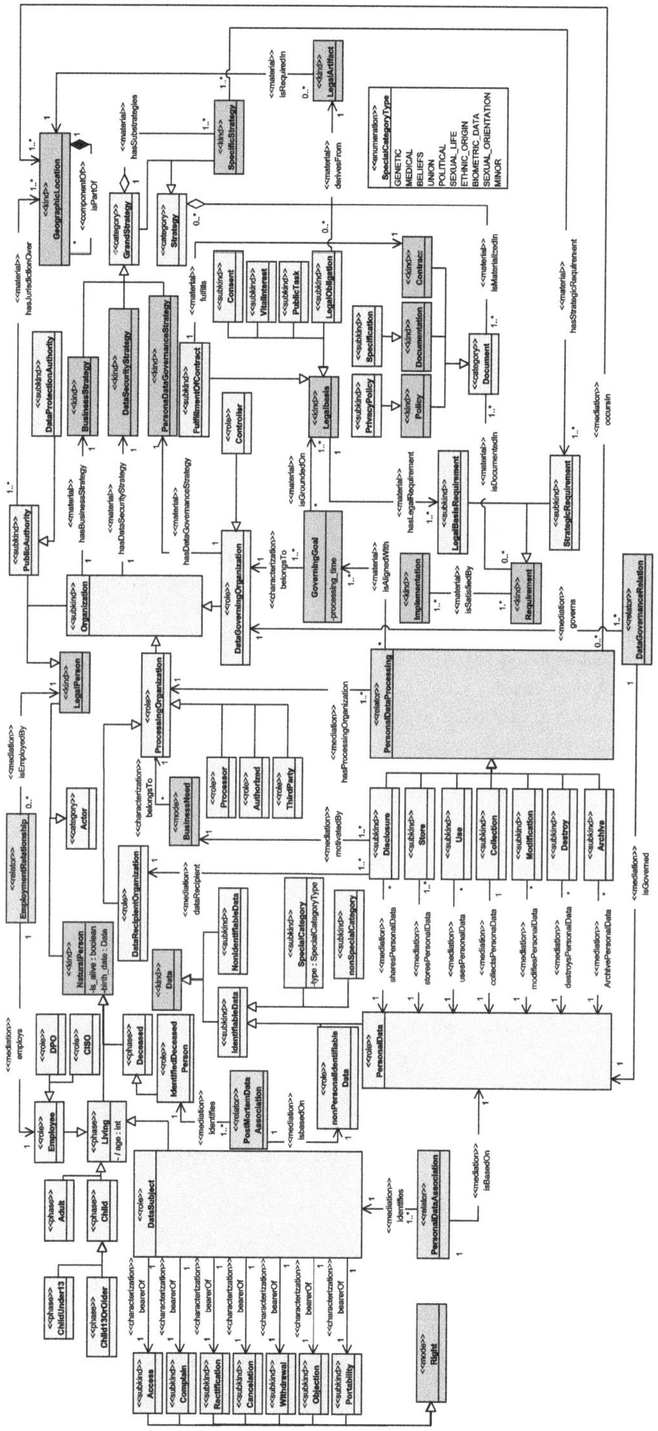

Fig. 1. The proposed Core ontology of privacy and personal Data Processing.

Table 1. Competency questions guiding the development of the ontology. The questions are organized into groups reflecting the main aspects of the domain addressed by the model.

ID	Competency Question	Main Concepts
Individuals and Personal Data		
CQ1	Can personal data exist independently of a data subject?	Personal data and data subject
CQ2	Under which conditions does a data qualify as identifiable data?	Data, identifiable data, and natural person
CQ3	Under which conditions does identifiable data qualify as personal data?	Identifiable data, personal data, natural person, data subject
Organizations and Data Governance Roles		
CQ4	Under which conditions does an organization act as a controller rather than a processor?	Organization, controller, and processor
CQ5	Which organizational roles are responsible for a given personal data processing activity?	Processing organization and personal data processing
CQ6	Which goals motivate a given personal data processing activity?	Personal data processing and goal
Personal Data Processing		
CQ7	Which types of operations constitute personal data processing?	Personal data, personal data processing, and processing organization
CQ8	Can multiple processing activities be performed on the same personal data?	Personal data and personal data processing
CQ9	Can multiple organizations participate in the same personal data processing activity?	Personal data, personal data processing, processing organization
Legal Basis and Data Subject Rights		
CQ10	Which rights hold for a data subject with respect to their personal data?	Personal data, data subject, and right
CQ11	Which types of legal basis can justify personal data processing?	Personal data, personal data processing, and legal basis
CQ12	Can a personal data processing activity be grounded on more than one legal basis?	Personal data, personal data processing, and legal basis
CQ13	Under which conditions can a legal basis be considered satisfied?	Legal basis, requirement, and fulfillment
CQ14	Can a legal basis exist independently from a goal?	Legal basis and goal
Data Governance, Security, and Traceability		
CQ15	What strategies structure personal data governance and security in an organization?	Strategy, personal data, governance, and security
CQ16	Which requirements operationalize personal data governance and security strategies?	Requirement, personal data, governance, and security
CQ17	How are governance and security requirements fulfilled in practice?	Governance, security, requirement, and fulfillment
CQ18	Under which conditions does a processing activity qualify as personal data sharing?	Personal data, personal data processing, sharing
CQ19	How can the motivations behind personal data processing be traced?	Personal data, personal data processing, motivation, and traceability

but as a role played by IDENTIFIABLEDATA when it refers to a DATASUBJECT. In turn, DATASUBJECT is modeled as a role played by a living natural person. This commitment captures that data qualifies as personal data only under a relational configuration involving identifiable data, a living data subject, and the governance and processing context in which that data is collected, stored, and governed. DATA can be of a special category, which we modeled as an enumeration because, within the scope of the ontology, its values constitute a closed set of mutually exclusive classification labels and do not bear additional properties or participate in distinct relations.

EMPLOYEE is grounded in an EMPLOYMENTRELATIONSHIP with a LEGALPERSON, whereas DPO and CISO additionally depend on organization-specific appointments.

6.2 Organizations and Data Governance Roles

The ontology represents institutional actors as LEGALPERSON, which is specialized into ORGANIZATION and PUBLICAUTHORITY. A PUBLICAUTHORITY has jurisdiction over a GEOGRAPHICLOCATION, which may be recursively structured through parthood, thereby avoiding a commitment to any jurisdiction-specific territorial taxonomy. DATAPROTECTIONAUTHORITY specializes PUBLICAUTHORITY and captures authorities whose relevance stems from supervisory and regulatory functions in data protection.

Organizational participation is modeled through roles, following established role-modeling principles [24]. PROCESSINGORGANIZATION is the role played by an organization when it participates in a personal data processing activity. PROCESSOR, AUTHORIZED, and THIRDPARTY are derived subroles, determined by how the organization participates in the processing configuration. For instance, a PROCESSOR acts on behalf of a CONTROLLER. DATARECIPIENTORGANIZATION, in turn, is characterized by receiving personal data through a DISCLOSURE. By contrast, DATAGOVERNINGORGANIZATION is the role played by an organization that governs personal data through a DATAGOVERNANCERELATION. CONTROLLER specializes DATAGOVERNINGORGANIZATION. Thus, controller and processor are not modeled as interchangeable labels: the former belongs to the governance dimension, whereas the latter belongs to the processing-participation dimension. A DATAGOVERNINGORGANIZATION also bears GOVERNINGGOAL(s), which orient processing activities to conform to its governance strategy.

6.3 Personal Data Processing

PERSONALDATAPROCESSING is modeled as a relator connecting personal data and the organization that processes it. It is specialized into COLLECTION, STORE, USE, MODIFICATION, DISCLOSURE, ARCHIVE, and DESTROY. These specializations capture the main types of operations required by the competency questions. They are modeled as classes because processing types have distinct relational structures and constraints. The ontology also commits to a minimal processing structure: each instance of PERSONALDATA participates in exactly one COLLECTION and in at least one STORE. Other forms of processing may occur depending on the case.

Disclosure is treated as a special form of personal data processing in which personal data is communicated. This requires the participation of a DataRecipientOrganization, modeled as a role specializing ProcessingOrganization. The ontology also relates Disclosure to a BusinessNeed, which captures the organizational motivation for extending the processing configuration beyond the original organization. Under this commitment, a processing activity qualifies as personal data sharing when it is a Disclosure involving a recipient organization and the disclosed personal data.

6.4 Legal Basis and Data Subject Rights

The ontology represents the legal layer of processing through LegalBasis, modeled as a kind and specialized into Consent, VitalInterest, PublicTask, LegalObligation, and FulfillmentOfContract. FulfillmentOfContract is associated with Contract, while LegalObligation is associated with LegalArtifact, whose applicability is situated with respect to a GeographicLocation. GoverningGoal(s) are grounded in LegalBasis, thereby making explicit that the goals orienting data governance must rest on juridical grounds.

The documentation layer is captured through Document, which is specialized into Policy, Documentation, and Contract, with Specification refining Documentation. These classes represent the artifacts through which legal bases, requirements, and implementations are expressed and stabilized.

Finally, Right is modeled as a mode inhering in DataSubject, with specializations such as Access, Rectification, Cancelation, Objection, Withdrawal, Complain, and Portability. These specializations are modeled as classes because they denote distinct types of legally dependent modes inhering in a DataSubject. Rights are therefore not isolated legal objects, but as dependent moments of the data subject within a governed personal-data configuration.

6.5 Data Governance, Security, and Traceability

The ontology captures the strategic layer via Strategy, which is specialized into GrandStrategy and SpecificStrategy. BusinessStrategy, DataSecurityStrategy, and PersonalDataGovernanceStrategy are modeled as grand strategies. The first two belong to Organization, whereas PersonalDataGovernanceStrategy belongs to DataGoverningOrganization, linking strategy directly to the governance roles introduced above.

A Requirement denotes a reified normative prescription with its own identity and identifiable prescriptive content. Requirements make explicit, at a finer level of granularity, normative conditions associated with a legal basis or prescriptions established by one or more specific strategies. Requirements can be referred to and traced independently of any particular Document or Implementation. Documents express or further specify requirements, whereas Implementations satisfy them. A Requirement remains the same across changes in its documentary representation or supporting implementations, provided that its prescriptive content remains unchanged. LegalBasisRequirement and StrategicRequirement are modeled as disjoint subkinds. Each LegalBasisRequirement arises from exactly one LegalBasis, preventing a single legal requirement from combining conditions associated with different legal justifications. By contrast, a StrategicRequirement arises from one or more SpecificStrategies, since different strategies may overlap and establish the same prescription.

The documentary layer is captured through Document, which is specialized into Policy, Documentation, and Contract, with Specification refining Documentation. This structure provides the basis for traceability: processing activities are aligned with governing goals; governing goals are grounded in legal bases; grand strategies are decomposed into specific strategies; legal bases and specific strategies give rise to requirements; and requirements are expressed or further specified in documents and satisfied by implementations. A processing configuration can therefore be traced across its organizational, legal, strategic, documentary, and implementation dimensions.

7 Evaluation

The ontology was evaluated in two steps, each addressing a different aspect of its adequacy. First, we verified whether it provides the internal conceptual requirements expressed by the competency questions. Second, we examined whether its distinctions remain coherent and understandable when used in representative privacy scenarios. These steps assess if the ontology covers its conceptual completeness and its applicability.

7.1 Competency Question-Based Verification

To assess whether the ontology satisfies its internal conceptual requirements, we conducted a competency question-based verification. The purpose of this step was to examine whether the ontology provides the classes, relationships, and constraints required to make explicit the conceptual distinctions presupposed by the competency questions defined in Sect. 5.2.

To this end, we systematically analyzed the defined competency questions by identifying, for each of them: **i)** the conceptual distinctions they presuppose and **ii)** the corresponding modeling constructs that make these distinctions explicit in the ontology. The full verification of all competency questions is available as openly accessible supplementary material on Zenodo for transparency [18]. Here, we focus on a representative subset to illustrate how the ontology supports different kinds of conceptual requirements.

CQ1: Can personal data exist independently of a data subject? This question requires the ontology to distinguish personal data from the subject to whom the data refers, and to make explicit the dependence that holds between them. The ontology addresses this question by modeling PersonalData and

DataSubject as roles connected through a relator (i.e., PersonalDataAssociation), thereby making explicit their existential dependence. Under this commitment, an instance of IdentifiableData instantiates the PersonalData role only insofar as it participates in a PersonalDataAssociation with a DataSubject. The underlying data item may persist without instantiating this role if that relational condition ceases to hold.

CQ18: Under which conditions does a processing activity qualify as personal data sharing? This question requires the ontology to make explicit what distinguishes personal data sharing from personal data processing in general, and under which conditions a processing activity instantiates that more specific type. It must therefore distinguish the general processing relation from the particular case in which personal data is communicated from one organization to another, while also representing the additional organizational role required for such communication to occur. The ontology addresses this question by modeling Disclosure as a specialization of PersonalDataProcessing. A Disclosure is characterized by the participation of a ProcessingOrganization that performs the activity and a DataRecipientOrganization to which the disclosed data is sent. Moreover, the ontology also associates the Disclosure with a BusinessNeed, making explicit the organizational motivation for that particular sharing. Under this commitment, a PersonalDataProcessing activity qualifies as personal data sharing when it instantiates the Disclosure subkind and includes a recipient organization to whom the personal data is communicated.

The full CQ-by-CQ verification, publicly available on Zenodo, provides evidence that the ontology contains the modeling constructs required to address the conceptual requirements captured by the competency questions.

7.2 Instantiation of a Representative Scenario

To complement the competency question-based verification, we instantiate the ontology for the following representative data-protection **scenario**:

Inkfold is a Portuguese startup that provides users with access to a catalog of Portuguese comic books through an online platform. Access to the platform is free, but requires users to consent to the processing of their personal data for the provision of its core functionalities. Inkfold also offers an optional purchasing feature, allowing users to buy comic books directly on the platform with a credit card. Since access to comics is tailored according to age, the platform distinguishes between child and adult users.

The scenario is analyzed through a specific case involving cross-border disclosure of personal data from Inkfold to Veridata, highlighting the ontology's ability to distinguish personal data processing in general from disclosure to a foreign organization.

Cross-Border Disclosure to a Foreign Organization. The instantiation of this scenario is shown in Fig. 2. Inkfold and Veridata are represented as

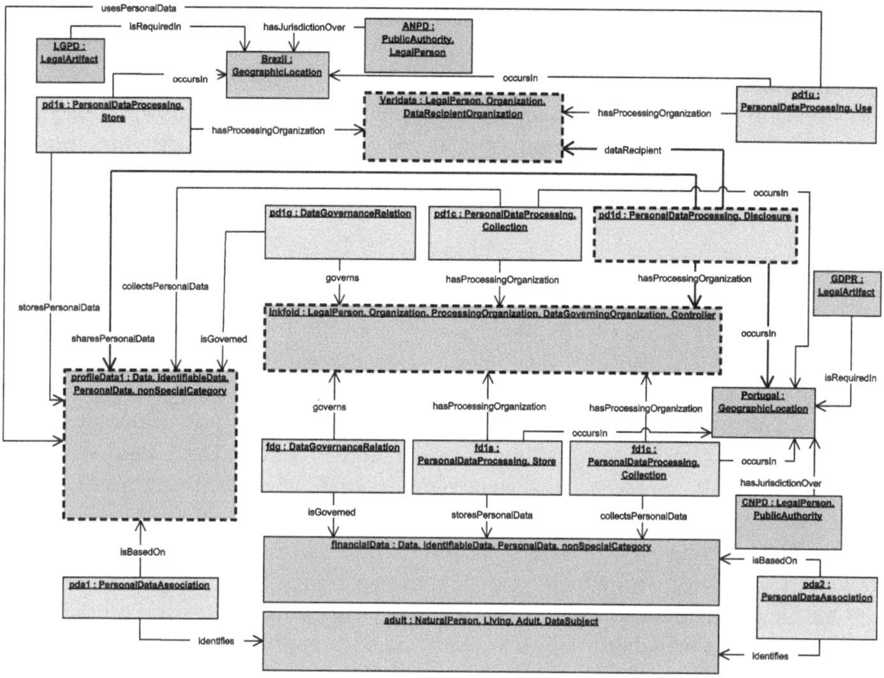

Fig. 2. Instantiation of the representative scenario: cross-border disclosure of personal data.

legal entities. Inkfold plays the roles of PROCESSINGORGANIZATION, DATAGOVERNINGORGANIZATION, and CONTROLLER, while Veridata plays the role of DATARECIPIENTORGANIZATION. These roles hold in virtue of their participation in specific personal data processing and governance relations. Portugal and Brazil are instantiated as GEOGRAPHICLOCATIONS, together with the corresponding legal artifacts and public authorities: the GDPR and the CNPD in the Portuguese/EU setting, and the LGPD and the ANPD in the Brazilian setting.

The disclosed data is represented as *profileData1*, an instance of DATA, IDENTIFIABLEDATA, PERSONALDATA, and NONSPECIALCATEGORY. This instance captures the user profile information that Inkfold disclosed to Veridata for storage in Brazil. By contrast, *financialData* is represented separately, since it is collected and stored by Inkfold but is not disclosed to Veridata.

The disclosure relation is represented by *pd1d*, an instance of PERSONALDATAPROCESSING specialized as DISCLOSURE. This relator mediates the disclosed personal data, the processing organization, and the recipient organization. The model clearly separates Veridata's participation in the processing of profile data received through disclosure from the financial data, which remains under Inkfold.

This instantiation shows that cross-border disclosure depends on a configuration involving a personal data item, a disclosure relator, participating organizations, and their locations in different jurisdictions. The compliance concern arises from this configuration as a whole: Inkfold governs and discloses personal data from the Portuguese/EU context, while Veridata stores and processes that data in Brazil. The instantiation illustrates how the model can make explicit the configuration in which a processing arrangement constitutes cross-jurisdictional disclosure and, consequently, the point at which applicable RDPRs may need to be reassessed.

8 Discussion

This work contributes to the identification and formalization of Regulatory Data Protection Requirements (RDPRs) through a jurisdiction-agnostic ontology grounded in UFO. The ontology distinguishes RDPRs from privacy requirements and provides a conceptual basis for analyzing transborder personal data flows. This distinction is important because RDPRs derive from legal and regulatory instruments, while privacy requirements may originate from broader organizational, technical, or user-centered concerns. In information systems engineering, conflating these two classes of requirements can obscure which obligations are legally grounded and which concerns belong to privacy design more generally.

Our contribution also differs from most existing data protection ontologies in its empirical and jurisdictional basis. The ontology is grounded in regulatory text and legal language, and informed by empirical research involving over 70 lawyers and multiple regulations. While other ontologies, such as PrOnto, are also based on legal sources, they typically focus on a single regulation. This work instead conceptualizes requirements common across regulations, making it one of the few jurisdiction-agnostic ontologies for regulatory data protection requirements.

The ontology addresses a recurring difficulty in translating data protection law into information system specifications by making explicit that several compliance-relevant notions are role-dependent, relational, and context-sensitive. A data item qualifies as personal data in virtue of its association with a data subject; its compliance relevance then depends on the governance and processing configurations in which it participates. Similarly, an organization qualifies as a controller, processor, data recipient, or data governing body based on its role in data governance or processing. These commitments are relevant because treating such notions as fixed labels can obscure their dependence on specific governance and processing configurations.

The same point applies to the processing of personal data. Modeling the processing as a relator makes the processing configuration itself the unit of analysis: an operation over personal data, performed by a processing organization, under a governance structure. This allows the ontology to distinguish collection, storage, use, and disclosure without reducing them to informal variants of data handling. It also allows processing to be connected to governing goals, legal bases, business needs, requirements, documents, and implementations. The relevant contribution is the explicit articulation of the chain from processing to purpose, from purpose to legal basis, and from legal basis to requirements and implementations.

The representative scenario illustrates how these ontological commitments structure the representation of a data protection situation. In the cross-border disclosure view, the relevant issue is the configuration that governs how Inkfold discloses profile data to Veridata, a recipient organization located in another jurisdiction. The model makes explicit the data disclosed, the processing organization, the recipient organization, the business need motivating the disclosure, and the jurisdictional context in which the disclosure occurs. In the governing-goal and legal-basis view, the same scenario shows that Inkfold processes profile data and financial data under different governing goals and legal bases: platform access is grounded in consent, whereas shopping is grounded in contract fulfillment. These distinctions make explicit several dimensions along which applicable RDPRs may differ: when data is disclosed to another organization, when processing is aligned with a different goal, or when that goal is grounded on a different legal basis.

From a requirements engineering and conceptual modeling perspective, the ontology provides an explicit conceptualization of the elements and relations involved in RDPRs. This conceptualization could serve as a shared reference for legal, organizational, and technical stakeholders, although its effectiveness in cross-functional and interdisciplinary settings remains to be evaluated. It provides an explicit account of the key elements that could inform activities across the requirements lifecycle, including which data is involved, who governs it, who processes it, what operation is performed, what goal motivates the processing, what legal basis grounds that goal, what jurisdictional context applies, and how the resulting requirements are documented and implemented.

The jurisdiction-agnostic character of the ontology is aligned with a two-level view of requirements for transborder personal data flows, as we proposed in [21]. At level 1, requirements common across jurisdictions are represented through a shared conceptual structure. At level 2, jurisdiction-specific requirements, interpretations, and constraints are introduced. This ontology contributes to level 1 by formalizing the common RDPR structures. In this sense, it provides a reusable foundation for comparing regulations and for identifying where jurisdiction-specific extensions are required. We acknowledge that local regulations may have different conceptualizations of specific aspects. These differences are part of the level 2 requirements.

The ontology can also serve as a conceptual baseline for compliance-oriented artifacts across regulations. It could serve as a conceptual basis for the future development of requirements catalogs, modeling patterns, regulatory comparison frameworks, ontology-based knowledge graphs, and tool-supported compliance representations. These artifacts should not be seen as replacements for legal analysis. Their value lies in preserving explicit ontological commitments when legal requirements are translated into technical and organizational specifications.

The evaluation conducted in this work supports claims about the ontology's conceptual coverage and representational applicability. The competency questions assess whether the ontology captures the intended domain distinctions, while the representative scenario illustrates how its concepts and relations can be instantiated to analyze a data protection situation. These evaluations provide initial evidence of the ontology's suitability as a conceptual foundation for requirements engineering and compliance-oriented applications. Further application-based evaluation could examine its use by practitioners and its integration into concrete requirements and compliance artifacts.

The main limitation of the ontology follows from its structural scope. The model focuses on identity, classification, dependence, mediation, governance, and traceability. It includes goals and business needs only insofar as they are needed to explain the motivation and justification of processing configurations. It does not yet provide a full account of events, temporal evolution, or compliance dynamics. Consequently, phenomena such as the execution of processing operations, the exercise of data subject rights, the creation and termination of obligations, and the satisfaction or violation of requirements over time remain outside the scope of the present model.

The modeling analysis suggests that ambiguity in regulatory data protection requirements may arise not only from terminology but also from underspecified ontological commitments. When stakeholders lack an explicit account of what personal data requirements are, such as actors, legal basis, rights, among others, they may appear to agree while relying on incompatible conceptualizations. The ontology provides an explicit basis for discussing, modeling, and formalizing RDPRs across jurisdictions. By making the adopted ontological commitments explicit, it is intended to help reduce conceptual ambiguity in requirements engineering and to support the development of more coherent information systems for transborder personal data flows.

9 Conclusions and Future Work

This paper presented a jurisdiction-agnostic reference ontology for Regulatory Data Protection Requirements (RDPRs) in transborder personal data flows. Grounded in UFO and developed following SABiO 2.0, the ontology distinguishes RDPRs from broader privacy requirements and provides a conceptual basis for representing requirements common across jurisdictions.

The main contribution is a set of explicit ontological commitments for representing RDPRs independently of any single regulation. These commitments support a precise account of how processing configurations are governed, justified, and traced to requirements and implementations. The ontology was evaluated using competency-question-based verification and a representative scenario. The evaluation showed that the ontology makes explicit distinctions that are often implicit or conflated in legal and technical discourse.

Future work will extend the ontology with an event-based layer for processing occurrences and compliance-relevant changes, and a refined normative layer for obligations, permissions, prohibitions, institutional acts, and satisfaction conditions. We will also operationalize the reference ontology and evaluate derived artifacts in application-based tasks involving legal and technical practitioners.

Use of AI. This paper used Grammarly for correcting orthography and grammar. All the decisions are ultimately of the authors. No other usage of AI is declared by the authors.

Data Availability statement and Acknowledgments. All the data is available at [18].
This work was supported by the Universitat Politècnica de València through grant PAID-06-24 and by the European Union through the Horizon Europe BETTER project (grant agreement No. 101136262) and the Horizon 2020 Marie Skłodowska-Curie Actions (grant agreement No. 101081455).

References

1. Bartolini, C.: Using ontologies to model data protection requirements in workflows. In: JSAI International Symposium on Artificial Intelligence, pp. 233–248. Springer, Heidelberg (2015). https://doi.org/10.1007/978-3-319-50953-2_17
2. Bradford, A.: The Brussels Effect: How the European Union Rules the World. Oxford University Press (2020)
3. Breaux, T.D.: Legal accountability as software quality: a us data processing perspective. In: 2022 IEEE 30th International Requirements Engineering Conference (RE), pp. 101–113. IEEE (2022)
4. Dalela, A.: A study on security and privacy practices in Danish companies. In: Proceedings of Usable Security on Privacy Symposium, pp. 1–9 (2022)
5. Devathasan, K., et al.: Empathy, self-determination and motivation: moderating diversity for enhanced performance in software development teams. Empir. Softw. Eng. **30**(3), 82 (2025)
6. for Economic Co-operation, O., Development: Cross-border data flows: taking stock of key policies and initiative (2022). https://doi.org/10.1787/5031dd97-en
7. El Ghosh, M.: Capturing the basics of the gdpr in a well-founded legal domain modular ontology. In: Formal Ontology in Information Systems, IOS Press (2021)
8. Falbo, R.D.A.: Sabio: systematic approach for building ontologies. In: CEUR (2014)
9. Falbo, R.A., de Menezes, C.S., da Rocha, A.R.C.: A Systematic approach for building ontologies. In: Coelho, H. (ed.) IBERAMIA 1998. LNCS (LNAI), vol. 1484, pp. 349–360. Springer, Heidelberg (1998). https://doi.org/10.1007/3-540-49795-1_31
10. for Fundamental Rights, E.U.A.: Handbook on European data protection law: 2018 Edition. Council of Europe (2018)
11. Gharib, M., et al.: An ontology for privacy requirements via a systematic literature review. J. Data Semant. **9**(4), 123–149 (2020)
12. Griffo, C., et al.: Conceptual Modeling of Legal Relations, pp. 169–183. Springer, Heidelberg (2018). https://doi.org/10.1007/978-3-030-00847-5_14
13. Guizzardi, G., et al.: Grounding software domain ontologies in the unified foundational ontology (ufo): the case of the ode software process ontology. In: Conferencia Iberoamericana de Software Engineering (2008). https://api.semanticscholar.org/CorpusID:32490124
14. Guizzardi, G., et al.: UFO: unified foundational ontology. Appl. Ontol. **17**(1), 167–210 (2022). https://doi.org/10.3233/AO-210256. https://journals.sagepub.com/action/showAbstract

15. Hadar, I., et al.: Privacy by designers: software developers' privacy mindset. Empir. Softw. Eng. **23**(1), 259–289 (2017). https://doi.org/10.1007/s10664-017-9517-1
16. Jureta, I.J., et al.: A core ontology for requirements. Appl. Ontol. **4**(3–4), 169–244 (2009). https://doi.org/10.3233/ao-2009-0069
17. Kuner, C.: Regulation of transborder data flows under data protection and privacy law: past, present, and future. TILT Law & Technology Working Paper (016) (2010)
18. Negri-Ribalta, C.: Obi-pia data set - ontology-based method for interdisciplinary data protection impact assessment (2026). https://doi.org/10.5281/ZENODO.15166882. https://zenodo.org/doi/10.5281/zenodo.15166882
19. Negri-Ribalta, C., et al.: Comparing and conceptualizing data protection requirements worldwide for privacy regulatory compliance (2026). https://arxiv.org/abs/2607.22270
20. Negri-Ribalta, C., et al.: Understanding the gdpr from a requirements engineering perspective—a systematic mapping study on regulatory data protection requirements. Requir. Eng. **29**(4), 523–549 (2024)
21. Negri-Ribalta, C.: Towards evidence-based conceptual modeling for international data protection requirements. In: 2025 IEEE 33rd International Requirements Engineering Conference Workshops (REW), pp. 233–242. IEEE (2025)
22. Ortiz Mesías, L., et al.: Repensando el derecho al olvido y la necesidad de su consagración legal en chile. Revista chilena de derecho y tecnología **10**(1), 77–109 (2021)
23. Palmirani, M., et al.: Pronto: privacy ontology for legal reasoning. In: Kő, A., Francesconi, E. (eds.) Electronic Government and the Information Systems Perspective, pp. 139–152. Springer, Cham (2018). https://doi.org/10.1007/978-3-319-98349-3_11
24. Prince, S.T., et al.: Anti-Patterns in Ontology-Driven Conceptual Modeling: The Case of Role Modeling in OntoUML. IOS Press (2016). https://doi.org/10.3233/978-1-61499-676-7-161
25. Renata, G., et al.: An Ontological Interpretation of Non-Functional Requirements. IOS Press (2014). https://doi.org/10.3233/978-1-61499-438-1-344
26. Sutcliffe, A.: Collaborative requirements engineering: bridging the gulfs between worlds. In: Intentional Perspectives on Information Systems Engineering, pp. 355–376. Springer, Heidelberg (2010). https://doi.org/10.1007/978-3-642-12544-7_20
27. Trade, U., (UNCTAD), D.: Global cyberlaw tracker (2026). https://unctad.org/topic/ecommerce-and-digital-economy/ecommerce-law-reform/summary-adoption-e-commerce-legislation-worldwide
28. Uschold, M., et al.: Ontologies: principles, methods and applications. Knowl. Eng. Rev. **11**(2), 93–136 (1996)
29. Voss, W.G.: Cross-border data flows, the gdpr, and data governance. Wash. Int'l LJ **29**, 485 (2019)
30. Werner, C.: The lack of shared understanding of non-functional requirements in continuous software engineering: accidental or essential? In: 2020 IEEE 28th International Requirements Engineering Conference (RE), pp. 90–101. IEEE (2020)

Foundational and Reference Ontologies

What Secrets Are: Toward a Formal Ontology of Secrecy

Alexandra Rowland[1,2](✉), Glenda Moura Amaral[1], Giancarlo Guizzardi[1], Tiago Prince Sales[1], and Rob Lemmens[1]

[1] University of Twente, Enschede, The Netherlands
a.c.s.j.rowland@utwente.nl
[2] Kadaster, Apeldoorn, The Netherlands

Abstract. Access control, privacy engineering, and confidentiality frameworks are fundamentally concerned with managing who knows what and depend on the ability to reason about the active maintenance of ignorance, yet none provides a formal ontological account of the social-intentional phenomenon that underpins them. Without this, these systems can specify the normative surface of concealment without being able to reason about the beliefs, goals, and commitments that constitute and sustain it. This gap is addressed by taking a social-intentional approach and modelling secrecy not as an epistemic state but as an actively produced and maintained condition grounded in the intentional and social structure of the agents involved. This paper presents a formal ontology of secrecy grounded in the Unified Foundational Ontology (UFO) and specified in OntoUML, supporting interoperability with existing ontologies for trust, value, risk, and prevention. The secret is modelled as a social-intentional relator constituted by a Consequential Belief, or the agent's goal-grounded assessment of the risk that revelation poses, and a commitment to maintaining nescience, situated within a trust structure derived from ONTrust and a risk and prevention structure grounded in COVER. The resulting ontology distinguishes Secret Owners, Holders, and Keepers; models weak and strong trust as grounding different levels of normative obligation; and characterises secret-keeping as a distributed preventive structure in which every Keeper contributes an antidote to the collective risk of revelation. The result is a reusable ontological module that fills a foundational gap in information systems design by providing the intentional structure that existing frameworks implicitly depend on but do not themselves supply.

Keywords: secrecy · trust · commitment · privacy · formal ontology · ontology driven conceptual modelling · information control

1 Introduction

Secrecy pervades information systems. Trade secrets govern what organisations disclose to competitors. Security clearances determine who may access classified information. Medical confidentiality constrains what clinicians may share

© The Author(s), under exclusive license to Springer Nature Switzerland AG 2027
A. Bernasconi et al. (Eds.): ER 2026, LNCS 17081, pp. 165–181, 2027.
https://doi.org/10.1007/978-3-032-40795-5_10

with third parties. Consent mechanisms regulate what data processors may do with personal information. In each case, some agents are actively maintaining the ignorance of others with respect to certain information and the correctness, robustness, and trustworthiness of these arrangements depends on the ability to reason precisely about this structure. Yet despite its pervasiveness, secrecy has received no formal ontological treatment that would render its structure precise, modular, and reusable across domains: existing frameworks operate at the normative surface, specifying what agents may or may not do with information without modelling the intentional and social structure through which it is actively concealed. A system so built can record that consent has been withdrawn without reasoning about what normatively remains, enumerate the parties to a processing chain without identifying which bear ungoverned Revelation Dispositions, and specify a confidentiality obligation without saying what it protects or why—so that privacy violations go undetected, insider threats remain invisible to access control, and withdrawal leaves residual obligations ungoverned, the intentional structure beneath them being unmodelled. This gap is addressed by presenting a formal ontology of secrecy, named SECRET, grounded in the Unified Foundational Ontology (UFO) [7] and specified in OntoUML; grounding modelling decisions and supporting formal interoperability with existing ontologies for trust, value, risk, and prevention.

The paper makes the following contributions: the secret modelled as a social-intentional «relator» constituted by a Consequential Belief and a commitment to maintaining nescience, extending Ismail and Shafie [15]; the Revelation Disposition as a present structural vulnerability grounded in COVER [19]; a trust and delegation structure derived from ONTrust [2]; and secret-keeping characterised as a distributed preventive structure in Baratella et al.'s [3] terms. Together, these establish a reusable ontological module positioning secrecy as the foundational intentional substrate for any formal account of information control.

The remainder of the paper is structured as follows. Section 2 introduces the relevant background on UFO and ontology-driven conceptual modelling. Section 3 surveys related work. Section 4 develops the formal ontology of secrecy in four stages: the secret core, sharing secrets, trust in secret-keeping, and prevention and concealment. Section 4.3 illustrates the ontology's applicability through a privacy specialisation and a concrete application to consent withdrawal. Section 5 discusses the implications of the analysis and identifies directions for future work. Section 6 concludes.

2 Background

Unified Foundational Ontology (UFO). UFO is a formal foundational ontology providing rigorous theoretical foundations for conceptual modelling [7]. UFO is organised into three incrementally layered strata. UFO-A provides an ontology of endurants—entities that persist through time—distinguishing between *substantials* (existentially independent entities) and *moments* (existentially dependent entities that inhere in other individuals). Moments are further divided into *intrinsic moments*, which depend on a single bearer, and *relators*, which depend on two or more distinct individuals simultaneously and serve as truth-makers of material relations. UFO-B [1,12] extends UFO-A with an ontology of events and introduces *dispositions*. These are modes whose manifestation under triggering conditions gives rise to events. UFO-C [8,13] builds on both layers to address intentional and social entities, covering beliefs, desires, intentions, goals, commitments, claims, and social relators. A *social relator* constitutes one or more commitment-claim pairs; the social moments that related agents acquire in virtue of their norm-governed relationship [7,8]. The formal analysis in this paper is conducted within the tradition of *ontology-driven conceptual modelling (ODCM)*, which employs ontological theories to develop engineering artefacts that make the ontological commitments of conceptual models explicit [11]. The central methodological practice applied here is *ontological unpacking* [10]: the analysis of a domain concept by exposing the ontological structure it presupposes. The modelling language used is OntoUML [9], an ontologically well-founded extension of UML whose stereotypes and constraints directly reflect the distinctions of UFO.

Philosophical and Sociological Foundations. Simmel's [20] foundational treatment identifies secrecy as an active social form, or the deliberate management of an epistemic gap, rather than a mere absence of knowledge, and identifies the structural impulse toward betrayal as an inherent feature of secret-keeping arrangements. Marx and Muschert [16] extend this framework into a sociology of information, characterising secrecy as an active relational practice of information control and drawing attention to the role of trust as a necessary condition for sharing information under incomplete knowledge. Bok [4] distinguishes secrecy from privacy on the grounds that secrecy is characterised by intentional concealment rather than a diffuse interest in controlling access to oneself, and argues that the moral weight of a secret derives from the potential harm its revelation would cause. Together, these works establish the concepts central to the formal analysis developed here: the distinction between the propositional content of a secret and the social structure surrounding it, the active and relational nature of concealment, the role of nescience, and the belief structure motivating concealment.

Ontological Treatments of Adjacent Phenomena. Two bodies of ontological work are directly relevant to the present analysis. On trust and social commitment, the social relator pattern foundational to this work originates in the ODE Software Process Ontology [8], which demonstrated how UFO-C's social commitments and claims can be bundled within relators to model norm-governed relationships between agents. The ONTrust framework [2] provides a comprehensive reference ontology of trust grounded in UFO-C, formally characterising trust as a mental moment inhering in a trustor with respect to a trustee's disposition or intention to perform an action. ONTrust distinguishes social trust, grounded in interpersonal assessment, from institution-based trust, mediated by formal agreements, and characterises trust as involving the trustor's willingness to be vulnerable to the trustee's behaviour. On risk, value and prevention, the Common Ontology of Value and Risk (COVER) [19] grounds risk in UFO, establishing that something can only be at risk if it is of value to some agent with respect to their goals, formalising a risk experience as involving a threat event with the potential to cause a loss event that negatively impacts an agent's goals. Baratella et al. [3] propose a UFO-based ontology of prevention, distinguishing active countermeasures from antidotes, which suppress a disposition entirely to prevent triggering. Both frameworks are applied in the present work to model the risk structure of secret-keeping and the preventive role of commitment.

3 Related Work

Formal Treatments of Secrecy. The most significant prior formal treatment of secrets to the present work is that of Ismail and Shafie [15], who formalise secrets as a five-way relation between a proposition, a group of Secret Keepers, a group of Nescients, a condition of secrecy, and a time point. The authors provide necessary and sufficient conditions for this relation to hold and develop a logical language incorporating belief, intention and revelation to derive a typology of secrets. A complementary tradition in computer science approaches secrecy as an information-flow property of multi-agent systems. Halpern and O'Neill [14] define secrecy in terms of an agent's knowledge using the runs-and-systems framework, capturing the epistemic surface of concealment through notions of non-deducibility and probabilistic independence. While this line of work provides precise tools for reasoning about information flow in computational systems, it treats secrecy as a property of system states rather than as a social-intentional structure. The present work takes Ismail and Shafie's logical treatment as its point of departure and provides the ontological grounding necessary for semantic interoperability, principled reuse and integration with broader ontological frameworks for social, intentional and normative phenomena.

Privacy and Confidentiality Ontologies. PrOnto [18] models the core conceptual structure of the GDPR, including agent roles, processing purposes and deontic operations for rights and duties, with the aim of supporting legal reasoning and compliance checking. The Ontology for Protection of Personal Data (OPPD) [5] takes a similar GDPR-oriented approach but grounds its modelling in UFO, applying ontology-based conceptual modelling practices and reusing patterns from UFO-L [6]. Both ontologies operate at the normative level, modelling the permissibility of information flows, and do not address the intentional and social structure through which agents actively maintain the ignorance of others. The present work operates at a more foundational level, providing the intentional substrate that such normative frameworks implicitly rely on.

4 SECRET: A Formal Ontology of Secrecy

Taking Ismail and Shafie's [15] five-way logical relation as its point of departure, the present analysis asks what kind of entity a secret is, what constitutes it, and how its components are ontologically structured.

4.1 The SECRET Core

Secretum vs. Secret. Implicit in Ismail and Shafie's definitions [15] is a distinction between the propositional content of a secret and the social structure that maintains it as needing to be concealed. The propositional content, the date of birth of a person, the contents of a military map, whether a patient has a certain condition, for example; is nothing inherently secret. What transitions a proposition from a statement of fact to a secret is the social-intentional structure surrounding it. Figure 1 presents the result of unpacking this structure.

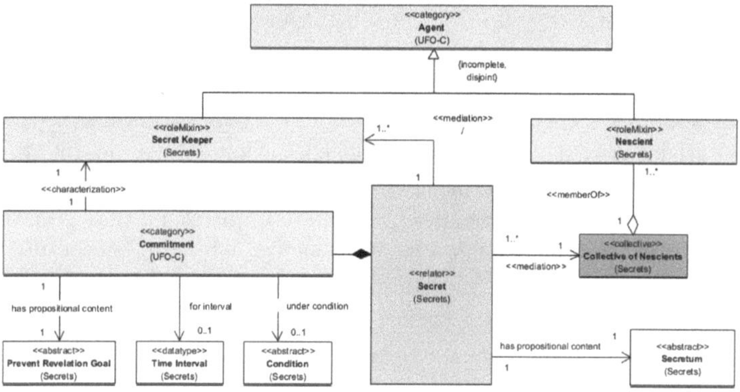

Fig. 1. Social-intentional structure of the secret core modelled in OntoUML.

The propositional content is modelled as an «abstract» entity, the *Secretum*, while the secret itself is modelled as a «relator». This is a first and important ontological commitment; the alternative of treating the proposition as playing the role of a secret relative to a surrounding social-intentional structure is unavailable because roles are relationally dependent constructs that presuppose this relator structure in this domain. The Secretum, as an abstract individual, exists outside of time and space and remains true or false independently of whether any agent believes it or acts on it. The proposition *Anna has received a serious medical diagnosis*, for example, existed before Anna formed any intention to conceal it and will continue to exist after the secret ceases to hold. The Secret, by contrast, is a concrete endurant. It comes into being, persists through time, and ceases to exist either when the Nescient collective is dissolved or when the Secret Owner in whom the Consequential Belief inheres ceases to exist: in the case of an individual, upon their death; in the case of an organisation, upon its dissolution. The same Secretum can ground multiple distinct secrets; Anna's friend and her employer may independently keep her diagnosis from different groups for different reasons, each with their own Keeper collective, Nescient collective, and motivating goals. This would be unrepresentable if secret and Secretum were the same entity.

Nescience. Ismail and Shafie [15] identify nescience as a necessary condition for a secret. A Nescient is an agent who does not believe the Secretum and whom the Keeper intends should not come to believe it; belief is taken here, rather than knowledge in the justified-true-belief sense, as the operative attitude throughout, the Secretum's truth value being bracketed, so that an agent who believes a false Secretum, or a true one without justification, is on this account no longer a Nescient. It is not sufficient that a collective happens not to believe the Secretum, for the Keeper must intend that they should not come to, and this intentional orientation is captured through a *commitment* inhering in the Secret Keeper, modelled as a «category» from UFO-C and composed into the Secret relator; in the minimal case internal, a self-directed intention made by the agent to themselves, and having as its propositional content the goal whose achievement consists in the non-occurrence of a revelation event, namely the *Prevent Revelation Goal.* This grounds Ismail and Shafie's condition of secrecy within an ontological structure rather than treating it as a logical predicate, the optional Time Interval and Condition capturing their time point and condition of secrecy as structured components. Crucially, it is the commitment that constitutes the Nescient collective as such, since the Keeper actively designates which agents should remain ignorant. As Marx and Muschert [16] observe, nescience is not the absence of information but a socially produced and intentionally maintained condition, so that a person toward whom Anna bears no intention of maintaining ignorance is not a Nescient but merely uninformed. Keepers, for their part, are not modelled as a collective, since each bears a separate Commitment individuating a distinct antidote, so that Keeper-hood is predicated individually whereas nescience is a condition of the group as such.

Disposition, Belief and the Stakes of Revelation. The model so far follows Ismail and Shafie's five-way relation closely. The present analysis now makes its most significant departure by introducing two concepts absent from their account: the *Revelation Disposition* and the *Consequential Belief.*

Any agent who knows the Secretum bears a Revelation Disposition. This is a real and present property inhering in the Secret Keeper by virtue of their knowledge of the Secretum. Following COVER [19] and Baratella et al. [3], this is a Vulnerability: a disposition whose manifestation under triggering conditions gives rise to a revelation event. This Vulnerability could manifest, for example, as a result of a Keeper being asked directly, feeling social pressure, or being placed under a normative obligation to reveal the secret. Modelling the Revelation Disposition as a present structural feature rather than a possible future event is a contribution over Ismail and Shafie's logical treatment, in which revelation is an operation that either holds or does not.

The *Consequential Belief* provides the motivational foundation for the Commitment. In UFO-C, any intention requires a motivational basis [7]. Following COVER [19], risk is irreducibly tied to value. Indeed, something is only at risk if it is of value to some agent with respect to their goals. The Consequential Belief is the agent's structured assessment of that risk: a «subkind» of Belief, modelled as a «mode», whose propositional content refers to a Goal. The «mode» stereotype denotes an intrinsic moment inhering in a single individual; it is this belief that motivates the adoption of the Prevent Revelation Goal and, therefore, the Commitment itself. Without it, there is no secret, only information that happens not to have been shared. This extends Ismail and Shafie's account and is consistent with Bok's [4] observation that harm is not incidental to secrecy but constitutive of it. Since the Consequential Belief refers to a Goal rather than to the Secretum, it may inhere in a collective agent as readily as in an individual one: an organisation has goals, and bears risk with respect to them in COVER's sense, without thereby grasping the propositional content whose concealment it requires. Belief in the Secretum admits of no such generality, being borne only by agents who can grasp that content, so that an organisation knows what it conceals only through its members; an asymmetry which, rather than any restriction on Ownership, distinguishes the institutional case.

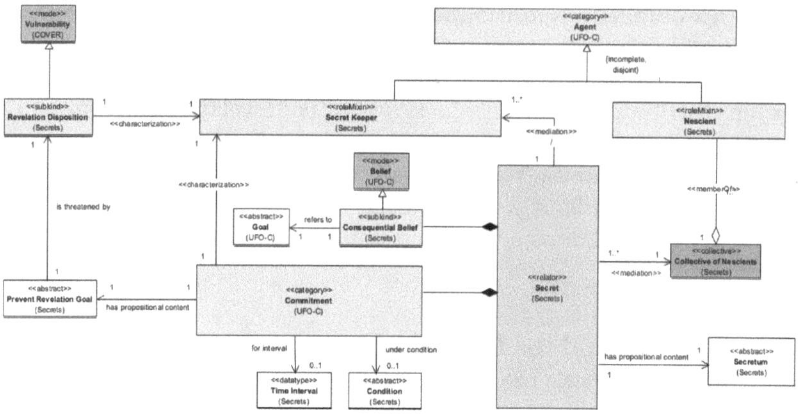

Fig. 2. Foundational secret model refined with Revelation Disposition and Consequential Belief in OntoUML.

Consider two agents who both know Anna's diagnosis. Anna holds a Consequential Belief that disclosure would harm her quality of life, and has formed a Commitment to maintaining her family's nescience. A colleague who learned of it in passing holds no such belief and has no basis for commitment. Both bear the Revelation Disposition. What distinguishes them is not their epistemic position but whether they hold a Consequential Belief that its manifestation would constitute a loss with respect to a goal-relevant value. Figure 2 introduces both concepts into the model.

4.2 Sharing Secrets

The previous section models the foundational structure of secrecy where a single agent plays all roles simultaneously. In practice, secrets are frequently shared, and the unified role structure gives way to a more complex arrangement in which distinct roles must be differentiated.

Secret Holders and the Revelation Disposition. When a secret is shared, at least one agent beyond the original Keeper comes to know the Secretum without necessarily having any commitment regarding it. Any agent exposed to the Secretum and who has come to know its propositional content is a *Secret Holder*, defined purely by their epistemic relation to the Secretum rather than by any commitment, goal, or intentional orientation. The Secret Holder is modelled as a «roleMixin», secret holding cutting across identity kinds since a person, collective, or organisation may all be Holders in virtue of that epistemic relation. The Secret Keeper is a specialisation of it. Every Keeper is necessarily a Holder, though not every Holder a Keeper, the Keeper adding a commitment to maintaining nescience where the Holder role captures the more general condition of knowing the Secretum with or without one. In the extended model (see Fig. 3), the Revelation Disposition inheres in any Secret Holder, being a structural feature of knowing the Secretum irrespective of whether the Holder has any commitment to suppress it, so that the risk of revelation is not confined to the Keeper but distributed across all who know it; the Revelation Disposition is thus the formal ontological grounding of Simmel's [20] observation that every secret carries a structural impulse toward betrayal present in every agent who holds it. A Secret Holder without a commitment, such as Anna's son, who accidentally reads her medical documents, is an unmanaged source of risk qualitatively different from Maria.

The Secret Owner and the Consequential Belief. The Secret Holder structure establishes who knows the Secretum and who bears the Revelation Disposition. What it does not capture is why the secret exists at all. When the secret is shared, the roles of originator and Keeper come apart: the agent who originates the secret does so based on a goal-grounded belief about the stakes of revelation, while a Keeper may maintain nescience purely based on a social commitment without sharing that belief. It is the originating agent, introduced here as the *Secret Owner*, whose motivational foundation needs to be formally introduced.

In the foundational model presented in the previous section, the Consequential Belief was introduced as a constitutive component of the secret without yet being connected to a specific role. When Owner and Keeper are differentiated, the Consequential Belief can be properly located as a property of the Owner, the agent whose goal-grounded belief originates the secret. Two distinct subtypes

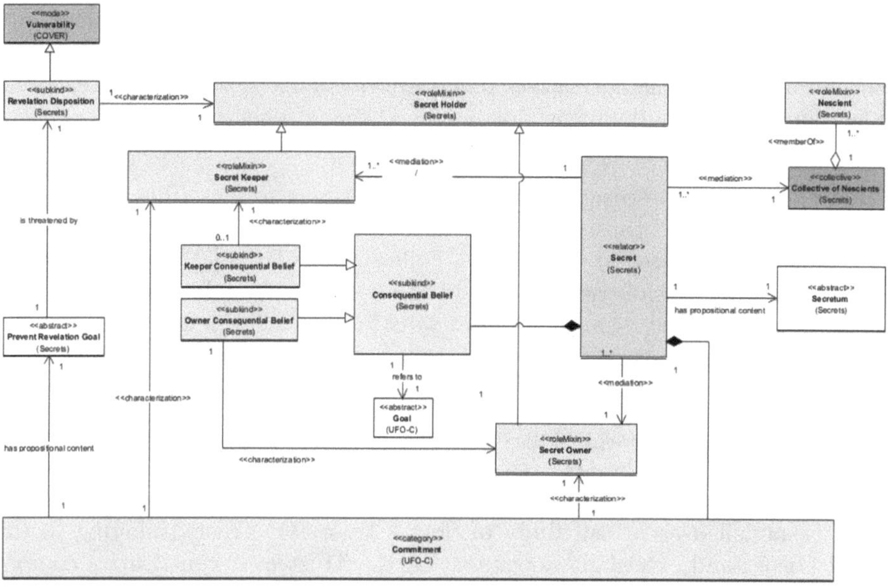

Fig. 3. Secret Holder and Owner structure with Consequential Belief modelled in OntoUML.

must be distinguished. The *Owner Consequential Belief* refers to the Owner's goals, motivates the original designation of the Nescient collective, and necessarily characterises the Secret Owner. The *Keeper Consequential Belief* refers to any goal the Keeper wishes to protect and optionally characterises the Secret Keeper. Without the Owner's Consequential Belief, there is no secret; without the Keeper's Consequential Belief, there may still be one, maintained purely based on a social commitment. Ownership is not determined by the subject matter of the secretum but by whose consequential belief grounds the secret, the Owner being that agent (individual or collective) in whom the belief sustaining it inheres. Figure 3 extends the models presented in previous figures by incorporating the Secret Owner.

Commitment and Social Structure. Both the Secret Owner and the Secret Keeper bear a commitment to maintaining nescience, modelled here as a «category» from UFO-C and internal in the minimal case; when the secret is shared, that structure must be extended to account for the social relationship sharing creates. In UFO-C a *social commitment* inheres in one agent but is existentially dependent on another, being directed toward that agent rather than self-directed [7], and associated with every such commitment is a *social claim*, the complementary moment inhering in the agent toward whom it is directed and representing their entitlement to the committed behaviour [8]. When Anna asks Maria to keep her secret and Maria agrees, they together constitute the normative structure of *trusted delegation* [2], Maria bearing a social commitment toward Anna,

Anna acquiring a social claim against Maria, this being the Owner's deliberate conferral of secret-keeping responsibility on the Keeper: an internal commitment can be revised without normative consequence, whereas a social one creates an obligation whose abandonment violates the Owner's social claim.

Trust in Secret-Keeping. The commitment structure describes how secret-keeping is constituted through trusted delegation, but does not account for why the Owner would share the secret at all. Following ONTrust [2], trust is a mental moment motivating the trustor to make themselves vulnerable to the trustee's behaviour. Without it, sharing a secret would introduce a new Revelation Disposition without any basis for confidence it would be suppressed.

Weak Trust. In its most primitive form, the trust that grounds secret-keeping is *weak trust*. This is the Owner's belief that a particular agent will maintain nescience without any formal agreement or normative obligation in place. Weak Trust is modelled as a «subkind» of Social Trust (ONTrust), inhering in the Secret Owner and externally dependent on the Trustee. A constitutive component is the *Secret Keeping Commitment Belief*; the Owner's unverified belief that the trustee will behave as if committed. The Weak Trust grounds a *Secret Keeping Delegation* mediating the Secret Owner as delegator and the Secret Holder as delegatee. Critically, in the weak trust case, the Holder has accepted no formal commitment. They bear the Revelation Disposition without any means to suppress it, and the secret's continued existence depends entirely on the Owner's Secret Keeping Intention. If the Owner's intention ceases, the secret ceases to exist. Figure 4 presents the formal model of the weak trust structure.

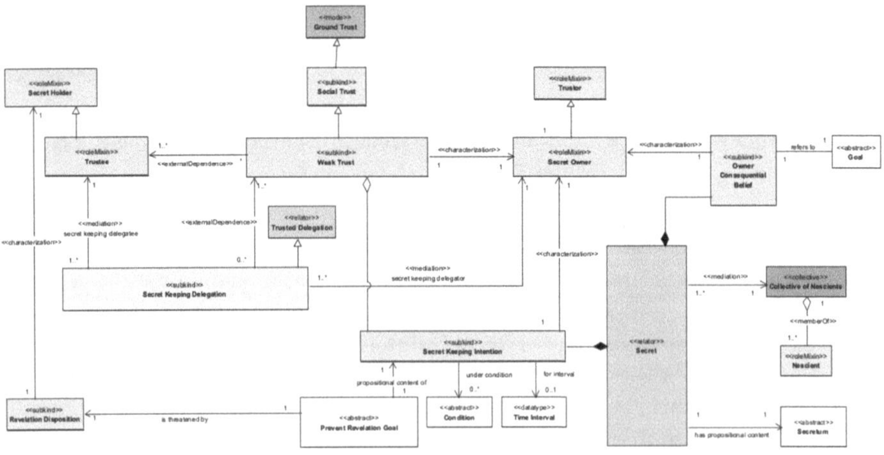

Fig. 4. Weak trust structure in secret-keeping modelled in OntoUML.

Strong Trust. Where weak trust is insufficient—where the Consequential Belief refers to goals of significant value, or the Owner needs to delegate to agents they do not know personally—a stronger normative foundation is required. Strong Trust is modelled as a «subkind» of Weak Trust (ONTrust), grounded on a *Secret Keeping Agreement*: a «relator» specialising ONTrust's agreement structure which comes into being when the Holder formally accepts the delegation, and which is constituted by the *Secret Keeping Commitment* (a «mode» inhering in the Keeper, externally dependent on the Owner) and the *Secret Keeping Claim* (a «mode» inhering in the Owner, externally dependent on the Keeper), counterpart moments grounded in the ODE social relator pattern [8] whose propositional content refers in both cases to the Prevent Revelation Goal. The Holder's acceptance transforms them into a Secret Keeper whose Revelation Disposition is now governed by a formal commitment, so that the secret's continued existence, no longer dependent solely on the Owner's intention, is sustained independently by the Keeper's; the model thereby accommodates both personal (Anna and Maria) and institutional (a defence organisation and cleared officers) arrangements within the same formal structure, what differs being not the structure but what grounds the trust beliefs. Figure 5 presents the formal model of the strong trust structure.

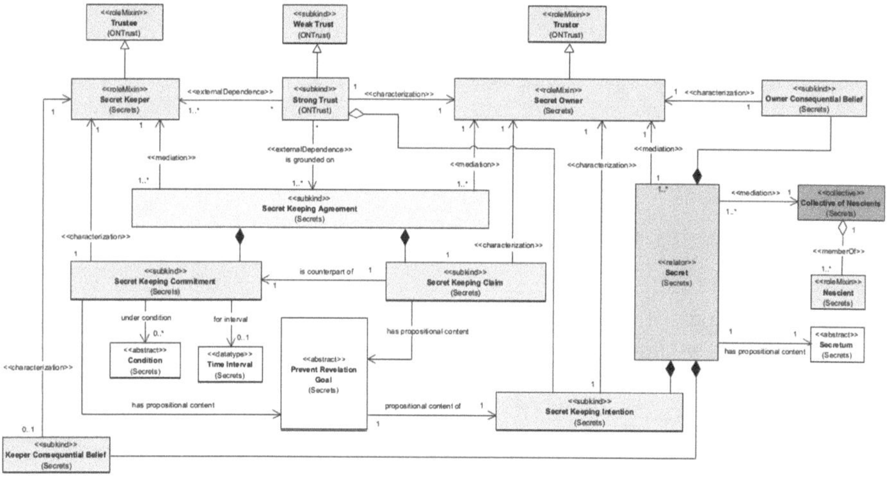

Fig. 5. Strong trust and Secret Keeping Agreement modelled in OntoUML.

Prevention and Concealment. The trust structure describes how the secret-keeping relationship is formalised. This section develops the ontological structure of the Keeper's commitment as a preventive mechanism, drawing on Baratella et al. [3] and COVER [19]. As shown in Fig. 6, the Revelation Disposition may be activated by a Revelation Trigger, a situation conducive to disclosure, and manifests as a Revelation event, a «subkind» of Threat Event (COVER), which causes a Loss Event frustrating the Secret Owner's goal. The Secret Owner is the Object at Risk in COVER's terms or the agent whose goal-relevant value is threatened by the Revelation Disposition. The full COVER chain, from vulnerability through threat event to loss event and goal frustration, is explicitly grounded in the structure of the secret.

The Keeper's Commitment functions as an antidote in Baratella et al.'s precise sense. It suppresses the Revelation Disposition entirely, preventing manifestation even when triggering conditions are present. This is what distinguishes active secret-keeping from passive non-disclosure and gives formal ontological grounding to Simmel's [20] observation that secrecy is not an epistemic state but an active social form. A preference for non-disclosure without a formal commitment is not an antidote; the disposition remains present and ungoverned. This is a contribution over Ismail and Shafie's account [15], in which the Keeper's intention is a logical predicate without the dispositional structure that distinguishes genuine commitment from mere preference. Active countermeasures, such as deflecting questions, denying knowledge, operate at the trigger level and complement the antidote when triggering conditions arise despite suppression.

The full preventive structure of a shared secret involves multiple antidotes operating in parallel, all directed at preventing the same Revelation Event. The maintenance of a shared secret is not a single act of suppression but a distributed preventive structure in which every Keeper contributes an antidote to the collective risk. The Revelation event only terminates the secret when the Nescient collective as a whole is dissolved. A single accidental exposure does not destroy the secret if the broader collective remains intact, though it introduces an unmanaged Revelation Disposition into the risk structure.

4.3 From Secrecy to Privacy and Confidentiality

Privacy, confidentiality, and access control each depend on reasoning about the active maintenance of ignorance, yet each generally operates at the normative surface, so that without an account of why an agent has an interest in concealment, what a normative agreement creates, or where ungoverned Revelation Dispositions exist in a processing chain, systems cannot reason about the intentional reality they are meant to govern. The account developed above supplies precisely that substrate.

To illustrate this, consider how the secrecy ontology grounds privacy. Privacy concerns a data subject's normative interest in controlling access to information about themselves. This is an interest grounded in a Consequential Belief: the data subject's assessment that disclosure would harm a goal they are committed to maintaining. In the present ontology, the Data Subject specialises the Secret Owner, Personal Data specialises the Secretum, and the Consent Agreement specialises the Secret Keeping Agreement, thus, creating a Secret Keeping Commitment in the Data Controller and a Secret Keeping Claim in the Data Subject. This grounding makes explicit what existing privacy ontologies, such as PrOnto [18] and OPPD [5] leave implicit.

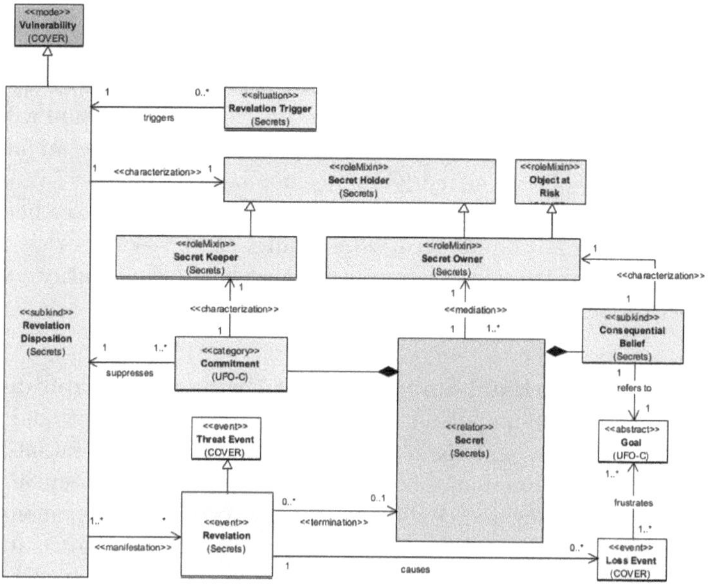

Fig. 6. Prevention and risk structure of secret-keeping modelled in OntoUML.

Consider consent withdrawal. When a data subject withdraws consent the Secret Keeping Agreement is dissolved and the controller's Secret Keeping Commitment ceases, the controller reverting to an uncommitted Secret Holder bearing an unmanaged Revelation Disposition, so that the secret's continued existence now depends solely on the Owner's intention rather than on any normative obligation. A system built on existing privacy ontologies can record that consent has been withdrawn but cannot reason about these ontological consequences, what obligations persist, which agents now bear ungoverned Revelation Dispositions, and how robust the remaining concealment structure is, which the present ontology supplies. Confidentiality and access control admit analogous specialisations; the full development of these is the subject of ongoing work.

5 Discussion

The formal analysis developed in this paper reveals several structural features of secrecy that have significant implications for information systems design and that are not captured by prior treatments.

Secrecy as Risk Management. The introduction of the Revelation Disposition as a present structural vulnerability, inhering in every agent who knows a Secretum, reframes secret-keeping as an inherently distributed risk management activity in which every agent brought into knowledge introduces a new vulnerability, and the commitment structure is a distributed preventive response; one antidote per Keeper, all directed at the same class of events. The implication for information systems design is direct: the security of a secret is determined not by the sensitivity of the information alone but by the completeness of the antidote structure, since a single uncommitted Holder, knowing the Secretum without any commitment to suppress their Revelation Disposition, constitutes an unmanaged risk that no number of committed Keepers can eliminate. Anna's son illustrates this precisely, for however robustly Maria's commitment suppresses her own disposition, he remains an unmanaged vulnerability in the secret's risk structure; systems reasoning about information control must be able to identify such agents and to assess the adequacy of the preventive structure as a whole.

Secrecy as a Foundational Component of Privacy and Confidentiality. The analysis reveals an important asymmetry between secrecy and adjacent concepts such as privacy and confidentiality. Secrecy is a social-intentional phenomenon; the active maintenance of ignorance grounded in Consequential Belief and commitment. Privacy and confidentiality are normative phenomena because they specify when and how the maintenance of ignorance is legitimate, obligatory, or protected. Privacy is not reducible to secrecy. A person may have a privacy interest in information they have never actively concealed, and surveillance concerns do not involve concealment at all. However, wherever privacy norms are actively enacted, the social-intentional structure modelled here is operative. Anna's interest in keeping her diagnosis from her family is not a privacy preference but is rather grounded in a consequential belief about what she values, sustained by commitments that create normative obligations, and threatened by Revelation Dispositions that no rule-based framework can identify or reason about. A formal account of secrecy is, therefore, a prerequisite for a formal account of privacy, not a substitute for it. Privacy ontologies require additional normative structure—rights, entitlements, contextual norms—beyond what the secrecy ontology provides. But they cannot be built on principled ground without the intentional foundation the present work establishes. This positions the present ontology not as a privacy ontology but as the foundational layer on which privacy ontologies can be built.

The Tension Between Personal and Institutional Secrecy. The model accommodates both personal and institutional secret-keeping within the same formal structure, the difference lying in what grounds the trust relationship" and dropping "but the analysis reveals a significant tension. In personal secrecy, the Owner and Keeper are typically known to one another, and the trust relationship is grounded in personal assessment. In institutional secrecy, the Owner is a collective agent which, while it bears the Consequential Belief that grounds the secret, cannot itself bear belief in the Secretum, and the trust relationship is grounded in institutional structure rather than personal assessment. The model accommodates this as a case of the shared structure developed above, the organisation occupying the Owner role while its officers, whose own Consequential Beliefs are not required, hold the Secretum and bear Keeper Commitments arising from institutional agreement; the office persists through the succession of its officers, and with it the secret. What remains beyond the present model is the elaboration of complex delegation chains and overlapping Nescient collectives, which constitutes an important direction for future work.

Limitations. The model assumes a well-defined Nescient collective, a single Secret Owner, and a Secretum that is a discrete proposition. In practice, nescience boundaries are fuzzy, secrets may have multiple originators with conflicting goals, and secret content is often a complex of interrelated information. Consider, for example, a scenario in which both Anna and her doctor independently originate secrets about the same diagnosis with different nescient collectives and different motivating goals. These limitations point to extensions rather than deficiencies in the foundational commitments.

6 Conclusion

This paper has presented a formal ontology of secrecy, SECRET, grounded in UFO and specified in OntoUML, extending Ismail and Shafie's logical treatment through an ontological unpacking methodology. The secret is modelled as a social-intentional relator constituted by a Consequential Belief and a commitment to maintaining nescience, situated within a trust and delegation structure derived from ONTrust and a risk and prevention structure grounded in COVER and Baratella et al.'s ontology of prevention.

The principal contributions are the modelling of the secret as a social-intentional relator grounded in Consequential Belief; the Revelation Disposition as a structural vulnerability distributed across all who know the Secretum; the Owner and Keeper Consequential Belief as distinct subtypes differing in necessity and reference; the Secret Keeping Delegation and Agreement as specialisations of ONTrust's trust and delegation structure; and the characterisation of secret-keeping as a distributed preventive structure; together a reusable module formally interoperable with existing frameworks for trust, value, risk, and prevention.

The analysis positions secrecy as a necessary foundational component of any formal account of information control, including privacy, confidentiality, and access control, not a substitute for the normative frameworks these domains employ, but the intentional substrate on which their formal modelling depends. The development of a full privacy ontology grounded in this foundation, incorporating Nissenbaum's contextual integrity framework [17] and aligning with GDPR role structures, is the primary direction of ongoing work.

References

1. Almeida, J.P.A., Falbo, R.A., Guizzardi, G.: Events as entities in ontology-driven conceptual modeling. In: Laender, A.H.F., Pernici, B., Lim, E.-P., de Oliveira, J.P.M. (eds.) ER 2019. LNCS, vol. 11788, pp. 469–483. Springer, Cham (2019). https://doi.org/10.1007/978-3-030-33223-5_39

2. Amaral, G., Sales, T.P., Baratella, R., Porello, D., Guizzardi, R., Guizzardi, G.: ONTrust: a reference ontology of trust (2026). https://doi.org/10.48550/ARXIV.2602.07662
3. Baratella, R., Fumagalli, M., Oliveira,., Guizzardi, G.: Understanding and modeling prevention. In: Guizzardi, R., Ralyté, J., Franch, X. (eds.) Research Challenges in Information Science, vol. 446, pp. 389–405. Springer, Cham (2022). https://doi.org/10.1007/978-3-031-05760-1_23
4. Bok, S.: Secrets: On the Ethics of Concealment and Revelation. Vintage, Westminster (2011)
5. El Ghosh, M., Abdulrab, H.: Capturing the basics of the GDPR in a well-founded legal domain modular ontology. In: Neuhaus, F., Brodaric, B. (eds.) Frontiers in Artificial Intelligence and Applications. IOS Press (2021). https://doi.org/10.3233/FAIA210378
6. Griffo, C., Almeida, J.P.A., Guizzardi, G.: Conceptual modeling of legal relations. In: Trujillo, J.C., Davis, K.C., Du, X., Li, Z., Ling, T.W., Li, G., Lee, M.L. (eds.) ER 2018. LNCS, vol. 11157, pp. 169–183. Springer, Cham (2018). https://doi.org/10.1007/978-3-030-00847-5_14
7. Guizzardi, G., Botti Benevides, A., Fonseca, C.M., Porello, D., Almeida, J.P.A., Prince Sales, T.: UFO: unified foundational ontology. Appl. Ontol. **17**(1), 167–210 (2022). https://doi.org/10.3233/AO-210256
8. Guizzardi, G., Falbo, R.D.A., Guizzardi, R.S.S.: Grounding software domain ontologies in the unified foundational ontology (UFO): the case of the ODE software process ontology. In: Lencastre, M., Cunha, J.F.e., Valecillo, A. (eds.) Memorias de la XI Conferencia Iberoamericana de Software Engineering (CIbSE 2008), Pernambuco, Brasil, 2008, pp. 127–140 (2008)
9. Guizzardi, G., Fonseca, C.M., Benevides, A.B., Almeida, J.P.A., Porello, D., Sales, T.P.: Endurant types in ontology-driven conceptual modeling: towards OntoUML 2.0. In: Trujillo, J.C., et al. (eds.) ER 2018. LNCS, vol. 11157, pp. 136–150. Springer, Cham (2018). https://doi.org/10.1007/978-3-030-00847-5_12
10. Guizzardi, G., Guarino, N.: Explanation, semantics, and ontology. Data Knowl. Eng. **153**, 102325 (2024)
11. Guizzardi, G., Wagner, G., Almeida, J.P.A., Guizzardi, R.S.: Towards ontological foundations for conceptual modeling: the unified foundational ontology (UFO) story. Appl. Ontol. **10**(3–4), 259–271 (2015). https://doi.org/10.3233/AO-150157
12. Guizzardi, G., Wagner, G., de Almeida Falbo, R., Guizzardi, R.S.S., Almeida, J.P.A.: Towards ontological foundations for the conceptual modeling of events. In: Ng, W., Storey, V.C., Trujillo, J.C. (eds.) ER 2013. LNCS, vol. 8217, pp. 327–341. Springer, Heidelberg (2013). https://doi.org/10.1007/978-3-642-41924-9_27
13. Guizzardi, R.S.S., Guizzardi, G.: Ontology-based transformation framework from TROPOS to AORML. In: Social Modeling for Requirements Engineering, pp. 547–570. The MIT Press (2010)
14. Halpern, J.Y., O'Neill, K.R.: Secrecy in multiagent systems. ACM Trans. Inf. Syst. Secur. **12**(1), 1–47 (2008). https://doi.org/10.1145/1410234.1410239
15. Ismail, H.O., Shafie, M.: A commonsense theory of secrets. In: Brodaric, B., Neuhaus, F. (eds.) Frontiers in Artificial Intelligence and Applications. IOS Press (2020). https://doi.org/10.3233/FAIA200662
16. Marx, G.T., Muschert, G.W.: Simmel on secrecy. In: Rol, C., Papilloud, C. (eds.) Soziologie als Möglichkeit, pp. 217–233. VS Verlag für Sozialwissenschaften, Wiesbaden (2009). https://doi.org/10.1007/978-3-531-91437-4_13
17. Nissenbaum, H.: Privacy in Context: Technology, Policy, and the Integrity of Social Life. Stanford University Press, Stanford (2010)

18. Palmirani, M., Martoni, M., Rossi, A., Bartolini, C., Robaldo, L.: PrOnto: privacy ontology for legal reasoning. In: Kő, A., Francesconi, E. (eds.) EGOVIS 2018. LNCS, vol. 11032, pp. 139–152. Springer, Cham (2018). https://doi.org/10.1007/978-3-319-98349-3_11
19. Sales, T.P., Baião, F., Guizzardi, G., Almeida, J.P.A., Guarino, N., Mylopoulos, J.: The common ontology of value and risk. In: Trujillo, J.C., et al. (eds.) ER 2018. LNCS, vol. 11157, pp. 121–135. Springer, Cham (2018). https://doi.org/10.1007/978-3-030-00847-5_11
20. Simmel, G.: The sociology of secrecy and of secret societies. Am. J. Sociol. **11**(4), 441–498 (1906). https://doi.org/10.1086/211418

ROCAP: A Reference Ontology for Cybersecurity Attack Planning

Antoine Leblanc[1,2](✉), Zequan Huang[1,2], Hervé Cholez[3], Jacques Robin[2], Sébastien Larinier[2], Giancarlo Guizzardi[4], Ítalo Oliveira[4], Tiago Prince Sales[4], Xavier Rousseau[5], Nourhène Ben Rabah[1], and Bénédicte Le Grand[1]

[1] Center for Research in Informatics (CRI), University Paris 1 Panthéon-Sorbonne, Paris, France
{zequan.huang,nourhene.ben-rabah,benedicte.le-grand}@univ-paris1.fr

[2] Engineering School of Informatics, Electronics and Automation (ESIEA), Paris, France
antoine.leblanc@univ-paris1.fr,
{jacques.robin,sebastien.larinier}@esiea.fr

[3] Luxembourg Institute of Science and Technology, Esch-sur-Alzette, Luxembourg
herve.cholez@list.lu

[4] Semantics, Cybersecurity, and Services Group, University of Twente, Enschede, The Netherlands
{g.guizzardi,i.j.dasilvaoliveira,t.princesales}@utwente.nl

[5] Gatewatcher, Paris, France
xavier.rousseau@gatewatcher.com

Abstract. Cybersecurity is a constantly-evolving domain, driven by the rapid emergence of new vulnerabilities and the continuous expansion of novel technological environments. Amidst this complexity, Security Operations Center (SOC) analysts must continuously assess the risks threatening their infrastructure by reconstructing attack scenarios from scattered signals. Cybersecurity ontologies support this by modeling core concepts and structuring Cyber Threat Intelligence data, yet existing proposals suffer from limited reuse beyond their original use-case and, critically, do not represent the attack plan as an entity that exists independently of the traces it produces. We propose the *Reference Ontology for Cybersecurity Attack Planning (ROCAP)*, which is grounded in the Unified Foundational Ontology (UFO) and aligned with MITRE's *de facto* industry standards. By formalizing the attack plan as an intentional structure, ROCAP is designed to be reused and adapted across the evolving landscape while easing interoperability with operational workflows. We demonstrate its practical utility for SOC analysts by answering Competency Questions derived from *ISO/IEC 27005* and *NIST CSF 2.0.*

Keywords: Cybersecurity · Ontology · Attack Planning · Risk Assessment · Security Operation Center

© The Author(s), under exclusive license to Springer Nature Switzerland AG 2027
A. Bernasconi et al. (Eds.): ER 2026, LNCS 17081, pp. 182–199, 2027.
https://doi.org/10.1007/978-3-032-40795-5_11

1 Introduction

Security Operations Center (SOC) analysts need to assess the risks threatening the Information and Communication Technology (ICT) infrastructure under their protection, in order to choose the most efficient countermeasures—a decision grounded in the system's resources, their vulnerabilities, and predefined attack scenarios. To do so, they must reconstruct attack scenarios from scattered signals observed across heterogeneous tools [39], at the intersection of risk and attack-planning reasoning.

Cybersecurity ontologies have emerged as the preferred approach [19]: they integrate narrow-scope tools at the conceptual rather than syntactic level, structure historical ***Cyber Threat Intelligence (CTI)*** data, and establish a shared communication framework. Attack trees and attack graphs also decompose an attacker's goal into ordered steps, but as instance-level artifacts tailored to one assessment they lack foundational grounding, exhibiting ambiguous terminology and limited semantic interoperability [28]. The limitations below therefore concern reference ontologies specifically, not attack-modelling techniques in general. A *first* limitation concerns expressive scope. While some ontologies model the causal chain of an attack—its stages, dependencies, and techniques—and sometimes its attacker's motivation, none formally represents the *attack plan* as an entity existing independently of the traces it produces. This matters operationally: the same credential reuse through phishing may serve data exfiltration or long-term persistence, and the defensive response differs accordingly. Capturing intention as a mere motivation label is therefore insufficient; distinguishing these cases requires representing the plan as an intention *bound to* a structured specification of the intended course of action—its ordered steps and dependencies—against which a partial execution can be interpreted [6]. A *second*, orthogonal limitation [19] is the lack of reuse beyond the original use-case: no operational ontology dedicated to attack planning is grounded[1] in a general-purpose foundational ontology such as the ***Unified Foundational Ontology (UFO)*** [13]—a structural flaw that limits consistency maintenance during evolution and extension, as shown for D3FEND [27].

We propose a ***Reference Ontology for Cybersecurity Attack Planning (ROCAP)*** grounded in UFO, bridging (i) theoretically-grounded reference ontologies—integrating and extending the UFO-based ***COVER*** [32] and ***ROSE*** [26]—and (ii) operationally-grounded industry standards—adapting ***MITRE D3FEND***[2] [18], ***CAPEC*** [22], and the ***Unified Kill Chain (UKC)*** [31]. Aligned with these standards to *ease* integration with SOC workflows, ROCAP is published as a FAIR-compliant [17] artifact[3] and was co-

[1] A reference ontology is a well-structured representation of a part of reality, designed for knowledge exchange and reuse, while an operational ontology is its concrete implementation.

[2] Which itself includes the MITRE digital asset ontology of attack targets and the MITRE ATT&CK taxonomy [36].

[3] All complementary code, ROCAP model and documents can be found here: https://github.com/AntoineLeblancFr/ROCAP.

designed with SOC analysts from a ***Network Detection and Response (NDR)*** vendor together with experts in cybersecurity standards and ontological engineering.

Our contributions are twofold. First, building on the planning concepts of UFO-C—the social and intentional layer of UFO—we provide a formal ontological definition of an attack plan that leverages the intentional dimension of cyberattacks, absent from current attack-planning ontologies. Second, adapting from industry-standard ontologies and taxonomies, we define a set of *mediating concepts* that bring operational artifacts and ontological commitments into a single coherent model.

We validate ROCAP's practical utility from a SOC-analyst perspective through *competency questions* derived by a cybersecurity-standard expert from ISO/IEC 27005:2022 [16] and NIST CSF 2.0 [25], answered over a Prolog instantiation of a real-life BlackSuit ransomware APT campaign [38] and a manually generated alternative.

The remainder of the paper is organized as follows. Section 2 introduces the ontological baseline and the related work. Section 3 presents ROCAP, our proposed ontology. Section 4 validates it from a SOC perspective and Sect. 5 concludes.

2 Related Work on Cybersecurity Ontologies

2.1 Ontological Baseline: Well-Grounded Ontologies

The Unified Foundational Ontology (UFO) [13], an ISO/IEC CD 21838-5 standard proposal, is a formal theory integrating formal ontology, cognitive psychology, and linguistics, providing domain-independent, reusable concepts for conceptual modeling. It is operationalized through OntoUML [8], a language implementing UFO's axioms as a precise, visually expressive syntax. Several ontologies build on it, including security ontologies COVER and ROSE.

The Common Ontology of Value and Risk (COVER) [32] conceptualizes `Value` and `Risk`, the latter grounded in ISO 31000:2018 [15]. COVER disambiguates `Risk` under three scopes: a measurable quantity (`Risk`); a chain of events (`Risk Event`) impacting an agent's goals (`Risk Experience`); and the relationship ascribing a risk quantity to uncertain future experiences (`Risk Assessment`).

The Reference Ontology for Security Engineering (ROSE) [26] reuses and refines COVER for ISO 31000:2018 security. It refines the `Risk Experience` with an `Attack` (an `Action` specializing `Risk Event`) and an `Attacker` (an agent whose `Threat Capability` creates `Attacks`).

2.2 Industry Cybersecurity Standard Ontologies and Taxonomies

Several institutional frameworks structure the cybersecurity knowledge that existing ontologies draw upon.

MITRE ATT&CK [36] is a taxonomy of adversary tactics and techniques observed in real-world intrusions, organized along a kill-chain-like matrix that has become the *de facto* reference vocabulary for describing attack behavior.

MITRE D3FEND [18] is an ontology defining defensive countermeasures to be applied complemented by its offensive counterpart—ATT&CK. D3FEND also introduces a sub-ontology of artifacts (physical or digital), as the basis for conceptualizing the relations between offensive techniques (ATT&CK) and defensive techniques (D3FEND), providing a solid reference for cyber risk treatment.

CAPEC (Common Attack Pattern Enumeration and Classification) [22], also from MITRE, complements ATT&CK at a lower abstraction level, cataloging attack patterns with prerequisites, consequences, and related weaknesses.

CVE (Common Vulnerabilities and Exposures) [23] provides a standardized identifier for publicly disclosed *vulnerability types*, while **CWE (Common Weakness Enumeration)** [24] classifies the underlying software *weakness types* that these vulnerability types specialize.[4] Together, the CAPEC→CWE→CVE chain enables a traceable path from abstract attack patterns to concrete exploitable weaknesses.

None of these frameworks, however, formalizes the intentional dimension of an attack: they catalogue the available offensive techniques, the vulnerabilities that enable them, and the defenses that counter them, yet none addresses the rationale underlying an attacker's choice of a specific technique sequence, nor the structure by which such a choice constitutes a coherent plan.

2.3 Cybersecurity Ontologies on Attack Planning

The formal representation of cybersecurity knowledge has produced a diverse landscape of ontologies and knowledge graphs, which we survey along four axes.

Foundationally-Grounded Proposals. Only PAPO [29] anchors its constructs in a foundational ontology, reusing the UFO-based COVER and ROSE to model attacker intentions in the phishing domain. It shows that UFO can support intentional reasoning about cyberattacks, but remains scoped to a single attack family and does not address multi-stage campaigns.

Attack-Sequencing Proposals Without Intentional Grounding. Most of the literature models the structural side of plans through attack-dependency formalisms. MulVAL [30], the APT attack ontology [40], WAVED [1], ATT&CK-Ont [2], TAON [21], and DDoS-Ont [5] encode multi-hop precondition–effect

[4] A weakness (CWE) is a general type of flaw in software code or design, whereas a vulnerability (CVE) is a more specific vulnerability type, bound to a particular product and version, that can be directly exploited to compromise a system. Neither is a particular: the actual vulnerability is the one borne by a concrete deployed system, which *instantiates* a CVE-catalogued type.

or kill-chain dependencies across ATT&CK tactics; others capture them only implicitly (CSKG4APT [34], KG-Reasoning [9]) or not at all (APTOnt [37], RMO [35]). The object of formalisation is invariably the *attack graph*: the space of possible attack paths. Such formalisms answer *what could happen*, not *what a specific adversary has committed to.*

Intentional Proposals Without Structured Plans. CSKG4APT [34] captures APT-group motivations and intent levels, and the Zachman-based attribution framework [33] analyses attacker motivations geopolitically. These contributions rightly treat attacks as goal-directed, but represent the attacker's intention only as an *end goal*—a motivation label satisfiable in many ways. Such a reading is legitimate in general, yet insufficient for *plan recognition*, which requires a *closed* intention [6,11]: one whose satisfaction is bound to the instantiation of a specific, structured course of action. It is this binding—not the goal alone—that these proposals leave unaddressed.

Explicit Planning Proposals. Only three proposals explicitly invoke planning. NAPO [7,14] targets network attack planning from a military perspective but lacks foundational grounding and standards integration; Liu & Guo's AG-PDO [20] treats a plan as a solver output on the defender side; and DDoS-Ont [5], despite its title *Attack Plan Detection*, encodes a conjunction of CAPEC-derived preconditions rather than an intentional structure.

A recent survey [19] identifies one structural reason for this fragmentation: the near-absence of foundational grounding. Our review reveals a second. Existing approaches capture either the attacker's intention—a goal label—or the execution as observed events. What lies *between* is left unrepresented: the plan itself—the intention committing the attacker to a specific, structured course of action—which gives content to the goal and provides the blueprint against which executions can be compared. This is the gap ROCAP is intended to fill.

3 A Reference Ontology for Cybersecurity Attack Planning

ROCAP reuses and extends the conceptual modeling of `Value` and `Risk` in COVER, together with that of security engineering in ROSE, and by integrating the above-mentioned industry adopted ontologies and taxonomies. Specifically, we focus on ***Advanced Persistent Threat (APT)***, a form of highly targeted, multi-stage cyber-attack conducted by well-resourced `Attacker` (ROSE), which represents one of the most impactful forms of cyber-threat in practice. From ROSE's perspective, an APT campaign can be considered as a `Risk Experience` constituted by interrelated `Risk Events`. This focus enables us to precisely characterize an `Attacker`'s intention and action by introducing the notion of `Attack Plan` (*cf.* Sect. 3.1).

In the rest of this paper, we use the following OntoUML representation conventions. External concepts are prefixed (*e.g.*, `Agent` from UFO is referred as `UFO::Agent`), and concepts defined or refined by us are highlighted with a thicker border and have no prefix. The color denotes the corresponding UFO categorization: pink for object types, blue for intrinsic aspect types, orange for situation types, yellow for event types, green for relators and purple for higher-order types. The same principle applies to all sub-ontologies introduced in the remainder of this paper.

3.1 Attack Plan Definition

The Attacker Model. ROCAP adopts an intentional model of the adversary grounded in UFO-C, COVER and ROSE. A `ROSE::Attacker` is a `UFO::Agent` characterized by three intrinsic aspects that jointly determine its behaviour: (i) a `COVER::Threat Capability`, the disposition capturing what the attacker is *able* to do (skills, tooling, resources); (ii) `UFO-C::Beliefs`, mental states representing the attacker's subjective perception of the target environment—its infrastructure, deployed defenses, and user behaviour; and (iii) `UFO-C::Intentions`, commitments to achieving an *objective*, where an objective is the goal that constitutes the propositional content of an intention. These aspects relate as follows: following the belief–desire–intention account of practical reasoning [6], the attacker forms an `Attack Plan` as a *closed* intention directed at an objective, selecting—on the basis of its `UFO-C::Beliefs`—a structured course of action it believes feasible, whose execution is in turn bounded by its `Capability`. `UFO-C::Beliefs` thus constrain which plans are *envisaged*; capability constrains which are *executable*. `COVER::Threat Capability` is detailed within the risk-assessment sub-ontology (Sect. 3.3); here it suffices that it is a property of the same attacker that bears the intention.

The Attack Plan Definition. In UFO-C, a `Plan` is an `UFO-C::Action Type` (or originally in [11] an `UFO-C::Action Universal`)—an `UFO-B::Event Type` whose instances are actions performed by an agent to satisfy an intention [11]. The temporal parts of such an instance—its individual steps—stand in `UFO-B::Historical Dependence`, a relation stronger than accidental precedence but weaker than strict causality [12], and the agent's commitment to realizing a specific plan is a `UFO-C::Closed Commitment`. Two readings of "plan" are admissible: a plan as an Action Type, or a plan as an *intention to instantiate* such an Action Type [6]. We adopt the latter, intentional reading, as it is the one relevant to attack *planning*: it lets us represent the attacker's commitment to a specific structured course of action as an entity that exists independently of whether that course is realized—so that partially observed, or entirely unexecuted, campaigns can still be reasoned about.

Accordingly, we define an ***`Attack Plan`*** as a closed intention, i.e., an `Intention` that is also a `UFO-C::Closed Commitment`. Such an intention is held by a `ROSE::Attacker`, constrained by its `UFO-C::Beliefs`,[5] and its propositional content is a malicious goal. Such an intention is *based on* a distinct `UFO-C::Complex Action Type` that specifies the structured course of action to which the attacker commits. `UFO-B::Historical Dependence` orders the temporal parts of the *instances* of that type—the individual attack steps of an actual campaign—not the parts of the type itself. An `ROSE::Attack` is then an `UFO-C::Action`—an actual, intentional occurrence in the world—that *instantiates* the `UFO-C::Action Type` and thereby *manifests* the `Attack Plan`.

3.2 Attack Plan Modelling

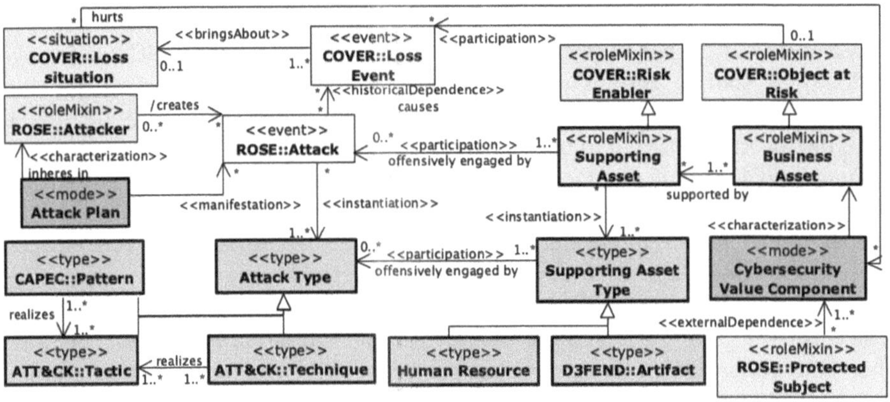

Fig. 1. The Attack sub-ontology of ROCAP.

Assets Under Attack. In **Fig.** 1, we present a UFO-based, COVER & ROSE-aligned conceptualization of the socio-technical system targeted by the `ROSE::Attacker`. We represent one socio-technical system as composed of many instances of `Business Asset` that each hold value for an organization and therefore qualify as `COVER::Objects At Risk`. A `Business Asset` is an organizational component bearing value for the organization—every `Business Asset` is a `UFO::Endurant`[6] and can instantiate more specific types, such as Business Workflow. We introduce the `Cybersecurity Value Component` (a `UFO::Mode`) that characterizes a `Business Asset` with respect to a `ROSE::Protected Subject`'s concerns. We name it a *value component*, rather than a *security property* or *principle*, to mark its grounding in `COVER::Value`: confidentiality, integrity,

[5] A `UFO-C::Belief` represents an intentional mental state of an agent that models their subjective perception of reality.

[6] `UFO::Endurants` are individuals that persist in time while maintaining their identity, i.e., they are wholly present at any given moment of their existence.

and availability are modelled here not as free-standing properties but as the value dimensions a `Business Asset` holds for a `Protected Subject`. Specific components—such as `Confidentiality`, `Integrity`, and `Availability`—specialize it; each individual component (*e.g.*, the confidentiality of a given patient record) inheres in the `Business Asset` and bears a value reflecting how strongly the `Protected Subject` requires it to be preserved. The bearer of these modes admits alternatives: the confidentiality level may instead be read as a belief of the Protected Subject—externally dependent on the asset's disposition to be exposed—or as a quality grading the protective capacities of the surrounding system, a design space analogous to the Trust/Trustworthiness distinction [3,4]. We retain inherence in the Business Asset, its subject-relativity marked by the external dependence on the Protected Subject (Fig. 1), as our impact analysis attaches loss to the asset's value components; aligning with belief- and obligation-based readings is left to future work. Furthermore, a `Business Asset` is supported by `Supporting Assets`—a functional dependence rather than parthood [10]: to deliver its value to the `ROSE::Protected Subject`, a `Business Asset` requires instances of `Supporting Asset` functioning as such. The dependence is contingent, meaning that a `Business Asset` can exist without supporting assets (e.g., a newly chartered department), but cannot realize its value without them. A `Supporting Asset` is a role played by an `Endurant`: either a technical resource characterized by a `D3FEND::Artifact`—physical or not (e.g., a physical server, an operating system, a virtual machine, a deployed business application)—or a `Human Resource`, a person in charge of the technical system. The payroll function, for instance, is supported by a deployed application, the server hosting it, and the administrators operating it.

A core design choice here is to decouple `COVER::Value` from `COVER::Vulnerability`. `Business Assets` hold `COVER::Value` for the organization through their `Cybersecurity Value Components`, whereas vulnerabilities attach at the supporting layer: `Supporting Asset` specializes `COVER::Risk Enabler` (ROSE) and therefore bears the `COVER::Vulnerabilities` that *characterize* a `Risk Enabler`. A `Supporting Asset` may thus bear one or more vulnerabilities (*e.g.*, unpatched software, or personnel with weak cyber awareness) that the `ROSE::Attacker` can exploit.

We acknowledge that a `Supporting Asset` such as a server also has value (*e.g.*, its monetary cost); we nonetheless attribute value at the `Business Asset` level and *distribute* a `Supporting Asset`'s value across the assets it supports. The reason is structural: our impact analysis reasons about loss through the `Cybersecurity Value Components` inhering in `Business Assets`, keeping the loss chain aligned with what the organization stands to lose; assigning intrinsic value to each `Supporting Asset`—the natural alternative—would double-count value already realized there. Symmetrically, a `Business Asset` bears `COVER::Vulnerabilities` only indirectly, through its `Supporting Assets`.

Attack Logic. To capture the `ROSE::Attacker`'s behavior, we align our model with the *de facto* ***Tactics and Techniques*** from [36].

An ROSE::Attack of a certain Attack Type is the manifestation of the ROSE::Attacker's COVER::Threat Capability and UFO::Intention meeting a COVER::Vulnerability of a Supporting Asset (Sect. 3.3). The specialization of Attack Type is centered on ATT&CK::Tactic, which represents a complex UFO::Event type that achieves high-level adversarial goal (*e.g.*, Initial Access). An ROSE::Attack instantiates an Attack Type categorized along two complementary axes: ATT&CK::Tactic, the adversarial goal it pursues (*e.g.*, Initial Access), and ATT&CK::Technique, the means employed—each technique *realizing* one or more tactics. A CAPEC::Pattern addresses the same offensive mechanism at a more abstract level: both are event types—repeatable across occurrences—of which the ATT&CK and CAPEC catalogue entries are mere descriptions; a Technique types the observable behaviour, a Pattern the underlying mechanism.

We further make two claims to refine the granularity of impact analysis : (1) We assume that an Attack does not directly engage a Business Asset. Instead, it offensively engages a Supporting Asset by exploiting its COVER::Vulnerabilities; (2) The Attack subsequently causes a COVER::Loss Event which impacts the Business Asset. This brings about an unwanted COVER::Loss Situation (*e.g. data leak*) that hurts the Cybersecurity Value Components (*e.g., confidentiality*) inhering in the impacted Business Asset, and thereby also hurts the Intention of a ROSE::Protected Subject (*cf.* Fig. 1)

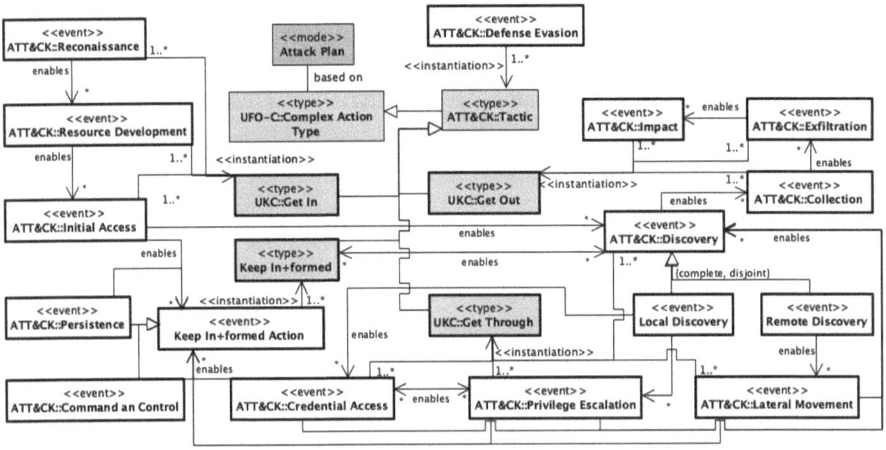

Fig. 2. The Attack Tactic dependency sub-ontology.

Attack Dependency. In **Fig.** 2 we define attack dependency by building on Tactics defined in ATT&CK [36], and the meta-tactics introduced in the Unified Kill Chain (UKC) [31]. UKC groups Tactics into three meta-Tactics—Get In, Get Through, and Get Out—which *subsume* ATT&CK::Tactic rather than aggregate its instances: a tactic such as Reconnaissance instantiates both ATT&CK::Tactic and Get In. Yet, UKC remains agnostic about temporal dependencies among the Tactics within each meta-tactic. Since UFO-B::Historical Dependence holds between individual events, the dependencies of Fig. 2 cannot themselves be UFO-B::Historical Dependence relations between Tactics. Following the pattern of defined domain relations in ROSE, we introduce *enables* between event types: *enables(B, A)* holds when instances of A typically *historically depend on* some instance of B. Since *enables* relates first-order event types only, dependencies targeting the Keep In+formed meta-tactic go through Keep In+formed Action, a base event type specialized by its Tactics. Guided by the SOC analysts involved in the co-design to be compliant with real world APT campaigns, we propose several necessary adaptations to ATT&CK and UKC:

- We include all Tactics in our dependency modeling, except ATT&CK::Execution, which we treat as an internal part of other Tactics, rather than a standalone one.
- UKC places ATT&CK::Persistence and ATT&CK::Command and Control (C2) under UKC::Get In. However, during Get Through, new instances of these Tactics may be required at both host and network levels. We thus extend UKC's tri-partite meta-Tactic structure by introducing a fourth called Keep In+formed to encompass both ATT&CK::Persistence and ATT&CK::C2.
- ATT&CK::Defense Evasion, which UKC places under Get In, is a *cross-cutting* Tactic: its instances serve to prevent detection by the defender. As this prevention relation targets the defensive sub-model, it lies outside the scope of Fig. 2.
- We split ATT&CK::Discovery into two sub-tactics: Local Discovery and Remote Discovery. Local Discovery refers to discovery within a system or network to which the Attacker already has access. Remote Discovery refers to discovery outside the Attacker's current access zone.

Figure 2 orders these Tactics within each meta-Tactic. Two dependencies are worth noting, as they are fixed neither by ATT&CK nor by UKC. Persistence and C2 are mutually enabling—trojan-based campaigns typically establish Persistence before C2, whereas web-shell intrusions reverse that order—and, in Get Out, both Exfiltration and Impact require Collection, which in turn depends on Discovery, since an attacker can only collect what it has already discovered.

3.3 Cybersecurity Risk Assessment

The initial risk assessment in ROSE and COVER is grounded in the COVER::Risk Experience, defined as the actual or potential interaction between an adversarial intent (UFO::Intention), a system COVER::Vulnerability, and an ROSE::Attacker.[7] In **Fig.** 3, ROCAP introduces Untreated Risk being

[7] More precisely its COVER::Threat Capability, a concept beyond the scope of this paper.

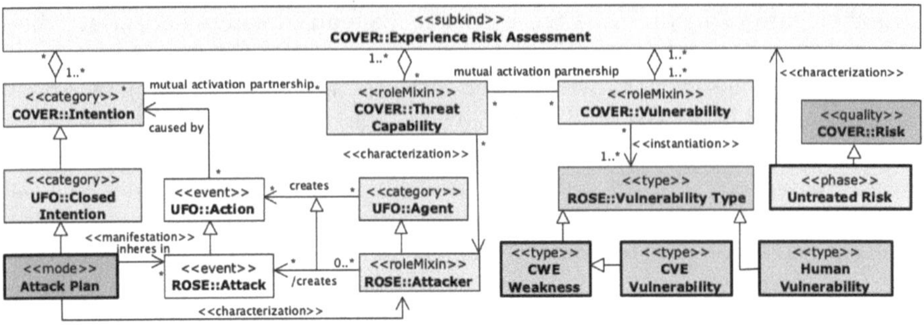

Fig. 3. The Cybersecurity Experience Risk Assessment sub-ontology.

the `COVER::Risk` assessed through `COVER::Experience Risk Assessment`. Following COVER, we quantify Untreated Risk along likelihood (triggering and causal) and severity (the impact of a `Loss Event` on the `Cybersecurity Value Component`), reflecting the current risk exposure of a `Risk Subject` given the existing defenses.

Vulnerability Classification. Figure 3 models the `COVER::Vulnerability` inhering in the aforementioned assets as either a *technical* vulnerability—a `CWE::Weakness` type or a `CVE::Vulnerability`—or a *human* vulnerability, a bias arising from an individual's dispositions or external influences [25], whereby the outcome of an action diverges from what the actor's cognitive capability anticipated.

4 Validation

4.1 Methodology

To be practical and reusable, ROCAP should support the tactical and operational activities that security analysts perform around attack planning. Our validation proceeded in four iterative stages. First, the ontology was progressively reviewed with both expert groups, who assessed its conceptual completeness, suggested missing concepts (such as `Cybersecurity Value Component` or `Untreated Risk`), and validated its alignment with operational practice and cybersecurity standards. Second, cybersecurity requirements were systematically extracted from **ISO/IEC 27005:2022** and **NIST CSF 2.0** and mapped to ontology concepts. Third, Competency Questions (CQs) were derived through an expert-driven process involving two complementary groups: SOC analysts from Gatewatcher, contributing operational expertise on attack investigation and incident response, and information security standardization experts—including a member of the ISO/IEC JTC 1/SC 27 Luxembourg national committee—contributing risk-management expertise. The CQs were refined until consensus, ensuring both standard coverage and SOC-operational relevance. Finally, they were implemented as Prolog queries and evaluated against the BlackSuit ransomware and Long-Term Espionage scenarios.[8] We present the most important CQs, related to `Attack Plan`, in Table 1.

4.2 Standards to Build Competency Questions

ISO/IEC 27005:2022 is the reference standard for information security risk management; its guidelines on identifying threats, vulnerabilities, and risk scenarios directly inform how an adversary operationalizes an attack. Crucially, it inherits the risk-management philosophy of ISO 31000:2018, already formalized in UFO terms by COVER and ROSE, letting us verify that ROCAP covers the standard's requirements consistently with its underlying ontological commitments. **NIST CSF 2.0** complements it by structuring the full threat-management life-cycle: defensive outcomes—notably within *Identify*, *Govern*, and *Detect*—must mirror and anticipate an attacker's tactical steps, and its outcome-driven rather than prescriptive character suits validating ROCAP's operational aspects.

Table 1. Selection of Competency Questions (CQs) derived from ISO/IEC 27005:2022 and NIST CSF 2.0.

CQ ID & References	Competency Question
CQ4 (ISO §7.2.1, ID.RA-03)	What threat sources and actors are identified and associated?
CQ5 (ISO §7.2.1, ID.RA-02)	What capabilities, intentions, and objectives characterize an attacker?
CQ6 (ID.RA-02, DE.AE-07)	What attack types, techniques, and patterns characterize a given plan?
CQ7 (ISO §7.2.1, DE.AE, RS.AN)	Given a partial trace, which attack plans is the adversary carrying out?
CQ8 (ISO §7.2.1, DE.AE, RS.AN)	Can identically looking attacks be distinguished by the adversary's goal?

4.3 Running Example: The BlackSuit Ransomware APT Campaign

We focus here on a Prolog implementation of ROCAP, two APT scenarios and the above competency questions. We chose Prolog for its expressivity to both represent and execute complex, historical dependencies in attack planning. An OWL version of ROCAP is also available here. **APT**

[8] The complete traceability matrix linking standard requirements, ontology concepts, and competency questions is provided in the accompanying online repository: https://github.com/AntoineLeblancFr/ROCAP.

Campaign. We instantiate ROCAP with a simplified real-world scenario[9] from a CTI report—*Fake Zoom Ends in BlackSuit Ransomware* [38]—in which the attacker compromises an organization through a malicious fake Zoom installer. As Fig. 4 shows, the `blacksuitOperator` is characterized by `blacksuitPlan_bs`, an `Attack Plan` whose committed course of action decomposes into four `Closed Intentions`: *gainInitialFoothold_bs*, *maintainPersistent_bs*, *locateValuableData_bs*, and *exfiltrateAndEncryptDataToExtortVictim_bs*. This course of action is a `Complex Action Type`; its eight instantiating `Attack` occurrences—the individual steps, chained by `Historical Dependence`—manifest the plan. The first step offensively engages `johnDoe` (a person playing the `Supporting Asset` role), exploiting a `Human Vulnerability`; the remaining steps engage `Supporting Assets` of various types. Each such vulnerability ultimately drives the loss chain hurting `victimCorpITDepartment`'s value components, modelled at the type level in Fig. 3. Traversing this path backwards, a SOC analyst can trace an adverse outcome to its originating vulnerability and threat source.

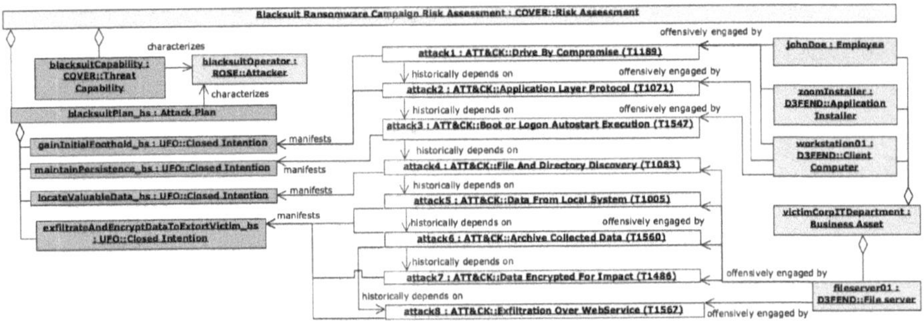

Fig. 4. Simplified Scenario from the BlackSuit Ransomware APT Campaign.

An Alternative Espionage Scenario. To demonstrate the operational value of plan reification, Fig. 5 introduces a second `Attack Plan`: a manually generated *Long-Term Espionage scenario*. The second plan shares the first three steps with the BlackSuit campaign, but diverges at a distinct `Closed Intention`. While the shared-prefix mechanics are visible in Fig. 5, anchoring the steps to separate intentions is what makes the plan/trace separation testable and allows the ontology to distinguish look-alike campaigns.

[9] For readability, Fig. 4 depicts only the elements needed to answer the competency questions selected in this paper (Sect. 4.4); the complete instance diagram, including the loss chain (`Loss Event`, `Loss Situation`, `Cybersecurity Value Component`) and the borne vulnerabilities, is provided in the repository.

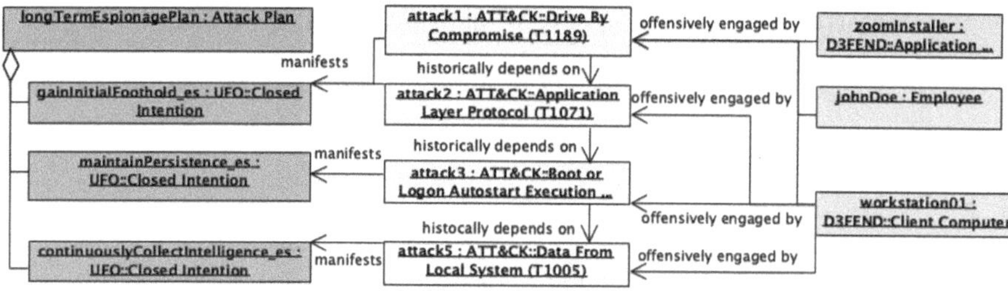

Fig. 5. Alternative Scenario from the BlackSuit Ransomware APT Campaign: Long-Term Espionage.

4.4 Answers to the Competency Questions

We now answer the competency questions of Table 1 on the running example, reporting for each what the corresponding Prolog query returns. To make the reasoning transparent rather than merely report success, we then detail CQ7: we give its codification as a Prolog rule and walk through the resolution that produces its answer. We single out CQ7 because it is the question that most directly exercises the reification of the plan—reasoning over a partial execution to determine which plan an adversary is carrying out—and thus best illustrates the white-box reasoning the ontology affords.

Threat Sources and Actors (CQ4—CQ5). CQ4 identifies each `ROSE::Attacker` along with their associated `Attack Plan` and `COVER::Threat Capability`. In our execution, it successfully binds the BlackSuit operator to its *ransomware deployment capability* and *plan*, and the second *espionage attacker* to a *long-term access capability*. CQ5 expands this by returning the four reified `Closed Intentions` (from *initial foothold* to *encryption-based extortion*) that define the BlackSuit operator's active objectives. This treats attacker objectives as structural ontological entities rather than plain-text labels.

Attack Plan (CQ6—CQ8). CQ6 maps the ordered attack steps of a plan to their corresponding `ATT&CK::Technique` types. CQ7 leverages the reification of the plan to reason over *partial* executions. Listing 1 gives its codification: each plan reifies the committed course of action it is based on as an ordered list of steps,[10] carried by the plan's `steps` attribute, and the rule succeeds through `append(Trace, Anticipated, Steps)` whenever the observed *Trace* is an ordered *prefix* of that sequence, binding *Anticipated* to the steps still to come.

[10] For readability, steps are identified by their ATT&CK technique code; the repository uses named step individuals. The step list reifies the content of the plan's `Closed Intention`—the course of action the attacker commits to.

Listing 1. Codification of CQ7 and the two candidate plans.

```
% CQ7: which plan is the adversary carrying out, given a partial trace?
% Succeeds when the observed Trace is an ordered prefix of the steps
% of the course of action the plan is based on.
cq7(Trace, cq7{plan:Plan, observed:Trace, anticipated:Anticipated}) :-
    instanceOf(Plan, attackPlan),
    attr(Plan, steps, Steps),
    append(Trace, Anticipated, Steps).
```

The engine derives the answers in Listing 2 as follows. For the observed prefix `[t1189,t1071,t1547]`, the engine enumerates candidate plans via `instanceOf(Plan, attackPlan)` and retrieves each plan's reified `Steps`. For *blacksuitPlan_bs*, `append` unifies the trace as a prefix of the eight-step sequence and binds *Anticipated* to `[t1083,t1005,t1560,t1486,t1567]`; on backtracking, the same holds for *longTermEspionagePlan*, binding *Anticipated* to `[t1005]`. Two solutions are returned—a state of *ambiguity*, each with its own anticipated continuation. When *File and Directory Discovery* (`t1083`) is additionally observed, `append` still succeeds for *blacksuitPlan_bs* (whose fourth step is `t1083`) but *fails* for *longTermEspionagePlan*, whose fourth step is `t1005`: the trace is no longer a prefix, so unification cannot proceed. The ambiguity collapses and *blacksuitPlan_bs* remains the sole answer.

Listing 2. CQ7 matching a partial trace against candidate `Attack Plans`.

```
% Ambiguous case: the observed techniques form a prefix shared by both
    plans
?- cq7([t1189, t1071, t1547], Answer).
Answer = cq7{anticipated: [t1083, t1005, t1560, t1486, t1567],
             observed: [t1189, t1071, t1547],
             plan: blacksuitPlan_bs} ;
Answer = cq7{anticipated: [t1005],
             observed: [t1189, t1071, t1547],
             plan: longTermEspionagePlan}.
% Disambiguated case: t1083 belongs only to the BlackSuit plan
?- cq7([t1189, t1071, t1547, t1083], Answer).
Answer = cq7{anticipated: [t1005, t1560, t1486],
             observed: [t1189, t1071, t1547, t1083],
             plan: blacksuitPlan_bs}.
```

CQ8 completes the picture by exercising the *intentional* layer: it isolates look-alike attacks that instantiate the same technique yet are anchored to separate, non-overlapping `Closed Intentions`. This is the distinction execution-oriented models cannot draw—two identical observations are told apart not by what is observed, but by the plan and intention they realize.

5 Conclusion

We presented ROCAP, a Reference Ontology for Cybersecurity Attack Planning grounded in UFO and integrating core ontologies (COVER, ROSE) with industry standards (D3FEND, CAPEC, Unified Kill Chain). By formalizing an `Attack Plan` as a `Closed Intention` bound to a `Complex Action Type`, ROCAP establishes a plan/trace separation that lets analysts reason about partially executed campaigns and distinguish identical early traces that diverge later—a capability unsupported by existing cybersecurity ontologies—and we validated it through competency questions derived from ISO/IEC 27005:2022 and NIST CSF 2.0 on a Prolog instantiation of the BlackSuit campaign. Future work will extend ROCAP into ROCADe (Reference Ontology for Cybersecurity Attack and *Defense* planning), supporting both defensive SOC and offensive red-teaming decision support, and fully align on UFO the concepts originating from D3FEND [27], particularly for automating risk analysis.

Acknowledgments. This work was supported by the French National Research Agency (ANR) (grant number ANR-23-CE39-0010) and the Luxembourg National Research Fund (FNR) (grant number INTER/ANR/23/18034502) under the ANCILE project. The authors thank the SOC analysts at Gatewatcher who participated in the co-design and validation of ROCAP.

Data Availability Statement. All complementary code, ROCAP model and Competency Questions traceability can be found here: https://github.com/AntoineLeblancFr/ROCAP.

References

1. Akbar, K.A.: The design and application of a unified ontology for cyber security. In: International Conference on Information Systems Security, pp. 23–41 (2023)
2. Akbar, K.A., et al.: The design of an ontology for ATT&CK and its application to cybersecurity. In: Proceedings of the Thirteenth ACM Conference on Data and Application Security and Privacy, pp. 295–297. ACM (2023)
3. Amaral, G.: Towards a Reference Ontology of Trust, pp. 3–21 (2019)
4. Amaral, G.: Trustworthiness requirements: the pix case study (2021)
5. Ansarinia, M.: Ontology-based modeling of DDoS attacks for attack plan detection. In: International Symposium on Telecommunications, pp. 993–998 (2012)
6. Bratman, M.: Intention, Plans, and Practical Reason. Harvard University Press (1987)
7. Chan, P.: An ontological knowledge base for cyber network attack planning. In: International Conference on Cyber Warfare and Security (2015)
8. Fonseca, C.M.: Ontology-driven conceptual modeling as a service. In: CEUR Workshop Proceedings, p. 2969 (2021)
9. Gilliard, E., et al.: Knowledge graph reasoning for cyber attack detection. IET Commun. **18**(4), 297–308 (2024)
10. Guizzardi, G.: The Problem of Transitivity of Part-Whole Relations in Conceptual Modeling Revisited, pp. 94–109 (2009)
11. Guizzardi, G.: Grounding software domain ontologies in the unified foundational ontology (UFO): the case of the ODE software process ontology. In: Conferencia Iberoamericana de Software Engineering (2008)
12. Guizzardi, G., Wagner, G., de Almeida Falbo, R., Guizzardi, R.S.S., Almeida, J.P.A.: Towards ontological foundations for the conceptual modeling of events. In: Ng, W., Storey, V.C., Trujillo, J.C. (eds.) ER 2013. LNCS, vol. 8217, pp. 327–341. Springer, Heidelberg (2013). https://doi.org/10.1007/978-3-642-41924-9_27
13. Guizzardi, G.: UFO: unified foundational ontology. Appl. Ontol. (2022)

14. van Heerden, R., et al.: Using an ontology for network attack planning. Int. J. Cyber Warfare Terror. **6**(3), 65–78 (2016)
15. International Organization for Standardization: ISO 31000:2018 – risk management: Guidelines (2018)
16. International Organization for Standardization: ISO/IEC 27005:2022 – guidance on managing information security risks (2022)
17. Jacobsen, A., et al.: Fair principles: interpretations and implementation considerations. Data Intell. **2**(1–2), 10–29 (2020)
18. Kaloroumakis, P.E., Smith, M.J.: Toward a knowledge graph of cybersecurity countermeasures. The MITRE Corporation, Technical report (2021)
19. Leblanc, A.: Rethinking cybersecurity ontology classification and evaluation: towards a credibility-centered framework. In: Enterprise Design, Operations, and Computing, pp. 284–299. Springer, Heidelberg (2026). https://doi.org/10.1007/978-3-032-15140-7_16
20. Liu, Y., Guo, Y.: Towards real-time warning and defense strategy AI planning for cyber security systems aided by security ontology. Electronics **11**(24), 4128 (2022)
21. Luh, R.: TAON: an ontology-based approach to mitigating targeted attacks. In: Proceedings of the 18th International Conference on Information Integration and Web-Based Applications and Services, pp. 303–312. ACM (2016)
22. MITRE Corporation: CAPEC – Common Attack Pattern Enumeration and Classification. https://capec.mitre.org/
23. MITRE Corporation: Common Vulnerabilities and Exposures (CVE). https://www.cve.org/
24. MITRE Corporation: Common Weakness Enumeration (CWE). https://cwe.mitre.org/
25. National Institute of Standards and Technology: The NIST Cybersecurity Framework (CSF) 2.0. Technical Report. NIST CSWP 29 (2024)
26. Oliveira, Í., et al.: An ontology of security from a risk treatment perspective. In: Conceptual Modeling – ER 2022, pp. 365–379. Springer, Heidelberg (2022). https://doi.org/10.1007/978-3-031-17995-2_26
27. Oliveira, Í., et al.: Boosting D3FEND: ontological analysis and recommendations. In: Proceedings of the FOIS 2023, pp. 334–348 (2023)
28. Oliveira, Í., et al.: An ontological lens on attack trees: toward adequacy and interoperability. In: Formal Ontology in Information Systems, vol. 409, pp. 151–165. IOS Press (2025)
29. Oliveira, Í., et al.: An ontological model of the phishing attack process. In: Enterprise, Business-Process and Information Systems Modeling. BPMDS 2025, EMMSAD 2025, vol. 558, pp. 274–289. Springer, Heidelberg (2025). https://doi.org/10.1007/978-3-031-95397-2_17
30. Ou, X., et al.: MulVAL: a logic-based network security analyzer. In: Proceedings of the 14th USENIX Security Symposium, pp. 113–128 (2005)
31. Pols, P.: The Unified Kill Chain. Fox-IT and HAN University of Applied Sciences, Technical report (2017)
32. Sales, T.P., Baião, F., Guizzardi, G., Almeida, J.P.A., Guarino, N., Mylopoulos, J.: The common ontology of value and risk. In: Trujillo, J.C., et al. (eds.) ER 2018. LNCS, vol. 11157, pp. 121–135. Springer, Cham (2018). https://doi.org/10.1007/978-3-030-00847-5_11
33. Putrevu, V.S.C.: A framework for advanced persistent threat attribution using Zachman ontology. In: Proceedings of the 2023 European Interdisciplinary Cybersecurity Conference (EICC '23), pp. 34–41. ACM (2023)

34. Ren, Y., et al.: CSKG4APT: a cybersecurity knowledge graph for advanced persistent threat organization attribution. IEEE Trans. Knowl. Data Eng. **35**(6), 5695–5709 (2023)
35. Scarpato, N., et al.: Reachability matrix ontology: a cybersecurity ontology. Appl. Artif. Intell. **33**(7), 643–655 (2019)
36. Strom, B.E.: MITRE ATT&CK: Design and Philosophy. The MITRE Corporation, Technical report (2020)
37. Sun, L., et al.: APTKG: constructing threat intelligence knowledge graph from open-source APT reports based on deep learning. In:2022 5th International Conference on Data Science and Information Technology (DSIT), pp. 01–06 (2022)
38. The DFIR Report: Fake Zoom Ends in BlackSuit Ransomware (2025). https://thedfirreport.com/2025/03/31/fake-zoom-ends-in-blacksuit-ransomware/
39. Vielberth, M., et al.: Security operations center: a systematic study and open challenges. IEEE Access **8**, 227756–227779 (2020)
40. Wang, F.: Ontology-based APT attack detection and defense countermeasures. In: International Conference on High Performance Big Data and Intelligent Systems (HDIS), pp. 27–33 (2022)

An Ontology Design Pattern to Represent the Selective Transitivity of Fluid Flow Connections

Fabrício H. Rodrigues[1(✉)], Nicolau O. Santos[2], Joel L. Carbonera[2], Haroldo R. S. Silva[2], Mara Abel[2], and João Netto[2]

[1] State University of New York at Buffalo (UB), Buffalo, USA
fr33@buffalo.edu

[2] Federal University of Rio Grande do Sul (UFRGS), Porto Alegre, Brazil
{nicolau.santos,joel.carbonera,hrssilva,marabel,netto}@inf.ufrgs.br

Abstract. Representing connectivity in fluid flow systems is a key requirement for ontologies across fields ranging from process engineering to urban infrastructure. The modeling of the dynamic relationship between parts of a complex system that allows data or material to flow across those components remains an open question. While the relation of flow connection is intuitively perceived as transitive and frequently behaves as such, engineering practice reveals numerous scenarios where this property fails to hold, either due to the internal structural isolation of components or their dynamic operational states. This context-sensitive behavior represents a substantial modeling challenge, imposing a trade-off among capturing valid indirect flow pathways, preventing spurious connections, and maintaining model parsimony. This paper proposes the notion of *selective transitivity* and, based on that, presents a novel Ontology Design Pattern (ODP) to account for this characteristic of the flow connection relation. The pattern is implemented using OWL and SWRL and supports the automated inference of indirect pathways while systematically avoiding unintended, structurally or operationally blocked connections and preserving parsimony. We illustrate the pattern's application in a case study in the Oil & Gas industry. Given the generality of the notion of selective transitivity, we argue that this ODP can be extended/adapted to other domains.

Keywords: Ontology · Ontology Design Pattern · Connection · Transitivity · Fluid Flow Systems · Oil and Gas

1 Introduction

Various fields heavily rely on controlling the flow of fluids through complex networks of pipes, valves, and similar components – from urban HVAC (Heating, Ventilation, and Air Conditioning) and water supply systems to chemical plants

© The Author(s), under exclusive license to Springer Nature Switzerland AG 2027
A. Bernasconi et al. (Eds.): ER 2026, LNCS 17081, pp. 200–216, 2027.
https://doi.org/10.1007/978-3-032-40795-5_12

and oil and gas pipelines. Managing such systems involves a range of challenging tasks, such as flow routes planning, safety monitoring, and failure diagnosis/response, requiring computer-based solutions for their effective operation.

Ontologies can play a major role in this context. As a formal, explicit specification of a shared conceptualization [7], an ontology enables the semantic integration and interoperability of data from different sources while supporting automated reasoning tasks. Several ontologies (*e.g.*, [3–5]) were proposed to represent relevant aspects of fluid flow systems, such as their functional composition and the flow connections between their components. Nevertheless, they present limitations when dealing with the nuanced behavior of the flow connection relation – *i.e.*, a relation between two objects that allows fluid to pass from one to the other – regarding transitivity.

Intuitively, the flow connection relation seems to be transitive. In simple flow systems, such as a series of connected pipes, it indeed behaves as a transitive relation. Still, engineering practice reveals numerous scenarios in which flow connection transitivity simply fails to hold (*e.g.*, when a component's internal structure prevents flow between other components connected to it) or is contingent upon the operational state of certain system components (*e.g.*, valves).

This context-sensitive behavior of the flow connection relation with respect to transitivity poses a representational challenge and imposes a trade-off among capturing valid indirect flow pathways, preventing the inference of spurious connections, and maintaining model parsimony. While a transitive characterization enables the inference of genuine indirect flow pathways, it will also yield spurious connections in cases of structural or operational flow interruptions. Conversely, a simple non-transitive approach avoids erroneous inferences but at the cost of failing to infer valid connections, which significantly constrains the system's reasoning capabilities. Finally, more elaborate strategies (*e.g.*, defining specialized relations to account for contextual variants, or relying on external procedural reasoning) may reconcile inferential completeness with correctness, but usually hinder model simplicity, reusability, and/or semantic clarity.

Accurately capturing this transitive-like character of flow connections is a requisite for various reasoning tasks, such as inferring reachability between components of a flow system, which is key for predicting and simulating flow propagation within the system. To address this issue, in this paper we propose an ontology design pattern (ODP), *i.e.*, a modeling solution to solve a recurrent ontology design problem [1]. The ODP from an ontological analysis of the nature of flow connections in fluid systems and implemented using the Web Ontology Language (OWL)[1] and the Semantic Web Rule Language (SWRL)[2], which are well established and widely supported languages for formal ontology representation. With that, we aim to provide a domain-independent, easily reusable solution that can be employed as a small standalone model, integrated into existing ontologies, or used to guide the development of new ontological models to represent fluid flow systems.

---

[1] www.w3.org/TR/owl2-syntax/.

[2] www.w3.org/submissions/SWRL/.

The contributions of this paper are threefold: (1) we present an ontological analysis of the flow connection relation, distinguishing its underlying static/structural and dynamic/operational aspects; (2) we introduce the general notion of *selective transitivity* for mediated relations; and (3) we propose an ontology design pattern that applies this notion to the case of flow connections.

In Sect. 2 we discuss the challenges of representing flow connections; in Sect. 3 we make an ontological analysis of the flow connection relation regarding transitivity and propose the notion of selective transitivity; in Sect. 4 we present the proposed ODP and apply it to a case study in the Oil & Gas industry in Sect. 5; finally, Sect. 6 discusses our results and brings our concluding remarks.

2 The Challenge of Representing Flow Connections

In this paper, we use the notion of flow connection to denote a relation of potential operational reachability between the interiors of two objects. More specifically, if there is a flow connection x–▸y[3], fluid can propagate from within x to within y. Now, to further explore the complexities of representing the flow connection relation, we will consider three scenarios (Fig. 1A-C) that exemplify typical configurations found in fluid flow systems. All such scenarios capture situations in which one entity has a flow connection to an intermediary entity, which in turn has a flow connection to a third entity. Nevertheless, they differ with respect to whether (and how) such a chain of flow connections gives rise to a further flow connection between the first and the third entities.

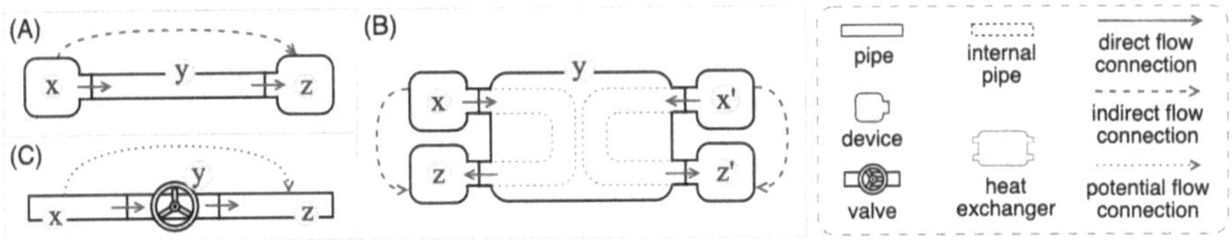

Fig. 1. Illustrative Scenarios

In scenario (A), a device x is connected to a pipe y that is connected to another device z, so that x can feed fluid to y and y to z. Also, x can feed z by feeding fluid to y, which then feeds it to z. Thus, we have the direct connections x–▸y and y–▸z, and the indirect connection x–▸z (in virtue of the chain x–▸y–▸z). In (B), a heat exchanger y receives hot fluid from x and sends it to z, while receiving cold fluid from x' and sending it to z'. Thus we have x–▸z via x–▸y–▸z and x'–▸z' via x'–▸y–▸z'. However, internally to y, hot and cold fluids flow through hydraulically isolated pipes (represented as dashed lines inside the heat exchanger in Fig. 1B) that allow heat exchange between fluids

[3] The symbol '–▸' will be used to represent a flow connection between two objects, *e.g.*, 'x–▸y' represents a flow connection between x and y.

without mixing them. With that, despite the chains $x \rightarrowtriangle y \rightarrowtriangle z'$ and $x' \rightarrowtriangle y \rightarrowtriangle z$, there are neither $x \rightarrowtriangle z'$ nor $x' \rightarrowtriangle z$. Finally, in (C), pipe x is connected to y and y to z, so that we have $x \rightarrowtriangle y$, $y \rightarrowtriangle z$, and a *potential* $x \rightarrowtriangle z$. That is, when y is *open*, fluid can flow from x to z through y, and then we have $x \rightarrowtriangle z$ via $x \rightarrowtriangle y \rightarrowtriangle z$. However, when y is *closed*, the chain $x \rightarrowtriangle y \rightarrowtriangle z$ remains, but $x \rightarrowtriangle z$ ceases to hold.

Together, these scenarios show that flow connection is not globally transitive: sometimes a chain $x \rightarrowtriangle y \rightarrowtriangle z$ gives rise to an indirect $x \rightarrowtriangle z$, but not always. Still, simply characterizing it as non-transitive does not reflect the full picture. Even though not globally transitive, we can treat the flow connection relation as transitive in certain constrained settings. Indeed, domain professionals consistently reason about the transitive behavior of flow connections based on their local context to identify indirect connections. This systematic, albeit tacit, treatment of flow connections points to an underlying regularity that knowledge representation systems could capture. Even so, capturing it declaratively in standard ontology languages remains non-trivial.

Declaring the flow connection relation as transitive enables the discovery of all existing indirect connections in a system. However, besides being ontologically incorrect, it leads to the spurious inference of numerous non-existent connections, since the reasoner cannot distinguish between connection chains that indeed constitute an open flow line and those that are structurally disconnected (*e.g.*, $x \rightarrowtriangle y \rightarrowtriangle z$ versus $x' \rightarrowtriangle y \rightarrowtriangle z$ in scenario B) or operationally blocked (*e.g.*, when valve y is closed in C). In contrast, simply declaring the relation as non-transitive prevents the inference of non-existent pathways, but sacrifices the ontology's expressivity, hindering the automated deduction of the indirect connections.

One alternative to remediate these limitations is to retain a non-transitive relation and delegate the inference of indirect connections to external mechanisms, *e.g.*, graph algorithms that incorporate heuristics to identify mediated connections or query templates that capture structural/operational patterns of indirect pathways. Although this approach can avoid the naïve transitive approach's spurious inferences while allowing the retrieval of real indirect connections, it moves part of the domain semantics to external resources. This leads to the recurrent issue that we call "*ontology outside the ontology*", *i.e.*, when a relevant part of the domain semantics – the *de facto* ontology – is not in the ontology artifact, but rather encoded elsewhere. Consequently, the quality of inferences and query results depends on resources other than the ontology artifact itself, reducing transparency, maintainability, reusability, and interoperability.

Another alternative is to 'tweak' the ontology to support some desired inferences while minimizing unintended consequences. Suppose that, in (B), y receives gas from x and liquid from x'. In this case, we could specialize flow connection ($\rightarrowtriangle$) into two transitive relations *feedsGasTo* ($\rightarrowtriangle_{(g)}$) and *feedsLiquidTo* ($\rightarrowtriangle_{(l)}$). Then, given $x \rightarrowtriangle_{(g)} y \rightarrowtriangle_{(g)} z$ and $x' \rightarrowtriangle_{(l)} y \rightarrowtriangle_{(l)} z'$, we would correctly infer $x \rightarrowtriangle_{(g)} z$ and $x' \rightarrowtriangle_{(l)} z'$, and then $x \rightarrowtriangle z$ and $x' \rightarrowtriangle z'$, without inferring $x \rightarrowtriangle z'$ or $x' \rightarrowtriangle z$.

Although useful, these workarounds tend to be tailored to specific applications rather than capturing general principles, which limits their reuse. Also, they introduce entities and relations for merely reasoning purposes without reflecting relevant ontological distinctions, leading to their proliferation as the number of scenario variations increases. *E.g.*, $\mathrel{-\!\!\triangleright}_{(g)}$ and $\mathrel{-\!\!\triangleright}_{(l)}$ do not capture any difference on how objects can be connected, which restrains its application: if y only worked with liquid streams, we would wrongly infer $x \mathrel{-\!\!\triangleright} z'$ and $x' \mathrel{-\!\!\triangleright} z$; if y was a device that heats incoming liquid until it evaporates or that mixes different incoming fluids and outputs their mixture, we would not be able to infer $x \mathrel{-\!\!\triangleright} z$. Besides that, complex scenarios (*e.g.*, chemical plants) would require specialized types of connections for various types of fluid (*e.g.*, oil, water, fuel, vapor).

The challenge is therefore to represent flow connection in a way that (1) infers valid indirect paths, (2) avoids spurious ones, (3) keeps the relevant semantics within the ontology artifact using standard technologies, (4) remains reusable, and (5) preserves domain fidelity. The next section makes an ontological analysis of contextual transitive behavior of flow connections and introduces the notion of *selective transitivity* to deal with this issue.

3 Selective Transitivity and Fluid Flow Connections

As we already discussed, the relation of flow connection is non-transitive, but not simply that. It is true that the existence of flow connections between x and y and between y and z does not necessarily entail the existence of a flow connection between x and z. Still, in certain circumstances, as the scenarios presented in fig. 1 exemplify, indirect flow connections like $x \mathrel{-\!\!\triangleright} z$ do *systematically* arise from chains like $x \mathrel{-\!\!\triangleright} y \mathrel{-\!\!\triangleright} z$. This is markedly different from the case of other non-transitive relations, *e.g.*, *loves*: if $loves(x, y)$ and $loves(y, z)$, it may or may not be the case that $loves(x, z)$; whether x *loves* z or not is, in principle, independent of whether x loves y and y loves z. Similarly to *loves*, if $x \mathrel{-\!\!\triangleright} y$ and $y \mathrel{-\!\!\triangleright} z$, it may or may not be the case that $x \mathrel{-\!\!\triangleright} z$. However, unlike *loves*, sometimes a flow connection $x \mathrel{-\!\!\triangleright} z$ is not established independently from $x \mathrel{-\!\!\triangleright} y$ and $y \mathrel{-\!\!\triangleright} z$, but rather *in virtue of* such a connection chain, in such a way that, *ceteris paribus*, if either $x \mathrel{-\!\!\triangleright} y$ or $y \mathrel{-\!\!\triangleright} z$ is terminated, $x \mathrel{-\!\!\triangleright} z$ will cease as well. In particular, this is the case when x is connected to z through an intermediary element y whose internal arrangement enables the flow from x to continue to z.

Therefore, although there is no *absolute* transitive law[4] for the relation of flow connection, there is a *selective* transitive law that conditions the supervenience of an additional, indirect relation $x \mathrel{-\!\!\triangleright} z$ upon $x \mathrel{-\!\!\triangleright} y \mathrel{-\!\!\triangleright} z$ on the status of the intermediary element y. That is, y's exhibition of certain properties[5] provides a local context in which the non-transitive flow connection relation behaves transitively.

In fact, this contextual transitive behavior is not exclusive to fluid flow connections, but rather constitutes a more general phenomenon characteristic of a broad range of mediate relations. It naturally applies to closely analogous domains, such as electrical systems, in which establishing an indirect connection

[4] www.britannica.com/topic/transitive-law.

[5] Here we use 'y exhibits a certain property' in a broad sense to cover cases in which y instantiates a category, bears a dependent entity (e.g., a quality or disposition), stands in a relation to another entity, and so on.

requires the intermediate entity to be in a permissive state. Similarly, in computer networks, an indirect connection between x and z via y depends on y's ability to translate between the protocols used by x and z. However, we can also find the same behavior in quite disparate domains. As an example we have the relation of *trust(x,y)*, meaning that x trusts y to carry out a certain type of task [2]. If we have the chain $trust(x, y) \wedge trust(y, z)$, we will only have $trust(x, z)$ if, besides being able to carry out the task, y also has referral competence, *i.e.*, is skilled in evaluating another party's ability to perform the task.[6] Also, in Moltmann's account for the part-whole, an additional $partOf(x, z)$ relation arises from $partOf(x, y)$ and $partOf(y, z)$ when y lacks integrity [6].[7]

To account for such a phenomenon, we propose the notion of ***selective transitivity***, *i.e., the property of a non-transitive relation that behaves as transitive depending on the status of the intermediary related entities that mediate the chain of relations.* Based on that, we define *selectively transitive relations* as follows:

Definition 1. ***(Selectively Transitive Relation)*** *A non-transitive relation* R *such that* $\forall x, y, z \; \exists K \; R(x, y) \wedge R(y, z) \wedge K(y) \rightarrow R(x, z)$, *where* $K(y)$ *means that* y *exhibits the collection of properties* K.

Different selectively transitive relations may be associated with different selective transitivity conditions K (*e.g.*, y's ability to translate between different network protocols in the case of network connections; y being an honest and reliable referrer in the case of *trust* relations). For fluid flow connections, we can identify two contextual factors that toggle its selective transitivity.

The first factor concerns the mediator's internal mereotopological complexity, which becomes evident when we contrast scenarios (A) and (B) from Sect. 2. In (A), the intermediary pipe's structure is rather simple, *i.e.*, two boundary openings and the pipe's internal self-connected spatial region that affords a path for any fluid that enters through one opening to reach the other. In contrast, the heat exchanger in (B) has internal components whose specific arrangement creates two isolated internal paths, so that the fluid that enters through one opening can only reach another specific opening. With that, the heat exchanger as a whole fails to license local transitive behavior for the flow connection relation, which is only manifested at the level of its internal pipes, whose individual structures assure that there are paths between each and every one of its openings. This shows that for an intermediary entity to function as a transparent link in a transitive chain, its internal mereotopology must ensure reachability between each and every one of its openings.

The second factor concerns the mediator's dynamic operational status, as observed in contrasting scenarios (A) and (C). Both the intermediary valve in (C) and the mediating pipe in (A) have a similar internal mereotopology – *i.e.*, two openings with a direct path between them – and neither faces the structural

[6] "*Trust in the ability to refer to a third party, which can be called referral trust, is precisely what allows trust to become transitive*" [2].

[7] "*the presence of integrity may block [...] transitivity for the ontological part structure of entities*" [6].

issues exemplified in (B). The relevant distinction here is the valve's ability to alternate between two operational states: one in which its internal path is unobstructed and another in which such a path is blocked. With that, similarly to scenario (A), there will invariably be a structural path between the openings of the mediating valve y in (C), but its effective availability will depend on the valve's operational state – *i.e.*, the flow connection relation will only locally behave as transitive when y is in the unobstructed state. In other words, the valve's internal contiguous space (delimited by the inner surface of the valve's body) remains, regardless of whether the valve's obturator occupies part of it.

In summary, for local transitivity to obtain for the flow connection relation, the mediating entity y must be both

1. ***fully internally connected***: having an internal topological structure such that there is a path between every one of its openings to every other of them (*i.e.*, having an internal self-connected spatial region that share boundaries with each of the object's openings); and
2. ***open to flow***: having all its openings and internal paths between its openings unobstructed (*i.e.*, having no immobile material object occupying its openings or internal contiguous spatial region).

The two properties combined constitute the conditions K that characterize the selective transitivity of the flow connection relation, which can be expressed by saying that the object is (3) ***fully open to flow*** (*i.e.*, being both *fully internally connected* and *open to flow*).

This explains why the flow connection relation behaves transitively in scenario (A): since the mediating pipe fulfills both conditions, it becomes 'transparent' to this relation. In effect, when an intermediary entity meets these two criteria, it establishes a continuous, confined, and unobstructed spatial region, delimited by inner surfaces of contiguous conduits, through which fluid can flow from within one entity to within another. The existence of such a contiguous space is the basis for the potential operational reachability between the two indirectly connected objects.

3.1 Obstructed Paths and Structural Path Connection

In scenario (C), the flow connection between x and z depends on the operational state of the valve y: when y is closed, it blocks the path from x to z, so that no flow connection is established. Despite that, x and z still remain, in some sense, connected. When we say that the "*path is blocked*", we commit to the existence of a "*path*" between those entities that persists in the face of the blockage imposed by y. That is, there still remains a structure that affords an internal contiguous and confined spatial region for fluid to flow through, upon which a flow connection is established once the blockage is removed – so that the inner surfaces of contiguous conduits can guide the flow of fluid from within an entity to within another.

To account for cases like this, we introduce the ***structural path connection*** relation, which holds when there is such a structural path between two entities, regardless of whether it is obstructed or not. The ***flow connection*** relation builds upon the structural connection one: the latter denotes a path; the former, an unimpeded one. Regarding selective transitivity, the structural connection relation only requires the mediating entities to be *fully internally connected*. If, on top of that, they also become *open to flow*, an effective flow connection arises.

In practical terms, the structural path connection relation represents the static *as-built* topological connectivity between the components of a fluid flow system, which remains invariant in face of their varying operational status. Moreover, by accounting for the notion of "*blocked flow paths*", this relation allows us to distinguish between active and inactive paths, which is relevant for identifying alternative flow routes. In the next section, we present an ODP that covers both flow and structural path connections.

4 An ODP for Selectively Transitive Flow Connections

In this section we propose an ODP to represent the selective transitivity of the relations of flow connection and structural path connection. It is implemented using OWL and SWRL, keeping the relevant domain semantics within the ontology to support the automated inference of indirect connections while systematically avoiding the unintended retrieval of blocked or interrupted pathways. With this ODP, we intend to provide a declarative framework to facilitate tasks related to reachability analysis and flow routing in fluid flow systems. Thus, it is conceived to assist in answering questions such as those listed in table 1, which includes questions focusing on effective flow connections (*e.g.*, CQ1), on structural flow paths between entities (*e.g.*, CQ4), and on their interaction (*e.g.*, CQ5).

Table 1. List of competency questions (CQs) for the ODP.

ID	Competency Question
CQ1	From/to which entities can x receive/send fluid?
CQ2	Can x receive/send fluid from/to z?
CQ3	Can x receive/send fluid from/to z if y is open/closed?
CQ4	Which entities have structural paths from/to x?
CQ5	Which entities are blocking the flow from x to reach z?

The OWL elements that compose the ODP (Table 2) include object properties to represent the relations of structural path connection (*i.e.*, $hasFlowpathTo$) and flow connection (*i.e.*, $feeds$), as characterized in Sect. 3.1. They also include the class $InternallyConnected$, whose instances meet the K selective transitivity conditions for *structural path connections* (*i.e.*, being *fully internally connected*), and its subclass $FullyOpen$, whose instances meet the

K conditions for *flow connections* (*i.e.*, being *fully open to flow*) – as characterized in Sect. 3. Finally, it also includes *hasDirectFlowpathTo* (subproperty of *hasFlowpathTo*) for non-mediated structural connections, and *partOf* for object composition.

The axioms in Table 3 complete the ODP. A1 and A2 formalize the selective transitivity of *feeds* and *hasFlowpathTo*. A3 and A4 allow inferring flow and structural connections from direct structural connections. By A4, if there is a direct structural path between two objects that are both open to flow (*i.e.*, fluid can enter/exit them), there is also a flow connection between them. The remaining axioms allow us to infer connections between whole objects from connections between their parts – *i.e.*, if there is a connection from/to a part of x, there is also a connection from/to x itself.

Table 2. OWL components of the ODP. We use upper camel case for owl:Class names (*e.g.*, *FullyOpen*) and lower camel case for owl:ObjectProperty names (*e.g.*, *partOf*).

ODP Element	Description
InternallyConnected	Class of objects that are fully internally connected.
FullyOpen	Class of objects that are both fully internally connected and open to flow.
feeds	Represents a flow connection.
hasFlowpathTo	Represents the structural path connection.
hasDirectFlowpathTo	A structural path connection not mediated by any intermediary entities.
partOf	The general relation of parthood.

Table 3. Axioms that compose the ODP (universal quantification is assumed for all free variables). All of them were implemented as SWRL rules, except for A3, which was represented using *rdfs:subPropertyOf*.

ID	Axiom
A1	$hasFlowpathTo(x, y) \wedge hasFlowpathTo(y, z) \wedge InternallyConnected(y) \implies hasFlowpathTo(x, z)$
A2	$feeds(x, y) \wedge feeds(y, z) \wedge FullyOpen(y) \implies feeds(x, z)$
A3	$hasDirectFlowpathTo(x, y) \implies hasFlowpathTo(x, y)$
A4	$hasDirectFlowpathTo(x, y) \wedge FullyOpen(x) \wedge FullyOpen(y) \implies feeds(x, y)$
A5	$hasDirectFlowpathTo(x, y) \wedge partOf(y, z) \implies hasDirectFlowpathTo(x, z)$
A6	$hasDirectFlowpathTo(y, z) \wedge partOf(y, x) \implies hasDirectFlowpathTo(x, z)$
A7	$hasFlowpathTo(x, y) \wedge partOf(y, z) \implies hasFlowpathTo(x, z)$
A8	$hasFlowpathTo(y, z) \wedge partOf(y, x) \implies hasFlowpathTo(x, z)$
A9	$feeds(x, y) \wedge partOf(y, z) \implies feeds(x, z)$
A10	$feeds(y, z) \wedge partOf(y, x) \implies feeds(x, z)$

The ODP's main goal is accounting for the selective transitivity of structural and flow connection relations. This is captured by a basic structure with three elements: an object property representing the selectively transitive relation, a class representing its selective transitivity conditions, and an axiom associating the relation with the class. Concretely, we have *hasFlowpathTo*, *InternallyConnected* and axiom A1 to handle structural connections, and *feeds*, *FullyOpen* and axiom A2 for the flow connections. With that, given the existence of chains of *hasFlowPathTo* or *feeds* relations, we can infer further, indirect relations.

Moreover, the ODP is intended to automate the inference of transient flow connections based on the invariant topological structure of a fluid flow system and on the operational states of its components. To relieve the modeler of the upfront burden of considering all indirect structural paths between the system's components, the ODP supports inferences of indirect structural connections based on local information. It provides *hasDirectFlowpathTo* to represent the system in terms of direct structural connections between its components, and *InternallyConnected* to indicate the components that afford mediated structural flow paths. Given this basic structure, axioms A1 and A3 allow inferring further structural connections. Then, with *FullyOpen* we can indicate the system's components that are in an operational state that affords indirect effective flow connections, which can be inferred via axioms A2 and A4.

In a sense, the ODP establishes a granularity level for analysis of the domain. Since its scope of inference is limited by the nature of the selective transitivity of flow and structural connections, it cannot be applied to arbitrarily complex objects, but just to those that are fully internally connected. That is, the ODP enables inferences about more complex entities, but only when applied at the appropriate level of abstraction. With that, the modeler is led to analyze the target flow system and identify the fully connected entities. If a key entity is not fully connected, the ODP leads us to analyze such an entity's internal structure, determine which of its components are relevant for flow purposes, and represent them explicitly in the system's model. In other words, the ODP guides the modeler to see through black boxes and discern the components that are ultimately involved in the flow phenomenon. Then, we can integrate such components back into the entities at higher abstraction levels via the *partOf* relation, and infer structural and flow connections between such larger entities via axioms A5-A10.

Figure 2a shows how to apply the ODP to scenario (B) from Sect. 2 and the structural path connections that can be inferred from this. First, we create instances for each entity, including the internal pipes p and p' that compose the heat exchanger y. Then, we classify p and p' as *InternallyConnected*, and use *partOf* to make them components of y. Finally, we assert the direct structural path connections from x to p, from p to z, from x' to p', and from p' to z' using *hasDirectFlowpathTo*.

The dashed lines in Fig. 2a represent the *hasFlowpathTo* relations inferred by running a semantic reasoner (*e.g.*, HermiT[8]) over this model. Given the *has-*

[8] www.hermit-reasoner.com.

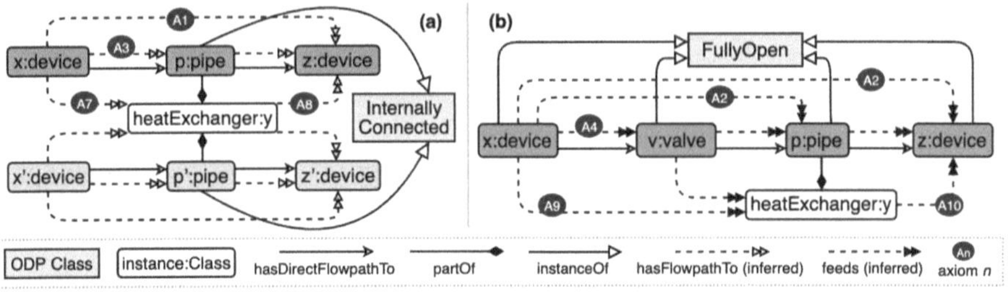

Fig. 2. Using the ODP to address the issues exemplified by the scenarios from Sect. 2. Solid lines between boxes represent asserted relations; dashed lines represent inferred ones. Blue ellipses indicate the axiom that leads to the inference of the marked relation.

DirectFlowpathTo relation $x \rightarrow p$[9], axiom A3 leads to the *hasFlowpathTo* relation $x \twoheadrightarrow p$. Analogously, A3 also allows us to infer $p \twoheadrightarrow z$, $x' \twoheadrightarrow p'$, and $p' \twoheadrightarrow z'$. Given $InternallyConnected(p)$, $x \twoheadrightarrow p$, and $p \twoheadrightarrow z$, axiom A1 leads to $x \twoheadrightarrow z$. Likewise, given $InternallyConnected(p')$, $x' \twoheadrightarrow p'$, and $p' \twoheadrightarrow z'$, A1 leads to $x' \twoheadrightarrow z'$. By A7, $x \twoheadrightarrow p$ and $partOf(p, y)$ lead to $x \twoheadrightarrow y$. Similarly, $x' \twoheadrightarrow p'$ and $partOf(p', y)$ lead to $x' \twoheadrightarrow y$. Finally, by A8, $p \twoheadrightarrow z$ and $partOf(p, y)$ lead to $y \twoheadrightarrow z$, whereas $p' \twoheadrightarrow z'$ and $partOf(p', y)$ lead to $y \twoheadrightarrow z'$. The isolation of the flow paths from x to z and from x' to z' is preserved because the model contains none of the following:

- $p \twoheadrightarrow p'$, which would create the chain $x \twoheadrightarrow p \twoheadrightarrow p' \twoheadrightarrow z'$ and allow A1 to erroneously infer $x \twoheadrightarrow z'$;
- $p' \twoheadrightarrow p$, which would create the chain $x' \twoheadrightarrow p' \twoheadrightarrow p \twoheadrightarrow z$ and allow A1 to erroneously infer $x' \twoheadrightarrow z$;
- $InternallyConnected(y)$, which would allow A1 to erroneously infer $x \twoheadrightarrow z'$ from $x \twoheadrightarrow y$ and $y \twoheadrightarrow z'$, as well as $x' \twoheadrightarrow z$ from $x' \twoheadrightarrow y$ and $y \twoheadrightarrow z$; and
- *partOf* relations between elements belonging to distinct flow paths, which would otherwise produce spurious *hasFlowpathTo* relations via A7 or A8.

In Fig. 2b we apply the ODP to a modified version of scenario (B) comprising y's hot fluid loop plus a valve v mediating x and p. It covers both mediator's mereotopological and operational aspects, so that we can show how the ODP handles inferences of flow connections in cases like (C). By A4, $FullyOpen(x)$, $FullyOpen(v)$ and $x \rightarrow v$ lead to $x \rightarrowtriangle v$. Similarly, by A4, we also infer $v \rightarrowtriangle p$ from $v \rightarrow p$ and $p \rightarrowtriangle z$ from $p \rightarrow z$. Given $x \rightarrowtriangle v$, $v \rightarrowtriangle p$ and $FullyOpen(v)$, A2 leads to $x \rightarrowtriangle p$ – and, for analogous reasons, also to $x \rightarrowtriangle z$ and $v \rightarrowtriangle z$. Given $x \rightarrowtriangle p$ and $partOf(p, y)$, A9 allows inferring $x \rightarrowtriangle y$ – as well as $v \rightarrowtriangle y$, given $v \rightarrowtriangle p$ and $partOf(p, y)$. Finally, by A10, $p \rightarrowtriangle z$ and $partOf(p, y)$ lead to $y \rightarrowtriangle z$. This representation allows us not only to infer all the existing flow connections, but also to avoid inferring spurious ones. *E.g.*, suppose we modify our model by removing the assertion $FullyOpen(v)$, meaning that v is closed. In this case, the model no longer fulfills

[9] We use '$x \twoheadrightarrow y$' to represent a *structural path connection* between x and y (*i.e.*, *hasFlowpathTo(x,y)*), '$x \rightarrow y$' to represent a direct structural path connection (*i.e.*, *hasDirectFlowpathTo(x,y)*), and '$x \rightarrowtriangle y$' to represent a flow connection (*i.e.*, *feeds(x,y)*).

the conditions to infer $x \rightarrow v$ from A4. Without $x \rightarrow v$, it does not meet the conditions for A2 either, so that $x \rightarrow p$ and $x \rightarrow z$ are not inferred. Lastly, without $x \rightarrow p$ the conditions for A9 are left unmet and we no longer infer $x \rightarrow y$. With that, the model suitably captures the system's behavior when we close valve v, ceasing certain flow connections while preserving their underlying structural paths.

5 Case Study: Wells and Offshore Oil Platforms

In offshore petroleum production systems, hydrocarbons are extracted from subsea reservoirs by *producer wells* and transported to a production *platform* through a network of pipelines, valves, and other fluid handling equipment.

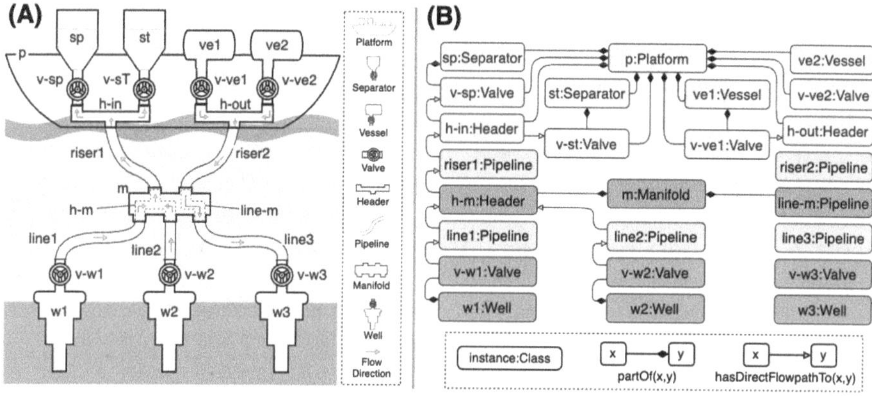

Fig. 3. Overview of an offshore oil production system connecting multiple wells to a production platform through subsea equipment and flowlines.

For our case study we will consider the simplified production system depicted on Fig. 3A. It consists of a platform p that operates two producer wells $w1$ and $w2$, and one injector well $w3$. The flow between p and the wells is mediated by the manifold m, which internally isolates the production flow – which goes through the header *h-m* – from the injection flow – which passes through the pipeline *line-m*. Produced fluids enter p through the inlet header *h-in* and can go into the production separator *sp* or the test separator *st*. Vessels $ve1$ and $ve2$ store different injection fluids, which exit p through the outlet header *h-out*. For simplicity, each well, separator, and vessel has a single master valve to control incoming/outgoing flows. Also, m has no flow controlling capacities. Finally, we are only considering flow interruptions due to operational interventions (*e.g.*, valve operation), disregarding abnormal incidents (*e.g.*, pipeline clogging).

5.1 Applying the ODP

To represent the described system[10], we created classes for the main types of artifacts, *i.e., Platform, Well, Manifold, Separator, Vessel, Header, Valve,* and *Pipeline*. Given the internal structure of valves, pipelines and headers, we defined their corresponding classes as subclasses of *InternallyConnected*. *Pipeline* and *Header* also specialize *FullyOpen*. Then, we created individuals for the named entities in Fig. 3A and classified them into the appropriate domain class.

We used *partOf* to link entities to their parts (*i.e.,* wells, separators and vessels to their valves, the platform to its topside equipment, and the manifold to its internal production header and injection pipeline). Finally, we used *hasDirectFlowpathTo* to connect the entities along the flow paths between topside and subsea structures, exclusively focusing on fully internally connected objects. Thus, instead of directly connecting flowlines to wells, we linked them to the wells' master valves – doing similarly to separators, vessels, and the platform itself. Regarding the manifold, we also went one level of abstraction down, connecting flowlines and risers to the manifold's internal components.

This representation of the system's structural configuration (Fig. 3B) enables the inference of structural connections from producer wells $w1$ and $w2$ to separators *sp* and *st*, and from vessels $ve1$ and $ve2$ to the injector well $w3$. Moreover, although both manifold m and platform p integrate production and injection flowpaths, no spurious connection is inferred from $w1$ or $w2$ to $w3$, which shows the ODP's success in logically isolating such paths. This allows discovering which wells the platform p operates, *i.e.,* those that have a *hasFlowpathTo* from/to p.

On top of that, we can infer the wells that are currently producing (*i.e.,* those with a *feeds* relation towards the production separator *sp*), or what type of fluid is being injected into the reservoir (*i.e.,* retrieving the vessel with a *feeds* relation with $w3$). If we close, *e.g.,* $w1$'s master valve *v-w1*, $feeds(w1, sp)$ will no longer be inferred, but the underlying $hasFlowpathTo(w1, sp)$ will remain – indicating that, although temporally inactive, $w1$ is still operated by p.

The model's ability to dynamically update flow connections in response to changes in valves' status is the basis for more complex tasks, *e.g.,* determining which valves to close/open to measure the production of individual wells. It also helps in cases of high-pressure incidents, such as gas kicks. When safety barriers like downhole safety valves are activated, the model can reflect the modified plant state in real time, providing an accurate overview of isolated sections and remaining risks, allowing for faster and more informed emergency responses.

6 Discussion and Concluding Remarks

In this paper, we presented an ODP to account for the elusive *selective transitivity* of fluid flow connections. It allows the inference of genuine indirect connections between components of a fluid flow system while avoiding the inference

[10] An example implementation is available at https://github.com/fabricio-henrique-rodrigues/selective-transitivity-ODP.

of spurious ones. It was conceived as a purely declarative solution that keeps the logic underlying flow connection within the ontology artifact, so as not to require external mechanisms for reasoning.

Previous works have attempted to handle fluid flow connections. Notably, the Flow Systems Ontology (FSO) [4] aims at representing energy and mass flow relations between systems and their components. Concerning fluid flow, FSO offers the non-transitive *fso:feedsFluidTo* object property to represent flow connections. It also captures systems' composition via the *fso:isComponentOf* property, which is used in property chains to infer that if a component of system x feeds fluid to a component of system y, then x feeds fluid to y.

However, with *fso:feedsFluidTo* being simply non-transitive, FSO does not support inferences of any additional flow connection, relying on query templates using SPARQL property path expressions to navigate through indirect connections – which results in the "*ontology outside the ontology*" issue discussed in Sect. 2. In contrast, our ODP maintains the logic underlying the selective transitivity of flow connections entirely as part of the ontology axiomatization, enabling the inference of a system's network of connections without depending on any external knowledge resource. This brings the 'intelligence' into the ontology artifact, transforming it from an inert data structure over which externally encoded expertise operates into a declarative framework for qualitative reasoning.

Besides, FSO query templates are still liable to retrieve spurious flow connections. To mitigate this, FSO relies on *fso:suppliesFluidTo* and *fso:returnsFluidTo*, subproperties of *fso:feedsFluidTo* that denote the logical supply and return of fluid between components or systems. Resembling the 'ontology tweaking' approach described in Sect. 2, this distinction is based on the entities' roles in a specified process, not on any particularity of the flow connection itself, which limits the reuse of the ontology. Conversely, the proposed ODP is based on an ontological analysis that untangles two aspects usually collapsed under the notion of flow connection: the structural path connection and the effective flow connection that builds upon it. As a result, the ODP provides means to distinguish between static topology and dynamic operational reachability, which translates into further reasoning capabilities.

First of all, by distinguishing these two layers of connection, the ODP can account for the persistence of a structural baseline even when valves are closed. That is, unlike FSO, it allows us to differentiate cases where no connection exists at all from scenarios in which the effective flow connection is merely temporally suspended. It also enables the inference of a system's global operational state at a given time based purely on local information, such as the connections between immediate neighbor components and the operational state of flow control devices. In large-scale industrial systems managed by multiple operators with highly compartmentalized domain expertise, such local data may be all that is accessible. In such scenarios, the ODP's ability to allow local updates on individual components to dynamically propagate their impacts across the entire system's network topology is a noteworthy benefit.

Such reasoning can also be used to support analyses such as HAZOP (Hazard and Operability study)[11], which examines how deviations from intended operating conditions propagate through a process, and FMEA (Failure Modes and Effects Analysis)[12], which traces how individual component failures affect the rest of a system. In both, the ability to distinguish the invariant structural paths (*hasFlowpathTo*) from the state-dependent effective connections (*feeds*) lets an analyst infer which downstream entities a given deviation or component failure can actually reach under a given pipeline configuration.

With respect to the notion of *selective transitivity*, our work has some parallels with [6]. At a more general level, Moltmann's *Transitivity Principle* for part structures can be understood as an earlier instance of what we call selective transitivity. Rather than introducing distinct part relations for different domains, Moltmann adopts a uniform weak part-whole relation (*i.e.*, $<$) whose transitive behavior is conditionally licensed by the lack of integrity of the intermediary entity. Her principle states that $x < y$ and $y < z$ entail $x < z$ whenever $\neg$*IntegratedWhole(y)*. This instantiates the general schema for selective transitivity – *i.e.*, '$<$' as R and '$\neg$*IntegratedWhole(y)*' as $K(y)$. Moltmann's principle can therefore be regarded as a conceptual precedent for the general schema we put forward, while our contribution lies in its abstraction as selective transitivity and its operationalization for fluid-flow systems.

Our work also has some limitations. The ODP's increased expressivity introduces certain computational trade-offs. It leads to a proliferation of inferred relations, increasing graph density and potentially degrading reasoning/querying performance. This augmented number of connections also tends to make certain types of queries more complex. For instance, retrieving the sequence of nodes that constitutes a specific flow path becomes challenging, as we cannot simply use a SPARQL property path to traverse the corresponding chain of connections and capture the entity reached at each sequential hop. Given the inference of a connection between every possible pair of nodes along the path, the originally asserted path is obscured by a dense web of virtual shortcuts. Still, we can mitigate this limitation by leveraging the distinction between direct and indirect connections to reconstruct the sequential path. Moreover, the intricacy of such queries does not arise from the nature of flow or structural connections themselves, but rather reflects specific analytical demands the user may have. Thus, it is reasonable to leave the additional complexity to the query structure, rather than burdening the ontology with extra-ontological sequencing logic.

The ODP was devised with only unidirectional flow connections in mind. We have not considered cases featuring bidirectional flow connections, which is left as future work. Besides, the ODP imposes a rather restrictive condition to allow inferring indirect flow connection, requiring every intermediary object in a pathway to be *fully open to flow*. For instance, consider a flow control device that has dozens of inlets/outlets and that allows individually opening/closing each of them: if even only a single such inlet/outlet is closed, the device as a whole would

[11] https://en.wikipedia.org/wiki/Hazard_and_operability_study.

[12] https://en.wikipedia.org/wiki/Failure_mode_and_effects_analysis.

not be *fully open to flow* and would not allow the inference of any of the dozens of indirect flow connections it is indeed mediating – a considerable drawback to the application of the ODP. Still, what the ODP offers is a rather basic necessary and sufficient condition that allows us to attribute a local transitive behavior of flow connection without further considerations. In this sense, as discussed in Sect. 4, this restriction is useful to guide the modeler in the process of identifying the suitable level of abstraction to account for the target system's complexity. A last source of limitation is the lack of further formal validation to guarantee inferential completeness and soundness, which is part of ongoing efforts that will be reported in future publications.

Finally, our work opens some research opportunities. The notion of selective transitivity that underlies our ODP is agnostic to the nature of the flowing entity. Be it fluid through valves, electrons through circuit breakers, vehicles through traffic junctions, or data packets through firewalls, the core requirement remains: transitivity must be licensed by the internal state of the intermediary component – which points to the possibility of extending the proposed ODP or deriving similar ones to such analogous domains.

Also, both layers of the notion of flow connection exhibit an affordance character. A structural path connection opens the possibility for an effective flow connection, requiring only that the connected components acquire a *FlowOpen* status. A flow connection, in turn, affords a fluid flow process, given the presence of fluid and a favorable pressure gradient. This dispositional cascade naturally paves the way for a third, processual layer: an *isFeedingFluidTo* relation to capture the actual transport of fluid between entities. We plan to explore this extension in future work, along with the alignment of the ODP with major top-level ontologies (*e.g.*, BFO, UFO, DOLCE).

Acknowledgments. The authors 2–6 would like to acknowledge Petrobras and the Brazilian National Agency of Petroleum, Natural Gas and Biofuels (ANP) for their financial support of the project ONTOKG through cooperation agreement No. (SIG-ITEC 2025/00193-0). Their research group is also supported by CAPES Finance Code 001 and by the Brazilian National Council for Scientific and Technological Development (CNPq), Grant No. 313367/2025-6.

Disclosure of Interests. The authors have not competing interests.

References

1. Gangemi, A., Presutti, V.: Ontology design patterns. In: Staab, S., Studer, R. (eds.) Handbook on Ontologies. IHIS, pp. 221–243. Springer, Heidelberg (2009). https://doi.org/10.1007/978-3-540-92673-3_10
2. Jøsang, A., Pope, S.: Semantic constraints for trust transitivity. In: 2nd Asia-Pacific Conference on Conceptual Modelling (APCCM'05), pp. 59–68 (2005)
3. Kitamura, Y., Ikeda, M., Mizoguchi, R.: A qualitative reasoning based on an ontology of fluid systems and its evaluation. In: 4th Pacific Rim International Conference on Artificial Intelligence (PRICAI'96), pp. 288–299 (1996)

4. Kukkonen, V., et al.: An ontology to support flow system descriptions from design to operation of buildings. Autom. Constr. **134** (2022)
5. Marquardt, W., et al.: OntoCAPE - A Re-Usable Ontology for Chemical Process Engineering. Springer-Verlag, Heidelberg (2010). https://doi.org/10.1007/978-3-642-04655-1
6. Moltmann, F.: Parts and Wholes in Semantics. Oxford University Press, Oxford (1997)
7. Studer, R., Benjamins, V., Fensel, D.: Knowledge engineering: principles and methods. Data Knowl. Eng. **25**, 161–197 (1998)

Business Process Discovery and Optimization

BPMN+OPT: A Conceptual Modeling Language for Business Process Optimization

Remco Dijkman[1], Arik Senderovich[2], and Stefanie Rinderle-Ma[3](✉)

[1] Eindhoven University of Technology, Eindhoven, The Netherlands
r.m.dijkman@tue.nl
[2] York University, Toronto, Canada
sariks@yorku.ca
[3] Technical University Munich, TUM School of Computation, Information and Technology, Garching, Germany
stefanie.rinderle-ma@tum.de

Abstract. Business processes often require optimization decisions, including resource assignment, case scheduling, and path routing. Such decisions are tightly coupled to process structure, resource availability, and uncertain activity durations. Yet the two communities that typically address such problems approach them from opposite directions: business process management (BPM) offers rich process models but limited optimization semantics, while operations research (OR) offers powerful solution methods but often abstracts away process structure early. We address this gap with BPMN+OPT, a BPMN-linked conceptual language that leaves the standard process structure unchanged and adds an optimization annotation layer. The layer identifies case and resource state used for optimization, stochastic behavior, controllable decision moments and variables, feasibility constraints, and objectives. We give BPMN+OPT an execution semantics based on Semi-Markov Decision Processes (SMDPs), supporting continuous-time, event-driven decision making with non-memoryless durations. This bridges process models and optimization-oriented execution. We demonstrate scheduling, resource assignment, and routing in one process and evaluate a proof-of-concept pipeline that maps BPMN+OPT models to SMDPs.

Keywords: Business Process Optimization · Conceptual Modeling · BPMN · Resource Allocation · Scheduling · Process Routing

1 Introduction

Business processes often require decisions that are optimization-driven rather than merely procedural: which resource should serve which case, when a case should be scheduled, or which path a case should follow when alternatives exist [3,15]. Such decisions arise in healthcare, logistics, manufacturing, and

© The Author(s), under exclusive license to Springer Nature Switzerland AG 2027
A. Bernasconi et al. (Eds.): ER 2026, LNCS 17081, pp. 219–235, 2027.
https://doi.org/10.1007/978-3-032-40795-5_13

service systems, where performance depends jointly on control flow, resource availability, stochastic activity durations, and operational objectives [1,15]. In outpatient chemotherapy, patients are scheduled into appointment slots, assigned staff and chairs, and routed according to clinical condition and operational load. These coupled decisions affect downstream availability, waiting, and congestion.

Despite their practical importance, such problems fall between two modeling traditions. Business Process Management (BPM) provides process models, such as BPMN, that are accessible to analysts and domain experts and that represent control flow, synchronization, and organizational roles [3,12], but often avoids 'solving' the underlying optimization problems. Operations Research (OR), in contrast, provides powerful models and solution methods for allocation, scheduling, routing, and other sequential decision making problems [1,15,17], yet OR formulations often begin from an already abstracted view of the system. As a result, information about where decisions occur, which alternatives are controllable, what information is available at the decision point, and how process execution affects future states is encoded outside the process model.

This paper addresses this gap by introducing *BPMN+OPT*, a conceptual modeling language for business process optimization problems. BPMN+OPT extends a BPMN-style process model with optimization-relevant information: case and resource attributes, stochastic behavior, controllability annotations, decision moments, decision variables, constraints, and objectives. The goal is not to replace either BPMN or OR formulations, but to provide an intermediate modeling layer that keeps the process structure visible while making the optimization structure explicit.

A central design choice is to give BPMN+OPT a *Semi-Markov Decision Process* (SMDP) execution semantics. This choice matches the target setting: processes evolve in continuous time, decisions are taken at event-driven epochs, and activity durations need not be memoryless. The SMDP view provides a state-based decision semantics in which feasible actions, stochastic transitions, holding times, and rewards are induced by the BPMN+OPT model [17,19]. In our proof of concept, a BPMN+OPT specification is compiled through a colored-Petri-net simulation backend while exposing SMDP-level states, actions, and transitions; the Petri net is an implementation mechanism, not the surface language or the contribution [5].

This paper contributes (i) a BPMN-linked conceptual language for business-process optimization, (ii) its abstract syntax and SMDP execution semantics, and (iii) proof-of-concept formulations and solution experiments for representative optimization problems. The remainder of the paper is organized as follows. Section 2 discusses the motivation and presents a running example. Section 3 defines BPMN+OPT and its SMDP semantics. Section 4 models the recurring optimization problems, and reports the proof-of-concept solution results. Section 5 discusses related work, and Sect. 6 concludes the paper.

2 Motivation

Business process optimization problems are rarely isolated from execution. Decisions such as assigning a resource, scheduling a case, or selecting a route are made while the process is running, depend on the current state of cases and resources, and affect future queues, workloads, and completion times. This creates a modeling gap: BPMN and related process modeling languages make control flow, synchronization, and organizational roles explicit, whereas Operations Research and sequential decision models optimize over states, actions, constraints, and objectives that are typically engineered outside the process model.

Running Example. We use an outpatient chemotherapy facility as a running example because it combines scheduling, assignment, and routing decisions in a single process. Patients are scheduled into appointment slots, arrive at the clinic, and proceed through several activities with uncertain durations that require both human and physical resources.

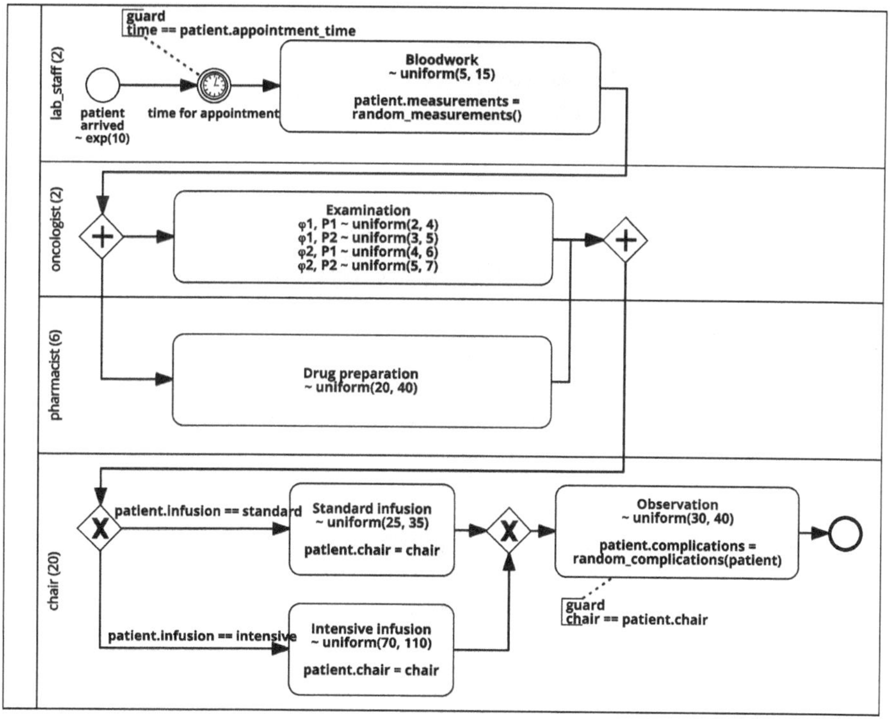

Fig. 1. Running example: standard BPMN process elements are shown in black; the BPMN+OPT optimization annotations are shown in orange. (Color figure online)

Figure 1 shows a typical pathway. At the patient's appointment time, blood work is performed by laboratory staff. The patient then undergoes an examination, the duration of which depends on the oncologist (ϕ_1 or ϕ_2) and the type of patient (P_1 or P_2). At the same time the pharmacy prepares the prescribed drug in parallel. Infusion can begin only after both examination and drug preparation are complete. The patient is then routed to either a standard or intensive infusion protocol, depending on clinical attributes such as measurements obtained earlier in the process. Finally, the patient remains under observation before discharge.

The example contains the ingredients of process-embedded optimization. Resource pools have capacities, activity durations are stochastic and may depend on case or resource attributes, and tasks may update attributes such as patient measurements. Conditions can then refer back to these attributes, for example when ensuring that observation uses the same chair assigned during infusion. The orange annotations in Fig. 1 are an illustrative concrete syntax for the abstract BPMN+OPT constructs defined below. The contribution of this paper is therefore the abstract syntax and SMDP interpretation, not a finalized graphical notation; a full notation and usability study are left to future work.

The process contains three interacting decision types. Patients must be scheduled into appointment times, waiting patients must be assigned to eligible resources, and patients must be routed between standard and intensive infusion. These decisions cannot be optimized independently, because they share resources and affect downstream states. BPMN+OPT is designed to represent these decisions at the process-model level before committing to a particular solver, simulation engine, or mathematical formulation.

3 BPMN+OPT: Syntax and SMDP Semantics

This section defines BPMN+OPT. We first give its abstract syntax: process elements, object types, attributes, and optimization annotations. We then define its execution semantics through a Semi-Markov Decision Process (SMDP), which provides the state-based interpretation needed for simulation and optimization.

The key design choice is to retain the BPMN process structure and add an optimization annotation layer. Standard BPMN tasks, events, gateways, sequence flows, data, and resource roles retain their usual modeling function [12]. The added layer identifies which choices are controllable, when they are made, which alternatives are feasible, how execution is stochastic, and which objective is optimized. These annotations provide the information needed to derive the SMDP states, actions, transitions, holding times, and rewards.

3.1 Abstract Syntax

Below, we provide the notations required to define the model, followed by a full abstract syntax specification for BPMN+OPT.

Domains, Expressions, and State Notation. We use the following notations throughout the remainder of the paper.

Let $\mathcal{L}$ denote the universe of attribute labels, $\mathbb{T}$ the universe of time values, $\mathbb{R}_{\geq 0}$ the universe of non-negative durations, $\mathcal{V}$ the universe of possible data values, and $\mathcal{D}$ the universe of data types. Each data type is interpreted as a set of admissible values, i.e., $D \in \mathcal{D} \Rightarrow D \subseteq \mathcal{V}$. An object type is defined by the attributes its objects may carry and the data type of each attribute. We therefore define the universe of typed attributes as $\mathit{Attr} \subseteq \mathcal{L} \times \mathcal{D}$, where $(l, D) \in \mathit{Attr}$ means that attribute l takes values from type D.

An object type O is a finite set of typed attributes, $O \subseteq \mathit{Attr}$. We distinguish object types from runtime objects. Object types specify admissible attributes and their data types, whereas runtime objects are concrete valuations of such attributes in a state. We use uppercase letters such as O, C, and R for object types, and lowercase letters such as o, c, and r for runtime objects. For example, a customer object type may be written as

$$O_{customer} = \{(id, str), (name, str), (age, int)\}.$$

We use expressions to specify conditions, derived quantities, constraints, and object-set aggregations. Let Expr denote the set of side-effect-free typed expressions generated from constants, attribute references, variables, operators, quantifiers over finite object sets, and aggregations:

$$e ::= v \mid l \mid u \mid f(e_1, \ldots, e_n) \mid \exists u \in Q : e \mid \forall u \in Q : e \mid \sum_{u \in Q} e,$$

where $v \in \mathcal{V}$ is a constant, $l \in \mathcal{L}$ is an attribute label, u is a bound variable ranging over a finite object set Q, and f is an operator or function symbol. Operators include arithmetic, comparison, logical, and domain-specific functions, such as $+$, $<$, $\wedge$, and $\neg$. Expressions are evaluated under an environment that binds object variables to runtime objects and interprets attribute references against the current state. For example, the concrete expression $\mathit{case.completion} < \mathit{case.start} + 10$ abbreviates a typed comparison over two attributes of a bound case object.

At any time $t \in \mathbb{T}$, the object state contains the currently existing objects and their attribute values. Given object types $\mathcal{O}$, we write

$$\mathcal{O}_t \subseteq \mathcal{P}(\mathit{Attr} \to \mathcal{V}),$$

where each element of $\mathcal{O}_t$ is a runtime object represented as a partial function from typed attributes to values. Partiality allows objects of different types to carry different attributes. Each object must satisfy its typing constraints: for every $o \in \mathcal{O}_t$, if $((l, D) \mapsto v) \in o$, then $v \in D$. When types are clear from context, we omit them and write, for example,

$$\mathcal{O}_t = \{\{id \mapsto \text{Alice}, age \mapsto 30\}, \{id \mapsto \text{Bob}, age \mapsto 42\}\}.$$

We write $\mathsf{Dist}(Y)$ for the set of probability distributions over Y, and Upd for possibly stochastic state-update rules. An update rule maps a current object valuation to a distribution over admissible successor valuations, capturing attribute updates caused by task completions, event occurrences, arrivals, and routing effects. We assume that every object has an attribute *id* whose value uniquely identifies it within the system, and let $\mathcal{I}$ denote the universe of identifiers. We use dot notation for object attributes: for example, *Alice.age* denotes the age of the object identified by Alice, and *customer.name* denotes the *name* attribute of a generic customer object.

Model Definition. As BPMN+OPT aims to unify business processes and their associated optimization problems in a single model, its abstract syntax has two parts: a BPMN-style process model and mathematical annotations that define the optimization problem. The process part uses a subset of BPMN [12] sufficient to express the problem classes identified in Sect. 2. Definition 1 specifies the information that can be expressed; it does not imply that every conforming model induces a finite or tractably solvable SMDP.

Definition 1 (BPMN+OPT Process). *A BPMN+OPT process is a tuple*

$$\mathcal{M} = (\mathcal{T}, \mathcal{E}, \mathcal{G}, \mathcal{F}, \mathcal{C}, \mathcal{R}, \mathsf{auth}, \mathcal{X}, \mathsf{Obj}, \mathsf{Con}, \mathsf{Mom}),$$

where:

- $\mathcal{T}$ *is a finite set of tasks. Each task* $T \in \mathcal{T}$ *is equipped with:*
  - *a condition* $\mathsf{cond}_T(r, c) \in \mathsf{Expr}$ *specifying for which combinations of resources r and cases c the task may occur;*
  - *a behavior* $\mathsf{beh}_T(r, c) \in \mathsf{Upd}$ *specifying a possibly stochastic update of the attributes of r, c, and other affected objects when T occurs; and*
  - *a processing-time function* $\mathsf{ptime}_T(r, c) \in \mathsf{Dist}(\mathbb{R}_{\geq 0})$ *returning the processing-time distribution for the given combination of r and c.*
- $\mathcal{E}$ *is a finite set of events. Each event* $E \in \mathcal{E}$ *is equipped with:*
  - *a type* $\mathsf{type}_E \in \{\mathsf{start}, \mathsf{intermediate}, \mathsf{end}\}$*;*
  - *if E is a start event, an interarrival-time distribution* $\mathsf{iat}_E \in \mathsf{Dist}(\mathbb{R}_{\geq 0})$ *and a generator* gen_E *specifying how case attributes are probabilistically initialized when a new case arrives; and*
  - *if E is an intermediate event, a processing-time function* $\mathsf{ptime}_E(c) \in \mathsf{Dist}(\mathbb{R}_{\geq 0})$ *and a behavior* $\mathsf{beh}_E(c) \in \mathsf{Upd}$*, analogous to tasks.*
- $\mathcal{G}$ *is a finite set of gateways. Each gateway* $G \in \mathcal{G}$ *has a type*

$$\mathsf{type}_G \in \{\mathsf{XOR}, \mathsf{AND}\} \times \{\mathsf{split}, \mathsf{join}\}.$$

- $\mathcal{F}$ *is a set of directed sequence flows between process elements. Each flow* $F \in \mathcal{F}$ *may have a condition* $\mathsf{cond}_F(r, c) \in \mathsf{Expr}$ *specifying for which combinations of resources and cases it may be traversed.*
- $\mathcal{C} \subseteq \mathcal{O}$ *is a set of case object types. Each case object type* $C \in \mathcal{C}$ *has:*
  - *an identifier attribute* $(id, \cdot) \in C$*; and*
  - *a location attribute* $(loc, \cdot) \in C$*, whose values indicate whether the case is waiting at a process element or being executed by a resource:*

$$(\{\mathsf{waiting}\} \times (\mathcal{T} \cup \mathcal{E} \cup \mathcal{G})) \cup (\{\mathsf{executing}\} \times (\mathcal{T} \cup \mathcal{E}) \times \mathcal{R}).$$

- $\mathcal{R} \subseteq \mathcal{O}$ *is a set of resource object types. Each resource object type* $R \in \mathcal{R}$ *has:*
  - *an identifier attribute* $(id, \cdot) \in R$*; and*
  - *a location attribute* $(loc, \cdot) \in R$*, whose values indicate whether the resource is idle or executing a task for a case:*

$$\{\mathsf{idle}\} \cup (\{\mathsf{executing}\} \times \mathcal{T} \times \mathcal{C}).$$

- $\mathsf{auth} \subseteq \mathcal{R} \times \mathcal{T}$ *specifies which resource object types are eligible to execute which tasks. A runtime resource object* r *is eligible for task* T *if* r *conforms to some resource type* R *with* $(R, T) \in \mathsf{auth}$.
- $\mathcal{X} \subseteq \mathcal{L} \times \mathcal{D}$ *is a set of decision variables, each defined by a label and a data type. These variables represent controllable quantities whose values are chosen by a decision maker or policy at decision moments.*
- $\mathsf{Obj} \subseteq \{\mathsf{min}, \mathsf{max}\} \times \mathsf{Expr}$ *is the set of optimization objectives. Each objective consists of an optimization direction and an expression evaluated over object attributes and, where relevant, decision variables.*
- $\mathsf{Con} \subseteq \mathsf{Expr} \times \{\leq, <, =, >, \geq\} \times \mathsf{Expr}$ *is the set of constraints over object attributes and decision variables. Each constraint is evaluated as a Boolean expression under the current object valuation and the chosen decision-variable valuation.*
- $\mathsf{Mom} \subseteq \mathsf{Expr}$ *is the set of decision moments, written as Boolean expressions over object attributes and, when needed, current decision-variable valuations. A decision may be taken in a state when at least one expression in* Mom *evaluates to true.*

Figure 2 illustrates how the abstract tuple is instantiated in a small resource-assignment fragment. The fragment contains the task

$$\mathcal{T} = \{\mathsf{Examination}\}.$$

For simplicity, we omit gateways from this fragment and use only the sequence flows needed to move a patient from arrival to examination and then to the next process step. The case object type represents patients:

$$C_{\mathsf{patient}} = \{(id, \mathcal{I}), (type, \{P_1, P_2\}), (loc, \mathcal{LOC}), (start, \mathbb{T}), (complete, \mathbb{T} \cup \{\bot\})\}.$$

where $\mathcal{I}$ denotes the universe of identifiers.[1] The resource object type represents oncologists:

$$R_{\mathsf{oncologist}} = \{(id, \mathcal{I}), (loc, \mathcal{LOC})\}.$$

In the fragment, this resource type is instantiated by two oncologist objects, for example

$$r_1 = \{id \mapsto \phi_1, loc \mapsto \mathsf{idle}\}, \qquad r_2 = \{id \mapsto \phi_2, loc \mapsto \mathsf{idle}\}.$$

[1] We use $\bot$ to denote an undefined or not-yet-assigned attribute value, such as a patient without an appointment time or an infusion route that has not yet been selected.

Thus,

$$\mathcal{C} = \{C_{\mathsf{patient}}\}, \qquad \mathcal{R} = \{R_{\mathsf{oncologist}}\}, \qquad \mathsf{auth} = \{(R_{\mathsf{oncologist}}, \mathsf{Examination})\}.$$

The task Examination may start when a patient is waiting for examination and an eligible oncologist is idle. Its processing time depends on both the patient type and the selected oncologist. The behavior of the task updates the patient and resource locations when the task starts, records the patient's completion time when the task completes, and releases the oncologist. This fragment is used again in Sect. 4, where we fully formulate the corresponding resource-assignment optimization problem.

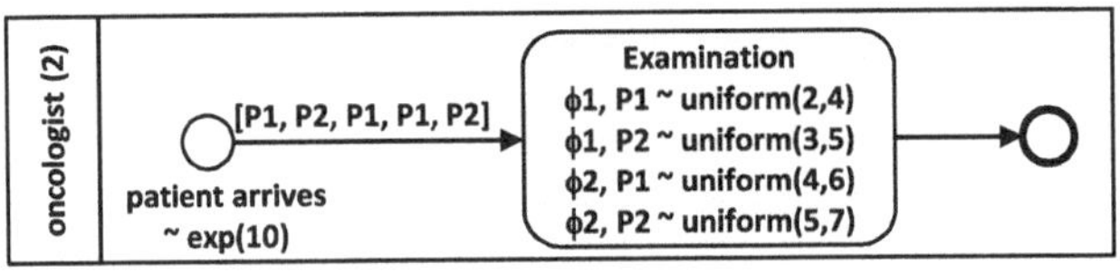

Fig. 2. Resource-Assignment Fragment: BPMN+OPT model.

Definition 2 (BPMN+OPT Execution State). *Let $\mathcal{M}$ be a BPMN+OPT process with case object types $\mathcal{C}$ and resource object types $\mathcal{R}$. At time $t \in \mathbb{T}$, the object valuation is $\mathcal{O}_t$, where $\mathcal{O} = \mathcal{C} \cup \mathcal{R}$. The execution state is $\sigma_t = (\mathcal{O}_t, \mathcal{Q}_t)$.*

The event calendar $\mathcal{Q}_t$ is part of the Markov execution state. It is available to the policy only for events whose occurrence times are operationally known; sampled but unrevealed arrival or completion times are latent, in which case the induced problem is partially observable and outside the present SMDP formalization.

The object valuation $\mathcal{O}_t$ records the currently existing case and resource objects together with their attribute values. The event calendar $\mathcal{Q}_t$ is needed only for execution semantics: it makes the induced decision process Markovian when processing times are non-memoryless or have already been sampled. When no confusion arises, we write expressions over $\mathcal{O}_t$ and leave $\mathcal{Q}_t$ implicit. We write $[\![e]\!]_{\sigma_t}$ for the value of expression e under the execution state. Some expressions, such as feasibility constraints, also refer to a temporary decision-variable valuation. For these, we write $[\![e]\!]_{\sigma_t,x}$, where x is used only as an evaluation context and is not itself an additional process-state component.

For example, in the resource-assignment fragment of Fig. 2, an execution state may contain one patient waiting for examination, two idle oncologists, and an event calendar recording pending future events:

$$\sigma_t = (\mathcal{O}_t, \mathcal{Q}_t),$$

where

$$\mathcal{O}_t = \{c_1 = \{id \mapsto 1,\ type \mapsto P_1,\ loc \mapsto (\mathsf{waiting}, \mathsf{Examination})\},\\ r_1 = \{id \mapsto \phi_1, loc \mapsto \mathsf{idle}\},\\ r_2 = \{id \mapsto \phi_2, loc \mapsto \mathsf{idle}\}\}$$

and, for instance,

$$\mathcal{Q}_t = \{(\mathsf{arrival}, t + \delta)\},$$

with δ denoting the residual time until the next scheduled arrival. In this simple state there are no pending task completions because no task is currently executing. The decision-moment expression

$$\exists c \in \mathcal{C}_t, \exists r \in \mathcal{R}_t : c.loc = (\mathsf{waiting}, \mathsf{Examination}) \wedge r.loc = \mathsf{idle}$$

therefore evaluates to true under σ_t. The event calendar is part of the execution state, but this particular decision moment depends only on the object valuation $\mathcal{O}_t$. By contrast, a feasibility constraint such as

$$x_t(c_1, r_1) + x_t(c_1, r_2) \leq 1$$

requires a temporary decision-variable valuation. Under

$$x = \{x_t(c_1, r_1) \mapsto 1,\ x_t(c_1, r_2) \mapsto 0\},$$

the constraint evaluates to true; under

$$x = \{x_t(c_1, r_1) \mapsto 1,\ x_t(c_1, r_2) \mapsto 1\},$$

it evaluates to false. Thus, the persistent execution state is object- and event-calendar-based, while decision-variable valuations are introduced only for checking feasibility and interpreting controllable choices.

3.2 SMDP Execution Semantics

We define the execution semantics of BPMN+OPT as a Semi-Markov Decision Process (SMDP). This matches the systems targeted by the language: processes evolve in continuous time, decisions occur at event-driven epochs, and activity durations need not be memoryless.

Definition 3 (SMDP). *An SMDP is a tuple (S, A, Rew, P, Θ), where S is a set of decision states, $A(s)$ is the set of actions admissible in state s, $P(s, a, s')$ is the probability that action $a \in A(s)$ leads to the next decision state s', $Rew(s, a, s')$ is the reward associated with the transition, and $\Theta(\cdot \mid s, a, s')$ is the holding-time distribution between s and s'.*

For a BPMN+OPT model $\mathcal{M} = (\mathcal{T}, \mathcal{E}, \mathcal{G}, \mathcal{F}, \mathcal{C}, \mathcal{R}, \mathsf{auth}, \mathcal{X}, \mathsf{Obj}, \mathsf{Con}, \mathsf{Mom})$, the induced SMDP is obtained by observing the execution only at decision epochs. Consequently, the state space contains the reachable execution states in which at least one decision moment is enabled:

$$S = \{\sigma_t \mid \exists m \in \mathsf{Mom} : [\![m]\!]_{\sigma_t} = \mathsf{true}\}.$$

States between decision epochs are not represented explicitly in S; their effects are summarized by transition probabilities, rewards, and holding times.

The admissible action set $A(s)$ contains the controllable choices available in state $s = \sigma_t$. Each primitive action is a pair (ξ, v), where ξ is a currently relevant decision-variable instance and v is the value assigned to it. Let $\mathsf{Inst}_{\mathcal{X}}(\sigma_t)$ denote the set of such instances, for example $x_t(c,r)$, $y_t(c)$, or $z_t(c)$ for assignment, scheduling, and routing, respectively. With $x[\xi \mapsto v]$ denoting the temporary valuation obtained by assigning v to instance ξ, we define

$$A(s) = \big\{(\xi, v) \bigm| \xi \in \mathsf{Inst}_{\mathcal{X}}(\sigma_t),\ v \in \mathsf{Dom}(\xi),\ \forall \gamma \in \mathsf{Con} : [\![\gamma]\!]_{\sigma_t, x[\xi \mapsto v]} = \mathsf{true}\big\}.$$

For example, suppose two patients c_1 and c_2 are waiting for Examination, oncologist ϕ_1 is idle, and oncologist ϕ_2 is busy. Then the currently relevant assignment instances are

$$\mathsf{Inst}_{\mathcal{X}}(\mathcal{O}_t) = \{x_t(c_1, \phi_1), x_t(c_2, \phi_1)\}.$$

The corresponding admissible actions are

$$(x_t(c_1, \phi_1), 1) \quad \text{and} \quad (x_t(c_2, \phi_1), 1),$$

which start Examination for the selected patient–oncologist pair. Instances such as $x_t(c_1, \phi_2)$ are not admissible in this state because ϕ_2 is not idle.

In this paper we use primitive sequential decision semantics: each primitive action assigns one value to one decision-variable instance, after which decision moments are re-evaluated. If another decision is enabled at the same simulation time, another primitive action is chosen immediately; otherwise, execution advances to the next event in $\mathcal{Q}_t$. This convention keeps the SMDP action space small and matches online settings in which decisions are committed one at a time. Joint decisions can still be represented by defining a decision-variable instance whose domain is a structured assignment, such as a matching between several cases and resources, but the proof of concept uses the primitive form.

Applying an action first performs the corresponding controlled update. A resource-assignment action enables a guarded task start for the selected case–resource pair. A scheduling action updates a case attribute, such as an appointment time. A routing action updates the case attribute that determines the outgoing branch of a gateway. Execution then proceeds autonomously by processing the earliest enabled item in $\mathcal{Q}_t$: task completions, arrivals, intermediate events, gateway routing, and stochastic behavior updates are applied until either a new decision moment becomes true or the evaluation horizon is reached. Thus, a controlled step followed by autonomous execution induces a transition

$$\sigma_t \xrightarrow{a,\ \tau,\ r} \sigma_{t+\tau},$$

where τ is the elapsed holding time and r is the reward accumulated during the autonomous segment.

For example, suppose patient c_1 is waiting for Examination, both resources ϕ_1, ϕ_2 are available and the next arrival is scheduled for $t + 10$. Figure 3 shows the possible transitions from this state, corresponding to assigning ϕ_1 and ϕ_2 to c_1. In both cases, the Examination will complete after a randomly drawn time interval and the reward is minus the cycle time of the patient. After completion, there is no waiting patient. Consequently, the next state of the SMDP is only after 10 time units, when the next patient arrives.

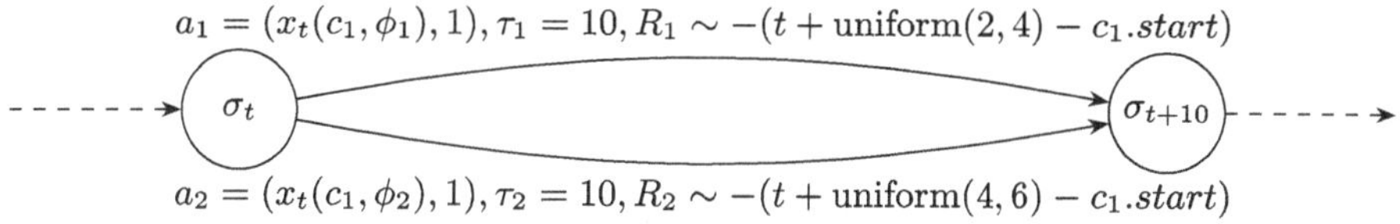

Fig. 3. Example SMDP.

The SMDP quantities P, Θ, and Rew are induced by the stochastic elements of the BPMN+OPT model: arrival distributions, processing-time distributions, routing conditions, behavior updates, and the state of the event calendar. When these quantities are analytically available, the SMDP can be constructed explicitly. More commonly, they are estimated by simulation: starting from state s and action a, the execution semantics are followed until the next decision state s' is reached, recording the elapsed time and accumulated reward. Repeating this experiment yields empirical estimates of $P(s, a, s')$, $\mathit{Rew}(s, a, s')$, and $\Theta(\cdot \mid s, a, s')$. The reward function is derived from Obj and may be terminal or accumulated over time; the experiments in Sect. 4.2 use accumulated flow-time rewards.

4 Modeling Optimization Problems in BPMN+OPT

We demonstrate BPMN+OPT using enactment-time problem classes identified in BPM–OR research: scheduling, resource allocation, and process navigation or action recommendation [7,16]. In our example, these correspond to case scheduling, resource assignment, and path routing. The three sub-problems below are part of a single BPMN+OPT model corresponding to Fig. 1. We formulate these problems at the modeling level and then use the induced SMDP semantics to execute and evaluate the resulting decision models. We developed a proof-of-concept implementation[2], which supports specifying BPMN+OPT problems in JSON, mapping them to the SMDP semantics, and solving the resulting SMDP.

[2] https://github.com/bpogroup/simpn/tree/bpmnopt/er_paper.

4.1 Problem Formulation

We now show how the three recurring optimization problems from the running example are represented in BPMN+OPT. Each problem is defined using the essential elements of an optimization problem outlined above: a decision moment identifies when control is handed to a policy, decision variables represent the controllable choice, constraints define feasibility, and the objective evaluates the resulting process performance.

Resource Assignment. We use the resource-assignment fragment from Fig. 2. For each waiting patient c and idle authorized oncologist r, the binary decision-variable instance

$$x_t(c, r) \in \{0, 1\}$$

indicates whether c is assigned to r.

The decision moment is enabled when a patient is waiting for Examination and an idle resource authorized for this task exists:

$$\exists c \in \mathcal{C}_t, \exists r \in \mathcal{R}_t : [\![c.loc]\!]_{\mathcal{O}_t} = (\mathsf{waiting}, \mathsf{Examination}) \ \wedge \ [\![r.loc]\!]_{\mathcal{O}_t} = \mathsf{idle},$$

where r is required to conform to a resource type R with $(R, \mathsf{Examination}) \in \mathsf{auth}$. Feasibility requires at most one oncologist per patient and at most one patient per oncologist:

$$\sum_{r \in \mathcal{R}_t} x_t(c, r) \leq 1 \quad \forall c \in \mathcal{C}_t, \qquad \sum_{c \in \mathcal{C}_t} x_t(c, r) \leq 1 \quad \forall r \in \mathcal{R}_t.$$

If $x_t(c, r) = 1$, the induced action starts $\mathsf{start}(\mathsf{Examination}, c, r)$. Under the sequential decision semantics of Sect. 3, multiple assignments at the same simulation time are made one by one, with the decision moment re-evaluated after each assignment.

Case Scheduling. The second problem is assigning appointment times to arriving patients. Patient objects are extended with an appointment-time attribute,

$$\mathcal{C} \subseteq \{\ldots, (appointment\_time, \mathbb{T})\}.$$

For a patient c without an appointment, the decision variable

$$y_t(c) = c.appointment\_time$$

selects the appointment time. The decision moment is enabled when a patient is waiting for an appointment and no appointment time has yet been assigned:

$$\exists c \in \mathcal{C}_t : [\![c.loc]\!]_{\mathcal{O}_t} = (\mathsf{waiting}, \mathsf{time\ for\ appointment}) \wedge y_t(c) = \bot.$$

The basic feasibility constraint is $y_t(c) \geq t$, so appointments cannot be scheduled in the past. Unlike resource assignment, the decision does not immediately start a task; it updates the patient's appointment-time attribute, which later enables the appointment event.

Path Routing. The third problem is deciding whether a patient follows the standard or intensive infusion path. Patient objects are extended with an infusion attribute,

$$\mathcal{C} \subseteq \{\ldots, (\mathit{infusion}, \{\mathit{standard}, \mathit{intensive}\})\}.$$

For a patient c reaching the infusion-choice point, the decision variable

$$z_t(c) = c.\mathit{infusion}$$

selects the branch. The routing decision is made after examination and drug preparation are both complete, when the patient reaches the XOR-split before infusion. Let G_{infusion} denote this gateway. The decision moment is

$$\exists c \in \mathcal{C}_t : [\![c.\mathit{loc}]\!]_{\mathcal{O}_t} = (\mathsf{waiting}, G_{\mathsf{infusion}}) \wedge z_t(c) = \bot.$$

The constraint is that exactly one admissible infusion type is selected, $z_t(c) \in \{\mathit{standard}, \mathit{intensive}\}$. The selected value then determines which outgoing branch of the XOR-split is taken.

Objective. All three decision types use the same finite-horizon performance objective: minimize cumulative patient flow time. For completed patients this coincides with completion time minus arrival time; for patients still in the system at the horizon, their elapsed time is counted:

$$\min \left(\sum_{\substack{c \in \mathcal{C}_t: \\ c.\mathit{complete} \neq \bot}} c.\mathit{complete} - c.\mathit{start} + \sum_{\substack{c \in \mathcal{C}_t: \\ c.\mathit{complete} = \bot}} t - c.\mathit{start} \right).$$

Equivalently, over an execution interval this objective can be represented as the area under the number-in-system curve,

$$\int n(u)\, du,$$

which is the reward representation used in Sect. 4.2. The examples cover these recurring enactment-time decisions, not all forms of business-process optimization. Design-time process redesign, strategic capacity or SLA planning, native batching, and tasks requiring several resources simultaneously are outside the present scope; alternative objective functions can be specified through *Obj* in Definition 1, while the evaluation horizon is supplied externally in the present formulation.

4.2 Solving the Induced SMDP

Section 3 defines the SMDP induced by a BPMN+OPT model. Enumerated decision states permit standard dynamic programming; larger processes require an executable generator because queues, resources, scheduled events, residual times, and case attributes make enumeration infeasible. Our JSON-based proof of concept compiles models into simulations that expose states, feasible actions, rewards, and holding times; Monte Carlo exploration yields an empirical SMDP for tabular methods.

Resource-Assignment Fragment. We first evaluate the fragment in Fig. 2. The abstract state records the number of waiting patients of each type and the idle oncologists,

$$\tilde{s} = (n_{P_1}, n_{P_2}, I), \qquad I \subseteq \{\phi_1, \phi_2\}.$$

Actions assign a waiting patient type to an idle oncologist; ties among patients of the same type are broken by longest waiting time. The reward is the negative area under the number-in-system curve,

$$r_k = -\int_{t_k}^{t_{k+1}} n(t)\, dt,$$

so maximizing reward minimizes cumulative flow time. We compare three heuristics against two SMDP-based methods: tabular Q-learning and empirical value iteration on the Monte Carlo-compiled SMDP.

Table 1. Resource-assignment fragment results ($H = 200$, $K = 5$; 95% CI).

Method	Avg. cycle time
FIFO	86.8 [84.5, 89.0]
SPT	86.7 [84.4, 89.0]
Random	96.5 [94.0, 99.1]
Q-learning	85.7 [81.6, 89.7]
Value iteration	85.7 [81.6, 89.7]

Table 1 reports results for horizon $H = 200$ with undiscounted cumulative reward ($\gamma = 1$), using $K = 5$ replications of 30 evaluation episodes. The two SMDP-based methods perform close to FIFO and SPT, while random assignment is clearly worse. The experiment is mainly a pipeline validation: the generated SMDP preserves decision-relevant distinctions, such as which oncologist is idle, that are needed to prefer faster resource–patient combinations.

Full Outpatient Process. We also applied the pipeline to Fig. 1, where scheduling, routing, and assignment interact. The experiment validates their exposure through a common SMDP interface with feasibility masks and cumulative flow-time rewards. It also shows the scalability limit of tabular methods: queue, resource, case, event, and time dimensions create sparse states, although the interface can support function approximation.

5 Related Work

BPMN+OPT relates to three streams of work. First, conceptual and formal process-modeling research has given process notations precise semantics and verification support. In BPM, formal work on BPMN has focused on giving the notation precise execution semantics, often through translations to Petri-net-based formalisms [2]. Workflow-pattern research has similarly characterized recurring control-flow and resource-allocation constructs in process-aware systems [18]. Language support for specific elements of decision making has also been developed, including the Decision Model and Notation (DMN), which provides a common notation for business decision requirements and decision models [13]; goal-oriented requirements approaches such as KAOS, which capture objectives and constraints [8], and declarative languages such as Declare [14], which can specify constraints over activities. These languages make process behavior, rules, goals, or constraints explicit, but they do not by themselves specify a sequential stochastic optimization problem. BPMN+OPT complements them by linking decision epochs, feasible actions, stochastic timing, and process-level objectives to the process model; an optimized policy may subsequently be represented or enacted using decision-management technology such as DMN [13].

Second, operations research provides mature models for scheduling, resource allocation, and service-system control [1,15]. BPMN+OPT therefore does not claim a new OR formulation or solution algorithm; its contribution is the process-linked specification from which solver-specific states, actions, constraints, and rewards can be constructed. Sequential decision making and reinforcement learning methods can also support runtime process adaptation once a suitable state and action representation has been fixed [11]. These methods are strong on solution quality, but they usually assume that the state space, action space, constraints, and rewards have already been engineered. BPMN+OPT is upstream of that step: it provides a conceptual language and mapping layer that keeps the optimization problem traceable to the process model before a particular solver or approximation method is chosen.

Third, process mining and performance-enrichment methods infer models, durations, waiting times, and congestion patterns from event data. They can therefore discover or calibrate BPMN+OPT parameters. Prescriptive process monitoring recommends interventions for ongoing cases and may optimize when to intervene [6,20]; BPMN+OPT instead specifies the process-level decision space, constraints, stochastic dynamics, and objective from which interacting policies can be derived.

Business-process simulation models arrivals, activity durations, routing probabilities, resource availability, and performance measures [10]. BPMN+OPT does not claim these stochastic ingredients as new; it distinguishes exogenous behavior from controllable choices and maps the latter, together with feasibility and objectives, to an SMDP. Decision-aware BPMN/DMN models and process-engine extensions already support executable decision logic and optimized task-specific resource allocation [4,9]. BPMN+OPT complements these approaches by specifying interacting scheduling, assignment, and routing decisions under stochastic timing and cumulative objectives; the resulting policy may be enacted through BPA/RPA [21].

6 Conclusion

This paper introduced BPMN+OPT, a BPMN-linked conceptual modeling language for process-embedded optimization problems. BPMN+OPT makes controllable decisions, feasible choices, constraints, objectives, stochastic behavior, and case/resource attributes explicit at the process-model level. Its SMDP semantics define how such models induce decision states, actions, transitions, rewards, and holding times while preserving traceability to process structure. An outpatient oncology example showed how scheduling, resource assignment, and routing decisions can be represented in one model. The proof-of-concept implementation demonstrated semantic executability: BPMN+OPT specifications can be compiled into executable decision environments for both small tabular SMDPs and larger simulation-based settings.

Future work will extend BPMN+OPT toward data-driven calibration using process mining and performance-mining techniques. We will also define the graphical notation more systematically and evaluate its understandability through a user study. Finally, although the SMDP semantics provide an analyzable execution model, the reachable state space can grow rapidly with the number of cases, resources, attributes, and pending events. We therefore aim to study decomposition and abstraction techniques that exploit process structure while preserving traceability between BPMN+OPT models and induced optimization problems.

References

1. Cayirli, T., Veral, E.: Outpatient scheduling in health care: a review of literature. Prod. Oper. Manag. **12**(4), 519–549 (2003)
2. Dijkman, R.M., Dumas, M., Ouyang, C.: Semantics and analysis of business process models in BPMN. Inf. Softw. Technol. **50**(12), 1281–1294 (2008)
3. Dumas, M., La Rosa, M., Mendling, J., Reijers, H.A.: Fundamentals of Business Process Management, 2 edn. Springer (2018)
4. Ihde, S., Pufahl, L., Völker, M., Goel, A., Weske, M.: A framework for modeling and executing task-specific resource allocations in business processes. Computing **104**, 2405–2429 (2022)
5. Jensen, K., Kristensen, L.M., Wells, L.: Coloured petri nets and CPN tools for modelling and validation of concurrent systems. Int. J. Softw. Tools Technol. Transfer **9**(3–4), 213–254 (2007)
6. Kubrak, K., Milani, F., Nolte, A., Dumas, M.: Prescriptive process monitoring: Quo vadis? PeerJ Comput. Sci. **8**, e1097 (2022)
7. Kunkler, M., Schumann, F., Rinderle-Ma, S.: Business process optimization: a systematic review of combining concepts from business process management and operations research. In: Proceedings of EDOC, pp. 61–83. Springer, Cham (2026)
8. van Lamsweerde, A.: Requirements Engineering: From System Goals to UML Models to Software Specifications. Wiley (2009)
9. de Leoni, M., Felli, P., Montali, M.: Integrating BPMN and DMN: modeling and analysis. J. Data Semant. **10**, 165–188 (2021)

10. López-Pintado, O., Dumas, M.: Business process simulation: probabilistic modeling of intermittent resource availability and multitasking behavior. Inf. Syst. **127**, 102471 (2025)
11. Metzger, A., Kley, T., Palm, A.: Triggering proactive business process adaptations via online reinforcement learning. In: Fahland, D., Ghidini, C., Becker, J., Dumas, M. (eds.) BPM 2020. LNCS, vol. 12168, pp. 273–290. Springer, Cham (2020). https://doi.org/10.1007/978-3-030-58666-9_16
12. Object Management Group: Business Process Model and Notation (BPMN), Version 2.0.2. OMG Specification formal/2013-12-09, Object Management Group (2013)
13. Object Management Group: Decision Model and Notation (DMN), Version 1.4. OMG Specification formal/23-03-01, Object Management Group (2023)
14. Pesic, M., Schonenberg, H., van der Aalst, W.M.P.: DECLARE: full support for loosely-structured processes. In: Proceedings of EDOC, pp. 287–300. IEEE Computer Society (2007)
15. Pinedo, M.L.: Scheduling: Theory, Algorithms, and Systems, 5 edn. Springer (2016)
16. Pufahl, L., Stiehle, F., Ihde, S., Weske, M., Weber, I.: Resource allocation in business process executions–a systematic literature study. Inf. Syst. **132**, 102541 (2025)
17. Puterman, M.L.: Markov Decision Processes: Discrete Stochastic Dynamic Programming. Wiley (1994)
18. Russell, N., van der Aalst, W.M.P., ter Hofstede, A.H.M., Edmond, D.: Workflow resource patterns: identification, representation and tool support. In: Pastor, O., Falcão e Cunha, J. (eds.) CAiSE 2005. LNCS, vol. 3520, pp. 216–232. Springer, Heidelberg (2005). https://doi.org/10.1007/11431855_16
19. Sutton, R.S., Precup, D., Singh, S.: Between MDPs and semi-MDPs: a framework for temporal abstraction in reinforcement learning. Artif. Intell. **112**(1–2), 181–211 (1999)
20. Teinemaa, I., Tax, N., de Leoni, M., Dumas, M., Maggi, F.M.: Alarm-based prescriptive process monitoring. In: Weske, M., Montali, M., Weber, I., vom Brocke, J. (eds.) BPM 2018. LNBIP, vol. 329, pp. 91–107. Springer, Cham (2018). https://doi.org/10.1007/978-3-319-98651-7_6
21. Wewerka, J., Reichert, M.: Robotic process automation—a systematic literature review and assessment framework (2020)

Discovering Sustainability-Aware Business Process Variants from Event Logs

Nathalie Wolf(✉), Holger Wittges, and Stefanie Rinderle-Ma

TUM School of Computation, Information and Technology, Technical University of Munich, Garching, Germany
{nathalie.wolf,holger.wittges,stefanie.rinderle-ma}@tum.de

Abstract. With growing demand for transparency in the sustainability performance of business processes, understanding how process variants shape sustainability outcomes becomes increasingly important. Process mining provides an empirical foundation for such analyses. However, formal methods for identifying sustainability-aware process variants are still lacking. To address this gap, the present article introduces a structured approach for sustainability-aware process variant discovery, which combines trace clustering with execution-level sustainability analysis. The approach is centered on a formal definition of sustainability-aware process variants and integrates sustainability as an additional analytical dimension into process variant analysis. It further enables statistical characterization of process variants and the derivation of sustainability-annotated process models, facilitating their structured comparison. An empirical evaluation on sustainability-annotated event logs demonstrates the applicability and analytical value of the proposed approach and highlights its potential to support sustainability-aware process analysis.

Keywords: Process Mining · Process Variant Discovery · Sustainability

1 Introduction

Driven by increasing regulatory requirements and growing stakeholder expectations, sustainability has become a core strategic concern for organizations, encompassing economic, environmental, and social aspects [9]. As the operational backbone of organizations, business processes directly affect overall sustainability performance and thus represent a key lever for achieving corporate sustainability objectives [3]. However, business processes are rarely executed in a uniform manner. Across varying contextual factors, process executions often differ considerably, resulting in distinct process variants [23]. As sustainability performance may vary significantly across these process variants, understanding such differences is essential for sustainability transparency [28].

Against this background, process mining provides an empirical basis for analyzing business processes [1,2] and thus represents a promising approach

© The Author(s), under exclusive license to Springer Nature Switzerland AG 2027
A. Bernasconi et al. (Eds.): ER 2026, LNCS 17081, pp. 236–252, 2027.
https://doi.org/10.1007/978-3-032-40795-5_14

for assessing sustainability-related characteristics (e.g., CO_2 emissions, renewable material usage) of process executions [10,13,15]. While initial research has begun to apply process mining to analyze sustainability in business processes (e.g., [6,13,14]), existing approaches only scratch the surface, as multi-perspective analyses of business process sustainability remain largely underexplored [10]. Furthermore, research on process variant analysis predominantly focuses on control-flow differences, while other perspectives, such as data and resource characteristics, receive limited attention [23]. Consequently, sustainability-aware process mining and process variant analysis remain largely disconnected, and approaches for systematically identifying process variants based on sustainability-related characteristics are still missing. To address this gap, this article proposes an approach for sustainability-aware process variant discovery (SaPVD), extending process variant analysis by incorporating sustainability as an additional analytical dimension. Accordingly, this article focuses on the following research question.

RQ How can sustainability-aware business process variants be formally defined and derived from event logs to enable their analysis and visualization?

Specifically, this article introduces (i) a formal definition of sustainability-aware process variants and proposes (ii) the SaPVD approach for their identification from sustainability-annotated event logs using sustainability-enriched trace clustering. Additionally, (iii) methods for the statistical characterization of the identified variants are provided, complemented by (iv) a first concept for sustainability-annotated process models that visualizes sustainability-related differences at the process structure level. Following [18], these contributions constitute knowledge of a new algorithmic task and a corresponding algorithmic design.

2 Sustainability-Aware Process Variants

Process mining focuses on the analysis of real-world executions of business processes with the objective to identify inefficiencies and systematically improve process performance [1,2]. The foundation of such analyses are event logs, which include the recording of business process executions based on data captured by information systems [1]. Following [1], an event log $L \subseteq C$ is a set of cases over a case universe C and an event universe E. Each case $c \in C$ represents a single process execution and is associated with a trace $\sigma \in E^*$, where E^* denotes the set of all finite sequences over E, and $\sigma = \langle e_1, e_2, \ldots, e_n \rangle$ with $e_i \in E$, each representing the execution of a specific activity within a business process.

From an analytical standpoint, process executions can be examined along multiple conceptually distinct dimensions, depending on the analysis objective [23]. In this contribution, process executions are analyzed from two complementary perspectives: a structural perspective and a sustainability perspective.

The structural perspective focuses on the order and execution of activities within a process execution. In this context, individual process executions are grouped into process variants. A process variant describes a set of process executions that are considered coherent based on selected structural criteria [17,23]. Process variants are not an inherent property of an event log. Rather, they form an analytical abstraction introduced for a specific purpose. Depending on the applied criteria, multiple equally valid variant compositions may exist for the same event log. A process variant, therefore, serves as a flexible instrument for grouping process executions to make them comparable [5,17,23].

Structural analyses of process executions can be enriched with sustainability-related attributes that capture their economic, environmental, and social characteristics. These sustainability attributes are modeled as attributes within the event log and can be assigned at log, case, or event level [28]. Sustainability attributes thus characterize individual process executions but do not represent structural process properties. Consequently, structurally identical process executions may exhibit different sustainability characteristics, e.g., due to variations in resource utilization, while structurally different executions may show comparable sustainability patterns. Against this background, sustainability is treated as a distinct semantic dimension at the execution level, which complements rather than replaces structural process analysis. Building on this conceptual separation, a sustainability-aware process variant is formally defined as follows.

Definition 1 (Sustainability-aware Process Variant). *A sustainability-aware process variant $V_i \subseteq C$ is a non-empty subset of cases such that:*

(a) all cases $c \in V_i$ are structurally coherent under a given structural abstraction,
(b) V_i exhibits systematic differentiation from other process variants V_j $(i \neq j)$ with respect to a sustainability attribute mapping $\phi : C \rightarrow \mathbb{R}^d$, capturing execution-level sustainability characteristics, and
(c) the set of process variants $\{V_i\}$ forms a partition of C for the considered process variant abstraction, i.e., $\bigcup_i V_i = C$ and $V_i \cap V_j = \emptyset$ for $i \neq j$.

The existence of sustainability-aware process variants cannot be assumed in advance, as not every event log contains structurally coherent variants that show meaningful sustainability-related differentiation. Structural diversity alone does not imply sustainability-related differentiation, since sustainability represents an additional, context-dependent semantic dimension. Their identification requires an integrated consideration of structural abstractions and sustainability attributes, while both perspectives remain analytically and conceptually distinct.

3 Sustainability-Aware Variant Discovery Approach

The primary objective of the SaPVD approach is the identification and analysis of sustainability-aware process variants, as defined in Sect. 2, by considering structural coherence and execution-level sustainability context.

Figure 1 illustrates the proposed five-step method for the identification and analysis of sustainability-aware process variants. The approach is structured into two consecutive phases: process variant identification (Subsect. 3.1) and process variant analysis (Subsect. 3.2). The first phase focuses on the identification of process variants by grouping process executions based on process-related and sustainability-related characteristics. The second phase centers on the interpretation and model-based representation of the identified process variants, assessing the differentiation along both dimensions.

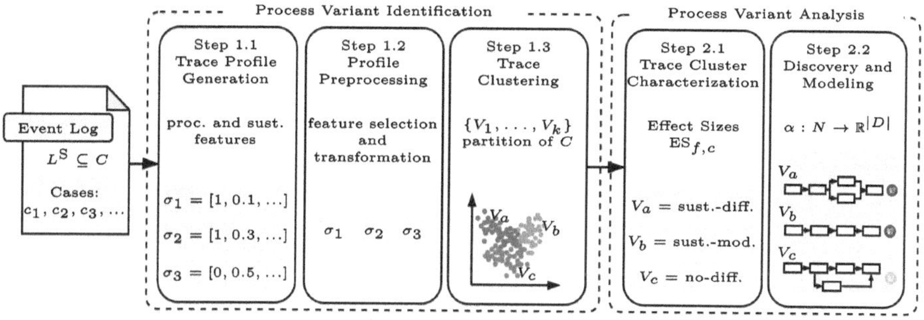

Fig. 1. Sustainability-aware Process Variant Discovery Approach (SaPVD).

The application of the SaPVD approach requires two essential prerequisites. First, a sustainability-annotated event log L^S must be available, which extends a standard event log L with sustainability attributes D capturing economic, environmental, and social characteristics [28]. Second, the event log must exhibit a sufficiently high data quality to ensure valid and interpretable results [29]. If necessary, appropriate preprocessing steps should be performed beforehand.

This section subsequently describes the individual steps of the SaPVD approach required to derive sustainability-aware process variants, excluding event log generation and preprocessing. To illustrate each step, a simplified excerpt of a sustainability-annotated procurement event log [27] is used as a running example throughout this section. Table 1 shows five representative cases $c_1, \ldots, c_5 \in C$ with their activity sequences and selected sustainability attributes from D.

Table 1. Running Example – Excerpt of a Sustainability-annotated Event Log

Case	Trace	Renewable Material	Material Quantity (ST)	Empl. Skill Level	CO_2 Emissions (KG)
c_1	⟨PR, PO⟩	true	16,000	expert	0
c_2	⟨PR, PO⟩	false	16,000	expert	0
c_3	⟨PR, PO, GR, SI, IR, FI, PA⟩	true	160,000	entry	1,364
c_4	⟨PR, PO, GR, SI, IR, FI, PA⟩	true	192,000	entry	1,636
c_5	⟨PR, PO, GR, SI, IR, FI, PA⟩	true	48,000	entry	600

PR: Create Purchase Requisition Item, PO: Create Purchase Order Item, GR: Create Goods Receipt, SI: Create Supplier Invoice, IR: Record Invoice Receipt, FI: Create Financial Invoice, PA: Payment.

3.1 Process Variant Identification

The first phase builds on trace clustering [24,29], a widely adopted approach for identifying process variants from event logs, and extends it by incorporating sustainability-related characteristics to derive coherent sustainability-aware process variants. It is organized into three steps: trace profile generation, profile preprocessing, and trace clustering.

Step 1.1 – Trace Profile Generation. The first step of the SaPVD approach establishes a trace-level representation of process executions based on the event log L. For this purpose, the approach builds upon the profiling concept introduced by [21], in which traces are characterized by profiles. A profile describes a set of items derived from a specific trace perspective. Each item corresponds to a metric that assigns a numerical value to a trace, for example to capture the frequency of individual activities. The resulting profiles are aggregated into trace-level vector representations, forming the feature space for subsequent steps.

Building on the existing profiling concepts, the SaPVD approach extends the profiles introduced by [21] by a sustainability-related profile that captures the sustainability characteristics of a trace. To this end, the sustainability-related attributes of the underlying event log are consolidated into a sustainability profile. The following definition formalizes the sustainability profile.

Definition 2 (Sustainability Profile). *Let L^{S} be a sustainability-annotated event log over C and E, and let $\mathcal{F} = \mathcal{F}^{\mathrm{Q}} \uplus \mathcal{F}^{\mathrm{L}} \uplus \mathcal{F}^{\mathrm{B}} \uplus \mathcal{F}^{\mathrm{K}}$ be a set of sustainability-related features derived from the annotation set D, where $\mathcal{F}^{\mathrm{Q}}$ denotes quantity features, $\mathcal{F}^{\mathrm{L}}$ level or score features, $\mathcal{F}^{\mathrm{B}}$ boolean features (where $\top$ denotes true), and $\mathcal{F}^{\mathrm{K}}$ categorical features, reflecting the semantic nature of sustainability-related attributes as specified in [28]. For a case $c \in C$, the sustainability profile $\varphi_{sust}(c) := \langle \varphi^{\mathrm{Q}}(c,f), \varphi^{\mathrm{L}}(c,f), \varphi^{\mathrm{B}}(c,f), \varphi^{\mathrm{K}}(c,f,v) \rangle$ is a numerical feature vector obtained by aggregating event-level sustainability features of c according to their feature type, i.e., $\mathcal{F}^{\mathrm{Q}}$, $\mathcal{F}^{\mathrm{L}}$, $\mathcal{F}^{\mathrm{B}}$, or $\mathcal{F}^{\mathrm{K}}$. To this end, let $E(c)$ denote the set of events belonging to case $c \in C$ and $\nu(e,f)$ the value of feature $f \in \mathcal{F}$ for event $e \in E$, and $\mathrm{dom}(f)$ the set of possible values of feature f. Then:*

$$\varphi^{\mathrm{Q}}(c,f) = \sum_{e \in E(c)} \nu(e,f), \qquad f \in \mathcal{F}^{\mathrm{Q}}, \tag{1}$$

$$\varphi^{\mathrm{L}}(c,f) = \frac{1}{|E(c)|} \sum_{e \in E(c)} \nu(e,f), \qquad f \in \mathcal{F}^{\mathrm{L}}, \tag{2}$$

$$\varphi^{\mathrm{B}}(c,f) = |\{e \in E(c) \mid \nu(e,f) = \top\}|, \qquad f \in \mathcal{F}^{\mathrm{B}}, \tag{3}$$

$$\varphi^{\mathrm{K}}(c,f,v) = |\{e \in E(c) \mid \nu(e,f) = v\}|, \qquad f \in \mathcal{F}^{\mathrm{K}}, v \in \mathrm{dom}(f). \tag{4}$$

The sustainability profile is instantiated using type-specific aggregation functions reflecting the semantic nature of sustainability attributes, operationalizing the mapping $\phi : C \to \mathbb{R}^d$ introduced in Definition 1. The aggregation functions are chosen to preserve the measurement scale of each feature type, e.g., summation for quantities ($\mathcal{F}^{\mathrm{Q}}$) and averaging for relative scores ($\mathcal{F}^{\mathrm{L}}$).

Applying Definition 2 to case c_3 of the running example, material quantity and CO_2 emission are aggregated as $\mathcal{F}^{\mathrm{Q}}$, renewable material usage as $\mathcal{F}^{\mathrm{B}}$, and employee skill level as $\mathcal{F}^{\mathrm{K}}$, yielding the sustainability profile $\varphi_{\mathrm{sust}}(c_3)$.

Step 1.2 – Profile Preprocessing. The second step prepares the feature space for trace clustering by improving the comparability and quality of the profile features. It includes feature transformation techniques to ensure metric comparability, as well as feature selection methods to control dimensionality and to address collinearity within the feature space [29]. The input to this step consists of trace-level vector representations, which are transformed into a refined feature space suitable for robust clustering.

The selection of appropriate preprocessing techniques depends on the structural and statistical properties of the underlying event log [29]. Consequently, no universal preprocessing strategy exists. To address this challenge, the proposed methodology specifies data-independent principles from which context-adaptable recommendations for preprocessing sustainability-related features are derived.

- **Domain knowledge-based protection rule.** During the application of feature selection techniques, sustainability-related features should be explicitly protected, as, e.g., variance-based criteria may eliminate infrequent yet semantically relevant characteristics.
- **Feature weighting.** As non-sustainability-related features may numerically dominate sustainability-related features, feature weighting can be treated as an experimental variable to investigate the influence of sustainability-related attributes on the resulting cluster structure.

Step 1.3 – Trace Clustering. The third step of the SaPVD approach applies suitable clustering algorithms to derive coherent process variants by grouping process executions with similar process-related and sustainability-related characteristics in the preprocessed feature space. In the context of trace clustering, various algorithms [24] may be employed, including hierarchical, partitioning, and density-based techniques. Since sustainability-related profiles often contain heterogeneous data types, including categorical and numerical features, a central challenge is the selection of clustering approaches capable of appropriately handling such heterogeneity [24]. To address this challenge, the SaPVD approach recommends applying multiple clustering methods and comparatively evaluating their suitability with respect to the underlying analytical objective [29].

In the running example, c_1 and c_2 are grouped into the same cluster, primarily due to their identical trace $\langle \mathrm{PR}, \mathrm{PO} \rangle$ and similar sustainability characteristics, while c_3 and c_4 form a separate cluster and c_5 a third cluster.

3.2 Process Variant Analysis

The second phase of the SaPVD approach builds on the trace clusters derived in Phase 1 and focuses on their classification into semantic variant types and derivation of sustainability-annotated process models. Following the classification by [23], the proposed approach can be categorized as a hybrid technique, as it combines the statistical characterization of sustainability-related differences with their model-based visualization. The phase is organized into two steps.

Step 2.1 – Trace Cluster Characterization. This step performs a statistical characterization of the trace clusters identified in Phase 1, using established statistical methods [11,26]. The objective is to construct a quantitative basis for comparing trace clusters along process-related and sustainability-related dimensions. Thus, each trace cluster is described by cluster-level feature statistics [11,25] reflecting systematic differences between clusters.

To quantify the differentiation between process variants, a normalized effect-size score is used, which captures the magnitude of deviation of a trace cluster relative to the ensemble. Effect sizes are well-suited, as they are independent of absolute feature scales and enable comparability across heterogeneous features [22]. For each active feature, a score is computed as follows: $\mathrm{ES}_{f,c} = {}^{|\tilde{x}_{f,c} - \tilde{x}_{f,\cdot}|}/_{\sigma_f}$, where $\tilde{x}_{f,c}$ denotes the median of feature f in variant c, $\tilde{x}_{f,\cdot}$ the global median of feature f across all variants, and σ_f the standard deviation of these variant medians. The median is used as a robust measure, as it is less sensitive to outliers than the mean [11]. Only active features with $\sigma_f > 0$ are considered, as constant features do not contribute to variant differentiation.

For each process variant, scores are aggregated separately for process-related and sustainability-related features by averaging effect-size values across all active features of the respective perspective. Based on predefined effect-size thresholds, adapted from [7], process variants are assigned to the following semantic cluster types that reflect the dominant source of differentiation.

Definition 3 (Sustainability-aware Process Variant Types). *A sustainability-aware process variant is characterized by its relative differentiation in process-related and sustainability-related attributes, quantified by the scores* Δ_{proc} *and* Δ_{sust}*, respectively. Based on the degree of differentiation along these two complementary dimensions, an identified trace cluster is classified into one of the following types:*

- ***Sustainability-differentiating:*** *The process variant exhibits systematic sustainability-related deviations* ($\Delta_{\text{sust}} \geq 0.5$) *without corresponding differentiation in process-related characteristics* ($\Delta_{\text{proc}} < 0.5$)*.*
- ***Sustainability-modulated:*** *The process variant exhibits systematic deviations in both process-related* ($\Delta_{\text{proc}} \geq 0.5$) *and sustainability-related attributes* ($\Delta_{\text{sust}} \geq 0.5$)*.*
- ***Process-driven:*** *The process variant primarily differs in process-related characteristics* ($\Delta_{\text{proc}} \geq 0.5$)*, while sustainability-related attributes do not show substantial deviations* ($\Delta_{\text{sust}} < 0.5$)*.*
- ***No-differentiation:*** *The process variant exhibits no pronounced process- or sustainability-related deviations* ($\Delta_{\text{proc}} < 0.5$, $\Delta_{\text{sust}} < 0.5$)*.*

In the running example, the cluster containing c_1 and c_2 is classified as *sustainability-modulated*, showing systematic deviations in both process-related and sustainability-related characteristics. The cluster of c_3 and c_4 is classified as *sustainability-differentiating*, driven by above-average renewable material usage and quantity. The cluster including c_5 exhibits no pronounced differentiation and is thus classified as *no-differentiation*. Process-driven and no-differentiation variants are intentionally retained, as the absence of sustainability-related differentiation is analytically meaningful.

Step 2.2 – Discovery and Modeling. The final step of the SaPVD approach translates the results of statistical trace cluster characterization into model-based representations to make sustainability-related differences explicit at the level of process-related characteristics. Therefore, a dedicated process model is discovered for each process variant and enriched with sustainability-related annotations, enabling systematic comparison and interpretation across process variants. Such a process model is defined as follows.

Definition 4 (Sustainability-annotated Process Model). *Let* $M = (N, R)$ *be a process model with elements* N *and relations* $R \subseteq N \times N$. *A sustainability-annotated process model extends* M *by an annotation function* $\alpha : N \rightarrow \mathbb{R}^{|D|}$ *that assigns a (possibly sparse) vector of sustainability attribute values to model elements, where zero entries indicate the absence of the corresponding sustainability attribute. The annotation reflects sustainability characteristics without altering the underlying process structure.*

The SaPVD approach recommends the instantiation of sustainability-annotated process models as directly-follows graph (DFG) $G = (\text{Act}, F)$ [1], where Act is a set of activities and $F \subseteq \text{Act} \times \text{Act}$ a set of directly-follows relations. DFGs are chosen as they provide a simple and widely adopted process representation [1], serving as a first visualization concept for sustainability-related differences across process variants. Sustainability annotations are attached to activity nodes $a \in \text{Act}$ as annotation vectors $\alpha(a) \in \mathbb{R}^{|D|}$, whose components correspond to sustainability attributes in D. Annotation values are derived from effect-size-based comparisons of execution-level sustainability features, as introduced in Step 2.1. Case-level features are aggregated at the variant level and associated with the process variant as a whole.

To support interpretability, the process model may optionally be enriched with a visual encoding [4,19], adapted to the sustainability context. Node color represents the direction and magnitude of deviation relative to the global, while annotation symbols indicate the sustainability dimension of the dominant feature. This supports an intuitive interpretation of sustainability-related differences within the process structure.

This step completes the SaPVD approach by making sustainability-related differences explicit at the process structure level.

4 Empirical Evaluation of the Approach

The proposed SaPVD approach is evaluated within an experimental setup grounded in an exploratory research design [18]. In the following, the experimental setup is outlined, and the resulting empirical findings are subsequently presented. The implementation and complete results are available in the associated repository[1].

4.1 Data and Set-Up

The evaluation is conducted on multiple event logs and considers different configurations of the SaPVD approach, including trace profiles, preprocessing options, and clustering algorithms. The experimental scheme is illustrated in Table 2.

Table 2. Experimental Setup of the Empirical Evaluation

Event Log	Trace Profile Config.	Feature Weighting	Dimension Reduction	Clustering Algorithm
Production	Process	No	No	k-means
P2P	Sustainability	Yes	PCA	AHC
M2S	Full			HDBSCAN
O2C				

All combinations result in 30 runs per event log. Feature weighting is applied only to the sustainability and full trace profile configurations, as only these include sustainability-related features.

The SaPVD evaluation uses four sustainability-annotated event logs published in [27], covering the economic, environmental, and social sustainability dimensions. The event logs include a synthetic production event log for wooden chair production and three event logs from a real-world ERP system, covering the processes procure-to-pay (P2P), make-to-stock (M2S), and order-to-cash (O2C) of a fictitious muesli-producing company. Table 3 summarizes key characteristics of the four event logs. As these represent the currently available case-centric sustainability-annotated event logs [28], they provide a suitable basis for an initial empirical assessment of the approach.

Table 3. Characteristics of the Sustainability-annotated Event Logs

Event Log	Cases	Events	Activities	Sustainability Attribute Categories
Production	250	3,300	7	Cost, Material, Waste, Water, Energy, Emission, Employee, Workplace, Safety
P2P	1,141	7,590	7	Material, Emission, Employee
M2S	577	11,934	12	Waste, Emission, Workplace
O2C	3,182	37,669	11	Emission, Employee, Safety

[1] https://github.com/nathalieTUM/SaPVD.

The evaluation setup defines five trace profiles: activity profiles capture the occurrence frequency of each activity, transition profiles the frequency of directly-following activity pairs, performance profiles case-level and inter-event duration metrics, and context profiles case- and event-level contextual attributes [21], complemented by a sustainability profile according to Definition 2.

Based on these, three trace profile configurations, represented as concatenated feature vectors, are derived for the experimental application. The process configuration includes the activity, transition, and performance profiles. The sustainability configuration extends this set by incorporating the sustainability profile, while the full configuration encompasses all five trace profiles. This setup enables a systematic assessment of the additional contribution of sustainability attributes beyond established process-related trace characteristics.

Based on an exploratory event log analysis, a unified preprocessing pipeline is defined as outlined in Step 1.2, including removal of constant and infrequent features, log-transformation of skewed features, robust scaling, and removal of highly correlated features, while sustainability features are explicitly protected from frequency-based feature selection. Additionally, the experimental setup introduces variations by assigning higher weights to sustainability features and by either applying principal component analysis (PCA) or omitting it prior to trace clustering. PCA is selected to reduce the dimensionality of the heterogeneous feature space while preserving its principal variance structure [29].

For the comparative analysis, three clustering algorithms are selected following Step 1.3. They represent complementary clustering strategies, namely partitioning (k-means), hierarchical (agglomerative hierarchical clustering (AHC)), and density-based (HDBSCAN), enabling a systematic comparison of their suitability for sustainability-enriched trace clustering [24]. Distances are computed on the resulting feature vectors using Euclidean distance. The number of clusters is determined in a preceding parameter analysis per event log.

For the qualitative interpretation of the clustering results, a statistical cluster characterization of all run configurations is performed as described in Step 2.1. Subsequently, for each event log, the run configuration is selected that meets a minimum clustering quality while maximizing the number of sustainability-aware process variants. The selected run configuration is then used for process discovery and modeling to make sustainability-related differences explicit at the level of process-related characteristics, as outlined in Step 2.2.

4.2 Results Process Variant Identification

This subsection evaluates the clustering quality of process variants identified across the experimental configurations (see Table 2), focusing on cluster cohesion and separation. The evaluation is primarily based on the silhouette score (SIL) [20], which measures cluster cohesion and separation, complemented by the Davies-Bouldin index (DBI) [8], which captures these from a different perspective. Structural properties of the identified clusters are additionally considered.

Out of 120 experimental runs across the four event logs, 112 runs yield complete process variant partitions, addressing condition (c) of Definition 1. The remaining eight runs correspond to configurations employing HDBSCAN on larger event logs (P2P and O2C) with more complex trace profiles. In these cases, all traces are classified as noise, preventing any process variant derivation. Table 4 summarizes the results by reporting the average SIL per event log, trace profile combination, and clustering algorithm, and the impact of feature weighting.

Table 4. Trace Clustering Evaluation Results

Event Log	Trace Profile Config.	k-means	AHC	HDBSCAN	Δ Weight.
Production	process	0.437	0.419	0.502	—
	sustainability	0.126	0.147	**0.282**	−0.014
	full	0.114	0.144	0.276	−0.009
P2P	process	1.000	0.251	0.982	—
	sustainability	0.261	0.244	**0.450**	+0.011
	full	0.197	0.179	0.358	+0.095
M2S	process	0.450	0.451	0.523	—
	sustainability	0.289	0.302	**0.687**	+0.120
	full	0.268	0.277	0.614	+0.147
O2C	process	0.691	0.741	0.862	—
	sustainability	0.132	0.129	**0.454**	+0.109
	full	0.128	0.110	—*	−0.053†

* All traces classified as noise, no valid clusters formed.

† Δ Weight for O2C/full based on k-means and AHC only. HDBSCAN produces no valid trace clusters.

The trace profile configuration is the dominant factor influencing the quality of the identified process variants. The process configuration consistently achieves the highest cluster cohesion (mean SIL = 0.61), as it captures the structural regularities of process executions. The sustainability configuration (mean SIL = 0.29) reduces cluster separability, reflecting the complementary nature of sustainability-related and process-related characteristics. The full configuration (mean SIL = 0.24) further increases dimensionality without enhancing the clarity of the process variant partition structure. This reflects an inherent trade-off. The inclusion of sustainability-related features required for sustainability-aware variant identification simultaneously reduces structural separability.

Moreover, the results indicate that neither feature weighting nor PCA-based dimensionality reduction has a robust influence on trace cluster quality. Weighting yields a noticeable improvement only for M2S (ΔSIL = +0.13), while effects are marginal or slightly negative across the remaining event logs. These results suggest that trace profile selection is the primary driver of variation in the resulting variant structures. Among the applied clustering algorithms, HDBSCAN achieves the highest cohesion (mean SIL = 0.52) but does not produce complete partitions for more complex configurations. In contrast, k-means and AHC yield consistently robust and complete partitions, achieving a mean SIL of 0.26.

Across all valid experimental runs, between 2 and 13 process variants per event log are identified (mean = 5.5), with k-means and AHC consistently producing 4–7 process variants across all configurations, while HDBSCAN yields varying numbers of process variants due to noise classification.

Overall, the results demonstrate that the SaPVD approach produces stable process variant partitions across heterogeneous event logs, with stability depending strongly on the chosen trace profile configuration. The SIL scores confirm sufficient internal cohesion, thereby satisfying condition (a) of Definition 1. The identified partitions form the basis for the subsequent process variant analysis.

4.3 Results Process Variant Analysis

This subsection focuses on the semantic characterization of the process variants identified in Subsect. 4.2 in the context of sustainability-aware process variants. Table 5 summarizes the distribution of semantic types (see Definition 3) across all four event logs, demonstrating the approach's transferability.

Table 5. Semantic Type Distribution of Sustainability-aware Process Variants

Event Log	#Variants	#Sust.-diff.	#Sust.-mod.	#Proc.-driven	#No-diff.
Production	5	3	2	–	–
P2P	7	4	1	–	2
M2S	6	1	4	–	1
O2C	4	2	2	–	–

The following analysis exemplarily uses the P2P event log, while detailed results for the remaining event logs are available in the referenced repository. Based on the criteria outlined in Sect. 4.1, the selected run comprises the sustainability profile configuration with no feature weighting, PCA, and k-means. Although HDBSCAN achieves higher cluster cohesion (see Sect. 4.2), a k-means configuration run is selected as it reliably produces complete partitions while maximizing the number of sustainability-aware process variants.

Figure 2 illustrates the effect sizes of the sustainability-related features for each trace cluster and enables a compact comparison of cluster-specific deviations relative to the overall population. Clusters with pronounced sustainability-related effect sizes indicate sustainability-related differentiation, though the distinction between *sustainability-differentiating* and *sustainability-modulated* variants additionally depends on the process-related differentiation score Δ_{proc} introduced in Step 2.1. Of the seven identified process variants, four are classified as *sustainability-differentiating* (IDs 2, 3, 4, and 6) and one as *sustainability-modulated* (ID 1), while two variants (IDs 0 and 5) exhibit no differentiation and

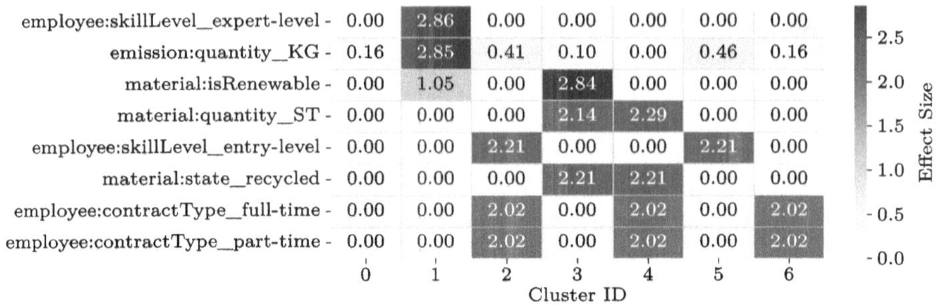

Fig. 2. Effect Sizes of Sustainability Features per Cluster for the P2P Event Log.

are excluded from the subsequent analysis. Across all trace clusters, eight sustainability features show significant effects, including material properties, employee attributes, and emission volume.

Three of the identified process variants are modeled in Fig. 3 as sustainability-annotated process models (see Definition 4) using a DFG representation. The models link process structure with sustainability semantics and highlight local sustainability differentiation. Node color and saturation encode the strength of the dominant attribute's deviation from the overall population, while annotation icons indicate the sustainability dimension of the attribute.

Variant 1 (*sustainability-modulated*, $n = 25$) shows high differentiation in both dimensions ($\Delta_{\text{proc}} = 2.86$, $\Delta_{\text{sust}} = 0.84$), driven by the absence of *Create FI Invoice* and further activities and an above-average proportion of employees with `skillLevel_expert`. Variant 3 (*sustainability-differentiating*, $n = 213$) is characterized by strong sustainability-related differentiation ($\Delta_{\text{sust}} = 0.91$) associated with material-related sustainability characteristics, while maintaining a stable control flow. Variant 4 (*sustainability-differentiating*, $n = 209$) exhibits the highest sustainability score ($\Delta_{\text{sust}} = 1.07$) driven by above-average material throughput (`quantity_ST`), near-zero control flow deviation ($\Delta_{\text{proc}} = 0.00$), indicating a purely sustainability-driven variant. The contrast between Variants 3 and 4 illustrates that different sustainability dimensions can yield structurally similar yet semantically distinct variants.

The identification of sustainability-differentiating and sustainability-modulated variants confirms that the identified process variants satisfy condition (b) of Definition 1, exhibiting systematic differentiation w.r.t. ϕ. The results demonstrate that the proposed approach enables the identification of process variants that systematically differ along sustainability-related dimensions, even without process-related differences. Although the resulting variant structures and semantic type distributions vary depending on the underlying process context, the evaluation across four event logs indicates applicability across multiple process types and sustainability dimensions. Nevertheless, further validation across additional domains and organizational settings remains necessary.

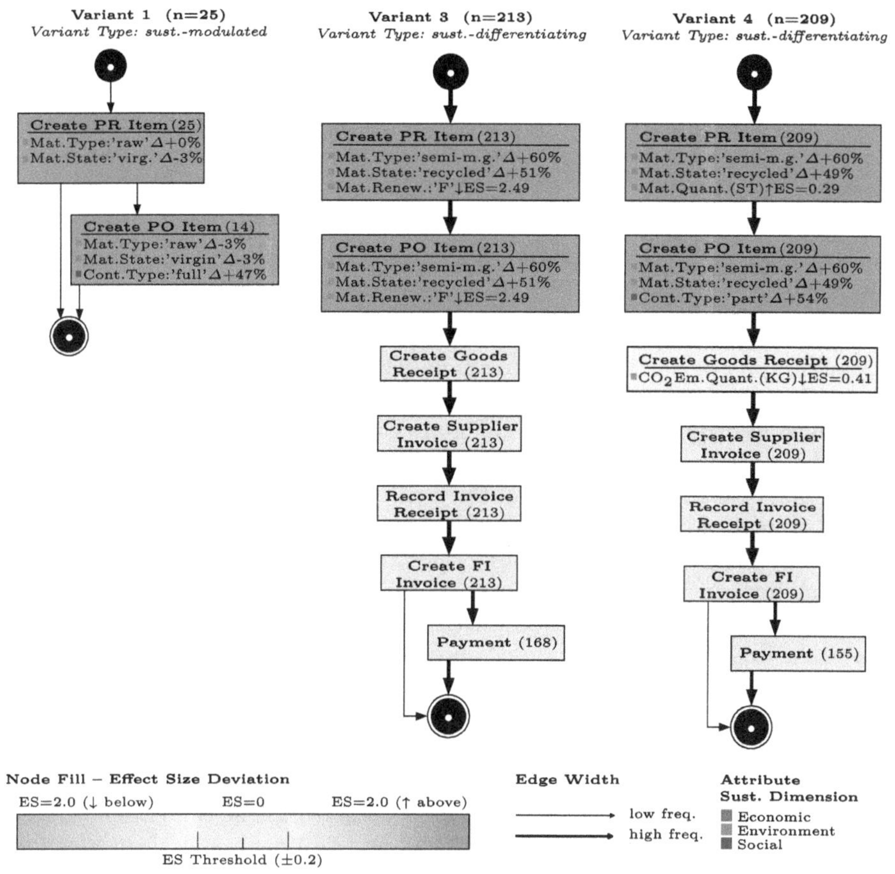

Fig. 3. Sustainability-annotated DFGs for Selected P2P Process Variants.

5 Related Work

The authors in [13] highlight the potential of process mining for sustainability analysis, noting that the field has not yet fully reached the sustainability domain. Recent research has explored this area, though existing approaches remain largely conceptual or focused on individual sustainability aspects such as emissions [6,15,16]. A first step towards multi-perspective sustainability analysis is taken by [12], exploring the object-centric perspective. In particular, [14] maps reporting indicators to process steps and enriches process models with sustainability metrics. Despite these advances, multi-perspective sustainability analysis at the process execution level remains largely underexplored [10].

A formal foundation is provided by [28], which specifies sustainability-annotated event logs and explicitly identifies the comparison of sustainability-aware process variants as a potential use case for sustainability-oriented process improvement. This need is further underscored by research on process variant analysis, where [23] identifies the comparison along additional perspectives beyond control-flow as an open challenge. While existing approaches address sustainability information, process variants, or multi-perspective process analysis individually, none provides a framework for systematically combining these perspectives to identify, characterize, and classify sustainability-aware process variants.

6 Conclusion

This article introduces sustainability-aware process variants as a formal concept and proposes SaPVD as a corresponding approach, contributing: (i) a formal definition of sustainability-aware process variants characterized by structural coherence and sustainability differentiation, (ii) a systematic identification method based on sustainability-enriched trace clustering, (iii) a sustainability-aware statistical characterization of the identified variants, and (iv) their visualization as sustainability-annotated process models. Together, these contributions address the article's guiding research question and the identified gap between sustainability-aware process mining and process variant analysis.

The empirical evaluation on four sustainability-annotated event logs demonstrates the feasibility of the proposed approach. The results indicate that sustainability-aware process variants emerge only under specific structural conditions. The approach explicitly treats their absence as a valid analytical outcome, confirming that sustainability is not a universal differentiating dimension of process-related characteristics. This is further reflected in the inherent trade-off between sustainability awareness and cluster quality observed in the evaluation.

This article establishes sustainability as an additional analytical dimension in process variant analysis, thereby connecting two previously disconnected research streams. Specifically, it addresses the need for multi-perspective sustainability analysis identified by [10] and responds to Challenge 1 of [23] by extending process variant analysis beyond control-flow differences. Furthermore, it operationalizes the process variant comparison use case proposed by [28]. Accordingly, the proposed approach provides a foundation for sustainability-oriented process improvement by enabling organizations to systematically identify and compare process variants along sustainability dimensions, supporting informed decision-making and targeted process optimization. Possible applications include sustainability benchmarking across process variants, prioritization of improvement measures, and monitoring of sustainability-related process changes over time.

While the proposed approach demonstrates its feasibility, several limitations remain. The identification of sustainability-aware process variants is sensitive to the choice of clustering configuration, as different parameter settings may yield varying variant structures. Furthermore, the approach identifies sustainability-related differences across process variants without establishing causal relationships. Additionally, sustainability-annotated event logs are not yet widespread in practice, though initiatives such as [28] provide a formal foundation for their generation. Incomplete sustainability information or the availability of only a limited subset of sustainability attributes may restrict the identification and characterization of sustainability-aware process variants. Therefore, the evaluation relies on research-based event logs, and empirical validation in real-world organizational settings remains open for future work. Future research should consequently focus on the practical application in real-world settings, the investigation of causal relationships between sustainability-related variant characteristics and process performance to better explain sustainability outcome differences across process variants, and methodological extensions of the approach, including refined visualization concepts, configuration selection strategies, and dimension-specific sustainability analyses. Furthermore, systematic approaches for weighting sustainability-related features, such as domain expert elicitation or sensitivity analyses, represent a valuable direction for future research.

In conclusion, the SaPVD approach represents a step toward integrating sustainability into process variant analysis. By providing a formal conceptualization and a systematic identification and analysis method, this article opens new avenues for improving sustainability transparency in business processes.

References

1. van der Aalst, W.M.P.: Process Mining. Springer, Heidelberg (2016)
2. van der Aalst, W.M.P., Carmona, J.: Process Mining Handbook. Springer (2022)
3. van der Aalst, W.M.P., Hinz, O., Weinhardt, C.: Sustainable systems engineering: opportunities and challenges. Bus. Inf. Syst. Eng. **65**(1), 1–6 (2023). https://doi.org/10.1007/s12599-022-00784-6
4. Bolt, A., de Leoni, M., van der Aalst, W.M.P.: A visual approach to spot statistically-significant differences in event logs based on process metrics. In: Nurcan, S., Soffer, P., Bajec, M., Eder, J. (eds.) CAiSE 2016. LNCS, vol. 9694, pp. 151–166. Springer, Cham (2016). https://doi.org/10.1007/978-3-319-39696-5_10
5. Bolt, A., de Leoni, M., van der Aalst, W.M.P.: Process variant comparison: using event logs to detect differences in behavior and business rules. Inf. Syst. **74** (2018). https://doi.org/10.1016/j.is.2017.12.006
6. Brehm, L., Slamka, J., Nickmann, A.: Process Mining for Carbon Accounting: An Analysis of Requirements and Potentials, pp. 209–244. Springer (2022)
7. Cohen, J.: Statistical Power Analysis for the Behavioral Sciences. Routledge (1988)
8. Davies, D.L., Bouldin, D.W.: A cluster separation measure. IEEE Trans. Pattern Anal. Mach. Intell. **2**, 224–227 (1979)
9. Elkington, J.: 25 years ago I coined the phrase "triple bottom line". Here's why it's time to rethink it. Harvard Bus. Rev. (2018)
10. Fritsch, A., Ullrich, M., Graves, N., Klessascheck, F., Nurkasanah, I.: Process science for sustainability: research gaps and research strategy. In: EMISA 2025. Gesellschaft für Informatik e.V. (2025). https://doi.org/10.18420/EMISA2025_17
11. Goswami, S., Chakrabarti, A.: Quartile clustering: a quartile based technique for generating meaningful clusters. J. Comput. (2012)
12. Graves, N., Fritsch, A., Hensen, R., Koren, I., van der Aalst, W.M.P.: Object-centric process mining for semi-automated and multi-perspective sustainability analyses. In: International Conference on ICT4S. IEEE (2025)
13. Graves, N., Koren, I., van der Aalst, W.M.P.: Rethink your processes! A review of process mining for sustainability. In: International Conference on ICT4S. IEEE (2023)

14. Hiziroglu, O.A., Dogan, O.: A framework for sustainability performance measurement through process mining. Systems **13**(7) (2025)
15. Joas, A., Gierlich-Joas, M., Bahr, C., Bauer, J.: Towards Leveraging Process Mining for Sustainability – An Analysis of Challenges and Potential Solutions, pp. 354–371. Springer (2024). https://doi.org/10.1007/978-3-031-70418-5_21
16. Kroeger, S., Streibel, L., Jordan, P., Klages, B., Soellner, C., Zaeh, M.F.: Sustainability assessment of production networks using simulation-data-based process mining. Procedia Comput. Sci. **237**, 493–501 (2024)
17. Li, C., Reichert, M., Wombacher, A.: Mining process variants: goals and issues. In: International Conference on Services Computing, pp. 573–576. IEEE (2008)
18. Mendling, J., Leopold, H., Meyerhenke, H., Depaire, B.: Methodology of algorithm engineering. ACM Comput. Surv. **58**(4), 1–38 (2025)
19. Nguyen, H., Dumas, M., La Rosa, M., ter Hofstede, A.H.M.: Multi-perspective comparison of business process variants based on event logs. In: Trujillo, J.C., et al. (eds.) ER 2018. LNCS, vol. 11157, pp. 449–459. Springer, Cham (2018). https://doi.org/10.1007/978-3-030-00847-5_32
20. Rousseeuw, P.J.: Silhouettes: a graphical aid to the interpretation and validation of cluster analysis. J. Comput. Appl. Math. **20** (1987)
21. Song, M., Günther, C.W., van der Aalst, W.M.P.: Trace clustering in process mining. In: Ardagna, D., Mecella, M., Yang, J. (eds.) BPM 2008. LNBIP, vol. 17, pp. 109–120. Springer, Heidelberg (2009). https://doi.org/10.1007/978-3-642-00328-8_11
22. Sullivan, G.M., Feinn, R.: Using effect size - or why the P value is not enough. J. Grad. Med. Educ. **4**(3), 279–282 (2012)
23. Taymouri, F., Rosa, M.L., Dumas, M., Maggi, F.M.: Business process variant analysis: survey and classification. Knowl.-Based Syst. **211** (2021)
24. Thaler, T., Ternis, S., Fettke, P., Loos, P.: A comparative analysis of process instance cluster techniques. In: Wirtschaftsinformatik, vol. 29 (2015)
25. Tukey, J.W.: Exploratory Data Analysis. Addison-Wesley (1977)
26. Vargha, A., Postáné Török, R.: A new method to interpret cluster analysis results in the presence of heterogeneous clusters. J. Person-Oriented Res. **12**(1), 1–12 (2026). https://doi.org/10.17505/jpor.2026.29047
27. Wolf, N., Wittges, H., Rinderle-Ma, S.: SuXXES event logs: synthetic and ERP-based process data with integrated sustainability data (2025). https://doi.org/10.5281/zenodo.17756035
28. Wolf, N., Wittges, H., Rinderle-Ma, S.: SuXXES: Integrating Sustainability Data Into Process Event Logs, pp. 213–229. Springer (2026)
29. Zandkarimi, F., Rehse, J., Soudmand, P., Hoehle, H.: A generic framework for trace clustering in process mining. In: International Conference on Process Mining. IEEE (2020)

Agent-Based Directly-Follows Graphs

Qingtan Shen[1(✉)], Timotheus Kampik[2,3], Nir Lipovetzky[1], and Artem Polyvyanyy[1]

[1] The University of Melbourne, Victoria 3010, Australia
{qingtan.shen1,nir.lipovetzky,artem.polyvyanyy}@unimelb.edu.au
[2] SAP, Walldorf, Germany
timotheus.kampik@sap.com
[3] Umeå University, Umeå, Sweden

Abstract. Agent system mining is a branch of process mining that adopts a bottom-up approach to data-driven analysis of socio-technical systems, such as organizations executing business processes. In this setting, a system is analyzed as a collection of autonomous agents, each with its own local state and behavior, that interact with one another and with the environment to contribute to the global behavior of the system. The state-of-the-art approach to discovering systems of agents constructs modular agent system models captured as Petri nets, but does not directly support the analysis of intra- and inter-agent handovers and their frequencies. This paper presents agent-based Directly-Follows Graphs (DFGs), a novel representation of systems of agents that captures the frequencies of intra- and inter-agent handovers and annotates edges with handback and agent availability information. This representation can support the analysis of agent-system behavior and identify opportunities for process improvements. Building on this representation, we propose a technique for discovering agent-based DFGs from event data recorded during the execution of business processes. The technique is evaluated using real-world event data by assessing the quality of discovered models in terms of precision and recall. We compare agent-based DFGs with existing representations and show how they can support agent-related analytics, including identifying potential handover-related bottlenecks and understanding collaboration patterns and task interruptions.

Keywords: Agent system mining · process mining · directly-follows graphs

1 Introduction

Process mining is a field that integrates concepts from data science and process science [1]. It aims to extract behavior patterns from event data recorded during process execution to guide improvements to the processes that generated the data. Process discovery, a core subarea of process mining, focuses on constructing process models from event data to facilitate process understanding [2,17]. Existing process discovery techniques [4,5,11,24] typically represent constructed processes as directly-follows graphs (DFGs), Business Process Model and Notation (BPMN) diagrams, or Petri nets, which capture activities and their control-flow relations. Complementary to control-flow, modern information systems often record information about agents that perform activities,

© The Author(s), under exclusive license to Springer Nature Switzerland AG 2027
A. Bernasconi et al. (Eds.): ER 2026, LNCS 17081, pp. 253–270, 2027.
https://doi.org/10.1007/978-3-032-40795-5_15

such as human workers or software components. This makes it possible to view business processes from an agent-based perspective [22], where agents perform activities and may interact with others through mechanisms such as the handover of work.

Analyzing handovers of work among agents alongside activity control-flow can reveal coordination structures and collaboration patterns [20]. Organizational mining techniques [3,21] exploit such patterns by capturing handover relations and activity-execution patterns among agents, typically generating social networks or organizational models. Although some techniques [7,25] incorporate relationships between activities and agents, this information is generally not explicitly integrated into visualizations of activity-level interactions and handovers. Agent system mining [22] extends this perspective by treating a system as a collection of autonomous agents, each with its own local state and behavior, that interact to shape the global behavior of the system. Agent Miner [23] discovers agent process models and agent interaction models from event data and integrates them into a multi-agent system (MAS) model. However, its Petri net representations do not directly reveal the frequencies of intra- and inter-agent handovers, nor the availability status of the agents (that is, busy or idle) during handovers. Such information is relevant to identifying potential bottlenecks associated with handovers and waiting times [10,15].

DFGs provide a natural basis for addressing this limitation because they directly represent activity-level relations and readily support frequency-based edge annotations. We therefore propose an agent-based DFG discovery technique that constructs DFGs from event logs enriched with representations of intra-agent behavior and inter-agent handovers. An input *event log* is a form of event data that is a collection of traces, each representing one process execution, with each trace constituting a sequence of recorded events, where each event holds information on the case identifier of the process execution, the process activity that triggered the event and the agent that executed the activity, and the timestamp at which the event was triggered or observed.

Concepts from agent-based DFGs support important analyses. Specifically, handover relations reveal coordination and collaboration patterns [3,20,21], handover and handback frequencies expose patterns relevant to potential bottlenecks, waiting times, setup effort, longer completion times, and reduced work quality [9,10,15], idle and busy handovers reveal resource availability and contention relevant to waiting-time inefficiencies [9,10], while continuation and interruption relations expose focused execution and possible task switching [14]. Experimental results show that the technique can generate high-quality agent-based DFGs, while the proposed visualizations expose agent-related information not directly represented by existing approaches.

This paper makes the following contributions:

- It introduces agent-based DFGs and proposes a technique for discovering agent-based DFGs from event logs.
- It presents visualizations of agent-based DFGs that emphasize agent-related information, including handovers, handbacks, and continuation and interruption behaviors. These distinctions expose information relevant to analyzing collaboration patterns, task interruptions, and potential handover- and waiting-time-related bottlenecks.

– It evaluates agent-based DFG discovery on industrial event logs and compares the information exposed by the proposed visualizations with that of existing approaches.

The paper proceeds as follows. Section 2 reviews existing work on DFG discovery and organizational mining techniques. Section 3 presents a motivating example by comparing an agent-based DFG with existing models. Section 4 introduces the concepts required to support subsequent discussions. Section 5 describes our techniques for discovering and visualizing agent-based DFGs. Section 6 evaluates the quality of the discovered models and illustrates their visualizations. Section 7 concludes the paper.

2 Related Work

This section reviews techniques for discovering DFGs, agent-based process analysis, and organizational mining.

Several existing techniques construct DFGs and annotate them with performance-related measures, such as waiting times or activity frequencies, often combined with filtering mechanisms to improve readability [13]. To enhance the expressiveness of DFGs, Pfahlsberger et al. [16] introduced path semantics and ways to represent allowed and prohibited process behaviors. DFG extensions also support practical process analysis, e.g., Inductive Visual Miner [12] enhances DFG visualization by showing how well different parts of a model fit the observed data. Alkhammash et al. [5] defined the stochastic semantics of DFGs by interpreting them as collections of traces together with the likelihoods of observing those traces during system execution. They also introduced GASPD, a genetic discovery technique for learning Stochastic Directed Action Graphs from event logs, which extend DFGs by allowing duplicate activity nodes. Zhian et al. [26] subsequently evaluated several metaheuristics for guiding the grammatical inference performed by GASPD toward the discovery of more accurate models.

Resource (i.e., agent instances) information in event logs has also been widely visualized in process mining. Existing techniques visualize agent performance using formats such as heatmaps [6] and represent agent interactions or organizational relationships through social networks [3]. Similarly, Song and van der Aalst [21] proposed organizational models that group agents with similar behavioral patterns into clusters. Yang et al. [25] proposed a technique for grouping resources by classifying execution contexts extracted from cases, activities, and temporal information. In addition, van Hulzen et al. [7] introduced a technique for discovering resource profiles across multiple activity-related dimensions, e.g., activity duration. However, these works primarily analyze agent-level interactions or organizational structures and do not integrate this information with control-flow in process models.

Other approaches aim to integrate agent information into control-flow models. For example, Rozinat et al. [19] discovered colored Petri nets that incorporate resource perspectives within process models. More recently, Agent Miner [23] groups agents into types and constructs MAS models that combine agent type behaviors and their interactions captured as Petri nets. Klijn et al. [8] proposed event knowledge graphs that capture which resources trigger specific events and label consecutive events executed by the same resource. Subsequently, they enriched DFGs with frequency annotations describing agent behaviors, including agent continuation patterns and idle or busy handovers [9]. However, the Petri net-based representations provide limited support for visualizing agent interaction characteristics, such as interruptions and busy handovers. Moreover, although event knowledge graphs and enriched DFGs support the analysis of agent behavior, they primarily operate at the individual agent level without considering higher-level organizational structures, such as groups of agents with similar behavioral patterns. This limits their effectiveness for understanding agent behavior within organizational interaction patterns.

3 Motivating Example

This section motivates MAS-DFGs, a type of agent-based DFGs proposed in this paper, by comparing them with conventional DFGs, MAS Petri net models produced by Agent Miner [23], and actor behavioral DFGs [9]. The comparison is based on the real-world BPIC2015-1 log[1] with 20 activities and 21 agents. Activities are extracted from the *concept:name* attribute using the subprocess-level prefix (e.g., *01-HOOFD*), which captures the subprocess category of each event. This abstraction enables the analysis of high-level patterns of agent interactions while avoiding overly fine-grained distinctions of activities. Agents are extracted using the *org:resource* attribute. This log features frequent interactions between agents across traces, making it well-suited to demonstrate the benefits of MAS-DFGs in capturing agent behavior and interactions.

Figure 1 shows a conventional DFG, where nodes represent activities and edges denote directly-follows relations annotated with their frequencies. While it captures activity-level frequency patterns, it does not include agent-related information and therefore cannot support agent-level analysis. Figure 2 shows the MAS Petri net discovered by Agent Miner, in which activities are colored by agent type: Type-1 (green) and Type-2 (purple). Agents are clustered into types based on behavioral similarity. For clarity, agent instances are denoted by identifiers such as R_1 and R_2. The Type-1 cluster comprises $\{R_{1\text{–}2}, R_4, R_6, R_8, R_{10\text{–}11}, R_{13}, R_{19\text{–}21}\}$, while the remaining agents belong to Type-2. This modular representation clarifies agent interactions within and across types. While the MAS model integrates agent and control-flow perspectives, it does not directly visualize interaction frequencies, distinguish intra- from inter-agent-type handovers, or support additional annotations. Moreover, representing the model as a Petri net can make it difficult to read and interpret in practice [13]. Figure 3 shows the actor behavioral DFG [9], where edges are annotated with continuation, interruption, handover-idle, and handover-busy frequencies derived from agent-level behavior. This representation exposes patterns, such as busy handovers, that may indicate potential execution inefficiencies. However, it does not capture organizational structure (i.e., groups of agents), and therefore cannot distinguish intra-group and inter-group behaviors.

Figure 4 shows the MAS-DFG discovered by the technique proposed in this paper. Agent types are first identified using a grouping approach similar to Agent Miner. The

[1] https://doi.org/10.4121/uuid:a0addfda-2044-4541-a450-fdcc9fe16d17.

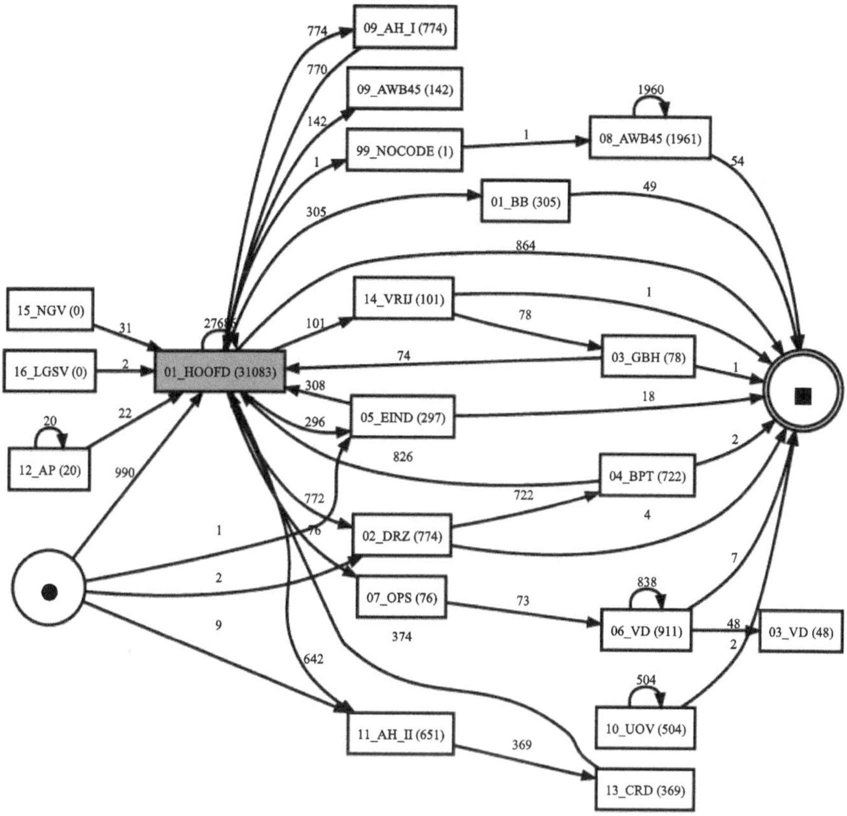

Fig. 1. Conventional DFG.

agent type behavioral complexity threshold is set to 0.1, retaining the 10% most frequent activities, while the interaction complexity threshold is set to 1 to capture all handovers. The resulting model has two agent types: Type-1 (orange) and Type-2 (purple). Edges are color-coded to represent intra-agent-type directly-follows relations (blue), inter-agent-type handovers (red), and start/end transitions (black). Each edge is annotated with its frequency, providing detailed insights into intra-agent-type behavior and inter-agent-type handover patterns. Prior work shows that handovers may increase completion times and reduce work quality [9,15]. Such patterns are present in Fig. 4. For example, the most frequent inter-agent-type handover occurs when Type-1 completes *01-HOOFD* and transfers it to Type-2, which then performs the same activity, occurring 52 times. To assess potential inefficiencies (cf. Sect. 5.2), we further classify inter-agent-type handovers as idle or busy.

MAS-DFGs integrate control-flow-level frequency information and agent interactions into a single representation. They make intra- and inter-agent-type relations directly visible while preserving the organizational groupings. This allows for the direct

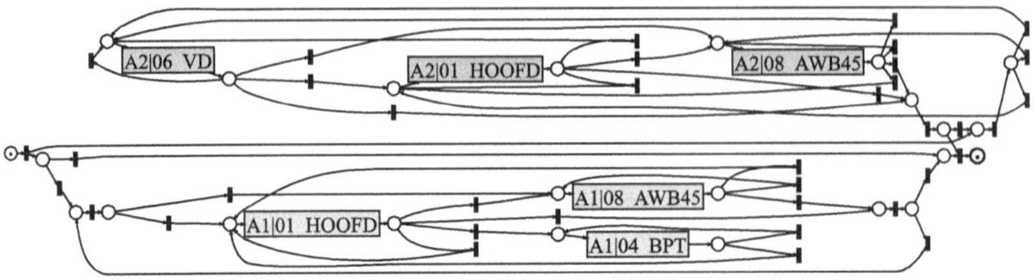

Fig. 2. MAS Petri net [23].

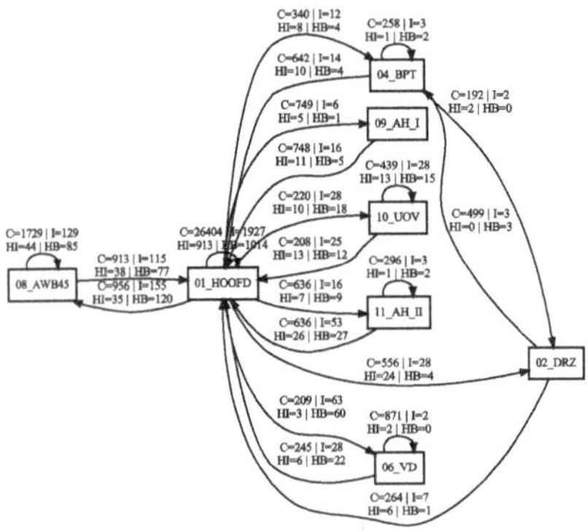

Fig. 3. Actor behavioral DFG [9].

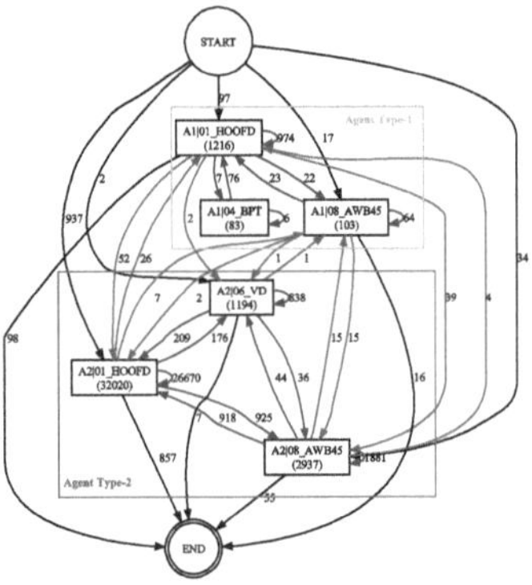

Fig. 4. Multi-agent system DFG.

identification of frequent interaction patterns and provides a basis for further annotations of handbacks, interruptions, and idle or busy handovers.

4 Preliminaries

Let $\mathcal{E}$ denote the universe of events. Each event $e \in \mathcal{E}$ is represented as a tuple $e = (c, a, t, r)$, where c is the identifier of a process *case*, or instance, for which the event was recorded, a is the *activity* that triggered the event, t is the *timestamp* when the event was recorded, and r is the instance of the *agent* that performed the activity. Let $AN = \{case, act, time, res\}$ be the set of all attribute names. For an event $e = (c, a, t, r)$ and attribute name $k \in AN$, $\#_k(e)$ denotes the value of attribute k for event e, defined by the mapping: $\#_{case}(e) = c$, $\#_{act}(e) = a$, $\#_{time}(e) = t$, and $\#_{res}(e) = r$. A *trace* is the sequence of all events with the same case identifier ordered by timestamps, while an *event log* is a collection of traces. For $k \in AN$ and trace $\sigma = \langle e_1, e_2, \ldots, e_n \rangle$, $\#_k(\sigma)$ denotes the sequence of attribute values $\langle \#_k(e_1), \#_k(e_2), \ldots, \#_k(e_n) \rangle$.

The classification framework for agent behavior analysis [14] defines four classes of agent interactions across two consecutive events in a trace.

- *Continuation (C)*: The same agent executes the activities that trigger both consecutive events and performs no other activity between them.
- *Interruption (I)*: The same agent executes the activities that trigger both consecutive events but performs one or more activities in another trace between them.
- *Handover Idle (HI)*: Different agents execute the activities that trigger the two consecutive events, and the agent responsible for the second event performs no other activity during the handover period.
- *Handover Busy (HB)*: Different agents execute the activities that trigger the two consecutive events, and the agent responsible for the second event performs one or more activities in other traces during the handover period.

Agent Miner [23] is the first approach for discovering MAS models from event logs. It clusters agents into types based on behavioral similarity, computed by comparing agent-level DFGs using overlapping edges, with each agent assigned to a single type. For each agent type, a process model is constructed from aggregated event sequences of its member agents. An interaction Petri net model is then discovered from transitions between consecutive executions of different agent types. These models are integrated into a MAS Petri net. The discovery is controlled by the thresholds (t_1, t_2), which govern the levels of detail in the constructed agent and interaction models, respectively.

5 Approach

This section introduces the agent-based DFG discovery technique, formally defines agent-based DFGs, and describes visualization methods. The overall pipeline is illustrated in Fig. 5. To illustrate the technique, we use a sample event log $L = \{\sigma_1, \sigma_2\}$, where $\sigma_1 = \langle e_1, e_2, e_3, e_4, e_5, e_6 \rangle$ and $\sigma_2 = \langle e_7, e_8, e_9, e_{10} \rangle$. The corresponding activity sequences are $\#_{act}(\sigma_1) = \langle a_1, a_2, a_1, a_2, a_2, a_3 \rangle$ and $\#_{act}(\sigma_2) = \langle a_1, a_2, a_2, a_3 \rangle$; the agent sequences are $\#_{res}(\sigma_1) = \langle r_1, r_1, r_2, r_2, r_1, r_3 \rangle$ and $\#_{res}(\sigma_2) = \langle r_2, r_2, r_1, r_1 \rangle$. Each event has a unique timestamp, ordered within its trace from t_1 to t_6 for σ_1 and from t_7 to t_{10} for σ_2. Using an agent type clustering approach, for example the one by AM, one can obtain a mapping τ from agents to agent types. For the running example, we assume $\tau(r_1) = \tau(r_3) = T_1$ and $\tau(r_2) = T_2$. Based on this mapping, we proceed to demonstrate the steps of our agent-based DFG discovery approach.

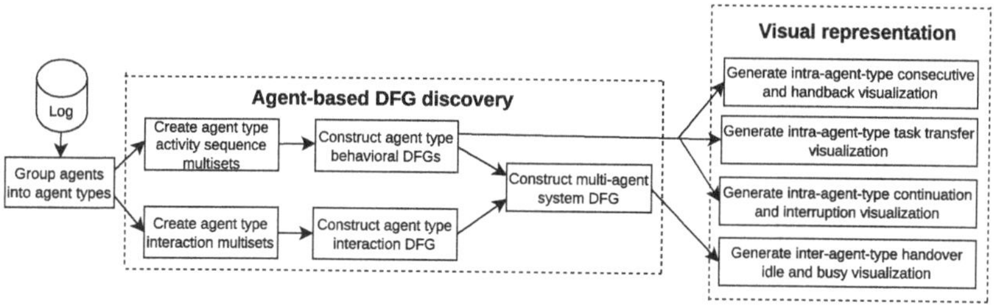

Fig. 5. The agent-based DFG discovery and visualization pipeline.

5.1 Agent-Based DFG Discovery

Next, we introduce and illustrate the key definitions of agent-based DFGs following the discovery phase in Fig. 5.

Agent Type Activity Sequence Multisets. For an agent type T and a trace σ, its activity sequence multiset, denoted by σ^T, consists of the maximal contiguous subsequences of activities in σ triggered by agents of type T. The *agent type activity sequence multiset* for agent type T in event log L, denoted by L^T, is obtained by aggregating all such subsequences (including repeated ones) across all traces in an event log L.

In the example, it holds that $\sigma_1^{T_1} = \{\langle a_1, a_2\rangle, \langle a_2, a_3\rangle\}$ and $\sigma_2^{T_1} = \{\langle a_2, a_3\rangle\}$. Trace σ_1 describes two agent type activity sequences as e_2 and e_5 are not consecutive in σ_1 and events e_3 and e_4 are triggered by r_2, which is of a different type. Applying the same procedure for T_2 yields $\sigma_1^{T_2} = \{\langle a_1, a_2\rangle\}$ and $\sigma_2^{T_2} = \{\langle a_1, a_2\rangle\}$, induced by events e_3 and e_4 in σ_1 and events e_7 and e_8 in σ_2. Finally, aggregating the results across all traces gives the log-level agent type sequences $L^{T_1} = \{\langle a_1, a_2\rangle, \langle a_2, a_3\rangle^2\}$ and $L^{T_2} = \{\langle a_1, a_2\rangle^2\}$.

Agent Type Behavioral DFGs (ATB-DFGs). The *ATB-DFG* of an agent type T is an edge-weighted directed graph $G^T = (V^T, E^T, w^T)$, where w^T maps edges E^T to weights in $\mathbb{N}$. The node set V^T consists of all activities that occur in at least one sequence in L^T and additional *Start* and *End* nodes that represent the start and the end of the sequences, respectively. An edge $(a, b) \in E^T$ is included in the graph if activity a is directly followed by activity b in at least one sequence in L^T. The weight of an edge $(a, b) \in E^T$ specifies how often activity a is directly followed by activity b across all sequences in L^T. In addition, starts and ends of sequences are captured by introducing edges from the *Start* node to all first activities in the sequences and from all last activities in the sequences to the *End* node. The weights of such edges represent the number of sequences that start and end with the corresponding activities. One can use a threshold $\theta_1 \in [0, 1]$ to retain the smallest set of the most frequent activities whose cumulative frequency accounts for at least θ_1 fraction of all activity occurrences in the activity sequences.

Figures 6a and 6b show the ATB-DFGs G^{T_1} and G^{T_2} constructed using the agent type activity sequences L^{T_1} and L^{T_2}, respectively. For instance, the weight of edge (a_2, a_3) in G^{T_1} is two because there are two sequences $\langle a_2, a_3\rangle$ in L^{T_1} in which activity a_2 is directly followed by activity a_3. As these are also the only two sequences in L^{T_1} that end with activity a_3, edge (a_3, End) has the weight of two in G^{T_1}.

Agent Type Interaction Multisets. For two consecutive events e_i and e_{i+1} in a trace triggered, respectively, by agent instances r_i and r_{i+1} of different types, that is, $\tau(r_i) \neq \tau(r_{i+1})$, we say that an *agent type interaction* occurs between the corresponding activity-agent type pairs. We denote the multiset of all such agent type interactions across all traces in the event log L by I^L. One can use a threshold $\theta_2 \in [0, 1]$ to retain the smallest collection of the most frequent interactions in I^L whose cumulative frequency accounts for at least a θ_2 fraction of all interaction occurrences in I^L.

In the example, the consecutive events in σ_1 involving different agent types are (e_2, e_3) and (e_4, e_5), yielding the interactions $(a_2, T_1) \Rightarrow (a_1, T_2)$ and $(a_2, T_2) \Rightarrow (a_2, T_1)$, respectively. In σ_2, the pair (e_8, e_9) yields the interaction $(a_2, T_2) \Rightarrow (a_2, T_1)$. Aggregating over the log, the resulting interaction set is $I^L = \{(a_2, T_1) \Rightarrow (a_1, T_2),\ (a_2, T_2) \Rightarrow^2 (a_2, T_1)\}$.

Agent Type Interaction DFGs (ATI-DFGs). The *ATI-DFG* of an event log L is an edge-weighted directed graph $G^{AT} = (V^{AT}, E^{AT}, w^{AT})$ that represents the interactions between agent types captured in L. The node set V^{AT} consists of all agent types and additional *Start* and *End* nodes. An edge (T_1, T_2) is in E^{AT} if there exist activities a_1 and a_2 such that $(a_1, T_1) \Rightarrow (a_2, T_2)$ is in I^L, indicating an interaction between these agent types. The weight (w^{AT}) of an edge between agent types captures how many interactions between the corresponding agent types exist in I^L. An edge is added from (to) the *Start* (*End*) node to (from) an agent type node if the agent type triggers the first (last) event in some trace in L. The weights of such edges reflect how many traces start or end with events triggered by the corresponding agent types.

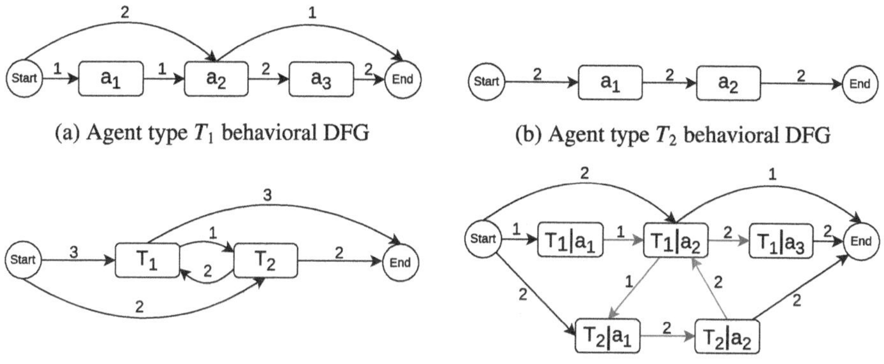

(a) Agent type T_1 behavioral DFG

(b) Agent type T_2 behavioral DFG

(c) Agent type interaction DFG

(d) Multi-agent system DFG

Fig. 6. Agent-based DFGs.

Figure 6c shows the ATI-DFG G^{AT} of the example log. G^{AT} summarizes inter-agent-type handovers aggregating them across all activity pairs. For example, it holds that $w^{AT}(T_2, T_1) = 2$, as there are two interactions between these agent types in I^L.

Multi-Agent System DFGs (MAS-DFGs). The *MAS-DFG* of an event log L is an edge-weighted directed graph $G^{MAS} = (V^{MAS}, E^{MAS}, w^{MAS})$ constructed by integrating the ATB-DFGs of all agent types and their interactions. The node set V^{MAS} consists of activity-agent type pairs (a, T) for each activity a appearing in L^T and additional *Start* and *End* nodes. The edge set E^{MAS} contains two types of edges (with the types left implicit, however). First, all intra-agent-type edges from each ATB-DFG are included, i.e., if an edge exists from activity a_1 to a_2 in (the edge set of) the ATB-DFG of agent type T, then it exists from (a_1, T) to (a_2, T) in E^{MAS}. Second, inter-agent-type edges are added based on the interaction relationship previously defined. For each interaction $(a_u, T_u) \Rightarrow (a_v, T_v) \in I^L$, an edge is added in the MAS-DFG from node (a_u, T_u) to (a_v, T_v), and its weight, as represented in w^{MAS}, is set to the frequency of the interaction across the log. Finally, the start and end edges are connected to the MAS-level *Start* and

End nodes to preserve trace boundaries, analogously to how we handled such edges above. Threshold-based filtering can be applied. In the case of MAS-DFGs, different thresholds can be applied for intra-agent-type and inter-agent-type interaction edges.

Figure 6d shows the MAS-DFG of the example event log. This MAS-DFG integrates agent type behaviors and their interactions into a single representation, keeping both intra-agent-type directly-follows relations and inter-agent-type handovers. For visual clarity, intra-agent-type edges are shown in blue and inter-agent-type edges in red.

5.2 Agent-Based DFG Visualization

Building on the generated agent-based DFGs, this subsection presents four visualization approaches shown in the visual-representation phase of Fig. 5.

Intra-Agent-Type Consecutive and Handback Visualization. For each ATB-DFG, we apply a visualization that explicitly distinguishes handback behavior from consecutive behavior for each agent type. Activities that occur consecutively in an agent type sequence are represented with solid edges. In contrast, a handback captures a delayed continuation of execution by the same agent type after at least one intervening event that is executed by another agent type. Handbacks are represented with dashed edges. The frequencies of solid and dashed edges are recorded separately for each activity pair across the log. We illustrate the visualization using the ATB-DFG of agent type T_1 in Fig. 6a, with the resulting representation shown in Fig. 7a. In trace σ_1, the solid edge $a_1 \rightarrow a_2$ occurs once (from e_1 to e_2), and $a_2 \rightarrow a_3$ occurs twice (from e_5 to e_6 and e_9 to e_{10}). The dashed edge forms a loop at a_2 due to the handback from e_2 to e_5 within σ_1. This visualization (Fig. 7a) distinguishes consecutive behavior from delayed handback behavior, with dashed edges highlighted in red. It enables analysts to identify both dominant workflows and recurrent intra-agent handovers, providing insights into both local and long-range dependencies.

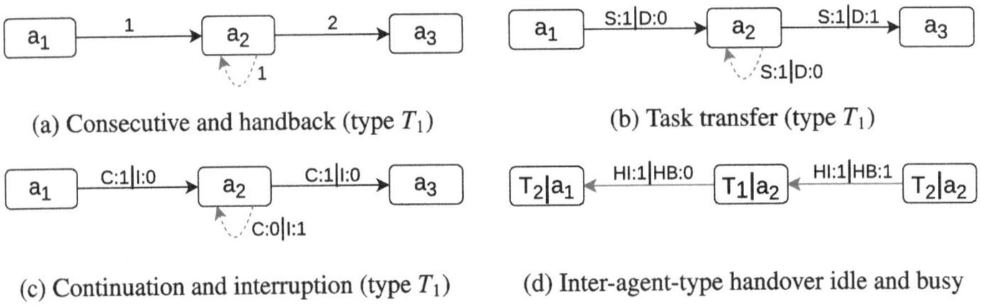

Fig. 7. Visualizations of agent type behaviors and inter-agent handovers.

Intra-Agent-Type Task Transfer Visualization. We apply a visualization at the agent type level by distinguishing whether consecutive and handback relations are performed by the same agent instance or by different agents within the same agent type. Given a trace, for each pair of activities connected by either a solid edge (immediate consecutive events) or a dashed edge (handback events), we examine the associated agents. If the same agent instance executes both events, the edge is labeled S (same); otherwise, it is labeled D (different). Frequencies are recorded separately for each combination of edge type (solid or dashed) and label (S or D). The visualization for agent type T_1 is presented in Fig. 7b. This visualization can enable analysts to identify patterns of individual responsibility versus collaborative execution, providing deeper insight into resource utilization and coordination within agent types.

Intra-Agent-Type Continuation and Interruption Visualization. We next consider the visualization of continuation and interruption behaviors for each agent type. This visualization is constructed from the activities in the ATB-DFGs, restricting attention to events executed by the same agent instance. For each pair of consecutive and handback behaviors executed by the same agent instance, we determine the agent's execution status according to the definitions of *continuation (C)* and *interruption (I)* introduced in Sect. 4. An agent status is determined as C if the agent continues processing without intervening events from other traces, and as I otherwise. Frequencies are aggregated separately for continuation and interruption behaviors, both consecutive and handback, and these counts are used to label the edges. The sample visualization for agent type T_1 is presented in Fig. 7c. It provides insights into agent availability and task execution patterns. Frequent continuations indicate that an agent focuses on a single task, whereas frequent interruptions may signal idle periods or task switching, enabling analysts to identify potential inefficiencies in resource utilization.

Inter-Agent-Type Handover Idle and Busy Visualization. We now focus on handovers between different agent types. For each inter-agent-type handover, the agent's status is evaluated according to the definitions of *handover idle (HI)* (where the receiving agent is idle during the handover period) and *handover busy (HB)* (where the receiving agent is busy with other traces) introduced in Sect. 4. In this visualization, nodes represent the activities retained from the MAS-DFG across all agent types. An edge from activity a_u executed by agent type T_u to activity a_v executed by agent type T_v ($T_u \neq T_v$) is annotated with the frequencies of HI and HB handovers observed in the log. The sample visualization for inter-agent-type handover is presented in Fig. 7d, where nodes without connecting edges have been omitted for clarity. This technique enables analysts to evaluate the efficiency of cross agent type coordination. Edges with high HB frequencies indicate that the receiving agent was already engaged, potentially causing delays or resource contention, whereas edges with high HI frequencies highlight idle periods that could be leveraged to improve throughput. By linking these handovers directly to activities, the visualization provides actionable insight into workflow dependencies and supports effective task allocation across agent types.

6 Evaluation

This section evaluates the quality of the Agent-based DFGs Discovery (ADD) technique from both technical and visualization perspectives. The implementations of the discovery and visualization techniques are publicly available.[2]

6.1 Datasets and Experimental Setup

We use eight real-world BPIC event logs (see Table 1) to evaluate the quality of agent-based DFGs based on the precision, recall, and size of MAS-DFGs. A variant-frequency filter is applied to remove infrequent traces, thereby focusing the analysis on representative behavior. Precision measures how well a model avoids producing behavior not observed in the log, while recall measures how well it captures the behavior recorded in the log. To compute precision and recall of MAS-DFGs, we follow the procedure of Leemans et al. [13], which converts DFGs into Petri nets and applies state-of-the-art conformance-checking measures that require sound Petri nets. We use the Entropia tool [18] to compute entropy-based precision and recall. To enable comparison with existing techniques, we apply two DFG-to-Petri net conversion strategies. The first strategy removes agent type distinctions by deduplicating activities across agent types. The resulting Petri nets are compared with those discovered by Inductive Miner (IM) [11], a state-of-the-art conventional process discovery technique. This comparison evaluates how well agent-based DFG discovery captures overall process behavior when agent type information is removed, providing a conventional process discovery baseline. The second strategy preserves duplicate activities across agent types, and the resulting Petri nets are compared with those discovered by Agent Miner (AM) [23], a state-of-the-art agent-based process discovery technique. This enables comparison with an existing agent-based discovery approach. For fair comparison, only activity labels are retained in the converted or generated Petri nets, without agent type labels. Model size is defined as the total number of nodes and edges. We report the size of each MAS-DFG and its converted Petri nets, and compare them with IM- and AM-generated models. For each log, we first apply the AM grouping technique with threshold $t = 1$ to identify agent types. We then generate MAS-DFGs using ten threshold pairs $(0.1, 1.0), (0.2, 0.9), \ldots, (1.0, 0.1)$ in ADD, where the first and second thresholds control filtering in ATB-DFGs and ATI-DFGs, respectively, before their integration into MAS-DFGs. Each MAS-DFG is converted into Petri nets using a PM4Py function.[3] For comparison, we construct Petri nets using IM with ten noise thresholds $0.1, 0.2, \ldots, 1.0$, and apply the same ADD threshold pairs when generating MAS models with Agent Miner. All models are evaluated using Entropia.

We next evaluate the visualization perspective. We first generate and collect visualizations for all datasets using two threshold settings and make them available (see footnote 2). We then select the agent-based DFGs generated from BPIC2015-1 with

[2] https://github.com/QINGTANS/Agent-Based-DFGs-Discovery-Code-and-Visual-Representations.

[3] https://pm4py-source.readthedocs.io/en/latest/_modules/pm4py/objects/conversion/dfg/variants/to_petri_net_invisibles_no_duplicates.html#Parameters.

Table 1. Quality comparison of ADD-derived Petri nets with deduplicated activities and Petri nets by Inductive Miner (IM), and of ADD-derived Petri nets with duplicated activities and MAS Petri nets by Agent Miner (AM). Precision, recall, and size are reported for the smallest model. “PR num.” denotes the number of models on the precision–recall Pareto front.

Log	Log properties			ADD DFGs	ADD Petri nets (dedup. labels)					IM Petri nets					ADD Petri nets (dup. labels)					AM MAS Petri nets				
	Filter	#Traces	#Ag.	Size range	Prec.	Rec.	Size	Size range	PR num.	Prec.	Rec.	Size	Size range	PR num.	Prec.	Rec.	Size	Size range	PR num.	Prec.	Rec.	Size	Size range	PR num.
BPIC2012	80%	225,412	68	65–548	0.28	**0.66**	**128**	128–985	4	**0.48**	**0.66**	144	141–428	2	**0.28**	**0.66**	223	223–1786	**2**	0.19	**0.66**	**141**	141–1425	0
BPIC2013	80%	6,143	593	23–107	**0.69**	**0.68**	**41**	41–174	6	0.35	0.61	64	64–102	2	**0.69**	**0.68**	**81**	81–349	**8**	0.61	**0.68**	106	106–316	0
BPIC2014	10%	140,101	195	68–707	**0.39**	0.68	**154**	154–1438	6	0.16	**0.84**	216	216–364	0	**0.39**	**0.68**	224	224–2225	**6**	0.31	**0.68**	**210**	210–1862	0
BPIC2015-1	80%	44,075	21	45–256	0.37	**0.95**	**84**	84–554	3	**0.44**	**0.95**	98	98–253	**5**	**0.37**	**0.95**	**151**	151–838	**4**	0.33	**0.95**	155	155–805	0
BPIC2015-2	80%	36,670	11	45–281	0.16	**0.86**	317	90–676	4	**0.24**	0.77	**244**	108–305	1	**0.16**	**0.87**	453	151–917	**4**	0.13	0.86	**445**	164–893	0
BPIC2015-3	80%	51,405	10	54–381	0.34	**0.95**	107	107–683	**5**	**0.4**	0.83	**101**	101–244	2	**0.35**	**0.95**	180	180–1227	**3**	0.3	**0.95**	**175**	175–1083	0
BPIC2015-4	80%	39,837	10	47–309	0.25	0.62	**101**	101–683	6	**0.34**	**0.76**	109	109–280	1	**0.26**	**0.61**	**159**	159–1021	**6**	0.19	**0.61**	175	175–1012	0
BPIC2015-5	80%	49,615	21	79–456	**0.26**	0.75	**87**	87–695	**5**	0.09	**0.95**	166	166–254	2	**0.26**	**0.75**	259	259–1480	**5**	0.22	**0.75**	**219**	219–1293	0

the AM grouping threshold $t = 1$ and the DFG construction threshold pair $(0.1, 1.0)$ as a representative example. Based on these models, we construct various visualization types introduced in Sect. 5.2. To assess visualization quality, we draw on prior studies showing that agent behavior can influence process efficiency, and examine whether such aspects can be represented visually. In particular, handovers have been associated with longer completion times and reduced work quality [15], while waiting times are closely related to process efficiency, with resource contention and resource availability being important contributing factors [9, 10]. We therefore compare MAS-DFG representations with conventional DFGs, Petri nets discovered by AM [23], and actor behavioral DFGs [9] to evaluate how well these aspects are supported.

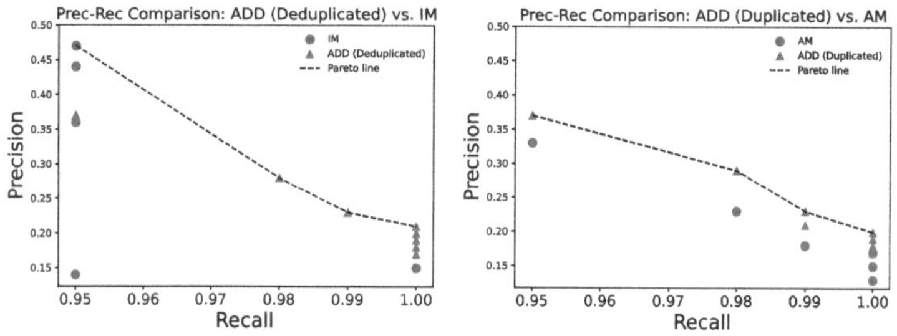

(a) ADD and IM model comparison (b) ADD and AM model comparison

Fig. 8. Precision–recall Pareto front plots for BPIC2015-1.

6.2 Results

Table 1 summarizes the evaluation results across eight logs. For each log, we construct ten deduplicated-activity Petri nets converted from MAS-DFGs and compare them with ten Petri nets discovered using IM. We also construct ten duplicated-activity Petri nets converted from MAS-DFGs and compare them with ten Petri nets discovered using AM, which also preserves duplicated activities. For each method, we select the model with the smallest size among those with non-zero precision and recall, and report its precision, recall, and model size. Higher precision and recall, together with smaller size, indicate better performance. In the deduplicated-activity setting, ADD achieves higher precision in 3 of 8 logs and higher recall in 5 of 8 logs than IM. In addition, ADD produces smaller models in 6 logs. These results indicate that ADD can generate simpler models while maintaining competitive behavioral coverage. To further analyze the trade-off between precision and recall, we study the Pareto front of the precision–recall space. Models on the top-right Pareto frontier represent better trade-offs. We count the number of models on the Pareto front for each method and log. The results show that ADD outperforms IM in 7 logs, while IM performs better in 1 log. Figure 8a is an example where ADD models are more frequently located in the top-right region. In the duplicated-activity setting, ADD achieves higher precision and recall in all logs. Although AM produces smaller models in 5 logs, ADD consistently achieves superior Pareto performance. In all logs, the Pareto fronts are fully occupied by ADD-generated models; an example is shown in Fig. 8b. Finally, the size of ADD-generated DFGs is consistently smaller than that of AM-derived Petri nets, indicating more interpretable structures. Overall, the results demonstrate that Petri nets derived from MAS-DFGs achieve superior precision and recall, particularly in the duplicated-activity setting.

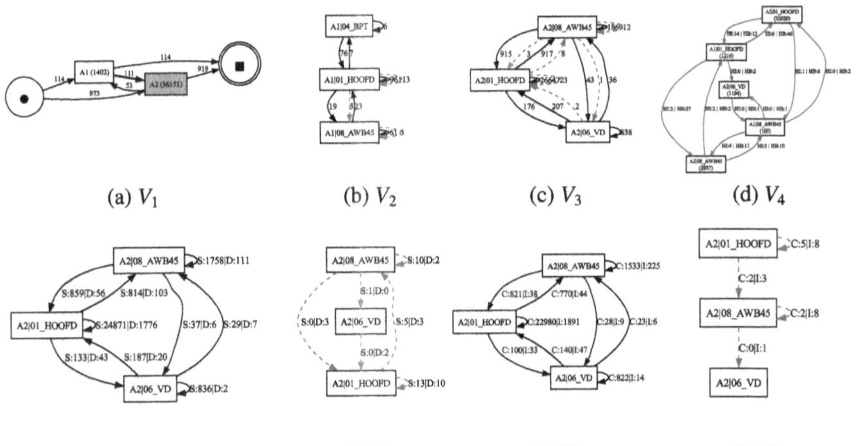

(a) V_1 (b) V_2 (c) V_3 (d) V_4

(e) V_5 (f) V_6 (g) V_7 (h) V_8

Fig. 9. Visual representations of BPIC2015-1.

We evaluate the visual representations using the BPIC2015-1 model with thresholds (0.9, 0), selected for its simplicity and clarity of presentation. Figure 9 presents the full set of visual representations, while its MAS-DFG is shown in Fig. 4. Figure 9a shows the interaction model, where handover frequencies between agent types are obtained by aggregating inter-agent-type edges in the MAS-DFG. Figure 9d extends this view by distinguishing inter-agent-type handovers into busy and idle frequencies. Figure 9b and Fig. 9c present intra-agent behavior for two agent types, capturing consecutive and handback patterns, where dashed red edges represent handbacks. Figure 9e and Fig. 9f focus on Type-2 and separately present consecutive and handback behaviors, together with the frequencies of task transfers to other agents within the same agent type. Figure 9g and Fig. 9h show interruption patterns for agent Type-2, considering cases where consecutive or handback behavior involves the same agent.

Table 2 compares our visual representations with baseline models across eight aspects. The first four capture handover related information relevant to bottleneck analysis, and the last four capture waiting time-related information based on agent status. Conventional DFGs and MAS models discovered by Agent Miner do not annotate these frequencies, providing limited visualizations. Actor behavioral DFGs capture control-flow handovers and interruption frequencies between activities connected by direct-follows relations, where control-flow handovers refer to handovers occurring between consecutive activity pairs in a trace. However, they do not distinguish intra- and inter-agent-type behaviors, limiting their support for organizational analysis. By contrast, our representations V_1 to V_8, together with the MAS-DFG, support broader analytical tasks. V_1 summarizes inter-agent-type handover frequencies and highlights which agent type initiates transfers most often; e.g., it shows that A_1 hands work over to A_2 111 times. V_4 refines this by showing detailed inter-agent handovers between activity pairs together with busy frequencies; e.g., *01-HOOFD* from A_1 to A_2 occurs 52 times, of which 46 are busy handovers, suggesting a potential waiting time-related bottleneck [9, 10]. V_2 and V_3 show intra-agent-type consecutive and handback frequencies. V_5 and V_6 further distinguish whether these transitions involve different individual agents within the same agent type. E.g., V_5 shows the consecutive transition *01-HOOFD* → *01-HOOFD* involves different agents 1776 times, while V_6 shows the handback transition occurs between different agents 10 times. Such intra-agent-type handovers and handbacks may cause waiting times and additional setup effort for the receiving agent, thereby increasing completion time [15]. V_7 and V_8 focus on interruptions when consecutive or handback behaviors involve the same agent, thereby supporting interruption frequency visualization; e.g., the transition *01-HOOFD* → *06-VD* has the highest interruption proportion among consecutive behaviors at 24.8%, while *08-AWB45* → *08-AWB45* has the highest interruption proportion among handback behaviors at 80%. These patterns suggest potential bottlenecks and opportunities to reduce unnecessary interruptions. Finally, the MAS-DFG can support these analyses through corresponding edge annotations. With activity labels and direct-follows relations, it supports control-flow handover analysis similar to actor behavioral DFGs. In addition, by incorporating agent type labels, it extends the analysis to intra- and inter-agent-type perspectives, supporting a broader range of analytical tasks than existing models.

In practice, the proposed visual representations can support five analytical tasks that are not directly supported by existing models: *(i)* analyze workload balance across agent types using V_1; *(ii)* identify frequent handbacks within agent types using V_2 and V_3; *(iii)* identify frequent intra-agent-type handovers using V_5 and V_6; *(iv)* identify frequent intra-agent-type interruptions using V_7 and V_8; and *(v)* identify frequent and busy inter-agent-type handovers using V_4. These tasks are of interest to workforce planners, process analysts, and process managers seeking to understand workload distribution and collaboration patterns and identify opportunities for process improvement. Further-

Table 2. Comparison of visual representations across handover and waiting time aspects; a checkmark indicates that the corresponding frequency can be obtained directly from the visual representation, while a cross indicates that it cannot.

Visual representations	Handover-related measures				Waiting time-related measures			
	Control-flow handover	Intra-agent-type handback	Intra-agent-type handover	Inter-agent-type handover	Control-flow interruption	Intra-agent-type interruption	Control-flow handover busy	Inter-agent-type handover busy
Conventional DFG (Fig. 1)	×	×	×	×	×	×	×	×
AM MAS model (Fig. 2)	×	×	×	×	×	×	×	×
Actor behavioral DFG (Fig. 3)	✓	×	×	×	✓	×	✓	×
Agent type interaction graph (V_1)	×	×	×	✓	×	×	×	×
Inter-agent handover graph (V_4)	✓	×	×	✓	×	×	✓	✓
Agent type behavioral graph (V_2 & V_3)	×	✓	×	×	×	×	×	×
Intra-agent task transfer graph (V_5 & V_6)	✓	×	✓	×	×	×	×	×
Intra-agent continuation graph (V_7 & V_8)	×	×	×	×	✓	✓	×	×
MAS-DFG (Fig. 4)	✓	✓	✓	✓	✓	✓	✓	✓

more, users can define agent types according to their analytical needs and adjust two filtering thresholds to control the complexity of the resulting visualizations. The first threshold filters infrequent activities in agent type behavioral models, while the second filters infrequent inter-agent-type interactions. These mechanisms help reduce visual clutter and allow users to focus on the most frequent behavioral and interaction patterns, particularly when data contains many activities, agent types, and interactions.

The experimental evaluation has several limitations. First, agent grouping is performed using the Agent Miner (AM) technique, and agent-based DFG discovery builds upon these groups; however, the absence of ground-truth agent types prevents the assessment of grouping quality. Second, precision and recall are computed on Petri nets derived from MAS-DFGs, as no ground-truth MAS-DFGs are available for direct comparison. Third, the conversion from DFGs to Petri nets relies on local frequency-based heuristics and therefore cannot reliably reconstruct global control-flow structures such as choices and concurrency, which implies that precision, recall, and size do not fully capture all dimensions of model quality. Additional metrics are required to assess structural properties of the resulting Petri nets. For visualization, the evaluation is based on aspects identified in prior work; user studies or industry interviews would provide stronger validation of practical usefulness. The proposed technique also has limitations. As a DFG-based approach, agent-based DFG discovery does not explicitly model concurrency or simultaneous execution by multiple agents, and may fail to capture long-term dependencies in agent behavior. In addition, the visual representations focus on agent type behaviors and do not identify specific agents responsible for interruptions or busy handovers. Future work includes developing an interactive visualization tool that supports user-defined agent grouping and multi-level exploration of discovered models.

The tool will enable hierarchical analysis from agent type behavioral models to individual agent behaviors, facilitating fine-grained performance analysis. User studies will also be conducted to assess the usability of the proposed visualization approach.

7 Conclusion

This paper introduces the concept of agent-based DFGs, which extend directly-follows graphs by incorporating agent type and frequency information to support the analysis of intra- and inter-agent-type behaviors. We further present an agent-based DFG discovery technique for constructing agent-based DFGs from event data. Experimental results show that Petri nets derived from MAS-DFGs to define their execution semantics achieve high precision and recall, comparable to those discovered by state-of-the-art conventional and agent-based discovery techniques. These results confirm that discovering models of interacting agents from event logs can yield insights that complement conventionally discovered control-flow models that assume centralized process control [20]. Moreover, the proposed visualizations expose information relevant to analyzing handover patterns and waiting-time inefficiencies and may help identify potential bottlenecks from both control-flow and organizational viewpoints. The results suggest that agent-based DFGs can support a range of analytical tasks beyond those enabled by existing models and can be discovered from event data. Future work may focus on developing interactive visualization tools and incorporating user-centered evaluations to enhance the practical applicability of agent-based DFGs.

References

1. van der Aalst, W.: Process Mining: Data Science in Action. Springer (2016)
2. van der Aalst, W.: Foundations of process discovery. LNBIP, vol. 448, Springer (2022)
3. van der Aalst, W., Reijers, H., Song, M.: Discovering social networks from event logs. CSCW **14**(6) (2005)
4. van der Aalst, W., Weijters, T., Maruster, L.: Workflow mining: discovering process models from event logs. IEEE Trans. Knowl. Data Eng. **16**(9) (2004)
5. Alkhammash, H., Polyvyanyy, A., Moffat, A.: Stochastic directly-follows process discovery using grammatical inference. In: CAiSE. LNCS, vol. 14663. Springer (2024)
6. Hoogmoed, A., Vidgof, M., Djurica, D., Rubensson, C., Mendling, J.: Visual representation of resource analysis insights for process mining. In: BPMDS. LNBIP, vol. 511. Springer (2024)
7. van Hulzen, G.A., Li, C.Y., Martin, N., van Zelst, S., Depaire, B.: Mining context-aware resource profiles in the presence of multitasking. Artif. Intell. Med. **134** (2022)
8. Klijn, E., Mannhardt, F., Fahland, D.: Aggregating event knowledge graphs for task analysis. In: ICPM Workshops. LNBIP, vol. 468. Springer (2023)
9. Klijn, E., Tentina, I., Fahland, D., Mannhardt, F.: Decomposing process performance based on actor behavior. In: ICPM. IEEE (2024)
10. Lashkevich, K., Milani, F., Chapela-Campa, D., Suvorau, I., Dumas, M.: Why Am I Waiting? Data-Driven Analysis of Waiting Times in Business Processes. Springer (2023)
11. Leemans, S.J.J., Fahland, D., van der Aalst, W.M.P.: Discovering block-structured process models from event logs containing infrequent behaviour. In: Lohmann, N., Song, M., Wohed, P. (eds.) BPM 2013. LNBIP, vol. 171, pp. 66–78. Springer, Cham (2014). https://doi.org/10.1007/978-3-319-06257-0_6

12. Leemans, S., Fahland, D., van der Aalst, W.: Process and deviation exploration with inductive visual miner. In: BPM Demos. CEUR Workshop Proceedings, vol. 1295 (2014)
13. Leemans, S., Poppe, E., Wynn, M.: Directly follows-based process mining: exploration & a case study. In: ICPM. IEEE (2019)
14. Leribaux, A., Oyamada, R., De Smedt, J., Bozorgi, Z.D., Polyvyanyy, A., De Weerdt, J.: Linking Actor Behavior to Process Performance over Time. Springer (2026)
15. Liu, B., et al.: What are the factors affecting the handover process in open source development? J. Syst. Softw. **153** (2019)
16. Pfahlsberger, L., Rubensson, C., Knoblich, S., Vidgof, M., Mendling, J.: Multi-perspective path semantics in process mining based on causal process knowledge. In: PoEM Companion, CEUR Workshop Proceedings, vol. 3645 (2023)
17. Polyvyanyy, A.: Notes of a process scientist: process discovery. In: Mining a Scientist's Process. LNCS, vol. 16480, pp. 368–383. Springer (2026)
18. Polyvyanyy, A., et al.: Entropia: a family of entropy-based conformance checking measures for process mining. In: ICPM Doctoral Consortium/Tools, CEUR Workshop Proceedings, p. 2703 (2020)
19. Rozinat, A., Mans, R.S., Song, M., van der Aalst, W.: Discovering colored Petri nets from event logs. Int. J. Softw. Tools Technol. Transf. **10**(1) (2008)
20. Shen, Q., Polyvyanyy, A., Lipovetzky, N., Kampik, T.: Applying organizational mining to discover agent systems from event data. Inf. Syst. **138** (2025)
21. Song, M., van der Aalst, W.: Towards comprehensive support for organizational mining. Decis. Support Syst. **46**(1) (2008)
22. Tour, A., Polyvyanyy, A., Kalenkova, A.: Agent system mining: vision, benefits, and challenges. IEEE Access **9** (2021)
23. Tour, A., Polyvyanyy, A., Kalenkova, A., Senderovich, A.: Agent miner: an algorithm for discovering agent systems from event data. In: BPM. LNCS, vol. 14159. Springer (2023)
24. Weijters, A., van der Aalst, W., De Medeiros, A.: Process Mining with the HeuristicsMiner Algorithm. BETA publicatie: Working Papers, Technische Universiteit Eindhoven (2006)
25. Yang, J., Ouyang, C., ter Hofstede, A., van der Aalst, W.: No Time to Dice: Learning Execution Contexts from Event Logs for Resource-Oriented Process Mining. Springer (2022)
26. Zhian, H., Buyya, R., Polyvyanyy, A.: Multi-objective metaheuristics for effective and efficient stochastic process discovery. In: BPM. LNCS, vol. 16044. Springer (2025)

Modeling Concepts and Modeling Practice

Beyond the Model Artifact

An Empirical Study of the Socio-Cognitive Value of Domain Modeling Activities

Isadora Valle[1(✉)], Tiago Prince Sales[1], Eduardo Guerra[2], Luiz Olavo Bonino da Silva Santos[1], Henderik A. Proper[3,4], and Giancarlo Guizzardi[1]

[1] University of Twente, Enschede, The Netherlands
{i.vallesousa,t.princesales,l.o.boninodasilvasantos, g.guizzardi}@utwente.nl

[2] Faculty of Engineering, Free University of Bozen-Bolzano, Bolzano, Italy
eduardo.guerra@unibz.it

[3] TU Wien, Vienna, Austria
henderik.proper@tuwien.ac.at

[4] HU University of Applied Sciences, Utrecht, The Netherlands

Abstract. Although previous studies have identified several goals associated with modeling activities and model use, recent discussions on AI-supported software development have reinforced the need to better understand how modeling generates value in practice. This study investigates how practitioners perceive the value generated throughout modeling activities. To this end, we conducted an empirical investigation combining an online survey and semi-structured interviews involving practitioners working with domain modeling across multiple project contexts. Based on an inductive thematic analysis, the findings suggest that modeling value also emerges from the socio-cognitive activities supported throughout modeling processes. Five major mechanisms through which modeling generates value were identified, revealing how modeling supports negotiation of meaning, cognitive externalization, sensemaking, and coordination throughout software and domain engineering activities. The study contributes empirical evidence regarding how the value of modeling is perceived in practice and advances a process-oriented perspective on modeling value beyond artifact-centric interpretations.

Keywords: Domain modeling · Value in modeling · Socio-cognitive

1 Introduction

Recent advances in artificial intelligence (AI) have intensified discussions regarding the role and value of domain modeling in software engineering practice [5,15,16,23]. As AI-supported development increasingly automates implementation and code generation activities, researchers and practitioners have questioned which aspects of domain modeling continue to be valuable.

© The Author(s), under exclusive license to Springer Nature Switzerland AG 2027
A. Bernasconi et al. (Eds.): ER 2026, LNCS 17081, pp. 273–289, 2027.
https://doi.org/10.1007/978-3-032-40795-5_16

Although research on domain modeling has traditionally emphasized the utility of models as representational artifacts [7,9,11,12,32], this artifact-centered perspective provides only a partial explanation of modeling value. These studies contribute to the notion of use value in modeling by advancing the understanding of modeling goals and the structural characteristics associated with achieving them. However, there is still a limited understanding of how modeling activities contribute to the realization of these goals in practice and which mechanisms give rise to the perceived value associated with domain modeling.

Understanding these mechanisms may help practitioners address the frequent difficulty of explaining and assessing the benefits of modeling [33,34], particularly in AI-supported development contexts. An empirical investigation is therefore essential for understanding why practitioners continue to invest in modeling activities even when the direct value of models remains difficult to measure [32]. Such evidence can also help bridge academia and industry regarding improvements in modeling methods, tools, and guidelines, while contributing to ongoing discussions on return on modeling effort (RoME) [22], qualitative assessment in modeling practices [35], and collaborative human-AI modeling approaches [17,28].

This study is therefore guided by the following research question: *How does domain modeling generate value in practice beyond the model artifact itself?* To address this question, we conducted an empirical investigation combining an online survey [30] and semi-structured interviews [1] involving professionals working with domain modeling across multiple project contexts.

The findings suggest that the perceived value of modeling also emerges from the socio-cognitive activities supported throughout modeling processes. Five major mechanisms were identified: establishing shared meaning among stakeholders, externalizing and structuring understanding, exploring and guiding action, navigating abstraction and perspectives, and coordinating across organizational and system boundaries. These findings indicate that modeling functions as a socio-cognitive mechanism that supports sensemaking, negotiation of meaning, cognitive externalization, and coordination throughout software and domain engineering activities. While prior work primarily identifies modeling goals and outcomes, this study investigates the underlying mechanisms through which these outcomes are achieved in practice.

The remainder of the paper is organized as follows. Section 2 presents the notion of modeling value. Section 3 details the empirical investigation process employed. Section 4 and 5 present and discuss the findings derived from the analysis. Section 6 addresses potential threats to validity. Section 7 positions the study in relation to the state of the art. Finally, Sect. 8 presents concluding remarks and directions for future research.

2 Modeling From a Value Perspective

The problem addressed in this study concerns how the value of modeling manifests in practice. Addressing this challenge first requires clarifying what is meant by "modeling value." The concept of value is used differently across disciplines and is often associated with utility, benefit, or usefulness. This study adopts the notion of use value, which concerns the practical utility an object provides relative to specific stakeholder needs [36]. From this perspective, modeling may generate value depending on how effectively modeling activities and artifacts support stakeholder goals.

Previous research has investigated the goals associated with the use of models and modeling activities. Empirical studies indicate that models are used in practice to achieve multiple functional goals, including intervention, communication, understanding, problem-solving, documenting, and learning [11,32]. Prior work also identified additional quality goals and structural model properties associated with achieving these goals [32]. These studies contribute to understanding what practitioners seek to achieve through modeling and which characteristics of models contribute to perceived usefulness.

More recently, researchers have started to investigate modeling value beyond an exclusively artifact-oriented perspective. In modeling contexts, value may emerge through different forms of action [22]. It may be generated during model (co-)creation, for example, by supporting shared understanding or negotiation; during model use, when models support analysis, communication, or decision-making; and through model transaction, when models are reused or shared across contexts. From this perspective, value is not restricted to the resulting artifact, but may also emerge throughout the activities performed around representations, such as exploration, negotiation, analysis, and coordination.

3 Methodology

The study employed a mixed-methods research approach [29] following a convergent parallel design that combined an online survey [30] with semi-structured interviews [1]. Participants could choose between completing the survey individually or answering the survey questions during an online interview conducted by the researchers. This approach provided flexibility for participants while allowing the collection of both structured responses and more detailed qualitative explanations regarding their modeling experiences. Study findings and supplementary materials are available in the replication package.

3.1 Questionnaire Design

The survey and interview protocols followed the same questionnaire structure, which underwent four iterative revisions involving three researchers before approval. The final version was composed of four sections: introduction, project profiling, reference model description, and model purposes breakdown.

The introductory section presented the study context and included the informed consent form. The project profiling section contained six questions covering: a fictitious project identifier, a brief project description, team size and participant role, number and domain of organizations involved, project budget, and a description of the models used or developed within the project context. Based on this information, participants selected one model to serve as the reference model for the remaining questions.

The reference model description section contained seven questions related to the selected model, including the model identifier, model type, modeling language, supporting tool, model source (developed or reused), and its main purposes. The model purposes question was closed-ended and allowed participants to select one or more purposes among the six functional modeling goals identified in previous work [32], or specify an alternative purpose.

The model purposes breakdown section was divided into seven subsections; however, participants answered only the subsections corresponding to the purposes previously selected. Each subsection contained three questions investigating: (i) the objects involved in the modeling activity, (ii) the stakeholders using the model, and (iii) how the model contributed to achieving the selected purpose. For each question, participants could provide up to three items. For example, when participants selected communication as a modeling purpose, they were asked to specify what was being communicated (e.g., rules, relationships, technical concepts), who used the model for this purpose, and how the model supported this communication activity. The latter question was particularly important for the analysis, as it directly captured participants' perceptions regarding how modeling generated value throughout practical activities. Most questions in the questionnaire were open-ended to encourage detailed descriptions of modeling experiences and practices. Whenever considered necessary, examples were provided to support questionnaire completion.

3.2 Data Collection

The survey was launched in February 2026 through posts published on the authors' LinkedIn profiles. These posts were subsequently shared in relevant LinkedIn groups and across the authors' professional networks. Direct invitation emails were also sent to professional contacts and researchers in the conceptual modeling community identified through Google Scholar.

The survey remained open until March 2026 and received 20 complete responses from modeling practitioners. Among these, six responses were collected during online interviews in which a researcher filled out the survey while interacting with participants. Additionally, four supplementary interviews were conducted and included as qualitative data sources. These interviews did not result in complete survey responses because participants preferred discussing their broader experiences with modeling rather than focusing on a single project.

The interviews were conducted via Microsoft Teams. With participants' consent, the platform transcription functionality was activated to support the questionnaire filling process and subsequent data analysis. Interview transcripts were anonymized and stored in a secure repository with restricted access granted to only one researcher. Any data not used in the study has already been deleted.

3.3 Data Analysis

The survey could be completed in any language; however, only responses in English and Portuguese were collected. Similarly, the interviews were conducted in either English or Portuguese, depending on participants' preferences. To minimize translation bias, the data were analyzed in their original language.

The analysis focused on understanding how models contributed to achieving stakeholders' purposes. Therefore, the analyzed data consisted of 10 interview transcriptions and 14 responses to subquestion 3 (the "how" question) from the model purposes breakdown section of the questionnaire. The data were analyzed through inductive thematic analysis [4]. In this approach, themes emerge from the data through iterative coding and interpretation rather than from pre-existing analytical categories. NVivo 12 was used to support the analysis process following the thematic analysis procedure proposed by Braun and Clarke [4].

The analysis began with repeated readings of the interview transcripts and survey responses to support familiarization with the data. Initial codes were then generated through the identification and labeling of relevant text references. These codes were progressively grouped into themes and subthemes through iterative comparison and refinement.

To support coding consistency and validation, a profile was created for each code, including: the core idea represented by the code, typical indicators, exclusion criteria, and representative examples. Based on these profiles, a large language model (LLM) was used as a supporting validation mechanism following a role-model prompt engineering strategy [10]. The LLM evaluator was instructed to: (i) determine whether the proposed code was semantically appropriate for the excerpt, (ii) evaluate whether the excerpt genuinely reflected the mechanism represented by the code, (iii) identify potential overlaps with other codes, (iv) distinguish primary from secondary mechanisms, and (v) avoid superficial validation based exclusively on keyword similarity.

The prompts were executed using ChatGPT 5.5 and Gemini 3 Flash. The validation process was performed in two stages. First, the LLMs analyzed possible overlaps between codes. The researcher manually reviewed the suggested overlaps and, when appropriate, merged or expanded existing codes. Second, the LLMs evaluated the compatibility between references and their assigned codes. Each reference received a validation rating classified as High, Medium, or Wrong. References evaluated as Wrong by both LLMs, or as Wrong by one and Medium by the other, were excluded from the final dataset. Consequently, only references receiving at least one High evaluation or two Medium evaluations were retained. The coding notebook, codebook guide, prompts, and final validation results are publicly available in the replication package.

4 Results

The analyzed sample comprised 20 projects involving modeling practices across multiple countries, application domains, and organizational structures, ranging from small-scale initiatives to large, distributed projects. The sample reflects heterogeneous modeling contexts sufficient to support the investigation of modeling value across different practical settings.

Projects Profiling. Most projects involved multifunctional teams and multiple stakeholders. Only one reported project was conducted individually. The teams included modelers (14), domain experts (16), product managers or product owners (14), software architects (13), software developers (10), project managers or scrum masters (10), business analysts (7), data specialists (7), UX/UI designers (7), and DevOps or operations engineers (4).

The projects spanned diverse organizational and geographical contexts. Based on the information provided by participants, it was possible to identify projects from the Netherlands (7), Norway (1), Germany (1), and Brazil (3). Reported domains included information technology (11), public sector (8), finance (4), transportation (4), manufacturing (3), energy and utilities (3), healthcare (2), education (2), and other sectors.

The analyzed projects also varied substantially in scale and investment. Reported budgets ranged from projects below USD 50,000 (3) to projects exceeding USD 10 million (1), while several participants either did not track project budgets (7) or preferred not to disclose them (4).

All projects reported the use of multiple model types and representational approaches, indicating heterogeneous modeling environments. Enterprise-related models were the most frequently mentioned (10), followed by process-oriented representations (9), conceptual and domain-oriented models (8), semantic and ontology-oriented models (5), data models (5), and behavioral representations (3). Participants also reported service-oriented models (3), governance and planning models (4), and informal or hybrid representations such as sketches and PowerPoint visualizations (3).

Reference Models Description. Although projects involved multiple models, participants selected one reference model to discuss in detail. The set included conceptual models (4), enterprise models (5), process models (4), ontologies (4), sequence diagrams (1), knowledge graphs (1), and service models (1).

The reported modeling languages and notations included ArchiMate (7), BPMN (2), UML (2), OntoUML/gUFO (2), CASE/Barker (2), OWL (1), logic-based representations (1), programming languages (1), and custom or evolving notations (2). This diversity reflects the broad range of organizational, technical, and analytical contexts represented in the study.

Participants also reported using a wide variety of modeling tools, including enterprise architecture platforms, diagramming tools, ontology engineering environments, whiteboards, presentation tools, and AI-supported environments. Among the most frequently mentioned tools were Bizzdesign (3), Visual Paradigm (3), Archi (2), Draw.io (2), and PowerPoint (3).

Most reference models (14) were developed within the context of the reported projects, while six corresponded to reused or adapted models. All analyzed models were associated with multiple modeling purposes, including creating or modifying systems (16), supporting understanding (15), solving problems (12), communication (14), documentation (14), and learning (4). This reinforces the multifunctional character of the modeling practices analyzed.

Thematic Analysis Overview. The final analysis was based on 178 coded references distributed across 21 subthemes and five themes. The themes defined in Table 1 describe recurring mechanisms through which participants perceived modeling as contributing to the achievement of different modeling purposes. The themes emerged inductively from their descriptions of how modeling supported communication, understanding, coordination, problem-solving, and learning activities throughout their projects.

Table 1. Themes of Modeling Value Mechanisms

Theme	Definition
Shared Meaning and Alignment	It captures how modeling supports the negotiation and establishment of shared meaning among participants.
Cognitive Externalization	It captures how modeling supports understanding by externalizing knowledge into manipulable representations.
Exploration and Decision Support	It captures how modeling supports exploration, reasoning, and intervention during problem-solving and system development.
Representational Flexibility	It captures how modeling supports transitions across representations, abstraction levels, and stakeholder perspectives.
Organizational Coordination	It captures how modeling supports coordination across teams, domains, systems, and organizational contexts.

Figure 1 illustrates the final thematic structure and presents the quantitative results from the coding process. During validation, 27 references were excluded.

5 Discussion

5.1 Shared Meaning and Alignment

Participants described **modeling as a mechanism for reducing ambiguity, aligning interpretations, and enabling collective understanding.** They noted that stakeholders frequently believe they agree on concepts or requirements while operating with different assumptions, interpretations, or levels of

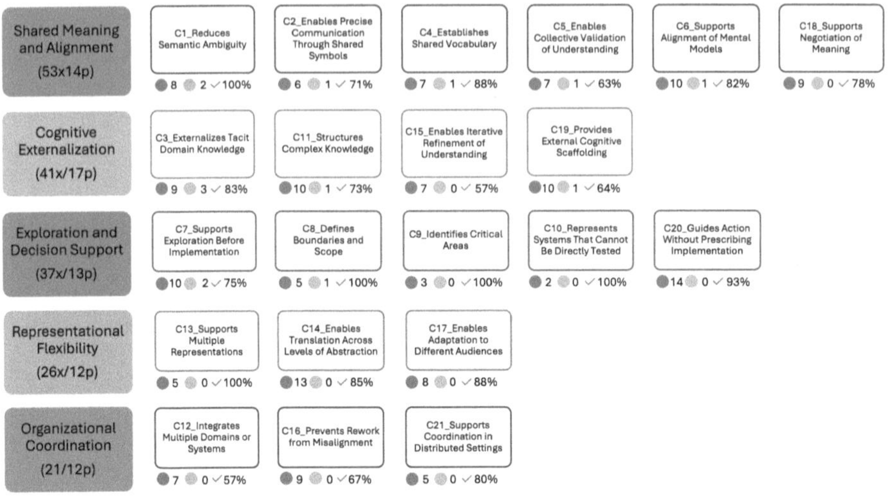

Fig. 1. Theme map. *The notation (x/p) indicates the number of coded references (x) and the number of participants who expressed the theme (p). The green circle represents references evaluated as High, the yellow circle represents references evaluated as Medium, and the check mark represents agreement between the two LLMs.* (Color figure online)

abstraction. In this context, where purely verbal communication becomes insufficient, modeling activities helped make these differences explicit and discussable. As one participant explained, *"we may, for example, agree on a specific phrase, understand it completely different, and still say we agree. But then if we draft it as a model, it turns out we did not mean the same."*

Participants also emphasized how modeling interactions supported precision and reduced semantic ambiguity. Shared notations and symbols were described as reducing dependence on individual interpretation during communication. One participant exemplified this by explaining that *"everybody in the industry understands what service roughness is, what it is, and that is the symbol. So you do not need to describe it."* Participants also noted that repeated interaction with models gradually introduced common concepts and terminology into discussions. These shared vocabularies were tied to collectively recognized structures represented in the model. In some cases, they referred to models as functioning similarly to domain-specific languages through which complex ideas could be communicated more consistently.

Modeling also played an important role in collaboratively validating and negotiating understanding. Participants described models being discussed, questioned, revised, and "*played back*" to stakeholders to verify whether the representation adequately captured the domain. Visual representations frequently served as shared reference points during discussions, helping participants ground disagreements and test interpretations. For example, one participant described how developers repeatedly returned to a UML diagram on a whiteboard during implementation to clarify missing details and maintain alignment between the model and the evolving system. Another participant emphasized the importance of explicit visual references during discussion: *"we need to make it explicit and be able to point to it. Do you agree with how I wrote it down or visualize it here?"* In this sense, shared understanding did not emerge through immediate consensus, but through progressive alignment around a persistent representation.

5.2 Cognitive Externalization

Participants described **modeling not simply as documenting knowledge, but as an active process through which understanding is developed, evaluated, and refined.** They emphasized that modeling supports understanding by organizing complex knowledge into forms that can be manipulated and explored. Rather than confronting complexity as an undifferentiated whole, participants used modeling to structure relationships, dependencies, and constraints in ways that supported inspection and reasoning. Several participants described using models to compare organizations, visualize multidimensional information, map dependencies across systems, or identify missing constraints.

Participants emphasized the role of modeling in externalizing tacit or difficult-to-articulate domain knowledge, explaining that certain aspects of a domain only became visible once represented explicitly. One participant noted that modeling *"helps to sort of extract those things and make them tangible that they actually exist because we can see them."* Another participant explained that modeling was often the first activity performed to understand the domain vocabulary and business processes before implementation activities began. Modeling, therefore, transformed fragmented or implicit understanding into tangible structures that could be jointly inspected, discussed, and refined.

Participants also described modeling as an iterative activity through which understanding evolved. Models were revised, extended, and restructured as participants identified missing constraints, reconsidered assumptions, or refined conceptual distinctions. One participant explained that *"the modeling brought to bear new knowledge that they didn't have, even when they thought they did."* This refinement process was tied to the iterative manipulation of representations throughout modeling, enabling participants to revisit decisions, stabilize understanding, trace reasoning, and refine interpretations as projects evolved.

Several participants also described how modeling activities contributed to the creation of representations that preserved organizational knowledge, supported continuity across time, and bridged conceptual understanding and implementation concerns throughout collaborative work. As one participant explained, *"you have to find this fine line where you are modeling enough for somebody to understand the machinery and then make the leap into the software and how the whole thing works."*

5.3 Exploration and Decision Support

Participants described **modeling as a way of investigating structures, anticipating consequences, and guiding decisions before implementation.** They described modeling as a means of *"reducing the guessing game"* by exploring the problem space before committing to technical solutions. Through modeling, participants reasoned about potential changes, evaluated alternatives, analyzed the implications of different decisions, and identified what belonged within a system's scope and what should remain outside its boundaries. As one participant explained, modeling iterations helped predict *"what happens if I change this, if I change that."* Another one illustrated how modeling supported implementation decisions by clarifying *"how the data should be modeled in the database,"* and *"how the code should then interact with that data."* Participants described this exploratory process as essential for understanding the domain, defining responsibilities, and clarifying interactions between systems and stakeholders.

Modeling was also used to identify critical areas, dependencies, and points of strategic importance. Participants described modeling to support the recognition of pain points, the prioritization of investments, and the identification of areas requiring additional analysis or refinement. One participant explained how modeling supported discussions about *"what could we automate"* and where optimization efforts should be prioritized. In some cases, modeling also enabled exploring situations in which direct experimentation was costly, impractical, or impossible. One participant, for example, described using modeling to simulate vehicle crashes and test stress conditions to reason about behaviors and consequences before real-world implementation.

Although participants emphasized the importance of modeling in supporting decision-making, they did not describe it as prescribing implementation in a rigid manner. Instead, modeling was used to guide action while preserving flexibility regarding how solutions would ultimately be realized.

5.4 Representational Flexibility

Participants described **modeling as enabling the transformation, reframing, and selective adaptation of representations depending on the problem context and audience.** They described moving between visual diagrams, code, textual descriptions, informal sketches, and formal modeling notations depending on the task being performed. In several cases, the same conceptual structure was represented differently across activities such as analysis, implementation, communication, or teaching. One participant illustrated this process by explaining how the team started with an information model and then *"translate[d] the information model into an object model."*

Participants also emphasized the importance of navigating different levels of abstraction throughout modeling activities. Modeling enabled them to shift between high-level overviews and detailed representations in order to focus attention on particular concerns without losing awareness of the broader system context. As one participant described, understanding evolved by moving *"from the satellite perspective to the plane perspective to the helicopter perspective."* Participants explained that different abstraction layers expose different aspects of a problem, making particular constraints, trade-offs, or decisions visible at specific moments of analysis. One participant noted that certain representations provide *"just enough information to highlight a specific problem or highlight a specific trade-off decision to be made."*

This flexibility was also closely connected to adapting representations to different audiences and collaborative contexts. Participants described modifying representations to match the knowledge, goals, and expectations of stakeholders. One participant explained that the same model required different versions for end users and developers. These representational shifts were not treated as disconnected views, but as interconnected perspectives that supported continuity across heterogeneous forms of reasoning.

5.5 Organizational Coordination

Participants described **modeling as a way of integrating heterogeneous structures and maintaining coherence in distributed development environments.** They emphasized its role in connecting multiple domains, systems, and organizational perspectives through shared representational structures. Participants explained that interoperability often depends on establishing common conceptual foundations across otherwise disconnected systems, processes, datasets, and stakeholder groups. Several participants referred to models as a form of *"common glue"* supporting coordination between technical and organizational elements. One participant further explained that interoperability between domain systems was *"always the goal"* in cross-domain initiatives.

Participants also described how modeling activities supported coordination across distributed organizational settings in which stakeholders maintained different partial perspectives of a system. As one participant explained, *"Everybody does some kind of modeling. If I talk with a business analyst, they usually have some business process models. If I talk to the product owner, they have some sort of a model of a product that they are defining."* In this sense, modeling supported the alignment of distributed perspectives without requiring complete domain expertise from all participants.

Another important aspect of modeling is preventing rework and duplication caused by fragmented understanding. Participants described situations in which insufficient modeling led to redundant effort, architectural inconsistencies, or costly redevelopment. One participant described a team that needed to *"redo their complete application"* because they lacked a shared understanding of the domain. In contrast, they explained that explicit representations helped teams identify integrations, reuse structures, and avoid *"reinventing the wheel."*

Several participants emphasized that these coordination benefits become increasingly important as organizational scale and complexity grow. While informal and implicit understanding may suffice in smaller settings, participants argued that larger distributed environments require more deliberate forms of modeling to maintain alignment, continuity, and interoperability over time.

5.6 Toward a Socio-Cognitive View of Modeling

The findings suggest that the value of modeling extends beyond the resulting model artifact and is also associated with the cognitive and collaborative activities supported throughout the modeling process. While models' utility remains important, the findings indicate that **a substantial portion of modeling value emerges from the socio-cognitive processes enabled through interaction with representations.**

Modeling supported iterative framing and reframing of problems, exploration of alternatives, and refinement of understanding. These activities suggest that modeling can be viewed as a sensemaking process. Sensemaking theory describes how individuals and groups construct understanding in situations characterized by ambiguity, uncertainty, or incomplete information [38]. From this perspective, meaning is progressively developed through interpretation and interaction. This view is particularly relevant in software and domain engineering contexts [27], where stakeholders frequently operate with evolving requirements, partial knowledge, and multiple perspectives on the same problem.

Modeling also supported exposing inconsistencies, clarifying assumptions, and negotiating meanings across stakeholders. By grounding discussions in structured representations, it enabled participants to externalize reasoning processes that would otherwise remain implicit in verbal communication alone. These observations align with theories of verbalization and articulation, which explain how external expression contributes to transforming implicit understanding into structures that can be discussed and collaboratively refined. Activities such as self-explanation, self-reflection, and teaching support reasoning by making assumptions, interpretations, and partially formed understandings more explicit and available for discussion [8,14].

Similarly, modeling supported iterative refinement, transitions across abstraction levels, coordination across teams, and preservation of understanding throughout development activities. Theories of external and distributed cognition explain how cognitive activities can be distributed across representations, artifacts, and social interactions [13,26]. From this perspective, modeling supports reasoning by stabilizing information, reducing memory demands, and enabling the manipulation of complex structures and relationships.

By evidencing that many important benefits of modeling emerge through socio-cognitive activities, the findings also contribute to ongoing discussions regarding the role of domain modeling in AI-supported development contexts [5,15,16,23]. The socio-cognitive processes observed throughout modeling activities resemble the slower and more deliberate reasoning associated with System 2 cognition, while current AI systems primarily operate through fast pattern-based generation mechanisms commonly associated with System 1 processes [17]. From this perspective, AI may be more valuable in supporting modeling activities and collaborative reasoning than in replacing modeling altogether [28].

6 Threats to Validity

This study is subject to limitations associated with retrospective reporting and participant perception. Since participants were asked to discuss projects selected by themselves, the results may be influenced by the rosy view phenomenon [18], leading participants to emphasize positive modeling experiences. This threat was partially mitigated by encouraging participants to discuss concrete situations and challenges, as well as by including ongoing projects in the interviews.

The use of online interviews may also represent a limitation. Although online settings can affect social presence and interaction dynamics [2], this threat was mitigated through the use of video communication and the interviewer's prior experience with semi-structured interviews. In addition, the study focused on the interpretation of participants' statements rather than behavioral observation.

Another limitation concerns the modest sample size and the transferability of the findings. Although the results are not intended to be statistically generalizable, the diversity of projects and the richness of the collected data contributed to the identification of recurring patterns. Furthermore, the sample size complied with the saturation criterion commonly associated with qualitative research [31].

The study may also be affected by researchers' interpretation bias, since thematic analysis involves subjective judgment during coding and theme interpretation. To mitigate this threat, the analysis was conducted iteratively and continuously grounded in empirical extracts from the interviews. Moreover, AI-assisted validation was used to support consistency checking. However, all coding and interpretation decisions remained under the researchers' responsibility.

Finally, the interpretation of the findings through the lenses of sensemaking, verbalization, and cognitive externalization represents one possible theoretical perspective on the observed phenomena. Alternative theoretical frameworks could lead to complementary interpretations of the data.

7 Related Work

7.1 Empirical Studies on Modeling Goals and Value

Several empirical studies have investigated the goals, motivations, and perceived benefits associated with domain modeling practices. Dobing and Parsons [9] investigated how different Unified Modeling Language (UML) [20] components are used in software development practice and for which purposes they are considered useful. Similarly, Ho-Quang et al. [12] analyzed the motivations and benefits associated with the use of UML models in software development teams. Consistent with the findings presented here, their results emphasize collaboration, communication, coordination, planning, and integration as important motivations and benefits associated with modeling activities.

Other studies investigate modeling value by identifying modeling goals, quality goals, and structural model properties associated with achieving these goals [11,32]. Davies et al. [7] additionally investigated practitioners' motivations for domain modeling activities. Although these studies identify important goals and benefits associated with modeling activities, they provide a limited understanding of how modeling contributes to the realization of these goals in practice.

7.2 Cognitive and Collaborative Perspectives on Modeling

From a cognitive perspective, existing literature presents two complementary research directions related to the findings of this study. The first investigates cognitive mechanisms involved in conceptual and domain modeling activities. The second investigates verbalization and reflective articulation in learning and problem-solving contexts. Together, these research directions support the view of modeling as a socio-cognitive activity that contributes to reasoning, understanding, coordination, and knowledge construction.

Research on conceptual and domain modeling has investigated cognitive activities involved in modeling practice, including relational reasoning, abstraction management, working memory demands [39,40], and cognitive complexity during model construction [24,25]. These studies emphasize the importance of structuring modeling activities to support reasoning and reduce cognitive overload.

A complementary line of research investigates how verbalization, explanation, and reflective articulation support understanding and problem-solving activities. Prior work shows that self-explanations and explanations directed toward others strategies contribute to knowledge construction and support complex tasks requiring abstraction and integration of new knowledge [6,8]. Pirolli and Recker [21] further show that explanations emphasizing abstract conceptual structures contribute to learning and problem-solving performance.

Studies on verbalization strategies have also investigated think-aloud protocols as mechanisms for externalizing reasoning processes during complex tasks. Wade [37] discusses their role in supporting reflective reasoning, while Blech et al. [3] and Noushad et al. [19] show how think-aloud activities expose intermediate reasoning steps and make complex thought processes more observable. Together, these studies reinforce the view that externalizing reasoning contributes to reflection, clarification, and understanding.

Although the cognitive and collaborative roles of modeling have already been discussed in the literature, existing work has focused on theoretical interpretations or isolated cognitive mechanisms associated with specific modeling or learning tasks. Limited attention has been given to understanding how these processes manifest throughout modeling practice in real-world software and domain engineering contexts. There is still limited empirical evidence regarding how practitioners themselves perceive the role of modeling in supporting collective sensemaking, negotiation of meaning, cognitive externalization, and coordination across stakeholders during practical modeling activities.

8 Conclusion

This study investigated how domain modeling generates value in practice beyond the resulting model artifact. While previous studies have contributed to understanding modeling goals and the structural characteristics associated with achieving them, there is still limited understanding of how modeling contributes to the realization of these goals throughout practice. Based on an empirical investigation combining surveys and semi-structured interviews with modeling practitioners, this work analyzed how models supported the achievement of different modeling purposes across real-world project contexts.

The results indicate that an important part of modeling value emerges throughout the socio-cognitive activities supported during modeling processes. Five major mechanisms through which modeling generates value were identified: establishing shared meaning, externalizing and structuring understanding, exploring and guiding action, navigating abstraction and perspectives, and coordinating across organizational and system boundaries.

These findings contribute empirical evidence regarding how practitioners perceive the value of modeling in practice and support a process-oriented perspective on modeling value beyond artifact-centric interpretations. The paper also relates these mechanisms to theories of sensemaking, verbalization, and cognitive externalization. In doing so, it helps explain why modeling remains valuable in complex, collaborative, and AI-supported software engineering contexts even when its direct value is difficult to measure. Future work may expand this investigation through larger empirical studies, quantitative evaluations, and the exploration of additional theoretical perspectives on modeling practice.

References

1. Adams, A., Lunt, P., Cairns, P.: A qualitative approach to HCI research (2008)
2. Basch, J.M., et al.: It takes more than a good camera: which factors contribute to differences between face-to-face interviews and videoconference interviews regarding performance ratings and interviewee perceptions? J. Bus. Psychol. **36**, 921–940 (2021)
3. Blech, C., Gaschler, R., Bilalić, M.: Why do people fail to see simple solutions? using think-aloud protocols to uncover the mechanism behind the einstellung (mental set) effect. Think. Reason. **26**(4), 552–580 (2020)
4. Braun, V., Clarke, V.: Using thematic analysis in psychology. Qual. Res. Psychol. **3**(2), 77–101 (2006)
5. Chen, K., Yang, Y., Chen, B., López, J.A.H., Mussbacher, G., Varró, D.: Automated domain modeling with large language models: a comparative study. In: 2023 ACM/IEEE 26th MODELS, pp. 162–172. IEEE (2023)
6. Chi, M.T.H., et al.: Eliciting self-explanations improves understanding. Cogn. Sci. **18**(3), 439–477 (1994)
7. Davies, I., et al.: How do practitioners use conceptual modeling in practice? Data Knowl. Eng. **58**(3), 358–380 (2006)
8. Dillenbourg, P., Self, J.A.: A computational approach to socially distributed cognition. Eur. J. Psychol. Educ. **7**(4), 353–372 (1992)

9. Dobing, B., Parsons, J.: How UML is used. Commun. ACM **49**(5), 109–113 (2006)
10. Federiakin, D., et al.: Prompt engineering as a new 21st century skill. In: Frontiers in Education, vol. 9, p. 1366434. Frontiers (2024)
11. Guizzardi, G., Proper, H.A.: On understanding the value of domain modeling. In: 15th International Workshop on Value Modelling and Business Ontologies (2021)
12. Ho-Quang, T.: Practices and perceptions of UML use in open source projects. In: International Conference on Software Engineering, pp. 203–212 (2017)
13. Hutchins, E.: The distributed cognition perspective on human interaction. In: Roots of Human Sociality, pp. 375–398. Routledge (2020)
14. Joseph, L.M., et al.: The effects of self-questioning on reading comprehension: a literature review. Read. Writ. Q. **32**(2), 152–173 (2016)
15. Krishna, M.: Using LLMs in software requirements specifications: an empirical evaluation. In: IEEE 32nd RE, pp. 475–483. IEEE (2024)
16. Lukyanenko, R.: Intelligent agile: conceptual modeling and AI for next-generation agile software development. Available at SSRN 5490008 (2025)
17. Lukyanenko, R., et al.: Software development and modeling in the age of artificial intelligence manifesto (2025)
18. Mitchell, T.R., et al.: Temporal adjustments in the evaluation of events: the "rosy view." J. Exp. Soc. Psychol. **33**(4), 421–448 (1997)
19. Noushad, B., et al.: Twelve tips for applying the think-aloud method to capture cognitive processes. Med. Teach. **46**(7), 892–897 (2024)
20. OMG: UML 2.0 superstructure specification – Final adopted specification. Technical Report PTC/03-08-02, Object Management Group (2003)
21. Pirolli, P., Recker, M.: Learning strategies and transfer in the domain of programming. Cogn. Instr. **12**(3), 235–275 (1994)
22. Proper, H.A., Guizzardi, G.: Modeling for enterprises; let's go to RoME ViA RiME. In: The Practice of Enterprise Modeling 2022 Forum, vol. 3327 (2022)
23. Romeo, J., et al.: UML is back. or is it? Investigating the past, present, and future of UML in open source software. In: 47th ICSE, pp. 2342–2354. IEEE (2025)
24. Rosenthal, K., Strecker, S., Pastor, O.: Modeling difficulties in data modeling. In: Dobbie, G., Frank, U., Kappel, G., Liddle, S.W., Mayr, H.C. (eds.) ER 2020. LNCS, vol. 12400, pp. 501–511. Springer, Cham (2020). https://doi.org/10.1007/978-3-030-62522-1_37
25. Rosenthal, K., Strecker, S.: Toward a taxonomy of modeling difficulties: a multimodal study on individual modeling processes (extended abstract). EMISA Forum **41**(1), 31–32 (2021)
26. Scaife, M., Rogers, Y.: External cognition: how do graphical representations work? Int. J. Hum. Comput. Stud. **45**(2), 185–213 (1996)
27. Seidel, S., Recker, J., Brocke, J.V.: Sensemaking and sustainable practicing: functional affordances of information systems in green transformations1. MIS Q. **37**(4), 1275–1300 (2013)
28. Silva Mercado, J.: AI assisted domain modeling explainability and traceability. In: Proceedings of the ACM/IEEE 27th MODELS, pp. 130–135 (2024)
29. Storey, M.D., et al.: Guiding principles for mixed methods research in software engineering. Empir. Softw. Eng. **30**(5), 138 (2025)
30. Sue, V.M., Ritter, L.A.: Conducting Online Surveys. Sage (2012)
31. Tong, A., Sainsbury, P., Craig, J.: Consolidated criteria for reporting qualitative research (coreq): a 32-item checklist for interviews and focus groups. Int. J. Qual. Health Care **19**(6), 349–357 (2007)

32. Valle, I.: What do I get from modeling? An empirical study on using structural conceptual models. In: Proper, H.A. (ed.) 27th EDOC2023, Proceedings, vol. 14367, pp. 21–38. Springer (2023)
33. Valle, I., et al.: Mapping the pain: how modelers experience and respond to common domain modeling frustrations. In: Gianola, A., et al. (eds.) 29th EDOC2025, Revised Selected Papers. LNCS, pp. 193–209. Springer (2025)
34. Valle, I., et al.: Unraveling the pain points of domain modeling. Inf. Softw. Technol. **183**, 107736 (2025)
35. Valle, I.: Modeling value canvas: a tool to rationalize the value of domain modeling. In: Fuentes, L. (ed.) CAiSE 2026, Proceedings. LNCS, vol. 16558, pp. 1–18. Springer (2026)
36. Vargo, S.L., et al.: On value and value co-creation: a service systems and service logic perspective. Eur. Manag. J. **26**(3), 145–152 (2008)
37. Wade, S.E.: Using think alouds to assess comprehension. Read. Teach. **43**(7), 442–451 (1990)
38. Weick, K.E., Weick, K.E.: Sensemaking in Organizations, vol. 3. Sage Publications, Thousand Oaks (1995)
39. Wilmont, I., et al.: Abstract reasoning in collaborative modeling. In: 45th HICSS2012), Proceedings, 4–7 January 2012, Grand Wailea, Maui, HI, USA, pp. 170–179. IEEE Computer Society (2012)
40. Wilmont, I., Hengeveld, S., Barendsen, E., Hoppenbrouwers, S.: Cognitive mechanisms of conceptual modelling. In: Ng, W., Storey, V.C., Trujillo, J.C. (eds.) ER 2013. LNCS, vol. 8217, pp. 74–87. Springer, Heidelberg (2013). https://doi.org/10.1007/978-3-642-41924-9_7

Modeling Temporal Requirements of Processes with $STNU^w$

Franziska S. Hollauf(✉) and Johann Eder

Department of Informatics-Systems, University of Klagenfurt, Klagenfurt, Austria
franziska.hollauf@aau.at, johann.eder@aau.at

Abstract. Time is a basic category for modeling a universe of discourse and reasoning about its properties. For processes, event-based temporal concepts allow the representation of admissible sequences of events and temporal constraints between events. Temporal constraint networks in various forms provide means for formally modeling temporal requirements of processes and for reasoning about possible conflicts between these requirements. $STNU$, Simple Temporal Networks with Uncertainty, express constraints between the timepoints of events and capture the temporal uncertainty of durations depending on external events. Recently, $STNUO$, Simple Temporal Networks with Uncertainty and Oracles, have been introduced to explicitly model the timepoint when these durations are known. Agile controllability, a generalization of the well-established notion of dynamic controllability, leverages this knowledge to ensure the absence of conflicts among temporal requirements. Here we introduce $STNU^w$, a subclass of $STNUO$ extending $STNU$ with the concept of weak contingent activities and timepoints, which is sufficient for modeling a plenitude of scenarios while it still admits checking agile controllability with polynomial complexity. We formally define $STNU^w$ and a procedure for efficiently and effectively checking agile controllability of $STNU^w$. A proof-of-concept implementation facilitates an evaluation of the scalability of the approach.

Keywords: Temporal Constraints · Requirement Analysis · Process Modeling

1 Introduction

As time is an essential basic concept for processes in information systems, the modeling of temporal aspects and requirements for process executions needs means for the representation of temporal aspects of the environment of an information system and the modeling of temporal goals, obligations, and permissions such as durations, deadlines, milestones, maximum reaction time, and minimum delay [6,19]. Here we report on research providing concepts for modeling these temporal aspects of processes, in particular different variants of temporal constraint networks (TCN), and developing notions and procedures for checking whether temporal process models are free of contradictions or conflicts.

© The Author(s), under exclusive license to Springer Nature Switzerland AG 2027
A. Bernasconi et al. (Eds.): ER 2026, LNCS 17081, pp. 290–305, 2027.
https://doi.org/10.1007/978-3-032-40795-5_17

Modeling processes mostly leverages event-based models, where events characterize the start and end of activities (tasks, process steps), and temporal requirements are therefore modeled as temporal constraints between these events [6,9,19]. Modeling languages for processes such as BPMN, UML activity charts, or event-driven process chains, which already feature concepts for basic temporal aspects representing precedence or admissible partial orders between events, are extended with concepts to express constraints such as durations of activities or minimum and maximum gaps between these events [19]. Here, we study different variants of temporal constraint networks as a basis for formally defining concepts for representing temporal constraints. Checking the feasibility of process models and their temporal requirements includes analyzing whether compliant executions of the process model are possible or whether the temporal requirements are - potentially - in conflict.

For process execution, we assume that a controller assigns timepoints to the start and end events of activities, ensuring that process executions comply with the temporal requirements. If all events can be determined by the controller, temporal requirements of processes can be modeled in a *Simple Temporal Network (STN)*, and a model is feasible if all constraints can be satisfied [7]. When processes communicate with the environment, however, some of these events are triggered by the environment and can only be observed, but not influenced by the process controller. *Simple Temporal Networks with Uncertainty (STNU)* allow for representing activities with externally triggered end events such that the duration of these so-called contingent activities is uncertain [4,21]. For example, if the delivery of an item is guaranteed to take 2–7 days, the actual delivery duration is only known when the parcel arrives. Checking feasibility requires avoiding the *hindsight fallacy*, i.e., that the decision of the controller to guarantee compliance will depend on future unknown timepoints of events set by the environment. Hence, satisfiability is not sufficient and, in consequence, different notions of controllability have been developed. In our example, the controller cannot schedule an event exactly one day before the unknown day the shipment will be received. Until recently, *dynamic controllability (DC)* was the most relaxed notion for temporal feasibility, which guaranteed that compliance was possible [4,21]. *DC* requires that the timepoint of an event may only depend on the values of smaller (= earlier) timepoints but not on timepoints of events which happen later. Several efficient techniques with polynomial complexity have been developed to check whether a process model is dynamically controllable [3,15,16,20,21].

Recently, oracles have been introduced as new concepts for representing when a controller has advanced information about external events [22]. For example, the exact duration of the shipment might be announced at least 2 days before the actual delivery. For these *Simple Temporal Networks with Uncertainty and Oracles (STNUO)*, a new advanced notion of temporal feasibility was proposed: *agile controllability (AC)* [13]. *AC* extends *DC* by taking into account the timepoint when a controller knows the actual duration of an activity ended by an external event, and hence decisions of the controller might depend on the timepoints of all events the controller already *knows* before, in contrast to all that *happened* before. In our example, it is feasible that based on the information about the day of delivery, the controller schedules some activity to start exactly one day before the item arrives. Checking AC, however, is known to have exponential complexity [13,22].

The contribution of this paper is to introduce $STNU^w$, a subclass of $STNUO$, enhancing $STNU$ with the concept of so-called *weak contingent* activities, which are activities whose duration is known when they start but cannot be influenced by the controller. Moreover, we present a procedure for checking AC of $STNU^w$ effectively and efficiently. $STNU^w$ are clearly more expressive than $STNU$ and allow modeling a wide array of relevant scenarios, as demonstrated in the next section, while still admitting checking procedures with polynomial complexity.

The remainder of the paper is organized as follows. In Sect. 2 we motivate the investigation of $STNU^w$ with examples. The basic concepts of $STNU^w$ and AC are formally defined in Sect. 3, and in Sect. 4 we propose a procedure to check AC for $STNU^w$. In Sect. 5, we discuss the characteristics of our approach and evaluate its efficiency using a proof-of-concept implementation. After contrasting the approach with related work in Sect. 6, we draw some conclusions in Sect. 7.

2 Motivation

In the following, we present a real-world use case that motivates our research [2]. Figure 1, adapted from [22], visualizes a rehabilitation process with physical and psychological activities, as common in multi-modal pain therapy [2], in BPMN with temporal constraints. The process begins by informing the patient about upcoming activities. Then, it splits into two parallel running threads. The lower path outlines the psychological activities, including administering a questionnaire and then providing psychotherapy for the patient. The upper thread represents the physical rehabilitation path, beginning with an initial physical status examination, based on which the duration of physiotherapy is decided, followed by the physical exercise sessions, which are monitored alongside. Finally, the patient is discharged.

We focus here on the activities with uncertain duration and adorn these activities with a duration attribute $[x, y]$ indicating the minimum and maximum time with $-\infty < x \leq y < \infty$, which an activity can take to transition from state "started" to "completed" [19].

How long the patient has to do physical exercise (T5) depends on the evaluation beforehand (T3 and T4), but we know it must be performed for at least 20 and up to 30 days (480 to 720 h). How long the psychotherapy will take is also uncertain. Task T7 is known to be offered for at least 14 days, up to 37 days (336 to 888 h).

Further, temporal constraints between some activities are included, representing the allowed time distance between their start and end timepoints, respectively. These inter-task constraints between the starting/ending events of two tasks can be expressed with the concept $E_1[u, v]E_2$ where the first task's starting (S)/ending (E) event is E_1 and E_2 stands for the starting (S)/ending (E)

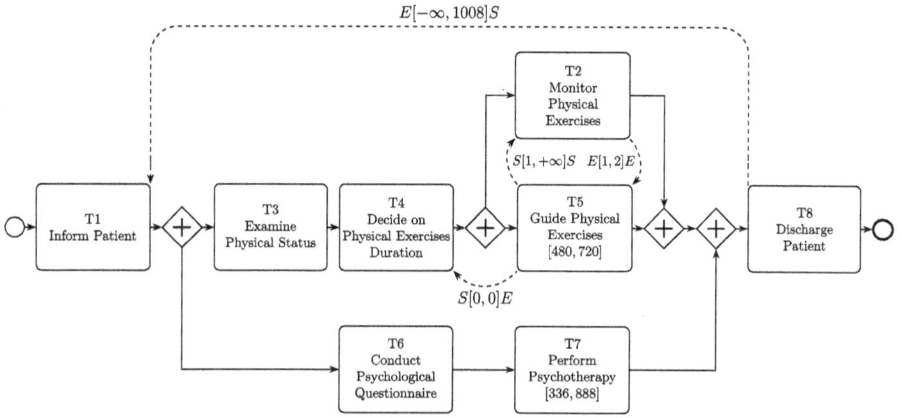

Fig. 1. BPMN diagram of rehabilitation process with temporal constraints

event of the second task [5]. In Fig. 1, the following temporal constraints of the process are illustrated: The patient must be discharged (T8) at the latest within 6 weeks (1008 h) after the start of therapy (T1), as the insurance does not allow for more. When the duration of the physical exercises is decided (T4), the exercises start immediately (T5). Task "Monitor Physical Exercise" (T2) has to start (at least) 1 h after the physical exercises start (T5) and has to end 1 to 2 h before the physical exercises (T5) end to avoid recording noisy data during the initial and final phase of the exercises.

Having designed such a process, the question is now whether these temporal requirements are (potentially) in conflict or whether the process can be surely executed without violating any temporal constraint. As this rehabilitation process involves uncertain activity durations (T5 and T7), we could use the concepts $STNU$ and DC to model and verify the absence of temporal requirement conflicts. Then, in our rehabilitation process, the uncertain duration of task T5 can only be observed at task termination. Hence, task T2 cannot be set to end at the required time distance before the end event of T5. So this $STNU$ is not dynamically controllable.

Nevertheless, the end event of T2 can be adequately set as early knowledge about the uncertain duration of T5 is available: at the end event of T4, the duration of T5 is determined. Hence, the scenario can be modeled with the concepts of $STNUO$ and AC. The most recent approach by Hollauf et al. [13] for checking whether $STNUOs$ are agile controllable, however, has two drawbacks: (1) exponential complexity, and (2) while positives are always true, negatives might be false, i.e., $STNUOs$ may be reported as not agile controllable although they are.

This work aims to address these shortcomings by motivating the investigation of a new concept class, a superclass of $STNU$, but a subclass of $STNUO$, which we introduce as $STNU^w$, which allows to represent situations when the earlier knowledge about the uncertain duration is received at the activity's start event, so-called *weak contingent durations*. Such weak contingent durations can be found frequently, and we provide a few examples:

- **Doctor's Appointment** A follow-up check should be made between two and six months after treatment. After the discharge examination, the doctor sets the date of the next appointment.
- **Traveling using a Navigation System** The navigation system communicates how long the drive will take based on current traffic conditions as one starts driving.
- **Traveling by Public Transport** Public transport offers different routes to reach the destination, using different metros, trams, or buses with varying speeds and frequencies, and hence, the duration of trips varies considerably. When the journey begins, an app computes the route and travel duration.
- **Delivery Process** Web shops announce a shipping time frame. However, they might notify their customers of the item's arrival within 2 days after placing the order.

In general, we are able to express constraints based on temporal variables [8] and temporal parameters [10] with the new formalism. Temporal variables are derived from the process environment as output of process activities or as parameters of received messages. They contain information about a timepoint in the future [8]. Temporal parameters are temporal variables assigned by the environment at the start of a process execution [10].

We formally define $STNU^w$ and present an approach to check whether an $STNU^w$ is agile controllable, which has polynomial-time complexity and is sound and complete, i.e., without any false positives or negatives. For the remainder of the paper, we will use the rehabilitation process as a running example to present our approach to AC for $STNU^w$.

3 Fundamental Concepts

This section formally presents the basic TCN concepts for representing uncertainty, $STNUO$ and $STNU$, and introduces $STNU^w$, a concept we propose for processes with weak contingent activities. As $STNUO$ is the most general concept, we first present its formal definition and then define $STNU$ and $STNU^w$ in terms of it. Further, their graphical representation and the concepts of dynamic and agile controllability are defined.

3.1 $STNUO$, $STNU$ and $STNU^w$

$STNUO$, Simple Temporal Network with Uncertainty and Oracles, offers modeling timepoints and temporal constraints between them, including timepoints at which the duration of contingent activities is revealed. Executable timepoints are assigned by the controller, and contingent timepoints by the environment.

Contingent timepoints are connected to an executable activation timepoint by a contingent link specifying the minimum and maximum duration between them. All other constraints are ordinary. Additionally, $STNUO$ includes oracles, executable timepoints associated with contingent timepoints, representing the timepoints at which their associated contingent duration is disclosed. $STNUO$ is thus defined as a quadruple of a set of timepoints, a set of ordinary constraints, and a set of contingent links, as well as a function that links a contingent timepoint with its oracle. To be self-contained, we repeat the formal definition from [13].

Definition 1 (STNUO [13]**).**
An STNU with Oracles (STNUO) is a quadruple $(\mathcal{T}, \mathcal{R}, \mathcal{L}, \mathcal{O})$*, where:*

- $\mathcal{T}$ *is a finite, non-empty set of real-valued variables called timepoints.* $\mathcal{T}$ *is partitioned into* $\mathcal{T}_X$*, the set of executable timepoints and* $\mathcal{T}_C$*, the set of contingent timepoints.* $\mathcal{T}_O \subseteq \mathcal{T}_X$*, is the set of oracle timepoints and* $\mathcal{T}_{CO} = \{C \in \mathcal{T}_C | \mathcal{O}(C) \in \mathcal{T}_O\}$ *is the set of contingent timepoints that have an oracle with* $\mathcal{T}_{CO} \subseteq \mathcal{T}_C$.
- $\mathcal{R}$ *is a set of binary (ordinary) constraints, each of the form* $Y - X \leq \delta$ *for some* $X, Y \in \mathcal{T}$ *and* $\delta \in \mathbb{R}$.
- $\mathcal{L}$ *is a set of* contingent links*, a special kind of constraints, each of the form* $x \leq C - A \leq y$*, where* $A \in \mathcal{T}_X, C \in \mathcal{T}_C$*, and* $x, y \in \mathbb{R} \mid 0 < x < y < \infty$*. A contingent link* $x \leq C - A \leq y$ *is also represented as* (A, x, y, C)*.* A *is called the* activation *timepoint;* C contingent *timepoint;* x *is the duration lower bound;* y *is the duration upper bound. If* (A_1, x_1, y_1, C_1) *and* (A_2, x_2, y_2, C_2) *are distinct contingent links, then* $C_1 \neq C_2$.
- $\mathcal{O}\colon \mathcal{T}_C \to \mathcal{T}_O \cup \{\bot\}$ *is a function that associates a contingent timepoint with its corresponding oracle, if any.*

Simple Temporal Network with Uncertainty ($STNU$) extends the STN concept with the possible representation of the concept of uncertain durations depending on external events, i.e., contingent durations [4,21]. As this concept is the base for $STNUO$, we formally defined $STNU$ in terms of $STNUO$ by omitting the oracle function $\mathcal{O}$.

Definition 2 (STNU). $S = (\mathcal{T}, \mathcal{R}, \mathcal{L})$ *is an* $STNU$*, iff* $S' = (\mathcal{T}, \mathcal{R}, \mathcal{L}, \emptyset)$ *be an* $STNUO$.

Next, we introduce *weak contingent* durations as contingent durations where the actual duration is revealed when the contingent activity starts. In the running rehabilitation process, T5 can be considered a weak contingent activity. *Simple Temporal Networks with Uncertainty and Weak Contingent Activities (*$STNU^w$*)* extend $STNU$ with weak contingent timepoints. We formally define $STNU^w$ as a subclass of $STNUO$, where all oracles are the activation timepoints of contingent links.

Definition 3 (STNU^w). *An* $STNUO$ $S = (\mathcal{T}, \mathcal{R}, \mathcal{L}, \mathcal{O})$ *is an* $STNU^w$*, iff* $\forall (A_i, x, y, C_i) \in \mathcal{L} : \mathcal{O}(C_i) \in \{A_i, \bot\}$.

3.2 Graph Representation

We define the distance graph of $STNUOs$, a common technique for visualizing $TCNs$.

Definition 4 (Distance Graph). *Each STNUO* $\mathcal{S} = (\mathcal{T}, \mathcal{R}, \mathcal{L}, \mathcal{O}))$ *can be expressed through its corresponding* distance graph $\mathcal{G} = (\mathcal{T}, \mathcal{E}_{\mathcal{R}} \cup \mathcal{E}_{\mathcal{L}})$. *The graph's nodes are the timepoints in* $\mathcal{T}$ *and the graph's edges, which are labeled and directed, are the constraints in* $\mathcal{R}$ *and* $\mathcal{L}$. *In particular:*

- $\mathcal{E}_{\mathcal{R}} = \{X \xrightarrow{\delta} Y \mid (Y - X \leq \delta) \in \mathcal{R}\}$
- $\mathcal{E}_{\mathcal{L}} = \{A \xrightarrow{c:x} C, C \xrightarrow{C:-y} A \mid (A, x, y, C) \in \mathcal{L}\}$

Each edge in $\mathcal{E}_{\mathcal{L}}$ indicates the uncontrollable possibility that the duration $(C - A)$ of its corresponding contingent link might take on its minimum value x/ maximum value y denoted as $A \xrightarrow{c:x} C / C \xrightarrow{C:-y} A$.

To indicate graphically, which nodes correspond to oracle timepoints (O) of contingent timepoints (C), we denote them in the following figures as O_C.

To demonstrate the graphical representation, we utilize our running example of the rehabilitation process. The mapping from a BPMN process model to a TCN model is described in [5], which, as a basic step, substitutes each activity with the corresponding start and end events; e.g., task T1 is expressed as $E_1 \xrightarrow{0} S_1$. As discussed in Sect. 2, this process includes a weak contingent activity (T5), and since the other contingent activity (T7) does not have an oracle, we can map it to an $STNU^w$. Consider that as S_5 is the oracle of E_5, we named this event O_{E5}. Accordingly, Fig. 2 visualizes the corresponding $STNU^w$ to the motivating example process in Fig. 1.

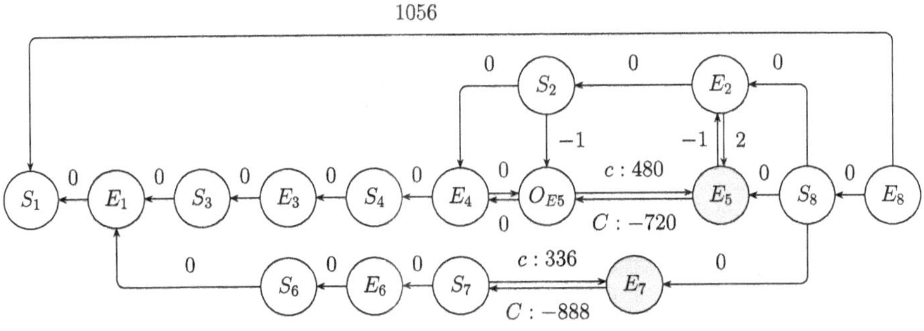

Fig. 2. $STNU^w$ of the motivating rehabilitation process

3.3 Controllability Concepts

Dynamic controllability (DC) has received the most attention for validating $STNU$. Based on knowing a contingent activity's duration only when it terminates, DC demands two properties: (1) A scenario in which later timepoints (greater assigned values) may depend on earlier timepoints (smaller assigned values) but not vice versa, and (2) such a scenario must be valid for all possible durations between the minimum and maximum known duration limit of a contingent activity [9,22].

To formally define DC, we recall some concepts from Hunsberger et al. [14].

- **Situation** A *situation* for an $STNU$ includes, for every contingent link, a *situation element* that expresses the link's actual duration assigned by the environment, which is a real value between the lower and upper bound defined with the contingent link.
- **Schedule** A *schedule* for an $STNU$ assigns a real value to each timepoint.
- **Execution Strategy** An *execution strategy* for an $STNU$ assigns a schedule for each possible situation.
- **Viable Execution Strategy** An execution strategy for an $STNU$ is *viable* if its schedule of each situation is a solution, i.e., an assignment that satisfies all the constraints.
- **History of a TCN** The set of contingent link durations observed up to and including a specific timepoint k is called *history* until k. An observed contingent link duration is, in other words, a situation element.
- **Dynamic Execution Strategy** An execution strategy for an $STNU$ is *dynamic* if for any two situations ω', ω'' and any non-contingent timepoint of the $STNU$ as k the following holds: If timepoint k is in the schedule assigned to situation ω' and if the history till timepoint k under situation ω' is the same as the history till timepoint k under situation ω'', then timepoint k is in the schedule assigned to situation ω''.

With these concepts, we can now define DC, which requires that assignments of timepoints depend only on earlier ones.

Definition 5 (Dynamic Controllability (DC) [14]). *An $STNU$ is* dynamically controllable *if there exists a viable dynamic execution strategy, that is, an execution strategy scheduling the controllable timepoints with the guarantee of satisfying all constraints, regardless of the specific duration (within the defined bounds) the contingent links will take during run-time.*

To check $STNUs$ for DC, several algorithms exist that are based on certain constraint propagation rules on the corresponding distance graph, according to which implicit constraints get derived from existing ones [3,15,16,20,21]. The DC checking algorithms propagate new edges until a *negative cycle* is found, indicating that the network is not dynamically controllable, or until no new constraints can be derived, signaling that the network is dynamically controllable.

In the following, we will use RUL, a constraint propagation system proposed by Cairo et al. [3,4]. If no execution strategies exist, RUL generates links in the distance graph which form a negative cycle [4].

Agile controllability (AC) was introduced as a more flexible notion of controllability based on $STNUO$ [13]. Now, timepoints may depend not only on earlier timepoints (see DC Definition 5), but also on those *known* earlier. It considers the knowledge that at a certain timepoint O (the oracle), the duration of a contingent activity C is revealed. To formally define AC, we first recall the definition of an *oracle-extended history* and the definition of an *agile execution strategy with oracles* from [13].

- **Oracle-extended History** It is still a set of contingent link durations observed up to and including a specific timepoint k, i.e., the contingent timepoint of the corresponding link was before or at the same time as timepoint k. But now it also includes all contingent links whose oracle was observed up to and including a specific timepoint k.
- **Agile Execution Strategy with Oracles** An execution strategy with oracles for an $STNUO$ is *agile* if for any two situations ω', ω'' and any timepoint of the $STNUO$ as k the following holds: If timepoint k is in the schedule assigned to situation ω' and if the oracle-extended history till timepoint k under situation ω' is the same as the oracle-extended history till timepoint k under situation ω'', then timepoint k is in the schedule assigned to situation ω''.

Based on these two concepts, we can formally define AC as stated in [13].

Definition 6 (Agile Controllability (AC)). *An $STNUO$ $\mathcal{N} = (\mathcal{T}, \mathcal{R}, \mathcal{L}, \mathcal{O})$ is* agile controllable *if it admits a viable agile execution strategy with oracles. We refer to agile controllability (AC) as the property of being agile controllable.*

4 Agile Controllability of $STNU^w$

To check whether an $STNU^w$ is agile controllable, we define a transformation from $STNU^w$ to an $STNU$, and prove that the transformation preserves AC. This allows us to apply algorithms for checking DC to determine the AC of weak contingent networks.

Figure 3 presents the essential transformation pattern of our proposed technique. The transformation has two steps: (I) transforming $STNU^w$ to a specific $STNUO$-pattern and (II) transforming such an $STNUO$ to $STNU$. The $STNU^w$ pattern on the left side of the figure consists of one weak contingent timepoint C and its activation timepoint A, which is also its oracle. The weak contingent duration is bound between m and M. In the first step, each weak contingent link is transformed into the pattern depicted in the middle. The idea for this transformation step is that, for any uncertain (contingent) activity duration, one knows for certain that it will at least take its minimal value m. Thus,

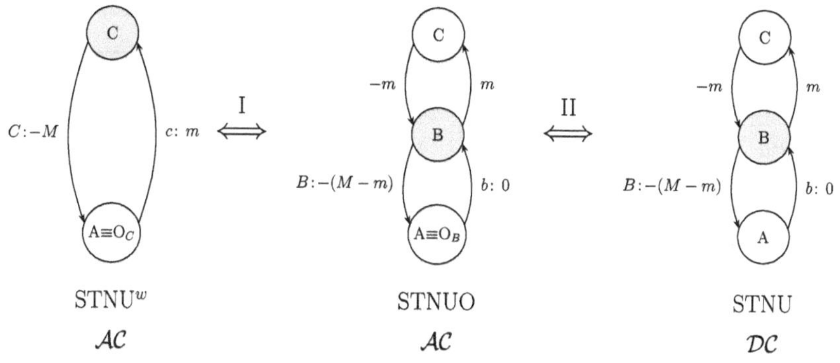

Fig. 3. Overview Proposed Transformation Technique

this transformed $STNUO$ pattern includes the same timepoints plus a new contingent timepoint B, whereas timepoint C is transformed into a non-contingent one. The new ordinary constraints between B and C express that the minimal duration m will always happen, and the new contingent link $(A, 0, M - m, B)$ represents the real uncertain time difference. Transforming step II from $STNUO$ to $STNU$ omits the oracle function and thus the oracles.

To apply DC checking algorithms to verify whether an $STNU^w$ is agile controllable, we must prove that transformation step I preserves AC and, for transformation step II, that, in this special case, AC and DC are equivalent. We prove step (I) by establishing mappings at the following three levels: situation, schedule, and execution strategy. The proof of step (II) uses the characteristic established by Cairo and Rizzi [4], namely that DC under RUL is preserved even if a contingent duration is revealed at any time between the activation timepoint plus the minimal duration and the contingent timepoint, rather than only at the contingent timepoint. Here, we present the proof sketches; the complete proofs can be found in a technical report publicly available in an online repository[1].

4.1 Transformation Formalization

First, we formally define the transformation between $STNU^w$s and $STNUO$s

Definition 7 (Transformation I $STNU^w$ to $STNUO$).
Let S be an $STNU^w$ with $(\mathcal{T}, \mathcal{R}, \mathcal{L}, \mathcal{O})$, with $\mathcal{T} = \mathcal{T}_X \cup \mathcal{T}_C$, $\mathcal{T}_O \subseteq \mathcal{T}_X$ is the set of oracle timepoints and $\mathcal{T}_{CO} = \{C \in \mathcal{T}_C | \mathcal{O}(C) \in \mathcal{T}_O\}$ is the set of contingent timepoints that have an oracle with $\mathcal{T}_{CO} \subseteq \mathcal{T}_C$. Let $\mathcal{B}$ be a function that creates new contingent timepoints and assigns one to each timepoint in $\mathcal{T}_{CO}$.

Let S' be an $STNUO$ with $(\mathcal{T}', \mathcal{C}', \mathcal{L}', \mathcal{O}')$, $\mathcal{T}' = \mathcal{T}'_X \cup \mathcal{T}'_C$ and $S' = \sigma(S, \mathcal{B})$ with the transformation σ defined as described in Algorithm 1.

For this transformation step, we have to prove the preservation of the AC property.

[1] https://github.com/ziss05/STNUW.

Algorithm 1: σ

Input: S **Output:** S' **Side Effect:** $\mathcal{T}', \mathcal{C}', \mathcal{L}', \mathcal{O}'$ are manipulated.

$\mathcal{T}_O' \leftarrow \mathcal{T}_O$
foreach $X \in \mathcal{T}_X \setminus \mathcal{T}_O$ **do** $\mathcal{T}_X' \leftarrow \mathcal{T}_X' \cup X$
foreach $X \in \mathcal{T}_{CO}$ **do** $\mathcal{T}_X' \leftarrow \mathcal{T}_X' \cup X$; $\mathcal{T}_C' \leftarrow \mathcal{T}_C' \cup \mathcal{B}(X)$
foreach $X \in \mathcal{T}_C \setminus \mathcal{T}_{CO}$ **do** $\mathcal{T}_C' \leftarrow \mathcal{T}_C' \cup X$
foreach $(Y - X \leq \delta) \in \mathcal{R}$ **do** $\mathcal{T}_R' \leftarrow \mathcal{T}_R' \cup (Y - X \leq \delta)$
foreach $(A, m, M, C) \in \mathcal{L} : A \in \mathcal{T}_O, C \in \mathcal{T}_{CO}$ **do**
    $\mathcal{T}_R' \leftarrow \mathcal{T}_R' \cup (C - \mathcal{B}(X) \leq m), (\mathcal{B}(X) - C \leq -m)$
    $\mathcal{L}' \leftarrow \mathcal{L}' \cup (A, 0, M - m, \mathcal{B}(C))$
foreach $(A, m, M, C) \in \mathcal{L} : A \notin \mathcal{T}_O$ **do** $\mathcal{T}_L' \leftarrow \mathcal{T}_L' \cup (A, m, M, C)$
foreach $C \in \mathcal{T}_C \setminus \mathcal{T}_{CO}$ **do** $\mathcal{O}'(C) = \mathcal{O}(C) = \bot$
foreach $C \in \mathcal{T}_{CO}$ **do** $\mathcal{O}'(\mathcal{B}(C)) = \mathcal{O}(C)$

Theorem 1. *Let S be an $STNU^w$, S' an $STNUO$ with $\sigma(S, \mathcal{B}) = S'$. If S is agile controllable, S' is agile controllable, and vice versa.*

Proof. Sketch. To prove the preservation of AC, we first establish mappings between situations and between schedules, which we then leverage to prove a mapping at the execution strategy level.

At the situation level, for a situation for S and a corresponding situation for S' we prove that for all contingent links without oracle the same situation elements are present in those two situations and that for the weak contingent links, if a situation for S has an element for a weak contingent link, the corresponding situation for S' includes the element for the derived new contingent link.

At the schedule level, the mapping is proved over subset relations based on the fact that a schedule for S' includes all timepoints of S as elements, plus computed values for the additional timepoints.

At the execution strategy level, we first prove that if a viable execution strategy exists for S, then one exists for S', and vice versa, by showing that all constraints are satisfied in both cases, leveraging the mappings proven at the situation and schedule levels and the transformation definition. Next, we prove that if S admits a viable agile execution strategy, S is agile controllable, and further, a viable agile execution strategy for S' exists, then S' is also agile controllable, and vice versa. The main revelation of this proof is that a specific OH of S is equal to a specific OH of S', as the newly introduced contingent nodes in S' for the weak contingent nodes in S have the same oracle as their corresponding contingent node pendant in S'.

□

Next, we define transformation step II from an $STNUO$ S' to an $STNU$ S'' and prove that in this case the AC of the input $STNUO$ is equivalent to the DC of the output $STNU$.

Definition 8 (Transformation II $STNUO$ **to** $STNU$**).**
Let S be an $STNU^w$. Let S'' be an $STNUO$ with $(\mathcal{T}',\mathcal{C}',\mathcal{L}',\mathcal{O}')$ such that $S' = \sigma(S,\mathcal{B})$, and S'' be an $STNU$ with $(\mathcal{T}'',\mathcal{C}'',\mathcal{L}'')$. The transformation $\sigma' : S' \rightarrow S''$ is defined as follows: $S'' = \sigma'(S)$ iff $\mathcal{T}'' = \mathcal{T}', \mathcal{R}'' = \mathcal{R}', \mathcal{L}'' = \mathcal{L}'$.

Theorem 2. *Let S be an $STNU^w$, S' an $STNUO$ and S'' an $STNU$ such that $S' = \sigma(S,\mathcal{B})$ and $\sigma'(S') = S''$. Iff there exists a viable dynamic execution strategy for S'' by applying RUL [4], there exists a viable agile execution strategy for S' and vice versa.*

Proof. The proof is based on the application of Corollary 20 in [4], which states that RUL remains correct, even if the duration of a contingent link is revealed already at the activation timepoint plus the minimal duration (or any time thereafter). S' and S'' have the same contingent links. All contingent links $(A, x, y, B) \in S'$ with $\mathcal{O}'(B) = A$ have a lower bound $x = 0$. Hence, the result of RUL applied to S'' holds if each duration of these links is revealed at the activation time A. Since $\mathcal{O}'(B) = A$: the duration for each contingent link $(A, x, y, B) \in S'$ with $\mathcal{O}'(B) = A$ will be revealed at timepoint A. So, if Σ'' is dynamically controllable, then Σ' is also dynamically controllable. And since an agile controllable execution strategy Σ' for S'' allows for timepoints to be dependent on earlier revealed ones, there exists a viable agile execution strategy for S'', if there exists a viable dynamic execution strategy for S'' by applying RUL [4] and vice versa.

□

The overall characteristic that must be proven is that S is agile controllable if and only if S'' is dynamically controllable under RUL.

Theorem 3. *Let S be an $STNU^w$, S' an $STNUO$, and S'' an $STNU$ with $\sigma(S,\mathcal{B}) = S'$ and $\sigma'(S') = S''$. S is agile controllable iff RUL applied to S'' determines that S'' is dynamically controllable.*

Proof. Follows directly from Theorem 1 and Theorem 2.

4.2 Transformation Example

As described in Sect. 3.2, the motivating example can be expressed by $STNU^w$, see Fig. 2. Therefore, we can apply our proposed technique to check whether this process is agile controllable. Applying the two transformation steps, the $STNU$ depicted in Fig. 4 results. Consider that the event O_{E5} is renamed to S_5 as $STNU$ does not have oracles. Utilizing now any of the available RUL-based algorithms for checking DC [3,15–17] of this $STNU$, the result would be positive. Thus, because of Theorem 3, since this $STNU$ is dynamically controllable, the original $STNU^w$ is agile controllable. Hence, the motivating rehabilitation process can be implemented so that the execution will be free of any temporal requirement conflicts.

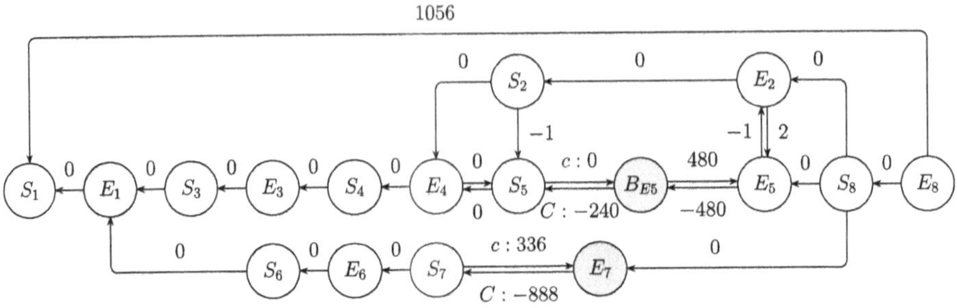

Fig. 4. *STNU* of the motivating rehabilitation process as output of σ

5 Evaluation and Discussion

In this section, we discuss the effectiveness and efficiency of our proposed approach. Since our transformation preserves the properties of RUL-based *DC* checking algorithms - which are proven to return only true positive or negative answers - our approach is inherently effective. Because the transformation has linear complexity, $O(n)$, the efficiency of the underlying *DC* algorithm is critical. We evaluate two variants: *RUL2021* [15], which performs significantly better in practice than its $O(mn + k2n + kn \log n)$ worst-case complexity, and *FindSRNC* [17], a variant that provides tracking conflicting constraints.

We conducted two separate experiments: first, a comparison of the runtimes between our implementation of the *RUL2021* and *FindSRNC* variants, and second, a comparison of our approach against the baseline *AC2025* [13] across varying $STNU^w$ sizes. Here, we present in the following only the baseline experiment. The comparison between the two *DC* variants is detailed in our technical report, which is available in an online repository[2], together with the full results and source code for both experiments.

The baseline experiment was conducted on an Apple M3 Pro (36 GB RAM). We used *STNURandomGenerator* via the *CSTNU-Tool*[3] to generate *STNU* instances, which we then adapted to construct $STNU^w$ instances, which are not *DC* but *AC*, resulting in 15 examples per category (node counts: 34, 44, 54, and 64, with 4, 5, 6, and 7 contingent nodes, respectively). The execution times in Fig. 5 represent the mean across these 15 instances per category, where each instance is the average of 10 independent runs. As shown in Fig. 5, our approach exhibits linear runtime, whereas the *AC2025* baseline is exponential. With execution times in the millisecond range, our approach is highly efficient.

6 Related Work

Using the concept of *TCN* for verifying the feasibility of process models under temporal constraints must be distinguished from research on compliance check-

[2] https://github.com/ziss05/STNUW.
[3] https://profs.scienze.univr.it/posenato/software/cstnu/index.html.

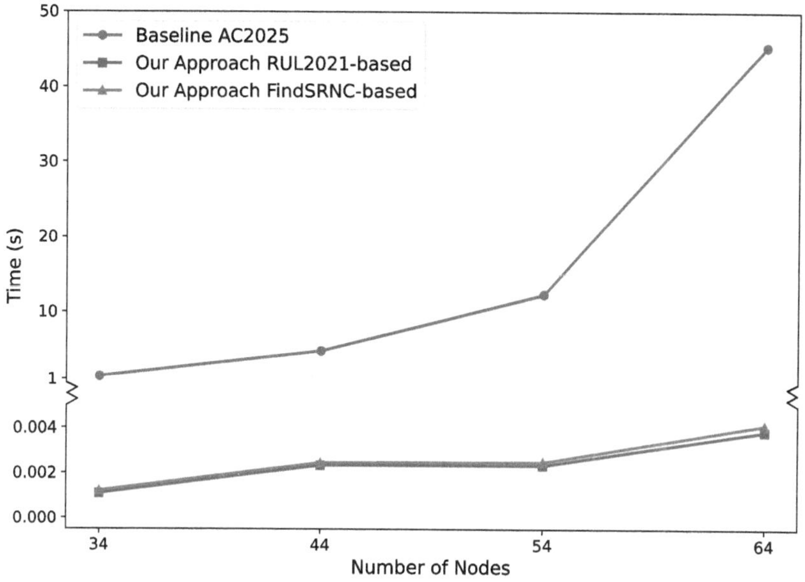

Fig. 5. Execution times in seconds for the three algorithms by node count

ing with conceptual models [18]. While compliance checks during the execution of processes, whether they adhered to the requirements, the research on TCN concepts aims to support the design of processes with temporal requirements, assuring the absence of conflicts among the temporal requirements.

The proposed approach for the subclass of weak contingent activities is distinguished from other approaches by how it represents when a contingent duration is revealed. While the duration of weak contingent tasks is known at the task's start, but set by the environment, the duration of semi-contingent tasks [11] is decided by the controller until the task begins. Another research direction focuses on the concept of *weak controllability* [25], in which all contingent durations are assumed to be known at the process start, and can be seen as a special case of AC. Temporal information may also be obtained from the process environment in the form of temporal variables [8]. Another approach to making contingent links more flexible is the concept of a guarded link: a contingent link whose duration is uncontrollable by the system but can be bounded by guards [23]. Another research direction investigates the degree of strong and dynamic controllability for $STNU$. Thus, *Probabilistic Simple Temporal Networks (PSTN)* are proposed in [1]. The work's focus is on determining the degree to which a network is controllable by proposing metrics for the approximation of how probable it is that offline (strong controllability) or online (dynamic controllability) dispatching is successful. The robustness of $PSTN$ is examined in [24]. The works [10,12] provide further flexibility by extending the concepts $STNU$ and $CSTNU$ (Conditional Simple Temporal Networks with Uncertainty), with temporal parameters. Parameters are assigned by the environment at the start of the process, i.e., their execution time is revealed at this event, and their occurrence is independent of that of any other timepoint.

7 Conclusion

This work contributes to exploring a basic concern of conceptual modeling: the trade-off between the expressiveness of a modeling language and the complexity of checking properties of models like consistency, conflicts, or, in this case, controllability. The new concept of weak contingent activities, where the duration of a contingent activity is known when the activity starts, leads to $STNU^w$, which extends the expressiveness of $STNU$ while the complexity of checking remains polynomial. It can also be seen as the identification of a subclass of $STNUO$ which admits efficient, scalable checking procedures. In a series of small examples, we demonstrated that the expressiveness is sufficient to model a large set of practically relevant scenarios. Ongoing research includes the identification of patterns in $STNUO$ models that can losslessly be mapped to $STNU^w$, leading to more efficient checking of agile controllability in many cases.

References

1. Akmal, S., Ammons, S., Li, H., Gao, M., Popowski, L., Jr, J.C.B.: Quantifying controllability in temporal networks with uncertainty. Artif. Intell. **289**, 103384 (2020)
2. Arnold, B., et al.: Multimodale Schmerztherapie. Der Schmerz **23**(2), 112–120 (2009)
3. Cairo, M., Hunsberger, L., Rizzi, R.: Faster dynamic controllability checking for simple temporal networks with uncertainty. In: 25th International Symposium on Temporal Representation and Reasoning (TIME 2018). LIPIcs, vol. 120, pp. 8:1–8:16 (2018)
4. Cairo, M., Rizzi, R.: Dynamic controllability of simple temporal networks with uncertainty: simple rules and fast real-time execution. Theoret. Comput. Sci. **797**, 2–16 (2019)
5. Combi, C., Gambini, M., Migliorini, S., Posenato, R.: Representing business processes through a temporal data-centric workflow modeling language: an application to the management of clinical pathways. IEEE Trans. Syst. Man Cybern. Syst. **44**(9), 1182–1203 (2014)
6. Combi, C., Pozzi, G.: Temporal conceptual modelling of workflows. In: Song, I.-Y., Liddle, S.W., Ling, T.-W., Scheuermann, P. (eds.) ER 2003. LNCS, vol. 2813, pp. 59–76. Springer, Heidelberg (2003). https://doi.org/10.1007/978-3-540-39648-2_8
7. Dechter, R., Meiri, I., Pearl, J.: Temporal constraint networks. Artif. Intell. **49**(1–3), 61–95 (1991)
8. Eder, J., Franceschetti, M., Köpke, J.: Controllability of business processes with temporal variables. In: ACM SAC 2019, pp. 40–47 (2019)
9. Eder, J., Franceschetti, M., Lubas, J.: Time and processes: towards engineering temporal requirements. In: Fill, H.G. (ed.) Proceedings of the 16th ICSOFT 2021, vol. 1, pp. 9–16. SciTePress (2021)

10. Franceschetti, M., Eder, J.: Checking temporal service level agreements for web service compositions with temporal parameters. In: 2019 IEEE International Conference on Web Services (ICWS), pp. 443–445. IEEE (2019)
11. Franceschetti, M., Eder, J.: Semi-contingent task durations: characterization and controllability. In: Rosa, M.L., Sadiq, S.W., Teniente, E. (eds.) Advanced Information Systems Engineering - 33rd International Conference, CAiSE 2021, Melbourne, VIC, Australia, June 28 - July 2, 2021, Proceedings. LNCS, vol. 12751, pp. 246–261. Springer (2021)
12. Franceschetti, M., Posenato, R., Combi, C., Eder, J.: Dynamic controllability of parameterized cstnus. In: Proceedings of the 38th ACM/SIGAPP Symposium on Applied Computing, pp. 965–973 (2023)
13. Hollauf, F.S., Posenato, R., Combi, C., Eder, J.: Modeling oracles in simple temporal networks with uncertainty. Inf. Comput. **307**, 105382 (2025)
14. Hunsberger, L.: Efficient execution of dynamically controllable simple temporal networks with uncertainty. Acta Informatica **53**, 89–147 (2016)
15. Hunsberger, L., Posenato, R.: Speeding up the RUL^- dynamic-controllability-checking algorithm for simple temporal networks with uncertainty. In: Proceedings of the 36th AAAI Conference on Artificial Intelligence, vol. 36, pp. 9776–9785. AAAI Press (2022)
16. Hunsberger, L., Posenato, R.: A faster algorithm for converting simple temporal networks with uncertainty into dispatchable form. Inf. Comput. **293** (2023)
17. Hunsberger, L., Posenato, R.: A faster algorithm for finding negative cycles in simple temporal networks with uncertainty. In: Sala, P., Sioutis, M., Wang, F. (eds.) 31st International Symposium on Temporal Representation and Reasoning (TIME 2024). LIPIcs, vol. 318, pp. 9:1–9:15. Schloss Dagstuhl – Leibniz-Zentrum für Informatik, Dagstuhl, Germany (2024)
18. Knuplesch, D., Reichert, M., Ly, L.T., Kumar, A., Rinderle-Ma, S.: Visual modeling of business process compliance rules with the support of multiple perspectives. In: Ng, W., Storey, V.C., Trujillo, J.C. (eds.) Conceptual Modeling, pp. 106–120. Springer, Heidelberg (2013)
19. Lanz, A., Reichert, M., Weber, B.: Process time patterns: a formal foundation. Inf. Syst. **57**, 38–68 (2016)
20. Morris, P.: Dynamic controllability and dispatchability relationships. In: Simonis, H. (ed.) CPAIOR 2014. LNCS, vol. 8451, pp. 464–479. Springer, Cham (2014). https://doi.org/10.1007/978-3-319-07046-9_33
21. Morris, P.H., Muscettola, N.: Temporal dynamic controllability revisited. In: 20th National Conference on AI, pp. 1193–1198 (2005)
22. Posenato, R., Franceschetti, M., Combi, C., Eder, J.: Introducing agile controllability in temporal business processes. In: Enterprise, Business-Process and Information Systems Modeling - 25th International Conference, BPMDS 2024, and 29th International Conference, EMMSAD 2024. LNBIP, vol. 511, pp. 87–99. Springer (2024)
23. Posenato, R., Lanz, A., Combi, C., Reichert, M.: Managing time-awareness in modularized processes. Softw. Syst. Model. **18**(2), 1135–1154 (2019)
24. Saint-Guillain, M., Vaquero, T., Chien, S.A., Agrawal, J., Abrahams, J.R.: Probabilistic temporal networks with ordinary distributions: theory, robustness and expected utility. J. AI Res. **71**, 1091–1136 (2021)
25. Vidal, T., Fargier, H.: Handling contingency in temporal constraint networks: from consistency to controllabilities. J. Exp. Theor. AI **11**(1) (1999)

Object or Resource? Capturing Conceptual Type Differences in Object-Centric Process Mining

Maximilian König[1(✉)], Arsalan Ghasemi[1], Simon Nowack[1], Anjo Seidel[1], Jan Niklas van Detten[2], and Mathias Weske[1]

[1] Hasso Plattner Institute, University of Potsdam, Potsdam, Germany
{maximilian.koenig,arsalan.ghasemi,anjo.seidel,mathias.weske}@hpi.de, simon-michael.nowack@student.hpi.de
[2] RWTH Aachen University, Aachen, Germany
n.vandetten@bpm.rwth-aachen.de

Abstract. Object-centric process mining enables comprehensive analysis of information systems by representing different perspectives on system behavior through object types. Such behavior is captured in object-centric event logs, where events are correlated via co-evolving objects of different types. Currently, these object types are treated as conceptually homogeneous in analyses, even though objects represent quite different entities involved in business processes, such as data objects and resources. Based on a literature survey, this paper argues that data objects and resources exhibit fundamentally different behavioral characteristics. These differences, along with organizational roles that resources can play, significantly hamper the analysis of object-centric event logs. To bring this perspective into object-centric process mining, we extend the metamodel of object-centric event logs with the concepts of resources and roles. Additionally, we introduce methods for identifying resources and roles in existing object-centric event logs, thereby enabling their transformation into the novel, extended metamodel. To evaluate the approach, we introduce a prototypical implementation and apply it to a set of publicly available event logs.

Keywords: Object-centric Process Mining · Organizational Mining · Metamodel Extension · Resource Discovery · Role Discovery

1 Introduction

Business processes describe the structured execution of activities in an organizational context to achieve a certain goal [27]. Traditionally, these business processes are considered from one dominant perspective, called a case notion, which groups recorded events into distinct process executions, called cases [20]. In an order management process, such a case notion could be the different orders so

© The Author(s), under exclusive license to Springer Nature Switzerland AG 2027
A. Bernasconi et al. (Eds.): ER 2026, LNCS 17081, pp. 306–322, 2027.
https://doi.org/10.1007/978-3-032-40795-5_18

that each case includes all activities executed from the placement to the delivery of a single order. However, looking at a process from a single perspective provides a limited view of its overall behavior.

To enable multi-perspective analysis, Object-centric Process Mining (OCPM) was introduced [20,21]. The paradigm proposes to consider all entities in a process as interacting objects with individual behavior. These objects are categorized into object types (e.g., orders, items, or employees) based on their shared attributes and roles in the system. To capture their interaction, events reference all involved objects. Therewith, each object type, or set of object types, may serve as a case notion, which enables grouping and analyzing events from multiple perspectives [3]. In the order management process, other perspectives include the individual items in an order or the employees executing the process, each resulting in different process representations and analysis aspects.

Several data formats, including object-centric event data (OCED) [8] and object-centric event logs (OCEL) [5], have been proposed to capture object-centric process instances. They are the foundation of the entire process mining pipeline that processes these logs to generate insights from real-world data. Steps in the pipeline include event log extraction [26], identifying case notions [3], process discovery [22,23], conformance checking [10,17], performance analysis [16], and what-if analysis through process simulation [13].

Current data formats and their corresponding analytical techniques fail to capture the conceptual differences between object types. In reality, resources, such as employees and software systems, exhibit characteristics distinct from those of non-resource objects, such as orders and documents, and are typically organized into roles, such as sales and logistics. For readability purposes, we will refer to non-resource objects as objects hereinafter. Disregarding these differences in the underlying data formats fundamentally impacts analyses based on them. While some OCPM approaches introduce individual distinctions for specific steps of the pipeline, e.g., identifying object-centric case notions [24] and process discovery [15,25], they are not yet integrated in other tasks [4,13,16,17].

To address this gap, we propose a behavioral characterization of resources and roles based on a literature survey and integrate these concepts with object-centric event logs. The contribution of this paper is twofold: (i) We extend the metamodel of object-centric event logs with the concepts of resources and roles to accommodate their characteristics in object-centric process mining. (ii) To provide backward compatibility with existing object-centric event logs, we define a set of metrics based on behavioral information present in current logs to automatically identify resource types. The practical feasibility is demonstrated by a prototypical implementation that applies the discovery and transforms existing event logs to match the extended metamodel.

The remainder of this paper is structured as follows: Sect. 2 introduces the current metamodel of object-centric event logs and presents a literature survey based on which characteristics of resource behavior and roles are discussed. Next, Sect. 3 presents the conceptual integration with object-centric event logs, while Sect. 4 presents our automated discovery approach to transform existing event logs to adhere to the extended metamodel. Section 5 evaluates our approach before Sect. 6 positions our work against existing literature and discusses our findings and Sect. 7 concludes the paper.

2 Background

In this section, we first introduce the metamodel of existing object-centric event log formats. Next, we motivate the distinction between resources and objects as well as the inclusion of roles in these data formats to support downstream analysis. Finally, we detail three characteristics identified in the literature that serve as indicators for resource-like behavior in object-centric event logs.

2.1 Object-Centric Event Logs

The metamodel for object-centric event logs defines which elements of a process are recorded and how they are related to one another. As such, it forms the conceptual basis for any implementation of object-centric event logs. The proposed metamodel is visualized in Fig. 1 as a UML class diagram. Recorded events represent an activity and have a timestamp as well as event attribute values belonging to an event attribute. Analogously, objects have an object type and object attribute values belonging to object attributes. Objects can have a qualified relation to other objects. Events are related to objects in a many-to-many relationship that may be refined through qualifiers.

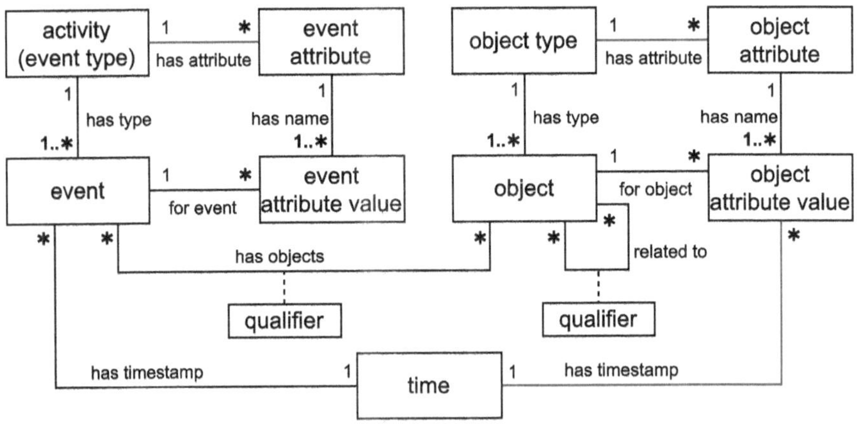

Fig. 1. Metamodel of object-centric event logs based on OCEL 2.0 [5] and OCED [8]. Black elements represent the overlap between both approaches; blue elements are part of OCEL 2.0 only; and green elements are specific to OCED. (Color figure online)

There are two main implementations of the metamodel, namely Object-centric Event Logs (OCEL) 2.0 [5] and Object-centric Event Data (OCED) [8].

Both agree on the core concepts while introducing some individual adaptations, as highlighted by the colored elements in Fig. 1. OCEL 2.0 assigns timestamps to object attribute values and explicitly links object and event attributes to the respective types. OCED requires at least one instance for each activity, object type, event attribute, and object attribute to exist in a log.

While the metamodel refers to an abstract schema, object-centric event logs represent the actual recordings in corresponding file format implementations. To formalize these logs, we assume the following universes to exist: $\mathbb{U}_e$ (events), $\mathbb{U}_o$ (objects), $\mathbb{U}_a$ (activities), $\mathbb{U}_{ot}$ (object types), and $\mathbb{U}_{time}$ (timestamps). Based thereon, we adapt the definition of an object-centric event log from [21]:

Definition 1 (Object-Centric Event Log). *An object-centric event log is a 6-tuple* $(E, O, A, OT, E2O, \mathsf{time})$ *where* $E \subseteq \mathbb{U}_e$ *is a set of events,* $O \subseteq \mathbb{U}_o$ *is a set of objects,* $A \subseteq \mathbb{U}_a$ *is a set of activities,* $OT \subseteq \mathbb{U}_{ot}$ *is a set of object types,* $E2O \subseteq E \times O$ *holds the relations between each event and its involved objects, and* $\mathsf{time} : E \to \mathbb{U}_{time}$ *is an injective function assigning each event a unique timestamp. Functions* $\mathsf{etype} : E \to A$ *and* $\mathsf{otype} : O \to OT$ *map events and objects to their activities and object types, respectively.*

Note that the formalization does not implement the entire metamodel but only the relevant concepts for this work. For abbreviation, we will use subscripts on sets to refer to certain subsets, i.e., $O_{ot} = \{o \in O \mid \mathsf{otytpe}(o) = ot\}$ for all objects of object type ot, $O_e = \{o \in O \mid (e, o) \in E2O\}$ for all objects in the $E2O$ relation of event e, and $E_a = \{e \in E \mid \mathsf{etype}(e) = a\}$ for all events of activity a.

An example log representing an order management process is shown in Fig. 2, together with a visualization of the process flow and relevant object types. The process involves four object types, namely *Order*, *Item*, *Package*, and *Employee*. Initially, an order is registered together with the ordered items. The individual items are procured before a set of items for an order is packed into a package. The package is delivered, potentially in several attempts. Concurrently, the order must be invoiced. Once delivery and invoicing are completed, the order can be archived. Each activity requires the participation of an employee.

2.2 Conceptual Type Differences in Downstream Analysis

Extracted from real-world processes, object-centric event logs typically move through a process mining pipeline consisting of preprocessing, process discovery, conformance checking, performance analysis, and simulation. In this section, we survey current literature structured along these pipeline steps to investigate how the missing object differentiation impacts these phases.

As shown in the metamodel depicted in Fig. 1, current object-centric event log standards treat all entities uniformly as objects. Hence, contemporary event log extraction approaches for object-centric event logs do not explicitly include resources and roles [26]. However, for event log preprocessing, van Detten et al. [24] leverage resource-like behavior to discover object-centric case notions based on which analyses can be conducted. In the discovery step, Liss et al.

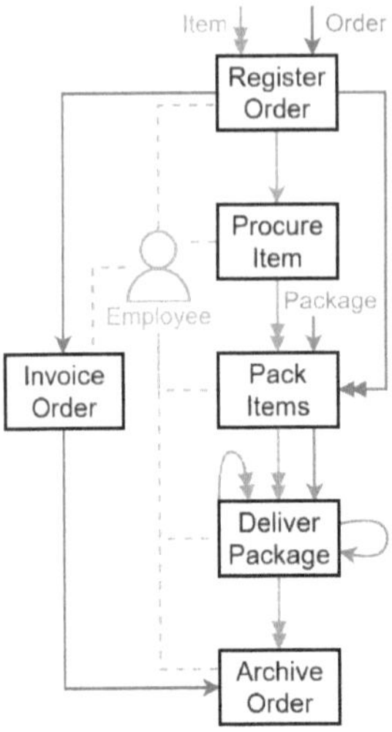

Event ID	Event Type	Timestamp	Related Objects
ev01	Register Order	2026-03-18 08:00	O1, I1, I2, E1
ev02	Procure Item	2026-03-18 09:00	I1, E1
ev03	Procure Item	2026-03-18 14:00	I2, E1
ev04	Register Order	2026-03-18 14:05	O2, I3, E1
ev05	Procure Item	2026-03-18 14:47	I3, E1
ev06	Invoice Order	2026-03-18 15:28	O2, E1
ev07	Pack Items	2026-03-18 16:00	O1, O2, I1, I2, I3, P1, E1
ev08	Invoice Order	2026-03-18 16:25	O1, E1
ev09	Deliver Package	2026-03-18 20:00	I1, I2, I3, P1, E3
ev10	Deliver Package	2026-03-19 07:00	I1, I2, I3, P1, E3
ev11	Archive Order	2026-03-19 08:00	O1, I1, I2, E2
ev12	Register Order	2026-03-19 08:25	O3, I4, I5, I6, E1
ev13	Archive Order	2026-03-19 08:55	O2, I3, E1
...	...	...	...
ev97	Invoice Order	2026-05-10 18:00	O8, E2
ev98	Deliver Package	2026-05-11 10:00	I27, I28, P9, E3
ev99	Archive Order	2026-05-11 11:00	O8, I27, I28, E1

Fig. 2. An informal process model depicting an order management process alongside an excerpt of an object-centric event log of the process. Colored edges differentiate the flow of different object types. Green, red, and blue edges indicate the flow of objects of types item, order, and package, respectively. Double arrowheads denote that several objects of that object type are involved in the same event corresponding to the activity. The dashed lines show the involvement of an employee in the respective activity. (Color figure online)

hierarchically structure processes derived from an event log based on resource-like behavior to improve the understandability of the resulting models [15]. To discover models with higher precision, SYSOC nets introduce a role-like concept, differentiating specializations in object types to group objects with similar behavior [25]. Current performance analysis techniques on object-centric event logs do not yet explicitly account for resource-specific aspects [17], thus not including performance measures that have been proposed for traditional process mining [7]. While the resource and role concepts are essential to case-centric process simulation and have received more attention recently [12], their lack of representation in object-centric event logs is mentioned as a limiting factor to object-centric process simulation approaches [13]. In addition, the application of OCPM for agent-based modeling and simulation has been proposed [4], which relies on the clear conceptual separation between autonomous agents and the objects they manipulate [9]. To facilitate the use of object-centric event logs in areas such as explainable AI, Adams et al. propose a feature extraction approach and highlight resources as a relevant dimension to consider [2].

The lack of distinction also highlights a gap between object-centric process modeling and process mining. Process modeling frameworks with the goal of model-driven engineering, such as PHILharmonicFlows [14] and fragment-based

Case Management [19], already incorporate a clear separation between resources with roles and objects that is not reflected in object-centric event logs.

2.3 Characteristics of Resource Behavior

The literature survey shows that several works along the OCPM pipeline either already utilize a resource-object differentiation or explicitly call for its introduction. In this section, we analyze approaches that introduce a notion of resource-like behavior to identify relevant characteristics that may be used for its automated discovery. Analogously, we examine existing role detection methodologies to inform our approach.

1. *Extended Object Lifetime.* Unlike objects that exist only for the duration of their processing, resources remain within an organization to handle numerous process instances. Consequently, their average lifetime, that is, the duration between their first and last appearance in an event log, is typically much longer than that of other objects. In process discovery, Liss et al. use this characteristic to better structure the complex behavior captured in object-centric event logs that may include execution data from several processes at the same time [15].
2. *Divergent Behavior.* Resources tend to be involved in several process instances. Thus, they execute the same activities multiple times, involving different sets of objects, which is called *divergence* [24]. For example, an employee may register several orders with different items. This results in single objects being hubs connected to many other objects. Therewith, it becomes difficult to identify otherwise disconnected groups of objects representing individual cases in object-centric event logs [24].
3. *Unstructured Individual Behavior.* While objects generally follow a strict, predefined lifecycle, resources are often involved in several cases concurrently. This results in individual behavior that is significantly less structured and more flexible than that of other objects. Therefore, object-centric modeling approaches that rely on the definition of individual object behavior tend to model resources as separate concepts instead of modeling highly connected object lifecycle graphs [14,19].

Roles. In object-centric event logs, a single object type may include several sets of specialized objects that exhibit different behavior. If that is not detected in process discovery, resulting models will be imprecise, since they allow for additional behavior that was not recorded in the log. To address that, SYSOC nets identify subsets among the objects of an object type that share the same behavior [25]. They explicitly incorporate this information in the discovered model to constrain process execution, thereby improving precision. While not specific to resources, the approach to group objects by the activities they are involved in is in line with *role* discovery approaches for traditional process mining [28]. From a modeling perspective, the differentiation according to capabilities also constitutes the main dimension along which roles are defined [14,19].

In summary, this survey shows the relevance of representing resource types and roles explicitly. Several approaches already define individual notions of resource-like behavior and roles tailored to their specific research objective. To unify these definitions, we propose extending the metamodel with these concepts, which will be addressed in Sect. 3. By leveraging the identified behavioral characteristics from these approaches, we can automatically detect resource-like object types and subsequently discover associated roles. This approach, detailed in Sect. 4, ensures backward compatibility between existing object-centric event logs and the extended metamodel.

3 Resources in Object-Centric Event Logs

In this section, we extend the object-centric event log metamodel to capture the distinction between resources and objects as well as the concept of roles. When extending the metamodel, a primary design goal is ensuring backward compatibility with existing approaches that do not utilize this differentiation. Hence, we introduce the classes *resource type* and *resource* as specializations of *object type* and *object*, respectively, thus making their use optional for existing approaches. Through this specialization, resource types and resources inherit the associations to object attributes, their corresponding values, and events. In addition, the association between events and resources signifies which resources an event was executed with.

As proposed in organizational mining approaches for traditional process mining [28], roles group resources according to their exhibited behavior, and resources may generally be part of several roles. Therefore, we introduce *role* as a separate class associated with resources through an `m:n` relationship. We set a lower bound of 1 on both ends to include only roles that contain at least one resource and to indicate that each resource belongs to at least one role. An `m:n` association between roles and resource types explicitly allows roles to include resources of several types. The resulting extended metamodel is depicted in Fig. 3 as a UML class diagram.

Formally, we represent an event log adhering to the extended metamodel and extending on Definition 1 as follows. We assume universes $\mathbb{U}_{rt} \subset \mathbb{U}_{ot}$ for resource types, $\mathbb{U}_r \subset \mathbb{U}_o$ for resources, and $\mathbb{U}_{rl}$ for roles.

Definition 2 (Object-Centric Event Log with Resources and Roles). *An object-centric event log with resources and roles is an 11-tuple* $(E, O, R, A, OT, RT, RL, E2O, E2R, R2RL, \mathsf{time})$ *where*

- $(E, O, A, OT, E2O, \mathsf{time})$ *is an object-centric event log,*
- $RT \subseteq \mathbb{U}_{rt}$ *is a set of resource types,*
- $R \subseteq \mathbb{U}_r$ *is a set of resources with* $\mathsf{rtype} : R \to RT$ *assigning each resource to exactly one resource type,*
- $E2R \subseteq E \times R$ *is the event-to-resource relation,*
- $RL \subseteq \mathbb{U}_{rl}$ *is a set of roles,*

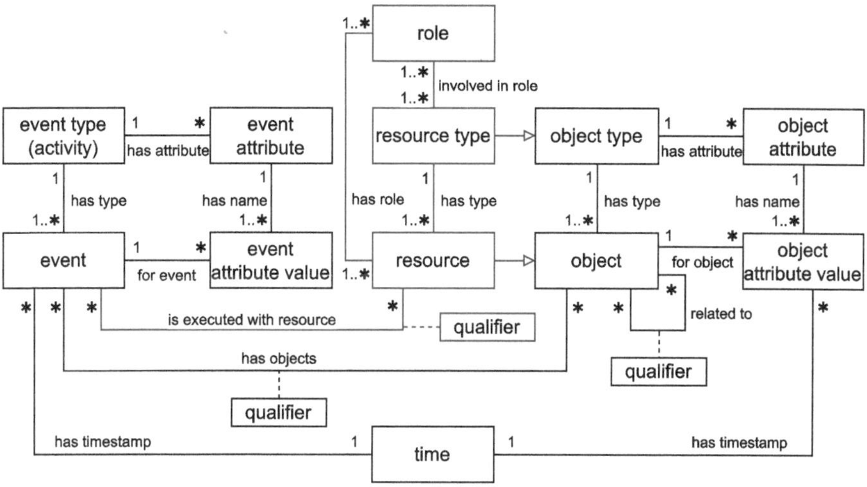

Fig. 3. Metamodel of object-centric event logs extended with resource-related concepts. Newly added elements are highlighted in red and include *resource*, *resource type*, and *role*.

- $R2RL \subseteq R \times RL$ *is the resource-to-role relation such that each resource is associated with at least one role and vice versa, i.e.,* $\forall r \in R, \exists rl \in RL : (r, rl) \in R2RL$ *and* $\forall rl \in RL, \exists r \in R : (r, rl) \in R2RL$*, and*
- $RT2RL \subseteq RT \times RL$ *is the resource-type-to-role relation such that each resource type is associated with at least one role and vice versa, i.e.,* $\forall rt \in RT, \exists rl \in RL : (rt, rl) \in RT2RL$ *and* $\forall rl \in RL, \exists rt \in RT : (rt, rl) \in RT2RL$

In the order management example in Fig. 2, only object type *Employee* classifies as a resource type. The event log includes three resources: $E1$, $E2$, and $E3$. Since employee $E3$ only ever executes *Deliver Package* activities, we can argue that they belong to a *Logistics* role.

4 Automated Log Transformation

In this section, we present our approach to automatically transform object-centric event logs into the new metamodel to preserve backward compatibility. Provided an object-centric event log as input, we compute a set of measures based on the behavioral characteristics identified in the literature survey in Sect. 2 and apply a threshold to identify resource types. Subsequently, we analyze each resource type to detect roles within them and, finally, incorporate both aspects into the event log to adhere to the extended metamodel presented in Sect. 3.

4.1 Discovering Resource Object Types

We propose three heuristics for the automatic detection of resource types that assign numerical scores to each object type based on the three characteristics defined in Sect. 2. These scores measure the extent to which a given object type conforms to each behavioral pattern. The decision is then finalized based on a threshold over the sum of the individual scores. We assume an object-centric event log $l = (E, O, A, OT, E2O, \mathsf{time})$ as defined in Definition 1 to be given.

Extended Object Lifetime. The first measure caters to the characteristic that resources are assets managed by an organization over a prolonged period of time, e.g., employees, machines, or software. Hence, the expectation is that resources have a longer average lifetime than objects that are processed only once.

To detect that, we compute the average lifetime of all objects for each object type $ot \in OT$. To determine an object's lifetime, we calculate the difference between the first and last event it occurs in. For a formal representation, we introduce the helper set $TS_o = \{t \in \mathbb{U}_{time} \mid \exists e \in E : o \in O_e \wedge t \in \mathsf{time}(e)\}$ containing the timestamps of all events related to an object $o \in O$, which allows us to compute the lifetime of o as $LT(o) = max(TS_o) - min(TS_o)$. For ot we then get $\overline{LT}(ot) = \frac{\sum_{o \in O_{ot}} LT(o)}{|O_{ot}|}$ as its objects' average lifetime. In general, the higher the lifetime, the more likely an object type is to be a resource type. To get a normalized score between 0 and 1, we divide the average object type lifetime by the total log duration. Hence, the lifetime score for an object type is computed as $LTS(ot) = \frac{\overline{LT}(ot)}{max(\{t \in \mathbb{U}_{time} | t = \mathsf{time}(e) \wedge e \in E\}) - min(\{t \in \mathbb{U}_{time} | t = \mathsf{time}(e) \wedge e \in E\})}$.

In Fig. 2, employee $E1$ is continuously involved in events, resulting in a lifespan of 55 days ($ev01$ to $ev99$), which equals the total log duration and a score of 1.0. In contrast, the lifespan of order $O1$ and its items $I1$ and $I2$ is one day, from registration ($ev01$) to archiving ($ev11$), resulting in a score of 0.018.

Divergent Behavior. As described in Sect. 2, resources tend to exhibit divergent behavior. They execute the same activities several times, each time involving a different set of objects.

Following the definition in [24], divergence is defined for a pair of object type and activity. An object type is divergent for an activity if (1) there occur two events of the activity involving the same object of the object type and (2) each of these events involves a different object of a second object type. To capture the number of divergent activities per object type $ot \in OT$, we define $DIV(ot) = |\{a \in A \mid \exists e', e'' \in E_a, e' \neq e'' : \exists o \in O : o \in O_{e'} \cap O_{e''} \wedge \exists ot' \in OT, ot \neq ot' : \exists o', o'' \in O_{ot'} : o' \in O_{e'} \wedge o'' \in O_{e''}\}|$. To normalize the value, we compute the ratio of divergent activities over the total number of activities an object type is involved in as the final divergence score, i.e., $DS(ot) = \frac{DIV(ot)}{|\{a \in A | \exists e \in E_a, o \in O_{ot} : e \in O_e\}|}$.

In the example, we can observe that employee $E1$ is involved in activities *Register Order*, *Procure Item*, *Invoice Order*, *Pack Items*, and *Archive Order*. For each activity, we observe at least two occurrences, each involving different objects of other types, i.e., different orders, items, or packages. Hence, object type

Employee is divergent for all of these activities. It is also divergent for *Deliver Package*, since $E3$ is involved in the delivery of different packages ($ev08$, $ev98$). Hence, the overall score is 1.0 for *Employee*. In contrast, orders participate in a maximum of one event for most activities, which precludes divergence. The sole exception is repeated delivery attempts ($ev08$ and $ev09$), which, in our example, involve the same objects and therefore do not indicate divergence.

Unstructured Individual Behavior. The third characteristic refers to the structuredness of the individual object behavior. For resources that are typically involved in several potentially concurrent cases, we can observe a high variability in their event sequences, while other objects tend to follow a stricter process.

To measure the structuredness of an object type's behavior, we analyze the directly-follows relations among the activities it is involved in. For a given object type, a directly-follows relation is established between two activities whenever an object is involved in an event of the first activity followed immediately by an event of the second. To compute the directly-follows relations for an object type $ot \in OT$, we define the relation $DFR_{ot} = \{(a, a') \in A \times A \mid \exists e \in E_a, e' \in E_{a'} : \exists o \in O_{ot} : o \in O_e \cap O_{e'} \wedge \mathsf{time}(e) < \mathsf{time}(e') \wedge \nexists e'' \in E : o \in O_{e''} \wedge \mathsf{time}(e) < \mathsf{time}(e'') < \mathsf{time}(e')\}$.

Because an object type may contain distinct subpopulations with completely isolated behavior, its overall set of activities $A_{ot} = \{a \in A \mid \exists e \in E_a, o \in O_{ot} : o \in O_e\}$ may contain disconnected clusters. To isolate these, we partition A_{ot} into a set of maximal disjoint subsets $\mathcal{A}_{ot} = \{A_1, ..., A_n\}$ such that no directly-follows relations span across them, i.e., $\forall (a, a') \in DFR_{ot} : \exists! A_i \in \mathcal{A}_{ot} : \{a, a'\} \in A_i$. For each subset $A_i \in \mathcal{A}_{ot}$, we compute its unstructured behavior score as the ratio of observed directly-follows relations over the maximum possible number of relations within that subset: $UBS(A_i) = \frac{|DFR_{ot} \cap (A_i \times A_i)|}{|A_i|^2}$. The final score of the object type is the average score across subsets, i.e., $UBS(ot) = \frac{\sum_{A_i \in \mathcal{A}_{ot}} UBS(A_i)}{|\mathcal{A}_{ot}|}$.

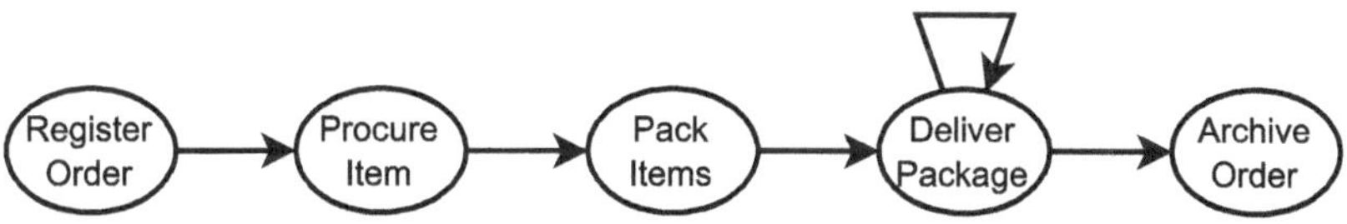

Fig. 4. DFG of the flattened process of object type *Item* based on the log in Fig. 2.

To illustrate this characteristic, the directly-follows graphs (DFGs) based on the identified relations for object types *Item* and *Employee* in Fig. 2 are depicted in Fig. 4 and Fig. 5, respectively. Each item follows a strict sequence of events, resulting in a linear structure and a score of 0.2. For type *Employee*, we identify two subgraphs, representing two groups of employees with distinct behavior. Both exhibit unstructured behavior, yielding a score of 0.86.

Finally, we compute the average of the scores for each characteristic for each object type and define a threshold T. Thus, the set of resource types $RT \subseteq OT$

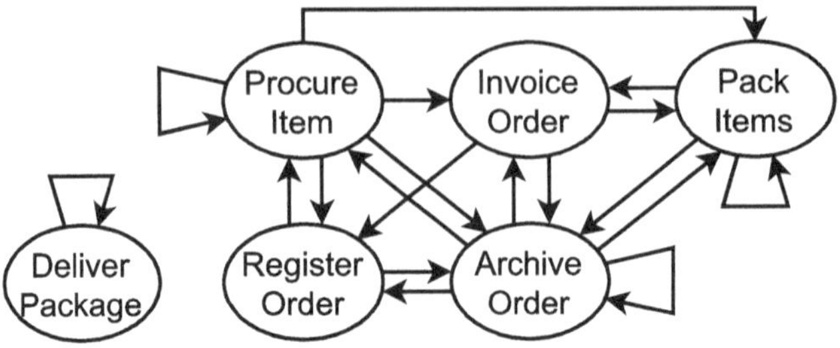

Fig. 5. DFG of the flattened process of object type *Employee* based on the log in Fig. 2.

for the input event log l is $RT = \{ot \in OT \mid (LTS(ot)+DS(ot)+UBS(ot))/3 \geq T\}$ and the set of resources $R \subseteq O$ comprises all objects of type $rt \in RT$, i.e., $R = \bigcup_{rt \in RT} O_{rt}$. The event-to-resource relation corresponds to the subset of the event-to-object relation involving resources, i.e., $E2R = E2O \cap (E \times R)$.

In the running example, object type *Employee* is identified as the only resource type with an overall score of 0.95.

4.2 Discovering Roles

Building upon the identified resource types, we next group the individual resources of one resource type into roles based on shared behavioral patterns. We closely follow the approach presented in [25] by discovering the sets of resources that have executed a given activity. Subsequently, we merge activities performed by identical sets of resources into a unified role.

To compute these shared activities, we define a function for each activity $a \in A_{rt}$ associated with a given resource type $rt \in RT$ that returns all resources of rt involved in at least one event of that activity, i.e., $RES(a, rt) = \{r \in R_{rt} \mid \exists e \in E_a : (e, r) \in E2R\}$. Based on that, we partition the set of activities into a set of maximal disjoint subsets $\mathcal{A}_{rt} = \{A_1, ..., A_n\}$ such that all activities within a subset are executed by the same set of resources, i.e., $\forall a, a' \in A_i : RES(a) = RES(a')$ for $i \in \{1, ..., n\}$.

To integrate the result into the metamodel, we define roles as tuples that pair a resource type with an activity partition. The complete set of roles RL for the input log l thus is $RL = \{(rt, A_i) \mid rt \in RT \wedge A_i \in \mathcal{A}_{rt}\}$. The resource-to-role relation maps each resource to the roles whose activities it is involved in, i.e., $R2RL = \{(r, (rt, A_i)) \in R \times RL \mid \mathsf{rtype}(r) = rt \wedge \exists a \in ET_i : r \in RES(a, rt)\}$.

An overview of the resource involvement with the different activities from the order management example is depicted in Table 1. By applying the described approach to resource type *Employee*, we discover three sets of activities that share the same resources, namely $\{$*Register Order, Procure Item, Pack Items*$\}$ with $E1$, $\{$*Deliver Package*$\}$ with $E3$, and $\{$*Invoice Order, Archive Order*$\}$ with $E1$ and $E2$. Hence, we end up with three roles that, based on domain knowledge, might refer to *Order Fulfillment*, *Logistics*, and *Accounting* in the order manage-

Table 1. Activity execution matrix for resource type *Employee* containing the number of occurrences for each resource-activity combination.

	Reg. Order	Proc. Item	Pack Items	Del. Package	Inv. Order	Arch. Order
E1	8	28	9	0	5	3
E2	0	0	0	0	3	5
E3	0	0	0	13	0	0

ment context. Each role contains one or several resources, and each resource is part of a role, thus fulfilling the requirements from the metamodel in Sect. 3.

5 Evaluation

In this section, we evaluate the feasibility of our approach. To that end, we apply our approach to eight public OCEL 2.0 event logs[1] to evaluate the overall performance in terms of runtime and correctness. We compare the results for each individual measure and the overall score. Our implementation, alongside detailed results for every log, is publicly accessible[2]. All experiments were conducted on a machine with an AMD Ryzen 7 7840U CPU and 32 GB RAM.

The aggregated results of our application are displayed in Table 2. For each log, we show the number of object types (#OT). From the provided event log documentations, we infer a set of resource types as a ground truth, displayed as the number of expected resource types (#RT). The following three columns list the results of the three individual measures: extended object lifetime (#M1), divergent behavior (#M2), and unstructured individual behavior (#M3). The numbers represent the number of object types that were identified as resource types by the measure. We identified thresholds of 0.85 for measures M1 and M2 and 0.75 for measure M3 to provide the best results. The value in parentheses shows the F1 score for each measure per log. The same information is shown for the aggregated score (#IRT) based on which we determined whether an object type is a resource type. Finally, the table includes the number of identified roles and the runtime per log, calculated as the average over ten runs. The largest logs have around 35,700 events and 14,000 objects (Logistics), and 3,850 events and 23,700 objects (Hinge Production).

Overall, our approach successfully discovered all expected resource types for seven out of eight logs. An additional resource type is discovered for the LRM P2P log, namely *Payment*. It exhibits both divergent (M2) and unstructured (M3) behavior according to our measures since it is related to a single activity that individual resources can repeatedly execute. However, this pattern matches with specialized resource types such as the *LabTechnician* in the LRM Hospital log and is therefore expected to be discovered as resource behavior.

[1] https://www.ocel-standard.org/event-logs/overview/.

[2] https://github.com/bptlab/Capturing-Conceptual-Type-Differences-in-OCPM.

Table 2. Overview of the results from applying our approach to public OCEL 2.0 event logs. We use the following abbreviations: OT = object types; RT = expected resource types; M1-3 = measures 1-3 (cf. Sect. 2.3); IRT = identified resource types. The numbers in parentheses show the F1 score of each measure.

Event Log	#OT	#RT	#M1	#M2	#M3	#IRT	#Roles	Runtime
Order Mgmt.	6	3	2 (0.8)	**3 (1.0)**	**3 (1.0)**	**3 (1.0)**	**6**	6 s
LRM Hiring	6	3	**3 (1.0)**	4 (0.86)	0 (0.0)	**3 (1.0)**	3	4 s
LRM Hosp.	8	7	2 (0.44)	**7 (1.0)**	6 (0.92)	**7 (1.0)**	**8**	3 s
LRM O2C	9	2	0 (0.0)	2 (0.67)	0 (0.0)	1 (0.67)	1	6 s
LRM P2P	6	1	**1 (1.0)**	2 (0.67)	2 (0.67)	2 (0.67)	2	2 s
Logistics	7	2	**2 (1.0)**	**2 (1.0)**	**2 (1.0)**	**2 (1.0)**	2	8 s
P2P	7	0	**0 (1.0)**	**0 (1.0)**	1 (0.0)	**0 (1.0)**	0	15 s
Hinge Prod.	12	5	4 (0.89)	3 (0.75)	**5 (1.0)**	**5 (1.0)**	**13**	11 s

Each of the three measures outperforms the others in some logs regarding the F1 score. M1 is a strong indicator on the LRM Hiring and LRM P2P logs, where resource types such as the *Worker* and *Facility* show a high average lifetime (M1) and unstructured (M3) but not divergent behavior (M2). However, it is less indicative of resource behavior, e.g., on the LRM Hospital log, where resource types such as *Nurse* and *DiagnosticEquipment* display lower lifetimes (M1) but highly divergent (M2) and unstructured behavior (M3). M3 is the only measure that correctly identifies the resources in the LRM O2C log, and M2 produces the best results on the Order Management log. Across all logs, M1 achieves the best precision, producing no false positives, while M2 correctly identifies most resource types but also yields the most false positives. Combining the three measures, the aggregated score improves the results of its individual components, resulting in an overall F1 score of 0.92 for our approach.

Regarding roles, only two logs contain information in their descriptions that can serve as a ground truth for the discovery. The hinge production log aggregates seven different types of machines and three types of workstations in the respective object types, which are correctly identified, leading to 13 roles for the log in total. The order management log includes a role attribute with three distinct values for the *employees* object type. Since two of these roles overlap in one activity, our approach correctly captures this structure in four roles with overlapping resources, resulting in six roles across all identified resource types.

In summary, our evaluation shows that the presented characteristics for resource behavior exist in object-centric event logs and that we can successfully discover them with the proposed approach. In addition, role structures can be distinguished among resources of the identified resource types, and the runtime performance of our implementation allows the application of our approach on standard end-user hardware.

6 Discussion and Related Work

In this section, we discuss our work in the context of existing approaches. To that end, we consider three research streams: metamodel extensions differentiating object types in OCPM, other notions of resource-like behavior and roles in OCPM, and the alignment between object-centric modeling and mining.

Graves et al. extend the metamodel to account for entities that do not have separate identifiers but whose quantity and state still impact the process execution [11]. To adapt OCPM to the IoT setting, the CORE metamodel [6] proposes further differentiating objects into *data sources* responsible for triggering events, *business objects* that are being impacted by events, and *general objects* that do not fall into either of the other two categories. In a sense, data sources constitute a category of resources, albeit with a limited scope. Although these approaches refine how object types are differentiated along structural and operational dimensions, they do not explicitly account for resource behavior or role structures. In the future, a conceptual integration with these approaches, along with the investigation of additional differentiation dimensions, should be considered.

Different works have introduced individual notions of resource-like behavior to address specific use cases in OCPM. Liss et al. group activities based on object lifetimes to hierarchically structure processes discovered from OCELs, thereby enhancing model understandability [15]. In the context of defining object-centric case notions, van Detten et al. utilize resource-like behavior based on divergence to establish cutoffs [24]; this prevents cases from becoming overly large and spanning the entire log, which has been a challenge in the field [3]. SYSSOC nets [25] aim to enhance discovered process models by capturing synchronization and specialization patterns in object-centric event logs in the form of silent object types that group objects and activity types. With our approach, we bring these notions together in a unified conceptualization of resources and roles in the context of OCPM to facilitate more differentiated downstream analyses. In addition, we build an automated discovery based on their characteristics of resource-like behavior and roles to detect these concepts in current event logs. While our evaluation shows that this approach can correctly discover them, we acknowledge several limitations. The proposed resource discovery relies on heuristic measures. Consequently, incorporating interactive domain knowledge could further refine the discovery results in complex scenarios, e.g., by determining suitable thresholds. Regarding role discovery, our implementation only differentiates roles within a single resource type; extending this to support type-spanning role discovery would fully realize the flexibility of our proposed metamodel.

Nevertheless, our work paves the way for the adoption of more advanced resource-related analyses from traditional process mining to the object-centric setting. For example, the concept of execution modes proposed in [28] could be extended to capture object properties as case types to discover more detailed interaction patterns. Further, the existence of several resource types in the same log opens up exploration potential for type-spanning social network analysis [18]. In addition, detecting resources is a preliminary step toward their inclusion in object-centric simulation approaches, where they are currently omitted [13].

Conceptualizations of resources vary across different business process metamodels [1]. In their consolidation of these metamodels, Adamo et al. propose the distinction between agentive and non-agentive resources, which is a dimension that is also represented in object-centric modeling frameworks [14,20]. However, since existing object-centric event log formats do not explicitly record event initiators, this cannot be captured by current OCPM approaches. Hence, future research endeavors should investigate an extension building on a unified terminology, such as the one proposed in [26], to align object-centric process modeling and mining in capturing the concept of resources and roles consistently.

7 Conclusion

In this paper, we propose a conceptual approach to integrate resources and roles into object-centric event logs by extending the current metamodel with resource types, resources, and roles. Based on a characterization of resource-like behavior and roles derived from existing literature, we develop an automated method to transform object-centric event logs into this extended format. As this transformation only extends existing data formats, the resulting event logs remain fully backward compatible with current OCPM techniques. Finally, we apply our method to publicly available event logs to demonstrate its practicality and its ability to correctly identify resources and roles.

References

1. Adamo, G., Francescomarino, C.D., Ghidini, C.: A business process meta-model: construction from the literature and ontological clarifications. Knowl. Eng. Rev. **40** (2025). https://doi.org/10.1017/S0269888925000049
2. Adams, J.N., Park, G., Levich, S., Schuster, D., van der Aalst, W.M.P.: A framework for extracting and encoding features from object-centric event data. In: ICSOC 2022. LNCS, vol. 13740, pp. 36–53. Springer (2022). https://doi.org/10.1007/978-3-031-20984-0_3
3. Adams, J.N., Schuster, D., Schmitz, S., Schuh, G., van der Aalst, W.M.P.: Defining cases and variants for object-centric event data. In: ICPM 2022, pp. 128–135. IEEE (2022). https://doi.org/10.1109/ICPM57379.2022.9980730
4. Bemthuis, R.H., Lazarova-Molnar, S.: Towards integrating process mining with agent-based modeling and simulation: state of the art and outlook. Expert Syst. Appl. (2025). https://doi.org/10.1016/J.ESWA.2025.127571
5. Berti, A., Koren, I., Adams, J.N.: OCEL (object-centric event log) 2.0 specification. CoRR (2024). https://doi.org/10.48550/ARXIV.2403.01975
6. Bertrand, Y., Imenkamp, C., Malburg, L.: An object-centric core metamodel for IoT-enhanced event logs. CoRR (2025). https://doi.org/10.48550/ARXIV.2506.21300
7. Dumas, M., Rosa, M.L., Mendling, J., Reijers, H.A.: Fundamentals of Business Process Management, 2nd edn. Springer (2018). https://doi.org/10.1007/978-3-662-56509-4

8. Fahland, D., Montali, M., Lebherz, J.: Towards a simple and extensible standard for object-centric event data (OCED) - core model, design space, and lessons learned. CoRR (2024). https://doi.org/10.48550/ARXIV.2410.14495
9. Garcia, A.F., da Silva, V.T., Chavez, C., de Lucena, C.J.P.: Engineering multi-agent systems with aspects and patterns. J. Braz. Comput. Soc. **8**(1), 57–72 (2002). https://doi.org/10.1590/S0104-65002002000100006
10. Gianola, A., Montali, M., Winkler, S.: Object-centric processes with structured data and exact synchronization - formal modelling and conformance checking. In: CAiSE 2025. LNCS, vol. 15702, pp. 185–202. Springer (2025). https://doi.org/10.1007/978-3-031-94571-711
11. Graves, N., Brockhoff, T., Koren, I., van der Aalst, W.M.P.: Extending process intelligence with quantity-related process mining. In: ICPM 2024 Workshops, pp. 337–349. LNBIP, Springer (2024). https://doi.org/10.1007/978-3-031-82225-4_25
12. Kirchdorfer, L., Blümel, R., Kampik, T., van der Aa, H., Stuckenschmidt, H.: AgentSimulator: an agent-based approach for data-driven business process simulation. In: ICPM 2024, pp. 97–104. IEEE (2024). https://doi.org/10.1109/ICPM63005.2024.10680660
13. Knopp, B., Pourbafrani, M., van der Aalst, W.M.P.: Discovering object-centric process simulation models. In: ICPM 2023, pp. 81–88. IEEE (2023). https://doi.org/10.1109/ICPM60904.2023.10271944
14. Künzle, V., Reichert, M.: PHILharmonicFlows: towards a framework for object-aware process management. J. Softw. Maint. Evol. Res. Pract. **23**(4), 205–244 (2011). https://doi.org/10.1002/smr.524
15. Liss, L., van der Aalst, W.M.P.: Process area extraction by multilevel resource detection for object-centric process mining. In: BPM 2026, pp. 197–214 (2026). https://doi.org/10.1007/978-3-032-02867-9_13
16. Park, G., Adams, J.N., van der Aalst, W.M.P.: OPerA: object-centric performance analysis. In: ER 2022. LNCS, pp. 281–292. Springer (2022). https://doi.org/10.1007/978-3-031-17995-2_20
17. Park, G., Adams, J.N., van der Aalst, W.M.P.: Conformance checking and performance analysis using object-centric directly-follows graphs. In: BPM 2024 Forum. LNBIP, vol. 526, pp. 179–196. Springer (2024). https://doi.org/10.1007/978-3-031-70418-5_11
18. Pika, A., Leyer, M., Wynn, M.T., Fidge, C.J., Hofstede, A.H.M.T., Aalst, W.M.P.V.D.: Mining resource profiles from event logs. ACM TMIS **8**(1) (2017). https://doi.org/10.1145/3041218
19. Seidel, A., Burghardt, P., König, M., Weske, M.: Extending case models to capture organizational aspects and time. In: ER Forum 2023. CEUR Workshop Proceedings. CEUR-WS.org (2023)
20. Seidel, A., Weske, M., Montali, M., et al.: Object-centric process management: a research manifesto. Inf. Syst. **141**, 102728 (2026). https://doi.org/10.1016/j.is.2026.102728
21. van der Aalst, W.M.P.: Object-centric process mining: dealing with divergence and convergence in event data. In: SEFM 2019. LNCS, vol. 11724, pp. 3–25. Springer (2019). https://doi.org/10.1007/978-3-030-30446-1_1
22. van der Aalst, W.M.P., Berti, A.: Discovering object-centric petri nets. Fundam. Informaticae **175**(1–4), 1–40 (2020). https://doi.org/10.3233/FI-2020-1946
23. van Detten, J.N., Schumacher, P., Leemans, S.J.J.: Discovering compact, live and identifier-sound object-centric process models. In: ICPM 2024, pp. 113–120. IEEE (2024). https://doi.org/10.1109/ICPM63005.2024.10680659

24. van Detten, J.N., Schumacher, P., Leemans, S.J.J.: A framework for advanced case notions in object-centric process mining. In: ICPM 2024 Workshops. LNBIP, vol. 533, pp. 402–414. Springer (2024). https://doi.org/10.1007/978-3-031-82225-4_30
25. van Detten, J.N., Schumacher, P., Leemans, S.J.J.: Object synchronizations and specializations with silent objects in object-centric petri nets. In: BPM 2024. LNCS, pp. 57–74. Springer (2024). https://doi.org/10.1007/978-3-031-70396-6_4
26. Verbruggen, C., Goossens, A., Smedt, J.D., Vanthienen, J., Snoeck, M.: iDOCEM: defining a common terminology for object-centric event logging and data-centric process modelling. Softw. Syst. Model. **24**(1), 9–33 (2025). https://doi.org/10.1007/S10270-024-01191-Z
27. Weske, M.: Business Process Management - Concepts, Languages, Architectures, 4th edn. Springer (2024). https://doi.org/10.1007/978-3-662-69518-0
28. Yang, J., Ouyang, C., van der Aalst, W.M.P., ter Hofstede, A.H.M., Yu, Y.: OrdinoR: a framework for discovering, evaluating, and analyzing organizational models using event logs. Decis. Support Syst. **158**, 113771 (2022). https://doi.org/10.1016/J.DSS.2022.113771

Advances in Ontology Engineering

LLM-Assisted Ontology Evolution for Hazards and Physical Threats — Continuous Identification and Integration of Emerging Threat Concepts

Servando V. Pizarro Martinez(✉), Timon T. Aldenhoff, Arnold F. Arz von Straussenburg, and Dennis M. Riehle

University of Koblenz – Institute for IS Research, Universitätsstraße 1, 56070 Koblenz, Germany
{pizarro,timonaldenhoff,arz,riehle}@uni-koblenz.de

Abstract. International aid organizations use hazard-and-threat ontologies to sort incident reports into shared categories for reporting and security-risk management. In volatile settings, these ontologies fall behind emerging threats such as drone incidents, maritime attacks, new violent actors, or early signs of political instability. We frame this as continuous adjustment: refining a deployed ontology over time based on new evidence, without rebuilding or directly editing it. Following Design Science Research, we design an LLM-assisted pipeline that extracts candidate concepts from incident emails, compares them against a read-only baseline ontology, and groups validated candidates into ranked review clusters by recurrence and evidence strength. A review application then lets domain experts accept, reject, or place a candidate on Watch, an intermediate state for recurring but unclear signals, so that human judgment stays between LLM output and any safety-related change. The artifact is evaluated through retrospective simulation over 37,204 incident emails at a European development cooperation organization.

Keywords: Ontology Evolution · Large Language Models · Conceptual Modeling · Crisis Response · Design Science Research

1 Introduction

Incident reports in international aid and development organizations increasingly describe operational patterns that existing classification schemes do not capture precisely, such as maritime incidents, aircraft warnings, service-dependency failures, or early signs of political instability. Beyond descriptive records, such reports trigger warning messages, dashboard updates, and coordination routines across field offices; organizations therefore use hazard-and-threat ontologies to map heterogeneous reports to shared categories before they enter these systems. These classification structures shape organizational routines, a role

© The Author(s), under exclusive license to Springer Nature Switzerland AG 2027
A. Bernasconi et al. (Eds.): ER 2026, LNCS 17081, pp. 325–341, 2027.
https://doi.org/10.1007/978-3-032-40795-5_19

long discussed in Information Systems (IS) and conceptual modeling research [9,29,30]. Crisis-management research similarly emphasizes ontologies for information sharing and interoperability in emergencies [17].

Once an ontology is embedded in operational routines, changes in the threat landscape become a maintenance problem. New threat types and shifting operational language can make existing labels too broad or misleading for current risk assessment. The issue becomes harder to ignore when the domain unit responsible for the ontology reports the coverage gap itself. In our case organization, practitioners reported that the existing domain-specific hybrid ontology no longer covers all relevant hazards and physical threats with sufficient precision. The ontology combines four elements: an Armed Conflict Location & Event Data Project (ACLED)[1]- and International Non-Governmental Organization Safety Organisation (INSO)[2]-inspired event taxonomy, an actor vocabulary, an administrative geographic hierarchy, and planned links between actors, events, locations, and organizational assets. Built from established external security-event data structures and internal organizational requirements, it already informs the standardization and template development of Global Incident Security systems. Consequently, ontology changes cannot be made as isolated modeling decisions; they may influence reporting practices and downstream security-risk-management processes.

The gap lies in maintaining a deployed ontology once emerging threat concepts begin to exceed its existing categories. Residual categories are acceptable for isolated reports; they become problematic when recurring or strategically relevant scenarios remain hidden under broad labels. Practitioners highlighted political instability as one such gap, since electoral violence and institutional instability can matter for security-risk management before they become classifiable incidents. Class-oriented gaps can also arise, for example when structured political-instability assessment contexts or critical service-dependency incidents physically block field operations. The maintenance challenge is therefore to decide whether observed or anticipated patterns justify adding a more specific concept or refining, renaming, merging, or removing existing categories. Unlike ordinary schema evolution, ontology evolution must preserve the meaning of categories while accounting for how they are used in operational reporting and downstream systems [4,22].

Consider a report about a prison break or jailbreak: at first sight, the wording suggests a missing crime-taxonomy value. The modeling question changes when the report links the event to armed actors, detainee releases, retaliatory violence, nearby unrest, or access restrictions. The relevant issue is then not only whether a new label is missing, but how the incident should connect to actors, consequences, and operational constraints. Such cases motivate an advisory workflow that preserves evidence and placement options instead of directly adding a new ontology term.

---

[1] https://acleddata.com/.
[2] https://ngosafety.org/.

We use continuous adjustment for the repeated, evidence-informed refinement of a deployed hazard-and-threat ontology whose categories already shape reporting routines and downstream systems. Because the ontology is safety-related, proposed changes must be reviewed by domain experts before they affect operational classifications. The expected outcome is a moderate set of additions or refinements rather than a complete redesign of the ontology. The artifact produces review material for domain experts—candidate concepts, refinements, mappings between reports and categories, and categories that may need reassessment—without directly modifying the operational ontology.

Expert review is difficult because incident information in the case organization is mainly available in internal incident emails that vary in structure, reliability, and context, combining semi-structured metadata, textual descriptions, current developments, and assessment or forecast sections. The broader corpus contains 37,204 incident records from April 2024 to April 2026, making manual post-deployment ontology maintenance difficult to sustain. Domain experts must still decide whether a candidate adjustment fits the ontology, reflects a meaningful threat scenario, and should enter the organizational governance process. Prior work on ontology learning and semi-automatic conceptual modeling shows that text-based and repository-based support can reduce this burden, but also that expert interpretation remains central [20,27]. In this study, recurrence, topicality, and expert-rated relevance serve as initial indicators for candidate prioritization.

Large Language Models (LLMs) can support this task by extracting candidate threat concepts from incident text and comparing them with the deployed ontology. Recent work has examined how LLMs can support ontology learning, conceptual model generation, and ontology-driven modeling assistance [1,8]. Less is known about post-deployment maintenance, especially how LLMs can identify coverage gaps in a deployed ontology and convert suggestions into traceable candidates for expert review. This matters because regenerating a deployed ontology would disrupt established classification routines. Candidate adjustments therefore need to fit the existing structure, be traceable to observed reports, and remain subject to stakeholder acceptance or rejection.

The research objective of this paper is to design and demonstrate an LLM-assisted artifact that continuously identifies emerging threat concepts in incident reports and prepares ontology adjustment candidates for governed expert review. We address this objective through two research questions:

RQ1: *How can incoming incident reports be compared with an existing ontology to identify insufficient conceptual coverage?*
RQ2: *How can ontology adjustment candidates and their rationales be generated and assessed in a human-in-the-loop review process?*

To answer these questions, we develop a two-stage pipeline that compares incoming incident reports with the current ontology and separates novelty detection from ontology-change governance. Stage 1 produces ontology-fit recommendations with source evidence. Stage 2 evaluates whether validated Stage 1 candidates have enough recurrent evidence to become advisory ontology changes.

A review application provides the human-in-the-loop mechanism through which domain stakeholders assess the generated proposals.

The empirical setting is a European organization active worldwide in international cooperation and sustainable development. The paper contributes to conceptual modeling by defining continuous adjustment as the repeated, evidence-informed refinement of a deployed hazard-and-threat ontology, and by showing how an LLM-assisted pipeline can generate traceable concepts, mappings, and rationales without directly modifying the operational ontology. Section 2 relates the study to ontology evolution, crisis-response ontologies, and LLM-supported ontology engineering. Section 3 describes the Design Science Research (DSR) process and artifact design; later sections report the results and discuss implications and limitations.

2 Background

2.1 Ontology Evolution

Ontology evolution refers to the timely, consistency-preserving adaptation of a deployed ontology to changes in the modeled domain, its conceptualization, or business and usage requirements [11,26]. It differs from ontology versioning, which manages the coexistence and interoperability of multiple variants of the same ontology [14]. In non-stationary settings, semantic and concept drift in incoming data challenge static knowledge representations [2,6,7].

In practice, this adaptation is a cyclic process of detecting change needs, suggesting and validating candidate changes, assessing their impact on dependent artifacts, and managing versions [26,31]. After deployment, the process must preserve downstream consistency and rely on expert-in-the-loop review [23]. Rather than autonomously rewriting the ontology, supporting tools typically present changes as candidates with rationales for human review before production [13]. These post-deployment conditions apply in crisis-response settings, where ontologies are embedded in Non-Governmental Organizations (NGOs) and emergency-management operations [17].

2.2 Crisis-Response Ontologies

Crisis-response ontologies provide a shared vocabulary for the events, actors, and response operations that emergency-management systems need to coordinate [17]. Examples include the Crisis Response Ontology (CROnto), covering crisis features, impacts, and response plans, intended as the knowledge model for downstream decision support [3]. A systematic review of the disaster domain identifies sixty-nine formal ontologies developed between 2010 and 2019 across all phases of the disaster management cycle, yet finds that infrastructure for managing evolving disaster knowledge is largely missing: most ontologies are neither published in dedicated repositories nor versioned to support comparison over time [21]. Existing automation populates a deployed crisis-management ontology with instances extracted from text, with expert validation at the end of the pipeline [5]. Structural adjustment of the deployed ontology, such as adding or refining concepts for recurring patterns in incoming reports, has received little attention in safety-critical settings. This gap connects to recent work on LLM-supported ontology engineering, where language models generate candidate ontology elements for expert review.

2.3 LLM-Supported Ontology Engineering

LLMs support tasks across the ontology engineering lifecycle, from requirements specification to maintenance, including domain modeling and evaluation [16]. Babaei Giglou, D'Souza, and Auer [1] decompose ontology learning into term typing, taxonomy discovery, and non-taxonomic relation extraction, while Lo *et al.* [18] fine-tune an LLM end-to-end to generate the taxonomic backbone of an ontology directly from text. Fathallah, Staab, and Algergawy [10] embed an LLM into an existing engineering methodology, guiding the model through requirement specification, conceptualization, and implementation in formal syntax.

For existing ontologies, Kollapally *et al.* [15] use an LLM to extract candidate concepts and place them in the hierarchy through lexical, semantic, and graph-based similarity, and Popa and Sîrbu [25] refine a knowledge graph by identifying disconnected components and proposing connections. Closer to ontology evolution, Jadhav *et al.* [13] use an LLM to propose new concepts and relationships from scientific literature for expert validation, and Bai *et al.* [2] drive test-time adaptation of temporal knowledge graphs under semantic drift. In the emergency-response domain, Lu *et al.* [19] construct event ontologies from text in a fully automated closed loop with incremental updates and without expert validation. Li, Garijo, and Poveda-Villalón [16] report that limitations are pronounced in domains where vocabularies are still evolving, and that expert validation remains essential in regulated or safety-critical settings. To our knowledge, the combination of a deployed safety-related ontology, stream-of-evidence input from incident reports, and explicit Watch-state governance has not been jointly addressed in prior LLM-supported ontology engineering work.

3 Research Design

Incoming reports reveal gaps in the deployed hazard-and-threat ontology; the research design therefore detects such gaps and prepares them for expert review. As Fig. 1 summarizes, the artifact separates evidence discovery from formal ontology change. Incident records enter the pipeline, Stage 1 produces validated handoff rows, Stage 2 consolidates them into advisory clusters, expert governance assigns review outcomes, and governed writeback occurs only for accepted candidates. The reference ontology remains read-only.

The study follows a DSR approach because the central contribution is an artifact that detects insufficient ontology coverage and prepares traceable adjustment candidates for expert review [12]. Echelon-based DSR framing delimits

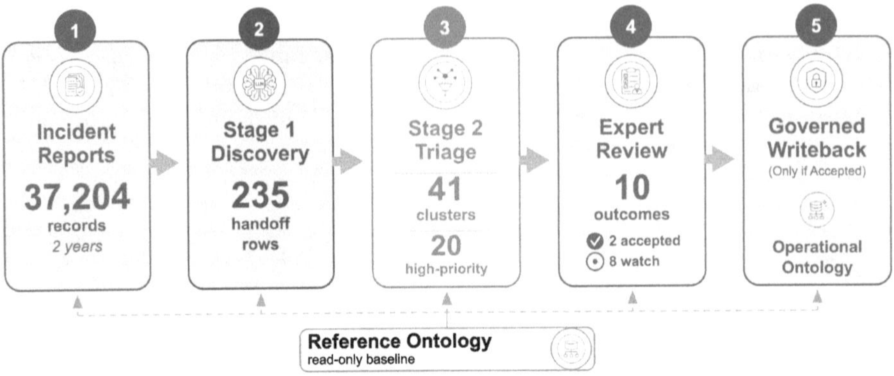

Fig. 1. LLM-assisted workflow for governed ontology adjustment.

this paper within the larger DSR project: it reports artifact development, retrospective demonstration, and embedded governance assessment, while operational integration into the organization's regular ontology-governance process remains a subsequent cycle [28]. The implementation is advisory-only: recommendations are stored as candidates and never written directly to the source ontology.

The case organization is a globally active European development cooperation organization whose security-risk-management processes depend on incident classification. The deployed ontology described in Sect. 1 serves as the baseline for generated candidates. Artifact objectives derive from the ontology, observed classification gaps, and practitioner accounts of missing or weakly represented threat concepts. These accounts also characterize the maintenance baseline: field offices adapt their security analysis to local conditions and resources, ranging from qualitative assessments to dedicated incident databases whose upkeep in a high-risk context alone takes several hours per week in addition to map production and reporting. The deployed ontology has accordingly been revised in a deliberate, demand-driven manner, three times since its first version, leaving room for the more continuous, evidence-based support the artifact targets. The artifact must therefore preserve structure, limit concept proliferation, attach report evidence, and support repeated expert review.

The data basis consists of internal incident emails available within the case organization. These records are organizational working material and are treated as confidential, although the cases they describe may also be reflected in public reporting. If structured explicitly, parts of these cases would resemble open event-data records such as ACLED incidents, with event types, actors, locations, consequences, and source-evidence cues. However, public event categories are not sufficient for the maintenance objective pursued here, because the deployed ontology also needs organization-specific distinctions for security-risk management, personnel safety, access constraints, and governance review. The artifact therefore does not reproduce an external event-data schema, but identifies ontology gaps and candidate categories from semi-structured and narrative email text.

For the evaluation, we replay the April 2024–April 2026 corpus of 37,204 incident records as a retrospective deployment simulation, treating the deployed ontology as the baseline for newly surfaced concepts. The current artifact processes text-only emails; image-bearing cases remain outside this iteration.

The artifact has two processing stages. Stage 1 inspects full email bodies, extracts candidate concepts, compares them with the baseline ontology, and writes validated handoff rows only where coverage is insufficient. It can emit typed operations such as category values, classes, subclasses, attributes, relations, or synonym mappings. Stage 2 consumes these rows in bimonthly cumulative advisory cycles: it compares recent and baseline windows, groups candidates by label, parent, and type, checks recurrence and source support, and produces propose, watch, or reject decisions with a draft patch artifact. In the retrospective simulation, Stage 1 processed the historical corpus in batches of 30 emails, while Stage 2 replayed bimonthly cumulative review cycles. In operational use, the same Stage 1 check is intended to run continuously as new incident emails arrive. In the final retrospective run, Stage 1 surfaced 235 validated handoff rows, and the final cumulative Stage 2 slice consolidated them into 41 advisory clusters for expert review. One semantic issue appeared as three structurally distinct modeling alternatives, retained in the full-review denominator to expose placement ambiguity. The artifact uses an OpenAI-hosted, Application Programming Interface (API)-based LLM endpoint and was developed with GPT-5.4 Mini. The LLM call is behind an OpenAI-compatible interface so later evaluations or deployments can replace the hosted model without changing the architecture.

The pipeline does not change the ontology directly; its outputs serve as stakeholder review material. An interactive web-based interface presents each candidate with evidence chains, coverage states, fit decisions, usefulness ratings, and shift metrics. Expert validation followed a three-session protocol with two domain experts, a field security officer and a central security manager. In individual walkthrough interviews, each expert examined the surfaced candidates and their incident evidence in the review application and recorded an initial assessment. A joint session then consolidated these assessments: both experts

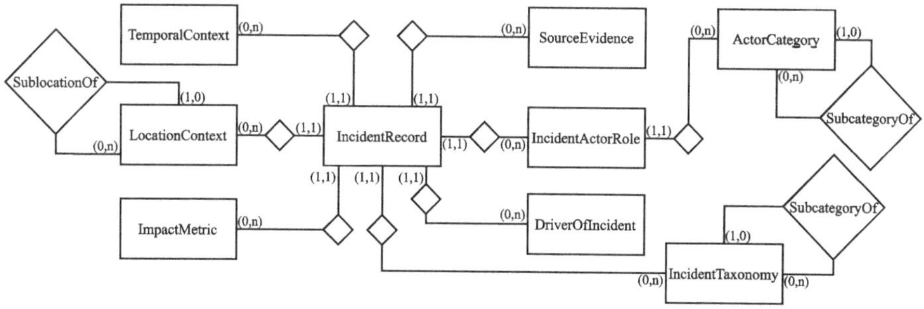

Fig. 2. Expert reference model used for ontology-fit assessment. The pipeline processes this deployed structure as a static JSON digest, evaluating gap candidates against designated extension surfaces to constrain unsupported ontology growth.

discussed source evidence, ontology fit, operational relevance, and governance implications for each candidate and recorded a consolidated governance outcome. Because ontology changes can affect safety-related information services, final integration remains subject to organizational approval.

An incident email reads like a short operational alert. Its subject line condenses the country, affected area, incident type, and immediate concern; the body adds anchors for location, coordinates, event date, incident type, and source reliability before narrative sections such as summary, background, developments, and assessment. For the artifact, this format provides initial classification signals and evidence about actors, triggers, consequences, uncertainty, escalation, and other operational details that must be mapped to the ontology or identified as insufficiently covered. Figure 2 shows the corresponding *IncidentRecord*-centered baseline, with taxonomy, actor, temporal, geographic, impact, driver, and source-evidence surfaces against which these extracted signals are assessed.

4 Results

The implemented artifact produced a reproducible reduction pipeline from operational incident reports to governed ontology-maintenance candidates. Its result is not an automatically modified ontology, but a traceable sequence of review artifacts. The pipeline is therefore interpretable as an ontology-maintenance filter: each retained item carries source evidence, a typed modeling operation, a placement hint, and a governance rationale.

4.1 Read-Only Baseline and Advisory Pipeline

The expert reference model in Fig. 2 provides the read-only conceptual baseline for ontology-fit assessment. It separates the deployed hazard-and-threat model into three structural areas. The *incident context* captures temporal, location, and impact-related information around a central *IncidentRecord* entity. The *operational core* links the record to source evidence, actor roles, and incident classifications. The *controlled vocabularies* provide governed value spaces for actor categories, incident taxonomy entries, and drivers of incident classification. Extracted signals are not treated as free labels: they are assessed against concrete ontology locations for existing coverage, controlled-vocabulary extension, incident or impact attributes, or broader class and relation proposals.

The pipeline implements this comparison as a typed and evidence-preserving contract. Each run persists the ontology digest, raw Stage 1 candidates, validation decisions, final handoff rows, clustered candidates, scored recommendations, optional agent-review notes, non-executed patch-operation drafts, and the review-app export. These artifacts make the reduction from email text to expert queue reproducible while keeping the operational ontology insulated from direct LLM mutation.

The agentic components are implemented as constrained orchestration modules using the Deep Agents SDK[3]. We refer to these two constrained pipeline

[3] https://docs.langchain.com/oss/python/deepagents/overview.

agents as DeepAgent components. In this artifact, they receive fixed prompts, typed Pydantic response schemas, and validation steps, but no ontology-write tools or autonomous editing authority. An online appendix [24] provides the prompt templates of both DeepAgent components, the Pydantic response schemas, the Stage 2 scoring weights and clustering rules, and synthetic example emails.

Stage 1 performs evidence discovery. The first DeepAgent component receives the full incident text and the persisted ontology digest, then applies two complementary extraction angles. The taxonomy pass checks whether report wording suggests a missing controlled value; the structural pass checks whether narrative facts such as counts, statuses, impact measures, or relations should become reusable structured fields. A validation pass then compares each candidate with the source email and baseline ontology. Only candidates accepted in the Stage 1 validation step become handoff rows for Stage 2; synonym mappings and rejected candidates remain traceable but do not enter the ontology-change queue.

Stage 2 converts these handoff rows into reviewable advisory clusters. It clusters by proposal type, normalized label, parent or field hints, and semantic-family patterns, while keeping structurally different modeling alternatives separate. Each cluster receives a placement hint and a score based on recurrence, source support, confidence, type consistency, structural fit, and follow-up penalties. After expert discussions clarified that the ontology should primarily support people- and personnel-security monitoring, the final Stage 2 variant applies a target-fit gate for harm, detention, rescue or release, access constraints, movement restrictions, and staff-safety relevance. The resulting recommendation tiers are reported against expert governance outcomes in Table 2. All clusters remain visible in the review interface, and the second DeepAgent component only adds advisory critique on evidence strength, existing coverage, merge-or-split issues, governance risk, and reviewer questions.

The *Jailbreak/Prison Break* cluster illustrates this advisory logic. Stage 1 surfaced the wording as a possible missing controlled value, and Stage 2 consolidated it into one advisory cluster with three linked source records and a tentative placement under the crime branch for confinement-related values. The cluster therefore became a review object with evidence, placement hint, and reviewer questions rather than an automatic ontology edit.

The resulting review artifacts are written into structured tables and exposed through an interactive web-based review interface. This interface gives experts direct access to the recommendations, source evidence, ontology-placement hints, and traceability information needed to inspect and document review decisions.

The final review queue shows that the artifact surfaces both classification and measurement gaps. Most candidates were mapped either to controlled values in the incident taxonomy or to impact-metric and *IncidentRecord* attributes. This distribution follows the source data: field reports often use local event labels that do not cleanly match existing taxonomy branches, and their prose contains recurring measurements not available as structured fields. Expert adjudication remained conservative. Of the 41 advisory groups, 2 were accepted for integration, 8 were placed on *Watch*, and 31 were rejected. The *Watch* outcomes are still governance-relevant because they preserve trace evidence for recurring or structurally ambiguous signals without prematurely expanding the deployed ontology.

5 Evaluation

5.1 Review Set and Outcome Definitions

The evaluation starts from the Stage 2 export rather than the raw corpus, keeping the focus on the artifact's governance function: turning incident-derived signals into a compact set of reviewable ontology-maintenance decisions.

We treat both *Accepted* and *Watch* as governance-relevant outcomes. *Accepted* refers to candidates selected for immediate integration. *Watch* keeps recurring, operationally relevant, or structurally ambiguous candidates visible for continued monitoring without yet changing the ontology. Usefulness ratings are kept separate as an interpretive signal rather than an independent gold standard.

The 41 exported advisory clusters form the full expert-review set, with 10 governance-relevant outcomes. Three rows referred to the same semantic issue, *Public health hazard/outbreak*, but represented different modeling alternatives as a controlled vocabulary value, a class, and an impact attribute; we retain all three in the denominator to expose placement ambiguity without counting them as independent semantic discoveries.

Evidence volume was not the primary determinant of acceptance: the two accepted candidates had evidence counts of 3 and 12, while the highest-evidence candidate, *Rescued/released persons count*, was placed on *Watch* because its structural placement as a quantitative metric required deliberation beyond the initial review cycle.

5.2 Expert Governance Outcomes

The three-session expert review produced conservative governance outcomes: two candidates were accepted for immediate integration, eight placed on *Watch*, and 31 rejected. This distribution is consistent with a mature baseline ontology and a conservative governance process: many recurring patterns were judged already covered, too narrow, or insufficiently actionable for new ontology commitment. This asymmetry is also intended: since overlooking an emerging threat concept is costlier here than reviewing an ultimately rejected candidate, the pipeline favors surfacing recurring candidates over aggressive pre-filtering; a high rejection rate reflects this recall-oriented triage function.

The full-review yield reached 24.4% when aggregating both *Accepted* and *Watch* outcomes. Usefulness ratings provided an additional signal of operational relevance, although we do not treat them as an independent gold standard for model correctness. In the consolidated review assessment, 20 review rows were rated as neutral or better (Likert ≥ 3); within this subset, governance-relevant density reached 50.0%. A stricter positive-only threshold (Likert > 3) increased this density to 64.3%, and the highest rating alone (Likert = 5) to 80.0%, suggesting that expert perceptions of usefulness are highly concentrated in the final governance-relevant set.

Table 1 classifies the 41 candidates by the ER operation their proposed change represents and the ontology component it would extend.

Table 1. Candidate gap surfaces by ER operation and ontology component.

ER operation	Ontology component	Gaps	Evid.	L≥3
Attribute extension	ImpactMetrics	20	1,351	6
Controlled-value ext.	IncidentTaxonomy	19	72	12
Class addition	IncidentRecord	2	3	2
Total		**41**	**1,426**	**20**

L≥3 denotes a mean usefulness rating of at least 3. Rows are candidate-level counts; the three *Public health hazard / outbreak* alternatives are counted separately by modeling operation.

This uneven distribution follows the structure of the incident reports and the reference model. *ImpactMetrics* received 20 attribute-oriented proposals, reflecting recurring quantitative and operational outcome signals such as casualty counts, displacement figures, movement restrictions, and response-related metrics. *IncidentTaxonomy* received 19 controlled-value proposals, which is expected because classification labels are the primary output of security-risk-management routines. Together, these two surfaces absorb 39 of the 41 candidates, suggesting that most surfaced gaps concern classification and impact representation rather than changes to the operational core.

The two *IncidentRecord*-level proposals are structurally more consequential and illustrate why candidate placement requires governance review. Temporal context, location context, source evidence, actor roles, and driver-of-incident values produced no review candidates in this run, an absence to interpret cautiously: the maintenance objective emphasized incident classification, impact attributes, access constraints, and personnel-security signals rather than systematic actor-vocabulary or causal-driver extension. The mapping therefore supports the paper's core claim: the artifact does not merely surface labels, but locates candidate gaps on specific ontology surfaces where different governance thresholds apply.

5.3 Advisory Recommendations and Expert Decisions

Table 2 compares Stage 2 advisory recommendations with final expert governance outcomes. The governance-relevant rate descends across priority tiers:

Propose-tier 50.0%, Watch-tier 42.9%, Reject-tier 16.7%. This gradient indicates partial discriminatory signal, but advisory priority alone did not determine governance relevance: five candidates classified as *Reject* by Stage 2 received governance-relevant outcomes, confirming that human adjudication remains necessary. The pipeline's primary role is to reduce volume and assemble evidence; the final determination of organizational meaning depends on expert judgment.

Table 2. Stage 2 advisory recommendations versus final expert governance outcomes.

Stage 2 rec.	Accepted	Watch	Rejected	Gov.-rel.
Propose	1	1	2	50.0%
Watch	0	3	4	42.9%
Reject	1	4	25	16.7%
Total	**2**	**8**	**31**	**24.4%**

$n = 41$. Gov.-rel. = (*Accepted* + *Watch*) / tier total. Results use the people-security variant.

Likert ratings further confirmed this distinction, with accepted candidates averaging 5.0 and rejected items 1.9. Automated scores and expert ratings aligned only partially: high-recurrence candidates such as *Smuggling* were rejected when they lacked a direct link to risk-management routines, while *displaced_persons* received a high usefulness rating despite a low advisory score.

5.4 Case Interpretations

The acceptance of *Cattle rustling* shows the importance of local domain knowledge in ontology maintenance: although general taxonomies might subsume such incidents under broader property-crime categories, experts treated cattle rustling as regionally salient because it can trigger retaliation, local unrest, or communal violence. Similarly, *Curfew/movement restriction status* was accepted because it captures strategic developments that directly affect operational access and staff safety, even in the absence of a physical attack.

The running example reappears in Fig. 3: the *Jailbreak/Prison Break* cluster received a high usefulness rating but was placed on *Watch* because, although operationally relevant, its correct placement remained unresolved. Additional evidence on involved actors, follow-on unrest, facility consequences, or access restrictions would determine whether to model it as a crime value, a broader unrest signal, a facility-related consequence, or an operational access concern. The case illustrates the value of *Watch*: the candidate stays visible with evidence and placement rationale while formal ontology commitment is deferred.

The case of *displaced_persons* highlights the system's role in governance normalization: although related concepts existed in previous ontology versions, the surfaced candidate allowed reviewers to confirm that the deployed model remained aligned with current field vocabulary.

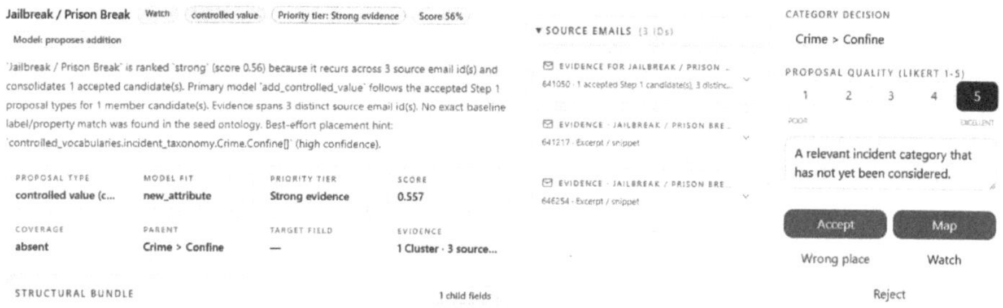

Fig. 3. Expert review interface for a deduplicated adjustment candidate. The example shows *Jailbreak/Prison Break* as a watch-listed controlled-value candidate with source evidence, coverage state, tentative category placement, usefulness rating, reviewer justification, and governance actions.

Cyberattack presents a more complex structural ambiguity: the pipeline produced four distinct candidates for cyber and digital threats, a class proposal directly under *IncidentRecord* and three controlled-value proposals across *Crime*, *IncidentCategory*, and *Strategic Development.* Reviewers rejected all four, but the cross-surface distribution reveals a genuine architectural tension: digital threats do not map cleanly onto the physical threat taxonomy, and no single placement commanded consensus. This is why the consolidation stage preserves structurally distinct alternatives rather than collapsing them into a single label; premature merging would have obscured the underlying modeling question.

The most instructive cross-surface ambiguity is *Public health hazard/outbreak*, which appeared as three simultaneous modeling alternatives: a controlled taxonomy value under *Natural Hazard*, a core class under *IncidentRecord*, and an impact attribute under *ImpactMetrics*; the joint review session assigned all three the same governance decision. The pipeline thus surfaces not only semantic gaps but also unresolved ontology-design decisions that only expert review can settle: whether a recurring phenomenon is a classifying label, a structural entity, or a quantitative attribute.

6 Discussion and Conclusion

The study addressed two research questions. For RQ1, the results show how incoming incident reports can be compared with a read-only ontology digest through typed extraction and validation passes, making candidate coverage gaps traceable without modifying the deployed ontology. For RQ2, the artifact shows how validated candidates can be clustered, scored, and routed through a structured review interface where domain experts adjudicate placement decisions under uncertainty.

The artifact should be read as an advisory pipeline rather than a formal ontology-repair algorithm. The *Watch* state is the clearest expression of this design, keeping operationally relevant but semantically unresolved signals visible until further evidence or deliberation supports a placement decision. *Jailbreak/Prison Break* illustrates this logic: the same signal may still resolve to any of the four candidate placements discussed in Sect. 5. Advisory scores therefore guide triage, while the final judgment about organizational meaning remains with domain experts. The relevance gate follows the same principle. In this setting, emphasizing human safety, personnel security, and access constraints aligned the review queue with protective decision-making, but such gates remain configurable maintenance objectives rather than fixed quality criteria. What is safety-specific is therefore the governance posture rather than the extraction logic: read-only insulation, conservative acceptance, and the *Watch* state address a setting in which misclassification can affect warnings and protective decisions, while their configurable nature lets the same workflow transfer to other evolving domain ontologies.

The evaluation supports the central premise that continuous ontology adjustment is primarily an organizational modeling problem rather than a technical extraction task. Conservative governance outcomes are consistent with a mature baseline ontology, and the cross-tabulation between Stage 2 recommendations and expert outcomes shows that automated priority carried a useful but incomplete signal. The artifact functions as a structured negotiation mechanism, presenting candidates with evidence, proposed placements, rationales, usefulness ratings, and governance actions. The replay reduced a historical incident-email corpus to a compact, evidence-linked advisory queue that two experts adjudicated in three review sessions, without delegating ontology change to the LLM. The pipeline and review application are reusable workflow artifacts that can be populated with new incident emails, though evaluated here only in retrospective replay. The contribution is therefore a governed process for making semantic uncertainty visible and actionable through read-only ontology insulation, configurable triage, and explicit deferred commitment.

The evaluation demonstrates contextual utility in one organizational setting and does not establish inter-rater reliability or generalizable decision accuracy. Its most important methodological limitation is the absence of an independent, corpus-wide expert reference set for the 37,204 incident emails. The results show which of the 41 pipeline-surfaced candidates experts accepted or placed on *Watch*, but not open-world recall or whether additional gaps were missed. Future work should therefore evaluate the workflow with additional reviewers and organizations, benchmark the LLM-assisted pipeline against simpler baselines such as keyword extraction or topic modeling, compare alternative model configurations and maintenance objectives, measure reviewer effort and runtime across cycles, and test whether the workflow transfers to open, news-based security-event streams. Global Database of Events, Language, and Tone (GDELT)[4] could serve as a next probe: its document-oriented layer provides richer narrative evidence around emerging events than coded event tables alone, and such an extension would test whether the artifact can integrate evidence across struc-

[4] https://www.gdeltproject.org/.

tured and unstructured sources while keeping maintenance decisions grounded in organization-specific reporting needs and ontology categories rather than inherited public event categories. A maintained staging ontology for accepted and watched candidates could also serve as a longitudinal reference for tracking how provisional gaps resolve before formal ontology mutation.

References

1. Babaei Giglou, H., D'Souza, J., Auer, S.: LLMs4OL: large language models for ontology learning. In: Payne, T.R., Presutti, V. (eds.) The Semantic Web - ISWC 2023. LNCS, vol. 14265, pp. 408–427. Springer, Heidelberg (2023)
2. Bai, H., Kang, S., et al.: Learning from surprise: fusing LLM-guided test-time adaptation for temporal knowledge graphs. Knowl.-Based Syst. **342**, 115867 (2026)
3. Bannour, W., Maalel, A., Ben Ghezala, H.H.: Ontology-based representation of crisis response situations. In: Nguyen, N.T., Chbeir, R. (eds.) Computational Collective Intelligence, pp. 417–427. Springer International Publishing, Cham (2019)
4. Buitelaar, P., Cimiano, P., et al.: Ontology-based information extraction and integration from heterogeneous data sources. Int. J. HumanComputer Stud. **66**(11), 759–788 (2008)
5. Chasseray, Y., Barthe-Delanoë, A.-M., Négny, S., Le Lann, J.-M.: Automated unsupervised ontology population system applied to crisis management domain. In: ISCRAM 2021 – 18th International Conference on Information Systems for Crisis Response and Management, pp. 968–981 (2021)
6. Chen, J., Lecue, F., Pan, J.Z., Chen, H.: Learning from ontology streams with semantic concept drift. In: Proceedings of the Twenty-Sixth International Joint Conference on Artificial Intelligence, pp. 957–963. International Joint Conferences on Artificial Intelligence Organization, Melbourne, Australia (2017)
7. Chen, J., Lécué, F., et al.: Knowledge graph embeddings for dealing with concept drift in machine learning. J. Web Semantics **67**, 100625 (2021)
8. Coutinho, M.L., Almeida, J.P.A., Guizzardi, G.: LLM-based modeling assistance for textual ontology-driven conceptual modeling. In: Companion Proceedings of the 44th International Conference on Conceptual Modeling: ER Forum, Special Topics, Posters and Demos. CEUR Workshop Proceedings. CEUR-WS.org, (2025)
9. De Alencar Silva, P., Weigand, H.: Enterprise Monitoring Ontology. In: Jeusfeld, M., Delcambre, L., Ling, T.-W. (eds.) Conceptual Modeling – ER 2011, pp. 132–146. Springer, Berlin, Heidelberg (2011)
10. Fathallah, N., Staab, S., Algergawy, A.: Taming hallucinations: a semantic matching evaluation framework for LLM-generated ontologies. In: Proceedings of the LLMs4OL Challenge @ ISWC 2025. CEUR Workshop Proceedings (2025)
11. Flouris, G., Manakanatas, D., et al.: Ontology change: classification and survey. Knowl. Eng. Rev. **23**(2), 117–152 (2008)
12. Hevner, A.R., March, S.T., Park, J., Ram, S.: Design science in information systems research. MIS Q. **28**(1), 75–105 (2004)
13. Jadhav, H., Heger, T., König-Ries, B., Algergawy, A.: ontology evolution in invasion biology using large language models: a hybrid approach. In: Proceedings of the LLMs4OL Challenge @ ISWC 2025. CEUR Workshop Proceedings (2025)
14. Klein, M., Fensel, D., Kiryakov, A., Ognyanov, D.: Ontology versioning and change detection on the web. In: Gómez-Pérez, A., Benjamins, V.R. (eds.) Knowledge Engineering and Knowledge Management: Ontologies and the Semantic Web, pp. 197–212. Springer, Berlin, Heidelberg (2002)

15. Kollapally, N.M., Geller, J., et al.: Ontology enrichment using a large language model: applying lexical, semantic, and knowledge network-based similarity for concept placement. J. Biomed. Inform. **168**, 104865 (2025)
16. Li, J., Garijo, D., Poveda-Villalón, M.: Large language models for ontology engineering: a systematic literature review. Semantic Web J. **20**, 1–45 (2026)
17. Liu, S., Brewster, C., Shaw, D.: Ontologies for crisis management: a review of state of the art in ontology design and usability. In: Comes, T., Fiedrich, F. (eds.) ISCRAM 2013 Conference Proceedings – 10th International Conference on Information Systems for Crisis Response and Management, pp. 349–359. Karlsruher Institut für Technologie, Baden-Baden, Germany (2013)
18. Lo, A., Jiang, A.Q., Li, W., Jamnik, M.: End-to-end ontology learning with large language models. In: Proceedings of the Advances in Neural Information Processing Systems 38: Annual Conference on Neural Information Processing Systems, p. 2024 (2024)
19. Lu, Z., Yang, J., et al.: EOAC-LLM: an LLM-driven event ontology automatic construction system. Intell. Syst. Appl. **30**, 200650 (2026)
20. Maedche, A., Staab, S.: Ontology learning for the semantic web. IEEE Intell. Syst. **16**(2), 72–79 (2001)
21. Mazimwe, A., Hammouda, I., Gidudu, A.: Implementation of FAIR principles for ontologies in the disaster domain: a systematic literature review. IJGI **10**(5), 324 (2021)
22. Noy, N.F., Chugh, A., Liu, W., Musen, M.A.: A framework for ontology evolution in collaborative environments. In: Cruz, I., Decker, S. (eds.) The Semantic Web - ISWC 2006, pp. 544–558. Springer, Berlin, Heidelberg (2006)
23. Noy, N.F., Klein, M.: Ontology evolution: not the same as schema evolution. Know. Inf. Sys. **6**(4), 428–440 (2004)
24. Pizarro Martinez, S.V., Aldenhoff, T.T., Arz von Straussenburg, A.F., Riehle, D.M.: Supplementary dataset: LLM-Assisted Ontology Evolution for Hazards and Physical Threats – Continuous Identification and Integration of Emerging Threat Concepts, (2026). [Dataset]. Zenodo. 45th International Conference on Conceptual Modeling (ER), St. John's, NL, Canada. https://doi.org/10.5281/zenodo.21594689
25. Popa, A., Sîrbu, T.-I.: From Fragmentation to Cohesion: An LLM-Based Iterative Approach to Ontology and Knowledge Graph Refinement. In: 2025 25th International Conference on Control Systems and Computer Science (CSCS), pp. 651–654. IEEE, Bucharest, Romania (2025)
26. Stojanovic, L., Maedche, A., Motik, B., Stojanovic, N.: User-driven ontology evolution management. In: Gómez-Pérez, A., Benjamins, V.R. (eds.) Knowledge Engineering and Knowledge Management: Ontologies and the Semantic Web, pp. 285–300. Springer, Berlin, Heidelberg (2002)
27. Thonggoom, O., Song, I.-Y., An, Y.: Semi-automatic conceptual data modeling using entity and relationship instance repositories. In: Jeusfeld, M., Delcambre, L., Ling, T.-W. (eds.) Conceptual Modeling – ER 2011, pp. 219–232. Springer, Berlin, Heidelberg (2011)
28. Tuunanen, T., Winter, R., vom Brocke, J.: Dealing with complexity in design science research: a methodology using design echelons. MIS Q. **48**(2), 427–458 (2024)
29. Wand, Y., Weber, R.: Research commentary: information systems and conceptual modeling-a research agenda. Inf. Syst. Res. **13**(4), 363–376 (2002)

30. Woo, C.: The Role of Conceptual Modeling in Managing and Changing the Business. In: Jeusfeld, M., Delcambre, L., Ling, T.-W. (eds.) Conceptual Modeling – ER 2011, pp. 1–12. Springer, Berlin, Heidelberg (2011)
31. Zablith, F., Antoniou, G., et al.: Ontology evolution: a process-centric survey. Knowl. Eng. Rev. **30**(1), 45–75 (2015)

From Ontological Violations to Explicit Witnesses: Level-Agnostic Diagnostics for OntoUML and MLT

Shilpi Gupta(✉), Mohammad Sadeghi, Monalisha Ojha, and Colin Atkinson

University of Mannheim, Mannheim, Germany
{gupta,sadeghi,ojha,atkinson}@uni-mannheim.de

Abstract. OntoUML and Multi-Level Theory (MLT) give conceptual models a checkable ontological semantics. However, the feedback produced when checking a model against these semantics is typically tied to the artifact that drives the check, such as class-level constraints, generated simulations, external counterexamples, or transformed Alloy and OWL representations. As a result, explanations become difficult to follow whenever the relevant evidence spans several classification levels and heterogeneous artifacts. We address this problem with a level-agnostic approach in which model content at every classification level, together with the structures that classify, specialise, and relate it, shares one typed graph, over which a safe, stratified Datalog layer derives both reusable semantic relations and diagnostic facts. Rather than returning only textual error messages, diagnostics are reported as explicit witness tuples whose arguments identify the authored model references, profile terms, and typed values that explain each warning or violation. The approach is illustrated using OntoUML well-formedness rules, the BinOver antipattern with an explicitly authored individual witness, non-adjacent classification errors, and MLT-style powertype and partition constraints.

Keywords: OntoUML · Multi-Level Modeling · Ontological Validation · Explainable Diagnostics · Datalog

1 Introduction

Conceptual models are most useful when their diagrams are not merely pictures, but disciplined engineering artifacts whose intended semantics can be checked and explained. OntoUML supports this goal by using the Unified Foundational Ontology (UFO) to distinguish categories of model elements, such as *kinds*, *roles*, and *mixins*, whose distinct properties give rise to well-formedness rules and anti-patterns [11,18,19,21]. Multi-Level Theory (MLT) extends this checkable foundation to higher-order conceptual modeling, in which some elements are both types and instances at the same time, by making notions such as *powertypes*, *categorisers*, and *partitions* first-class citizens [1,7,8].

© The Author(s), under exclusive license to Springer Nature Switzerland AG 2027
A. Bernasconi et al. (Eds.): ER 2026, LNCS 17081, pp. 342–358, 2027.
https://doi.org/10.1007/978-3-032-40795-5_20

OntoUML and MLT diagnostics are supported by numerous editors and tool integrations, including OLED, current OntoUML tooling, and ML2 [7,10,20]. Their feedback is useful, but sometimes difficult to follow because the justification for an identified problem may span multiple artifact types and classification levels. For example, a rule may be checked over a type model, a class-level anti-pattern may be confirmed by an individual, a higher-order structure may be encoded as profile metadata, and a reasoning service may be applied to Alloy, OWL, or RDF artifacts derived from the explicitly authored model [2,5].

To address this problem, we make the diagnostics themselves *level-agnostic* by allowing rules to operate over one single model representation in which individuals, first-order types, and higher-order classifiers, as well as relationships, categorisations, and annotations, are all first-class elements. Classification levels remain explicit, but an individual diagnostic may refer to elements from any of them in a uniform way within a single result.

We realize this approach using PAMoLa[1] (Poly-Aligned Modeling Language), our multi-level, typed graph substrate, with Datalog providing its deductive semantic layer. This means that validation rules operate directly over the same graph in which models are authored, using recursive predicates to compute derived relations such as specialisation closure and partition membership, and stratified negation to support absence-sensitive checks. Since diagnostic rules retain the values bound by their variables, every finding emerges as a witness tuple containing references to the authored model elements involved, together with any profile terms, reasons, or scalar values needed to state the finding precisely. Human-readable messages can then be rendered from these records, while the structured references remain available for navigation, highlighting, grouping, and further processing.

Using Datalog over generic or level-agnostic model representations is not new. The Telos family—O-Telos/ConceptBase, DeepTelos, and MLT-Telos—uses a universal proposition representation [13–15,17], while the Uni-Level Description similarly flattens data model, schema, and data into a single first-order representation queried with Datalog [4]. Both therefore recover the distinctions they need from facts laid over one generic form. PAMoLa, in contrast, takes a "carrier-canonical" approach in which a small catalog of typed element kinds, each with a defined structural role and applicable property vocabulary, is fixed in the substrate itself and made available for modeling over multiple classification levels in the style of the Orthogonal Classification Architecture [3]. This shared catalog acts as a semantic normal form that allows object-oriented kernels, relational and graph stores and Datalog fact views to rely on the same structural distinctions. Moreover, since rules are themselves stored as ordinary model elements whose head arguments are named, these names directly supply the roles reported in witness tuples. Fixing the catalog in this way reduces encoding freedom, but avoids inventing a fresh graph vocabulary for each diagnostic program.
The paper makes four contributions:

[1] https://pamola.net.

1. level-agnostic OntoUML and MLT diagnostics as explicit witness tuples over PAMoLa's carrier-canonical graph;
2. executable Datalog rules for *kind* constraints, the BinOver anti-pattern, partition checks, non-adjacent classification and partition specialisation;
3. an integrated violation-seeded model whose MLT backbone adapts the ML2 examples of Fonseca et al. [7]; and
4. structured feedback and project-specific extension through named rule-head arguments and additional rule content.

Section 2 explains the problem in more depth, Sect. 3 introduces the representation, Sect. 4 presents the rule layer, Sect. 5 gives the examples, and Sects. 6–7 discuss implications and related work.

2 OntoUML, MLT and Level-Bound Diagnostics

When a model violates a constraint, the key question addressed in this paper is not whether the violation can be detected, since existing tools already do this well, but whether the evidence for it can be presented in terms of the explicitly authored elements that the modeler can recognize and act upon.

2.1 OntoUML Constraints and Anti-patterns

OntoUML categories constrain how classes may specialize and relate. For example, a *kind* supplies an identity principle, *roles* and *phases* are anti-rigid sortals, and *mixins* abstract across sortal hierarchies [11,19]. These classifications of classes support structural rules whose justification concerns the individuals classified by the types. For example, a *kind* should not specialize another sortal, because its instances would then receive a second identity supplier. Although such a rule is evaluated purely over the type hierarchy, what it enforces is a claim about the nature of the classified individuals, so its meaning is ontological rather than merely syntactic.

The BinOver anti-pattern makes the need for explicit evidence particularly visible. It concerns a binary relation whose end types may overlap [18]. Relevant evidence includes the relation, its endpoint types, the structural reason for possible overlap, and, when instance content is present, an individual inhabiting both endpoint extensions. A *diagnostic witness* is therefore an ordered, role-labeled tuple of authored model references together with any profile terms, reason terms, or scalar values needed to state a finding precisely.

2.2 MLT and Higher-Order Modeling

MLT introduces higher-order types, *powertypes*, *categorisers*, and *partitions* for cases in which a type's instances are themselves types [1,7]. In the fragment used in this paper, a categorizer classifies types specializing a designated base, a powertype relates a higher-order type to the base's subtypes and a partition adds complete, disjoint coverage, so every base individual belongs to exactly one branch. Thus `PersonTypeByGender` may partition `Person` through first-order members, `Man` and `Woman`, whose instances are ordinary individuals. One diagnostic may consequently need to name a higher-order classifier, its first-order members, and an individual. High-order OntoUML provides related support for types of types, powertypes, and categorizers [8].

2.3 From Level-Bound to Level-Agnostic Diagnostics

In common toolchains, diagnostic evidence is often distributed across heterogeneous technical representations, such as class-level models, anti-pattern reports, Alloy worlds [5], OWL or gUFO consequences [2], and profile annotations for higher-order constructs [8]. Each approach is useful in its own right, but may separate a finding from some of the elements that explain it. In BinOver, for example, the suspicious relation is type-level, the reason involves specialisation and identity provision, confirmation may involve an individual, and higher-order classifications may reside in profile metadata. A result produced at one stage therefore often names only part of the explanation, which the modeler must reconstruct across artifacts.

In contrast, in our approach we compute diagnostics over one level-agnostic graph. Explicit semantic predicates define specialisation, classification, endpoint typing, and partition membership while diagnostic predicates return role-labeled witnesses over model references and typed values. The analysis is fixed-model deduction in the sense that it derives consequences of the finite explicitly authored model, but neither synthesizes missing individuals nor searches for a possible world. Alloy's bounded instance and counterexample generation is therefore complementary rather than equivalent.

3 A Level-Agnostic Graph-Based Substrate

The multi-level graph substrate used to represent models and evaluate validation rules is PAMoLa[1], which is designed to be a general-purpose multi-level modeling platform rather than a tool focused on validating MLT and/or OntoUML models.

3.1 Model Representation Approach

The running model in Fig. 1 adapts the person-type example and ordered-type scaffold shown in Figs. 3 and 4 of Fonseca et al. [7]. We extend this backbone with researcher-status classifications, OntoUML interpretations, and the `worksFor` relation, and then introduce the deliberately invalid structures and individuals needed to exercise the diagnostics.

In particular, `Bob` is typed by `Man`, `Casey` by `ManWomanOverlap`, and `Taylor` by `PersonTypeByGender`, while `Alex` deliberately has both `Manager` and `Researcher` as direct classifiers. The concrete syntax is based on the Level-Agnostic Modeling Language (LML) [16].

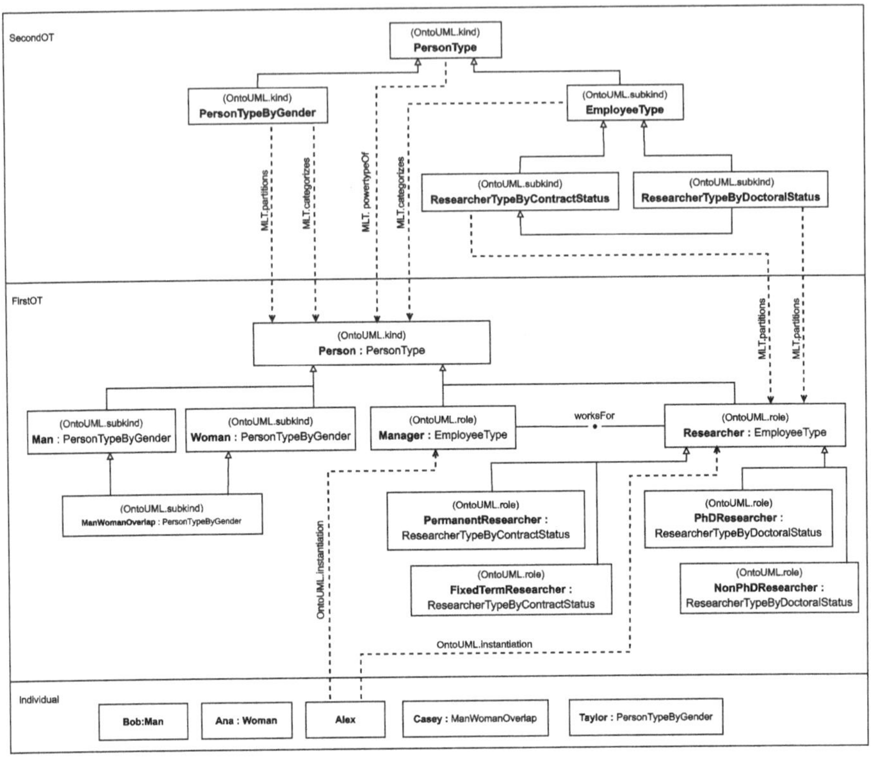

Fig. 1. Violation-seeded model adapted from Fonseca et al. [7]. The source labels `SecondOT`, `FirstOT`, and `Individual` denote ordinary custodian containers, not fixed meta-model levels. Parenthesized labels are Marker tags while dashed arrows are Marker references.

Every construct in this diagram is represented by one of a small number of information "carriers", which are PAMoLa's fixed, typed structural forms. More precisely, every model element is an *ordium* (an identity- and information-bearing unit with exactly one linguistic carrier kind) which determines the property vocabulary applicable to it. Method-level concepts such as OntoUML categories and MLT references then travel as content over these forms rather than becoming new kernel metaclasses, a commitment stronger than an arbitrary graph encoding but weaker than hardening every method concept into the kernel. Properties are optional, and HUTN may omit values supplied by defined defaults when their explicit presence is not significant. Table 1 summarizes the PAMoLa carriers used in this paper.

For example, every named rectangle in Fig. 1 is an `Entity`, whether it denotes the individual `Bob`, the first-order type `Person`, or the higher-order classifier `PersonTypeByGender`. The domain relation `worksFor`, in contrast, is a `Relationship`, whose two `Participation` wards identify the endpoint Entities through the property `hasRelatum`. Generalisation sets are reified in the same style, as a `Categorisation` with `Intercalation` endpoints, where `isGeneralisation` distinguishes the general endpoint from the special ones. `Intercalation` is PAMoLa-specific terminology for the `Categorisation` analogue of a `Participation`. In other words, instead of pointing directly to its generalisation and specialisation types, a `Categorisation` is the custodian of several addressable `Intercalations` (one for each end) and each `Intercalation` refers to its endpoint through its `hasRelatum` property. This gives each end an unambiguous location for end-specific information and allows generalisation sets with arbitrary numbers of specialisations.

Table 1. PAMoLa carrier kinds used or referenced in the examples.

Core family	Carrier kind	Role in this paper
`Clabject`	`Entity`	Individuals, types, and higher-order classifiers.
`Clabject`	`Relationship`	Domain relationships such as `worksFor`.
`Mediation`	`Participation`	Identity-bearing Relationship endpoint.
`Mediation`	`Intercalation`	Identity-bearing Categorisation endpoint.
`ImmanentOrdium`	`Categorisation`	Reified generalisation-set.
`Moment`	`Attribute/Method`	Feature occurrences.
`TranscendentOrdium`	`Marker`	OntoUML/MLT tags and references.
`BehaviouralOrdium`	`Atom`, `Parameter`, `Argument`	Rules and ordered predicate arguments.

The family column of Table 1 groups the carrier kinds by their structural roles. For example, `Entity` and `Relationship` are `Clabjects` and can therefore participate in ontological classification, while `Participation` and `Intercalation` are `Mediations`, generic carriers for endpoint occurrences that make each end addressable. The family names reflect related ideas in multi-level modeling and UFO, but they denote structural carrier roles rather than automatic ontological classifications. In particular, `Clabject` captures the class/object duality of multi-level modeling. `Participation` and `Intercalation` are `Mediation` carriers because they make the ends of reified structures independently addressable, while `Moment` is the generic family for feature occurrences associated with another ordium.

The purpose of this small, fixed catalog is to act as a minimal semantic commitment between model content and technical realizations, so that independently implemented backends and tools, whether object-oriented, relational, graph-based, or deductive, agree on one canonical structural interpretation. Domain classifiers and profile terms remain ordinary content, so their evolution does not require adding new carrier kinds.

The PAMoLa core defines seven universal properties, namely `hasName`, `hasPID`, `hasFQN`, `hasNote`, `hasCustodian`, `follows`, and `hasLinguisticType`, while `Clabjects` additionally admit `hasDeclaredType` and `hasPotency`. The carrier-specific properties used here include `hasTag`, `refersTo`, `hasRelatum`, and `isGeneralisation`. Of the universal properties, `hasCustodian` has one deliberately narrow meaning, identifying each non-root ordium's unique structural parent and thereby placing it in the model's locality tree. As a result, a `Marker` is a ward of the element it annotates, a `Participation` is a ward of its `Relationship`, and an `Intercalation` is a ward of its `Categorisation`. However, the semantic role of each ward is determined by its carrier kind and properties, since custody alone denotes neither annotation, participation, specialisation, nor classification. The transitive closure of the wards rooted at any ordium forms its *clade*, which provides a common scope for FQN construction, loading, projection, and rule execution. An ordium's PID gives it a stable lifetime identity, while its unique FQN is derived from its name and custodian path.

A `Marker` carries a tag and optionally a reference. It expresses OntoUML interpretations such as `OntoUML.kind` and MLT relations such as `MLT.partitions` using referenceable profile terms rather than free-form strings, while, in the examples considered here, the annotated element remains linguistically an `Entity`. This avoids adding a kernel category for every external stereotype and permits several profiles to interpret the same ordium. These mechanisms serve different purposes. `hasLinguisticType` fixes the PAMoLa carrier kind of an ordium, `hasDeclaredType` expresses classification within the represented domain, and a `Marker` records an interpretation supplied by an external or domain-specific profile. Representing `OntoUML.kind` as an ordinary declared type would conflate the OntoUML vocabulary with the domain's own classification hierarchy.

Ordinary direct ontological classification uses `hasDeclaredType`. In the OntoUML profile used here, a reference `Marker` tagged `OntoUML.instantiation` is reserved for deliberate multiple direct classification, as in the case of `Alex`. The rule layer normalizes both representations into the shared `iof` relation.

3.2 Textual HUTN View

PAMoLa models can also be serialized and exchanged textually using a Human-Usable Textual Notation (HUTN). Figure 2 uses two-letter carrier badges and nesting for custody, which makes the locality tree visible without repeatedly stating `hasCustodian`. It shows `Marker` tags and declared types, together with `Categorisations` and their `Intercalations`. It also shows the corresponding `Relationship` and `Participation` structure and `Alex`'s two instantiation `Markers`.

The right-hand fragment makes the distinction between custody and semantic references explicit by showing how ward-to-custodian edges organize the clade while `hasRelatum` links point to the relationship endpoints. For example, the nested `researcherEnd` and `managerEnd` blocks are wards of `worksFor`, corresponding to the solid ward-to-custodian arcs in the graph fragment, whereas their dashed `hasRelatum` arcs point separately to `Researcher` and `Manager`. The elided HUTN subtrees repeat these same representation patterns.

4 Rule-Based Semantics and Diagnostic Witnesses

The rule layer gives operational meaning to the explicitly authored graph. Its authoritative form is reified model content, represented using PAMoLa `Atom`,

```
EN {hasName "Violation_Seeded_Model",
  EN {hasName "SecondOT",
    EN {hasName "PersonType",
      MK {hasName "stereotype_kind", hasTag OntoUML.kind},
      MK {hasName "powertypeOf_Person", hasTag MLT.powertypeOf, refersTo FirstOT.Person}
    },
    ...
  },
  EN {hasName "FirstOT",
    ...
    EN {hasName "Manager", hasDeclaredType SecondOT.EmployeeType,
      MK {hasName "stereotype_role", hasTag OntoUML.role}
    },
    EN {hasName "Researcher", hasDeclaredType SecondOT.EmployeeType,
      MK {hasName "stereotype_role", hasTag OntoUML.role}
    },
    CA {hasName "EmployeeRoles", isDisjoint false,
      IC {hasName "general_Person", isGeneralisation true, hasRelatum Person},
      IC {hasName "special_Manager", isGeneralisation false, hasRelatum Manager},
      IC {hasName "special_Researcher", isGeneralisation false, hasRelatum Researcher}
    },
    RE {hasName "worksFor",
      PA {hasName "researcherEnd", hasRelatum Researcher},
      PA {hasName "managerEnd", hasRelatum Manager}
    },
    ...
  },
  EN {hasName "Individual",
    ...
    EN {hasName "Alex",
      MK {hasName "instantiates_Researcher", hasTag OntoUML.instantiation, refersTo FirstOT.Researcher},
      MK {hasName "instantiates_Manager", hasTag OntoUML.instantiation, refersTo FirstOT.Manager}
    },
    ...
  }
}
```

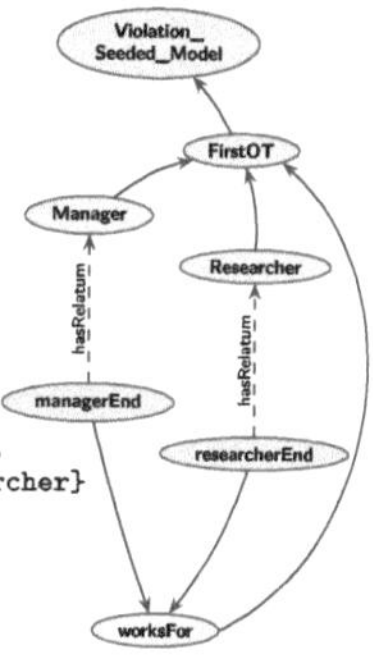

Fig. 2. Abridged HUTN view (left) and typed graph interpretation of its `worksFor` fragment (right). Ellipses omit subtrees and nesting denotes custody, solid arrows point from ward to custodian, while dashed arrows carry `hasRelatum` references.

`Parameter`, and `Argument` elements and executed directly by the internal rule engine, while the Datalog listings excerpted in the remainder of this section are generated projections intended for inspection and independent execution.

The language is safe, function-free Datalog with positive recursion, stratified negation-as-failure, equality, inequality, and binary arithmetic. It has no existential heads or aggregates [6]. Every variable in a negated or comparison literal also occurs in a positive body atom, so the rules are range restricted. Listings use Nemo syntax [12], with `?`-prefixed variables (so that model identifiers can appear unquoted) and `~` for negation. Evaluation starts from the explicitly authored facts (i.e., the declared rather than derived ones) and proceeds stratum by stratum to the least fixed point over this finite model. The resulting fixed-model, closed-world reading permits absence-sensitive checks such as partition completeness.

The profiles and diagnostic rules are loaded into the same kernel as the model so that FQN references resolve uniformly, but the subject fact view is fenced, meaning that domain facts come only from the selected model clade, augmented by ground program facts. As a result, reified rule `Atoms`, `Parameters`, `Arguments`, and profile metadata cannot accidentally become model subjects, a separation that is important in a homoiconic substrate where rules and the content they check coexist in one address space. The rule program itself is organized in three layers. Representation predicates such as **markedRef** and **endType** recover facts from PAMoLa's carrier structures, semantic predicates such as **specialisesPlus**, **iofPlus**, and **partitionMember** then compute reusable domain closure over them, and exported diagnostic predicates finally select the combinations that constitute findings and retain them as witnesses. Sections 4.1 and 4.2 introduce the first two layers, while Sect. 5 describes the exported diagnostics.

4.1 Markers, Specialisation, and Classification

Generic Marker navigation hides the annotation representation from later rules. The same predicates apply to OntoUML category tags, MLT references, and explicit additional classifications:

```
marked(?X, ?Tag) :-
    Marker(?M), hasCustodian(?M, ?X), hasTag(?M, ?Tag).
markedRef(?X, ?Tag, ?Y) :-
    Marker(?M), hasCustodian(?M, ?X), hasTag(?M, ?Tag), refersTo(?M, ?Y).
```

Specialisation is derived from the general and special `Intercalations` of reified `Categorisations` and then transitively closed, while classification combines ordinary declared typing with explicit instantiation `Markers` and follows specialization for its indirect cases. Defining these relations once lets every diagnostic reuse the same semantic closure.

```
specialises(?S, ?B) :-
    categorisationGeneral(?C, ?B), categorisationSpecial(?C, ?S).
specialisesPlus(?S, ?B) :- specialises(?S, ?B).
specialisesPlus(?S, ?B) :- specialises(?S, ?M), specialisesPlus(?M, ?B).

iof(?X, ?T) :- hasDeclaredType(?X, ?T).
iof(?X, ?T) :- markedRef(?X, OntoUML.instantiation, ?T).
iofPlus(?X, ?T) :- iof(?X, ?T).
iofPlus(?X, ?S) :- iof(?X, ?T), specialisesPlus(?T, ?S).
```

specialisesPlus is distinct from the core predicate **ancestor**, which denotes custodial ancestry.

4.2 Relationship and MLT Predicates

Relationship endpoint types are obtained from custodied `Participations` rather than from invented source/target annotations. This makes role occurrences, rather than arbitrary edge orientation, the stable basis for endpoint diagnostics:

```
endType(?R, ?P, ?T) :- Relationship(?R), Participation(?P),
    hasCustodian(?P, ?R), hasRelatum(?P, ?T).
relationEndPair(?R, ?A, ?B) :- endType(?R, ?P1, ?A),
    endType(?R, ?P2, ?B), ?P1 != ?P2.
```

MLT relations are represented by profile `Markers` that refer from a higher-order `Entity` to a base type. The first three rules recover powertype, categoriser, and partition relationships from those `Markers`. Since a partition is a categoriser with additional completeness and disjointness conditions, the fourth rule exposes this implication, while `partitionMember` connects a partition declaration to its first-order members:

```
powertypeOf(?P, ?B) :- markedRef(?P, MLT.powertypeOf, ?B).
categorizes(?C, ?B) :- markedRef(?C, MLT.categorizes, ?B).
partitions(?P, ?B) :- markedRef(?P, MLT.partitions, ?B).
categorizes(?P, ?B) :- partitions(?P, ?B).
partitionMember(?P, ?M) :- partitions(?P, ?B), iof(?M, ?P), specialisesPlus(?M, ?B).
```

4.3 Predicate Summary and Witness Signatures

Table 2 summarizes the main representation, semantic, and helper predicates used below, including the OntoUML taxonomy predicates `sortal` and `identityProvider`.

Table 2. Main semantic and helper predicates.

Predicate	Meaning
`marked(X,T); markedRef(X,T,Y)`	Marker tag, optionally with referenced target.
`ontoKind(X); sortal(T); identityProvider(X)`	OntoUML interpretations and stereotype families.
`specialisesPlus(S,B)`	Direct or indirect specialisation.
`iof(X,T); iofPlus(X,T)`	Direct and specialisation-closed classification.
`relationEndPair(R,A,B)`	Types of two distinct Relationship ends.
`binOverCase(A,B,S,R)`	Possible overlap, support `S`, and reason `R`.
`partitions(P,B); partitionMember(P,M)`	Partition base and member.
`baseIndividual(X,B)`	Potency-zero `X` classified by base `B`.
`partitionBranch(P,M); coveredBy(P,X)`	Top-level branch and individual coverage.
`effectivePotency(X,N)`	Explicit potency, or LML default zero.

A ground diagnostic tuple retains the references and typed values explaining a result. However, a predicate name and arity alone do not tell the modeler which role each position plays. PAMoLa's reified head `Atom` therefore contains ordered, identity-bearing `Arguments` whose names define these roles, while severity and an explanatory note belong to the predicate declaration. For head Arguments $a_1, \ldots, a_n$, the result signature is $\Sigma(p) = \langle severity(p), \langle name(a_1), \ldots, name(a_n)\rangle\rangle$. Ground values are paired with these roles, without a parallel result schema or message-template language. Thus the five terms returned by `warn_bin_over_case` can be presented as `relation`, `firstEndpointType`, `secondEndpointType`, `support`, and `reason`, while retaining direct references to the implicated model elements.

5 Worked Examples over the Diagnostic Model

The diagnostics below are evaluated together over Fig. 1, so global evaluation also exposes problems created by interactions among the explicitly authored assertions, not only the cases introduced to exercise individual rules.

5.1 Kind Constraint

We first introduce the rule style using a *kind* constraint. PersonTypeByGender and its ancestor PersonType are both marked OntoUML.kind, an intentionally invalid combination; following high-order OntoUML, higher-order classifiers may carry OntoUML category Markers. The profile predicate sortal supplies the forbidden ancestor family.

```
forbiddenKindAncestorTag(?Tag) :- sortal(?Tag).
err_kind_bad_ancestor(?Kind, ?Ancestor, ?Tag) :- ontoKind(?Kind),
    specialisesPlus(?Kind, ?Ancestor), marked(?Ancestor, ?Tag),
    forbiddenKindAncestorTag(?Tag).
```

For the running model, these rules derive the following diagnostic record.

err_kind_bad_ancestor:
kind = PersonTypeByGender, *ancestor* = PersonType, *forbiddenTag* = OntoUML.kind.

5.2 BinOver with an Explicit Individual Witness

worksFor relates Researcher and Manager, both of which are roles whose identity is supplied by Person. Since the categorization containing these endpoint types is not declared disjoint, their extensions may overlap, giving rise to the common-identity-provider form of BinOver. The OntoUML catalog distinguishes several BinOver variants. The example-relevant profile slice used here retains the common-identity-provider variant exercised by the running model, together with the generic disjointness rules needed to interpret it correctly.

```
warn_bin_over_case(?R, ?A, ?B, ?S, ?Reason) :-
    relationEndPair(?R, ?A, ?B), binOverCase(?A, ?B, ?S, ?Reason).
warn_bin_over_witness(?R, ?A, ?B, ?X) :-
    warn_bin_over_case(?R, ?A, ?B, _, _), iofPlus(?X, ?A), iofPlus(?X, ?B).
```

For the running model, the first rule derives this structural diagnostic record.

warn_bin_over_case:
relation = worksFor, *firstEndpoint* = Manager, *secondEndpoint* = Researcher, *support* = Person, *reason* = commonIdentityProvider.

Since Alex is also classified by both endpoint types, the second rule derives this individual-witness record.

warn_bin_over_witness:
relation = worksFor, *firstEndpoint* = Manager, *secondEndpoint* = Researcher, *individualWitness* = Alex.

5.3 Partition Overlap and Induced Subtype Overlap

PersonTypeByGender partitions Person through top-level branches Man and Woman while ManWomanOverlap specializes both branches, and Casey, typed by that subtype, consequently instantiates both.

```
err_partition_overlap(?P, ?X, ?M1, ?M2) :- partitions(?P, ?B),
    baseIndividual(?X, ?B), partitionBranch(?P, ?M1),
    partitionBranch(?P, ?M2), ?M1 != ?M2,
    iofPlus(?X, ?M1), iofPlus(?X, ?M2).
err_partition_subtype_overlap(?P, ?T, ?M1, ?M2) :-
    partitionBranch(?P, ?M1), partitionBranch(?P, ?M2), ?M1 != ?M2,
    specialisesPlus(?T, ?M1), specialisesPlus(?T, ?M2).
err_partition_missing(?P, ?B, ?X) :-
    partitions(?P, ?B), baseIndividual(?X, ?B), ~coveredBy(?P, ?X).
```

Here, `partitionBranch` excludes nested members from the top-level branch set. The first two rules derive these individual- and type-level diagnostic records.

`err_partition_overlap:`
partition = `PersonTypeByGender`, *focus* = `Casey`, *firstMember* = `Man`, *secondMember* = `Woman`.

`err_partition_subtype_overlap:`
partition = `PersonTypeByGender`, *focus* = `ManWomanOverlap`, *firstMember* = `Man`, *secondMember* = `Woman`.

The global run also derives the three missing-partition findings for `Alex` in Table 3.

5.4 Non-adjacent Higher-Order Classification

`Taylor` has potency zero but is directly typed by potency-two `PersonTypeByGender`, skipping the required one-step transition.

```
err_non_adjacent_iof(?X, ?T, ?PX, ?PT) :- iof(?X, ?T),
    effectivePotency(?X, ?PX), effectivePotency(?T, ?PT), ?PT != ?PX + 1.
```

For `Taylor`, the rule derives this diagnostic record.

`err_non_adjacent_iof:`
element = `Taylor`, *directType* = `PersonTypeByGender`, *elementPotency* = `0`, *typePotency* = `2`.

The generic LML layer also derives `violation(Taylor,potencyStep)`, although presentation uses the richer record. Likewise, the partition-specific member finding refines the corresponding general categorizer finding for Taylor.

5.5 Partition Specialization

`ResearcherTypeByDoctoralStatus` and `ResearcherTypeByContractStatus` both partition `Researcher`, but the model specialises the former under the latter.

```
err_partition_specialisation(?P1, ?P2, ?B) :-
    partitions(?P1, ?B), partitions(?P2, ?B), ?P1 != ?P2,
    specialisesPlus(?P1, ?P2).
```

The rule derives this purely higher-order diagnostic record.

`err_partition_specialisation:`
specialPartition = `ResearcherTypeByDoctoralStatus`, *generalPartition* = `ResearcherTypeByContractStatus`, *baseType* = `Researcher`.

5.6 Artifact and Diagnostic Summary

The complete model, profiles (with their vocabulary and rules), reified rules, generated Datalog, executable test, and expected results are available in the accompanying artifact[2]. The model contains 24 `Entity` ordia, one `Relationship`, two `Participations`, 11 `Categorisations`, 26 `Intercalations`, and 23 `Markers`. Its

[2] https://github.com/shilpi-gupta-mzn/Level-Agnostic-Diagnostics.

self-contained execution projection contains 408 model facts and 56 statements selected from the core and profiles, giving 464 logical statements before export directives. The repository supplies the corresponding example-relevant core and profile slices in paired HUTN and Datalog forms.

The run derives 16 diagnostic tuples and one generic LML violation. Four pairs arise twice because endpoint and partition-member order is semantically irrelevant. The feedback projection orders those pairs canonically, presents the richer non-adjacent record instead of the generic potency message, and prefers the partition-specific member record over its general categorizer counterpart. These presentation decisions produce the 11 records in Table 3, while all 17 raw facts remain queryable in support of alternative renderings or later provenance analysis. The three missing-partition diagnostics for `Alex` are valid because, as a `Researcher` and `Manager`, `Alex` is also a `Person` but has no member classification for the one Person partition or the two Researcher partitions.

6 Discussion

The examples show three benefits of level-agnostic diagnostics. First, findings retain the references and typed values that explain them. For example, BinOver reports a relation, endpoint types, structural support, and a machine-readable reason, while a separate predicate names an individual witness. Partition specialisation instead reports two higher-order classifiers and their base type. A human-readable note may accompany these fields, but does not replace the structured record needed for navigation, highlighting, grouping, deduplication, and further processing. Text is therefore a presentation of the diagnostic rather than its only representation.

Second, one semantic vocabulary spans all classification levels. Predicates such as `specialisesPlus`, `iofPlus`, `partitions`, and `partitionMember` apply whether a witness contains an individual, first-order type, or higher-order classifier. The rules do not need separate encodings for a class model, object model or higher-order profile artifact.

Third, the deductive layer is built for extension. Once a project has stable relations for specialization, classification, endpoints, identity provision, and partition membership, project-specific checks can compose them with local profile terms. Recursive closure is defined once, stratified negation adds absence-sensitive conditions, and every new diagnostic can use the same role-labeled result convention. Individual checks could also be expressed in OCL, SHACL/SPARQL, or Cypher. Datalog's shared deductive layer nevertheless supports systematic extension because new checks can reuse the same derived predicates, compose under one semantics, and report witnesses in the same form.

Table 3. The 11 normalized diagnostics for the integrated model, obtained from the 17 raw findings by collapsing symmetric pairs and eliding subsumed findings.

Predicate	Severity	Normalized witness
err_kind_bad_ancestor	Error	PersonTypeByGender, PersonType, OntoUML.kind
warn_bin_over_case	Warning	worksFor, Manager, Researcher, Person, commonIdentityProvider
warn_bin_over_witness	Warning	worksFor, Manager, Researcher, Alex
err_partition_missing	Error	PersonTypeByGender, Person, Alex
err_partition_missing	Error	ResearcherTypeByContractStatus, Researcher, Alex
err_partition_missing	Error	ResearcherTypeByDoctoralStatus, Researcher, Alex
err_partition_overlap	Error	PersonTypeByGender, Casey, Man, Woman
err_partition_subtype_overlap	Error	PersonTypeByGender, ManWomanOverlap, Man, Woman
err_non_adjacent_iof	Error	Taylor, PersonTypeByGender, 0, 2
err_partition_bad_member	Error	PersonTypeByGender, Person, Taylor
err_partition_specialisation	Error	ResearcherTypeByDoctoralStatus, ResearcherTypeByContractStatus, Researcher

Rule evaluation and feedback presentation are intentionally separated, so the feedback layer can canonicalize symmetric pairs and prefer the more informative of overlapping records while preserving all raw facts, as Sect. 5 illustrated.

The evaluation is deliberately small and batch-oriented. It establishes executable agreement for the reported model and rules, but not industrial-scale performance, incremental maintenance, automated repair, or complete derivation provenance, and the witness tuples identify the elements making a rule true rather than full proof trees. Practical adoption also requires governed profile vocabularies, reusable rule libraries, and editors that hide raw Datalog and reified rule structures from ordinary modelers.

7 Related Work

OntoUML validation has a long history. Its anti-pattern catalog and tooling identify recurring error-prone structures [18,21], while OLED and current tools support syntax checking, anti-pattern detection, simulation, transformation, and model analysis [10,20]. Alloy transformations provide bounded instances and counterexamples [5], while gUFO and OWL/RDF approaches connect OntoUML to ontology-engineering infrastructure [2]. The present work focuses on deriving one role-labeled witness record from a fixed explicitly authored model when its explanation spans several classification levels.

Constraint- and graph-based validation is established more broadly. OCL and USE evaluate constraints over UML models [9], SHACL defines graph constraints and standardized validation-result objects [22], and SPARQL, Cypher, and related languages can express many individual checks. Our contribution is not a new query operator, but the combination of a shared level-agnostic representation, reusable deductive closure, and source-model witnesses with intrinsic role names. Alloy addresses a different analysis mode by searching for bounded possible worlds rather than deriving consequences from one fixed model.

MLT and ML2 provide the nearest conceptual-modeling foundation [1,7]; high-order OntoUML also supports types of types, powertypes, and categorizers [8]. The diagnostic rule set presented here combines selected interpretations from those traditions, rather than proposing another theory of higher-order classification.

The closest deductive relatives are in the Telos family. O-Telos represents explicit propositions through the identity-bearing base relation $P(o, x, l, y)$, and ConceptBase applies Datalog rules and integrity constraints across arbitrary abstraction levels [13,17]. DeepTelos adds deep characterization through most-general instances [15], while MLT-Telos reconstructs MLT* deductively, derives implicit facts, and detects modeling errors [14]. These systems demonstrate that deductive, level-agnostic validation over a universal proposition substrate is well established.

PAMoLa occupies a different point in this design space. O-Telos obtains broad scope through *propositional reduction*, in which diverse explicit content uses one proposition form and distinctions are recovered through classes and axioms. PAMoLa instead uses *carrier canonicalization*, in which its finite typed core fixes selected `Clabject`, `Mediation`, `Moment`, `Marker`, value, and behavioral structures in one PID/FQN-addressable clade space. The stronger commitment reduces representational freedom but gives object, relational, graph, textual, and deductive realizations a shared structural contract. Reified rule heads additionally provide the witness roles used here.

8 Conclusion

In this paper we have shown that ontological diagnostics for OntoUML and MLT can be made level-agnostic by evaluating them over a single carrier-canonical graph in which individuals, types, higher-order classifiers, and the rules themselves are all ordinary model content. Perhaps the most important lesson from this exercise is that explanation quality depends as much on representation as on checking. Once every element involved in a violation is addressable within one substrate, role-named witnesses follow directly from the representation. By contrast, reconstructing the same evidence across heterogeneous artifacts becomes more difficult with every additional level and tool. The approach also shows that the choice need not be between a completely generic representation and one that hard-codes every method concept. In the examples studied here, a small canonical catalog supports the selected OntoUML and MLT diagnostics without hard-wiring either method into the substrate. In future work we therefore plan to grow the diagnostic rules into governed, reusable libraries, to add incremental evaluation and provenance services above the same semantic predicates, and to investigate how far the witness-role convention can serve as a general contract between modeling tools and emerging AI-based assistants.

Acknowledgments. This work was funded by the German Research Foundation (DFG) – CRC 1608 – 501798263.

Disclosure of Interests. The authors have no competing interests to declare.

References

1. Almeida, J.P.A., Fonseca, C.M., Carvalho, V.A.: A comprehensive formal theory for multi-level conceptual modeling. In: Mayr, H.C., Guizzardi, G., Ma, H., Pastor, O. (eds.) ER 2017. LNCS, vol. 10650, pp. 280–294. Springer, Cham (2017). https://doi.org/10.1007/978-3-319-69904-2_23
2. Almeida, J.P.A., Guizzardi, G., Falbo, R.A., Sales, T.P.: gUFO: a lightweight implementation of the unified foundational ontology. In: Proceedings of the Joint Ontology Workshops (2019)
3. Atkinson, C., Kühne, T.: The essence of multilevel metamodeling. In: Gogolla, M., Kobryn, C. (eds.) UML 2001. LNCS, vol. 2185, pp. 19–33. Springer, Heidelberg (2001). https://doi.org/10.1007/3-540-45441-1_3
4. Bowers, S., Delcambre, L.M.L.: Using the uni-level description (ULD) to support data-model interoperability. Data Knowl. Eng. **59**(3), 511–533 (2006). https://doi.org/10.1016/j.datak.2005.10.007
5. Braga, B.F.B., Almeida, J.P.A., Guizzardi, G., Benevides, A.B.: Transforming OntoUML into Alloy: towards conceptual model validation using a lightweight formal method. Innov. Syst. Softw. Eng. **6**, 55–63 (2010)
6. Ceri, S., Gottlob, G., Tanca, L.: What you always wanted to know about Datalog (and never dared to ask). IEEE Trans. Knowl. Data Eng. **1**(1), 146–166 (1989). https://doi.org/10.1109/69.43410
7. Fonseca, C.M., Almeida, J.P.A., Guizzardi, G., Carvalho, V.A.: Multi-level conceptual modeling: theory, language and application. Data Knowl. Eng. **134**, 101894 (2021). https://doi.org/10.1016/j.datak.2021.101894
8. Fonseca, C.M., Guizzardi, G., Almeida, J.P.A., Sales, T.P., Porello, D.: Incorporating types of types in ontology-driven conceptual modeling. In: Conceptual Modeling - ER 2022. LNCS, vol. 13607, pp. 18–34. Springer (2022)
9. Gogolla, M., Büttner, F., Richters, M.: USE: a UML-based specification environment for validating UML and OCL. Sci. Comput. Program. **69**, 27–34 (2007)
10. Guerson, J., Sales, T.P., Guizzardi, G., Almeida, J.P.A.: OntoUML Lightweight Editor: a model-based environment to build, evaluate and implement reference ontologies. In: IEEE 19th International Enterprise Distributed Object Computing Workshop (EDOCW), pp. 144–147. IEEE (2015)
11. Guizzardi, G.: Ontological foundations for structural conceptual models. Ph.D. thesis, University of Twente (2005)
12. Ivliev, A., Gerlach, L., Meusel, S., Steinberg, J., Krötzsch, M.: Nemo: your friendly and versatile rule reasoning toolkit. In: Proceedings of the 21st International Conference on Principles of Knowledge Representation and Reasoning, pp. 743–754 (2024). https://doi.org/10.24963/kr.2024/70
13. Jarke, M., Gallersdörfer, R., Jeusfeld, M.A., Staudt, M., Eherer, S.: ConceptBase: a deductive object base for meta data management. J. Intell. Inf. Syst. **4**(2), 167–192 (1995). https://doi.org/10.1007/BF00961873
14. Jeusfeld, M.A., Almeida, J.P.A., Carvalho, V.A., Fonseca, C.M., Neumayr, B.: Deductive reconstruction of MLT* for multi-level modeling. In: Proceedings of the 23rd ACM/IEEE International Conference on Model Driven Engineering Languages and Systems: Companion Proceedings. ACM (2020). https://doi.org/10.1145/3417990.3421410

15. Jeusfeld, M.A., Neumayr, B.: DeepTelos: multi-level modeling with most general instances. In: Comyn-Wattiau, I., Tanaka, K., Song, I.-Y., Yamamoto, S., Saeki, M. (eds.) ER 2016. LNCS, vol. 9974, pp. 198–211. Springer, Cham (2016). https://doi.org/10.1007/978-3-319-46397-1_15
16. Lange, A., Atkinson, C.: Multi-level modeling with MELANEE. In: Proceedings of the MODELS 2018 Workshops. CEUR Workshop Proceedings, vol. 2245, pp. 653–662. CEUR-WS.org (2018)
17. Mylopoulos, J., Borgida, A., Jarke, M., Koubarakis, M.: Telos: representing knowledge about information systems. ACM Trans. Inf. Syst. **8**(4), 325–362 (1990). https://doi.org/10.1145/102675.102676
18. OntoUML Community: BinOver: Binary relation with overlapping end types (2025). https://ontouml.readthedocs.io/en/latest/anti-patterns/BinOver/index.html
19. OntoUML Community: OntoUML specification documentation (2025). https://ontouml.readthedocs.io
20. OntoUML Community: OntoUML Tooling (2026). https://ontouml.org/ontouml/tooling/
21. Sales, T.P., Guizzardi, G.: Ontological anti-patterns: empirically uncovered error-prone structures in ontology-driven conceptual models. Data Knowl. Eng. **99**, 72–104 (2015). https://doi.org/10.1016/j.datak.2015.06.004
22. World Wide Web Consortium: Shapes constraint language (SHACL). W3C Recommendation, W3C (2017). https://www.w3.org/TR/shacl/

Towards Ontological Support for Governance, Risk and Compliance of Enterprise AI

Jasmine Hong[1(✉)], Surabhi Nigam[1], Ida Asadi Someh[1], Sonja Zillner[2], and Shazia Sadiq[1]

[1] The University of Queensland, QLD, Brisbane, Australia
jasmine.hong@student.uq.edu.au, {surabhi.nigam, i.asadi}@business.uq.edu.au, s.sadiq@uq.edu.au
[2] Siemens AG and Technical University of Munich, Munich, Germany
sonja.zillner@siemens.com

Abstract. The rapid adoption of enterprise AI has been accompanied by a fragmented and evolving landscape of regulations, standards, and policy frameworks. Although these instruments often overlap in intent, they diverge in terminology, scope, and enforceability across jurisdictions, creating significant governance, risk, and compliance (GRC) challenges for organisations. This paper proposes a conceptual model that can provide ontological support for enterprise AI GRC. Following a Design Science Research approach, we analyse thirteen global AI regulations and standards to systematically examine how GRC concepts are covered. Using thematic analysis and structured abstraction, we derive a coherent set of governance, risk, and compliance dimensions that underpin the model. The resulting artefact aims to enhance semantic cohesion, clarify attribution to source instruments, and support cross-jurisdictional reasoning.

Keywords: Enterprise AI · Governance Risk and Compliance · Ontology

1 Introduction

The last decade has witnessed a rapid acceleration in the development and deployment of artificial intelligence (AI) technologies across virtually all sectors of the economy. Advances in machine learning, deep learning, and generative AI have enabled organisations to embed AI into core business functions and public services at unprecedented scale and speed, giving rise to a plethora of Enterprise AI applications. *Enterprise AI* refers to AI technologies developed to address business and organisational needs, in both public and private enterprises, and contrasts with *Consumer AI*, which is designed for use by individuals, enhancing convenience in everyday tasks [1].

Alongside these technological advances has come growing recognition of the risks associated with AI systems, including concerns related to safety, bias, accountability, transparency, privacy, and broader societal impact. As a result, governments, standards bodies, and international organisations have responded with an expanding landscape of

© The Author(s), under exclusive license to Springer Nature Switzerland AG 2027
A. Bernasconi et al. (Eds.): ER 2026, LNCS 17081, pp. 359–368, 2027.
https://doi.org/10.1007/978-3-032-40795-5_21

regulations, standards, ethical guidelines, and policy frameworks intended to govern the responsible design, deployment, and use of AI.

This regulatory and standards ecosystem has grown both rapidly and unevenly, resulting in a dilemma [23]. On the one hand, jurisdictions around the world are introducing AI-specific legislation, sectoral regulations, and non-binding policy instruments, often informed by different regulatory philosophies and risk priorities. On the other hand, while these initiatives share common goals, they frequently differ in scope, terminology, and levels of enforceability resulting in a complex and evolving governance environment [12]. Different regions stipulate different yet overlapping compliance requirements that organisations must navigate as they adopt and operationalise AI systems, causing downward pressure on AI innovation. This fragmentation obscures traceability between obligations making compliance activities manual, fragmented, and duplicated [9]. The result is an enterprise AI GRC burden that is simultaneously error-prone and inefficient, increasing both compliance risk and organisational cost. These challenges reveal a need for formal mechanisms that can systematically represent and align AI GRC concepts across heterogeneous regulatory and standards regimes.

In this paper our research objective is to motivate, design and interrogate the utility of a conceptual model that can formally represent AI GRC concepts in a machine-interpretable knowledge structure with a view to providing ontological support to deliver accurate, context-sensitive GRC guidance across regulatory jurisdictions. We posit that by systematically analysing how GRC concepts are represented across AI regulations and standards and structuring these concepts into a coherent, navigable conceptual model, we can facilitate a shared, structured understanding of obligations and risks, and provide the semantic foundation to reason coherently about cross-jurisdiction AI GRC.

We present our contributions as below: in Sect. 2, we highlight prior works from both academia and industry towards creating structured ontologies for AI GRC. We outline our approach based on design science research in Sect. 3 for developing an artefact, namely a conceptual model as a means of providing ontological support for AI GRC. Section 4 and 5 presents the comparative analysis of 13 global AI regulations and standards that form the conceptual foundations for modelling AI GRC and the resulting conceptual encoding. We conclude the paper in Sect. 6.

2 Related Work

Recent years have seen growing interest in the development of ontologies and structured vocabularies to support aspects of GRC for AI systems. This body of work reflects the increasing need to formalise regulatory requirements, risk concepts, governance policies, and documentation artefacts. However, existing contributions tend to address specific slices of the AI GRC problem space rather than offering an integrated, enterprise-level, and cross-jurisdictional perspective.

One prominent line of work focuses on AI risk representation. The AI Risk Ontology (AIRO) provides a formal vocabulary for expressing risks associated with AI systems [7], grounded in established risk management standards such as ISO 31000 [11] and ISO/IEC 23894 [10], as well as regulatory constructs from the EU AI Act [6]. AIRO supports the modelling of AI systems and enables reasoning for regulatory classifications such as "high-risk" AI under Annex III of the EU AI Act [7]. As such, AIRO offers a strong foundation for the "risk" dimension of AI GRC but does not explicitly address governance structures, compliance obligations, or organisational evidence management. The AI Risk Atlas Nexus [2] provides a complementary approach through a collection of open-source tools that leverage ontologies to bridge the gap between mitigation strategies. Another contribution for AI risk management is the open vocabulary for risks (VAIR) [8], that directly targets the EU AI Act's hierarchy of risks to assist with AI risk assessments.

The modelling of regulatory controls has been widely studied in the context of business process compliance research [19], with contributions both on modelling and reasoning. For AI regulation, the Trustworthy AI Requirements (TAIR) ontology [9] aims to extract and formalise concepts derived from normative statements in legal texts and technical standards. TAIR focuses on requirements modelling and traceability and addresses the compliance dimension of AI GRC, but it remains primarily concerned with requirements representation rather than governance processes [8].

In the governance and policy domain, the W3C Open Digital Rights Language (ODRL) provides a vocabulary for representing permissions, prohibitions, and obligations [22]. ODRL is particularly relevant for modelling governance policies and control rules [5], however, it does not capture AI-specific risk constructs or regulatory classifications. Additional work such as the Model Card Report Ontology (MCRO) formalises the structure of model cards, enabling transparency artefacts to be represented in RDF/OWL for indexing and aggregation [16]. MCRO supports governance reporting and evidence generation [16] but operates at the artifact level rather than at the enterprise GRC integration level.

Beyond ontologies, governance frameworks such as the National Institute of Standards and Technology (NIST) AI Risk Management Framework [17] are widely used as conceptual backbones for organisational AI governance programs. While not formal ontologies, such frameworks are frequently used to support operationalisation. The ISO/IEC 42001 [8] is a significant global initiative towards responsible development and use of AI systems. Recent work [6, 8] identifies the challenge of determining the degree to which conformance to standards can also help achieve regulatory compliance, highlighting the overlapping yet inconsistent landscape.

Together, these efforts demonstrate significant progress towards the development of ontology components for AI GRC. However, they remain fragmented, addressing discrete GRC concerns. Currently, no integrated, enterprise-level ontology harmonises these elements to support coherent, cross-jurisdictional AI GRC.

3 Methodology

This study adopts a Design Science Research (DSR) methodology to develop and evaluate a conceptual model that provides ontological support for enterprise AI GRC. DSR enables problem solving through the design of an artefact, often producing design knowledge in the process [21]. We use the widely adopted Design Science Research methodology process model [18] to build the conceptual model as the key artifact. Our work is motivated by a growing problem of an AI governance landscape where regulations and standards can overlap in intent and concepts while remaining inconsistent in terminology, resulting in a semantic disparity that substantially increases the compliance burden for enterprises addressing multiple regulations across jurisdictions.

Accordingly, the solution objective of our design artefact is to provide structured support for organisations to navigate a large corpus of heterogenous regulations and standards. To evaluate the utility of the artefact [13] we identify four criteria of (1) semantic cohesion: artefact's ability to respectively organise dispersed GRC knowledge into a coherent structure, (2) attribution clarity: enable traceability to source regulations, (3) cognitive navigability: support effective exploration and interpretation across a multitude of regulatory requirements, and (4) representational completeness: provide assurance of coverage and consequently compliance.

Our aim therefore is to develop a conceptual model by systematically analysing the representation of GRC concepts across AI regulations and standards, and structuring these concepts into a coherent, navigable model. To undertake the design and development of the model we first conduct a knowledge acquisition step to identify representative AI regulations and standards from 13 countries during the last six years.

1. Interim Measures for the Management of Generative Artificial Intelligence Services (China - CN)
2. AI Guidelines for Business (Japan - JP)
3. An Act promoting the development and regulation of Artificial Intelligence in the Philippines (Philippines - PH)
4. Voluntary AI Safety Standard (Australia - AU)
5. Bill of Law No. 21 (Brazil - BR)
6. European Union Artificial Intelligence Act (European Union - EU)
7. Generative Artificial Intelligence Technical and Application Guideline (Hong Kong - HK)
8. Model AI Governance Framework for Generative AI (Singapore - SG)
9. Artificial Intelligence Risk Management Framework (NIST United States - US)
10. Regulation of Law No. 31814 (Peru - PE)
11. Recommendation on the Ethics of Artificial Intelligence (UNESCO - UN)
12. Responsible AI Guidance for the Public Service: Gen AI (New Zealand - NZ)
13. Basic Act on the Development of Artificial Intelligence and Establishment of Trust (South Korea - SK)

Our semantic analysis is anchored in the Uschold and King ontology-building methodology [20], which provides structured guidance for ontology construction from domain analysis. To enhance the semantic foundation, we explicitly adopt foundational ontology principles by grounding our derived concepts in risk and governance frameworks from 13 countries, thereby mitigating subjectivity by ensuring concept derivation is traceable to normative source documents rather than interpretive choice. Subsequently, following an iterative process we conduct an analysis of the corpus using the Braun and Clarke's thematic analysis approach [3] enabling the derivation of first-order concepts and second-order themes. We then draw upon the Gioia method [15], to abstract the second-order themes into a third tier of aggregate dimensions. This additional layer of abstraction, enables a more navigable interpretation of the underlying narratives within the corpus. The results as presented in Sect. 4, identify 11 aggregated dimensions across the three pillars of governance, risk and compliance. These concepts and the detailed comparisons expose scope, overlaps and redundancies and thereby form the foundation for the conceptual model which is presented in Sect. 5.

Overall, our approach encapsulates five key steps faithful to the DSR methodology: (1) articulating a solution objective and associated evaluation criteria; (2) knowledge acquisition; (3) semantic analysis; (4) structured abstraction into aggregate dimensions; and (5) conceptual encoding. We posit that these five steps not only enable a systematic development of the key artefact (Fig. 1) but also provide process guidance on how ontological support for AI GRC can be conceptualized and maintained.

4 Comparative Analysis

We formed the initial codes by identifying text excerpts in the corpus that encapsulated meaningful, interesting features [3], making use of Nvivo. This requires some extent of the coder's judgement and interpretation to determine the relevance and significance of an extract. Researcher bias was mitigated by continuous discussions between multiple coders of the research team. An example of coding excerpts is seen in Table 1.

Table 1. Example development of first order code "*Disclosure about AI capabilities and limitations*".

Source	Excerpt
Australia	"Document the scope for each AI system, including intended use cases, **capabilities, limitations..**." (Item 9.2.2)
EU	"Detailed information about the monitoring, functioning...of the AI system, in particular with regard to: **its capabilities and limitations in performance**, including the degrees of accuracy for specific persons or groups of persons on which the system is intended to be used..." (Annex IV, Item 3)
Japan	"provide and explain information...**Capabilities and limitations of the AI system or service**, and proper/improper use by AI business users" (pg. 17)
USA	"**Limitations of the generalizability** beyond the conditions under which the technology was developed are documented." (Measure 2.5)

Following the identification of first order codes, the second order themes were developed. Whilst higher coding frequencies may be indicative of an emerging theme, literature stresses that the approach should not be regarded as a quantitative study [14], and it is essential to recognize that themes are not objectively existent in the data, instead, the narrative is actively constructed by the researcher based on their unique interpretation of the different codes [4]. An example of second order codes to form themes is presented in Table 2.

The abstraction of the second order themes into aggregate dimensions [15], identified 11 dimensions associated with the three pillars of Governance, Risk, and Compliance. This extensive and interactive process provided us with the necessary concepts, relationships, and properties to construct the conceptual model. Table 3 depicts the total number

Table 2. Example development of first order codes.

First order Code	Second order theme
Disclosure about AI capabilities and limitations	Model Quality
Disclosure about AI testing results	
Disclosure about AI Risks	

of references coded under each aggregate dimension across the corpus of 13 countries that we included in our comparative analysis.

Table 3. Summary of comparative analysis of 13 countries

GOVERNANCE													
	CN	JP	PH	AU	BR	EU	HK	SG	US	PE	UN	NZ	SK
Sustainability	3	8	6	0	9	8	1	1	1	6	12	4	9
Oversight	0	2	6	2	1	26	2	0	1	13	6	2	11
Transparency	2	20	2	13	1	27	11	8	9	3	8	10	2
Values	4	21	6	20	3	26	6	3	10	14	35	13	13
Trustworthiness	5	16	3	17	4	14	25	14	16	10	17	6	3
RISK													
	CN	JP	PH	AU	BR	EU	HK	SG	US	PE	UN	NZ	SK
Categorisation	0	0	1	5	0	16	10	3	10	5	1	1	4
Forecast	0	4	0	0	1	7	6	3	1	2	1	3	7
Protection	1	3	0	1	0	1	0	0	3	0	2	0	0
Accountability	0	2	0	0	1	1	0	0	2	4	2	1	0
COMPLIANCE													
	CN	JP	PH	AU	BR	EU	HK	SG	US	PE	UN	NZ	SK
Enforcement	2	1	4	0	0	32	1	0	3	1	5	1	4
Standardisation	2	3	1	3	1	4	4	1	0	5	2	2	0

Although the dimensions present a comprehensive coverage across all 13 jurisdictions, within each dimension there is significant variability in scope, terminology, and levels of enforceability. Due to space limitations, we provide the summary of one aggregate dimension as an example of the analysis: **Transparency under the Governance pillar**.

Themes

under Transparency are discussed to a comparable extent across the corpus. Generally, jurisdictions focused on declaring *what* transparency requirements were necessary, rather than how to operationalise them. For example, Australia's standard discusses 'Model intention' themes by mandating the disclosure of *"the scope for each AI system, including intended use cases"* (Item 9.2.2), whilst similarly, the EU AI Act mentions disclosing *"the tasks that the [general-purpose] AI model is intended to perform"* (Annex 11, Sect. 1.1). Likewise, the EU AI Act discusses disclosure of 'Model quality', including transparency about *"the overall expected level of accuracy in relation to its intended purpose"* (Annex 4.3), whilst Australia's standard refers to communication with suppliers about the known *"issues"* and *"faults"* of the model (Item 8.1.2). Several regulations make references to 'Model implementation' reflected through transparency declarations of the model's in-built technical components. For example, mandates to *"provide insights into the decision-making process"* (Hong Kong, pg. 29) and disclose *"Safety measures implemented (e.g., bias correction techniques and safeguarding the exfiltration of sensitive data)"* (Singapore, pg. 14). In addition, transparency surrounding 'AI use' focussed on what needed to be declared (e.g. that *"synthetic audio, image, video or text"* is undeniably distinguishable for *"natural persons concerned [to be] informed that they are interacting with an AI system"* (EU AI Act, Article 50)). Although Hong Kong's framework elaborates on this theme to a marginally greater extent by further stating how to operationalise AI detectability through watermarking (pg. 26) and labelling (pg. 17).

5 Developing the Conceptual Model for Ontological Support

These concepts and the detailed comparisons expose scope, overlaps, and redundancies and thereby form the foundations for the conceptual model presented below. The conceptualisation task is guided by an ontology-building methodology introduced by Uschold and King [20], where we encode the concepts and their definitions, relationships and properties captured through the comparative analysis into a model using a common representation for ontology documentation, namely the Web Ontology Language (OWL) as represented in Fig. 1.

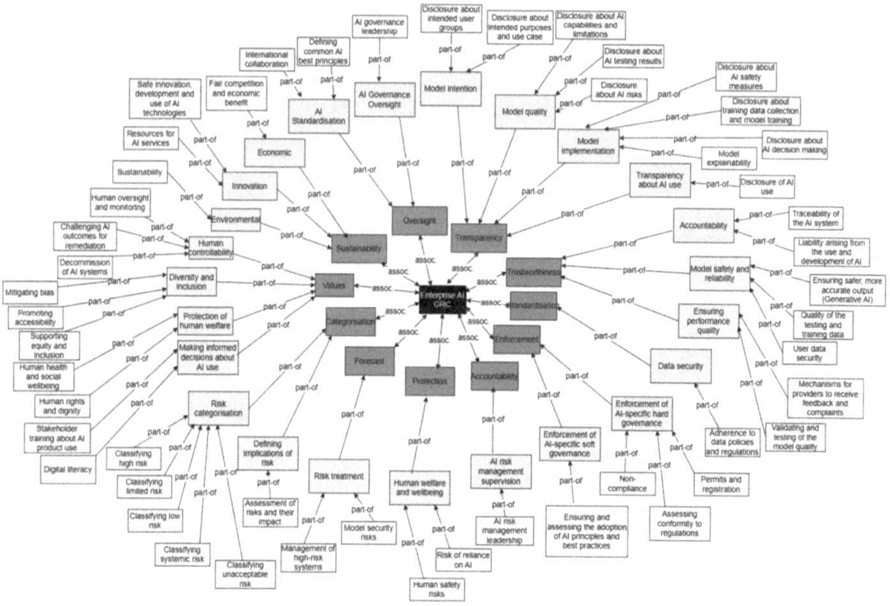

Fig. 1. Conceptual encoding of Governance, Risk and Compliance for Enterprise AI

We provide an instantiation of the conceptual model in Fig. 2 to demonstrate how the conceptual model can be utilized in practice to provide ontological support. The example is focused on the aggregate dimension, "Transparency", encapsulating a variety of second-order themes. A compliance officer may need to understand transparency stipulations across the European Union Artificial Intelligence Act (EU AI Act), Australia's Voluntary AI Safety Standard and the United States' Artificial Intelligence Risk Management Framework (AI RMF). Through such a 'view' of the overall model, the compliance officer will be able to group semantically disparate clauses across regulations into a unified view of "Transparency", serving as a minimum benchmark for Governance adherence across multiple regulatory frameworks.

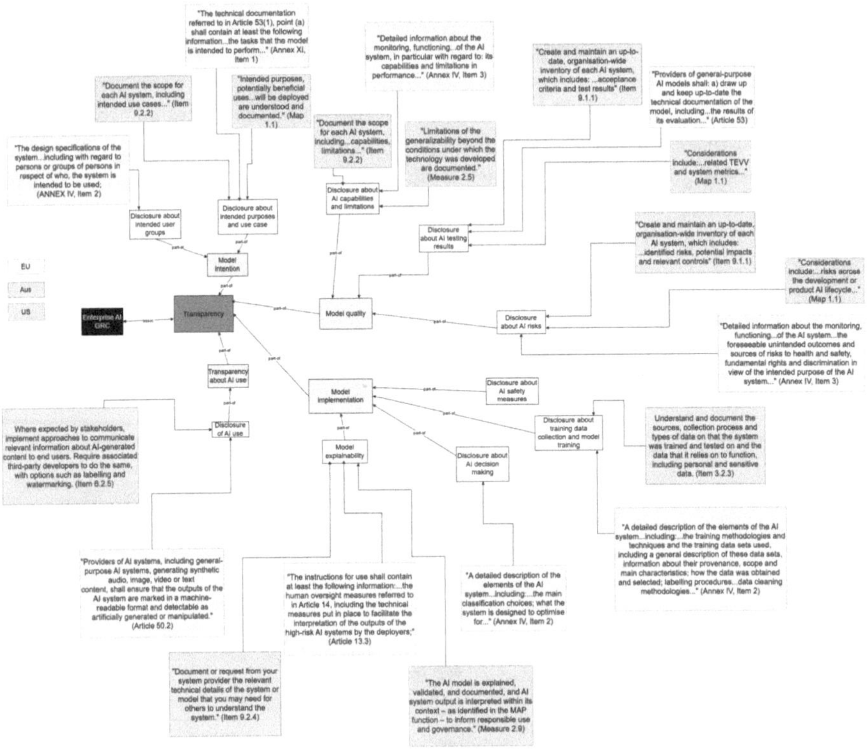

Fig. 2. Instantiation of the model with regulations from EU, US and Australia

6 Conclusions

An increasingly complex and fragmented GRC landscape for Enterprise AI applications is creating a dilemma for organisations wanting to adopt AI safely and responsibly, yet finding the regulatory and standards regimes negatively impacting their AI innovation ambitions due to excessive compliance burden. In this paper, we present a 5-step approach grounded in design science research methodology for developing a conceptual model that can provide essential ontological support for navigating the AI GRC landscape. Our approach provides the methodological guidance for developing and maintaining the conceptual model. The systematic approach we followed allows extensions to further regulations as well as changes to existing ones, while the proposed model, developed through a systematic analysis of 13 global regulations and standards, provides proof of concept for how to achieve this support.

Our work is not without limitations. We have outlined four criteria for evaluating the utility of the model (in Sect. 3), but the results of the evaluation are not part of this short paper. Our work is supported by a large GRC team deploying industrial AI at a global manufacturing organisation, and the first part of our future work is to conduct an empirical evaluation of these criteria (as well as broader validity measures [13]) with the team. The second part of our future work is to build a knowledge graph from the evaluated conceptual model to enable a machine-interpretable foundational layer for a natural language query and recommendation tool that leverages large language models (LLMs) and retrieval-augmented generation (RAG) to respond to practitioner queries. The tool is intended to provide a testbed to investigate the effectiveness of ontological support for cross-jurisdiction GRC of Enterprise AI applications.

Acknowledgments. This work is partly funded by the ARC Training Centre for Information Resilience.

Disclosure of Interests. The authors have no competing interests to declare that are relevant to the content of this article.

References

1. Australian Research Alliance for Enterprise AI: Australian Research Alliance for Enterprise AI. https://enterpriseai.org.au/. Accessed 01 May 2026
2. Bagehorn, F., et al.: AI Risk Atlas: Taxonomy and Tooling for Navigating AI Risks and Resources. https://arxiv.org/abs/2503.05780 (2025). https://doi.org/10.48550/arXiv.2503.05780
3. Braun, V., Clarke, V.: Using thematic analysis in psychology. Qual. Res. Psychol. **3**, 77–101 (2006). https://doi.org/10.1191/1478088706qp063oa
4. Byrne, D.: A worked example of Braun and Clarke's approach to reflexive thematic analysis. Qual. Quant. **56**, 1391–1412 (2021). https://doi.org/10.1007/s11135-021-01182-y
5. De Vos, M., Kirrane, S., Padget, J., Satoh, K.: ODRL policy modelling and compliance checking. In: Lecture Notes in Computer Science, pp. 36–51. Springer, Cham (2019). https://doi.org/10.1007/978-3-030-31095-0_3
6. European Union: Regulation (EU) 2024/1689 laying down harmonised rules on artificial intelligence (Artificial Intelligence Act). https://eurlex.europa.eu/eli/reg/2024/1689/oj. Accessed 01 May 2026
7. Golpayegani, D., Pandit, H.J., Lewis, D.: AIRO: an ontology for representing AI risks based on the proposed EU AI act and ISO risk management standards. In: Hitzler, P., et al. (eds.) Towards a Knowledge-Aware AI. Studies on the Semantic Web, vol. 49, pp. 51–65. IOS Press, Amsterdam (2022). https://doi.org/10.3233/SSW220008

8. Golpayegani, D., Pandit, H.J., Lewis, D.: To Be High-Risk, or Not To Be—Semantic Specifications and Implications of the AI Act's High-Risk AI Applications and Harmonised Standards. In: Proceedings of the 2023 ACM Conference on Fairness, Accountability, and Transparency (FAccT '23),Chicago, IL, USA, June 12–15, 2023, pp. 905–915. ACM, New York (2023). https://doi.org/10.1145/3593013.3594050
9. Hernandez, J., Golpayegani, D., Lewis, D.: An open knowledge graph-based approach for mapping concepts and requirements between the EU AI act and international standards. AI and Ethics. **5**, 4463–4474 (2025). https://doi.org/10.1007/s43681-025-00708-6
10. International Organization for Standardization : International Electrotechnical Commission: ISO/IEC 23894:2023 Information Technology – Artificial Intelligence – Guidance on Risk Management. ISO/IEC, Geneva (2023). https://www.iso.org/standard/77304.html
11. International Organization for Standardization: ISO 31000:2018 Risk management – Guidelines. ISO, Geneva (2018). https://www.iso.org/standard/65694.html
12. Kornutick, L.: Global AI regulations fuel billion-Dollar market for AI governance platforms. Gartner (2026). https://www.gartner.com/en/newsroom/press-releases/2026-02-17-gartner-global-ai-regulations-fuel-billion-dollar-market-for-ai-governance-platforms. Accessed 1 May 2026
13. Larsen, K.R., et al.: Validity in design science research. In: Hofmann, S., Müller, O., Rossi, M. (eds.) Designing for Digital Transformation. CoCreating Services with Citizens and Industry, pp. 272–282. Springer International Publishing, Cham (2020). https://doi.org/10.1007/978-3-030-64823-7_25
14. Lochmiller, C.: Conducting thematic analysis with qualitative data. Qual. Rep. **26**, 2029–2044 (2021). https://doi.org/10.46743/2160-3715/2021.5008
15. Magnani, G., Gioia, D.: Using the Gioia methodology in international business and entrepreneurship research. Int. Bus. Rev. **32**, 102097 (2023). https://doi.org/10.1016/j.ibusrev.2022.102097
16. Mitchell, M., et al.: Model cards for model reporting. In: Proceedings of the ACM Conference on Fairness, Accountability, and Transparency (FAccT '19). ACM, New York, NY, USA (2019). https://doi.org/10.1145/3287560.3287596
17. National Institute of Standards and Technology: Artificial Intelligence Risk Management Framework (AI RMF 1.0). NIST, Gaithersburg, MD (2023). https://doi.org/10.6028/NIST.AI.100-1
18. Peffers, K., Tuunanen, T., Rothenberger, M.A., Chatterjee, S.: A design science research methodology for information systems research. J. Manag. Inf. Syst. **24**, 45–77 (2007). https://doi.org/10.2753/mis0742-1222240302
19. Sadiq, S., Governatori, G., Namiri, K.: Modeling control objectives for business process compliance. In: Alonso, G., Dadam, P., Rosemann, M. (eds.) Business Process Management, pp. 149–164. Springer, Berlin Heidelberg, Berlin, Heidelberg (2007). https://doi.org/10.1007/978-3-540-75183-0_12
20. Uschold, M., King, M.: Towards a methodology for building ontologies. In: Workshop on Basic Ontological Issues in Knowledge Sharing, IJCAI-95, Montreal, Canada (1995)
21. vom Brocke, J., Hevner, A., Maedche, A.: Introduction to design science research. In: vom Brocke, J., Hevner, A., Maedche, A. (eds.) Design Science Research. Cases, pp. 1–13. Springer International Publishing, Cham (2020). https://doi.org/10.1007/978-3-030-46781-4_1
22. World Wide Web Consortium: Open Digital Rights Language (ODRL) Information Model 2.2. W3C, Geneva (2018). https://www.w3.org/TR/odrlmodel/
23. Wu, W., Liu, S.: Dilemma of the artificial intelligence regulatory landscape. Commun. ACM. **66**, 28–31 (2023). https://doi.org/10.1145/3584665

Requirements Engineering and Modeling Foundations

Trustworthiness Requirements for Decentralized Digital Identity Ecosystems: A Conceptual Model

Walid Fdhila[1,2](✉)

[1] University of Vienna, Vienna, Austria
[2] SBA Research, Vienna, Austria
walid.fdhila@univie.ac.at

Abstract. Digital identity wallets are becoming critical infrastructure. The European Digital Identity Wallet (EUDIW), mandated by eIDAS 2.0 and its implementing acts, is expected to serve hundreds of millions of European citizens. Yet neither the core regulation nor its supporting technical frameworks (e.g., ARF) provide a consolidated view of the trustworthiness requirements such systems entail. We present a conceptual model of trustworthiness requirements for decentralized digital identity ecosystems, instantiated for the EUDIW. The meta-model organizes the requirements into seven interdependent trust domains, connected through a typed relation language, all grounded in international standards and specifications. The taxonomy comprises and cross-validates 199 requirements with 81 typed relation instances.

Keywords: Trustworthiness · digital identity · trust · EUDIW

1 Introduction

Regulation (EU) 2024/1183 (eIDAS 2.0)[1], applicable across all 27 Member States, mandates that each Member State offer citizens a conformant European Digital Identity Wallet (EUDIW), and establishes certification and governance obligations on all ecosystem participants. The Architecture Reference Framework (ARF)[2], a Commission technical specification, defines the ecosystem architecture. The EUDIW follows the issuer–holder–verifier model formalized in W3C Verifiable Credentials [16]: an issuer signs a credential into the holder's wallet, and the holder presents a derived verifiable presentation to a relying party who validates it cryptographically, without contacting the issuer. A credential presentation involves multiple actors, protocols, cryptographic paradigms, and governance frameworks; failures at one layer can affect others, so trustworthiness must be established across technical, organizational, and regulatory dimensions.

[1] https://eur-lex.europa.eu/eli/reg/2024/1183/oj/eng.
[2] https://eudi.dev/2.8.0/.

© The Author(s), under exclusive license to Springer Nature Switzerland AG 2027
A. Bernasconi et al. (Eds.): ER 2026, LNCS 17081, pp. 371–381, 2027.
https://doi.org/10.1007/978-3-032-40795-5_22

The distinction between *trust* and *trustworthiness* is foundational to our assessment. Trust is a relationship: an actor A trusts an actor B for a property P if A acts as if P holds for B without independently verifying it [9]. Trustworthiness is a system property: B is trustworthy for P if P actually holds and can be verified. A system can be trusted without being trustworthy, and a trustworthy system that nobody trusts provides no value. Digital identity wallets need both, but our model targets trustworthiness: what properties must the ecosystem actually have, to what extent, and based on which evidence? Currently, obligations are fragmented across regulation, standards, and threat-modeling literature, and no practitioner, evaluator, or researcher can answer "is this wallet system trustworthy?" from any single authoritative source. Existing work either focuses on individual layers or organizes requirements by actor and credential category, obscuring the structural couplings that drive system-level trust behavior. **RQ:** we ask: *how can trustworthiness requirements of a regulated decentralized identity ecosystem be organized into a conceptual model that supports cross-domain structural analysis and clause-level traceability?* Concretely, we present: **C1)** a meta-model that organizes trustworthiness requirements into seven trust domains, a typed inter-requirement relation language, and six modeling principles, **C2)** a 199-requirement EUDIW instantiation grounded in standards and references, and **C3)** a four-stage construction methodology documented for potential adaptation to other regulated decentralized identity ecosystems.

Paper Organization. Section 2 positions the work; Sect. 3 presents the conceptual model; Sect. 4 the construction methodology; Sect. 5 the EUDIW instantiation; Sect. 6 validates the model; Sect. 7 concludes.

2 Related Work

Early trustworthiness-requirements work focused on IdP-centric architectures [9]; Decentralized identity redistributes trust across wallets, issuers, and verifiers, creating a different requirement space. Self-sovereign identity (SSI) surveys review the landscape and identify open challenges [12,14]. [7] derive 18 IAM requirements at category granularity; and [8] provide a comparative requirements analysis while [10] identifies 16 actor-role properties and three posture models; our work derives a substantially larger requirement set with structural classifications and a formal relation language.

Methodologically, KAOS [11] contributes goal refinement and conflict links, the NFR Framework [3] provides typed contribution links between softgoals, and [6] extend these for trust and security objectives. We adopt the typed-relations approach but apply it to *trust-property requirements* of a *decentralized identity ecosystem*: the schema is trust-specific, standards-derived, and organized by standards-body alignment rather than goal decomposition.

The work in [2] introduces a six-pillar trustworthiness framework for centralized digital identity management. We instead model the structural foundation of trustworthiness assessment for regulated decentralized identity ecosystems. The ARF defines 650+ high-level requirements, but is an architecture specification, not a trust taxonomy. ENISA's Draft EUDIW Certification Scheme [4] and Security Requirements [5] specify implementation-testable certification requirements, whereas our taxonomy captures ecosystem-level trust properties. Threat-centric works [1,15] ask "what can go wrong?"; we ask "what must be true?", using threat catalogues only as construction evidence.

3 Trustworthiness Requirement Conceptual Model

3.1 Meta-Model and Trust-Domain Stack

The principal entity is a typed *trustworthiness Requirement*: a verifiable normative property that a component or actor in the ecosystem must possess for the trust placed in it to be warranted, distinct from functional requirements (what a component does) and conformance requirements (whether it follows a protocol). Each Requirement is composed into a three-level hierarchy, linked to one or more *Standards* through a typed *Traceability* association (mapping type *direct*, *derived*, *implied*, or *original*), and related to other Requirements through a typed *Relation* language of six types (Fig. 1(a)).

The **requirement schema** carries seventeen typed attributes (Fig. 1(a)): fourteen textual or controlled-vocabulary, and three enumerated structural classifications. *Structural Criticality (SC)* records the cascade impact of a requirement's failure (*High*: failure invalidates requirements across distinct domains; *Medium*: degrades assurance within its subcategory; *Low*: self-contained). SC is derived, computed by closing the Dependency sub-relation (Sect. 3.2) under transitivity; it captures graph-theoretic cascade reach, not necessarily run-time behavioral cascade. *Trust Dimension (TD)* classifies the inter-party nature of the obligation: *Pure* (verifiable by a single actor without counterparty interaction), *Relational* (bilateral trust between specific actor types), or *Infrastructure* (depends on shared infrastructure on which all participants rely). *Regulatory Deontic (RD)* records the obligation level (SHALL, SHOULD, or NOT ADDRESSED, with compound values for conditional applicability). Requirements are organized through a three-level compositional hierarchy above the leaf entity: *Domains* (L1) partition the universe of trust concerns; *Subcategories* (L2) group by analytical purpose; *Requirement Classes* (L3) capture a coherent technical mechanism, and each class contains one or more Requirements. The branching factor is the smallest depth at which within-domain heterogeneity is resolved without producing single-requirement classes.

3.2 The Relation Language

We make inter-requirement structure explicit through a typed set of six relations. Each has a defined semantics over an abstract satisfaction predicate sat(·) (and, where applicable, an assurance-degree function assur(·)), a directionality, and a documented role in model navigation. The 6 types were sufficient to classify all

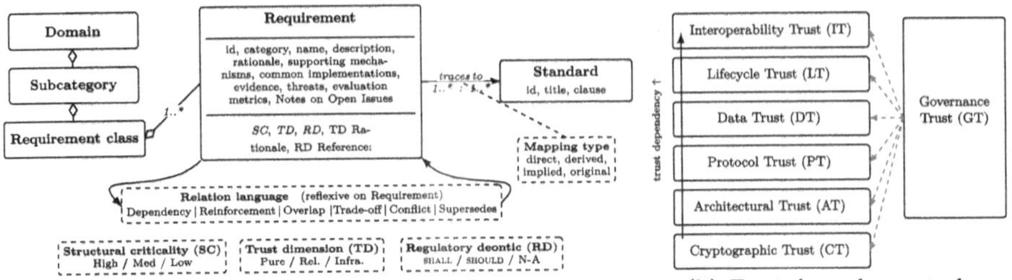

(a) Meta-model: entities and relation language. (b) Trust dependency stack.

Fig. 1. The conceptual model.

inter-requirements during construction; we do not claim the set is closed under all possible future extensions, but no candidate edge required a seventh type.

Dependency ($A \to B$)**:** $\neg\,\text{sat}(A) \Rightarrow \neg\,\text{sat}(B)$. Target B cannot be meaningfully satisfied unless source A is. Primary cascade relation, closed under transitivity for SC. Example: CT-KM-2 (storage protection) → CT-KM-3 (non-exportability).

Reinforcement ($A \to B$)**:** $\text{assur}(B \mid \text{sat}(A)) > \text{assur}(B \mid \neg\,\text{sat}(A))$. A raises the assurance of B but is not required for B to hold. Defence-in-depth. Example: CT-EC-4 (end-to-end encryption) → CT-EC-1 (transport encryption).

Overlap ($A \leftrightarrow B$)**:** $\exists M : \text{sat}(M, A) \wedge \text{sat}(M, B)$. The same mechanism instance M, canonical for A and B in the target architecture, satisfies both, viewed from different domains. (Stronger than mere co-satisfiability.) Example: CT-EC-1 (transport encryption) ↔ PT-TP-1 (remote transport security) (both TLS).

Trade-off ($A \leftrightarrow B$)**:** $\exists$ design points where increasing sat-degree of A decreases the achievable sat-degree of B, but admissible balance points exist where both hold to acceptable levels. Example: DT-SD-3 (zero-knowledge predicate proofs) ↔ DT-SD-1 (selective-disclosure granularity).

Conflict ($A \leftrightarrow B$)**:** $\neg\exists I : \text{sat}(I, A) \wedge \text{sat}(I, B)$ under current technology; no admissible balance point exists. Distinct from Trade-off by non-existence of balance. Example: AT-SS-5 (backup) ↔ CT-KM-3 (non-export).

Supersedes ($A \to B$)**:** A semantically replaces B; B is retained for traceability and historical reference; new edges go to A.

The relation language supports three analyzes: cascade impact via Dependency closure; design-tension identification via Trade-off and Conflict; defense-in-depth via Reinforcement. The predicates *mechanism* (Overlap), *design point* (Trade-off), and *admissible balance* are instantiation-defined primitives. These analyzes support, but do not automate, design activities such as identifying conflict clusters, tracing cascades from [BLOCKER] requirements, and checking whether reinforcement edges provide sufficient defense-in-depth.

3.3 The Seven-Domain Trust Dependency Stack

A *domain* is a group of requirements sharing an implementation layer: the same components satisfy them, the same standards tradition governs them, and the same type of professional or certification body assesses them. A candidate domain was accepted when three convergent criteria held: architectural decomposition, standards-body alignment, and threat-vector distinctness; the criteria co-vary (standards bodies organize around architectural layers, and threat catalogues follow standards. The seven domains are as follows.

Cryptographic Trust (CT) is the foundational layer: all other trust claims ultimately assume correct cryptographic operation. CT covers cryptographic primitives, key management, signature and verification, encryption, and agility. ***Architectural Trust*** **(AT)** covers component isolation, secure storage, wallet attestation, and trust-anchor management; the execution environment bridging CT primitives to PT protocols (concerns environmental isolation, not cryptographic correctness). ***Protocol Trust*** **(PT)** covers issuance and presentation flows, session integrity, transport (data in transit). ***Data Trust*** **(DT)** covers the credential as a data artifact: integrity, selective disclosure, privacy-preserving properties, data minimisation, and schema. It is one of the largest domains because the credential is the primary trust carrier; privacy is cross-cutting and spans DT, PT, LT, and GT rather than forming its own domain.
Lifecycle Trust **(LT)** covers credential state transitions, including issuance quality controls, revocation, renewal and re-issuance, and wallet recovery and deactivation. LT captures the temporal dimension of credentials as stateful artifacts, distinct from GT's organizational state machine. ***Interoperability Trust*** **(IT)** covers cross-system properties such as format conformance, protocol negotiation, and trust-framework federation. Unlike PT, which asks whether a protocol is secure, IT asks whether conformant implementations interoperate. ***Governance Trust*** **(GT)** covers certification, trusted-list governance, supervisory operations, audit, and transparency. The seven domains form an ordered stack (Fig. 1b): each layer presupposes the soundness of those below it. GT uniquely breaks the linear ordering by both *depending on* the operational correctness of every other domain and *exerting authority over* them, justifying its status as a domain.

3.4 Modeling Principles

Six principles govern the construction and adjudicate contested placements. **P1 (Cascade)**: domains are ordered such that each presupposes those below. **P2 (Bidirectional governance)**: GT combines bottom-up dependence with top-down authority. **P3 (Audit-surface coherence)**: a subcategory may deviate from strict layer alignment only when a coherent assessment surface justifies it.

P4 (Lifecycle separation): state transitions are a distinct trust concern from runtime correctness; obligations go in LT even when the mechanism is cryptographic or architectural. **P5 (Cross-system distinction)**: IT is reserved for obligations whose semantics involve more than one participant. **P6 (Atomic primary-domain assignment)**: each requirement has exactly one primary domain; cross-cutting is captured by Relation edges, not by duplication.

4 Construction Methodology

The conceptual model of Sect. 3 was constructed through a four-stage process. **1) Corpus and snapshot.** The model is grounded in a corpus of over 100 items: standards, specifications, regulations, and implementing acts (IETF RFCs:38; ETSI:9; W3C:4; NIST/FIPS:18; OpenID/credential formats:8; EU regulations and implementing acts:29; ARF 2.8) plus foundational academic references. We iteratively extracted trust-relevant obligations from each standards body into the working taxonomy. We do not claim formal saturation: [4,5] identified four additional obligations after our snapshot. **2) Synthesis.** Rather than extracting requirements from a single standard, we synthesize trust properties across overlapping standards. Extraction inherits source-specific structures (e.g., the ARF's actor–credential organization), duplicating cross-cutting concerns. Synthesis instead defines each trust property once and captures cross-cutting through relations. A property is included only if it is standard-independent, supported by at least two corpus standards, and not purely functional. Where standards differ, the canonical formulation prioritizes layer-correctness and ecosystem-agnosticism, while the Traceability association preserves links to source requirements. **3) Iterative refinement.** The taxonomy was hardened through four review phases against the modeling principles of Sect. 3.4. **R1 (Structural)** inspected the domain partition, hierarchy depth, and relation graph for orphan requirements and unjustifiable placements. **R2 (Deontic)** verified that every Regulatory Deontic claim is supported by a specific ARF or implementing regulation clause. **R3 (Completeness)** examined coverage against external threat catalogues ([1,15]). **R4 (Integration)** examined cross-artifact consistency. **4) Cross-artifact traceability.** Every Requirement is linked to its evidence through an IEEE 29148-compliant traceability matrix recording the requirement, source clause, obligation text, and a *mapping type*.

Table 1. Requirement example: one Dependency edge, one trade-off scenario.

Attribute	`DT-PE-1` Presentation Unlinkability
Domain/Class	DT/Privacy Engineering/Unlinkability
Obligation	Repeated presentations of a credential **shall not** be linkable by colluding verifiers beyond what disclosed attributes reveal.
Rationale	Prevents profiling under selective disclosure (GDPR Art. 25).
Mechanisms	BBS+, anonymous credentials, token diversification.
Adversaries	Colluding verifiers; passive network linkage.
SC/TD	High/Infrastructure
RD	SHALL (outcome, GDPR)/SHOULD (mechanism, ARF 2.8)

Dependency. `CT-SV-8` (Unlinkable Signature) → `DT-PE-1`: unlinkability holds only if the underlying signature scheme is itself unlinkable across presentations.

Trade-off. `DT-PE-1` ↔ `LT-RV-2` (Privacy-Preserving Revocation): unlinkable schemes impede per-credential revocation lookup; mitigations include short-lived credentials and accumulator-based revocation.

5 EUDIW Instantiation

This section reports the EUDIW instantiation at the ARF 2.8 snapshot of the meta-model of Sect. 3. Table 1 shows an abbreviated example requirement.

5.1 Numerical Overview

The instantiation comprises 199 requirements: CT 28, AT 29, PT 24, DT 36, LT 23, IT 20, GT 39. Figure 2 shows the full domain, subcategory, class, requirement structure with counts. GT is the largest domain (the institutional framework is broad); DT is second-largest (privacy engineering decomposes into narrowly-scoped obligations); IT is smallest (concentrated cross-system properties). The Structural Criticality distribution is 102 High, 75 Medium, 22 Low, concentrated in CT, AT, PT, and GT. The Trust Dimension distribution is 33 Pure, 79 Relational, 87 Infrastructure; IT contains *zero* Pure requirements. The Regulatory Deontic (RD) is three-valued (SHALL/SHOULD/NOT ADDRESSED) with 31 compound values encoding conditional applicability.

Fig. 2. Trustworthiness Requirements Taxonomy.

5.2 Exemplar: Data Trust and the Audit-Surface Exception

DT is the privacy-engineering domain and the principled exception to the layer-alignment convention (P3). Its 36 requirements occupy five subcategories, the most distinctive being DT-PE (privacy-preserving properties, 8 requirements). Four of the eight DT-PE requirements concern properties realised by mechanisms in other domains: presentation unlinkability (`DT-PE-1`, Table 1) is mechanically supported by unlinkable signatures in CT; communication unobservability (`DT-PE-4`) depends on network-layer mechanisms in PT; participation undetectability (`DT-PE-5`) is partly architectural. A layer-aligned taxonomy would scatter these across CT, PT, and AT, leaving no single subcategory to which a privacy assessor could turn when evaluating GDPR Art. 25 compliance. DT-PE is organized by privacy-engineering discipline rather than enforcement layer to preserve a coherent audit surface: the principled exception under P3.

6 Model Validation

We evaluate the artifact against the five system dimensions of the evaluation criteria for design-science IS artifacts [13], denoted here **D1–D5**: **D1** Goal (efficacy, generality), **D2** Environment (consistency with organization and technology; utility for people), **D3** Structure (consistency, completeness, homomorphism), **D4** Activity (consistency of methodology stages), **D5** Evolution (robustness, learning capability). **D2** criteria of utility for people, understandability, and ease of use require empirical studies with practitioners and are out of scope.

6.1 Internal Consistency: Structure and Classification

Three checks address structural consistency and completeness. **The Dependency sub-relation is near-acyclic** (satisfies **D3** consistency). Of the 50 Dependency edges, two mutual-prerequisite pairs (CT-KM-2 ↔ AT-CI-4, representing co-dependence between key-storage protection and hardware-security boundaries; and one pair involving a superseded requirement) form 2-cycles representing genuine co-dependence rather than modeling errors. The two strongly-connected components are collapsed to shared SC values; the remaining 46 directed edges form a DAG, licensing the cascade-reach computation underlying Structural Criticality. **Atomic primary-domain assignment is upheld** (satisfies **D3** consistency + P6). No requirement appears as a primary member of more than one domain, making the relation graph load-bearing rather than redundant with the partition. **Coding-fidelity check for principle P5.** P5 says interoperability obligations involve more than one participant; the Trust-Dimension value *Pure* is defined as verifiability by a single actor without counterparty interaction. By construction, $IT \cap Pure$ should be empty: this is a definitional entailment of the two definitions, not an empirical prediction. The 20 IT requirements are coded 3 Relational, 17 Infrastructure, 0 Pure. P5 was articulated prior to the final Trust-Dimension coding pass, so coders had access to the principle when classifying: this is a sanity check on coding fidelity, not a construct-validation of the principle. The four-stage construction methodology was applied uniformly across all 199 requirements (satisfies **D4**).

6.2 Homomorphism with External Normative Artifacts

ENISA's Draft EUDIW Certification Scheme [4,5] was developed in parallel. ENISA produces *testable certification criteria*; we model *trustworthiness requirements* and their structural relations. As both derive substantially from ARF 2.8, joint findings reflect regulatory alignment under partially overlapping inputs, not independent re-discovery (satisfies **D3** homomorphism) between our taxonomy and ENISA's artifact. Two kinds of cross-evidence emerge: i) regulatory alignment: five cross-cutting concerns (data minimisation (DT-DM), wallet-attestation integrity (AT-WA), trust-anchor management (AT-TA), supervisory operations (GT-SO), and audit/transparency (GT-AT)) appear independently in ENISA under different rubrics. ii) construct deficit and extensibility: four ENISA obligations our instantiation did not initially capture (supply-chain security, fraud-management, provider-termination, and protocol-orchestration integrity) now accepted as candidate extensions (`GT-GO-7`, `GT-AT-9`, `LT-DR-7`, `PT-SP-5`). Corpus grounding in ARF, eIDAS, and implementing acts (**D2** consistency with organization) and explicit incorporation of SD-JWT, BBS+, and OID4VCI/VP (**D2** consistency with technology) further support environment alignment.

6.3 Efficacy: Structural Diagnostics from the EUDIW

Efficacy (whether the artifact produces its desired effect) is demonstrated by the ecosystem-level structural diagnostics the model yields (satisfies **D1** efficacy). Twenty-nine requirements carry a [BLOCKER] annotation marking that the assembled corpus is silent, the technology is immature, or normative codification has not caught up. The clustering is informative. *Wallet attestation* (subcategory AT-WA) accounts for six of the 29 blockers (`AT-WA-1, 2, 4, 5, 7, 8`); six of eight AT-WA requirements are blocked. *Certification and trusted-list governance* (GT-CA and GT-TL) accounts for a further six (`GT-CA-1, 3, 7, 12`; `GT-TL-1, 2`). *Privacy-preserving cryptography and selective disclosure* (`CT-SV-8, DT-SD-3, DT-PE-1, DT-PE-2`) accounts for four. The remaining thirteen distribute across interoperability (5), lifecycle and revocation (4), cryptographic agility (2), and architectural integrity (2). The Protocol Trust domain contains *zero* blockers in the corpus-coverage sense, reflecting the maturity of OID4VCI, OID4VP, and ISO 18013-7 relative to the rest of the framework (this refers to specification coverage, not freedom from known security issues such as relay and cross-modal attacks in OID4VP). The EUDIW's remaining specification work lies not in protocols but in attestation, governance, and privacy-preserving primitives; the ecosystem-level diagnosis the conceptual model is built to support. *Generality* is partial (partially satisfies **D1** generality): the meta-model is designed for regulated decentralized-identity ecosystems broadly, but only the EUDIW instantiation is demonstrated here. The meta-model absorbs corpus evolution (ARF revisions, ETSI publications, implementing-act updates) through re-instantiation without structural change (satisfies **D5** robustness), and the four ENISA-identified extensions above demonstrate learning from external institutional review (satisfies **D5** learning capability).

7 Conclusion

We have presented a conceptual model of trustworthiness requirements for decentralized digital identity ecosystems, instantiated for the EUDIW with 199 requirements across seven trust domains. The model's structural services (e.g., cascade-reach analysis, cross-domain tension detection) produce ecosystem-level diagnostics that flat catalogues cannot. The homomorphism check against the ENISA certification scheme shows regulatory alignment under partially overlapping inputs and demonstrates the model's extensibility under independent institutional review. Future work extends the model with an actor-level trust graph, a deontic-coherence analysis, and an assessment-framework derivation.

Acknowledgment. This work was supported by the Vienna Science and Technology Fund (WWTF) under Grant ICT23-051, and SBA Research (SBA-K1 NGC), a COMET Center funded within the COMET – Competence Centers for Excellent Technologies Programme and by BMIMI, BMWET, and the federal state of Vienna. The COMET Programme is managed by FFG.

References

1. Abelán Álvarez, I., Hölzmer, P., Sedlmeir, J.: Privacy evaluation of the European digital identity wallet's architecture and reference framework. Comput. Secur. **160**, 104707 (2026). https://doi.org/10.1016/j.cose.2025.104707
2. Bottarelli, M., Epiphaniou, G., Mahmood, S., Hooper, M., Maple, C.: Assessing the trustworthiness of electronic identity management systems: framework and insights from inception to deployment (2025)
3. Chung, L., Nixon, B.A., Yu, E., Mylopoulos, J.: Non-Functional Requirements in Software Engineering. SOFT, vol 5, Springer (2000). https://doi.org/10.1007/978-1-4615-5269-7
4. ENISA: Draft candidate EUDIW cybersecurity certification scheme (2026). https://certification.enisa.europa.eu/publications/
5. ENISA: Wallet-related service provider security requirements (2026). https://certification.enisa.europa.eu/publications/
6. Giorgini, P., Massacci, F., Mylopoulos, J., Zannone, N.: Requirements engineering for trust management: model, methodology, and reasoning. Int. J. Inf. Secur. **5**, 257–274 (2006). https://doi.org/10.1007/s10207-006-0005-7
7. Glöckler, J., Sedlmeir, J., Frank, M., Fridgen, G.: A systematic review of identity and access management requirements in enterprises and potential contributions of self-sovereign identity. Bus. Inf. Syst. Eng. (2023)
8. Grüner, A., Mühle, A., Gayvoronskaya, T., Meinel, C.: A comparative analysis of trust requirements in decentralized identity management. In: Advanced Information Networking and Applications, pp. 200–213 (2020)
9. Jøsang, A., Fabre, J., Hay, B., Dalziel, J., Pope, S.: Trust Requirements in Identity Management, pp. 99–108. ACSW (2005)
10. Krul, E., Paik, H.Y., Ruj, S., Kanhere, S.S.: SoK: trusting self-sovereign identity. In: Proceedings of the Privacy Enhancing Technologies (PoPETs), pp. 297–313 (2024)
11. van Lamsweerde, A.: Requirements Engineering: From System Goals to UML Models to Software Specifications. Wiley, Chichester, UK (2009)
12. Mazzocca, C., Acar, A., Uluagac, S., Montanari, R., Bellavista, P., Conti, M.: A survey on decentralized identifiers and verifiable credentials. IEEE Commun. Surv. Tutorials **27**(6), 3641–3671 (2025)
13. Prat, N., Comyn-Wattiau, I., Akoka, J.: A hierarchy of evaluation criteria for information systems artifacts. Eur. J. Inf. Syst. **24**(3), 229–250 (2015). https://doi.org/10.1057/ejis.2014.2
14. Satybaldy, A., Ferdous, M.S., Nowostawski, M.: A taxonomy of challenges for self-sovereign identity systems. IEEE Access (2024)
15. Sharif, A., et al.: Protecting digital identity wallet: a threat model in the age of EIDAS 2.0. In: Risks and Security of Internet and Systems, pp. 89–106 (2025)
16. Sporny, M., Longley, D., Chadwick, D., Herman, I.: Verifiable credentials data model v2.0. W3c recommendation, W3C (2024)

Goal Model-Based Requirements Engineering for Robotic AI Systems

Meenakshi Manjunath(✉) and Marian Daun

Center for Robotics, Technical University of Applied Sciences Würzburg-Schweinfurt, Schweinfurt, Germany
meenakshi.manjunath@study.thws.de, marian.daun@thws.de

Abstract. Robotic applications increasingly integrate AI-based components to expand system autonomy and enable more flexible operation in new environments. However, these capabilities also introduce fundamental challenges for requirements engineering, regarding limited explainability and ever-evolving operational conditions. In particular, AI-based components often behave as black boxes, making it difficult for humans to understand why a system acts in a certain way or why a specific decision was made. This lack of transparency becomes especially critical in human-robot interaction, where humans and robots operate in close proximity and depend on each other during shared collaborative tasks. Therefore, safety concerns resulting from AI use need to be identified and sufficiently mitigated during requirements engineering. To support in this, we propose a goal modeling extension that integrates safety and explainability modeling for collaborative robotic AI systems. Use case based investigations show the applicability of our approach and shed light onto the interplay between robotic AI-components, safety, and explainability, which can improve future safety assessment of robotic systems.

Keywords: Requirements Engineering · Robotics Software Engineering · Robotics · Model-Based Engineering · Safety · Explainability

1 Introduction

Robotic systems are becoming increasingly intelligent, adaptive, and deeply integrated into human-centered environments. From industrial assembly and warehouse automation to healthcare assistance and service robotics, modern robotic applications rely heavily on artificial intelligence (AI) based components for perception, decision-making, and autonomous behavior [1].

However, the integration of AI into robotic systems also introduces new challenges for requirements engineering (RE). Unlike traditional software systems, robotic AI systems are not fully predictable or strictly deterministic. Their behavior depends on training data, confidence-based decisions, environmental conditions, and interactions with humans in real time [2]. A perception error, a

© The Author(s), under exclusive license to Springer Nature Switzerland AG 2027
A. Bernasconi et al. (Eds.): ER 2026, LNCS 17081, pp. 382–391, 2027.
https://doi.org/10.1007/978-3-032-40795-5_23

low-confidence classification, or an incorrect autonomous decision may not only affect system performance, but can directly lead to safety hazards, reduced trust, and accountability concerns in collaborative workspaces [3,4].

Traditional RE approaches primarily assume static system boundaries, clearly defined functional behavior, and predictable cause-effect relationships [5,6]. These assumptions are often insufficient for robotic AI systems, where uncertainty and adaptation are fundamental characteristics rather than exceptions [6]. As a result, important concerns such as safety and explainability are frequently addressed late in development leading to integration risks, limited traceability, and insufficient mitigation of AI-induced hazards [2].

This paper contributes a model-based RE approach that integrates XAI and safety elements in goal modeling, enabling AI-supported behavior, safety hazards, and mitigation tasks in collaborative robotic systems to be represented within a shared requirements goal model.

2 Related Work

Requirements Engineering for Robotics. As robotics becomes increasingly software-defined, RE plays a central role in specifying system behavior, assumptions, and operational boundaries [5]. Consequently, RE for robotics relies heavily on formal and model-based approaches to improve traceability, validation, and early assurance [7]. In addition to technical functionality, robotic requirements are often shaped by domain-specific safety regulations and standards.

Goal-oriented and stakeholder-driven modeling approaches further improve traceability between stakeholder expectations and system design decisions, particularly in model-based RE and MBSE contexts [8,9]. More recently, explainability-oriented requirement patterns have also been introduced for human-robot teamwork, emphasizing transparency and trust in autonomous decision making [10].

Requirements Engineering for Artificial Intelligence. Research in the direction of RE for AI-enabled systems, where RE methods are applied to specify, analyze, validate, and assure systems that incorporate AI-based components. In such systems, traditional assumptions of determinism, repeatability, and complete behavioral specification are often no longer valid, creating new challenges for requirements specification and verification [11].

A particularly relevant research area within RE for AI-enabled systems is the adaptation of traditional requirements modeling approaches such as i*, KAOS, and other goal-oriented methods for representing AI-specific system behavior and dependencies. These approaches aim to capture not only functional goals, but also assumptions, explainability needs, and human oversight requirements associated with machine learning components. Barrera et al. investigate how i* can support conceptual modeling for machine learning by representing actors, dependencies, and decision-making processes introduced by AI components [12].

For explainability, Navarro et al. [13] propose an i*-based approach for requirements modeling and elicitation for XAI, focusing on how stakeholder goals and explanation needs can be captured during early requirements analysis.

Requirements Engineering for Safety-Critical Systems. Safety has long been recognized as a fundamental concern in RE, particularly in systems where failures may lead to physical harm, financial loss, or severe operational consequences [14]. Safety requirements specify intended functionality constraints that prevent hazardous behavior and ensure acceptable system operation under abnormal conditions. For human-robot interaction this is a challenging task as safety threats result from the system, the human operator, as well as the collaboration between those actors [15]. In previous work, goal-oriented approaches have been proposed to support the specification of safety requirements [16,17]. By extending traditional goal models, safety constraints can be represented alongside functional goals, making dependencies, conflicts, and mitigation strategies more explicit [18]. Similarly, i*-based approaches for safety-critical systems model how safety responsibilities are distributed among actors, components, and organizational stakeholders, improving reasoning about accountability and system dependencies [19].

3 Goal Modeling for Safety-Critical Robotic AI System

This section introduces our goal modeling approach for safety-critical robotic AI systems. We propose an extension of goal-oriented modeling that integrates safety-related and XAI-related concepts into a shared requirements model. The purpose of the extension is to support the early modeling of collaborative robotic systems in which AI-based components influence perception, decision-making, and human-robot interaction.

We illustrate the approach using an industrial human-humanoid collaboration scenario. The figures in this paper show selected excerpts and scaled versions of the goal models to fit the page layout and improve readability.

3.1 Use Case

In the chosen industrial use-case, three main actors interact: a humanoid robot, a human operator, and an AI-enabled monitoring system. The humanoid shares the same physical workspace with a human operator and assists during assembly, material handling, and workstation support tasks. The shared workspace is monitored by an AI-enabled monitoring system that observes human activity, humanoid behavior, and workspace conditions during task execution.

The *Human operator* performs the primary assembly task and collaborates with the humanoid through shared activities such as tool handovers, assembly parts handover, and cooperative manipulation, and workspace coordination. The human depends on the humanoid for support during material handling and on the monitoring system for workspace information and hazard warnings.

The *Humanoid robot* assists the human during assembly, material handling, and workstation support tasks. Its role includes retrieving tools and assembly components, transporting parts from storage areas, handing over required objects, holding heavy components during assembly, and monitoring the workspace. To perform these tasks, the humanoid relies on physical subsystems for locomotion, balance, manipulation, force control, and collision avoidance, as well as AI-based perception and decision-making components. Its computer vision system supports local object detection, part classification, and human detection, while its decision-making system supports task prioritization, adaptive planning, and collaboration management under dynamic conditions.

The *AI-enabled monitoring system* acts as a continuous safety system. It observes robot actions, human activity, and workspace conditions. When potential hazards are detected, the system provides alerts for unsafe situations.

3.2 Modeling Safety Requirements of Human-Robot Collaboration

Using extended goal modeling concepts for safety based on our previous work [17,18], Fig. 1a presents an excerpt of the safety goal model focusing on the humanoid's tool-provision tasks. In the safety goal model, a *hazard* represents a potentially unsafe condition that may obstruct the achievement of a goal or a task. A *hazard origin* captures a possible source or contributing factor that can lead to a hazard. A *safety task* represents an action or strategy introduced to prevent, reduce, or control the effect of a hazard. A *safety resource* represents information, sensor input, or system state data required to detect, evaluate, or respond to a hazard (see Fig. 2). Examples include model confidence levels, picking coordinates, gripper sensor data, robot stability information, and workspace monitoring data.

On the humanoid side, several hazards may arise while the robot provides tools to the human operator. For example, the task *identify the required tool* may be obstructed by the hazard *incorrect tool identified.* This is modeled as a hazard as the identification result directly influences subsequent robot actions, including retrieval, transport, and handover. If the humanoid identifies the wrong tool as the required one, it may retrieve and bring an unsuitable tool to the human operator. This can disrupt the assembly sequence, lead to incorrect tool use, cause confusion for the human operator, or require them to intervene unexpectedly. Upon analyzing the origins of the hazards, it mainly originates from a *misclassification*, which could be from bad lighting conditions, failure of the computer vision pipeline, or an under-fitted computer vision model. The safety resource *model confidence levels* is the data that needs an evaluation for a reliable tool identification result. As safety tasks, the model includes re-running the identification process, retraining the computer vision pipeline, procuring additional training data, and requesting human assistance. These mitigation actions reduce the likelihood of the humanoid continuing with an incorrect tool selection.

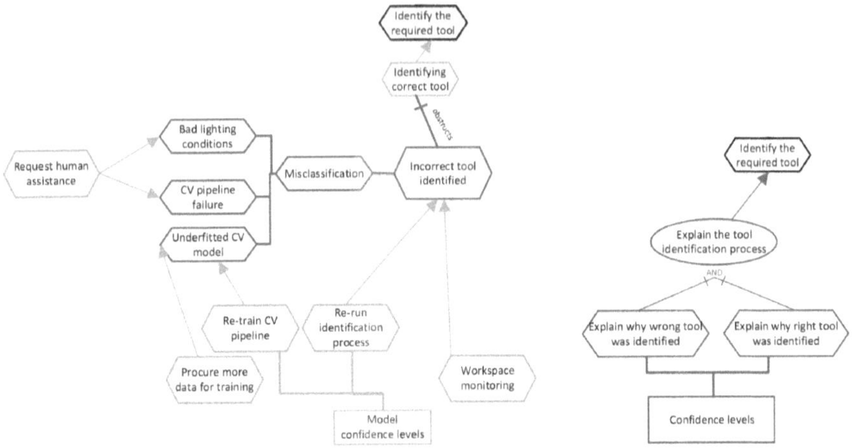

(a) Safety Goal Model (b) XAI Goal Model

Fig. 1. Goal Model Excerpts for Safety and XAI of the Use Case.

3.3 Modeling AI Requirements of Human-Robot Collaboration

The humanoid relies on AI-based perception to identify tools and parts, determine picking positions, and interpret workspace conditions. Similarly, the workspace monitoring system uses AI-supported observations to interpret human behavior, humanoid proximity, and coordination-relevant movements in the shared workspace. These AI-components must therefore be accounted for explicitly in the requirements model.

To model these AI-related requirements, we build on the XAI-oriented goal modeling approach proposed by Navarro et al. [13], which extends i* with concepts for representing explainability goals, explanation tasks, and XAI resources. An *XAI goal* captures what needs to be made understandable to the human operator, such as the reason behind a tool selection or a change in robot behavior. An *XAI task* describes the explanation-producing activity that operationalizes this goal, for example explaining why a certain tool was identified or why the humanoid changed its transport behavior. An *XAI resource* represents the information required to generate the explanation, such as confidence levels, picking coordinates, humanoid stability, or human motion data. We use these concepts to model how AI-supported behavior in the humanoid and the workspace monitoring system can be made understandable to the human operator.

As in Fig. 1b, on the humanoid side, explainability is required because several assistance tasks depend on AI-supported perception and decision-making. The human operator observes the humanoid's actions in the shared workspace, but cannot directly infer why the humanoid identified a specific object, selected a particular picking position, or changed its behavior during transport. Without explicit explanation support, these AI-supported actions may appear unpredictable or difficult to interpret. Therefore, the model introduces XAI tasks that make the humanoid's internal decision basis accessible to the human operator.

One of the explainability point concerns the task *identify the required tool*. Since this task relies on AI-based computer vision and classification, the humanoid must determine which tool is required for the current assembly step based on training data, captured image data, model confidence, and environmental conditions. Therefore, we introduce the XAI goal *explain the tool identification process*, which is decomposed into XAI tasks explaining why the right tool was identified or why a wrong tool may have been identified. The XAI resource *confidence levels* provides the information required to explain the reliability and certainty of the AI-based perception decision.

The XAI extension is not limited to retrospective explanations. XAI tasks may be triggered before or during execution to communicate confidence, the rationale for an intended action, or the reason for a behavioral change. This allows the human operator to verify the situation, request clarification, or interrupt an unsafe action. Several XAI resources, such as *confidence levels* and *picking coordinates*, also serve as safety resources, providing the basis for connecting explainability with runtime hazard mitigation in the integrated model.

3.4 Integrating Safety and AI Requirements in the Goal Models

The safety-oriented model and the XAI-oriented model provide two complementary views on the same collaborative robotic system. The safety model captures hazards, their origins, mitigation tasks, and safety-relevant information, whereas the XAI model captures explanation goals, tasks, and resources. In robotic AI systems, these views overlap because information used to explain AI-supported behavior may also be required to detect and respond to safety-critical situations. The integrated model therefore makes these relationships explicit.

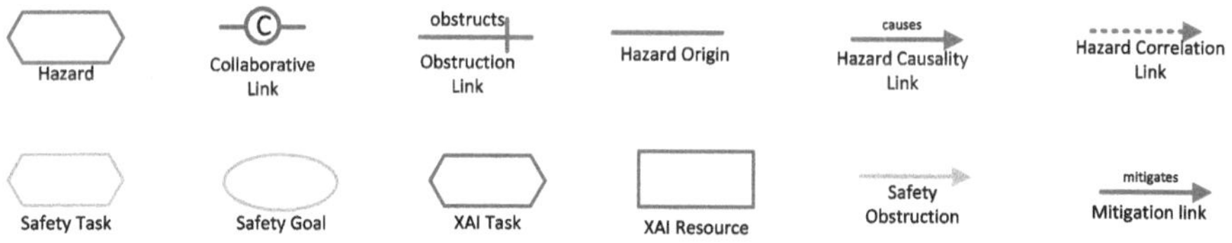

Fig. 2. All Goal Modeling Elements for Robotic AI system.

Figure 2 summarizes the modeling elements used in the final integrated goal model. In addition to the previously introduced safety elements from our previous work and XAI elements from Navarro et al. [13], the integrated model introduces two additional relation types. First, the ***hazard causality link*** captures a direct causal relation between hazards. For example, identifying the wrong tool leads to picking the wrong tool. Implicitly one can also say that, due to misclassification, a wrong tool was identified which leads to picking the wrong tool. Second, the ***mitigation link*** captures that an XAI task helps mitigate a hazard. This relation is essential for representing XAI not only as a transparency mechanism, but also as a support mechanism for safety-related decisions and actions.

Figure 3 shows the integrated goal model for the industrial assembly use-case. The model showcases how our extension can be applied to the industrial use-case. For the humanoid, the task *provide required tools* is used to illustrate how safety and XAI concerns interact. The task *identify the required tool* may be obstructed by the hazard *incorrect tool identified.* This hazard, as mentioned in Sect. 3.2 can be caused by misclassification, which may originate from bad lighting conditions, failure of the computer vision pipeline, or an under-fitted computer vision model. In the safety-oriented model, this hazard is addressed only through safety tasks such as re-running the identification process, retraining the computer vision pipeline, procuring more data, or requesting human assistance. In the integrated model, the XAI task *generate warning and mitigating instructions* additionally supports the mitigation of this hazard by using the XAI resource *low confidence levels.* Thus, the explanation does not only describe that the identification is uncertain, but also supports the decision to re-run the identification process or involve the human operator, if necessary. The same integration pattern is applied to tool retrieval and transport. Picking information and robot stability data support both the evaluation of hazards such as *picking wrong tool* and *tool falls down*, and explanations of why an action should be recalculated, paused, or stopped.

At the collaboration level, the central safety goal *safety of human operator* may be obstructed by *physical injury*, *strain*, and *lack of communication and coordination.* For example, unsafe proximity may lead to physical injury. The measured distance between the human and the humanoid, together with the safety threshold x_{safety}, supports both evaluation of this hazard and an explanation of why movement must be paused or adapted. One can also note that, implicitly, a tool falling down could also be the cause of physical injury of the human operator. The XAI task *generate warning based on predictions and mitigating instructions* supports the safety task *maintain safe proximity.* In this case, the explanation helps the human understand why the proximity condition is unsafe and what action is required to restore a safe interaction state.

For collaboration-related hazards, the model captures *lack of communication and coordination*, which may originate from inconsistent shared task state, conflicting task timing, missed previous warnings, unexpected movements, or uncoordinated movements or from strain. The XAI task *explain coordination mismatch and generate instructions for next action* mitigates this hazard by explaining why the current interaction state is inconsistent and by supporting safety tasks such as updating the task status or pausing action under coordination uncertainty. This shows that XAI is not restricted to explaining internal AI predictions, but can also be used to explain interaction-level mismatches in human-robot collaboration.

Figure 3 demonstrates that XAI and safety modeling overlap through shared resources and mitigation relations. By introducing explicit mitigation links, the

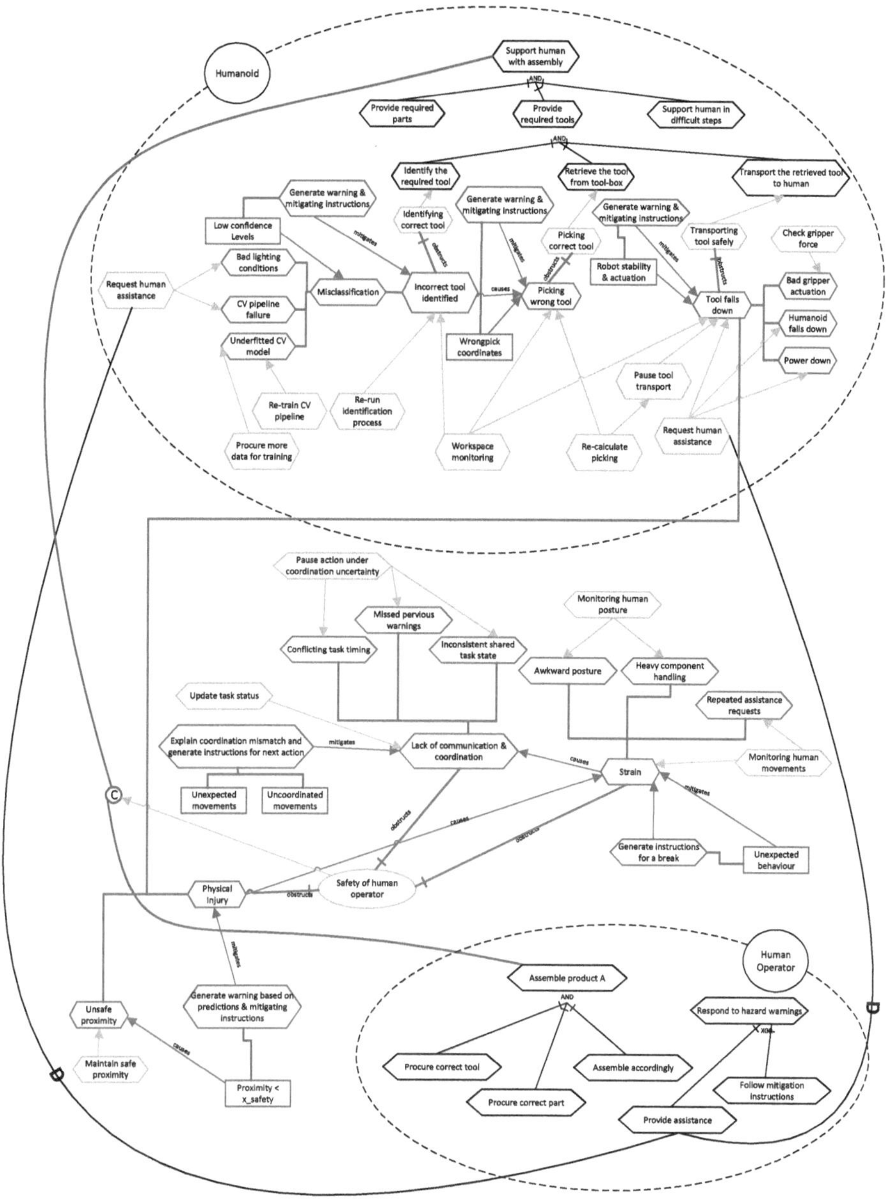

Fig. 3. Goal model of the industrial use case with Safety and AI-components.

model shows how XAI tasks can support safety tasks without replacing them. In this sense, XAI is modeled as a safety-supporting mechanism: it explains unsafe or uncertain situations, provides context for mitigation actions, and helps the human operator understand why a certain intervention is required. The safety-oriented model (Fig. 1a) makes explicit how hazards may obstruct functional tasks and safety goals within a system. Followed by the XAI-oriented model (Fig. 1b), it captures the explanation needs that arise from AI-supported perception, manipulation, and coordination. Finally, the integrated model (Fig. 3) combines these views by linking XAI tasks and resources to safety-relevant hazards and mitigation tasks.

4 Conclusion

Robotic AI systems challenge traditional requirements modeling because their behavior is shaped by dynamic environments, real-time human interaction, and AI-based components that are often difficult to understand. In collaborative robotic settings, this lack of transparency becomes safety-critical, since incorrect AI-supported behavior can directly affect the human operator and the shared task execution. This paper proposed a model-based requirements engineering approach that integrates explainability into safety-oriented goal modeling for collaborative robotic AI systems. Using an industrial humanoid assembly scenario, we showed how goal models can be extended to integrate the safety and AI-components requirements.

A central observation from the integrated model is that XAI is not limited to a post-hoc transparency mechanism. In the industrial scenario, explanations are relevant before and during mitigation. For example, confidence levels do not only support the explanation of an uncertain tool identification result, but also indicate when the identification process should be repeated or when human assistance should be requested. Similarly, picking coordinates information is not only technical data used by the humanoid, but also resources that support explanations for unreliable picking or unsafe transport behavior. This demonstrates that XAI resources can serve a dual role: they support human understanding and provide safety-relevant information for evaluating whether a task should continue, be adapted, or be stopped.

References

1. Chen, Y., et al.: AI-empowered intelligence in industrial robotics: technologies, challenges, and emerging trends. Intell. Robot. **6**(1), 1–18 (2026)
2. Ahmad, K., Bano, M., Abdelrazek, M., Arora, C., Grundy, J.: What's up with requirements engineering for artificial intelligence systems? In: 2021 IEEE 29th International Requirements Engineering Conference (RE), pp. 1–12, IEEE (2021)
3. Setchi, R., Dehkordi, M.B., Khan, J.S.: Explainable robotics in human-robot interactions. Procedia Comput. Sci. 176, 3057–3066 (2020). Knowledge-Based and Intelligent Information & Engineering Systems: Proceedings of the 24th International Conference KES2020
4. Shrivastava, A., Hussein, L., Singh, N., Yaday, K., Karuna, G., Dwivedi, S.P.: Human–robot collaboration: explainable AI models for safe industrial co-robotics. In: 2025 IEEE 5th International Conference on ICT in Business Industry & Government (ICTBIG), pp. 1–6, IEEE (2025)

5. Albuquerque, D., Castro, J., Ribeiro, S., Heineck, T.: Requirements engineering for robotic system: a systematic mapping study. In: Workshop on Requirements Engineering (WER) (2017)
6. García, S., Strüber, D., Brugali, D., Berger, T., Pelliccione, P.: Robotics software engineering: a perspective from the service robotics domain. In: Proceedings of the 28th ACM Joint Meeting on European Software Engineering Conference and Symposium on the Foundations of Software Engineering, pp. 593–604 (2020)
7. Heineck, T., Gonçalves, E., Sousa, A., Oliveira, M., Castro, J.: Model-driven development in robotics domain: a systematic literature review. In: Brazilian Symposium on Software Components, Architectures and Reuse, pp. 151–160, IEEE (2016)
8. Feng, Y., Gao, G., Wang, P., Fu, M., Zhang, Z.: Towards model-based requirements engineering: Construction method of stakeholder value networks model based on mbse. Comput. Ind. Eng. **195**, 110398 (2024)
9. Raja, J.J., Manjunath, M., Daun, M.: Towards a goal-oriented approach for engineering digital twins of robotic systems. In: ENASE, pp. 466–473 (2024)
10. Taylor, H.M., Mavridou, A., Farrell, M., Dennis, L.A.: Explainability pattern specifications for human-robot teamwork. In: 2025 IEEE Engineering Reliable Autonomous Systems (ERAS), pp. 1–8, IEEE (2025)
11. Qayyum, S., Qureshi, A.: A survey on machine learning based requirement prioritization techniques. In: CIIS '18, p. 51–55 (2018)
12. Barrera, J.M., Reina, A.R., García-Ponsoda, S., Trujillo, J., et al.: Use of AI* extension for machine learning: a real case study (2022)
13. Navarro, Á., Lavalle, A, Maté, A., Trujillo, J.: Requirements modeling and elicitation for explainable artificial intelligence based on I. In: iStar@ER, pp. 3–12 (2024)
14. Martins, L.E.G., Gorschek, T.: Requirements engineering for safety-critical systems: overview and challenges. IEEE Softw. **34**(4), 49–57 (2017)
15. Manjunath, M., Kranz, P., Tenbergen, B., Daun, M.: Taxonomy for early safety analysis of human-robot interaction. In: International Conference on Conceptual Modeling Companion Proceedings (2025)
16. Navarro, E., Sanchez, P., Letelier, P., Pastor, J.A., Ramos, I.: A goal-oriented approach for safety requirements specification. In: IEEE International Symposium and Workshop on Engineering of Computer-Based Systems, pp. 8–pp, IEEE (2006)
17. Manjunath, M., Raja, J.J., Daun, M.: Early model-based safety analysis for collaborative robotic systems. IEEE Trans. Autom. Sci. Eng. **22**, 17523–17534 (2024)
18. Daun, M., Manjunath, M., Raja, J.J.: Safety analysis of human robot collaborations with GRL goal models. In: International Conference on Conceptual Modeling, pp. 317–333, Springer (2023)
19. Ribeiro, M., Castro, J., Pimentel, J.: ISTAR for safety-critical systems., In: iStar@ ER, p. 8 (2019)

Defining the Kinematic Requirements for a Model-Based Capability Evaluation

Jeshwitha Jesus Raja(✉) and Marian Daun

Technical University of Applied Sciences Würzburg-Schweinfurt, Schweinfurt, Germany
jeshwitha.jesusraja@study.thws.de

Abstract. Modern robotic systems are designed to perform a range of tasks, making their early and precise requirement specification essential. At the same time, current robotic systems heavily rely on standardized robotic hardware, i.e., an application is developed for a specific already existing off-the-shelf robot. While system requirements are typically defined early in the design process, kinematic considerations are often only introduced at later stages, which can lead to infeasible designs and costly redesigns. Therefore, in this paper, we propose the early specification of kinematic robot requirements. Kinematic requirements are derived from high-level system requirements, the technical robot specification containing kinematic properties, and general robot capabilities. This approach allows for early assessment of a robot's motion capabilities, helping to identify potential limitations before physical development. We evaluate our approach by applying it to a current industry challenge as use case.

Keywords: System Requirements · Kinematic Requirements · Capabilities · Goal Model · SysML

1 Introduction

In recent years, huge advances in the field of robotics have been made, allowing the deployment of more and more complex industrial robots [20], service robots [18], and even humanoids mimicking the behavior of humans [19]. These advances are due to a standardization of robotic hardware [2]. In industry automation, for instance, collaborative robots (cobots) can be bought off-the-shelf and then adapted and programmed for the specific industry use case. Thereby, the focus of development in robotic applications has shifted from developing robotic hardware to software.

A brief requirements engineering phase focuses on the user needs and the capabilities to be achieved from a high-level perspective [21]. However, a robot's capabilities are often limited by its kinematic properties, which impose specific constraints on its motion. Despite their relevance, kinematic properties are typically considered only later in the development process. The late consideration

© The Author(s), under exclusive license to Springer Nature Switzerland AG 2027
A. Bernasconi et al. (Eds.): ER 2026, LNCS 17081, pp. 392–402, 2027.
https://doi.org/10.1007/978-3-032-40795-5_24

of the kinematic factors can result in robots that fail to perform their intended tasks, often leading to costly redesigns [10]. Therefore, integrating robot kinematics with system requirements at an early stage aids in evaluating the feasibility of requirements based on the robot's capabilities before its physical development and deployment, and refining the requirements or properties based on the outcome [7]. To address the disconnect between requirements engineering and kinematics, this paper proposes (a) the explicit derivation of kinematic requirements, (b) the explicit specification of kinematic capabilities of the robotic hardware, and (c) feasibility checking between kinematic requirements and kinematic capabilities.

The paper is outlined as follows: Sect. 2 discusses the related work and Sect. 3 presents the approach for specification of kinematic requirements and early model-based capability evaluation. The approach is then evaluated in Sect. 4. Finally, Sect. 5 concludes the paper with directions for future work.

2 Related Work

Robot kinematics describes the geometric and motion relationships between a robot's joints and its end-effector, independent of the forces involved [9]. These relationships determine the reachable workspace, attainable orientations, and motion constraints, thereby introducing fundamental constraints on the physical capabilities of a robotic system. Kinematic models are typically expressed using formulations such as Denavit–Hartenberg parameterizations [15] or homogeneous transformation matrices [13]. However, these representations are generally introduced during detailed design or control development rather than at the requirements phase, resulting in a disconnect between high-level capability requirements and the structural parameters that enable or restrict them.

During requirements engineering, robotic system requirements are traditionally expressed in textual form, which makes it difficult to trace dependencies between user goals, design decisions, and system elements as complexity increases [16]. This is particularly problematic as functional objectives of robotics applications are deeply intertwined with structural and physical constraints.

Goal modeling is a well-established response to this problem [22] as it represents stakeholder or system goals within their context and highlights hierarchical decomposition, contributions, and dependencies [11]. The Goal-Oriented Requirements Language (GRL) captures such objectives using goals, tasks, soft goals, and resources held by actors [1], enabling engineers to model not only what a robot shall accomplish, but why certain constraints are introduced. GRL and iStar have already proven useful for modeling robotic systems in early development phases [4,8,12].

Overall, several studies have integrated model-based techniques into robotic system development. Ohara et al. [14] showed how Systems Modeling Language (SysML) diagrams such as Use Case and Block Definition Diagrams (BDD) can structure requirements analysis for manipulation tasks, representing kinematic calculations as dedicated architectural components. Sekar et al. [17] coupled

SysML models with executable simulations to verify that manipulation capabilities satisfy task-level requirements. These approaches confirm the feasibility of combining structural models with simulation-based validation, but they treat kinematics as implementation-level detail introduced after requirements are defined, or as verification artifacts used to test predefined requirements. However, without a common modeling approach for describing robotic structure, systematic comparison of alternative designs against capability requirements remains difficult [5].

3 Systematic Derivation of Kinematic Requirements

In this section, we present a methodology for systematically defining and evaluating kinematic requirements within robotic system development. The approach bridges the gap between high-level system requirements and the kinematic feasibility of robotic motion by explicitly integrating requirements engineering with kinematic modeling. We introduce kinematic requirements as intermediate artifacts that connect system goals with the structural robot specifications.

3.1 Existing Artifacts in Robotics

Currently, in the field of robotics, several artifacts are typically available at different stages of development:

- **High-level Requirements Specification.** In robotics, high-level requirements are typically defined at the beginning of development as natural-language statements describing what is expected from the robot and its environment. In our approach, we specify these high-level requirements using GRL/iStar goal models [3,6] to allow for better traceability with the kinematic properties.
- **Kinematic Specification.** For existing robotic systems, e.g., off-the-shelf robotic hardware, kinematic models exist and they are commonly used for tasks such as motion planning and collision checking, often at later stages of system development. However, these models are typically far too detailed and at a too low level of granularity to be directly linked to the requirements.
- **Robotic Capabilities.** In the robotics community there is a fundamental understanding of general robotic capabilities. These are partly made explicit, for instance through specifications such as accuracy, velocity limits, or payload capacity, but largely remain part of the stakeholders' knowledge.

3.2 Feasibility Evaluation Using Kinematic Requirements

Figure 1 presents an overview of the proposed approach for the definition and evaluation of kinematic requirements in the context of existing artifacts in robotics. Two new structured artifacts are introduced: a kinematic requirements specification and a model-based kinematic robot specification. The kinematic requirements are derived by refining high-level requirements. And in parallel, the robot's existing kinematic model is formalized into a traceable SysML-based kinematic robot specification that captures its structural and motion-related properties. This integration occurs through a systematic feasibility checking step, where the newly derived kinematic requirements are evaluated against the formalized kinematic robot specification. This creates a direct traceability link between system objectives and physical motion constraints. If inconsistencies are identified, the approach then enables iterative refinement of either the requirements or the kinematic configuration, ensuring alignment between intended capabilities and kinematic feasibility.

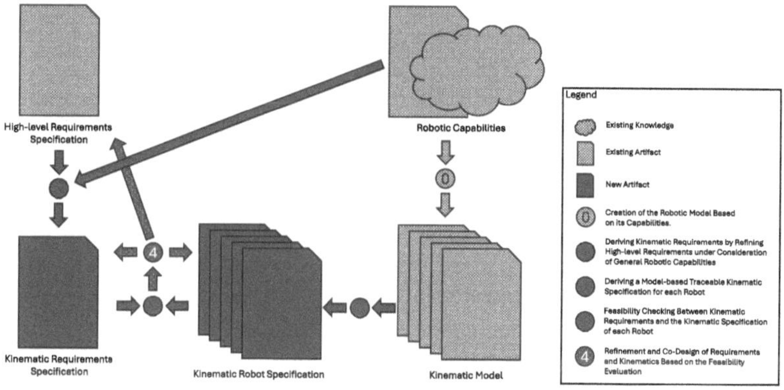

Fig. 1. Overview of the Approach.

Kinematic requirements can be explicitly derived from the high-level requirements taking into account general robotic capabilities. While system requirements define what the robot shall achieve, the kinematic specification defines how these tasks can physically be realized. Therefore, kinematic requirements emerge at the intersection of task demands and motion-related constraints. Here, every operational task imposes specific geometric and positional expectations on the robot, while the robot's kinematic structure defines what motions are physically possible. The task specifies what shall be achieved, whereas the kinematic model defines the limits within which motion can occur. By analyzing a task and identifying which kinematic attributes directly influence its execution, the qualitative task objective can be translated into an explicit kinematic requirement which formalizes the condition under which the task becomes physically executable. The derivation of kinematic requirements uses inputs from three primary sources, namely, system tasks and goals, relevant kinematic attributes (e.g., joint limits), and general robot capabilities.

These elements collectively contribute to the formulation of acquirable and verifiable kinematic requirements. Each kinematic requirement represents a formalized motion-related constraint that must hold for a task to be physically feasible. This approach establishes a direct traceability link between high-level system objectives and low-level physical motion constraints. Once the kinematic requirements are defined, they can be used for feasibility assessment and iterative refinement. Considering a simple pick-and-place example, a task like "Move the robot arm from point A to point B" can be analyzed using this structured derivation process. The task is selected from the goal model, and relevant kinematic attributes are identified. For example, the reachability determines whether points A and B lie within the robot's workspace dimensions, DoF affects achievable orientation, and joint limits constrain admissible configurations. By combining the task-level objective with these attributes, explicit kinematic requirements can be formulated, such as ensuring both points lie within the reachable workspace and that the required orientation can be achieved without violating joint limits. These requirements can then be evaluated against the robot's current kinematic specification to assess feasibility, thereby transforming abstract tasks into measurable motion-related constraints.

To model the robot's kinematic structure and motion-related properties, the identified kinematic attributes are translated into SysML diagrams, namely, BDD, Internal Block Diagrams (IBD), and parametric diagrams. Here, blocks represent the structural components of the robot, while their associated properties define the relevant kinematic attributes such as joint limits, link lengths, reachability, and repeatability. The fundamental elements of robot kinematics are generally well-established and standardized within the robotics community. The structures for elements such as link lengths, joint types, DoF, joint limits, and transformation matrices follow widely accepted modeling conventions. However, the specific numerical values and structural configurations of these elements are uniquely defined for each individual robot.

Once the kinematic requirements have been derived, they are systematically compared with the robot's kinematic specification. The feasibility checking process determines whether the robot's geometric and motion-related properties satisfy the task-level constraints, thereby enabling early stage kinematic feasibility assessment.

4 Evaluation

For the evaluation of the approach, the approach is applied to an industry use case which involves a UR5e robotic system (a collaborative robot) performing an automated assembly task. The wiring harness assembly challenge[1] focuses on automating the manual production of a hybrid automotive wiring harness module using robotics in an efficient, reliable, and standards-compliant manner, with particular emphasis on short cycle times and robust, flexible operation. The module consists of multiple automotive terminals and wires, thereby reflecting realistic industrial production conditions. Flexible wire manipulation remains one of the most demanding problems in robotics, particularly for stationary single-arm manipulators operating within constrained workspaces. As a result,

[1] https://www.leitungssatz-hub.de/en/robotik-challenge/robotik-challenge-2026/.

wire harness assembly is still predominantly manual and highly repetitive, motivating the introduction of this industrial challenge. The task therefore demands precise kinematic control, accurate orientation and insertion, and reliable execution within strict cycle-time limits.

4.1 Requirements Specification

Figure 2 presents the high-level goal model of the UR5e robot and its decomposition into operational tasks that are required to achieve autonomous wire harness assembly. The goal, Perform Automated Wire Harness, is refined into five major task groups representing the different phases of the assembly process. Several of these tasks are further decomposed into sub-tasks that shall be completed sequentially.

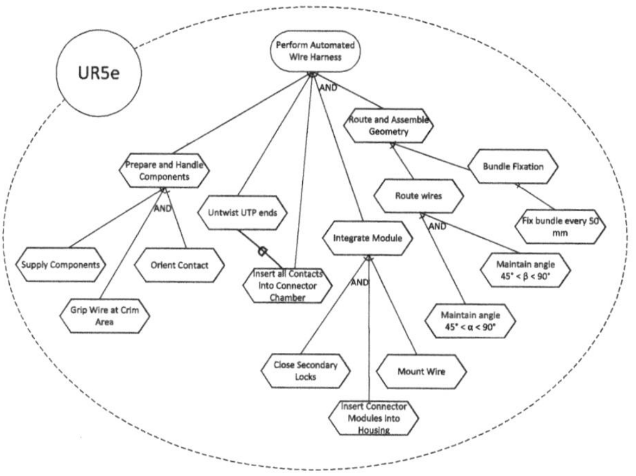

Fig. 2. GRL Goal Model visualizing UR5e's high-level objectives.

Figure 3 shows an excerpt of the BDD for the UR5e robotic system, capturing its structural decomposition and kinematic specification. The robot and its subsystems, such as the kinematic structure, joints, end-effector, control box, and communication interfaces, are modeled as blocks. Each block defines relevant properties, including physical parameters (e.g., mass, reach, payload), kinematic attributes (e.g., joint limits, link lengths, pose repeatability), and operational characteristics (e.g., TCP speed, power consumption).

Structural relationships between components are represented using associations and aggregations, reflecting how subsystems such as the joints and motors contribute to the overall kinematic structure. The diagram also includes parameter blocks, such as the DHParameterSet and TransformationMatrix, which formalize the mathematical representation of the robot's forward and inverse kinematics. Together, these elements define the structural and parametric foundation required for evaluating kinematic feasibility.

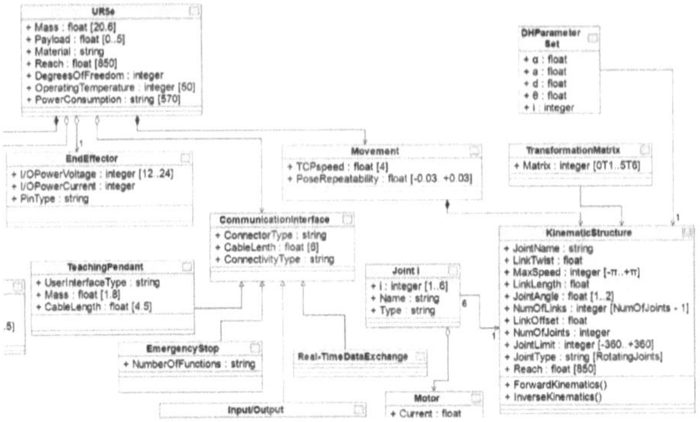

Fig. 3. Excerpt of BDD visualizing UR5e's kinematic and structural properties.

4.2 Feasibility Evaluation

In the goal model (shown in Fig. 2), the high-level tasks and, in particular, the operational sub-tasks are constrained by specific kinematic properties. To derive the corresponding kinematic requirements, these properties are first identified based on whether they directly influence the physical feasibility of task execution. Then, by explicitly associating these kinematic properties as constraints on the tasks and sub-tasks in the goal model, the high-level requirements can be translated into kinematic requirements. For example, for the task "Route Wires" under the goal "Perform Automated Wire Harness", the following kinematic attributes are relevant:

- **Workspace and Reachability:** The robot shall be capable of reaching all routing waypoints and fixture positions across the assembly board.
- **DoF:** At least six DoF are required to position and orient the TCP.
- **Orientation Capability:** The wrist configuration shall allow continuous orientation adjustments to satisfy geometric constraints.
- **Pose Repeatability:** TCP repeatability shall remain within the tolerance required for accurate wire placement.
- **Joint Limits and Motion Constraints:** All required routing trajectories shall lie within allowable joint ranges and avoid singular configurations.
- **Motion Smoothness and Velocity Control:** Controlled TCP velocity and acceleration are necessary to prevent oscillations or unintended displacement of the wire.
- **Payload Capacity:** The combined mass of the end-effector and manipulated wire shall remain within the rated payload capacity of the robot.

Based on the identified attributes, the kinematic requirements are derived. Table 1 shows the derived kinematic requirements along with their related kinematic attributes and corresponding high-level requirements.

For the kinematic requirements that have been derived, the required kinematic attributes can now be systematically compared with the existing kinematic

Table 1. Derived Kinematic Requirements.

Req. ID	Kinematic Requirement	Related Kinematic Attributes	Related High-Level Requirement
1.1	The robot shall provide a **reachable workspace** that includes all predefined routing waypoints on the assembly board.	Workspace and Reachability; DoF; Joint Limits and Motion Constraints	Route Wires
1.2	The robot shall maintain **TCP orientation capability** sufficient to satisfy the angular routing constraints $45° < \alpha < 90°$ and $45° < \beta < 90°$.	Orientation Capability; DoF; Joint Limits and Motion Constraints	Route Wires
1.3	The robot shall achieve a **pose repeatability** within the **tolerance** required for accurate placement of flexible wires into fixtures.	Pose Repeatability	Route Wires
1.4	The robot shall execute routing trajectories without exceeding **joint limits** or entering **singular configurations**.	Joint Limits and Motion Constraints; Workspace and Reachability; DoF	Route Wires
1.5	The robot shall ensure **controlled TCP motion** to prevent dynamic disturbance of flexible wires during routing operations.	Motion Smoothness and Velocity Control; Payload Capacity	Route Wires

properties of the robot. This step establishes whether the physical motion capabilities of the robot are sufficient to fulfill the defined task-level constraints. If all required kinematic constraints are satisfied, the task is considered kinematically feasible. If one or more constraints are violated, the task is classified as infeasible under the current robot configuration. This structured comparison ensures that high-level system goals are validated against the robot's actual physical motion capabilities before implementation. For example, the SysML-based kinematic model specifies that the UR5e has a maximum reach of 850 mm. If a task requires the robot to reach a point located 500 mm from its base, the requirement is considered kinematically feasible. However, if the task requires a reach of 1000 mm, the requirement is classified as kinematically infeasible, since it exceeds the robot's maximum reach and therefore cannot be physically accomplished.

Table 2 summarizes the kinematic requirements derived from the goal model for the task 'Route Wires' and evaluates their feasibility with respect to the UR5e robot's kinematic properties. The required kinematic attribute is compared with the corresponding UR5e kinematic value from the SysML model.

Table 2. Kinematic Requirements and Feasibility Evaluation for 'Route Wires'.

Kinematic Attribute	Required Value	Robot Value	Admissible Range	Feasibility
Workspace Reachability	All routing points reachable	850 mm reach	$\geq$ Required reach	Feasible
Orientation Capability	$45° < \alpha < 90°$	$\pm 180°$ wrist rotation	Within constraint	Feasible
Pose Repeatability	≤ 0.2 mm	± 0.03 mm	$\leq$ Required tolerance	Feasible

5 Discussion and Conclusion

Kinematics is a fundamental element in robotics as it defines the geometric feasibility of motion and therefore directly constrains what tasks a robot can realistically perform, making it essential to reflect kinematic limitations explicitly within system requirements. Therefore, in this paper, we highlighted the importance of incorporating kinematic considerations into the requirements engineering phase of robotic system development.

In requirements engineering, model-based specification improves formalization, traceability, and consistency by systematically linking stakeholder intentions to structural and technical system properties while reducing ambiguity inherent in textual descriptions. Addressing kinematics at a conceptual level enables earlier and more structured reasoning about capability feasibility, elevating kinematic parameters from purely mathematical artifacts to traceable requirement-level elements connected to stakeholder goals and capability definitions. To bridge the identified gap, this paper proposed a structured model-based methodology that integrates goal-oriented capability modeling with SysML-based structural modeling to derive kinematic constraints directly from capability objectives. By embedding kinematic properties within a traceable system model, the approach supported early feasibility assessment and strengthened alignment between functional intent and geometric realization.

This approach, therefore, enabled capability-driven comparison of alternative robotic architectures before detailed implementation. Additionally, it improves traceability by linking capability goals directly to structural parameters. Furthermore, the defined models can be refined if infeasible kinematic requirements are identified. This bidirectional refinement ensures consistency between intended system objectives and the robot's physical motion capabilities. Consequently, either the system goals are adapted to fit available hardware, or hardware modifications are specified early in the development process. As future work, a qualitative evaluation with experts and users is needed to assess the effectiveness and understandability of the approach.

References

1. Amyot, D., Ghanavati, S., Horkoff, J., Mussbacher, G., Peyton, L., Yu, E.: Evaluating goal models within the goal-oriented requirement language. Int. J. Intell. Syst. **25**(8), 841–877 (2010)
2. Bi, Z.M., Miao, Z., Zhang, B., Zhang, C.W.: The state of the art of testing standards for integrated robotic systems. Robot. Comput. Integr. Manuf. **63**, 101893 (2020)
3. Dalpiaz, F., Franch, X., Horkoff, J.: Definition and use of istar 2.0. In: Social Modeling Using the i* Framework: Essays in Honour of Eric Yu, pp. 65–81. Springer (2024)
4. Daun, M., Manjunath, M., Jesus Raja, J.: Safety analysis of human robot collaborations with GRL goal models. In: International Conference on Conceptual Modeling, pp. 317–333. Springer (2023)
5. Huckaby, J., Christensen, H.I.: A case for SySML in robotics. In: IEEE International Conference on Automation Science and Engineering, pp. 333–338. IEEE (2014)
6. ITU-T, R.Z.: ITU-T, recommendation z. 151 (11/18): user requirements notation (URN)-language definition (2018)
7. Raja, J., Daun, J., M.: Kinematic feasibility evaluation of robot requirements. In: International Conference on Research Challenges in Information Science, pp. 509–524. Springer (2026)
8. Raja, J., Manjunath, J., Daun, M., M.: Towards a goal-oriented approach for engineering digital twins of robotic systems. In: ENASE, pp, 466–473 (2024)
9. Kucuk, S., Bingul, Z.: Robot kinematics: Forward and inverse kinematics, vol. 1. INTECH Open Access Publisher London, UK (2006)
10. Kuo, C.H., Dai, J.S., Dasgupta, P.: Kinematic design considerations for minimally invasive surgical robots: an overview. Int. J. Med. Robot. Comput. Assist. Surg. **8**(2), 127–145 (2012)
11. van Lamsweerde, A.: Goal-oriented requirements engineering: a guided tour. In: Proceedings Fifth IEEE International Symposium on Requirements Engineering, pp. 249–262 (2001). https://doi.org/10.1109/ISRE.2001.948567
12. Manjunath, M., Jesus Raja, J., Daun, M.: Early model-based safety analysis for collaborative robotic systems. IEEE Trans. Autom. Sci. Eng. (2024)
13. Martínez, O., Campa, R.: Comparing methods using homogeneous transformation matrices for kinematics modeling of robot manipulators. In: International symposium on multibody systems and mechatronics, pp. 110–118. Springer (2020)
14. Ohara, K., Takubo, T., Mae, Y., Arai, T.: SysML-based robot system design for manipulation tasks. In: International conference on advanced mechatronics: toward evolutionary fusion of IT and mechatronics, pp. 522–527. The Japan Society of Mechanical Engineers (2010)
15. Patil, A., Kulkarni, M., Aswale, A.: Analysis of the inverse kinematics for 5 DOF robot arm using dh parameters. In: 2017 IEEE International Conference on Real-time Computing and Robotics (RCAR), pp. 688–693. IEEE (2017)

16. Rahman, M.A.A., Mizukawa, M.: Model-based development and simulation for robotic systems with SysML, Simulink and Simscape profiles. Int. J. Adv. Rob. Syst. **10**(2), 112 (2013)
17. Sekar, P.K.M., Baras, J.S.: Model-based systems engineering simulation framework for robot grasping. In: INCOSE International Symposium, vol. 32, pp. 82–89. Wiley Online Library (2022)
18. Sharma, G.D., Kharbanda, A., Parihar, J.S., Dawar, G., Taheri, B.: Navigating the robotics revolution: a review of research on service automation in shaping the future of tourism and hospitality. Int. J. Contemp. Hosp. Manag. **38**(13), 49–69 (2026)
19. Tong, Y., Liu, H., Zhang, Z.: Advancements in humanoid robots: a comprehensive review and future prospects. IEEE/CAA J. Automatica Sinica **11**(2), 301–328 (2024)
20. Urrea, C., Kern, J.: Recent advances and challenges in industrial robotics: a systematic review of technological trends and emerging applications. Processes **13**(3), 832 (2025)
21. Van Lamsweerde, A.: Requirements engineering in the year 00: a research perspective. In: 22nd International Conference on Software Engineering, pp. 5–19 (2000)
22. Van Lamsweerde, A.: Goal-oriented requirements engineering: a guided tour. In: International Symposium on Requirements Engineering, pp. 249–262. IEEE (2001)

How Systems Change: A Preliminary Ontological Account

Rodrigo F. Calhau[1(✉)], João Paulo A. Almeida[2], Giancarlo Guizzardi[3], and Victorio A. Carvalho[1]

[1] LEDS Research Group, Federal Institute of Espírito Santo, Espírito Santo, Brazil
{calhau,victorio}@ifes.edu.br
[2] Ontology and Conceptual Modeling Research Group (NEMO), Federal University of Espírito Santo, Espírito Santo, Brazil
jpalmeida@ieee.org
[3] Semantics, Cybersecurity and Services, University of Twente, Enschede , The Netherlands
g.guizzardi@utwente.nl

Abstract. Systems are usually conceived of as 'complex' (or 'organized' wholes) composed of 'connected' (or interacting) elements. They are dynamic entities whose composition, structure, aspects, and environment may change over time. In this paper, we take a step towards ontological foundations for modeling system change. Building on the Unified Foundational Ontology (UFO), we account for different dimensions of system variation over time inspired on Bunge's CESM model. The proposed foundations contribute to system change understanding and provide a conceptual base for future applications in system modeling approaches and languages.

Keywords: System · System change · System evolution · System situation · Ontology · Systems modeling

1 Introduction

Systems such as organizations, software systems, and cyber-physical systems are inherently dynamic entities that undergo continuous structural, compositional, environmental, and aspectual changes over time [1,4,8]. Such changes may involve the addition or removal of components, changes in their relationships, the emergence or dissolution of aspects, the variation of qualities and capabilities, and as a result of the latter, modifications in the possible interactions between the system and its environment. To properly understand and model these different dimensions of change in fields such as systems engineering, software engineering, and enterprise architecture, we need a proper understanding of this phenomenon.

This work proposes a preliminary account of system change by extending a core system ontology proposed in our previous work [5–7]. Our aim is to provide

© The Author(s), under exclusive license to Springer Nature Switzerland AG 2027
A. Bernasconi et al. (Eds.): ER 2026, LNCS 17081, pp. 403–413, 2027.
https://doi.org/10.1007/978-3-032-40795-5_25

an ontological foundation for system change based on the Unified Foundational Ontology (UFO) [9] and inspired by Bunge's CESM model [4].

The remainder of this paper is organized as follows. Section 2 presents the ontological baseline covering briefly the foundational ontology and the *system core ontology* [5–7], both of which are employed in Sect. 3 to develop the ontological foundation for system change; Sect. 4 discusses implications in system modeling, and presents final considerations and future works.

2 Ontological Baseline

Unified Foundational Ontology (UFO). UFO [9] is a Foundational Ontology, i.e., an axiomatic system of domain-independent ontological theories. UFO classifies entities into *individuals* and *types*. Individuals can be *situations*, *events*, and *endurants*. *Situations* are specific arrangements of a particular portion of reality. *Events* are individuals that "occur" or "happen" across time (e.g., the FIFA 2026 World Cup Final). *Endurants* are individuals which persist in time and may undergo qualitative changes without losing their identity. *Endurants* fall into two categories: *objects* and *aspects*. *Objects* are endurants that exist independently (such as the Moon, the Statue of Liberty). Of particular importance to account for systems is the notion of *functional complex*. A *functional complex* is an object composed of multiple parts that play functional roles with respect to the whole (e.g., an organization, the human body, a computer). Aspects, on the other hand, depend on other individuals to exist. A *relator* is a specific type of *aspect* that can mediate two or more things (e.g., John Lennon and Yoko Ono's marriage). Material relations are those derived from relator types (e.g., in the way "being married to" is derived from Marriage, or "enrolled at" is founded on Enrollment). In contrast to a relator, an *intrinsic aspect* is existentially dependent on a single individual. An intrinsic aspect can be a *mode* or a *quality*. *Qualities*, like color, height, weight, etc., may be directly projected into a value space. *Modes* are dispositional entities that are manifested through events, and which can have aspects of their own.

In contrast to *individuals*, *types* are entities that define common properties that are shared by their instances. The UFO taxonomy of types is organized into *endurant types* (e.g., "Car"', "Partnership"), *event types* (e.g., "Live Concert"', "Birth"), *object types* (e.g., "Person"', "Organization"), *aspect types* (e.g., "Age"', "Enrollment"), *situation types* (e.g., "Battery Level is Low"), etc. Endurant types are further classified according to their modal metaproperties (concerning rigidity and sortality). Rigid types, like *kinds* (e.g., "Car") and *subkinds* (e.g., "Ferrari"), are those that apply to their instances necessarily (and hence, apply throughout their instances existences). Anti-rigid types are those that classify their instances "dynamically". These include *roles* and *phases*. *Roles* are relationally-dependent ("Student", "Spouse") and *phases* classify their instances according to (mutable) intrinsic characteristics, e.g., "WorkingCar", "BrokenCar". Sortals are those endurant types that supply or carry a principle of identity for their instances (e.g., the object kind "Car", "Person", and the relator kind "Marriage"), while non-sortals are those (also called *dispersive types*) which abstract common features of sortals which different identity criteria (e.g., the *category* “Physical Object” is a rigid type subsuming “Car” and “Person”). Non-sortals that apply necessarily to some instances but contingently to others are called *mixins.*

Core Ontology of Systems (*COSy*). COSy[1] is a core ontology inspired by the CESM model [4] and grounded on the Unified Foundational Ontology (UFO). A portion of this ontology (represented in the UFO-based modeling language OntoUML [9]) is shown in Fig. 1. Systems are functional complexes with at least two proper parts (*components*), connected to external entities, and characterized by *system intrinsic aspects.* Components can be *units, modules, interfaces,* etc. For Bunge [4], *structure* is captured via *bonding relations* (connections). Relations that are bonding are “material”. They can be used to connect components within the same system (“is internally connected with”), or connect a system or a system component with *external entities,* i.e., entities in the environment (“is externally connected with”). The reification of internal connections, external connections, and system connections are *relator categories* in Fig. 1. The ontology addresses global properties [4] through *system intrinsic aspects* (including *dispositions* and *qualities*). A *System intrinsic aspect* “arises from” (i.e., ‘emerges from’ or ‘results from’) *component intrinsic aspects* (including *dispositions* and *qualities*). Intrinsic aspects of systems manifest themselves through *system events.* System events (e.g., internal events, interaction with the environment, etc.) can be triggered by *system situations,* potentially generating a new *system situation* as an outcome. System events are constituted by *component events* (e.g., component internal events, component internal interaction, component external interaction). *Component intrinsic aspects* manifest themselves through *component events.*

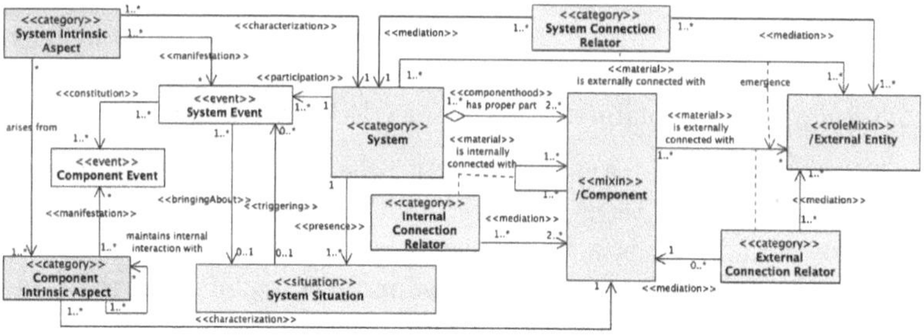

Fig. 1. Fragment of *COSy*: a Core Ontology of Systems, proposed in [5–7].

3 Ontological Foundations for System Change

This section presents the proposed extension of the system ontology. This ontology was built following the Systematic Approach for Building Ontologies

[1] https://github.com/nemo-ufes/cosy.

(SABiO) [3]. The ontology is modeled using OntoUML and transformed into an OWL implementation (based on the UFO implementation called gUFO [2]), shared using FAIR principles.

In this ontology, systems are considered entities subject to change, i.e., that can vary over time. When a system changes, it changes to a new *situation* – a certain configuration of parts and properties in a given time interval. This idea is illustrated in Fig. 2: the system s is formed by four system situations: ss_1 (from t_0 to t_1), ss_2 (from t_1 to t_2), ss_3 (from t_2 to t_3), and ss_4 (from t_3 to t_4), each corresponding to a different configuration of s in a different period of time.

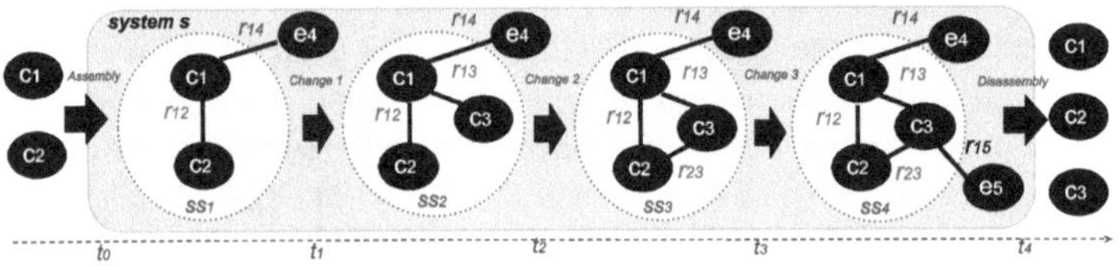

Fig. 2. An illustration of a system changing across different situations (configurations).

Figure 3 reveals *system situation* as a complex situation formed by the following parts: *Compositional Situation*, *Structural Situation*, *Environmental Situation* and *Aspectual Situation*, which are inspired in Bunge's *CESM (Composition, Environment, Structure, Mechanism)* model. In the original model, the *composition(t)* of system s is formed by the set of components that are parts of s at time t; the *environment(t)* is formed by all external entities that are connected to system s at time t; the *structure(t)* of system s is formed by all the connections between the components (internal or external) of system s at time t; finally, the *mechanism* is formed by the types of "processes" or "events" in which system s can participate. In what follows, these different dimensions of the CESM model are reconstructed and explained in terms of UFO elements.

Compositional Change. At a particular time interval, the components of a system stand in what we term *Compositional Situation.* For example, suppose system s shown in Fig. 2 is a "supervision system" initially composed of two components, the supervisor c_1 and the supervisee c_2, its composition in the period between t_0 and t_1, in system situation ss_1. With changes in the system, new situations are generated and new compositions can arise when components are added to or removed from the system. System s undergoes a change at time t_1 (Fig. 2) in which a new component c_3 (a new supervisee) is added, generating a new composition consisting of c_1, c_2, and c_3, and hence, a new compositional situation.

Structural Change. A system structural situation includes the (system and component) *connection relators* which reify the (internal and external) connections existing in a system at a given time interval. Consider the supervision system s in situation ss_2 (Fig. 2). At this moment, the system is formed by three

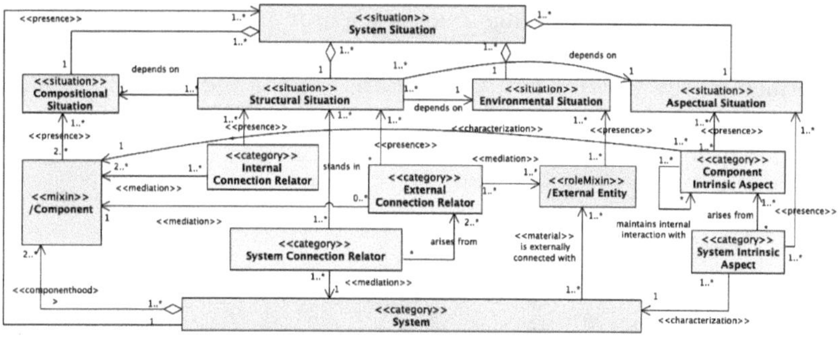

Fig. 3. An extension to the COSy Ontology with types of situations representing the CESM dimensions in which a system can change.

components: a supervisor (c_1) and two supervisees (c_2 and c_3). The supervisor has a "supervision" connection with each of the two supervisees (who initially are not related). These (internal) connections are mediated by the relators r_{12} and r_{13}, as illustrated. Supervisor c_1 is also (externally) connected to an external researcher e_4, through relator r_{14}. Thus, the structure of the system in the situation ss_2 is formed by r_{12} and r_{13}, corresponding to the supervision connections between the supervisor and the supervisees, and by r_{14} corresponding to an external connection. Just as the composition of a system can "change", so can the structure. In the example, supervisees c_2 and c_3 are connected only to the supervisor c_1 in situation ss_2. However, suppose that the two supervisees c_2 and c_3 start collaborating with each other as well. As a result, a new collaboration connection arises between them, mediated by the *relator* r_{23} (Fig. 2). Due to this change, a new system structure is generated in system situation ss_3, formed by the (internal) *relators* r_{12}, r_{13}, and r_{23}, and by the (external) relator r_{14}.

Aspectual Situation. The aspectual situation corresponds to a situation formed by (i) system and component aspects, including *intrinsic modes* and *qualities*; (ii) corresponding *quality values* that a system's (and components') aspects possesses in a given period of time. This is shown in Fig. 3, in which *component aspects* and *system aspects*, from a same system, stands in a *aspectual situation*. Examples include the *fuel level* of a car at a given moment, the *geographical position* of this car, and the *engine temperature* at that same moment. In the case of system s (Fig. 2), in situation ss_2, there is no collaboration connection between c_2 and c_3 because the level of collaboration capability, cc_2 and cc_3, of each supervisee is low. Consider the system undergoes an aspectual change and the collaboration capability cc_2 and cc_3 of each supervisee c_2 and c_3 increase, generating a new aspectual situation in situation ss_3.

Environmental Situation. In a system environmental situation, we have standing in all external entities connected to the system Fig. 3. In the example of system s (Fig. 2), the external researcher e_4 is an example of an external entity that is part of the environment in the situation ss_3. Similarly to the other types of situations, a"change" can transform an environmental situations to another. In the example of system s, the environment of system s in situation ss_3 is formed by the external entity e_4. As the system undergoes a change, situation ss_4 is brought about, including the external collaborator e_5 connected to the system through the supervised c_3.

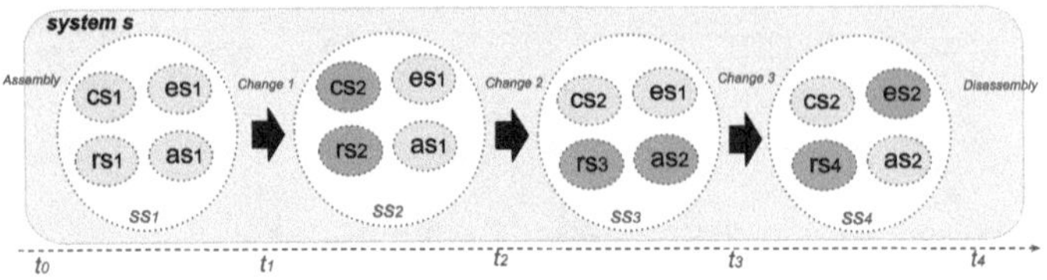

Fig. 4. System Change - Illustration (cs_x: compositional situation; rs_x: structural situation; es_x: environmental situation; as_x: aspectual situation).

Multidimensional Change. An important aspect is that although the previous examples focused only on changes in a single dimension, changes generally occur in more than one dimension of the system. This is because all these dimensions of a system are directly or indirectly interconnected. For example, the (internal) structure of a system is defined on the basis of its composition. Thus, a change in the composition of a system can cause a change in its structure. Analogously, changes in the external structure of a system and in its environment can mutually influence each other. The structure is also based on the aspectual situation, since the system's connections result from the (dispositional) aspects of the components. In short, the structural situation "depends" on compositional, environmental, and aspectual situations (Fig. 3). Thus, changes in these dimensions of the system will impact its structure. Figure 4 illustrates the dynamics of multidimensional change in the system's situations, from the running example. As illustrated, change 1 occurs because there is a change in composition (cs_1 to cs_2) which triggers a change in the system's structure (from rs_1 to rs_2), generating the situation ss_2. Change 2 occurs due to a change in aspectual situation (as_1 to as_2) which also triggers a change in structure (rs_2 to rs_3), generating the system's ss_3 situation. Change 3 occurs due to a change in environment (es_1 to es_2) which again triggers a change in structure (rs_3 to rs_4), generating the system's ss_4 situation.

System Change Event. Based on the previous definitions of system situations, we consider a system change to be an event (in UFO terms) that generates a new system situation. System events are triggered by system situations, and generate another system situation as an outcome, except for assembling and disassembling events (Fig. 5). Based on the dimensions presented earlier, we define two main types of change in a system: *aspectual change* and *configuration change*. The first type corresponds to a change in the "state" of the system, that is, a change in the values of the aspects (properties) of the system. For example, a car can be turned

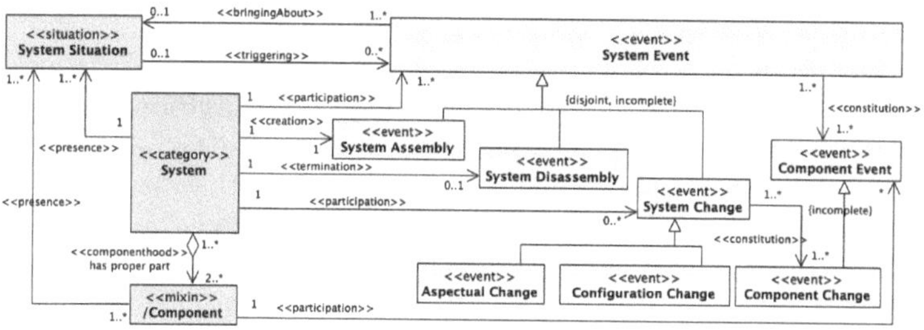

Fig. 5. System Situation Sub-Ontology Fragment: System Change (in OntoUML).

on, turned off, accelerated, braked, etc. The second type of change, configuration change, involves change in at least one non-aspectual dimension, namely, composition, structure, and environment. Consequently, a configuration change may also involve a change in the system's aspectual situation, but an aspectual change does not necessarily involve direct changes to composition, structure, and environment. Examples include changing a tire on a car, adding a tracking device to the car, or replacing a faulty radiator. Systems are composed of components, and therefore, system events are constituted by component events as well (Fig. 5). This means that a system change necessarily also involves changes in its parts, including the relationships between them, and also in the aspects of the system or components.

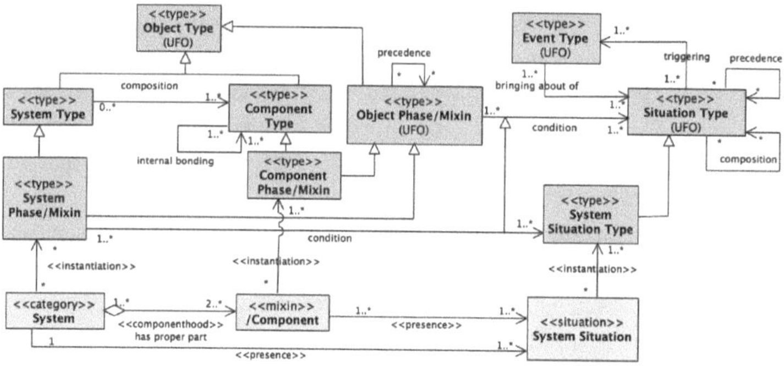

Fig. 6. System Situation Type - Sub Ontology (in OntoUML).

System Situation Type Sub-Ontology. We also present a sub-ontology at the type level as illustrated in Fig. 6. This sub-ontology is based on some essential UFO distinctions such as *object type*, *event type*, *situation type*, and *object phase / mixin* (an *object type* that specialize a *phase* or *phaseMixin*). As shown, instances of an *event type* 'bring about of instances of a'*situation type*, which instances, in turn, 'trigger' an *event type* instances. *Object types* can have different (sub) types of *object phase/mixin*, that include both *object phase* (with just one identity criteria) and *object phase mixin* (with distinct identity criteria). *Object phases/mixin* are, then, anti-rigid types that classify instances of *object types* dynamically, based on intrinsic and relational conditions represented by situation types. In this way, *object phases/mixin* have *situation types* as a condition, as illustrated. For example, a car instantiates the phase "fueled" if its situation instantiates the situation type "the car has gas level greater than zero". In summary, *object phases/mixin* are dynamic classifications of *objects* (e.g., systems) based on *situation types*, which are universal situations that condition the instantiation of such *object phases/mixin*. *Object types* include *system types* and *component types*, which are linked by a 'composition' relation [7]. So, as a result, *object phases/mixin* include *system phase/mixins* as well as *component phases/mixins*. The *system phase/mixins* have the *component phase/mixins* as 'condition', as illustrated. For example, the "out of gas" phase of car type depends on the "empty" phase of the gas tank type. A *system phase/mixin*, as a phase, also has *system situation types* as conditions. For example, the "out of gas" phase of car type has the "tank with no gas" system situation type as a condition. This means, a car can just instantiate the "out of gas" phase if its gas level is zero, i.e., it instantiates different phases based on the current system situation.

Ontology Illustration. We apply here the ontology to model the *robot vacuum cleaner* scenario. This system comprises a number of components, such as a rotating brush (br_1), dustbin (db_1), battery (ba_1), main circuit board (cb_1), sensor system (se_1), among others not shown, such as wheels, propulsion motor, etc. The robot can have different phases: at rest, cleaning, at standby, stuck or with an error. The components also have phases. For example, the battery can be *full* or *dead* (static phase); the battery can also be *charging* (when it is in the dock) or *discharging*, when it is in use (active phase); the brush can be *good for use* or *worn*; the dustbin can be *empty* or *full*. The instantiation of these phases depends on aspectual conditions and quality values associated with the robot and its components. The robot has qualities like its current position, a map of the environment, etc. The robot's components have aspects as: the dustbin has a dirt level; the battery has a charging level; the brush has a usage time, meaning it can be good for use or worn out (needing to be replaced). Regarding the robot's basic structure, the components mentioned above are connected to the main circuit board (cb_1). Concerning the environment, the robot interacts with different external entities such as the user (us_1)—directly or through a smartphone—, the dock (do_1), and obstacles. Figure 7 shows different changes undergone by the robot vacuum cleaner (ro), focusing on *configuration changes*. Changes in aspects will not be illustrated in the figure but will be addressed in the text. In the robot's structure in system situation ss_1 (Fig. 7), the rotating brush (br_1), dustbin (db_1), battery (ba_1), and sensor system (se_1) components are connected to the main circuit board (cb_1). In this situation (configuration), the robot has one external entity as part of its environment, the dock (do_1), connected to the robot's battery (ba_1). As depicted, a configuration change from situations ss_1 and ss_2 occurs in the system since the composition, environment, and structure of the system are modified. In this case, a mobile application is configured to access and control the robot vacuum cleaner remotely, Âăand as a result, the user (us_1) becomes connected to the robot through its mobile application (environmental and structural change). In addition, the mop module (ma_1) is added to mop the house (compositional and structural change).

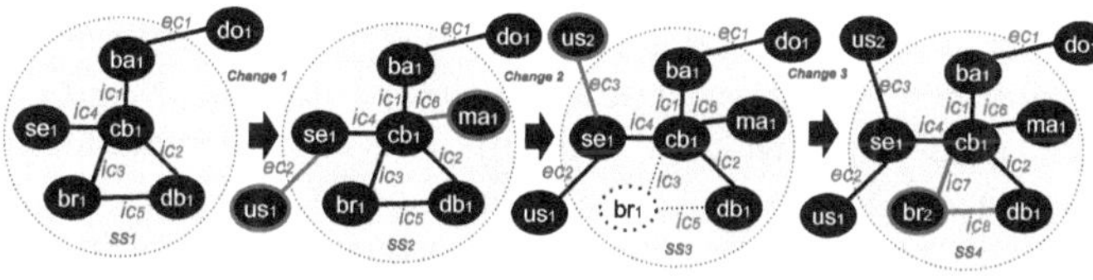

Fig. 7. Robot Vacuum Cleaner Situations Illustration.

Concerning the aspectual situation, robot operation generates multiple aspectual changes, and creating distinct aspectual situations and corresponding phase transitions. For example, the robot's battery is charged (aspectual change) by placing it in the dock, and battery get full (phase transition); robot changes its phase from resting to cleaning (phase transition) and starts cleaning the environment with the activation event, at a predefined time; robot returns to the dock with lower battery level and the higher dirt level after finishing cleaning (aspectual change) and start sleeping (phase transition), and so on. Figure 8 illustrates an example of an aspectual change in the robot. After cleaning the house, the battery level drops to zero (system situation) and the robot's battery becomes empty (component phase). Consequently, the robot becomes discharged (system phase), triggering a recharge (system event) that brings the battery level to full (system situation). As a result of this aspectual change, the robot becomes charged.

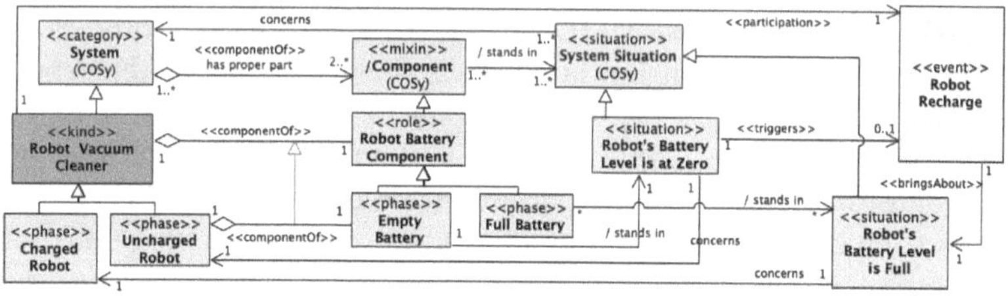

Fig. 8. Extending *COSy* to Illustrate the Robot Vacuum Cleaner Phases, Situations and Aspectual Change (in OntoUML).

These aspectual changes affect only aspect values (e.g., robot position, battery level, level of dirt in the compartment, etc.), without modifying necessarily system configuration (composition, structure, or environment). However, aspectual changes can also stimulate changes in the system configuration. Suppose the brush exceeds 300 h of use, surpassing its limit. The brush usage time changes (aspectual change), then it becomes worn (phase transition) and is blocked by the system, ceasing to respond to commands and interact with other components. This is shown in Fig. 7 where, in the situation ss_3, the brush (br_1) loses connection with the other components and becomes non-functional (structural change). As illustrated, the new situation ss_3 also included a new user (us_2) that becomes an external entity to the robot (environmental change). The brush degradation then induces another system configuration change involving the brush replacement (compositional and structural change). This change is made, in which the brush (br_1) is replaced by a new brush (br_2), generating a new situation ss_4. Brush replacement restores the robot's operational capability in situation ss_4. This example illustrates bidirectional dependency between aspectual and configurational changes.

4 Implications and Final Remarks

The proposed ontology provides ontological foundations for integrating these perspectives across multidimensional systems situations and change events. Class diagrams in UML or block/part diagrams in SysML generally focus on the structural perspective in isolation. Similarly, state-based diagrams in UML or SysML generally lack proper integration with other perspectives. Thus, when a change occurs in the system represented in a state diagram, it is unclear what the impacts of such a change are on the structure, composition, etc. In many state-based modeling approaches, states are represented as atomic labels, without an explicit ontological commitment to the underlying situation (e.g., configuration) of the system. The ontology enables to relate a phase of a system to a specific structure or configuration of the system. With the proposed ontology, it is possible to ground the phases of the system based on different types of situations proposed in this work. For example, a system cannot instantiate a "cleaning" phase if the cleaning brush is disconnected. Another important aspect is related to the term "state". In notations like UML/SysML, the meaning of "state" is ambiguous. As presented, systems instantiate phases that are grounded on aspectual or configurational situations of the system. That is, what is called "state" in such notations can actually be mapped to the system's phase, which is a dynamic classification of it grounded on its current situation. Furthermore, the ontology also allows to understand how phases of the part and the whole relate, enabling improved precision and expressiveness in state-based models. Beyond this integration of simultaneous phases, the type level, with its proposed hierarchy of phases, contributes to a global understanding of system behavior, allowing for the creation of taxonomies or hierarchies of system phases. In general, the proposed ontology contributes to a more integrated and semantically grounded representation of system change, allowing for explicit relationships between structure, behavior, environment, and aspects in distinct system situations.

Final Remarks. This work presented an ontological foundation for system change. System situations were categorized based on different dimensions of a system, drawing on Bunge's work. This categorization served as a basis for understanding different types of system change involving one dimension, such as aspectual changes, or multi-dimensional changes, such as configurational changes. The ontology also addressed the type level, where phases of a system were approached based on situation types. One aspect that needs further development concerns the system's and component's function, which can change.We implicitly included the system's function within the system situation, but in the future it may give rise to an exclusive sub-situation for the *functional situation*. Our focus in this work was greater on static situations (e.g., configuration); however, a relevant future work is to better explore ongoing "behavioral situations in systems" (while they manifest a capability), relating to active phases of the system, e.g., the performance of tasks and activities of a system. Finally, in this work we briefly addressed relationships between situations; however, it would be interesting to conduct a more in-depth investigation in the future into how situations relate ontologically. In general, the proposed ontology provides a basis for understanding system change as multidimensional and time-based, enabling future investigations into the ontological dependencies between emergent situations, phases, capabilities, and properties.

Acknowledgments. This study was financed in part by CNPq (443130/2023-0, 313412/2023-5) and FAPES (2026-PPX8T).

References

1. Ackoff, R.L.: Towards a system of systems concepts. Manage. Sci. **17**(11) (1971)
2. Almeida, J.P.A., Guizzardi, G., Falbo, R., Sales, T.P.: gufo: a lightweight implementation of the unified foundational ontology (ufo) (2019). http://purl.org/nemo/doc/gufo
3. de Almeida Falbo, R.: Sabio: systematic approach for building ontologies. In: Proceedings of the 1st JOWO on FOIS 2014. CEUR Workshop Proceedings, RJ (2014)
4. Bunge, M.: Treatise on Basic Philosophy. Ontology II: A World of Systems. Springer Netherlands, Dordrecht, Netherlands (1979)
5. Calhau, R.F.: Exploring system behavior in a system ontology. In: 42nd International Conference on Conceptual Modeling, ER 2023. CEUR (2023)
6. Calhau, R.F.: A system core ontology for capability emergence modeling. In: International Conference on EDOC, pp. 3–20. Springer (2023). https://doi.org/10.1007/978-3-031-46587-1_1
7. Calhau, R.F.: Towards an ontology of type-level phenomena for system modeling. In: International Conference on RCIS, pp. 121–139. Springer (2025). https://doi.org/10.1007/978-3-031-92474-3_8
8. Fine, K.: Things and their parts. Midwest Stud. Philos. **23**, 61–74 (1999)
9. Guizzardi, G.: Ontological Foundations for Structural Conceptual Models. No. 15 (2005)

LLMs and Multi-agent Systems

Tropos$^+$: Tropos Extended in the Days of Large Language Models

Paolo Bresciani[1], Paolo Giorgini[2], John Mylopoulos[2,3], Anna Perini[4], and Angelo Susi[4](✉)

[1] Trento, Italy
[2] University of Trento, Trento, Italy
paolo.giorgini@unitn.it
[3] University of Toronto, Toronto, Canada
jm@cs.toronto.edu
[4] FBK, Trento, Italy
{perini,susi}@fbk.eu

Abstract. Agent-Oriented Software Engineering methodologies such as Tropos were developed under assumptions inherited from symbolic models of agency, including stable goal interpretations, explicit reasoning, and a clear separation between design time and run time. The emergence of Agentic AI challenges these assumptions. LLM-based agents interpret goals at runtime, adapt through interaction and feedback, and exhibit behaviour that cannot be completely specified during design. In this paper, we argue that these changes require revisiting the conceptual foundations of Tropos rather than replacing its intentional perspective. We introduce a set of conceptual extensions, including the distinction between design-time and run-time intentionality, normative goals, delegation of reasoning authority, residual responsibility, and dynamic autonomy. We then discuss how these concepts may influence the interpretation of the Tropos development process and outline a research agenda for extending goal-oriented requirements engineering towards Agentic AI systems. Rather than presenting a complete methodology, this work aims to stimulate discussion on how intentional modelling should evolve to support adaptive, accountable, and continuously evolving intelligent systems.

Keywords: Goal-Oriented Requirements Engineering · Agentic AI · LLMs

1 Introduction

Agent-Oriented Software Engineering (AOSE) methodologies emerged in the late 1990s and early 2000 s to address the growing complexity of software systems operating in open, distributed, and socio-technical environments [13]. By

P. Bresciani—Independent researcher

© The Author(s), under exclusive license to Springer Nature Switzerland AG 2027
A. Bernasconi et al. (Eds.): ER 2026, LNCS 17081, pp. 417–427, 2027.
https://doi.org/10.1007/978-3-032-40795-5_26

modelling software in terms of autonomous actors, goals, and social dependencies, they introduced intentionality as a first-class engineering concept, enabling developers to reason not only about how a system should behave, but also why such behaviour is required. Among these methodologies, Tropos has played a prominent role by systematically exploiting intentional concepts—such as actors, goals, softgoals, and dependencies—throughout the software development lifecycle [1,2]. The success of Tropos is rooted in assumptions inherited from classical symbolic models of agency, most notably the Belief–Desire–Intention (BDI) paradigm [8]. Within this perspective, agents are intentional entities whose goals, reasoning strategies, and interactions can be explicitly modelled. Goals are assumed to have stable interpretations, reasoning processes can be anticipated at design time, and autonomous behaviour remains within boundaries established during requirements analysis and design. These assumptions provide the foundations for traceability, accountability, and verification, which have long been central objectives of goal-oriented requirements engineering [4,14].

The emergence of Agentic AI fundamentally challenges these assumptions. Large Language Model (LLM)-based agents, which we refer to as *agentives*, no longer rely exclusively on reasoning structures defined at design time. Instead, their behaviour emerges from the interaction between foundation models, prompting, external tools, memory, and continuous human feedback [12]. Consequently, the same organisational goal may be operationalised differently depending on execution context, interaction history, or subsequent learning. Recent research has produced increasingly powerful frameworks supporting planning, tool use, collaboration, and software engineering tasks [3,5–7,9–11,15–17]. These approaches demonstrate remarkable reasoning capabilities, yet they remain primarily concerned with *how* agents behave rather than with *why* they should behave in a certain way or how such behaviour should remain aligned with organisational intentions. From this perspective, the challenge posed by Agentic AI is not technological but conceptual. Stable goal semantics, explicit reasoning models, predictable enactment, fixed delegation structures, and the traditional separation between design time and run time can no longer be taken for granted. Yet, what requires reconsideration is therefore not the intentional perspective of Tropos itself, whose relevance is not under discussion, but the assumptions under which that perspective was originally interpreted. The central question is not how to replace Tropos, but how to evolve its conceptual foundations so that they remain applicable to systems combining traditional software agents and LLM-based agentives.

This paper presents Tropos$^+$ as a first step in this direction. Rather than introducing a complete methodology, we propose a conceptual perspective on how goal-oriented requirements engineering should evolve in the era of Agentic AI. We identify a small set of conceptual extensions that we believe are necessary for reasoning about adaptive and interpretative agents, including the distinction between design-time and run-time intentionality, normative goals, delegation of reasoning authority, residual responsibility, and dynamic autonomy. We then discuss how these concepts may influence the interpretation of the

Tropos development process and outline a research agenda for extending goal-oriented requirements engineering towards adaptive, continuously evolving, and accountable intelligent systems.

The remainder of the paper is organised as follows. Section 2 introduces the conceptual foundations underlying Tropos$^+$ and discusses the main conceptual shifts required by Agentic AI. Section 3 examines how these concepts influence the interpretation of the Tropos development process. Section 4 outlines the main research challenges that remain open. Finally, Sect. 5 concludes the paper.

2 Conceptual Foundations for Tropos$^+$

The previous section argued that the emergence of Agentic AI challenges some of the assumptions on which classical goal-oriented and agent-oriented methodologies were originally built. If goals are no longer interpreted in a stable way, reasoning cannot be fully specified at design time, and autonomy evolves during system operation, then the conceptual foundations of intentional modelling must also evolve. Rather than prescribing runtime behaviour, intentional models provide the conceptual basis for governance. They support the identification of goal drift, justify escalation to human actors when necessary, and preserve alignment between adaptive behaviour and organisational objectives. This governance role reflects the fact that the correctness of an agentive system can no longer be established exclusively through design-time specification, but must also be maintained throughout system operation. These concepts are intended as an initial conceptual foundation for discussing how goal-oriented requirements engineering may evolve while preserving the intentional perspective that characterises Tropos.

2.1 Challenges for Agent-Oriented Methodologies

Agentive behaviour introduces a set of conceptual challenges that go beyond implementation concerns and affect the foundations of agent-oriented modelling.

C1 **From explicit reasoning to interpretative behaviour.** Agent-oriented methodologies assume that reasoning follows structures that can be explicitly modelled, such as plans or rules. In agentive systems, behaviour depends on learned statistical models and run-time interaction context. As a result, the same goal may be operationalised differently depending on input phrasing or interaction history, even when the design-time model is unchanged.

C2 **Goal stability and goal drift.** Goals are traditionally treated as stable artefacts with fixed meaning across the lifecycle. In agentive systems, goals are interpreted at run time, and their operational meaning may vary across contexts. Over time, this may lead to *goal drift*, where behaviour progressively diverges from the original stakeholder intention.

C3 **Blurring the boundary between design time and run time.** Classical methodologies rely on a clear separation between design-time modelling and run-time execution. In agentive systems, planning and decision-making occur dynamically during execution, making it difficult to anticipate behaviour at design time. Decisions such as escalation or negotiation strategies may emerge at run time rather than being fully specified in advance.

C4 **Opacity and post-hoc rationalisation.** Symbolic agents provide explicit representations of beliefs, goals, and plans that support inspection and justification. Agentive systems, in contrast, often produce explanations only after decisions have been made. These explanations may be coherent but do not necessarily reflect the underlying reasoning process, limiting their usefulness for accountability.

C5 **Autonomy beyond predefined boundaries.** Autonomy in classical methodologies is typically defined at design time through roles and permissions. Agentive systems may generate novel actions or strategies that exceed predefined boundaries. Without explicit constraints, such behaviour may conflict with organisational expectations and governance requirements.

Taken together, these challenges suggest that the impact of Agentic AI is not merely technological. Rather, it affects the assumptions on which intentional and organisational modelling were originally grounded, including stable goal semantics, predictable enactment, fixed delegation structures, and design-time reasoning. The remainder of this section introduces a set of conceptual extensions that address these challenges while preserving the intentional perspective of Tropos.

2.2 Dual Intentionality and Normative Goals

The challenges discussed above suggest that extending Tropos is not simply a matter of introducing new modelling constructs. Rather, they require revisiting how intentionality, delegation, and autonomy are understood in systems whose behaviour is only partially determined at design time. In this section we introduce a set of conceptual extensions that, in our view, provide an initial foundation for reasoning about Agentic AI systems.

Classical methodologies implicitly rely on a single notion of intentionality. In agentive systems, however, intentionality must be understood at two distinct but related levels (*Dual intentionality*).

Definition 1 (Design-time intentionality). *Let A be a set of actors and G a set of goals. Design-time intentionality is a relation $I_d \subseteq A \times G$ such that $(a, g) \in I_d$ denotes that actor a is intentionally committed, at design time, to goal g.*

Design-time intentionality captures the commitments established during requirements analysis and represents the intentional perspective traditionally adopted by Tropos. For example, in a Meeting Scheduler System, the meeting initiator delegates to the system the goal of organising a meeting. This commitment exists independently of how the system will eventually fulfil it.

Definition 2 (Run-time intentionality). *Run-time intentionality captures how an agent operationalises goals in a specific context and at a specific time. It* *depends on the operational context and may vary over time through interaction and feedback.*

Run-time intentionality complements design-time intentionality by capturing the situated enactment of goals. While design-time intentionality specifies what an agent is expected to achieve, run-time intentionality reflects how those goals are interpreted and enacted in concrete execution contexts. The same meeting request, for example, can be operationalised differently depending on participants' preferences, organisational policies, or previous interactions, illustrating how the enactment of the goal becomes context dependent.

Because agentives evolve through interaction and feedback, goals cannot always be treated as fixed prescriptions. Instead, they must also be understood as evolving reference points against which behaviour can be evaluated.

Definition 3 (Normative goal). *A normative goal is a goal $g(t)$ where t is a discrete time dimension, $g(t_0)$ is the initial interpretation of g, and $g(t)$ is the interpretation of g at time t. Each normative goal has an associated rule that specifies how $g(t+1)$ is obtained from $g(t)$ through learning-by-being-told. In Tropos$^+$, we introduce learning goals (l-goals) which can be viewed as a particular class of normative goals whose operational interpretation evolves through learning and human feedback over time.*

Normative goals define what counts as acceptable behaviour without uniquely determining how that behaviour should be achieved. Unlike classical goals, whose satisfaction conditions are assumed to remain stable throughout the software lifecycle, normative goals act as evaluative reference points whose operational interpretation may evolve (through learning and feedback) while preserving the underlying organisational intention they represent. Consider the goal "preserve participants' trust". At design time, this expresses an organisational objective. At runtime, however, its operational interpretation may evolve as users provide feedback about acceptable negotiation strategies, privacy expectations, or escalation policies. The goal remains the same, but its operational interpretation changes over time. This reinterpretation makes explicit the possibility of *goal drift*, where the operational meaning of a goal progressively diverges from its initial interpretation. In this perspective, normative goals provide intentional anchors that support alignment between organisational values and adaptive system behaviour, even when operational decisions cannot be completely anticipated at design time.

Because design-time models cannot anticipate all situations, delegation must also account for interpretative decision-making.

Definition 4 (Delegation of reasoning authority). *Delegation of reasoning authority is a relation $auth \subseteq A \times G$ such that $(a, g) \in auth$ denotes that agent a is authorised to determine how goal g is operationalised at run time.*

This notion extends classical delegation relationships in Tropos. In traditional settings, delegation concerns the execution of predefined tasks or plans.

In agentive systems, delegation also concerns interpretative authority, namely the authority to determine how goals should be operationalised in contexts that could not be completely anticipated during design. In the Meeting Scheduler, delegating the organisation of meetings does not necessarily imply delegating the authority to relax organisational policies or privacy constraints. Delegation (of reasoning authority) therefore concerns not only execution, but also the authority to interpret goals.

Delegation does not eliminate accountability.

Definition 5 (Residual responsibility). *Residual responsibility is the principle according to which accountability for the enactment of a delegated goal remains assigned to human or organisational actors, even when an artificial agent is authorised to interpret and operationalise that goal at run time.*

Residual responsibility complements delegation of reasoning authority by making explicit that the authority to interpret goals does not imply the transfer of ultimate accountability. This distinction is particularly important in Agentic AI systems, where autonomous behaviour must remain aligned with organisational objectives, legal obligations, and human oversight. Even when the system autonomously negotiates meeting times, accountability for unfair or non-compliant decisions remains with the organisation.

Autonomy can no longer be regarded as a fixed design-time characteristic.

Definition 6 (Dynamic autonomy). *Dynamic autonomy is the degree of independent decision-making that an agent is permitted to exercise in a given context and at a given time.*

Dynamic autonomy implies that the degree of autonomy may vary according to context, organisational policies, perceived risk, or observed behaviour. Consequently, autonomy becomes a governable property that can be monitored, revised, and adapted throughout the operational lifecycle rather than a fixed attribute established once during system design. Routine scheduling may be performed autonomously, whereas situations involving conflicting organisational policies or sensitive participants may require reduced autonomy and human intervention.

Although introduced separately, these concepts are not independent. Normative goals require run-time intentionality because their operational interpretation cannot be fixed at design time. Delegation of reasoning authority defines who is allowed to perform this interpretation, while residual responsibility preserves accountability for its consequences. Dynamic autonomy determines how much discretion an agent may exercise when interpreting and enacting organisational goals.

Taken together, these concepts extend the intentional perspective underlying Tropos without abandoning its core principles. Design-time intentionality captures stakeholder commitments, while run-time intentionality reflects their situated enactment. Normative goals provide evolving evaluative references that support alignment between organisational intentions and adaptive behaviour. Delegation of reasoning authority distinguishes operational interpretation from ultimate accountability, while dynamic autonomy recognises that the level of decision-making authority exercised by an agent may itself evolve over time. These concepts do not yet constitute a complete extension of Tropos. Rather, they provide an initial conceptual foundation for discussing how intentional modelling should evolve in the presence of Agentic AI. In the next section, we discuss how these ideas may influence the evolution of the Tropos development process and the role of its modelling artefacts across the software lifecycle.

3 Implications for the Tropos Development Process

The conceptual extensions introduced in the previous section do not replace the Tropos development process. Rather, they change how its modelling artefacts are interpreted and used. The phases of Tropos remain largely unchanged, but their role evolves in the presence of agentive systems whose behaviour cannot be completely specified at design time. From this perspective, requirements models are no longer static artefacts consumed during development. They become persistent intentional structures that guide architectural decisions, support runtime governance, and preserve alignment between adaptive behaviour and organisational intent.

Requirements: Identifying Normative Goals. Requirements analysis continues to identify stakeholders, goals, softgoals, and dependencies. What changes is the interpretation of these artefacts. In particular, Tropos$^+$ distinguishes between goals whose operational meaning can be specified at design time and goals whose interpretation necessarily depends on context and may evolve through interaction, learning and feedback (see Definition 3). This distinction motivates the introduction of design goals (d-goals) and learning goals (l-goals). D-goals (i.e., the traditional goals of Tropos) can be operationalised through conventional software components or traditional agents. L-goals correspond to normative goals whose operational interpretation cannot be completely anticipated at design time and therefore requires runtime judgement. Requirements analysis therefore acquires an additional responsibility: it identifies where adaptive interpretation may be required, without assuming that agentive solutions are always necessary.

Architecture: Deciding Where Agentives are Needed. The decision to introduce an agentive should not be regarded as a requirements decision but as an architectural one. Once potentially normative goals have been identified, architectural design determines whether their interpretation can still be realised through conventional software components or whether it requires adaptive reasoning. Tropos$^+$ therefore promotes mixed architectures in which deterministic components coexist with agentives. Conventional components remain preferable whenever behaviour can be specified through predefined rules, workflows, or optimisation procedures. Agentives become justified only when contextual interpretation, negotiation, or evolving goal semantics cannot be adequately captured at design time. From this perspective, architectural design no longer concerns only system decomposition. It also establishes the boundaries within which agentives are allowed to interpret organisational goals.

Runtime: From Design Artefacts to Governance Artefacts. Perhaps the most significant change introduced by Agentic AI concerns the role of intentional models after deployment. In classical software engineering, requirements models primarily support development activities and traceability. Once implementation is completed, their role becomes largely documentary. In systems including agentives, this assumption no longer holds. Because goals are interpreted at runtime and their operational meaning may evolve, intentional models continue to play an active role throughout the operational lifecycle. Normative goals become reference points against which behaviour can be evaluated, delegation relationships define the limits of reasoning authority, and autonomy becomes a property that may be monitored and revised over time. Rather than prescribing runtime behaviour, intentional models provide the conceptual basis for governance. They support the identification of goal drift, justify escalation to human actors when necessary, and preserve alignment between adaptive behaviour and organisational objectives.

The three perspectives discussed above should not be interpreted as independent extensions to the Tropos process. Rather, they describe a continuous intentional lifecycle linking design-time decisions to runtime behaviour. Requirements analysis identifies organisational intentions and distinguishes goals that can be fully operationalised at design time from those requiring contextual interpretation. Architectural design then determines where adaptive reasoning is appropriate and explicitly delegates reasoning authority to agentive components, while preserving organisational accountability. During operation, intentional models continue to guide governance by monitoring how delegated reasoning is performed, detecting potential goal drift, and supporting interventions whenever adaptive behaviour diverges from organisational objectives. Viewed in this way, the principal contribution of Tropos$^+$ is not the addition of new modelling constructs, but a reinterpretation of the role played by intentional models throughout the software lifecycle. Instead of being consumed once implementation begins, they become persistent artefacts that connect requirements, architectural decisions, and runtime governance within a single conceptual framework. This continuity between design time and runtime reflects the central premise of Tropos$^+$: while the operational interpretation of goals may evolve, the organisational intentions that motivate them should remain explicit, traceable, and governable throughout the lifetime of the system.

These observations suggest that the contribution of Tropos$^+$ does not primarily lie in defining a new development methodology. Instead, it lies in reinterpreting the role of intentional modelling in the presence of Agentic AI. The phases of Tropos remain largely unchanged, but the meaning of the resulting artefacts evolves. Goals become normative reference points, delegation distinguishes execution from reasoning authority, and intentional models remain active beyond deployment as governance artefacts rather than static design documentation.

This reinterpretation should be regarded as an initial conceptual framework rather than a complete methodology. It identifies how existing Tropos concepts may evolve in the presence of adaptive agents while leaving several important questions open, including formal semantics, modelling notation, runtime reasoning, and empirical validation. These questions define the research agenda outlined in the next section.

4 Research Challenges and Future Directions

The conceptual extensions discussed in this paper should not be interpreted as a complete extension of Tropos. Rather, they identify a number of research directions that, in our view, are necessary for evolving goal-oriented requirements engineering in the era of Agentic AI. While the proposed concepts provide an initial vocabulary for reasoning about adaptive and interpretative agents, substantial work remains before they can be integrated into a mature engineering methodology.

- **RQ1: Formal semantics.** The notions of dual intentionality, normative goals, delegated reasoning authority, and dynamic autonomy require a formal semantic foundation. In particular, future work should investigate how normative goals can be formally represented, how their evolution over time can be characterised, and how phenomena such as goal drift can be analysed and detected.
- **RQ2: Metamodel and modelling notation.** The concepts introduced in this paper should eventually be reflected in an explicit metamodel and corresponding modelling notation. Such extensions would allow analysts to distinguish design goals from learning goals, represent delegation of reasoning authority explicitly, and capture governance concerns within existing Tropos models while preserving backward compatibility.
- **RQ3: Runtime governance.** Unlike traditional software systems, agentive systems continue to evolve after deployment. This raises new questions concerning runtime governance, including how intentional models should support monitoring, alignment assessment, autonomy modulation, and controlled adaptation throughout the operational lifecycle.
- **RQ4: Empirical evaluation.** The ideas presented in this paper require systematic empirical validation. Future work should investigate whether the proposed concepts improve requirements analysis, architectural decisions, governance, and traceability when compared with existing approaches. Industrial case studies, controlled experiments, and comparative evaluations will all be needed to assess their practical usefulness.
- **RQ5: Tool support.** Finally, extending Tropos towards Agentic AI will require appropriate tool support. Existing goal modelling environments could evolve to support the new concepts introduced in this paper, enabling the analysis of normative goals, runtime monitoring, governance mechanisms, and traceability between design-time intentions and runtime behaviour.

A broader challenge emerging from all these directions concerns the relationship between requirements engineering and runtime AI governance. Traditionally, requirements models have primarily supported design activities and traceability. Agentic AI suggests a different perspective: intentional models should remain active throughout system operation, providing the conceptual framework through which adaptive behaviour can be monitored, justified, and continuously aligned with organisational objectives.

Taken together, these challenges suggest that the contribution of Tropos^{+} should be understood primarily as a research agenda rather than as a complete methodology. Rather than replacing existing goal-oriented methodologies, we argue that Agentic AI requires revisiting some of their underlying assumptions while preserving their intentional perspective. We hope that the concepts introduced in this paper provide a useful starting point for this discussion and stimulate further research on how goal-oriented requirements engineering can evolve to support adaptive, accountable, and continuously evolving Agentic AI systems.

5 Conclusions

Agentic AI fundamentally challenges several assumptions that have traditionally underpinned goal-oriented requirements engineering. Stable goal semantics, explicit reasoning models, and fixed notions of autonomy can no longer be taken for granted when systems include adaptive LLM-based agents whose behaviour continues to evolve after deployment. Rather than proposing a complete extension of Tropos, this paper identifies a set of conceptual foundations that we believe are necessary for evolving its intentional perspective. We introduced the notions of design-time and run-time intentionality, normative goals, delegation of reasoning authority, residual responsibility, and dynamic autonomy, and discussed how these concepts may reshape the interpretation of the Tropos development process. From this perspective, intentional models evolve from design-time specifications into persistent artefacts supporting alignment, governance, and accountability throughout the operational lifecycle of Agentic AI systems. The contribution of Tropos^{+} should therefore be understood primarily as a research agenda. Future work includes the definition of formal semantics, metamodelling constructs, graphical notation, runtime governance mechanisms, empirical validation, and tool support. More broadly, we believe that the future of goal-oriented requirements engineering lies not in replacing its intentional foundations, but in reinterpreting them as persistent governance mechanisms for adaptive intelligent systems.

References

1. Bresciani, P., Perini, A., Giorgini, P., Giunchiglia, F., Mylopoulos, J.: Tropos: an agent-oriented software development methodology. Auton. Agents Multi Agent Syst. **8**(3), 203–236 (2004)

2. Giorgini, P., Mylopoulos, J., Nicchiarelli, E., Sebastiani, R.: Reasoning with goal models. In: Spaccapietra, S., March, S.T., Kambayashi, Y. (eds.) ER 2002. LNCS, vol. 2503, pp. 167–181. Springer, Heidelberg (2002). https://doi.org/10.1007/3-540-45816-6_22
3. Guo, T., Chen, X., Wang, Y.: Large language model based multi-agents: a survey of progress and challenges. In: Proceedings of the Thirty-Third International Joint Conference on Artificial Intelligence (IJCAI) (2024)
4. Henderson-Sellers, B., Giorgini, P.: Agent-Oriented Methodologies. IGI Global (2005)
5. Hong, S., et al.: Metagpt: meta programming for a multi-agent collaborative framework. In: International Conference on Learning Representations (ICLR) (2024)
6. Jin, D., Jin, Z., Chen, X., Wang, C.: Mare: multi-agents collaboration framework for requirements engineering. arxiv preprint arXiv:2405.03256 (2024)
7. Jin, D., et al.: iredev: a knowledge-driven multi-agent framework for intelligent requirements development. arXiv:2507.13081 (2025)
8. Rao, A.S., Georgeff, M.P.: BDI agents: from theory to practice. In: Proceedings of the First International Conference on Multiagent Systems, pp. 312–319. The MIT Press (1995)
9. Schick, T., Dwivedi-Yu, J., Dessì, R.: Toolformer: language models can teach themselves to use tools. In: Advances in Neural Information Processing Systems (2023)
10. Shinn, N., Cassano, F., Berman, E.: Reflexion: language agents with verbal reinforcement learning. In: Advances in Neural Information Processing Systems (2023)
11. Wang, G., Xie, Y., Jiang, Y.: Voyager: an open-ended embodied agent with large language models, arXiv preprint (2023). arXiv:2305.16291
12. Wang, L., Ma, X., Zhang, W.: A survey on large language model based autonomous agents. Artif. Intell. Rev. (2024)
13. Wooldridge, M.: Reasoning about Rational Agents. MIT Press (2000)
14. Wooldridge, M.: An Introduction to MultiAgent Systems. John Wiley & Sons (2009)
15. Wu, Q.: Autogen: enabling next-gen llm applications via multi-agent conversation framework, arXiv preprint (2023). arXiv:2308.08155
16. Yang, J., et al.: Swe-agent: Agent-computer interfaces enable automated software engineering. In: Advances in Neural Information Processing Systems (NeurIPS) (2024)
17. Yao, S., Zhao, J., Yu, D.: React: synergizing reasoning and acting in language models, arXiv preprint (2022). arXiv:2210.03629

Towards Orchestrating LLM-based Multi-Agent Systems with SysML v2

Léna Bamouh[1(✉)], Jean-Marie Mottu[2], Hugo Bruneliere[1], and Massimo Tisi[1]

[1] IMT Atlantique, LS2N (CNRS), Nantes, France
{lena.bamouh,hugo.bruneliere,massimo.tisi}@imt-atlantique.fr
[2] Nantes Université, LS2N (CNRS), Nantes, France
jean-marie.mottu@univ-nantes.fr

Abstract. The engineering of large and complex systems often involves many heterogeneous and sometimes repetitive tasks. Thus, technical solutions are needed to automate such tasks and related workflows. The advent of Large Language Models (LLMs), associated with task-specific agents, offers promising opportunities. However, the orchestration of workflows that involve the use of multiple (LLM-based) agents can be challenging: How can we precisely model such workflows and execute them in practice? In this paper, we propose relying on a specialization of SysML v2 to support the definition of multi-agent workflow orchestrations. We envision a generic orchestration framework that allows for the execution of these SysML v2 models and underlying workflows. In the context of the MOSAICO project, we show that our SysML v2-based orchestration language is expressive enough to model different workflows in various domains. We present initial experiments on such an orchestration framework to execute these workflows by calling LLMs whenever needed.

Keywords: Model-Based Engineering · Multi-Agent Systems · Large Language Models · Orchestration · SysML

1 Introduction

LLM-based agents are widely used to perform complex software and system engineering activities [6]. They are autonomous entities, using LLMs as central cognitive controllers, that are capable of perceiving their environment and taking actions to achieve specific goals [1]. However, they often face limitations in areas requiring expertise across multiple domains and tasks [11]. LLM-based Multi-Agent Systems (LMASs) have been proposed to overcome the limitations of individual agents while still benefiting from their specialized characteristics [5]. The goal is also to encourage divergent thinking, enhance reasoning capabilities, and facilitate text or code generation [4,8].

© The Author(s), under exclusive license to Springer Nature Switzerland AG 2027
A. Bernasconi et al. (Eds.): ER 2026, LNCS 17081, pp. 428–438, 2027.
https://doi.org/10.1007/978-3-032-40795-5_27

Several formalisms are already used in academia and industry to represent and execute workflows in the context of LMASs [5]. We argue that these formalisms do not fulfill all the expected requirements, particularly when LLMs are used to generate, analyze, or (partially) execute the modeled workflows. Such requirements are 1) *Expressiveness:* Provide sufficient constructs to represent the essential aspects of LMAS workflows; 2) *Textual notation:* Come with a native notation that is familiar to engineers and suitable for LLMs; 3) *Formal semantics:* Have a well-defined formal semantics for precise interpretation by orchestrator(s).

Given these requirements, we propose the use of action flows from SysML v2 as an LMAS workflow modeling and orchestration language. In this paper, we intend to address two main related research questions: *RQ1* – Is SysML v2 expressive enough to be used as a modeling and orchestration language for LMASs? *RQ2* – Can LMAs workflows modeled in SysML v2 be executed in practice?

To answer RQ1, we designed a *SysML v2-based language* for modeling and orchestrating LMAS. It is a specialization of SysML v2 focusing on a subset of Behavior (actions) and Structure (parts) elements. It comes with a *library* that specifies how an action should be executed and whether this action leverages an LLM-based agent. To answer RQ2, we implemented an initial *generic orchestration framework*. Its runtime engine uses an internal workflow-execution language that considers only the relevant information. Thus, we also implemented a transformation from our SysML v2-based language to this internal execution language. All the source code and experimental data are made available as open-source from the MOSAICO project's repository.[1]

The paper is structured as follows. First, Sect. 2 motivates our work via a running example. Then, Sect. 3 introduces our solution and its two main contributions. Section 4 describes our initial experiments with our solution. Finally, Sect. 5 reviews the related work and Sect. 6 opens on future work.

2 Running Example

To motivate our work, we introduce a collaborative requirement elicitation workflow in Fig. 1. It describes how an initial, informal system description is iteratively transformed into a validated set of requirements through the coordinated efforts of various specialized agents.

The process begins when a coordinating agent receives a system description from a user (*Get system description from user*). Then, it enters an iterative phase (*Decompose*) in which a generation agent analyzes the description and proposes a new requirement. To ensure quality, this requirement is subjected to three parallel evaluations conducted by distinct validation agents. The first agent verifies its correctness against the original system description (*Check correctness*). The second agent checks for redundancy against the list of already accepted requirements (*Check non redundancy*). The third agent evaluates whether this requirement can

[1] https://gitlab.eclipse.org/eclipse-research-labs/mosaico-project (cf. the two Orchestrator sub-projects in particular).

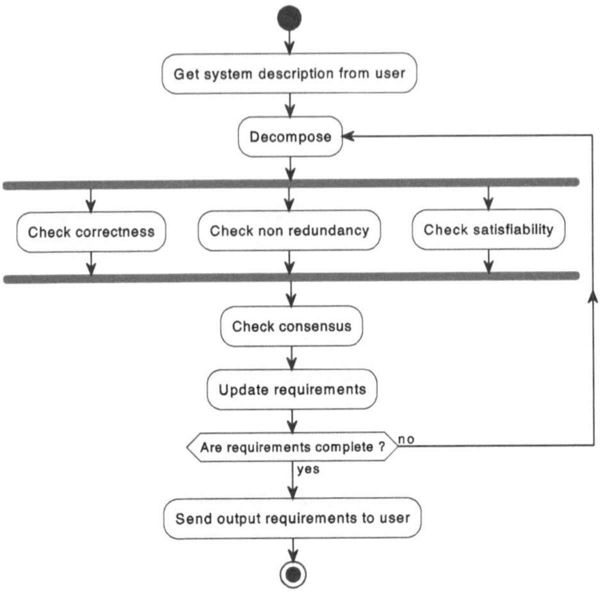

Fig. 1. Activity diagram representing our requirement elicitation workflow.

be logically satisfied (*Check satisfiability*). Once all the checks are completed, a consensus agent determines whether the new requirement should be accepted based on the answers of the three previously mentioned agents (*Check consensus*). A manager agent then updates the global requirement list (*Update requirements*) and assesses whether the overall set of requirements is complete or not (*Are requirements complete?*). If not, the process loops back (to *Decompose*) and prompts the generation agent again to propose additional requirements. Finally, once reaching a complete state, the final list of requirements is returned to the user (*Send output requirements to user*).

3 Contributions

3.1 An Overall Solution for LLM-Based Multi-agent Orchestration

The solution we propose has two main complementary components, as illustrated in Fig. 2: 1) A *Transformation* that provides semantics to our SysML v2-based orchestration language by transforming input models to MOSAICO Internal Orchestration Language (MIOL) models, and 2) A *Runtime Engine* dedicated to executing the multi-agent workflow models once expressed in MIOL.

The process begins when the user specifies her workflow (*Get User Input*) as a model expressed in our SysML v2-based language (*SysML v2 Workflow Code*). Based on the open-source SysML v2 Pilot Implementation[2], the *Transformation*

[2] https://github.com/Systems-Modeling/SysML-v2-Pilot-Implementation.

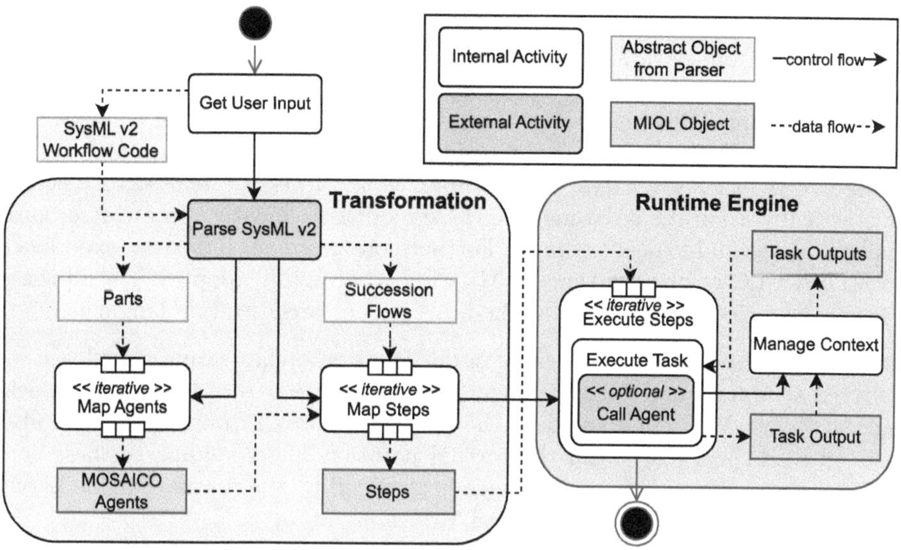

Fig. 2. Overview of our multi-agent orchestration solution.

component processes the input model to extract the different abstract syntax tree (AST) elements (*Parse SysML v2*). In particular, it allows identifying structural *Parts* and behavioral *SuccessionFlows*. Our transformation then performs two sequential actions. First, an iterative mapping block (*Map Agents*) translates the structural parts into concrete agent instances (*MOSAICO Agents*) in MIOL. Second, an iterative block (*Map Steps*) processes the succession flows, using the newly instantiated agents to generate a sequence of executable *Steps*.

Once the MIOL workflow model is fully constructed, it can be provided as input to the *Runtime Engine*. The workflow model is navigated via an iterative loop (*Execute Steps*). For each step, the engine evaluates the underlying logic (*Execute Task*). If the step requires LLM inference, the engine delegates the task by making an external request (*Call Agent*, marked as optional to account for deterministic assignment tasks). The resulting data (*Task Output*) is captured and forwarded to a collaboration agent in charge of managing the global context (*Manage Context*). This manager updates a global repository of *Task Outputs*, feeding the produced runtime data back into the execution loop. Finally, once all steps have been successfully executed, the process terminates.

3.2 SysML v2 as an Orchestration Language (Addressing RQ1)

The Systems Modeling Language (SysML)[3] v1 was adopted two decades ago by the Object Management Group (OMG) as the modeling standard for Model-Based Systems Engineering. SysML v2 was recently released and is now based

[3] https://www.omg.org/spec/SysML.

on a simpler core language, the Kernel Modeling Language (KerML), rather than the full Unified Modeling Language (UML)[4]. Moreover, it introduces a new programming-like textual syntax that is close to what engineers are accustomed to manipulating. This makes SysML v2 a natural candidate in our context. The fact that SysML v2 now comes with explicit formal semantics is also an advantage compared to other languages. For example, while LLMs can be used to generate syntactically accurate UML models, these models frequently contain structural hallucinations and logical errors [3]. Furthermore, from our industrial experience in MOSAICO, we observe that SysML v2 can be rapidly adopted. For all these reasons, we selected SysML v2 as the basis for our orchestration language.

Language Specification. Because of our focus on orchestrating workflows, we selected structural and behavioral constructs that are part of the Activity package of the SysML v2 metamodel. The concrete syntax of our language is also defined as a specialization of the textual notation corresponding to these constructs. The semantics of our language is provided by the runtime engine in our orchestration framework (cf. Section 3.3).

For *structural modeling*, as shown in Listing 1.1, we use the `part` and `part def` constructs to establish reusable agent templates and globally instantiate concrete agent entities. By inheriting (`specializes`) from our custom MOSAICO library (introduced right after), complementary to property redefinitions (`redefines`), we can precisely model the identity, role, and behavioral rules of each agent.

For *behavioral modeling*, the core orchestration logic is captured using the `action` and `action def` constructs. As shown in Listing 1.2, atomic tasks are defined as actions while data flows between these tasks are implicitly managed using typed parameters (`in`, `inout`, `out`). To support complex processes, we also consider several control flow constructs: strict sequential dependencies (`first`, `then`), concurrent execution branches (`fork`, `join`), dynamic conditional routing (`if`, `else`), and cyclic refinement processes (`loop...until`, `while`).

MOSAICO Library. SysML v2 does not provide constructs directly intended to characterize LLM-based agents. Thus, we introduce the MOSAICO library partially shown in Listing 1.1 and specified using our SysML-based textual notation. Its goal is to propose reusable types of agents and related task execution.

An `Agent` is generically defined by an identifier, version number, license(s), and operational skills. This way, the orchestration framework can dynamically retrieve, assess, and deploy the most suitable agents at runtime, allowing users to provide custom definitions for their agents. The MOSAICO library introduces a more specialized `ReferenceAgent` dedicated to managing human-in-the-loop inputs and front-end interactions, along with other agents types not detailed in this paper (e.g., `CollaborationAgent`, `SupervisionAgent`, `SolutionAgent`). Task execution is supported by specializing a standard `Step` into an `AgentStep`, thus linking an assigned agent with a `description` that serves as the LLM prompt. This construct is further refined into a `ReferenceStep` that automat-

[4] https://www.omg.org/spec/UML.

Listing 1.1. Specification of our MOSAICO library (excerpt).

```
package MOSAICO {
  // STRUCTURAL DEFINITIONS
  part def Agent {
    attribute id : String[0..1];
    attribute version : String[0..1];
    attribute licences : String[0..*];
    attribute skills : String[0..*];
  }
  part def ReferenceAgent specializes Agent {
    redefines id = "reference-agent-type";
    redefines version = "1.0";
  } // Other agent types can be defined...
  // BEHAVIORAL DEFINITIONS
  action def Step {
    attribute description : String[0..1];
  }
  action def AgentStep specializes Step {
    ref agent : Agent[0..1];
  }
  action def ReferenceStep specializes AgentStep {
    redefines agent : ReferenceAgent;
  } // Other agent behaviors can be defined...
}
```

ically delegates the execution of designated user-facing actions to a `Reference Agent`, thus ensuring that external interactions are properly managed.

To illustrate our example from Fig. 1, Listing 1.2 first defines specialized agent types, e.g., `RequirementManagerAgent`, by inheriting from the MOSAICO library and using `:>` to redefine identifiers and constraints. Then, the tasks are typed as `AgentSteps`, binding the LLM prompt (`description`) to an executor (`agent`). This highlights how data flows are established using `in` and `out` parameters, and how SysML v2 control flows (e.g., `loop...until` and `fork`/`joinNode`) are leveraged to model (and execute) iterative and parallel workflows.

3.3 Orchestration Framework (Addressing RQ2)

MOSAICO Internal Orchestration Language (MIOL). To decouple our orchestration engine from SysML v2, we introduce MIOL as a smaller pivot language to streamline execution plans. Workflows are structured as directed graphs of `Steps` linked via `next` references. A `Step` encapsulates a `Task` defined by a `taskName`, `taskDescription`, context (`dependencies`), and input/output data schemas (`Channels`). `Task` has been specialized for hybrid execution. An `AgentTask` indicates the LLM-based agent responsible for execution (`bestAgent`). An `AlgorithmicTask` indicates the deterministic `Statement` to be executed. Different kinds of `Step` are proposed. `ParallelStep` provides simultaneous execution of multiple independent `Steps`. `LoopStep` manages iterative workflows by evaluating a `Condition` using a specific `LoopKind`. `IfStep` enables workflow branching by evaluating a `Condition` that contains an `Expression` providing its logic.

Listing 1.2. SysML v2 version of the workflow from Figure 1 (excerpt).

```
package RequirementManagementAgentsNoParams {
  private import MOSAICO::*; // More imports...
  part def RequirementManagerAgent specializes Agent {
    :>> id = "requirement-manager-agent-type.v1";
    constraint { licences->includes("MIT") }
  }
  myRequirementManagerAgent : RequirementManagerAgent; // More definitions + instantiation...
  action def GenerateRequirementsProcess {
    first start;
    then action userInput : AgentStep {
      :>> description = "Get a system description from the user.";
      :>> agent = myRequirementManagerAgent; // Agent assignment
      out systemDescription : String;
      out requirements : String;
    }
    then loop action constructRequirementList {
      // More actions (decompose) here...
      then fork;
        then checkCorrectness;
        then checkNonRedundancy;
        then checkSatisfiability;
      action checkCorrectness : AgentStep {
        :>> description = "Checks whether the new Requirement is correct based on ...";
        in newRequirement : String;
        in systemDescription : String;
        out isCorrect : Boolean;
      }
      then joinNode; // More actions (checkNonRedundancy, checkSatisfiability) here...
      join joinNode; // More actions (checkConsensus, updateRequirements) here...
    } until constructRequirementList.updateRequirements.isComplete; // More actions here...
    then done;
  }
}
```

Transformation. We specified a set of SysML v2-to-MIOL mapping rules. `Part` definitions and instantiations are translated into agent types (`MOSAICO-AgentType`) and concrete agents (`MOSAICOAgent`), respectively. Atomic SysML v2 actions (`ActionUsage`) are encapsulated into executable `AgentTasks`, while control flows (e.g., successions, forks, loops, and transitions) are directly mapped to their corresponding execution nodes: `Step.next`, `ParallelStep`, `LoopStep`, and `IfStep`. Finally, the execution parameters and data flows are established by mapping SysML v2 redefinitions to concrete properties, constraints to embedded conditions, and action inputs/outputs to typed `Channels`.

Runtime Engine. At runtime, our orchestration engine consumes the head `Step` and then dynamically routes the control flow based on its specific type. For a standard `Step`, the underlying task is executed sequentially before advancing to the `next` step. For a `ParallelStep`, the constituent tasks within its body are dispatched concurrently. The orchestrator suspends the parent execution thread until all nested branches, including subsequent `next` steps, are fully resolved. When encountering an `IfStep`, the engine evaluates the runtime condition to route the control flow to the `then` branch or `else` branch (optional). For a `LoopStep`, the orchestrator traverses the encapsulated `headStep` and its subsequent `next` steps. This continues until a leaf node is reached, i.e., the termination condition is evaluated to indicate whether the iteration repeats or exits.

4 Initial Experiments

In addition to our running example from Sect. 2, which demonstrates iterative, parallel, and conditional workflows, we consider other models based on use cases from our industrial partners in MOSAICO. We authored the models, which were subsequently reviewed and validated by the partners to ensure accuracy and relevance: *Requirements Generation* orchestrates the creation of a validated software requirement list based on an initial system description; *Metamodel Generation* uses specialized agents to produce source code for a metamodel derived from a high-level domain description (this model contains conditional and cycling workflows); *3D Asset Generation & Optimization* generates, filters, and optimizes 3D assets from a mood-board to construct a graphical scene (this model contains iterative and parallel workflows). As visible in Table 1, we executed these different LMAS workflow models with our orchestration framework by considering GPT 4[5] as our underlying LLM.

Table 1. Summary of our first results. Between parenthesis is the number of additional coordination agents instantiated by the orchestrator. *hi* means human interaction, *ae* means agent execution, *o* means orchestration.

Application	RQ1 Metrics				RQ2 Metrics	
	LOCs	Actions + Nodes	SysML Elements	Agents	LLM calls	Execution Time (ms)
Requirements Generation	117	11	ForkNode, JoinNode, AssignmentAction, LoopAction, Constraint	6	≥ 7	**8,615** hi: 1,699 ae: 6,185 o: 731
Metamodel Generation	92	14	DecisionNode, MergeNode, AssignmentAction, Constraint	3 (+1)	≥ 4	**12,666** hi: 4,545 ae: 6,412 o: 1,709
3D Asset Generation & Optimization	293	32	ForkNode, JoinNode, LoopAction, Constraint	1 (+3)	≥ 4	**11,362** hi: 3,748 ae: 5,672 o: 1,942

Expressiveness of our SysML v2-Based Orchestration Language (RQ1). We show that our language allows modeling workflows belonging to different application domains, resulting in models of various sizes. This ranges from relatively small models of 92 lines (with only 11 to 14 steps) to larger models of 293 lines (with 32

[5] https://openai.com/index/gpt-4/.

steps). The modeled workflows rely on a heterogeneous number of agents, ranging from 2 to 6 for the scenarios in which these agents were explicitly specified.

Executability of our LMAS Workflow Models (RQ2). The collected execution traces reveal that our orchestration workflow strictly enforces the modeled control flows (e.g., loops, conditionals, parallel forks). It also accurately resolves inter-task dependencies, and instantiates the expected agents which then call the LLM whenever needed (from 4 to 7 times depending on the case). The execution times show that the overhead resulting from the use of our orchestration framework is rather limited in all cases. For example, orchestration only represents 13,5% of the total execution time in the least efficient case (i.e., *Metamodel Generation*).

General Conclusion. Our initial experiments highlight that SysML v2's native behavioral constructs, when appropriately specialized with our library, provide the necessary elements to model the target workflows. By transforming these SysML v2-based models into an executable intermediate representation, we show the applicability of our associated orchestration framework in this LMAS context. Considering the current capabilities of LLMs, and their frequent improvements, our experimental data confirms that the modeled LMAS workflows can be executed with a reasonable orchestration overhead.

5 Related Work

LMAS frameworks such as LangGraph, AutoGen, and CrewAI [12] or ChatDev [10], often constrain engineers to static hard-coded workflows that restrict their dynamic adaptability at runtime. To overcome this, more recent advances with frameworks such as Pydantic AI[6], and Google ADK[7], introduce graph-based execution states and dynamic handoff protocols. These already offer programmatic flexibility but usually demand a steep learning curve and require extensive programming expertise. As a result, they can cause substantial development and orchestration overheads. These approaches are also LLM-centric and do not seamlessly integrate traditional deterministic agents. Moreover, these code-centric frameworks embed the workflow logic directly into source code or rely on proprietary black-box configurations. This forces engineers to manage low-level details rather than focus on the conceptual workflows to be modeled.

Academic frameworks such as AgentMesh [7] deploy a cooperative architecture with a fixed topology of four specialized agents to automate code generation from software specifications. Similarly, the MAO framework [9] uses multi-agent orchestration to synthesize process models and employs structured phases (e.g., iterative refinement and testing) to mitigate LLM hallucinations. However, these frameworks are constrained by their reliance on static agents and predefined execution pipelines. As a consequence, they lack the flexibility required to model custom workflows and to adapt dynamically to different orchestration patterns.

[6] https://pydantic.dev/.
[7] https://adk.dev/.

Finally, we are not aware of any approach applying UML or SysML to LMAS workflows. The closest approach is SHERPA [2] which relies on UML Statecharts for the definition of internal workflows within a single LLM-based agent. By allowing to model and orchestrate LMASs directly in a SysML v2-based language, our solution decouples the collaborative logic from the execution environment.

6 Future Work

In the next steps, we plan to apply our solution in the context of more industrial use cases and related LMAS workflows coming from the MOSAICO project. This way, we can experiment in other application domains with even larger workflows involving numerous (i.e., thousands of) agents and underlying LLM calls. Moreover, we want to extend our solution to also support more complex hierarchical workflows, where macro-actions require decomposition and internal orchestration by sub-workflows. Finally, we want to assess the capability of current LLMs to automatically generate workflow models in our SysML v2-based language from natural language specifications provided by engineers.

Acknowledgments. This research work has been funded by Horizon Europe through the project MOSAICO (grant agreement No. 101189664). We would also like to thank our colleague Julien Cohen for the precious engineering support he provided in the context of this work.

References

1. Bouzenia, I., Devanbu, P., Pradel, M.: RepairAgent: An autonomous, LLM-based agent for program repair. In: ICSE 2025, pp. 2188–2200 (2025)
2. Chen, B., Chene, K., López, J.A.H., Mussbacher, G., Varró, D., Feizpour, A.: SHERPA: a model-driven framework for large language model execution. In: MODELS 2025, pp. 197–208. IEEE (2025)
3. De Bari, D., Garaccione, G., Coppola, R., Torchiano, M., Ardito, L.: Evaluating large language models in exercises of UML class diagram modeling. In: ESEM 2024, pp. 393–399 (2024)
4. Du, Y., Li, S., Torralba, A., Tenenbaum, J.B., Mordatch, I.: Improving factuality and reasoning in language models through multiagent debate. In: ICML 2024 (2024)
5. He, J., Treude, C., Lo, D.: Llm-based multi-agent systems for software engineering: Literature review, vision, and the road ahead. ACM TOSEM **34**(5), 1–30 (2025)
6. Hou, X., Zhao, Y., Liu, Y., Yang, Z., Wang, K., Li, L., Luo, X., Lo, D., Grundy, J., Wang, H.: Large language models for software engineering: A systematic literature review. ACM TOSEM **33**(8), 1–79 (2024)
7. Khanzadeh, S.: Agentmesh: a cooperative multi-agent generative ai framework for software development automation (2025). https://arxiv.org/abs/2507.19902v1
8. Liang, T., et al.: Encouraging divergent thinking in large language models through multi-agent debate. In: EMNLP 2024. pp. 17889–17904 (2024)

9. Lin, L., Jin, Y., Zhou, Y., Chen, W., Qian, C.: MAO: a framework for process model generation with multi-agent orchestration. IEEE TSC **18**(6), 3987–4000 (2025)
10. Qian, C., et al.: Chatdev: communicative agents for software development. In: ACL 2024, pp. 15174–15186 (2024)
11. Schick, T., et al.: Toolformer: language models can teach themselves to use tools. NeurIPS **36**, 68539–68551 (2023)
12. Taulli, T., Deshmukh, G.: Building Generative AI Agents Using LangGraph, AutoGen, and CrewAI. Springer (2025)

Assessing Semantic Fidelity of LLM-Generated BPMN 2.0 Process Models via Round-Trip Transformation

Luca Franziska Hörner(✉), Maximilian Möller, and Manfred Reichert

Ulm University, James-Franck-Ring 1, 89081 Ulm, Germany
luca.hoerner@uni-ulm.de

Abstract. Large language models (LLMs) have shown substantial potential for generating BPMN 2.0 process models from textual process descriptions. However, systematically assessing whether generated models preserve the underlying process semantics remains challenging due to the limited availability of scalable semantic evaluation approaches. This work proposes a round-trip transformation approach based on bidirectional text-to-model and model-to-text transformations to operationalize semantic fidelity in LLM-generated BPMN 2.0 process models. The approach combines complementary text- and process-model-based analyses to assess semantic completeness and semantic correctness. An empirical study comprising 180 generated process models indicates consistently high semantic completeness, while preserving temporal and logical ordering relations remains considerably more challenging. Furthermore, semantic fidelity proved robust across the evaluated LLM- and prompting-based generation settings, although prompting strategies significantly affected precision-related semantic completeness. Overall, the proposed approach enables systematic and comparatively scalable semantic fidelity evaluations of automated process model generation.

Keywords: Semantic Fidelity · Large Language Models · BPMN 2.0 Process Model Generation · Round-Trip Transformation

1 Introduction

Business Process Model and Notation (BPMN 2.0) is the de facto standard for representing business processes in a precise, formalized, and executable manner [14]. However, creating BPMN 2.0 process models often requires substantial modeling expertise and manual effort. Recent advances in large language models (LLMs) have therefore sparked growing interest in the automatic generation of BPMN 2.0 process models from natural language process descriptions [5,7,8]. These approaches have the potential to reduce modeling effort, support non-expert users, and accelerate the formalization of organizational process knowledge [11,17]. Consequently, research attention is increasingly shifting from process model generation toward assessing how faithfully generated BPMN 2.0 process models preserve process semantics. Semantic fidelity refers to the extent to

© The Author(s), under exclusive license to Springer Nature Switzerland AG 2027
A. Bernasconi et al. (Eds.): ER 2026, LNCS 17081, pp. 439–449, 2027.
https://doi.org/10.1007/978-3-032-40795-5_28

which a process model preserves the meaning and intent expressed in the original process description. Although recent work has evaluated LLM-generated BPMN 2.0 process models from perspectives such as syntactic correctness, usability, understandability, and expert-perceived quality [4,13], systematic and scalable semantic fidelity assessment remains an open challenge, as existing evaluations predominantly rely on expert-based assessments. To address this limitation, this work proposes a systematic and comparatively scalable round-trip evaluation approach for assessing semantic fidelity in LLM-generated BPMN 2.0 process models. The approach leverages transitivity by transforming an original process description into a BPMN 2.0 process model through a text-to-model (TtM) transformation and subsequently transforming the generated process model back into a textual process description via a model-to-text (MtT) transformation. Semantic fidelity is assessed through complementary text- and process-model-based analyses covering semantic completeness and semantic correctness. The proposed approach is implemented using BPMNGen, an LLM-based chatbot supporting both TtM and MtT transformations [8]. Based on this approach, we conducted an empirical study comprising 180 generated BPMN 2.0 process models across different process descriptions, LLMs, and prompting strategies to investigate the preservation and robustness of semantic fidelity. Accordingly, this work addresses the following research questions:
RQ1: To what extent is semantic fidelity preserved in LLM-generated BPMN 2.0 process models when assessed through semantic completeness- and semantic correctness-related indicators?
RQ2: How robust are semantic completeness- and semantic correctness-related indicators of semantic fidelity across different LLM- and prompting-based generation settings?

The paper is organized as follows. Section 2 introduces the background, Sect. 3 reviews related work, Sect. 4 presents the study design, Sect. 5 reports the results, and Sect. 6 and 7 discuss limitations and conclude the paper.

2 Backgrounds

2.1 LLM-Based BPMN 2.0 Process Modeling with BPMNGen

Recent advances in LLMs have enabled the automatic generation of BPMN 2.0 process models from natural language process descriptions through text-to-model (TtM) transformations [10]. LLMs can extract process-semantic information from textual descriptions and map it to BPMN 2.0 process elements and control-flow structures. Complementarily, model-to-text (MtT) transformations generate textual process descriptions from BPMN 2.0 process models. This work builds on BPMNGen (https://bpmngen.de), an LLM-based framework supporting both TtM and MtT transformations [8]. Its bidirectional transformation capability provides the foundation for the proposed round-trip approach by enabling systematic comparison between original and generated process descriptions. BPMNGen further provides a controlled and reproducible research environment through configurable LLMs and prompting strategies.

2.2 Semantic Quality and Semantic Fidelity of Process Models

The quality of process models can be analyzed from syntactic, semantic, and pragmatic perspectives. The SEQUAL framework by Krogstie et al. [12] conceptualizes these dimensions through syntactic correctness, semantic quality, and pragmatic interpretability. To operationalize SEQUAL's notion of semantic quality, we introduce *semantic fidelity*, i.e., the extent to which a generated process model preserves the meaning, process-semantic information, and semantic relations of the original process description. Semantic fidelity is assessed through complementary indicators of semantic completeness and semantic correctness (cf. Section 4.2).

2.3 Transitivity as Conceptual Base for Round-Trip Transformations

The proposed round-trip evaluation is conceptually based on transitivity [6]. Let A denote the original process description (OPD), B the BPMN 2.0 process model generated through a text-to-model (TtM) transformation, and C the generated process description (GPD) obtained through a subsequent model-to-text (MtT) transformation. If the generated process model B preserves the semantics of A and the MtT transformation preserves the semantics of B, C is expected to preserve the semantics of A. Accordingly, similarities and deviations between OPD and GPD provide an operational approximation of the semantic fidelity of the generated BPMN 2.0 process model (cf. Fig. 1).

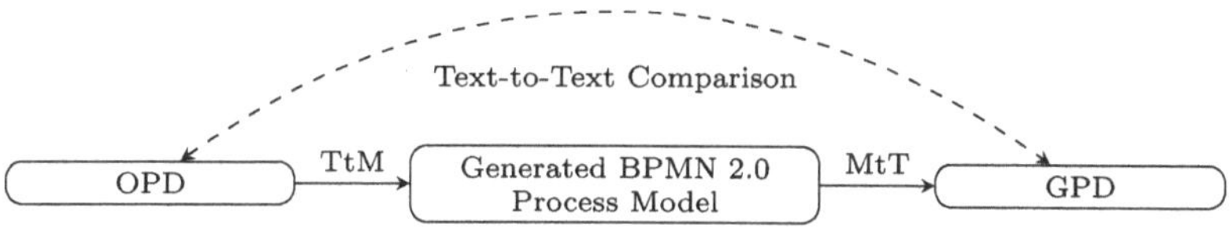

Fig. 1. Conceptual illustration of the round-trip transformation approach.

3 Related Work

Recent advances in LLMs have stimulated research on the automatic generation of BPMN 2.0 process models from natural language process descriptions [5,10]. Existing research has demonstrated that LLMs can extract process-semantic information from textual descriptions and map it to BPMN 2.0 process elements and control-flow structures [8,15]. Existing approaches improve BPMN 2.0 process model generation through hybrid architectures, structured intermediate representations, advanced prompting strategies, and conversational modeling support [5,8,11,13]. Existing evaluations mainly focus on syntactic correctness, understandability, usability, soundness, or expert-perceived semantic quality [4,8,16,17]. However, these evaluations predominantly rely on expert-based or qualitative assessments, limiting scalability, reproducibility, and comparability. Recent work has also explored MtT transformations, primarily evaluating the quality of generated textual descriptions [9]. In contrast to prior work, which either evaluates generated process models through expert-based assessments or focuses on generated textual descriptions, this work leverages bidirectional TtM and MtT transformations to enable a systematic and comparatively scalable round-trip assessment of semantic fidelity. The proposed approach jointly considers semantic completeness, semantic correctness, and textual similarity.

4 Study Context and Settings

4.1 Study Design and Materials

The study[1] follows a controlled round-trip experimental design to assess the semantic fidelity of LLM-generated BPMN 2.0 process models (cf. Fig. 2).

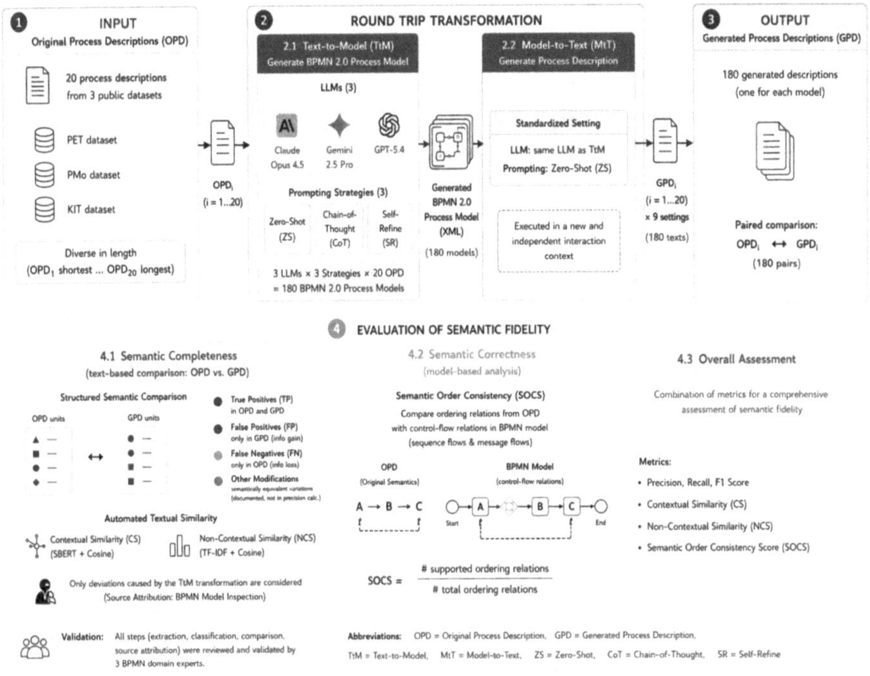

Fig. 2. Round-trip study design and materials.

(1) Input. We selected 20 textual process descriptions (OPD) from three public datasets (PET [1], PMo [2], and KIT [3]), covering different sources and

[1] All study materials, detailed results, Python scripts, and BPMNGen settings are publicly available at: https://doi.org/10.5281/zenodo.21806165.

description lengths. Furthermore, three state-of-the-art LLMs and three prompting strategies were evaluated.
(2) Round-Trip Transformation. Each OPD was transformed into a BPMN 2.0 process model through a TtM transformation and subsequently transformed back into a GPD through a MtT transformation using BPMNGen.
(3) Output. The round-trip results in paired instances of original and generated process descriptions (OPD–GPD), which form the basis for subsequent analysis.
(4) Evaluation of Semantic Fidelity.

(4.1) Semantic Completeness. To assess semantic completeness, process-semantic information was extracted from the OPD and the GPD using a Python-based script, mapped to corresponding BPMN 2.0 process elements (type and textual label), and compared through a structured semantic comparison. To isolate the impact of the TtM transformation, all deviations were manually traced back to their source via process model inspection, and only TtM-related deviations were considered. In addition, semantic completeness was complemented by contextual (SBERT) and non-contextual (TF-IDF) textual similarity measures.

(4.2) Semantic Correctness. Semantic correctness was assessed through semantic order consistency (SOCS) by comparing ordering relations derived from the OPD with the control-flow relations represented in the generated BPMN 2.0 process model. A Python-based analysis script automatically matched corresponding activities using exact, similarity-based, and token-overlap-based matching techniques before performing a reachability analysis to determine whether temporal and logical ordering relations were preserved. The reachability analysis additionally considered intermediate BPMN 2.0 events and gateways to determine valid paths between related activities.

(4.3) Overall Assessment. The overall evaluation combined structured semantic comparison metrics (precision, recall, F1), textual similarity measures (CS, NCS), and semantic order consistency (SOCS) to assess semantic fidelity. All automated evaluation steps were reviewed and validated by three BPMN domain experts. In addition, a subset of 45 generated process models was independently evaluated by separate BPMN domain experts, who assessed semantic completeness and semantic correctness using five-point Likert scales, where 1 indicated very poor and 5 excellent preservation of the respective dimension.

4.2 Study Metrics

To assess semantic fidelity, semantic completeness was measured using (i) *structured semantic comparison metrics* and (ii) *textual similarity metrics*, and semantic correctness using (iii) the *semantic order consistency metric.*

Structured Semantic Comparison Metrics

- **Precision.** Measures the proportion of units in the GPD that correctly correspond to the units contained in the OPD. Precision decreases when the GPD contains additional units that are not present in the OPD, i.e., FP.

$$\text{Precision} = \frac{TP}{TP + FP} \quad (1)$$

- **Recall.** Measures the proportion of units contained in the OPD that are preserved in the GPD. Recall decreases when units present in the OPD are missing in the GPD, i.e., FN.

$$\text{Recall} = \frac{TP}{TP + FN} \quad (2)$$

- **F1 Score.** Combines precision and recall into a single measure by balancing the effects of information gain (FP) and information loss (FN).

$$F1 = \frac{2 \cdot TP}{2 \cdot TP + FP + FN} \quad (3)$$

Automated Textual Similarity Metrics

- **Contextual Similarity (CS).** Measures the semantic similarity between OPD and GPD by considering the contextual meaning of words and phrases. CS was computed using cosine similarity over sentence embeddings generated by the pre-trained SBERT model `all-MiniLM-L6-v2`.
- **Non-contextual Similarity (NCS).** Measures the lexical similarity between OPD and GPD based on term overlap. NCS was computed using the statistical measure *TF-IDF* representations combined with cosine similarity.

Semantic Order Consistency Metric

- **Semantic Order Consistency Score (SOCS).** Measures the proportion of temporal and logical ordering relations derived from the OPD that are supported in the generated BPMN 2.0 process model.

$$SOCS = \frac{\#\,\text{supported ordering relations in generated process model}}{\#\,\text{total ordering relations in OPD}} \quad (4)$$

5 Study Results and Discussion

5.1 Overall Preservation of Semantic Fidelity (RQ1)

Results. Table 1 summarizes the overall results across all evaluated LLM- and prompting-based generation settings.

Discussion. The results of RQ1 indicate that semantic fidelity is largely preserved in LLM-generated BPMN 2.0 process models, particularly regarding semantic completeness. The high precision indicates that only limited additional

Table 1. Overall results of semantic fidelity preservation

	Semantic Completeness					Semantic Correctness
	Precision	Recall	F1	CS	NCS	SOCS
M	0.951	0.928	0.936	0.847	0.791	0.777
SD	0.066	0.085	0.056	0.064	0.082	0.185

process-semantic information (FP) was introduced, whereas the lower recall indicates that semantic fidelity degradation occurred more frequently through omitted information (FN). This behavior is plausible, as transforming natural language into formal BPMN 2.0 models inherently requires abstraction, particularly when process descriptions contain implicit assumptions, ambiguities, or underspecified control-flow dependencies. The high F1-scores indicate a strong balance between preserved and incorrectly transformed process-semantic information. Likewise, the combination of high CS and lower NCS indicates that semantic fidelity is primarily reflected in preserved process semantics rather than lexical similarity despite linguistic reformulations. In contrast, the lower SOCS values indicate that preserving temporal and logical ordering relations remains considerably more challenging because these relations are often implicit, ambiguous, or distributed across multiple sentences. The expert-based assessment confirmed these findings, yielding higher ratings for semantic completeness ($M = 4.11$, $SD = 0.56$) than for semantic correctness ($M = 3.18$, $SD = 0.89$). Kendall's coefficient of concordance further indicated statistically significant interrater agreement for both dimensions ($W = 0.243$ and $W = 0.204$, respectively; $p < 0.001$).

Answering Research Question 1. Semantic fidelity was largely preserved in the generated BPMN 2.0 process models. While semantic completeness remained consistently high for all metrics, preserving temporal and logical ordering relations proved substantially more challenging, as reflected by lower SOCS values.

5.2 Semantic Fidelity Robustness Across Generation Settings (RQ2)

Results. Table 2 summarizes the results regarding the robustness of semantic fidelity across all evaluated LLM-based generation settings.

To examine whether the observed descriptive differences were statistically meaningful, Friedman tests were conducted (cf. Table 3). The results did not reveal statistically significant differences across the evaluated LLMs. Furthermore, Kendall's coefficient of concordance (W) indicated weak effect sizes for all metrics ($W < 0.1$), indicating only minimal variation in semantic fidelity.

Table 4 summarizes the results regarding the robustness of semantic fidelity across all evaluated prompting-based generation settings.

To examine whether the observed differences between prompting-based generation settings were statistically significant, we conducted Friedman tests and

Table 2. Descriptive statistics across different LLM-based generation settings

LLM	Precision		Recall		F1		CS		NCS		SOCS	
	M	*SD*	*M*	*SD*	*M*	*SD*	*M*	*SD*	*M*	*SD*	*M*	*SD*
Claude	0.945	0.077	0.944	0.076	0.941	0.056	0.861	0.063	0.784	0.082	0.757	0.183
Gemini	0.966	0.052	0.907	0.101	0.931	0.060	0.828	0.071	0.797	0.076	0.781	0.182
GPT	0.944	0.064	0.935	0.073	0.937	0.053	0.852	0.053	0.792	0.087	0.777	0.185

Note: Claude = Claude Opus 4.5, Gemini = Gemini 2.5 Pro, GPT = GPT-5.4.

Table 3. Friedman Test results across different LLM-based generation settings

Metric	Test Statistics				Mean Ranks		
	χ^2	df	*p*	*W*	Claude Opus 4.5	Gemini 2.5 Pro	GPT-5.4
Precision	1.684	2	0.431	0.042	1.80	2.20	2.00
Recall	3.294	2	0.193	0.082	2.10	1.70	2.20
F1	0.692	2	0.707	0.017	2.08	1.85	2.08
CS	3.700	2	0.157	0.092	2.15	1.65	2.20
NCS	0.900	2	0.638	0.023	1.85	2.15	2.00
SOCS	0.592	2	0.744	0.015	1.88	2.10	2.03

post-hoc Wilcoxon signed-rank tests with Bonferroni correction ($\alpha = 0.0167$) (cf. Tables 5 and 6). The Friedman tests revealed statistically significant differences for precision and F1. However, after Bonferroni correction, statistically significant pairwise differences remained only for precision.

Discussion. The results of RQ2 indicate that semantic fidelity remains robust across different LLM- and prompting-based generation settings. The absence of statistically significant differences between the evaluated LLMs indicates that preserving process semantics is a stable capability of current LLM-based BPMN 2.0 process modeling approaches rather than a strength of a specific LLM. In contrast, the consistently lower and more variable SOCS values indicate that preserving temporal and logical ordering relations remains challenging, likely because implicit temporal dependencies, synchronization constraints, and

Table 4. Descriptive statistics across different prompting-based generation settings

Prompting Strategy	Precision		Recall		F1		CS		NCS		SOCS	
	M	*SD*	*M*	*SD*	*M*	*SD*	*M*	*SD*	*M*	*SD*	*M*	*SD*
CoT	0.967	0.049	0.927	0.080	0.944	0.048	0.846	0.067	0.785	0.085	0.775	0.177
SR	0.926	0.077	0.931	0.088	0.925	0.060	0.842	0.068	0.791	0.082	0.804	0.168
ZS	0.961	0.062	0.927	0.088	0.940	0.058	0.853	0.056	0.798	0.079	0.751	0.207

Note: CoT = Chain-of-Thought, SR = Self-Refine, ZS = Zero-Shot.

Table 5. Friedman Test results across prompting-based generation settings

Metric	Test Statistics				Mean Ranks		
	χ^2	df	p	W	CoT	SR	ZS
Precision	10.055	2	**0.007**	0.251	2.33	1.45	2.23
Recall	0.758	2	0.685	0.019	2.00	2.13	1.88
F1	7.811	2	**0.020**	0.195	2.43	1.58	2.00
CS	3.600	2	0.165	0.090	2.00	1.70	2.30
NCS	0.900	2	0.638	0.023	1.85	2.15	2.00
SOCS	2.986	2	0.225	0.075	1.73	2.23	2.05

Note: CoT = Chain-of-Thought, SR = Self-Refine, ZS = Zero-Shot.

Table 6. Post-hoc Wilcoxon Signed-Rank Tests

Metric	Comparison	Z	p
Precision	CoT vs. SR	−3.058	**0.002**
Precision	CoT vs. ZS	−0.827	0.408
Precision	ZS vs. SR	−2.696	**0.007**
F1	CoT vs. ZS	−1.198	0.231
F1	CoT vs. SR	−1.972	0.049
F1	ZS vs. SR	−1.546	0.122

Note: CoT = Chain-of-Thought, SR = Self-Refine, ZS = Zero-Shot.

branching semantics must be translated into explicit BPMN 2.0 control-flow structures. Although overall differences between LLMs were small, their error patterns differed. Gemini 2.5 Pro produced fewer hallucinations ($FP = 0.60$) but omitted more semantic information ($FN = 2.18$), GPT-5.4 introduced more additional semantics ($FP = 1.00$) while omitting fewer process elements ($FN = 1.30$), and Claude Opus 4.5 remained comparatively balanced ($FP = 0.86$, $FN = 1.35$). Across prompting strategies, Self-Refine produced significantly more hallucinated information ($FP = 1.23$) than Chain-of-Thought ($FP = 0.53$) and Zero-Shot prompting ($FP = 0.68$), whereas omitted semantic information remained stable ($FN \approx 1.6$), indicating that prompting primarily influences semantic elaboration, whereas omitted information reveals a more fundamental challenge of translating process descriptions into formal BPMN 2.0 process models.

Answering Research Question 2. Semantic fidelity remained robust across all generation settings. Only Self-Refine prompting produced significantly more hallucinated process-semantic information than the other prompting strategies.

6 Limitations and Threats to Validity

Several limitations should be considered when interpreting the results. Semantic fidelity was assessed through indicators of semantic completeness and semantic correctness based on structured semantic comparison, textual similarity, and semantic order consistency. Although this enables systematic and scalable evaluation, semantic fidelity is inherently multifaceted. Furthermore, the round-trip evaluation assumes that semantic deviations introduced during TtM transformation remain observable after the subsequent MtT transformation, although compensating transformation errors cannot be excluded. The structured semantic comparison depends on the extraction and mapping of process-semantic information, and minor variations in semantic interpretation may influence the results. Moreover, semantic correctness was operationalized through semantic order consistency, excluding aspects such as gateway appropriateness, exception handling, and behavioral soundness. Finally, the findings are limited to the evaluated process descriptions, BPMNGen, LLMs, and prompting strategies.

7 Conclusions and Future Work

This work presented a systematic round-trip evaluation approach for assessing semantic fidelity in LLM-generated BPMN 2.0 process models. Based on an empirical study comprising 180 generated process models, the results indicate that current LLM-based approaches largely preserve process-semantic information, while preserving temporal and logical ordering relations remains considerably more challenging. Furthermore, semantic fidelity proved robust across the evaluated LLM- and prompting-based generation settings, with prompting strategies mainly influencing hallucinated process-semantic information. Future work may extend the proposed approach to additional process domains, modeling languages, and generation settings, as well as investigate further process-model-based semantic correctness metrics beyond order consistency.

Disclosure of Interests. The authors have no competing interests to declare that are relevant to the content of this article.

References

1. https://huggingface.co/datasets/patriziobellan/PET, Accessed 21 April 2026
2. https://zenodo.org/records/15857589, Accessed 21 April 2026
3. https://huggingface.co/datasets/bis-aifb-kit, Accessed 21 April 2026
4. Drakopoulos, P., Malousoudis, P., Nousias, N., Tsakalidis, G., Vergidis, K.: Do LLMs speak BPMN? an evaluation of their process modeling capabilities based on quality measures. Computation (2026). https://doi.org/10.3390/computation14010010
5. Eldin, A.N., Assy, N., Anesini, O., Dalmas, B., Gaaloul, W.: Nala2BPMN: automating BPMN model generation with large language models. In: CoopIS, pp. 398–404. https://doi.org/10.1007/978-3-031-81375-7_27

6. Enderton, H.B.: A mathematical introduction to logic. Elsevier (2001). https://doi.org/10.1016/C2009-0-22107-6
7. Grohs, M., Abb, L., Elsayed, N., Rehse, J.R.: Large language models can accomplish business process management tasks. In: BPM, pp. 453–465. Springer (2023). https://doi.org/10.1007/978-3-031-50974-2_34
8. Hörner, L.F., Möller, M., Reichert, M.: Automatically generating BPMN 2.0 process models from natural language process descriptions: challenges, framework, quality assessment. Business & Information Systems Engineering, pp. 1–25 (2026). https://doi.org/10.1007/s12599-025-00983-x
9. Klievtsova, N., Mangler, J., Kampik, T., Rinderle-Ma, S.: Utilizing process models in the requirements engineering process through model2text transformation. In: Int. Requirements Engineering Conference (RE), pp. 205–217. IEEE (2024). https://doi.org/10.1109/RE59067.2024.00028
10. Köpke, J., Safan, A.: Efficient LLM-based conversational process modeling. In: Gdowska, K., Gómez-López, M.T., Rehse, JR. (eds) BPM 2024. LNBIP, vol. 534. Springer, Cham (2024). https://doi.org/10.1007/978-3-031-78666-2_20
11. Kourani, H., Berti, A., Schuster, D., van der Aalst, W.M.: Process modeling with large language models. In: van der Aa, H., Bork, D., Schmidt, R., Sturm, A. (eds.) BPMDS EMMSAD 2024 2024. LNBIP, vol 511. Springer, Cham. (2024). https://doi.org/10.1007/978-3-031-61007-3_18
12. Krogstie, J., Sindre, G., Jørgensen, H.: Process models representing knowledge for action: a revised quality framework. EJIS **15**(1), 91–102 (2006). https://doi.org/10.1057/palgrave.ejis.3000598
13. Licardo, J.T., Tanković, N., Etinger, D.: BPMN assistant: an LLM-based approach to business process modeling. Appl. Sci. **16**(5), 2213 (2026). https://doi.org/10.3390/app16052213
14. Object Management Group: BPMN 2.0: Business process model and notation (2011). https://www.omg.org/spec/BPMN/2.0/, Accessed 21 April 2026
15. Safan, A., Köpke, J.: BPMN-chatbot++: LLM-based modeling of collaboration diagrams with data. In: Proceedings of the BPM (2025)
16. Safan, A., Köpke, J.: A framework for LLM-based conceptual modeling: application to BPMN collaboration diagrams (2025)
17. Vidgof, M., Bachhofner, S., Mendling, J.: Large language models for business process management: Opportunities and challenges. In: Int. Conf. on BPM, pp. 107–123. Springer (2023). https://doi.org/10.1007/978-3-031-41623-1_7

From Regulatory Text to Conceptual Models: Generating Organizational Models, Role-Task Mappings and Process Descriptions

Anastasiya Damaratskaya, Catherine Sai, and Stefanie Rinderle-Ma(✉)

TUM School of Computation, Information and Technology, Technical University of Munich, Garching, Germany
{anastasiya.damaratskaya,catherine.sai,stefanie.rinderle-ma}@tum.de

Abstract. Regulatory texts often include process-relevant and organizational information, such as decision logic, duties, and actor relations. However, prior research in legal information extraction seldomly addresses organizational structures, and current text-to-process methods are not designed for raw regulatory text. Unlike process descriptions, regulatory documents exhibit greater linguistic complexity and non-sequentiality, often applying implicit actors and cross-references that hinder information retrieval. This paper presents a framework that automatically extracts organizational and process-relevant information from regulatory texts and generates machine-readable artifacts, such as organizational models, role-task mappings, and process descriptions. Thus, the approach yields process-oriented representations from legal text while capturing the organizational context necessary to operationalize regulatory requirements. The quality of the generated artifacts and their utility for downstream process model generation tools are evaluated for ten European regulatory documents. The results indicate that the approach outperforms LLM-only baselines, improves the usability of regulatory text, and enables the extraction of organizational and process-relevant information with promising quality for further automation and analysis.

Keywords: Legal Information Extraction · Large Language Models · Process Information Extraction · Organizational Information Extraction

1 Motivation

Organizations must ensure compliance between business processes and evolving regulatory requirements [9,28]. The challenge grows with regulatory scope, frequent updates, and complexity, affecting procedures, responsibilities, and compliance controls [21,28]. Research in process compliance and legal information extraction highlights that compliance analysis remains a complex and resource-intensive task, particularly for interpreting regulatory constraints and maintaining alignment with internal processes [9,21,28]. Real-world examples illustrate

© The Author(s), under exclusive license to Springer Nature Switzerland AG 2027
A. Bernasconi et al. (Eds.): ER 2026, LNCS 17081, pp. 450–460, 2027.
https://doi.org/10.1007/978-3-032-40795-5_29

the importance of regulatory requirements and the impact of non-compliance: OpenAI was fined EUR 15 million in 2024 for breaching privacy rules[1].

Process models are essential for communication, analysis, execution, and compliance. While recent work explores process model generation from textual descriptions using Natural Language Processing (NLP) and ML techniques [15,17], these approaches typically assume structured, procedural input. Regulatory documents, however, are written for legal interpretation and often lack explicit activities and actors [27]. This mismatch highlights the difficulty of using regulatory text in process-oriented applications and increases the need to transform regulatory text into structured, process-relevant representations [21,28].

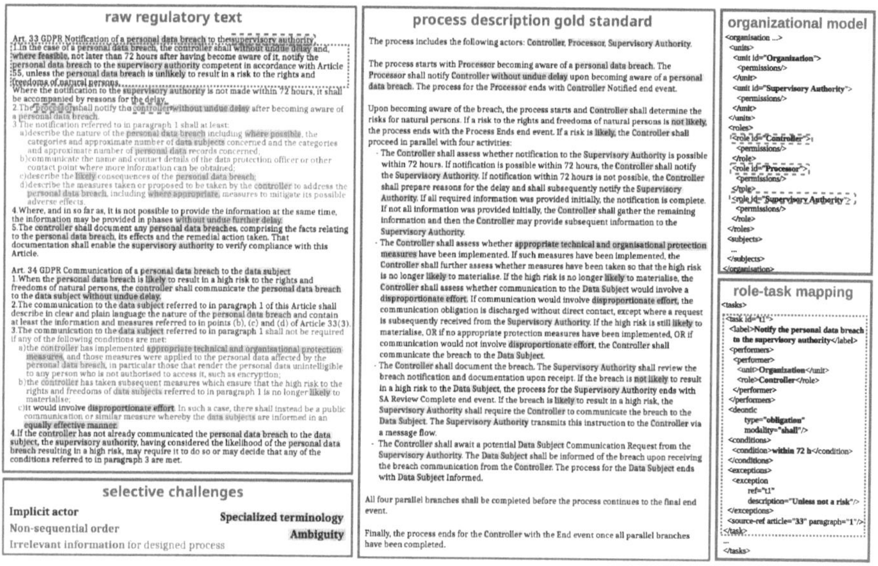

Fig. 1. Example transformation of GDPR articles.

Figure 1 contrasts a raw regulatory text passage from the GDPR[2] with its corresponding process description, organizational model, and role-task mapping. While retaining specialized terminology, the process description resolves structural challenges such as non-sequential ordering, implicit actors, and extraneous information. Additionally, the organizational components explicitly capture hierarchies and responsibilities, which standard BPMN 2.0 (bpmn.org) constructs such as pools and lanes often struggle to represent [6,26], and which legal extraction approaches typically overlook [21]. Converting regulatory texts into machine-processable representations yields three main benefits: first, it reduces interpretive complexity for non-legal stakeholders [9]; second, it enables direct

[1] https://tinyurl.com/5n8en4mv.
[2] General Data Protection Regulation, https://gdpr.eu/.

compliance analysis against internal documents, event logs, or process models [28]; and third, it provides structured inputs for downstream applications like BPMN generation [5]. Overall, raw legal text cannot be directly used in BPM applications, underscoring the need for an automated framework to extract organizational and process information for compliance analysis.

Section 2 reviews related work, Sect. 3 outlines the proposed approach, Sect. 4 presents the evaluation of the approach, and Sect. 5 concludes the paper.

2 Related Work

Legal NLP research primarily focuses on tasks like classification, summarization, and named entity recognition, leaving procedural and organizational information extraction largely unexplored [8,25]. Hassani et al. [10] argue that sentence-level and classification-based compliance automation is too narrow, advocating for context-aware Large Language Model (LLM) approaches. Existing frameworks like LexNLP [3] perform entity extraction but lack procedural or organizational awareness, while GraphCompliance [7] builds policy graphs for compliance reasoning, emphasizing relational representations. Despite studies stressing that compliance requires explicit duties, governance, and role definitions [16,18], automated extraction of organizational structures remains limited. Early work extracted normative elements without higher-level actor hierarchies [13], while conceptual models define roles and rules without automating their extraction [16]. Similarly, automated process model generation is shifting toward LLM-based methods [2,29]. However, existing rule-based and LLM approaches struggle on complex documents [1], depend heavily on input clarity [11], and often omit essential process elements [4]. Tools like `AutoBPMN.ai` [14] require structured inputs that raw regulatory texts fail to provide. This underscores the need to extract organizational structures and generate structured process descriptions for downstream LLM reasoning and legal practice.

3 Approach

This paper presents a structured, methodologically grounded approach that leverages NLP and LLMs to extract organizational and process-relevant information from regulatory text[3]. As shown in Fig. 2, regulatory text is first preprocessed, then used for organizational information extraction, role-task mapping, and process description generation, producing artifacts at each stage.

[3] https://github.com/AnastasiyaDmrsk/from-reg-text-to-models.

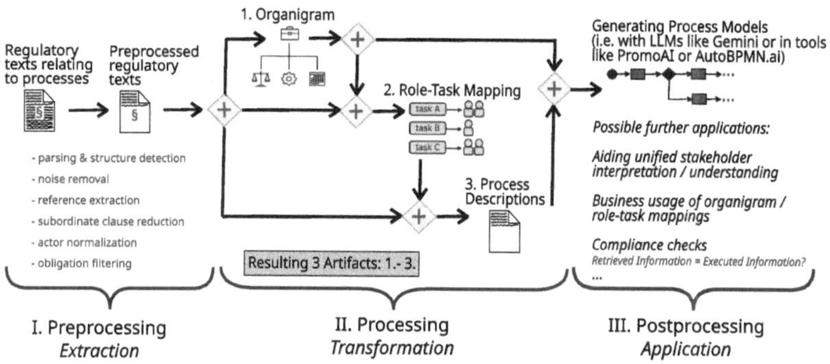

Fig. 2. Approach overview.

3.1 Preprocessing

Raw regulatory texts require normalization because they often contain complex syntax, cross-references, implicit actors, and non-sequentiality. These characteristics can cause LLMs and modeling tools to omit relevant obligations, duplicate activities, misidentify gateways, or generate process models at an unsuitable level of granularity. Thus, we apply a multi-stage preprocessing pipeline that transforms raw regulatory text into a structured, process-oriented representation.

The pipeline first identifies the *document structure* using regular expressions, splits the text into processable units, and assigns *position identifiers* for reference tracking. Legal filler phrases that usually do not affect procedural meaning, such as "inter alia", are removed, and whitespace, line breaks, and punctuation are *normalized.* To improve gateway identification, conditional openings such as "If" and task conjunctions such as "and" and "or" are normalized. *List items* are treated as parallel tasks by default, and a leading sentence is attached to each item to ensure independence. Sentences without *deontic modality* such as "shall", "should", and "must" [28] are removed. *Cross-references* are extracted into a CSV file with their location and reference and removed from the text if not part of the input. This preserves traceability while preventing unresolved references from being silently ignored during LLM-based processing. To isolate the core obligation, the pipeline also removes *non-obligatory subordinate clauses* using benepar [12] where available and a regex fallback otherwise. Before removal, clauses are verified to carry no critical information, e.g., actors, duties, or conditions, and are preserved otherwise. To address implicit actors, bare pronouns are replaced with the preceding actor where possible, while *passive constructions* without explicit actors are extended with a "by [actor]" phrase. Finally, the processed clauses are *represented linearly*: each article starts with its number and heading, followed by numbered paragraph clauses and lettered list items, while multiple articles are separated by "—".

The output is actor-explicit, deontic-filtered, gateway-aware, and, where identifiable, position-indexed, supporting reference tracking and further processing.

3.2 Processing

The processing stage uses preprocessed text to generate three artifacts, each building on previous output (cf. Fig. 2): (1) an organigram with actors and hierarchies; (2) a role-task mapping with tasks, obligations, performers, conditions, exceptions, and sources; and (3) a process description explaining task series per actor. While organizational information extraction and role-task mapping generation apply NLP techniques for explicit structures extraction and LLMs for deeper insights, process description generation is performed fully by LLMs. Each LLM generation can be validated by an additional LLM, with prompts specifying output format and examples to enhance accuracy.

Organizational Information Extraction: Organizational information is represented using the organizational model proposed in [23] for the Cloud Process Execution Engine (CPEE). We distinguish between three actor levels: **unit**, an independent institution with its own legal identity or autonomous resources (BPMN pool); **role**, a functional position or organ operating within a unit with an active part in the process (BPMN lane); **subject**, a concrete resource under an assigned role within a unit (cf. Fig. 1, upper right). As regulatory texts rarely assign tasks to individuals, subjects serve as placeholders for later substitution, clarifying resource allocation while distinguishing structure from execution.

Creating an organigram includes actor extraction and hierarchy identification subtasks. *Actor extraction* uses rule-based NLP (phrase matching, named-entity recognition, dependency parsing, and optionally GLiNER [30] for domain-specific actors) to identify potential candidates. The resulting list is passed to an LLM to correct and extend it. A second LLM then validates the candidates, looking for hallucinations, incorrect types, passive or missing actors. *Hierarchy identification* passes the final list to an LLM to identify **unit–unit**, **role–role**, and **role–unit** relationships. Then, a validating LLM checks for constraint violations and missing relations before producing a final model.

Role-Task Mapping Generation: Role-task mapping generation uses the preprocessed text and subject list as input and applies NLP techniques to identify candidate tasks and their locations, allowing indexing for later verification in the regulatory source. First, deontic markers are detected and mapped to modalities such as obligation ("shall"), prohibition ("shall not"), permission ("may"), or recommendation ("should"). The governing verb is identified and the verb phrase reconstructed as the task label. To address implicit tasks, such as delegated obligations (in which one actor ensures that another acts) and request-based tasks (triggered by a request), the pipeline extracts both governing and delegated activities as separate entities, assigns them the same modality, and marks request-based tasks as conditional. As for other conditions, clauses introduced by "if", "when", and "unless" are extracted. After completing the candidate list, the pipeline submits potential tasks to a generating LLM to extend the list with missing duties and details, as well as split compound entries. Lastly, a validating LLM reviews task candidates before producing the final representation.

Process Description Generation: The final step produces a structured process description from the role-task mapping and preprocessed text to support BPMN generation. A generating LLM orders tasks, assigning one per sentence, and explains the process end-to-end based on the predefined schema. A validating LLM ensures all relevant details, actors, and exceptions are accurately represented, checks execution order, and performs an additional validation for parallel gateways, which are particularly challenging for LLMs [19].

3.3 Postprocessing

The pipeline generates three standalone artifacts usable by downstream tools. A key use case is *process model generation*. Tools like `AutoBPMN.ai` [14] and ProMoAI [17] require process descriptions and are not optimized for raw regulatory text. Moreover, they primarily visualize control flow, while organizational information is handled separately in workflow, emphasizing the need for independent organigrams and role-task mappings. Alternatively, SOTA LLMs can be prompted to generate BPMN 2.0-supported files directly. All prompts are included in the project repository, enabling users to create process models via an LLM chat interface or API call. Beyond process visualization, organigrams *define authority hierarchies*, *support governance analysis*, and *facilitate onboarding in organizational and compliance contexts*, whereas role-task mappings provide *machine-readable tasks overview*, enabling *responsibility matrices*, *audit trails*, and *compliance monitoring* frameworks such as RACI charts.

4 Evaluation

This chapter evaluates the proposed framework by assessing each artifact individually. As a baseline, we selected ten regulatory documents from various domains,

Table 1. Dataset overview

#	Document	Type	Sector	CELEX	Art.	#Tokens	#Actors	#Tasks
1	AI Act	R	Technology	32024R1689	62	360	8	17
2	GDPR	R	Data Protection	32016R0679	33, 34	649	3	11
3	Driving License	D	Transport	32025L2205	11	725	4	17
4	Health Care	R	Health	32013R0604	–	473	5	14
5	CDD	D	Finance	32015L0849	–	414	9	11
6	eIDAS	R	Technology	32014R0910	17–19	1319	7	46
7	NIS2	D	Cybersecurity	32022L2555	23	1493	10	49
8	Medical Device	R	Health	32017R0745	10	1632	11	55
9	DSA	R	Information	32022R2065	22	679	5	19
10	Cybersecurity	R	Cybersecurity	32019R0881	48	492	5	21

each with multiple actors and process-relevant information, and manually created gold standards through detailed annotation. Then, the gold standards were independently reviewed by process modeling experts to ensure accuracy and completeness. Given the high cost of multiple LLM calls, evaluations were conducted manually using the chat interfaces of *Claude* and *Gemini* models[4]. Each task was run three times per document due to the non-deterministic nature of LLMs. For role-task mapping and process description evaluation, gold standards were used as input to ensure independence of the evaluation results. We also compared process models generated from preprocessed vs. raw regulatory text to evaluate the impact of preprocessing. Finally, the primary goal is to assess the approach's accuracy and whether models produced from generated process descriptions outperform those built from LLMs processing raw regulatory text.

Dataset. We evaluated the approach using 10 European regulatory documents from EUR-Lex[5], including both regulations (R) and directives (D) from diverse domains with varying numbers of tokens, actors, and tasks (Table 1). The second, fourth, and fifth documents were adopted from the CARB benchmark [24], while the rest were selected according to the following criteria: a) is in force, b) contains process-relevant information, and c) involves multiple actors and hierarchies. Overall, the dataset offers a representative testing environment that ensures a balanced mix of diversity, varying lengths, and structural complexity.

Organizational Information Extraction. Organizational information extraction is evaluated across unit, role, and actor detection, hierarchy identification, and subject binding. Unit, role, and actor extraction are measured with precision, recall, and F1 by matching predicted and gold-standard entities one-to-one based on textual similarity at a threshold of 0.8. Hierarchy reconstruction is evaluated separately for unit–unit and role–role relations. Subject binding evaluates complete unit–role–subject assignments using SBERT-based pair matching [22]. To isolate role assignment from unit naming inconsistencies, we additionally report role-only binding F1 and role coverage, i.e., the fraction of gold roles represented in at least one subject binding.

Across models, unit and role extraction obtain solid F1 scores (*unit*: Gemini 0.73, Claude **0.81**; *role*: Gemini **0.78**, Claude 0.70; *actor (general)*: Gemini **0.80**, Claude 0.73), indicating that the approach is suitable for detecting major actors. Regarding hierarchies, unit–unit relations are reliably retrieved (Gemini 0.87, Claude **1.0**), whereas role hierarchy detection (0.53) and subject binding ($\approx$0.60) yield lower scores, as semantically similar or overlapping actor terms often lead to merged terms rather than parent-child roles. For example, a specific role such as "Driving License Holder" who applies for renewal may be merged into the broader role "Applicant" rather than detecting a role–role relation. Subject binding is similarly affected by naming inconsistencies between units and roles, although role-level binding (Gemini: **0.80**, Claude: 0.73) and role coverage (Gemini: **0.92**, Claude: 0.73) show that many relevant role assignments are still captured.

[4] Claude Opus 4.6 Extended, claude.ai. Gemini 3.1 Pro, gemini.google.com.

[5] https://eur-lex.europa.eu/.

Throughout the evaluation, Gemini achieves higher recall, whereas Claude outperforms in precision, yielding similar F1 scores and indicating that both models are viable options for organizational extraction. Overall, the findings confirm that the framework reliably extracts units, roles, and unit hierarchies, regardless of the model selected.

Role-Task Mapping Generation. For role-task mapping evaluation, we use organigram gold standards with the preprocessed text to create the mappings and compute five metrics: task identification, which matches predicted tasks to gold tasks; performer correctness for verifying the correctness of assigned actors; deontic F1 to assess deontic modality correctness; and condition F1 and exception F1 to evaluate the extraction of triggering conditions and exceptions. The assessment shows that task identification achieves high F1 scores ($\approx$0.85) for both models, indicating that the approach captures relevant duties. Performer assignment ($\approx$0.80) and deontic modality detection ($\approx$0.80) also reach usable levels, suggesting that the generated mappings are sufficiently informative for downstream analysis and compliance-oriented applications. However, condition (Gemini: 0.56, Claude: **0.63**) and exception (Gemini: 0.52, Claude: **0.61**) detection remains challenging, since these elements are often nested or distributed across sentences, complicating the retrieval. Additionally, lower scores may result from representational differences: gold standards may assign one exception per role, whereas LLMs merge these roles into a single exception. Although the information is present, the evaluation does not account for such differences.

Again, Gemini achieves higher recall and performs marginally better on performer and deontic modality retrieval, while Claude obtains higher task precision and better condition and exception scores. Overall, the results are broadly comparable and support the feasibility of role-task mapping across both models.

Process Description Generation. Process descriptions are evaluated in two ways: first, by comparing descriptions generated directly by Gemini and Claude chats, as well as the approach's description to gold standards; second, by generating BPMN models directly from raw text using the CARB prompt [24] and from produced process descriptions with the process-description-to-BPMN prompt. We reuse the metrics introduced by CARB [24], specifically completeness (all required elements are present) and correctness. Process descriptions generated by the approach and Claude achieve the highest scores, outperforming the baseline, with an actor F1 score of **0.94** (vs. 0.64), a task F1 score of **0.87** (vs. 0.84), and a deontic F1 score of **0.72**, where the deontic metric, calculated only for matched tasks, is affected by extraction errors. On the other hand, the approach using Gemini also improves over the chat baseline, with actor F1 increasing from 0.63 to 0.93, task F1 from 0.78 to 0.83, and deontic F1 from 0.67 to 0.69. Furthermore, the approach yields shorter descriptions (Gemini: **981** vs. 1280, Claude: 1118 vs. 1293), which is beneficial as prior work shows that LLM performance is sensitive to input length [20]. In summary, our approach reduces output verbosity and enhances accuracy, demonstrating that the pipeline design provides a model-independent improvement over chat-generated process descriptions.

Application. To assess how preprocessing and process descriptions impact BPMN 2.0 file generation compared to raw text input, we compute completeness and correctness scores for both LLMs, presented in Table 2. Across LLMs, the table demonstrates that preprocessed regulatory text consistently improves BPMN quality, especially in activity and parallel gateway identification. The "Approach" rows in both tables show the results when preprocessed text is converted to process descriptions using the approach and entered into Gemini chat to produce BPMN files. We also compare the models produced by the `AutoBPMN.ai` [14] by applying Gemini 2.5 Flash Lite for raw text vs. the generated process description.

Table 2. Macro-averaged **completeness** (left) and **correctness** (right)

Model	I	Actor	Activity	Events	Cond.	AND	XOR	Model	I	Actor	Assign.	Contr. F	Decis. L	Cond. L
Gemini	P	0.68	0.52	0.14	0.01	0.87	0.02	Gemini	P	0.41	0.08	0.00	0.22
Gemini	R	0.66	0.41	0.16	0.01	0.30	0.02	Gemini	R	0.35	0.06	0.01	0.19
Claude	P	0.65	0.59	0.20	0.13	**0.90**	0.20	Claude	P	0.47	0.12	0.12	0.38
Claude	R	0.62	0.49	0.25	0.10	0.50	0.20	Claude	R	0.43	0.11	0.16	0.35
Approach	P	**0.78**	**0.80**	**0.26**	**0.25**	0.70	**0.87**	Approach	P	**0.74**	**0.22**	**0.35**	**0.63**
AutoBPMN	R	0.00	0.44	0.07	0.00	0.30	0.76	AutoBPMN	R	0.00	0.04	0.00	0.53
AutoBPMN	A	0.00	**0.60**	0.07	**0.01**	**0.67**	**0.89**	AutoBPMN	A	0.00	**0.08**	0.00	**0.66**

I = Input, P = Preprocessed, R = Raw, A = Approach, F = Flow, L = Logic.

Our approach achieves the overall best performance, attaining the highest completeness and correctness scores for actors, activities, conditions, control flow, and logic, and outperforming LLM-only baselines. Using generated process descriptions in `AutoBPMN.ai` [14] also yields enhanced models with more activities and gateways, improving scores compared to raw text input.

5 Conclusion

This work transforms unstructured regulatory texts into a set of valuable artifacts: (i) machine-readable organizational charts with explicit hierarchies, (ii) machine-readable role-task mappings with process-relevant information, and (iii) human-readable process descriptions detailing each actor's task sequence. Our main contribution lies in preprocessing regulatory by clarifying actors and activities, reducing redundancy, and structuring the text, along with integrating organizational, role-task, and process layers into a single pipeline. While organigrams and role-task mappings provide a more comprehensive, structured representation of actors and their responsibilities, process descriptions generated by the approach serve as an intermediary between complex regulatory text and visualized process models and improve actor assignment, task detection, and gateway modeling for both Gemini 3.1 Pro and Claude 4.6 Opus models. Additionally, the description provides a structured summary that facilitates legal-text interpretation and compliance reviews. *Conditions and exceptions* remain challenging to identify and require specialized extraction. The completeness and correctness scores are also lower for *events and data objects*, suggesting areas for future improvement. Other enhancements include direct model generation and integration into existing tools supporting workflow functionality, such as `AutoBPMN.ai`.

References

1. Bellan, P., Dragoni, M., Ghidini, C.: Process extraction from text: state of the art and challenges for the future. CoRR abs/2110.03754 (2021)
2. Bettencourt, J., Guerreiro, S.: Large language models to enhance business process modeling: past, present, and future trends (2026)
3. Bommarito, I.I., Katz, M.J., Detterman, D.M., E.M.: Lexnlp: natural language processing and information extraction for legal and regulatory texts. In: Research Handbook on Big Data Law, pp. 216–227. Edward Elgar Publishing (2021)
4. Boujmil, I., Chebil, W.: Improving BPMN model generation from texts through a prompt-guided fusion of NLP and LLM approaches. In: Knowledge Capture Conference, pp. 165–169. ACM (2025)
5. Capuzzimati, F., Violato, A., Baldoni, M., Boella, G.: Business process management for legal domains: supporting execution and management of preliminary injunctions. In: Legal Knowledge and Information Systems, pp. 149–152 (2015)
6. Carpella, C., Geist, V.: A layered approach for actor modelling in business processes. Bus. Process. Manag. J. **19**, 917–932 (2013)
7. Chung, J., et al.: Graphcompliance: aligning policy and context graphs for LLM-based regulatory compliance abs/2510.26309 (2025)
8. Conrad, J.G., Ganguly, D., Ghosh, K., Ghosh, S.: Introduction to the special issue on applications and evaluation of large language models in the legal domain (2025)
9. Hashmi, M., Governatori, G., Lam, H.-P., Wynn, M.T.: Are we done with business process compliance: state of the art and challenges ahead. Knowl. Inf. Syst. **57**(1), 79–133 (2018). https://doi.org/10.1007/s10115-017-1142-1
10. Hassani, S., Sabetzadeh, M., Amyot, D., Liao, J.: Rethinking legal compliance automation: opportunities with large language models. In: RE, pp. 432–440 (2024)
11. Hörner, L.F., Möller, M., Reichert, M.: Automatically generating BPMN 2.0 process models from natural language process descriptions: challenges, framework, quality assessment. Bus. Inf. Syst. Eng. **68**(1), 59–83 (2026)
12. Kitaev, N., Cao, S., Klein, D.: Multilingual constituency parsing with self-attention and pre-training. In: Computational Linguistics, pp. 3499–3505 (2019)
13. Kiyavitskaya, N., et al.: Automating the extraction of rights and obligations for regulatory compliance. In: Conceptual Modeling, pp. 154–168. Springer (2008)
14. Klievtsova, N., Ehrendorfer, M., Mangler, J., Rinderle-Ma, S.: Autobpmn.ai: conversational process modeling and automation. In: BPM (Demos/Resources Forum), pp. 304–311. CEUR Workshop Proceedings (2025)
15. Klievtsova, N., Kampik, T., Mangler, J., Rinderle-Ma, S.: Conversational process model redesign. Int. J. Cooperative Inf. Syst. **35**(1), 2650004:1–2650004:37 (2026)
16. Kornyshova, E., Boutal, L., Benramdane, M.K.: Digital business ecosystems: organizational model, roles, and governance towards flexibility. Procedia Comput. Sci. **225**, 4621–4630 (2023)

17. Kourani, H., Berti, A., Schuster, D., van der Aalst, W.M.P.: Promoai: process modeling with generative AI. In: IJCAI, pp. 8708–8712 (2024)
18. Koutsopoulos, G., Vannerus, J., Karlsson, L., Ureta, F.I.Q.: Implementing EU acts in organizations: requirements for a modeling framework. In: Practice of Enterprise Modeling. CEUR Workshop Proceedings (2024)
19. Lê, P.N., Schneider-Depré, C., Goossens, A., Stevens, A., Leribaux, A., De Smedt, J.: Leveraging machine learning and enhanced parallelism detection for BPMN model generation from text. arXiv:2507.08362 arXiv preprint (2025)
20. Paulsen, N.: Context is what you need: the maximum effective context window for real world limits of LLMS. arXiv preprint arXiv:2509.21361 (2025)
21. Premasiri, D., Ranasinghe, T., Mitkov, R., El-Haj, M., Frommholz, I.: Survey on legal information extraction: current status and open challenges. Knowl. Inf. Syst. **67**(12), 11287–11358 (2025)
22. Reimers, N., Gurevych, I.: Sentence-Bert: sentence embeddings using Siamese Bert-networks. In: Empirical Methods in Natural Language Processing (EMNLP) (2019)
23. Rinderle-Ma, S., Mangler, J., Ritter, D.: Fundamentals of Information Systems Interoperability: Data, Services, and Processes. Springer (2024)
24. Sai, C., Rinderle-Ma, S.: Agentic generation of process models from regulatory texts. In: Cooperative Information Systems, pp. 370–387 (2025)
25. Siino, M., Falco, M., Croce, D., Rosso, P.: Exploring LLMS applications in law: a literature review on current legal NLP approaches. IEEE Access (2025)
26. Skouti, T., Seiger, R., Furrer, F., Strahringer, S.: RBPMN: the value of roles for business process modeling. SoSyM **23**, 1375–1406 (2024)
27. Wang, H.J., Zhao, J.L., Zhang, L.: Policy-driven process mapping (PDPM): discovering process models from business policies. DSS **48**(1), 267–281 (2009)
28. Winter, K., van der Aa, H., Rinderle-Ma, S., Weidlich, M.: Assessing the compliance of business process models with regulatory documents. In: Conceptual Modeling, pp. 189–203 (2020)
29. Woensel, W.V., Motie, S.: NLP4PBM: a systematic review on process extraction using natural language processing with rule-based, machine and deep learning methods. Enterp. Inf. Syst **18**(11) (2024)
30. Zaratiana, U., Tomeh, N., Holat, P., Charnois, T.: Gliner: generalist model for named entity recognition using bidirectional transformer. In: North American Chapter of the Association for Computational Linguistics, pp. 5364–5376 (2024)

Process Modeling and Compliance

Stream an REA-MERODE Transaction Status Specification

Wim Laurier[1] (✉) and Satoshi Horiuchi[2]

[1] UCLouvain Saint-Louis, Boulevard du Jardin botanique 43, 1000 Brussels, Belgium
wim.laurier@uclouvain.be

[2] CHUO University, 742-1 Higashinakano, Hachioji-shi, Tokyo 192-0393, Japan
satoshi.55g@g.chuo-u.ac.jp

Abstract. Business transactions are fundamental to contemporary information systems, yet their operational implementation often lacks a precise, executable specification of transaction states and lifecycles. Although the Resource–Event–Agent (REA) ontology provides a strong semantic foundation for modeling economic phenomena, it offers limited support for representing dynamic state changes and end-to-end transaction behavior. This paper introduces STREAM (Status of Transaction REA–MERODE), a comprehensive transaction status specification that formalizes business transaction lifecycles as a synchronized set of finite state machines grounded in REA and implemented using the MERODE model-driven engineering methodology. STREAM explicitly defines transaction states and transitions across all phases identified in ISO/IEC 15944—planning, identification, negotiation, actualization, and post-actualization. In contrast to prior REA- or ISO-based approaches, the specification systematically incorporates iterative offer–counteroffer negotiation as well as unsuccessful transactions, rollbacks, and restarts. The resulting model could serve as a reusable and extensible template for developing standardized, interoperable, and ontology-driven business information systems.

Keywords: Business Transaction · Transaction Status · State Machine · MERODE · Resource-Event-Agent

1 Introduction

The recording of business transactions should not be limited to the stage at which the transfer of rights and obligations between trading partners is completed. Instead, it is necessary to capture the entire trajectory leading to the establishment of a transaction, and the transaction process data (e.g., proposals, negotiation, usage, and evaluation). By doing so, the latent informational value of transaction data can be enhanced, thereby supporting more advanced decision-making and judgment. Additionally, the existence of a standardized transaction framework that can be shared across entities and accessed rapidly could facilitate the selection and reconfiguration of trading partners.

The standard business transaction model defined in ISO/IEC 15944–4 [1] can be used as such a standardized framework. In this standard, business transactions are

© The Author(s), under exclusive license to Springer Nature Switzerland AG 2027
A. Bernasconi et al. (Eds.): ER 2026, LNCS 17081, pp. 463–472, 2027.
https://doi.org/10.1007/978-3-032-40795-5_30

defined based on the REA (Resource-Event-Agent) ontology, and its transaction process is structured into five phases: Planning, Identification, Negotiation, Actualization, and Post-actualization, enabling the integrated capture and sharing of business events leading to transaction completion. As a result, compared to approaches that focus solely on the actualization phase, it becomes feasible to capture information related to the entire transaction process, including unsuccessful negotiations and customer interactions.

The mechanism for managing such transaction processes, as defined in ISO/IEC 15944–4, is referred to as the Business Transaction State Machine (BTSM). BTSM provides a foundation for transaction processing systems (TPS) by enabling the integrated management of transaction states that evolve based on business events defined within a pre-specified transaction process. However, although REA provides a robust framework for representing the structural aspects of business transactions, it is fundamentally a static model that describes entities (i.e., resources, events, and agents) and their relationships. Consequently, it does not explicitly incorporate mechanisms for consistently representing and managing state changes of these entities. As a result, when constructing BTSM-based systems with REA, state management and transition logic must be designed separately, which makes it difficult to ensure their validity and consistency.

To overcome this limitation, this paper introduces the STREAM (Status of Transaction REA–MERODE) specification, a comprehensive transaction status model. STREAM defines a synchronized set of finite state machines (FSMs) for business transactions grounded in the REA ontology and implemented using the MERODE (Model-driven Enterprise Object-Relationship Development Environment) methodology. By leveraging MERODE's integrated treatment of object lifecycles, event propagation, and state synchronization, the proposed model captures the full spectrum of transaction behavior, including iterative negotiations, counteroffers, successful completions, and so-called "unhappy path" scenarios in which transactions fail or are restarted. Specifically, we propose a design method that allows for integrating negotiation processes and state transitions with the static structure of the REA ontology.

This paper's research question is: How can negotiation processes and state transitions be integrated into transaction structures based on the REA ontology? The main contribution of this study is the development of a model that integrates business events and state transitions in the negotiation and actualization phases.

The remainder of this paper is structured as follows. Section 2 presents the STREAM model, detailing its static and behavioral components as expressed in MERODE. Section 3 illustrates the model through an archetypal business transaction scenario, and Sect. 4 concludes the paper.

2 Model Description

In MERODE, FSMs defined for individual business object types do not operate independently. Each business event defined in the Object Event Table (OET) can act as a business event shared between business objects of different types. These shared events can simultaneously change the states of multiple directly or indirectly related objects. MERODE refers to this mechanism as event propagation [2]. The FSMs of related objects are synchronized through this event propagation mechanism, which guarantees maintaining overall consistency of object states regardless of their type. The forementioned object types are shown in an existence dependency graph (EDG). An EDG is a type of class diagram, specific to the MERODE methodology, in which object types relate to each other through existence dependency relationships.

The following subsections present the static and behavioral components of the MERODE transaction status model. The object types, business events and state machines presented below define states and state transitions for tracking transaction status based on the catalog order example described in ISO 15944-4 [1].

2.1 Static Conceptual Model: Existence Dependency Graph

Fig. 1 shows the EDG of the business transaction model. Each class in fig. 1 corresponds to a type of object that is essential for executing the business transaction phases of ISO 15944-1 (i.e., planning, identification, negotiation, actualization, and post-actualization). Where the presented model aims at being generic by avoiding class attributes, it is easily feasible to add relevant attributes or transaction states to it for real-world testing. All arrows between classes in fig. 1 are one-to-many associations between classes, in which the participation on the one side (i.e., the circle symbol) is mandatory, and the participation on the many side (i.e., the arrowhead) is optional.

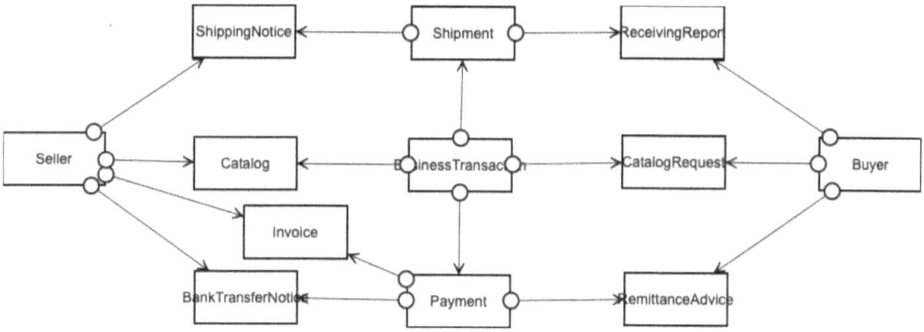

Fig. 1. Business transaction status EDG (existence dependency graph)

The `BusinessTransaction` class is the central class in this model. All remaining classes — except for the `Seller` and `Buyer` class, which are roles of economic agents — represent objectified messages that depend on the agent role that sends them or receives them in case they are issued by a third party. Buyers issue a `CatalogRequest` and `ReceivingReport` and receive a `RemittanceAdvice` from the bank. Sellers send a `Catalog`, `ShippingNotice` and `Invoice` and receive a `BankTransferNotice` from the bank. A `CatalogRequest` is the message the prospective buyer sends to the prospective seller (e.g., ordering a catalog on the seller's web page). The `Catalog` is the seller's answer to this request either as a tangible object, a visit of a sales representative or an electronic message. When a product is shipped, the seller prepares a `ShippingNotice` for the buyer and the buyer a `ReceivingReport` for the seller. After receiving the receiving report, the buyer sends out an `Invoice`, which results in a payment. When a payment is made the seller sends a `RemittanceAdvice` to the buyer as a proof that the payment has been made, where the seller receives a `BankTransferNotice` as a confirmation from the bank. Since the presented conceptual model aims at being generic and application independent, no attributes have been modeled. For example, the `RemittanceAdvice` and `BankTransferNotice` classes don't contain an attribute for the amount transferred or the date of the transfer.

2.2 Behavioral Conceptual Model: the BusinessTransaction class's FSMs

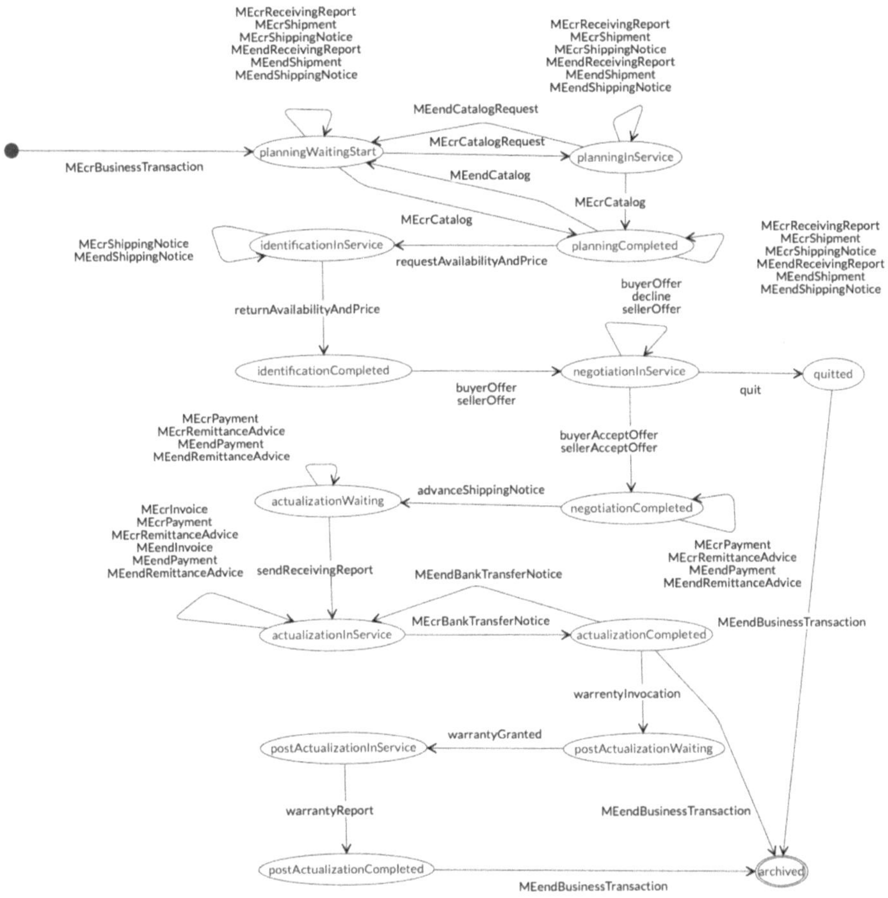

Fig. 2. FSM for Business Transaction objects

Fig. 2 elaborates the "UML activity graph for collaboration" and also an approach to "determine collaboration status by total effect of business events on object states" from the REA monograph [3], respectively fig. 6-3 and 6-4, and fig. 6-6 in the monograph.

The initial state of a `BusinessTransaction` object is `planningWaitingStart`. The planning phase involves sending and requesting a catalog. In contrast with the monograph and ISO standard, which contain a mandatory catalog request, fig. 2 adds flexibility by allowing for the creation a catalog object without prior request. Creating a catalog is the exclusive right of a prospective seller, which is represented by the existence dependency of a `Catalog` object on a `Seller` object in the EDG. Similarly, creating a catalog request is the exclusive right of a prospective buyer. Once a catalog request has been sent, the `BusinessTransaction` object's state becomes `planningInService`, and once a catalog has been sent, the `BusinessTransaction` object's state becomes `planningCompleted` regardless of whether a catalog request was sent.

	BusinessTransaction	Buyer	Seller	Shipment	Payment	ShippingNotice	ReceivingReport	RemittanceAdvice	BankTransferNotice	Invoice	Catalog	CatalogRequest
EVcrBusinessTransaction	O/C											
EVendBusinessTransaction	O/E											
requestAvailabilityAndPrice	A/M	A/M		A/M			O/M					
returnAvailabilityAndPrice	A/M		A/M	A/M		O/M						
warrantyInvocation	A/M	A/M		A/M			O/M					
EVcrBuyer		O/C										
EVendBuyer		O/E										
EVcrSeller			O/C									
EVendSeller			O/E									
buyerOffer	A/M	A/M		A/M			O/M					
buyerAcceptOffer	A/M	A/M		A/M			O/M					
sellerOffer	A/M		A/M	A/M		O/M						
sellerAcceptOffer	A/M		A/M	A/M		O/M						
EVcrShipment	A/M			O/C								
EVendShipment	A/M			O/E								
EVcrPayment	A/M				O/C							
EVendPayment	A/M				O/E							
EVcrShippingNotice	A/M		A/M	A/M		O/C						
EVendShippingNotice	A/M		A/M	A/M		O/E						
EVcrReceivingReport	A/M	A/M		A/M			O/C					
EVendReceivingReport	A/M	A/M		A/M			O/E					
EVcrRemittanceAdvice	A/M	A/M			A/M			O/C				
EVendRemittanceAdvice	A/M	A/M			A/M			O/E				
EVcrBankTransferNotice	A/M		A/M		A/M				O/C			
EVendBankTransferNotice	A/M		A/M		A/M				O/E			
EVcrInvoice	A/M		A/M		A/M					O/C		
EVendInvoice	A/M		A/M		A/M					O/E		
advanceShippingNotice	A/M		A/M	A/M		O/M						
sendReceivingReport	A/M	A/M		A/M			O/M					
EVcrCatalog	A/M		A/M								O/C	
EVendCatalog	A/M		A/M								O/E	
EVcrCatalogRequest	A/M	A/M										O/C
EVendCatalogRequest	A/M	A/M										O/E
warrantyGranted	A/M		A/M	A/M		O/M						
warrantyReport	A/M	A/M		A/M			O/M					
decline	A/M			O/M								
quit	A/M			O/E								

Fig. 3. OET for the MERODE Business Transaction Status Model

After completing the planning phase, fig. 2 continues with the identification phase. It shows that a business transaction object's identification phase is initiated by a prospective buyer's availability and price request (i.e. `requestAvailabilityAndPrice`) and completed with the return of availability and price information by the prospective seller (i.e., `returnAvailabilityAndPrice`). The OET in Fig. 3 shows with the presence of an "A/M" that sending such a request is the exclusive right of a buyer object and returning availability and price information that of a seller object. The OET also shows that in the STREAM model, these request and return events are events that modify the state of `ReceivingReport` and `ShippingNotice` objects respectively, which have been conceptualized respectively as the buyer and seller version of the shopping chart in online shopping applications.

The FSM in Fig. 4 also shows that the negotiation phase has an impact on the status of `Shipment` objects. The prospective buyer's availability and price request (i.e. `requestAvailabilityAndPrice`) changes the status of a `Shipment` object to `requested`, and the prospective seller's answer (i.e., `returnAvailabilityAndPrice`) changes its status to `identified`.

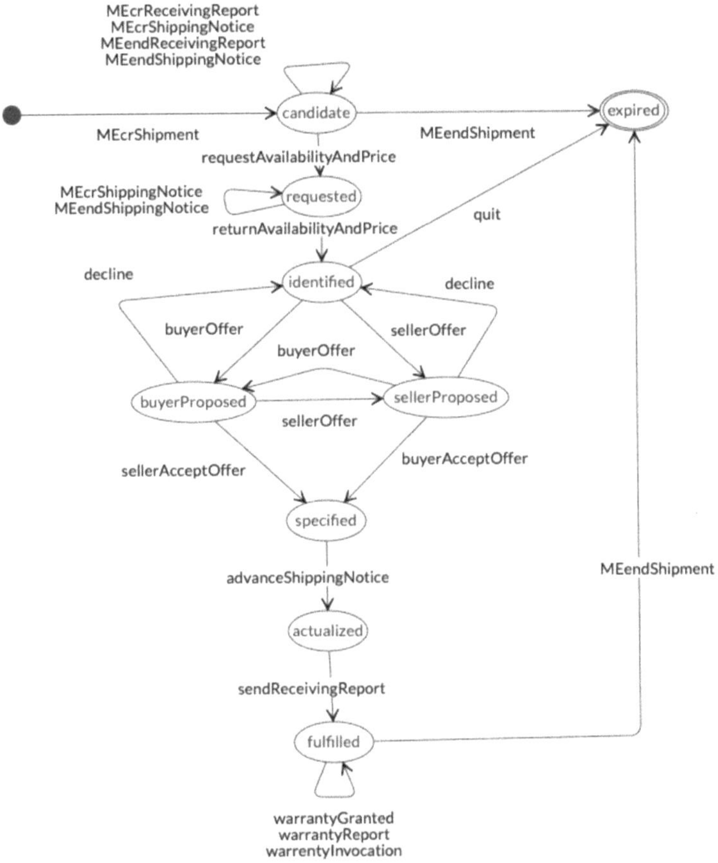

Fig. 4. FSM for shipment objects

The negotiation phase starts with an offer from either the buyer (i.e., `buyerOffer`) or the seller (i.e., `sellerOffer`). The OET shows with an A/M in the column of the `BusinessTransaction` and `Shipment` class that both the seller and buyer offer can change the state of business transaction and shipment objects. The ability of both the seller and buyer to initiate the negotiation phase is inspired by the colored Petri-net model of Horiuchi and Shimizu [4, 5] and resolves a limitation Hunka's [6] model. Where the `BusinessTransaction` object remains in the `inService` state until one of the trading-partners accepts the other partner's offer (i.e., sellerAcceptOffer or buyerAcceptOffer). It is imperative that a trading-partner cannot accept its own offer. Therefore, the state machine of Shipment objects in Fig. 4 keeps track of which partner made the last offer with the buyerProposed and sellerProposed object states. The chosen implementation allows for an infinite number of counteroffers without imposing a single counteroffer. When the prospective seller made the last offer (i.e., sellerProposed), only the prospective buyer can accept (i.e., buyerAcceptOffer) and vice versa. Once an offer has been accepted by the buyer or seller (i.e., buyerAcceptOffer or sellerAcceptOffer), the negotiation phase is completed (see fig. 2), and the shipment specified (see Fig. 4).

Consequently, the actualization phase starts with advancing a shipping notice (i.e., advanceShippingNotice), which changes the state of the transaction to actualizationWaiting. This state is followed by sending a receiving report (i.e., sendReceivingReport), which changes the state to actualizationInService. In this minimalistic model, the creation of a remittance advice does not change the state of the transaction. The actualization phase is then completed by the creation of a bank transfer notice (i.e. crBankTransferNotice), which changes the state of the BusinessTransaction object to actualizationComplete.

When the actualization phase is complete, the buyer has the option to invoke a warranty (i.e. warrantyInvocation), which can be granted by the seller (i.e., warrantyGranted), after which the buyer can acknowledge a correct execution of the warranty (i.e., warrantyReport). Granting a warranty gives rise to new business transactions that each progress through their own identification, negation and actualization phases, independently of the business transaction that gave rise to the warranty.

2.3 Behavioral Conceptual Model: the Shipment and Payment class's FSMs

Where the business transaction object is the central entity in this model, the Shipment and Payment class each received their own state machine as it is necessary to track their state individually. Part of the innovation of the presented model resides in the fact that these state-machines are synchronized with the business transaction state machine through MERODE's event propagation mechanism. In this MERODE model a shipment object refers to the future shipment of an economic resource.

Fig. 4 elaborates fig. 6-2 from the monograph, which is the "UML state machine diagram for Economic Resource Type". It shows that Shipment objects start their lifecycle in the candidate state. Once an availability and price request is sent out, the shipment's state is requested, and when the availability and price information is returned, it is in the identified state (cf. supra). Subsequently, the state machine keeps track of offers and counteroffers (cf. supra), until an offer is accepted. After offer acceptance, the Shipment object is in specified state. A shipment is actualized once a shipping notice is sent out by the seller and fulfilled once the receiving report is sent out by the buyer. Post-actualization has no impact on the state of the initial shipment. Hence the warranty events do not change the state of shipment objects. Where all prior states of the Shipment object align with ISO 15944-4, the fulfilled state is an extension of the ISO state machine in line with the monograph.

Additionally, DEMO's `quit` and `decline` events [7] were added to the `Shipment` class's state machine in response to REA's "happy path" bias. When an offer has been made by either the seller or the buyer, it can be declined by the counterparty or withdrawn by the proposer with the `decline` event, which regresses the `Shipment` object to the `identified` state. From this state new offers can be made, or the negotiations can end through the `quit` event, which bypasses the actualization and post-actualization phases of the according business transaction object (see Fig. 2).

Fig. 5 shows the finite state machine for `Payment` objects. It shows that a newly created `Payment` object starts its lifecycle in a `proposed` state. Once an invoice has been created, which is considered equivalent to sending an invoice in this minimalistic model, the `Payment` object is in the `specified` state. When a remittance advice is issued, the `Payment` object is `inService`, and when the `BankTransferNotice` is received, the `Payment` object is `fulfilled`.

Fig. 5. FSM for payment objects

3 Illustrative Example: Archetypal Business Transaction Scenario

Fig. 6 shows a 'happy path' scenario (i.e., the best scenario possible) for an archetypical business transaction, which elaborates on fig. 4–19 from the monograph, which shows "an example exchange process with phases". It lists a sequence of business events (i.e., the first column of Fig. 6 from top to bottom) that lead a business transaction from the planning stage to the (post-) actualization stage. The purpose of the scenario in Fig. 6 is to illustrate how MERODE's event propagation mechanism automates the synchronization of object states throughout the order process. The event propagation throughout the EDG is shown in the OET (Fig. 3). The scenario in Fig. 6 illustrates this synchronization by showing objects that are created by or states that change because of the execution of a business event in red.

Merode Event	Seller	Buyer	Business Transaction	Catalog Request	Catalog	Shipment	Receiving Report	Shipping Notice	Payment	Invoice	Remittance Advice	Bank Transfer Notice
crSeller	Elmo: exists											
crBuyer	Elmo: exists	Monster: exists										
crBusinessTransaction	Elmo: exists	Monster: exists	Cookie4Cash: planningWaitingStart									
crCatalogRequest	Elmo: exists	Monster: exists	Cookie4Cash: planningInService	CookiesR: exists								
crCatalog	Elmo: exists	Monster: exists	Cookie4Cash: planningCompleted	CookiesR: exists	CookiesC: exists							
crShipment	Elmo: exists	Monster: exists	Cookie4Cash: planningCompleted	CookiesR: exists	CookiesC: exists	CookieT: candidate						
crReceivingReport	Elmo: exists	Monster: exists	Cookie4Cash: planningCompleted	CookiesR: exists	CookiesC: exists	CookieT: candidate	CookieP: exist					
requestAvailabilityAndPrice	Elmo: exists	Monster: exists	Cookie4Cash: identificationInService	CookiesR: exists	CookiesC: exists	CookieT: requested	CookieP: exist					
crShippingNotice	Elmo: exists	Monster: exists	Cookie4Cash: identificationInService	CookiesR: exists	CookiesC: exists	CookieT: requested	CookieP: exists	CookieN: exists				
returnAvailabilityAndPrice	Elmo: exists	Monster: exists	Cookie4Cash: identificationCompleted	CookiesR: exists	CookiesC: exists	CookieT: identified	CookieP: exists	CookieN: exists				
sellerOffer	Elmo: exists	Monster: exists	Cookie4Cash: negotiationInService	CookiesR: exists	CookiesC: exists	CookieT: proposed	CookieP: exists	CookieN: exists				
buyerAcceptOffer	Elmo: exists	Monster: exists	Cookie4Cash: negotiationComplete	CookiesR: exists	CookiesC: exists	CookieT: specified	CookieP: exists	CookieN: exists				
advanceShippingNotice	Elmo: exists	Monster: exists	Cookie4Cash: actualizationWaiting	CookiesR: exists	CookiesC: exists	CookieT: actualized	CookieP: exists	CookieN: exists				
sendReceivingReport	Elmo: exists	Monster: exists	Cookie4Cash: actualizationInService	CookiesR: exists	CookiesC: exists	CookieT: fulfilled	CookieP: exists	CookieN: exists				
crPayment	Elmo: exists	Monster: exists	Cookie4Cash: actualizationInService	CookiesR: exists	CookiesC: exists	CookieT: fulfilled	CookieP: exists	CookieN: exists	CashT: proposed			
crInvoice	Elmo: exists	Monster: exists	Cookie4Cash: actualizationInService	CookiesR: exists	CookiesC: exists	CookieT: fulfilled	CookieP: exists	CookieN: exists	CashT: specified	CashI: exists		
crRemittanceAdvice	Elmo: exists	Monster: exists	Cookie4Cash: actualizationInService	CookiesR: exists	CookiesC: exists	CookieT: fulfilled	CookieP: exists	CookieN: exists	CashT: inService	CashI: exists	CashR: exists	
crBankTransferNotice	Elmo: exists	Monster: exists	Cookie4Cash: actualizationComplete	CookiesR: exists	CookiesC: exists	CookieT: fulfilled	CookieP: exists	CookieN: exists	CashT: fulfilled	CashI: exists	CashR: exists	CashB: exists
warrantyInvocation	Elmo: exists	Monster: exists	Cookie4Cash: postActualizationWaiting	CookiesR: exists	CookiesC: exists	CookieT: fulfilled	CookieP: exists	CookieN: exists	CashT: fulfilled	CashI: exists	CashR: exists	CashB: exists
warrantyGranted	Elmo: exists	Monster: exists	Cookie4Cash: postActualizationInService	CookiesR: exists	CookiesC: exists	CookieT: fulfilled	CookieP: exists	CookieN: exists	CashT: fulfilled	CashI: exists	CashR: exists	CashB: exists
warrantyReport	Elmo: exists	Monster: exists	Cookie4Cash: postActualizationComplete	CookiesR: exists	CookiesC: exists	CookieT: fulfilled	CookieP: exists	CookieN: exists	CashT: fulfilled	CashI: exists	CashR: exists	CashB: exists

Fig. 6. Illustrative business transaction scenario

4 Conclusion

This paper introduced STREAM, a transaction status specification grounded in the REA ontology and implemented through the MERODE model-driven engineering methodology. By defining a synchronized set of FSMs for business transactions and their related artifacts.

The primary contribution of STREAM lies in its explicit and complete specification of transaction lifecycles across all phases identified in ISO 15944, including planning, identification, negotiation, actualization, and post-actualization. Unlike prior approaches, STREAM provides formal state machines not only for successful transaction completion but also for failed negotiations, rollbacks, and transaction restarts. Through MERODE's event propagation mechanism, the model guarantees consistent state synchronization across transactions, shipments, and payments, thereby unifying artifact-centric and process-centric perspectives within a single coherent framework.

Beyond serving as an implementation of existing standards, STREAM contributes back to REA's body of knowledge by refining and extending transaction state semantics where ISO 15944-4 remains underspecified. In particular, the inclusion of explicit actualization and post-actualization state machines, as well as support for iterative offer–counteroffer negotiation, positions STREAM as a pragmatic yet theoretically grounded reference model for future REA-based systems.

Finally, STREAM is intentionally designed as a reusable and extensible template rather than a closed solution. Its role within a broader research agenda — most notably the ontology weaving [8] of independently developed REA aspect models such as REA^2 [9] — underscores its potential to function as a foundational building block for interoperable, standardized business information systems. As such, STREAM represents a step toward executable REA specifications that are not only conceptually sound, but also directly applicable in modern, distributed digital infrastructures.

Acknowledgments. **Jesper Kiehn**, for proofreading an earlier version of this manuscript.

This work was supported by the Fund for the Promotion of Joint International Research (Fostering Joint International Research (B)) of the Japan Society for the Promotion of Science (JSPS) under Grant Number **19KK0037**.

Disclorsure of interests.

The authors have no competing interests to declare that are relevant to the content of this article.

References

1. ISO/IEC: Information technology - Business Operational View Part 4: Business transaction scenario - Accounting and economic ontology (2007)
2. Snoeck, M.: Enterprise Information Systems Engineering: The MERODE Approach, 1st edn. Springer (2014)
3. McCarthy, W.E., Geerts, G.L., Gal, G.: The REA Accounting Model as an Accounting and Economic Ontology (2022)
4. Shimizu, S.: Rethinking counter-offers in the negotiation transaction process (in Japanese). CHUO Business Review. **45**, 59–74 (2024)
5. Horiuchi, S.: Amplifying business transaction state machine with LAP: through complementary using of DEMO and REA. J. Inf. Manag. **40**(4), 56–71 (2020)
6. Hunka, F., Zacek, J.: A new view of REA state machine. Appl. Ontol. **10**(1), 25–39 (2015)
7. Dietz, J.L.G.: The atoms, molecules and fibers of organizations. Data Knowl. Eng. **47**(3), 301–325 (2003)
8. Scheller, C.V.. Hruby, P.: No-code application development using ontology weaver. In: Proceedings of the 16th International Workshop on Value Modeling and Business Ontologies (VBMO2022), CEUR (**1613**), 73, Leuven (2022)
9. Laurier, W., Horiuchi, S., Snoeck, M.: An executable axiomatization of the REA^2 ontology. J. Inf. Syst. **35**(3), 133–154 (2021)

A Conceptual Model to Enhance Process Mining Analysis with Provenance

Álvaro Bernal-Caunedo[1](✉), Marco Franceschetti[1], Hagen Völzer[1], Manuel Resinas[2], and Barbara Weber[1]

[1] University of St. Gallen, St. Gallen, Switzerland
{alvaro.bernalcaunedo,marco.franceschetti,hagen.voelzer, barbara.weber}@unisg.ch
[2] Universidad de Sevilla, Seville, Spain
resinas@us.es

Abstract. Process mining relies on event data to analyze and improve business processes. The exploratory and non-linear nature of these analyses makes it difficult to understand, validate, compare, and communicate how findings are produced, limiting their business value. Existing provenance techniques focus on data lineage but lack support for systematic comparison of analyses, modular reuse of analysis steps, and comprehensive execution tracking. To address these limitations, we systematically derive a set of requirements and acceptance criteria based on established analytic provenance purposes. We further contribute a structured comparison of state-of-the-art provenance models, revealing critical gaps in comparative capabilities, reusability, and execution tracking. Based on these insights, we propose a conceptual provenance model tailored to exploratory process mining that supports branching analysis paths, comparison of analysis histories and states, reusability of analysis steps, and transparent representation of data evolution.

Keywords: Exploratory Process Mining · Analytic Provenance · Conceptual Model

1 Introduction

Process mining is widely used to analyze and improve processes based on event data [10]. In practice, analyses are rarely linear, requiring analysts to iteratively filter event logs, adjust parameters, apply different techniques, and compare alternative results [14]. This exploratory nature makes it difficult to understand, validate, and communicate how analysis outcomes (e.g., business rule violations, temporal constraint deviations) are produced.

Provenance techniques address these challenges by capturing analysis history and supporting analytical needs such as recalling prior steps, replicating results, exploring alternative paths, and communicating findings [8]. Building on these established provenance purposes, this work derives requirements tailored

© The Author(s), under exclusive license to Springer Nature Switzerland AG 2027
A. Bernasconi et al. (Eds.): ER 2026, LNCS 17081, pp. 473–483, 2027.
https://doi.org/10.1007/978-3-032-40795-5_31

to exploratory process mining. Acceptance criteria operationalize these requirements, ensuring they are conceptually grounded and practically verifiable.

Applying these criteria in a literature review shows that existing approaches focus primarily on basic data lineage and linear workflows. They exhibit critical gaps in four areas: comprehensive execution tracking (i.e., tracking the agent and execution environment of each operation), which limits reliable reproducibility, systematic comparison of alternatives, inspection of how intermediate data states evolve over time, and seamless reuse of analytical steps. Furthermore, branching support relies on informal mechanisms [2,4,7,11].

Based on these insights, we propose a conceptual provenance model tailored to exploratory process mining. The model explicitly supports branching analysis paths, systematic comparison of analysis histories and states, reuse of analysis steps, and transparent representation of data evolution. In doing so, it addresses the limitations of existing approaches and enables more effective exploration, validation, and communication of analysis processes.

The paper is structured as follows. Section 2 introduces core concepts like analytic provenance and its purposes, and formalizes the requirements, mapping them to provenance purposes and establishing acceptance criteria to compare provenance models. Section 3 reviews literature to identify gaps based on these requirements. Section 4 introduces our provenance model and its creation methodology. Section 5 discusses limitations and concludes with future work.

2 Requirements and Acceptance Criteria

To systematically derive a provenance model that meets the needs identified above, we first ground our understanding in analytic provenance and its objectives. Analytic provenance adapts general provenance principles to explicitly capture the analysis history, recording the sequence of analysis steps and their corresponding findings during exploratory data analysis [8]. In such settings, analysts iteratively refine their approach, compare alternative paths, and examine how data evolves over time. These activities motivate the need to understand the objectives of analytic provenance. We therefore ground our approach in an established classification of six analytic provenance purposes [8] that apply broadly to data analysis rather than specifically to exploratory process mining: *recall* (recovering awareness of current and previous analysis states), *presentation* (communicating insights to external stakeholders), *meta-analysis* (reviewing the analytic process to improve it), *replication* (reproducing a previous analysis), *action recovery* (undo/redo and branching of actions), and *collaborative communication* (sharing the analysis with others). Their full definitions are provided in the online appendix [1]. Within these purposes, our approach is scoped to objective operational data, excluding the subjective facets such as free-text annotations detailing the analyst's reasoning, hypotheses, or intents.

Based on these purposes, we derive a set of requirements for a provenance model tailored to exploratory process mining. To ground them, we first define the core structural components of an analytical workflow. An *analysis state* captures a complete snapshot at a specific point (data objects, intermediate results, parameters, and context). Workflows transition between states via an *operation* (the abstract definition of a task), whose concrete execution by an agent or system is recorded as an *analysis step*. The set of alternating states and steps forms an *analysis history* that may diverge into independent *branches* that share a common origin but maintain distinct subsequent states and dependencies.

To derive the requirements, we operationalize the mechanics necessary to fulfill each purpose in an exploratory environment. For example, action recovery (the user's need to undo actions and explore alternatives) is operationalized into *Traceability of Analysis Steps* and *Branching Capability*. Mapping these purposes to the workflow components yields the following core requirements:

R1: Traceability of Analysis Steps. The provenance model shall trace every step and state back to its originating data through the complete set of dependencies and the ordering of analysis steps, including all intermediate states, operations, parameter configurations and the agents or systems involved.

R2: Reproducibility. The provenance model shall capture all required components (input data versions, parameter configurations, and the execution environment) to enable the reliable re-execution of an analysis in identical conditions to obtain equivalent results.

R3: Branching Capability. The provenance model shall represent branching analysis histories by capturing independent analysis paths, their divergence points, and their ancestry relationships, ensuring that subsequent states and dependencies remain distinct across branches while preserving their common origin.

R4: Reusability of Analysis Steps. The provenance model shall represent a set of analysis steps as parameterizable pipelines and capture their structure (including operations, their ordering, dependencies, and configurations) to enable their identification, referencing for reuse and adaptation to different contexts.

R5: Support for Comparison of Analysis Histories. The provenance model shall represent analysis histories in a structured and transparent manner, including abstraction levels that group or categorize detailed analysis steps. This representation shall enable the systematic identification of similarities and differences in data selection, operations, and parameter configurations between multiple analysis histories, supporting meta-analysis through structured, side-by-side examination across histories that are not directly identical.

R6: Support for Comparison of Analysis States. The provenance model shall represent analysis states and defined abstractions of these states to enable the comparison of similarities and differences in their associated data. These abstractions shall capture relevant aspects or summaries (e.g., aggregated metrics, distributions, or feature-based representations) to support comparison when direct comparison is impractical due to complexity or dimensionality.

R7: Data Evolution Transparency. The provenance model shall represent the transformation lifecycle of data objects, such that each state transition can be examined in terms of the applied operations and the resulting changes in the data (e.g., event logs, models, KPIs).

As detailed in Table 1, each provenance purpose is supported by a specific subset of our requirements: foundational goals such as recall and presentation rely primarily on traceability and data evolution transparency, whereas operational functions like action recovery and collaborative communication additionally depend on branching and history comparison. More complex objectives such as meta-analysis and replication require reproducibility, reusability, and the comparison of states or histories.

Table 1. Correlation between provenance purposes and model requirements.

Purpose	Requirements
Recall	Traceability, Data Evolution Transparency
Presentation	Traceability, Comparison of Analysis States, Data Evolution Transparency
Meta-analysis	Traceability, Reusability of Analysis Steps, Comparison of Analysis Histories, Comparison of Analysis States
Replication	Reproducibility, Branching Capability, Reusability of Analysis Steps
Action Recovery	Traceability, Branching Capability
Collaborative Communication	Traceability, Comparison of Analysis Histories

To perform an analytical comparison of the provenance models, each requirement is operationalized through a set of acceptance criteria defined as verifiable conditions. For example, one criterion for *Traceability of Analysis Steps* requires that, *given an analysis step, the provenance model must capture and link the exact operations performed and their precise parameter configurations to the corresponding step*. The complete set of 20 acceptance criteria for all remaining requirements is provided in [1]. These criteria are used to verify whether existing approaches meet the established requirements.

3 Literature Review and Comparative Analysis

To systematically identify and analyze relevant state-of-the-art approaches, our literature review was guided by the established methodology proposed by Kitchenham [5]. It was driven by the research question: to what extent do existing provenance models satisfy the requirements for exploratory process mining analysis? Using Scopus with the keywords "Provenance Model" and "Analytic Provenance", the search yielded 57 occurrences; after a screening phase and a manual snowballing search [12], we obtained a final corpus of 48 papers. To ensure reproducibility and transparency, the detailed source selection, exclusion criteria, and snowballing procedure are provided alongside a BPMN model of the entire review procedure in [1].

Following the initial retrieval, a rigorous screening phase was conducted to isolate the studies most pertinent to our research objectives. We applied strict exclusion criteria to (i) discard papers that focused exclusively on domain-specific applications of provenance, (ii) surveys or semantic integration studies lacking concrete provenance models, and (iii) any articles where the full text was not available. After applying these filters, the remaining 32 papers advanced to the detailed data extraction stage. To ensure the comprehensiveness of our review and to capture foundational or highly relevant works potentially missed by the primary query, we complemented our methodology with a manual snowballing search [12]. This iterative process of examining references and citations identified an additional 16 papers, which were re-evaluated using the same screening and verification procedures to ensure full compliance with our requirements before being synthesized into the final analytical corpus.

With the final corpus of 48 papers established, we systematically assessed the state-of-the-art against our derived requirements. Because two of these papers were direct extensions of other works within the corpus, our evaluation ultimately focused on 46 distinct models. Each proposed approach was evaluated and classified for every requirement as either "Fully Supported", "Partially Supported" or "Not Supported". Specifically, if a model satisfies all acceptance criteria of a requirement, it is considered "Fully Supported". If it meets at least one acceptance criterion but fails others (e.g., when checking the traceability of analysis steps, the model tracks the sequence but lacks agent tracking or distinct parameter configurations), it is classified as "Partially Supported". If it meets none of the acceptance criteria, it is considered "Not Supported". To mitigate subjectivity, all classifications were independently reviewed by a second author, and disagreements were resolved through discussion. Detailed justifications and the underlying evidence for these classifications are provided in [1]. To visually synthesize these findings, Table 2 presents a comparison of our proposed model alongside the six approaches that most comprehensively fulfill the requirements, ordered by their overall degree of fulfillment. This table utilizes Harvey Balls to represent the classification levels (a filled circle indicates full support, a half-filled circle indicates partial support, and an empty circle signifies no support). The extended table detailing the evaluation of all 46 approaches is provided in [1].

Table 2. Partial comparison of approaches based on provenance requirements (● = fully supported; ◐ = partially supported; ○ = not supported)

Requirement	**Our model**	[13]	[9]	[2]	[6, 7]	[4]	[11]
Traceability of A. Steps	●	●	●	●	●	●	●
Reproducibility	●	◐	◐	●	◐	●	○
Branching Capability	●	●	◐	◐	●	◐	●
Reusability of A. Steps	●	◐	●	◐	◐	●	○
Support for Comparison of A. Histories	●	●	●	●	◐	○	○
Support for Comparison of A. States	●	●	◐	◐	◐	○	●
Data Evolution Transparency	●	◐	◐	◐	◐	◐	●

The review reveals that Traceability of Analysis Steps is the most consistently supported feature (20 of 46 fully, 26 partially), whereas the model's headline capabilities remain weakly supported across three fronts. First, comparison is the most critical gap: comparing analysis states is supported only by 16 of 46 models (only 7 full), as models represent states without the schemas or structural constructs needed to compare high-dimensional data, and comparison of full histories is likewise largely unsupported (18 none, 7 full), since models lack the structural abstractions to represent multiple paths for systematic, side-by-side comparison. Second, reusability is a major gap (21 none, 8 full): many models function strictly as logging tools for past executions, with no mechanisms to represent uninstantiated, parameterizable pipelines that analysts could extract and reuse. Third, comprehensive execution tracking is poorly supported (only 7 of 46 fully support reproducibility and a mere 3 provide full data evolution transparency) as models log operations and parameters but lack mechanisms to capture the complete runtime environment for reliable replay or to record the incremental, step-by-step changes between data states. Branching is only partially addressed, typically through annotations to track divergent decisions rather than an inherent ability to manage independent branches. Overall, because existing models act primarily as passive logging mechanisms, they misalign with the iterative, non-linear nature of exploratory process mining, leaving analysts unable to branch alternative hypotheses, compare divergent states, or handle the high-dimensional data that characterizes process mining analyses. To address these gaps, the next section presents our conceptual model, purposefully designed to satisfy our derived requirements and enable complex exploratory workflows.

4 A Conceptual Model to Enhance Process Mining Analysis with Provenance

This section presents the conceptual model for capturing analytic provenance in exploratory process mining. Section 4.1 derives the model's components from the requirements, Sect. 4.2 defines the core analytical entities, and Sect. 4.3 presents the formalized model with its structural mechanics and relationships.

4.1 Methodology

We employed a grammar-based derivation to transition from textual requirements to a conceptual model. Prior research indicates that applying such grammatical analysis to requirements engineering artifacts can significantly improve the completeness and accuracy of derived conceptual models [3]. Accordingly, nouns and noun phrases identified candidate entities and attributes, while verbs and relational expressions informed interactions and dependencies; this initial derivation was then refined by domain-specific modeling decisions.

This enabled traceable extraction of domain objects; for example, *R3* nouns ("analysis histories", "branches", "states"), informed entities like *AnalysisHistory*, *AnalysisBranch*, *AnalysisState* and *ArtifactState*, while verbs and relational phrasing yielded the model's structural relationships. This parsing ensured the extraction of the model's core objects (defined in Sect. 4.3). Furthermore, we iteratively refined this derivation process to achieve a comprehensive model.

4.2 Core Entities

The core of our conceptual provenance model is anchored by the *AnalysisHistory*, which encapsulates the entire lifecycle of an analytical process. To address *R3*, this history is structurally decomposed into independent *AnalysisBranch* paths. The progression within each branch is recorded as a sequence of immutable *AnalysisState* instances, which are bridged by active *AnalysisStep* executions. Each step represents the concrete application of a specific *Operation* (e.g., filters, attribute derivations), which is further classified by an *OperationType* and a broader *StepCategory* (e.g., log enrichment, process discovery). These operations are performed by an *Agent* within a precisely captured *RuntimeEnvironment*. To satisfy *R1* and *R2*, every step documents the exact configuration applied, linking concrete *ParameterValue* instances to their overarching *Parameter* definitions.

At the granular data level, an *AnalysisState* represents a holistic snapshot of the overall analysis at a specific point in time. It acts as a container that can encompass one or more *ArtifactState* instances, which are themselves immutable snapshots of specific artifacts (e.g., event logs, process models) utilized or generated during the analysis. To support *R7*, the model employs a *Delta* construct, designed as an abstract class to accommodate various subclasses (e.g., *DataFrameDelta*). These subclasses explicitly capture the specific, incremental structural modifications and transformations occurring between states by linking a root *ArtifactState* to an updated *ArtifactState*. By establishing this direct link, the model facilitates the generation of artifact-specific deltas, allowing for precise tracking of changes tailored to the type and structure of each artifact. Additionally, the diagram visually abstracts *Delta* as a single conceptual entity, omitting its underlying artifact-specific subclasses (e.g., *DataFrameDelta*). Direct comparison of raw analysis states is frequently impractical due to their size, complexity, and heterogeneity. To address this challenge and support *R5* and *R6*, the model introduces *StateAbstraction*, which provides comparable summaries or aggregated representations (e.g., trace variant distributions, performance metrics, or feature-based representations) of distinct states and overarching histories. Finally, to fulfill *R4*, sets of operations can be combined into modular *PipelineFragment* entities. Rather than treating an entire reusable workflow as a single, rigid sequence, utilizing fragments allows analysts to capture and reuse interchangeable sets of independent analysis steps, which can even be drawn from different branches. Furthermore, fragments extracted from several distinct analysis histories can be flexibly aggregated to compose a single pipeline. Within a pipeline of reusable steps, the specific operations executed are managed by explicit *Version* entities, ensuring that the lineage, structural integrity, and adaptability of reusable components are maintained across diverse execution contexts.

4.3 Conceptual Model

The formalized conceptual model is depicted as a UML class diagram in Fig. 1. This model is designed to capture the dynamic nature of exploratory analysis, enforcing an immutable and tree-based execution flow. We focus on a tree structure because it accurately reflects the chronological and step-by-step branching history of the analysis, providing a natural representation of how an analyst investigates alternative hypotheses over time without overwriting previous steps. In essence, an *AnalysisHistory* acts as the root container, aggregating one or more *AnalysisBranch* entities. This composition allows the model to capture parallel analysis paths without overwriting previous work (*R3*), with each branch explicitly tracking its structural origin via a *startsAt* relationship to its originating analysis state. Within a given branch, the analytical progression is modeled as a composition of static *AnalysisState* nodes and active *AnalysisStep* transitions.

The model differentiates between input and output (made possible by explicit relationships between *AnalysisStep* and *AnalysisState*) to maintain a traceable exploratory process mining workflow (*R1*). An *AnalysisStep* consumes exactly one source *AnalysisState* and produces exactly one target *AnalysisState*. To document the evolution of the data (*R7*), the step produces instances of *Delta* entities. To capture the exact transformation, this abstract entity is extended into artifact-specific subclasses (e.g., *DataFrameDelta*). Each *AnalysisState* encapsulates data through *ArtifactState* objects, acting as snapshots of overarching conceptual *Artifact* entities and utilizing specific metadata (*checksum*, *sizeBytes*, *contentRef*, and *mimeType*) to enable precise tracking and retrieval of data. Additionally, each state defines *StateAbstraction* entities, which use designated *functions* to facilitate comparison (*R5* and *R6*).

To support reproducibility (*R2*), every *AnalysisStep* is linked to the *Agent* that performed it and the *RuntimeEnvironment* (capturing specific *toolVersion* and *libraryVersions*). The underlying functional logic is encapsulated by an *Operation*, which is structurally classified by an *OperationType* (e.g., attribute derivation) and a broader *StepCategory* (e.g., enrichment). Operations are tightly coupled with their configurations: an *Operation* aggregates an ordered set of *Parameter* definitions (specifying data *type*, *required* flags, and *default* values), which are concretely instantiated by the precise *ParameterValue* entities logged during a specific *AnalysisStep*. For readability, the specific parameters used as inputs for an *AnalysisStep*, such as an *ArtifactState*, are not shown.

Reusability (*R4*) is structurally enforced through a composite workflow design. Rather than representing workflows as rigid monoliths, a *Pipeline* orderedly aggregates *PipelineFragment* entities. These fragments define specific sets of *AnalysisStep*s that function as reusable templates within a *Pipeline*. While *AnalysisStep*s are typically associated with *AnalysisState*s through input and output relationships, these associations are optional within fragments. This

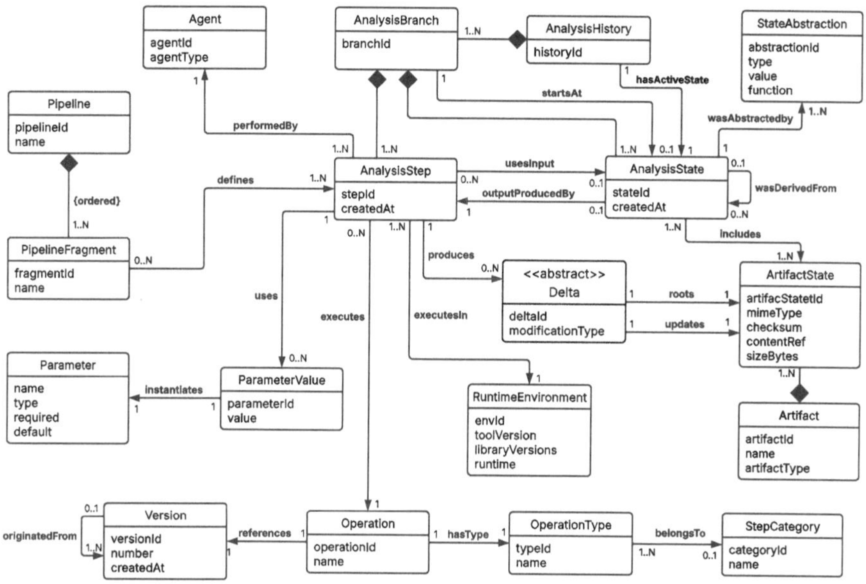

Fig. 1. Provenance Conceptual Model for Exploratory Process Mining.

allows independent steps from different branches to be grouped without enforcing a rigid internal sequence. It is only within the overarching *Pipeline* that these fragments are strictly ordered. This design allows granular analytical subroutines to be independently reused and adapted across different pipelines. Governance over both individual operations and pipelines is maintained by referencing *Version* entities, which capture creation timestamps and hierarchical lineage (*originatedFrom*).

5 Conclusion and Future Work

The proposed conceptual model provides a new understanding of analytic provenance by formalizing the highly iterative and non-linear realities of exploratory process mining. Designed to fulfill all derived requirements, it addresses gaps identified in the literature regarding the comparison of analysis histories and states, the modular reuse of analysis steps, and comprehensive execution tracking. While our approach shares similarities with models such as Flowris [9], FORSETI [11], Chimera [4], and Urbanite [6], and directly adapts mechanisms from related branching research [13], it extends that branching mechanism with dedicated structural constructs for the modular reuse of pipeline fragments and the systematic comparison of analysis histories and states (capabilities absent from these prior models). Future interactive tools built on this model will elevate provenance from a static log into an active structural enabler.

Despite these advancements, several limitations guide our future research. First, we will implement this conceptual foundation into a tool and carry out a thorough validation, including a qualitative evaluation with process mining experts to assess the usefulness and completeness of the captured provenance, together with comparative studies against existing tools. We will further extend it to process-specific operations such as discovery and alignment, and to Object-Centric Event Logs (OCEL). Second, we will enhance the model's practical utility by integrating human-centric annotations so analysts can record alternative hypotheses, and by embedding the model within an assisted approach that lowers its adoption complexity through explainability and reuse-based guidance. Additionally, we will develop tree pruning algorithms, which are necessary to simplify complex exploratory paths and communicate findings clearly to stakeholders. By satisfying requirements grounded in fundamental analytic provenance purposes, this work provides the necessary structural foundation to support transparency and rigor in complex exploratory workflows.

Acknowledgments. The work of M. Resinas is part of the project PID2024-156482NB-I00 funded by MICIU/AEI/10.13039/501100011033 and by ERDF/EU.

References

1. Bernal-Caunedo, Á., Franceschetti, M., Völzer, H., Resinas, M., Weber, B.: A conceptual model to enhance process mining analysis with provenance (2026). https://doi.org/10.5281/zenodo.21373047
2. Chapman, A.P., Jagadish, H.V., Ramanan, P.: Efficient provenance storage. In: Proceedings of the 2008 ACM SIGMOD International Conference on Management of data, pp. 993–1006 (2008)
3. Dalpiaz, F., Gieske, P., Sturm, A.: On deriving conceptual models from user requirements: an empirical study. Inf. Softw. Technol. **131**, 106484 (2021)
4. Foster, I., Vockler, J., Wilde, M., Zhao, Y.: Chimera: a virtual data system for representing, querying, and automating data derivation. In: Proceedings of 14th International Conference on Scientific and Statistical Database Management, pp. 37–46. IEEE (2002)
5. Kitchenham, B., Charters, S.: Guidelines for performing systematic literature reviews in software engineering. Tech. Rep. EBSE-2007-01, Keele University and University of Durham (2007)
6. Moreira, G., Ferreira, L., Veiga, C., Hosseini, M., Miranda, F.: Urbanite: a dataflow-based framework for human-AI interactive alignment in urban visual analytics. IEEE Trans. Vis. Comput. Graph. **32**(1), 1065–1075 (2026)
7. Moreira, G., et al.: Curio: a dataflow-based framework for collaborative urban visual analytics. IEEE Trans. Vis. Comput. Graph. **31**(1), 1224–1234 (2025)
8. Ragan, E.D., Endert, A., Sanyal, J., Chen, J.: Characterizing provenance in visualization and data analysis: an organizational framework of provenance types and purposes. IEEE Trans. Vis. Comput. Graph. **22**(1), 31–40 (2015)
9. Sun, J., Wang, J., Chen, Y., Qin, X.: Flowris: managing data analysis workflows for conversational agent. In: Lecture Notes in Computer Science. vol. 13946 LNCS, pp. 724–728 (2023)
10. Van Der Aalst, W.: Process mining: overview and opportunities. ACM Trans. Manag. Inf. Syst. **3**(2), 1–17 (2012)

11. Wang, B., et al.: Forseti: a visual analysis environment enabling provenance awareness for the accountability of e-autopsy reports. Visual Inform. **6**(3), 69–80 (2022)
12. Wohlin, C.: Guidelines for snowballing in systematic literature studies and a replication in software engineering. In: Proceedings of the 18th International Conference on Evaluation and Assessment in Software Engineering (2014)
13. Zerbato, F., Burattin, A., Völzer, H., Becker, P.N., Boscaini, E., Weber, B.: Supporting provenance and data awareness in exploratory process mining. In: International Conference on Advanced Information Systems Engineering, pp. 454–470. Springer (2023)
14. Zerbato, F., et al.: Initial insights into exploratory process mining practices. In: International Conference on Business Process Management, pp. 145–161. Springer (2021)

Optimizing Compliance Violation Resolution in Business Process Models

Marisol Barrientos[1(✉)], Karolin Winter[2], and Stefanie Rinderle-Ma[1]

[1] School of Computation, Information and Technology, Technical University of Munich, Garching, Germany
{marisol.barrientos,stefanie.rinderle-ma}@tum.de

[2] Department of Industrial Engineering and Innovation Sciences, Eindhoven University of Technology, Eindhoven, The Netherlands
k.m.winter@tue.nl

Abstract. Ensuring regulatory compliance of business process models remains challenging, with existing approaches focusing primarily on violation detection rather than resolution. To address this gap, this paper presents the Process Tree Repair (PTRepair), a framework for generating, applying, and assessing resolution strategies for compliance violations in business process models. PTRepair combines Large Language Model-based generation of candidate resolution strategies with rule-based process model transformations to ensure consistent and reproducible adaptations of process trees. The generated strategies are then assessed based on structural and behavioral soundness, resolution effectiveness, contextual consistency, change cost, and change location, enabling users to compare and select the most suitable alternative. An evaluation across business process models from different application domains demonstrates that PTRepair generates valid, high-quality resolution strategies that support compliance-aware process redesign.

Keywords: Business Process Compliance · Process Change Patterns · Process Compliance Optimization · Compliance Violation Resolution

1 Introduction

Business process compliance refers to ensuring that business processes satisfy compliance requirements and includes tasks such as compliance modeling, checking, analysis, and enactment [13]. Research has predominantly focused on representing [28] and verifying compliance requirements, more recently leveraging Large Language Models (LLMs) [5]. While these techniques effectively identify compliance violations, comparatively less attention has been given to resolving them [18]. Many approaches resolve violations only during or after execution, when operational, financial, or legal consequences may already have occurred, motivating design-time compliance resolution.

Design-time compliance resolution has been addressed through planning-based restructuring [2, 19], model-checking and pattern-based repair [8, 10], Petri-net repair and synthesis [20], logic-based repair [21], and process adaptation

© The Author(s), under exclusive license to Springer Nature Switzerland AG 2027
A. Bernasconi et al. (Eds.): ER 2026, LNCS 17081, pp. 484–494, 2027.
https://doi.org/10.1007/978-3-032-40795-5_32

techniques [23]. However, these approaches exhibit four major limitations. First, they primarily address control-flow compliance while providing limited support for data-, resource-, and temporal-related perspectives, potentially introducing inconsistencies (e.g., deleting an activity whose produced data is still required elsewhere). Second, they typically generate only a single repair alternative and often restrict changes to simple insert or delete operations, despite multiple valid resolutions frequently existing for the same violation. Third, they provide limited automated assessment of repair quality, making it difficult to compare alternative resolutions with respect to change cost, structural preservation, and compliance effectiveness. Finally, they often assume that suitable change locations or process states are already known, offering limited semantic support for identifying where modifications should be applied and reducing applicability in dynamic regulatory environments with evolving regulations or previously unseen activities.

Recent advances in LLMs have enabled conversational process redesign from natural-language requests [14]. Motivated by this progress, this paper proposes PTRepair, an LLM-assisted framework for design-time compliance violation resolution. PTRepair combines LLM-based generation of alternative resolution strategies with deterministic validation, automatic application of process model changes, and quality assessment metrics to ensure applicability, preserve structural and behavioral soundness, and compare candidate repairs. Specifically, this paper addresses the following research questions: **RQ1:** How can LLMs generate resolution strategies for compliance violations? **RQ2:** How can generated resolution strategies be automatically validated and applied to business process models? **RQ3:** How can resolution strategies be automatically assessed using quality metrics? The required background concepts are introduced in Sect. 2, PTRepair is presented in Sect. 3, the evaluation is reported in Sect. 4, and concluding remarks are given in Sect. 5.

2 PTRepair: Background

PTRepair represents business processes as Process Structure Trees (PSTs) [25] for their formal guarantees and precise change localization:

Definition 1 (Process Structure Tree). *A PST is a finite, rooted, ordered tree* $PST = (N, E, r, \lambda)$*, where:* N *is a finite set of nodes,* $E \subseteq N \times N$ *is a set of parent-child edges,* $r \in N$ *is the root,* $\lambda : N \rightarrow T$ *is a labeling function assigning each node a node type from the set* $T = \{activity, sequence, exclusive, parallel, loop\}$. *Nodes may store data elements, assigned resources, and temporal constraints.*

A *compliance requirement* (CR) specifies a condition that a process must satisfy. Compliance requirements are represented as Abstract Syntax Trees (ASTs) [16], encoding compliance patterns (e.g., `directly_follows`, `absence`, `activity_sends`) and process elements evaluated over a PST. Evaluating an AST over a PST determines whether the process complies with the requirement or identifies one or more compliance violations. Formally, a compliance violation is defined as $CV_{PST} := (CR, AE, desc)$, where CR is the violated requirement, AE the affected process elements, and $desc$ a explanation. Table 1 presents the running example as a PST fragment together with its description.

Table 1. Fuel Process as a Process Structure Tree

Process Structure Tree	Description

`sequence`
`|- act: Measure Quality`
`|- xor [type = regular]`
`| |- act: Regular Vendor`
`| |- act: Emergency Vendor`
`|- act: Send Payment`
	The process first performs *Measure Quality*, then selects either a *Regular* or an *Emergency Vendor*, and finally *Sends Payment*. The requirement that *Measure Quality* follows *Emergency Vendor* is violated because *Measure Quality* precedes it.

Compliance violations are detected using the Process Tree Verifier (PTV) [16]. Once detected, they can either be reported to users or addressed by repairing the process model. In this work, we consider the latter and define a *resolution strategy* as a sequence of process change operations op that transforms a process tree PST into a compliant process tree PST', i.e., $op(PST, params) = PST'$. For example, `insert(PST,{X,serial,A})` inserts activity X serially after activity A. Process trees are particularly suitable for such transformations because soundness can be verified locally on tree fragments. A total of 22 process change operations supported by the PTRepair are presented in Table 2.

Table 2. Process change operations

Category	Operation Label (ID)
Activity-Level	insert (cp1), delete (cp2), move (cp3), swap (cp5), copy (cp14), merge (cp16), split (cp15), rename (LP6)
Control-Flow	sequence to parallel (cp9), parallel to sequence ($cp9^{-1}$), embed in conditional branch (cp10), remove branch (cp17), embed pre-loop (cp8.1), embed post-loop (cp8.2), remove loop embedding ($cp8^{-1}$), modify conditional branch / loop (cp13)
Data	modify read (opd1), modify write (opd2), add write (opd3), remove write (opd4)
Resource	modify resource (opr1)
Temporal	modify timeout (opt1)

The framework adopts all activity- and control-flow-related operations from [14], except *Replace Process Fragment* (cp4), which requires semantically appropriate replacement fragments and user interaction; *Extract Sub Process* (cp6) and *Inline Sub Process* (cp7), which affect process modularization rather than compliance behavior; *Add Control Dependency* (cp11), *Remove Control Dependency* (cp12), and *Leave Single Branch* (cp18), whose effects can be expressed through supported operations; and *Replace Gateways* (cp19), which combines multiple control-flow modifications. Instead, PTRepair represents gateway adaptations through the explicit operations *sequence to parallel* (cp9) and *parallel to sequence* ($cp9^{-1}$), and introduces *remove loop embedding* ($cp8^{-1}$) to represent loop removal. The framework further extends the taxonomy with data- [22], resource-, and temporal-related operations. The original operations are derived from the change patterns in [26]. In Table 2, adopted operations are shown without highlighting, whereas newly introduced operations are highlighted in yellow .

A *resolution strategy* for a compliance violation CV of process tree PST is defined as a sequence of process change operations $RS_{CV} = \langle op_1, \ldots, op_n \rangle$, yielding the repaired process tree $PST' = op_n(\cdots op_2(op_1(PST))\cdots)$. Table 3 illustrates three alternative strategies for the running example. Although all restore compliance, they differ in their effects on the process. For example, RS1 measures quality only for emergency vendors, RS2 performs unnecessary measurements, and RS3 may introduce new compliance or functional violations. PTRepair therefore considers a *resolution context RC*, which specifies constraints that must be preserved during process adaptation.

Table 3. Candidate resolution strategies and updated PSTs

<table>
<tr><th>Resolution Strategy 1</th><th>Resolution Strategy 2</th><th>Resolution Strategy 3</th></tr>
<tr><td>Delete ‘Measure Quality’, embed ‘Measure Quality’ in the xor after ‘Emergency Vendor’</td><td>Move ‘Measure Quality’ before ‘Send Payment’</td><td>Move ‘Measure Quality’ after ‘Send Payment’</td></tr>
<tr><td>sequence
|~~act: Measure Quality~~
|- xor [type = regular]
| |- act: Regular Vendor
| |- sequence
| |- act: Emergency Vendor
| ‘- act: Measure Quality
|- act: Send Payment</td><td>sequence
|~~act: Measure Quality~~
|- xor [type = regular]
| |- act: Regular Vendor
| |- act: Emergency Vendor
|- act: Measure Quality
|- act: Send Payment</td><td>sequence
|~~-act: Measure Quality~~
|- xor [type = regular]
| |- act: Regular Vendor
| |- act: Emergency Vendor
|- act: Send Payment
|- act: Measure Quality</td></tr>
</table>

A *resolution context* (*RC*) specifies compliance requirements and process constraints that must remain preserved during process adaptation. It is represented as ASTs describing compliance requirements other than the violated one and additional business process constraints. In the running example, $RC = precedence(\text{Measure Quality}, \text{Send Payment})$, making Resolution Strategies 1 and 2 valid, whereas Resolution Strategy 3 violates the resolution context.

3 PTRepair: Framework

Figure 1 illustrates PTRepair. The framework takes as input a process model represented as a PST, compliance requirements, detected compliance violations, a resolution context, process change operations (Table 2), and compliance patterns [16]. It then generates candidate resolution strategies using an LLM-based heuristic planning approach (Sect. 3.1), applies and validates them to ensure operation consistency and preserve structural and behavioral soundness (Sect. 3.2), and finally evaluates valid strategies using quality metrics such as resolution effectiveness, contextual consistency, change cost, and change location (Sect. 3.3).

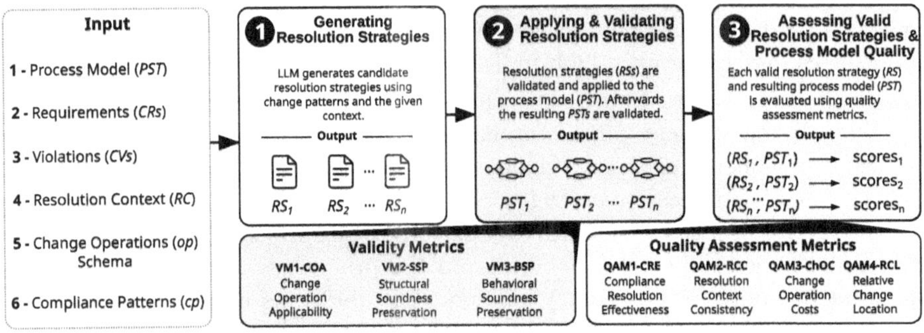

Fig. 1. Process Tree Repair (PTRepair) Framework.

3.1 Step 1: Generating Resolution Strategies

Compliance violations detected by the Process Tree Verifier (PTV) [16] form the basis for generating resolution strategies. PTRepair formulates this task as a planning problem that transforms a non-compliant PST into a compliant one through process change operations while preserving structural, behavioral, and contextual correctness. Unlike symbolic planners [2], which require predefined states and activities, compliance resolution often involves missing activities and semantically identifying suitable change locations. Recent work has shown that LLMs can effectively support planning through semantic reasoning [7]. PTRepair therefore employs an LLM as a heuristic planner, followed by rule-based validation and application of the generated strategies (Sect. 3.2).

Pre-processing PST. Before generating resolution strategies, the input process model is automatically converted into a simplified PST representation for LLM processing. The conversion preserves the hierarchical control-flow semantics and contextual information (activities, data, resources, and temporal annotations), while removing auxiliary structural wrappers and collapsing redundant hierarchy to reduce token consumption and structural noise.

LLM-Based Compliance Resolution. After pre-processing, PTRepair generates candidate resolution strategies using an LLM-based heuristic planner. The LLM receives the simplified PST representation, the detected compliance violation, process change operations, compliance pattern semantics, and generation instructions. These constrain the LLM to predefined change operations, promote minimal and localized modifications, preserve operation validity, and require machine-readable JSON output. The complete prompt, its iterative evolution, prompt engineering guidelines, and the ablation study evaluating the impact of process change operations and compliance patterns are available in the online repository[1]. The generated strategies are subsequently validated and deterministically applied to the PST (Sect. 3.2).

3.2 Step 2: Validating and Applying Resolution Strategies

This section describes how the change operations of generated resolution strategies are validated and sequentially applied to the PST. Each successfully applied operation produces an updated PST that serves as the basis for validating and applying the subsequent operation. Consequently, later operations may become invalid due to earlier changes. If any validation step fails, the strategy is invalid.

Validating and Applying Resolution Strategies. PTRepair first verifies the change operation applicability (**VM1-COA**) by checking that each change operation is supported and references existing process elements. Resolution strategies containing invalid operations are rejected. Valid strategies are then applied deterministically to the PST through the sequential execution of their process change operations (Table 2), producing an updated PST after each operation, as recommended in [14]. Depending on the operation, this may modify activity nodes, restructure control-flow fragments, or update process-related information. After all changes are applied, PTRepair automatically removes redundant control-flow constructs (e.g., empty XOR blocks or single-branch parallel blocks) before structural and behavioral validation.

Validating the Resulting PST. Resolution strategies generated by the LLM may introduce structural or behavioral soundness problems. Therefore, after each change operation, PTRepair validates whether the resulting PST preserves both properties, since process modifications may introduce unintended structural consequences beyond the intended repair [1]; otherwise, the resolution strategy is rejected. Structural soundness preservation (**VM2-SSP**) is ensured by verifying that the PST remains block-structured. For example, operations involving multiple activities (e.g., parallelization or fragment extraction) require compatible scopes and a common parent fragment, while loop embedding requires contiguous fragments within the same hierarchical level. Consequently, changes across incompatible branches, parallel scopes, or unrelated loop regions are rejected. Behavioral soundness preservation (**VM3-BSP**) analyzes the resulting PST for behavioral anomalies, including unreachable XOR branches, XOR blocks without executable alternatives, non-terminating loops, and terminate activities inside parallel blocks, which may cause synchronization anomalies or incomplete execution.

[1] https://github.com/marisol-barrientos/PTRepair, LA: 06 August 2026fn:repo.

3.3 Step 3: Assessing Valid Resolution Strategies and PST Quality

As shown in Table 3, multiple valid resolution strategies may exist for the same compliance violation, differing in resolution effectiveness, resolution context consistency, change operation cost, and relative change location. PTRepair assesses generated resolution strategies using the following quality metrics:

- **Resolution Effectiveness (QAM1-CRE).** After applying the change operations, the updated PST is verified using PTV [16]. The effectiveness is 1 if the targeted violation is resolved and 0 otherwise.
- **Resolution Context Consistency (QAM2-RCC).** The consistency score is $\text{ContextConsistency}(RS_{CV}) = 1 - \frac{|V_{new}|}{|CR_{context}|}$, where V_{new} is the set of newly introduced violations and $CR_{context}$ is the set of compliance requirements in the resolution context. Values are normalized to $[0, 1]$, where 1 indicates no additional violations.
- **Change Operation Cost (QAM3-ChOC).** It is defined as $\text{StrCost}(RS) = \sum_{op_i \in RS} w(op_i)$, where $RS = \langle op_1, \ldots, op_n \rangle$ and $w(op_i)$ is the predefined weight of operation op_i. The weights are: $w = 1$ (semantic edits), $w = 2$ (structural edits), $w = 3$ (control-flow transformations), and $w = 4$ (loop embeddings).
- **Relative Change Location (QAM4-RCL).** For $PST = (N, E, r, \lambda)$, the relative location of op_i is $\text{RCL}(op_i) = \text{Position}(n)/|N_{\text{activity}}|$, where n is the affected activity node and $N_{\text{activity}} \subseteq N$ is the set of activity nodes. The value lies in $[0, 1]$, with lower values indicating earlier changes in the process.

These metrics enable an assessment of alternative resolution strategies.

4 Evaluation

This section evaluates PTRepair. The prototype was implemented in Python 3.11, using GPT 5.5 to generate structured JSON-based process change operations and PTV [16] for compliance verification. Section 4.1 describes the evaluation dataset, and Sect. 4.2 presents the analysis of the results. The source code, dataset, prompts, evaluation results, and analysis of related work is publicly available online.[2] The evaluation was conducted in a single run. Assessing the stability of the results through multiple runs is left for future work.

4.1 Dataset

The evaluation dataset comprises 15 business process models and 57 compliance requirements. Of these requirements, 39 exhibit at least one compliance violation. Violating requirements contain an average of 2.6 violations (min. 1, max. 5). The dataset consolidates examples from previous compliance-resolution approaches and the evaluation corpus of PTV [16] (Table 4).

[2] https://github.com/marisol-barrientos/PTRepair, LA: 06 August 2026.

Table 4. Compliance patterns present in the dataset

Compliance Pattern(s)	Reference
exists; absence; parallel	[2], [6], [24], [27]; [20]; [8]
directly_follows	[2], [8,16]
leads_to	[2], [15], [9], [6,28]
precedence	[20], [10], [2], [9,24]
executed_by	[8], [10], [24,28]
timed_alternative; activity_receives	[27]; [6,24]
condition_directly_follows	[11,12]
condition_eventually_follows	[10], [2], [8,11]

Datasets were excluded if they used non-descriptive activity labels, specified unsupported compliance patterns, or defined constraints over UML class models rather than process behavior. Likewise, unsupported patterns (e.g., `max_time_between`) and datasets in which no compliance violations were detected were omitted. All process models and requirements were manually transformed into PST and AST representations. Future work will integrate automated translations to both representations [4]. Among temporal patterns, only `timed_alternative` is included, while failure-related patterns are excluded because their resolution depends on scenario-specific runtime semantics.

4.2 Analysis of Results

TResolver automatically evaluates generated resolution strategies and their corresponding updated process models using the validity and quality assessment metrics introduced in Sect. 3.2 and Sect. 3.3: change operation applicability **(VM1-COA)**, structural soundness preservation **(VM2-SSP)**, behavioral soundness preservation **(VM3-BSP)**, compliance resolution effectiveness **(QAM1-CRE)**, resolution context consistency **(QAM2-RCC)**, and change operation cost **(QAM3-ChOC)**. The relative change location metric **(QAM4-RCL)** is omitted because the dataset process models offer few alternative change locations. It remains relevant for runtime adaptation, where applying changes later in the process can preserve the execution of already running instances. Table 5 summarizes the evaluation results across all validation and quality assessment metrics.

A total of 147 candidate resolution strategies were generated for the 39 evaluated compliance violations, corresponding to an average of $\frac{147}{39} \approx 3.76$ resolution strategies per violation. The effectiveness of resolution strategies varied by process change operation. `swap`, `merge`, `parallelize`, `modify_loop_condition`, and `remove_write` resolved all evaluated violations, as they largely preserve the original process structure while changing localized behavioral or semantic aspects. In contrast, `copy_after`, `remove_loop`, `embed_post_loop`, and

Table 5. Summary of evaluation results and observations

Metric	Results and analysis
Change Operation Applicability (VM1-COA)	100% of generated strategies satisfied the predefined process change operations. This demonstrates that constrained prompting effectively prevents syntactically invalid process adaptations.
Structural Soundness Preservation (VM2-SSP)	**92%** of generated strategies were structurally applicable. Unsuccessful cases were mainly caused by missing structural elements (e.g., XOR branches, loops, termination nodes) [2,12,15].
Behavioral Soundness Preservation (VM3-BSP)	**85%** of generated strategies preserved behavioral soundness. Remaining cases involved behavior-sensitive modifications (e.g., loop changes or sequentialization of parallel) [2,28], showing that structural validity does not guarantee behavioral correctness.
Compliance Resolution Effectiveness (QAM1-CRE)	**73%** of violations were successfully resolved. Remaining failures were attributed to limitations of the compliance verifier (e.g., handling combined conditions [11,24] or strict resource/data matching [6,28]), rather than incorrect repairs.
Resolution Context Consistency (QAM2-RCC)	Among the successful repairs, **88%** preserved all previously compliant requirements, while **12%** introduced new violations. More than half of these were caused by overlapping requirements.
Change Operation Cost (QAM3-ChOC)	Complex compliance violations required more numerous and diverse change operations [2,11,24] than simpler violations. This indicates that repair effort is driven by both the structural complexity of the process model and the semantic complexity of the violated requirement.

`modify_read` were less effective because they depend more strongly on compatible structural regions and contextual assumptions. Frequently used operations such as `insert_after`, `insert_before`, `rename`, and `modify_resource` achieved moderate repair rates, showing that their effectiveness depends on the structural and semantic quality of the underlying process model.

5 Conclusion

This paper presented PTRepair, a framework for resolving compliance violations in business process models through LLM-based generation, deterministic process model adaptation, and quality assessment. PTRepair supports compliance-aware process redesign by generating and evaluating alternative resolution strategies. The evaluation demonstrates the effectiveness of the proposed approach in producing valid, high-quality resolution strategies. Future work will evaluate user acceptance, the usefulness of the quality metrics, and effective visualization of repairs. It will also investigate causal links between legal changes and process repairs [3], address overcompliant process models [17], and extend PTRepair with conversational violation resolution.

Acknowledgments. This work has been funded by the Deutsche Forschungsgemeinschaft (DFG) under project number 514769482.

References

1. Andree, K., Deigner, F., Stupp, F., Kuzmin, I., Pufahl, L.: Automatic support in process redesign: Structural impact analysis of change operations. In: Research Challenges in Information Science. Springer, Cham (2026)
2. Awad, A., Smirnov, S., Weske, M.: Resolution of compliance violation in business process models: a planning-based approach. In: OTM (2009)
3. Barrientos, M., Loebbecke, J., Winter, K., Rinderle-Ma, S.: Taming the complexity of legal change for business process compliance. BISE (2026)
4. Barrientos, M., Winter, K., Rinderle-Ma, S.: Automatic extraction and formalization of temporal requirements from text: a survey. In: EDOC (2024)
5. Barrientos, M., Winter, K., Rinderle-Ma, S.: Impact analysis of regulatory requirement changes on business process compliance. IST (2026)
6. Bernal, Á., Montero, F., Cabanillas, C., Fernandez, P., Resinas, M.: STATUS: a low-code business process compliance management system. In: the Best Dissertation Award (2024)
7. Cao, P., et al.: Large language models for planning: a comprehensive and systematic survey. CoRR (2025)
8. Elgammal, A., Türetken, O., van den Heuvel, W.: Using Patterns for the Analysis and Resolution of Compliance Violations. Int. J. Cooperative Inf, Syst (2012)
9. Förster, A., Engels, G., Schattkowsky, T., Straeten, R.V.D.: Verification of business process quality constraints based on visual process patterns. In: First Joint IEEE/IFIP Symposium on Theoretical Aspects of Software Engineering (2007)
10. Ghose, A., Koliadis, G.: Auditing business process compliance. In: ICSOC – Fifth International Conference (2007)
11. Governatori, G., Rotolo, A.: A conceptually rich model of business process compliance. In: Conceptual Modelling (2010)
12. Haarmann, S., Holfter, A., Pufahl, L., Weske, M.: Formal framework for checking compliance of data-driven case management. J. Data Semant. (2021)
13. Kharbili, M.E.: Business process regulatory compliance management solution frameworks: a comparative evaluation. In: Eighth Asia-Pacic Conference on Conceptual Modelling (2012)
14. Klievtsova, N., Kampik, T., Mangler, J., Rinderle-Ma, S.: Conversational Process Model Redesign. Int. J. Cooperative Inf, Syst (2026)
15. Letia, I.A., Goron, A.: Model Checking as Support for Inspecting Compliance to Rules in Flexible Processes. J. Vis. Lang, Comput (2015)
16. Loebbecke, J., Mangler, J., Rinderle-Ma, S.: Tree-based compliance verification: Bridging the gap between compliance requirements and process execution. In: ER - 44th International Conference (2025)
17. Loebbecke, J., Rinderle-Ma, S.: A framework for assessing overcompliance and undercompliance in business processes. In: CoopIS (2025)
18. López, H.A., Hildebrandt, T.T.: Three decades of formal methods in business process compliance: a systematic literature review. CoRR (2024)
19. Maggi, F.M., Marrella, A., Capezzuto, G., Armas-Cervantes, A.: Explaining non-compliance of business process models through automated planning. In: ICSOC - 16th International Conference (2018)
20. Masellis, R.D., Francescomarino, C.D., Ghidini, C., Laponin, A., Maggi, F.M.: Rule propagation: adapting procedural process models to declarative business rules. In: 21st IEEE International EDOC Conference (2017)

21. Oriol, X., Giacomo, G.D., Estañol, M., Teniente, E.: Embedding Reactive Behavior Into Artifact-centric Business Process Models. Future Gener. Comput, Syst (2021)
22. Rinderle, S., Reichert, M., Dadam, P.: Flexible support of team processes by adaptive workflow systems. Distributed Parallel Databases (2004)
23. Seyffarth, T., Kühnel, S.: Maintaining Business Process Compliance Despite Changes: A Decision Support Approach Based on Process Adaptations. J. Decis, Syst (2022)
24. Sun, X., Yang, S., Zhao, C., Yu, D.: Design-time business process compliance assessment based on multi-granularity semantic information. J. Supercomput. (2024)
25. Vanhatalo, J., Völzer, H., Koehler, J.: The Refined Process Structure Tree. Data Knowl, Eng (2009)
26. Weber, B., Rinderle, S., Reichert, M.: Change patterns and change support features in process-aware information systems. In: Information Systems Engineering (2013)
27. Winter, K., van der Aa, H., Rinderle-Ma, S., Weidlich, M.: Assessing the compliance of business process models with regulatory documents. In: 39th ER (2020)
28. Zasada, A., Hashmi, M., Fellmann, M., Knuplesch, D.: Evaluation of compliance rule languages for modelling regulatory compliance requirements. Softw. (2023)

PETALE: A Fine-Grained Evaluation Framework for Process Modeling Methods

Clara Kowalczyk[1,2,3(✉)], Alexis Brissard[1,2,3], Frederic Cuppens[1,3], and Amal Zouaq[1,2]

[1] Polytechnique Montreal, Montreal, Canada
{clara.kowalczyk,alexis.brissard,frederic.cuppens,amal.zouaq}@polymtl.ca
[2] LAMA-WeST Lab, Montreal, Canada
[3] LabCys, Montreal, India

Abstract. Evaluating the quality of business process models generated by Large Language Models (LLMs) is critical, yet existing approaches rely on *ad hoc* metrics or comparison to a gold-standard model. We argue this assumption is restrictive, as multiple process models can accurately represent the same process. We propose **PETALE**, a fine-grained evaluation framework that extract both process models and natural-language description into fine-grained semantic units (tasks, actors, etc.), and aligns them via semantic similarity to enable precise, reference model-free identification of errors and omissions. To support framework validation, we introduce TaskPET, a dataset of 45 manually-annotated processes using this units representation. Benchmark of state-of-the-art automated process modeling approaches against human expert baseline on TaskPET reveals modeling deficiencies of existing holistic metrics: while most methods reach near-human performance at task-level, they tend to fall short in identifying finer-grained elements such as actors or resources.

Keywords: Business Process Modeling · PMo Evaluation · Information Extraction · BPMN

1 Introduction

As automated Process Modeling (PMo) approaches gain wider adoption thanks to recent advances in natural language processing, evaluation of generated process models has become critical. Current evaluation approaches lack precision and standardization, relying on *ad hoc* metrics or heterogeneous frameworks that are difficult to compare. Most existing methods evaluate a generated model by comparing it against a gold-standard model [12], but this assumption is too restrictive. Indeed, a business process can be represented by multiple equally valid models differing in abstraction level, structure, or modeling perspective [1,22]. Additionally, these methods provide only a global quality score without identifying sources of error. To address these limitations, this

© The Author(s), under exclusive license to Springer Nature Switzerland AG 2027
A. Bernasconi et al. (Eds.): ER 2026, LNCS 17081, pp. 495–505, 2027.
https://doi.org/10.1007/978-3-032-40795-5_33

paper introduces **PETALE** (**P**rocess model **E**valuation with **T**ask **A**ttribute **L**LM-based **E**xtraction), a novel evaluation framework that compares a process model directly to the textual description it originated from, to obtain fine-grained insights beyond a single global score. We investigate the following research questions:

RQ1: Can process modeling approaches be evaluated in a fine-grained manner directly from their description, without relying on a gold standard model?

RQ2: How do automated process modeling methods compare to human experts when evaluated with PETALE?

To address these questions, this paper proposes several contributions.

1. **Process Information Task**, a new semantic annotation framework bridging the gap between process descriptions and process model formalisms.
2. **TaskPET**, a validation dataset extending the 45 processes descriptions from the PET dataset [2] with 505 annotated Process Information Tasks and 35 expert-created process models to support reproducible evaluation.
3. **PETALE**, an evaluation framework relying on Process Information Tasks to assess the fidelity of process models directly against their descriptions from a data and resource perspective.
4. **Benchmark** of several state-of-the-art LLM-based BPMN generation approaches against expert and automated baselines, uncovering novel limitations invisible to coarser metrics.

Section 2 reviews the literature on process model evaluation. Section 3 introduces the Process Information Task scheme, the TaskPET dataset, and the PETALE evaluation pipeline. Section 4 uses PETALE to benchmark state-of-the-art process modeling approaches. Section 5 concludes with limitations and future directions.

2 Related Work

Existing approaches for evaluating generated process models can broadly be divided into two categories: *model-to-model* and *model-to-text* evaluation.

Model-to-Model Evaluation. Most process model evaluation methods assess a generated model by comparing it to a reference (gold) model through similarity metrics, capturing its semantic, structural, or behavioral aspects [8]. Existing work of the PMo literature adopts a wide variety of similarity measures, rather than defining a standardized evaluation protocol: node-matching similarity [8], tuple comparison [12], expert assessment [23], Dice-coefficient adaptations [26], Graph Edit Distance and its variants [8,17,27], graph embeddings [6], simulation footprints [3], and conformance checking [15].

Although these metrics capture complementary details of process models, they all rely on a restrictive assumption: that there exists a single correct reference model. Yet, a business process can be correctly represented by multiple distinct models [1,22]. Variations in abstraction level, modeling perspective, or structural organization may still accurately describe the same process [12], while consequently leading to low similarity scores.

Model-to-Text Evaluation. A smaller body of work evaluates process models directly against the original textual description, avoiding reliance on a gold reference model. Round-trip approach converts the model back into text and compares it to the input description using embedding similarity [21], while LLM-as-a-judge methods directly prompt a model to estimate semantic similarity [4].

While these approaches address some limitations of model-to-model evaluation, they remain coarse-grained, offering limited insight into which process aspects are correctly captured. In addition, LLM-as-a-judge methods raise concerns regarding reproducibility and standardization in expert domains [9,25].

To address these limitations, we propose PETALE, a fine-grained evaluator of process models against textual descriptions, as positioned in Table 1.

Table 1. Comparison of different process model evaluation methods

Process Model Evaluation Method	Gold-Model -Free	Semantic Matching	Fine Grained
Model-to-model		(✓)	✓
Model-to-text	✓	✓	
PETALE	✓	✓	✓

3 PETALE Framework

An overview of PETALE is presented in Fig. 1. Rather than comparing against a gold model, PETALE identifies semantic units (introduced in Sect. 3.1) in both the textual description and the process model, then computes similarity scores reflecting their alignment. Extraction procedure of these units is described in Sect. 3.2, while matching method is detailed in Sect. 3.3.

3.1 TaskPET Dataset

Since processes are essentially sequences of tasks, we bridge the gap between natural language and process models by adapting Bellan et al.'s PET annotations [2] to tasks. We introduce a new annotation scheme called Process Information Tasks, referred to simply as tasks hereafter.

Definition 1 (Process Information Task). *A Process Information Task represents a single action described by exactly one Activity (the verb or action being performed) and zero or more instances of attributes associated to the action. These attributes are Activity Data (the object, data or system that the* *activity acts upon), Actor Performer (the person, role, department or organization that executes or initiates the activity) and Actor Recipient (the person, role, department or organization, that is affected by the activity or who the activity acts upon). Natural language description of the task is referred to as its verbalization.*

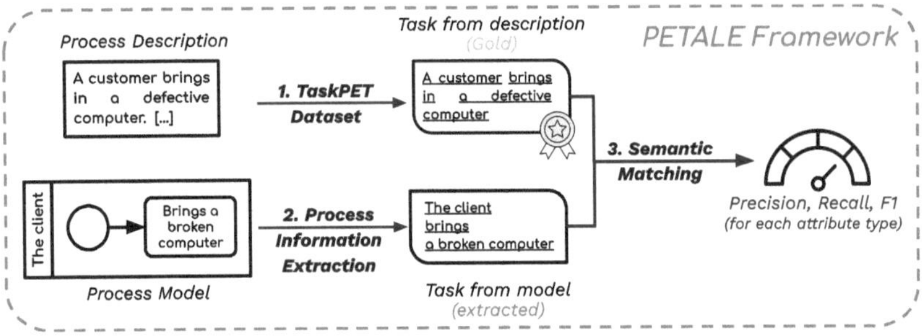

Fig. 1. Overview of the PETALE Framework.

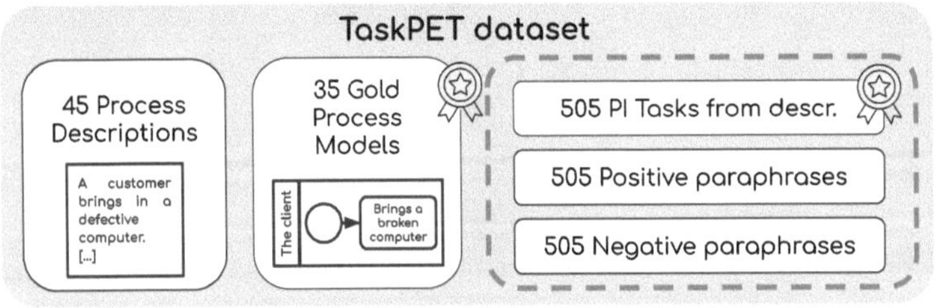

Fig. 2. Overview of the TaskPET dataset.

Bellan et al. [2] annotated the well-known 45 process descriptions from [10] using their PET scheme, resulting in the PET dataset. Despite detailed guidelines, this annotation scheme is limited as annotation decisions remain sometimes ambiguous: for instance, the distinction between *Activity Data*, *Actor*, and *Further Specification* is often left to annotator judgment, and no rules govern particle inclusion. Due to these inconsistencies, we disambiguated their annotation guidelines and re-annotated the same 45 process descriptions, resulting in 505 Process Information Tasks. Annotation methodology, guidelines, and details on the positive/negative paraphrases are provided in the complementary material (available in our repository : https://github.com/LAMA-WeST-Lab/PETALE). We also includes 35 expert-created process models provided by [7], resulting in the TaskPET dataset (see Fig. 2).

3.2 Task Attribute Extraction

PETALE evaluates process model fidelity by comparing tasks extracted from the model with those derived from its description. This first step, *Task Attribute Extraction* (TAE), aims to extract semantic information from process model elements, most of which is conveyed through textual labels. We address this by prompting an LLM to extract information directly from these labels, following a standard prompt engineering approach: role specification and contextual framing anchor the model in its task, a precise task definition constrains what counts as extractable information, and additional instructions handle edge cases. Strict output formatting constraints and few-shot examples are included to ensure consistent and parseable outputs.

While the extraction procedure described above is generic, its application requires mapping model-specific textual and structural elements to Process Information Task attributes. Implementation in BPMN 2.0,[1] a standard representation in process modeling, along with dataset and complementary material are available in the following repository: https://github.com/LAMA-WeST-Lab/PETALE.

3.3 Semantic Matching

To evaluate semantic similarity, it is first necessary to identify which extracted tasks correspond to which gold tasks, as this correspondence is not explicit from the textual descriptions alone. PETALE's Semantic Matching Module matches extracted and gold elements, following a procedure similar to [8,24].

Matching elements between two sets can be formulated as an Assignment Problem (see [5]), using a similarity metric to quantify the similarity of all possible pairs. *Greedy matching*, which sorts all candidate pairs in decreasing order of similarity and iteratively assigns the highest-similarity pair whose elements are still unmatched, until no valid pairs remain, is a standard solving algorithm of this problem among the process modeling community [8].

In PETALE, matched pairs are True Positives (TP); unmatched extracted and gold tasks are respectively False Positives (FP) and False Negatives (FN) (see Fig. 3). Precision, Recall, and F1 are derived from these counts.

Task-Level vs Attribute-Level Matching. Extracted tasks include their attributes, which are matched after task alignment for finer similarity analysis. For instance, a gold task "the CRS repairs the hardware" matched with "repair the computer" counts as a False Negative *Actor Performer* (absent from the process model). Attribute-level metrics thus expose missing or hallucinated elements invisible at task-level, offering detailed metrics from a data and resource perspectives.

[1] See https://camunda.com/bpmn/reference/ for more details about BPMN2.0.

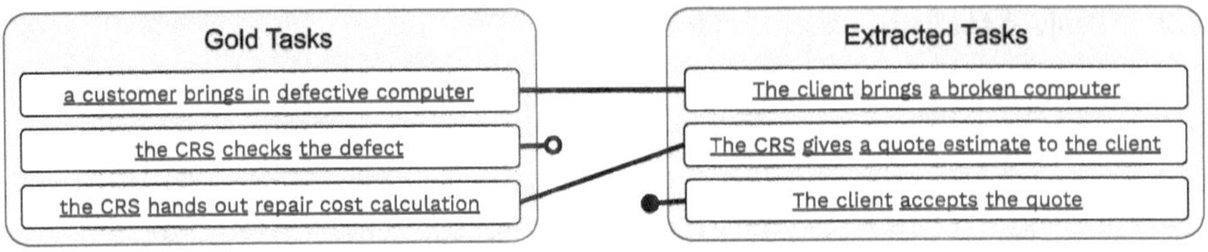

Fig. 3. Matching of gold and extracted tasks. Matched pairs are TP; unmatched gold tasks (○) are FN; unmatched extracted tasks (●) are FP.

4 Benchmark of PMo Approaches

4.1 Experimental Setup

We now use PETALE to evaluate manual and automated PMo methods.

Dataset. Each approach generates 35 BPMN models from the TaskPET process descriptions, which we evaluate using TaskPET's gold annotations.

Candidates. For manual process modeling, we use the 35 BPMN models made by human experts from [7]. For automated modeling, we select *PromoAI* [14] ran on GPT-4o-mini, as it is a standard PMo baseline, alongside recent open-source approaches : *AutoBPMN.AI* [13], *BPMN-Chatbot++* [20] and *BPMNGen* [11] all ran on GPT-4.1, and *BPMN Assistant* [16] with GPT-4o. Due to input size limitations or generation errors, *BPMNGen* and *ProMoAI* produced respectively 33 and 25 models. All approaches are evaluated in single-step generation to ensure reproducibility.

Metric and PETALE Configuration. BPMN models are evaluated with PETALE's F1 scores. Macro-averaged F1 across attribute types is also reported for global comparison. Complementary experiments conducted on PETALE's extraction and matching modules (provided in the repository[2]) compared respectively state-of-the-art LLMs and embedding models, to check their reliability. As a result, we adopt the following configuration: *Qwen2.5-72B-Instruct* [19] for extraction, *Greedy matching* algorithm with *RoBERTa cross-encoder*[3] similarity at task-level[4] for matching.

4.2 Results and Analysis

Human Experts Results and PETALE Validation. Results are shown in Table 2. Regarding human experts baseline, task-level results (0.89 F1) confirm expert model quality. Attribute-level scores are lower, but remain above

[2] https://github.com/LAMA-WeST-Lab/PETALE.
[3] https://huggingface.co/cross-encoder/stsb-roberta-large, accessed 19/04/2026.
[4] At attribute-level, where semantic distinctions are simpler, the lighter model *Octen-8B-Embedding* [18] with cosine similarity is used. A threshold τ=0.3 is used to filter out low-similarity pairs and avoid spurious matches during matching.

0.50. These lower scores may be partially due to errors propagating through PETALE's modules, for instance, matching errors from task to attribute levels, since attributes of unmatched tasks cannot be matched either. However, we argue they might also reflect a natural deviation of expert models from strict textual fidelity. Indeed, process model experts often condense details, rename actors, or infer plausible process logic beyond what is explicitly stated. These choices reflect domain expertise rather than modeling errors, but fidelity-focused metrics like PETALE tend to penalize them.

While these results demonstrate PETALE's ability to assess the fidelity of a process model to its description, they also highlight that semantic fidelity captures only one dimension of model quality. A broader discussion on the matter is provided in Sect. 5.

Automated Results. At task-level, most approaches perform competitively, with *AutoBPMN.AI* achieving the best F1 (0.92), narrowly outperforming human and automated baselines. *BPMNGen* and *BPMN Assistant* follow closely behind, while *BPMN-Chatbot++* is notably below both baselines (0.71).

At attribute level, task-level performance does not consistently transfer :*AutoBPMN.AI* and *BPMN Assistant*, which matched human experts at the task level, maintain their lead for *Activity* and *Activity Data*, but collapse for *Actor Performer*, likely due to their lack of pool and lane support. Similarly, *ProMoAI* shows weak performance for *Actor Performer* and *Activity*, suggesting that its task-level performance does not reflect a deeper understanding of process attributes. In contrast, *BPMNGen* (0.84 task-level F1) outperforms all automated approaches on *Actor Performer* (0.68). Despite this, all methods struggle with *Actor Recipient*, indicating general difficulty in modeling this attribute type.

Macro-averaged F1 scores of all automated approaches fall below the human expert baseline of 0.70, with *BPMNGen* standing out as the most balanced one (0.67). They also exceed the automated baseline *ProMoAI* (0.53), suggesting progress in capturing finer-grained details among recent open-source frameworks. However, this gap should be interpreted cautiously, as *ProMoAI* was only

Table 2. F1-scores for various PMo approaches. Highest results are in bold.

	Experts (Human Baseline)	PromoAI (Auto. Baseline)	Auto BPMN AI	BPMN Gen	BPMN Assistant	BPMN Chatbot ++
Generated BPMNs	35/35	25/35	35/35	33/35	35/35	35/35
Task-level	0.89	0.89	**0.92**	0.84	0.88	0.71
Activity	0.86	0.70	**0.92**	0.84	0.88	0.69
Activity Data	0.67	0.71	**0.79**	0.69	0.76	0.63
Actor Performer	**0.74**	0.16	0.19	0.68	0.19	0.59
Actor Recipient	0.51	0.55	0.58	0.48	**0.62**	0.47
Attribute Macro-F1	**0.70**	0.53	0.62	0.67	0.61	0.60

evaluated on 25/35 processes (as ProMoAI failed to generate them), making a definitive conclusion difficult.

Overall, the narrow spread among recent automated approaches (0.60–0.67) could suggest performance differences owe more to the underlying LLM than to the PMo framework itself. While automated approaches capture overall process structure fairly well at task level, they consistently struggle with finer-grained attributes such as actors and data.

5 Conclusion

This work introduces PETALE, a novel evaluation framework for process models built on the Process Information Task annotation scheme. By grounding evaluation in annotations shared between natural-language descriptions and process models, PETALE operates without a gold process model while offering fine-grained analysis through task attributes. Benchmarking state-of-the-art process modeling approaches confirms both the relevance of the framework and the value of fine-grained metrics. While task-level scores suggest that automated methods such as *ProMoAI*, *AutoBPMN.AI* or *BPMNGen* reach human performance, attribute-level analysis reveals systematic difficulties with finer-grained details such as recipient actors or data objects that coarser metrics would miss.

Our results also show that semantic fidelity to a textual description is not a sufficient quality indicator. As Beerepoot et al. [1] note, process model quality is inherently context-dependent: for instance, a process model intended for a manager should not have the same granularity or vocabulary as one for a technician. Fidelity to a source description is therefore one dimension of quality among many. This is further reflected in the imperfect scores obtained by expert-produced process models on PETALE, which we attributed to a mix of evaluation pipeline errors and legitimate divergences in human modeling choices.

Disentangling these factors precisely requires a systematic error analysis which we identify as a priority for future work. We expect it to further clarify PETALE's limitations, some of which are as follow. Evaluation ignores element ordering, which could be addressed drawing on structural similarity or control-flow conformance checking techniques. Process Information Task does not yet cover all information types expressed in natural-language descriptions, such as contextual details (i.e. place, time, manner). PET scheme broadly grouped them under *Further Specification* attribute, but we hope for future work to refine and disambiguate interpretation of these concepts to support more precise evaluation. The matching module is also sensitive to duplicated information, occasionally leading to spurious penalization. Coreference resolution may mitigate this issue. More broadly, extending PETALE to account for context-dependent quality criteria would better align it with real-world process model evaluation, where fitness to purpose matters as much as fidelity to a description.

Acknowledgments. This study was funded by MITACS (grant number IT32670). Computational resources for this research were provided by the Digital Research

Alliance of Canada. Regarding third-party assets, icons used in Figs. 1 and 2 are made by Puckung from www.flaticon.com and used under their free-use license.

Disclosure of Interests. The authors have no competing interests to declare that are relevant to the content of this article.

References

1. Beerepoot, I., Di Ciccio, C., Reijers, H.A., Rinderle-Ma, S., Bandara, W., et al.: The biggest business process management problems to solve before we die. Comput. Ind. **146**, 103837 (2023). https://doi.org/10.1016/j.compind.2022.103837
2. Bellan, P., Dragoni, M., Ghidini, C., Ponzetto, S., van der Aa, H.: Process extraction from natural language text: the PET dataset and annotation guidelines. In: Nozza, D., Passaro, L.C., Polignano, M. (eds.) Proceedings of the Sixth Workshop on Natural Language for Artificial Intelligence (NL4AI 2022). CEUR Workshop Proceedings, vol. 3287, pp. 177–191. CEUR-WS.org (2022). https://ceur-ws.org/Vol-3287/
3. Berti, A., Kourani, H., Antonov, A., Aalst, W.M.P.V.D.: Knowledge-driven hallucination in large language models: an empirical study on process modeling. TechRxiv **2025**(0904) (2025). https://doi.org/10.36227/techrxiv.175695580.03540927/v1
4. Berti, A., Wang, X., Kourani, H., Van der Aalst, W.M.: Specializing large language models for process modeling via reinforcement learning with verifiable and universal rewards. Process Sci. **2**(1), 26 (2025). https://doi.org/10.1007/s44311-025-00034-4
5. Burkard, R.E., Çela, E.: Linear Assignment Problems and Extensions. In: Du, D.Z., Pardalos, P.M. (eds.) Handbook of Combinatorial Optimization: Supplement Volume A, pp. 75–149. Springer US, Boston, MA (1999). https://doi.org/10.1007/978-1-4757-3023-4_2
6. Colonna, J.G., Fares, A.A., Duarte, M., Sousa, R.: Process mining embeddings: Learning vector representations for Petri nets. Intell. Syst. with Appl. **23**, 200423 (2024). https://doi.org/10.1016/j.iswa.2024.200423
7. Costa, A., Wimmer, A., Pufahl, L.: LLM4BPMNGen: A Tool for BPMN Generation with LLMs. In: Marcel, P., Polacsek, T., Karlapalem, K., Jean, S., Wang, H. et al. (eds.) Companion Proceedings of the 44th International Conference on Conceptual Modeling: Industrial Track, ER Forum, 8th SCME, Doctoral Consortium, Tutorials, Project Exhibitions, Posters and Demos. CEUR Workshop Proceedings, vol. 4099, pp. 333–337. CEUR (2025)
8. Dijkman, R., Dumas, M., van Dongen, B., Käärik, R., Mendling, J.: Similarity of business process models: metrics and evaluation. Inform Syst **36**(2), 498–516 (2011). https://doi.org/10.1016/j.is.2010.09.006
9. Dorner, F.E., Nastl, V., Hardt, M.: Limits to scalable evaluation at the frontier: LLM as judge won't beat twice the data. In: Yue, Y., Garg, A., Peng, N., Sha, F., Yu, R. (eds.) International Conference on Learning Representations, vol. 2025, pp. 26467–26491 (2025). https://proceedings.iclr.cc/paper_files/paper/2025/file/4264ee4376776907c0b87ed70b959585-Paper-Conference.pdf
10. Friedrich, F., Jan Mendling, Mendling, J., Frank Puhlmann, Puhlmann, F.: Process model generation from natural language text. In: International Conference on Advanced Information Systems Engineering, pp. 482–496. Springer (2011). https://doi.org/10.1007/978-3-642-21640-4_36

11. Hörner, L.F., Möller, M., Reichert, M.: Automatically Generating BPMN 2.0 Process Models from Natural Language Process Descriptions: Challenges, Framework, Quality Assessment. Bus. & Inf. Syst. Eng. (2026). https://doi.org/10.1007/s12599-025-00983-x
12. Klievtsova, N., Benzin, J.V., Kampik, T., Mangler, J., Rinderle-Ma, S.: Conversational Process Modeling: Can Generative AI Empower Domain Experts in Creating and Redesigning Process Models? (2024). https://doi.org/10.48550/arXiv.2304.11065
13. Klievtsova, N., Ehrendorfer, M., Mangler, J., Rinderle-Ma, S.: AutoBPMN.AI: Conversational Process Modeling and Automation. In: Reijers, H., Marrella, A., del Río Ortega, A., Rinderle-Ma, S., Depaire, B. et al. (eds.) Joint Proceedings of the Best Dissertation Award, Doctoral Consortium, and Demonstration & Resources Forum at BPM 2025. CEUR Workshop Proceedings, vol. 4032, pp. 304–311. CEUR-WS.org (2025). https://ceur-ws.org/Vol-4032/paper-40.pdf
14. Kourani, H., Berti, A., Schuster, D., van der Aalst, W.M.P.: ProMoAI: Process Modeling with Generative AI (2024). https://doi.org/10.48550/arXiv.2403.04327
15. Kourani, H., Berti, A., Schuster, D., van der Aalst, W.M.P.: Evaluating large language models on business process modeling: framework, benchmark, and self-improvement analysis. Softw. Syst. Modeling (2025). https://doi.org/10.1007/s10270-025-01318-w
16. Licardo, J.T., Tanković, N., Etinger, D.: Bpmn assistant: an LLM-based approach to business process modeling. Appl. Sci. **16**(5) (2026). https://www.mdpi.com/2076-3417/16/5/2213
17. Montani, S., Leonardi, G., Quaglini, S., Cavallini, A., Micieli, G.: A knowledge-intensive approach to process similarity calculation. Expert Syst. with Appl. **42**(9), 4207–4215 (2015). https://doi.org/10.1016/j.eswa.2015.01.027
18. Octen Team: Octen series: optimizing embedding models to #1 on RTEB leaderboard (2025). https://octen-team.github.io/octen_blog/posts/octen-rteb-first-place/
19. Qwen Team: Qwen2.5: a party of foundation models (2024). https://qwenlm.github.io/blog/qwen2.5/
20. Safan, A., Köpke, J.: BPMN-Chatbot++: LLM-Based Modeling of Collaboration Diagrams with Data. In: Proceedings of the Best BPM Dissertation Award, Doctoral Consortium, and Demonstrations & Resources Forum co-located with the 23rd International Conference on Business Process Management (BPM 2025). CEUR Workshop Proceedings, vol. 4032. CEUR-WS.org (2025). https://ceur-ws.org/Vol-4032/
21. SAP, S.: SAP-samples/LLM-round-trip-correctness. SAP Samples (2025)
22. Schoknecht, A., Thaler, T., Fettke, P., Oberweis, A., Laue, R.: Similarity of Business Process Models—A State-of-the-Art Analysis. ACM Comput. Surv. **50**(4), 52:1–52:33 (2017). https://doi.org/10.1145/3092694
23. Sholiq, S., Sarno, R., Astuti, E.S.: Generating BPMN diagram from textual requirements. J. of King Saud Univ. - Comput. and Inf. Sci **34**(10), 10079–10093 (2022). https://doi.org/10.1016/j.jksuci.2022.10.007. Part B
24. Sonbol, R., Rebdawi, G., Ghneim, N.: A machine translation like approach to generate business process model from textual description. SN Comput. Sci. **4**(3), 291 (2023). https://doi.org/10.1007/s42979-023-01742-z

25. Szymanski, A., Ziems, N., Eicher-Miller, H.A., Li, T.J.J., Jiang, M., Metoyer, R.A.: Limitations of the LLM-as-a-judge approach for evaluating LLM outputs in expert knowledge tasks. In: Proceedings of the 30th International Conference on Intelligent User Interfaces, pp. 952–966. IUI '25, Association for Computing Machinery (2025). https://doi.org/10.1145/3708359.3712091
26. Voelter, M., Hadian, R., Kampik, T., Breitmayer, M., Reichert, M.: Leveraging Generative Vision Models for Extracting Process Models from Documents. In: Gdowska, K., Gómez-López, M.T., Rehse, J.R. (eds.) Business Process Management Workshops, pp. 271–282. Springer Nature Switzerland, Cham (2025). https://doi.org/10.1007/978-3-031-78666-2_21
27. Waspada, I., Sarno, R.: An Improved Method of Graph Edit Distance for Business Process Model Similarity Measurement. In: 2020 4th International Conference on Informatics and Computational Sciences (ICICoS), pp. 1–6 (2020). https://doi.org/10.1109/ICICoS51170.2020.9299037

Author Index

© The Editor(s) (if applicable) and The Author(s), under exclusive license to Springer Nature Switzerland AG 2027

A. Bernasconi et al. (Eds.): ER 2026, LNCS 17081, pp. 507–508, 2027.
https://doi.org/10.1007/978-3-032-40795-5

FSC
www.fsc.org
MIX
Papier | Fördert gute Waldnutzung
FSC® C083411

Kolibri 360 GmbH
Ferdinand-Jühlke-Straße 7
99095 Erfurt, Deutschland
produktsicherheit@kolibri360.de